Concepts in Human Geography

Concepts in Human Geography

Edited by
Carville Earle,
Kent Mathewson,
and
Martin S. Kenzer

Rowman & Littlefield Publishers, Inc.

ROWMAN & LITTLEFIELD PUBLISHERS, INC.

Published in the United States of America
by Rowman & Littlefield Publishers, Inc.
4720 Boston Way, Lanham, Maryland 20706

3 Henrietta Street
London WC2E 8LU, England

Library of Congress Cataloging-in-Publication Data

Concepts in human geography / edited by Carville Earle, Martin Kenzer,
and Kent Mathewson.
p.   cm.
Includes bibliographical references and index.
1. Human geography.   I. Earle, Carville.   II. Kenzer, Martin S.,
1950–   .   III. Mathewson, Kent.
GR43.C66   1995   304.2–dc20   95-702   CIP

ISBN 0-8476-8104-1 (cloth: alk. paper)
ISBN 0-8476-8105-X (pbk.: alk. paper)

Printed in the United States of America

 ⊗ ™ The paper used in this publication meets the minimum requirements of American National Standard for Information Sciences—Permanence of Paper for Printed
Library Materials, ANSI Z39.48–1984.

Contents

vi   Contents

Illustrations

Preface

It has been said that the Empire State Building in New York City was built in less than a year. Books usually take longer, and this one on human geography's key concepts is very much a case in point. The construction of this anthology of sixteen original essays has consumed the better part of seven years, though the really hard work did not begin until 1993. One could, of course, blame our desultory progress on the curse of interesting times—when scholarship entered the postmodern turn, when the Soviet Union collapsed, and when history seemed at either an end or a new beginning—but the truth of the matter is that these were more nearly an explanation for the fast pace of construction after 1993 than an excuse for the rather languorous pace thereto. Like most everyone else in the late 1980s, we (the editors and authors of this volume) found ourselves spinning in a vortex that we neither anticipated nor knew quite how to control. The paradox is that these unsettling events had curiously calming and contemplative effects.

The need for a volume of human geography's key concepts seemed to us evermore pressing the further we moved into the 1990s. In an intellectual world in flux, it was somehow reassuring to know that the edifice of human geography was constructed of durable and rather remarkably resilient materials, that geographical inquiries on humanity's relations with earthbound places and environs were of an ancient and honorable design, and that these inquiries were built on the rock of classical, medieval, modern, and postmodern scholarship. But that said, the key concepts dealt with here are not of the sort that resemble rigid pilings driven deeply into the earth; they resemble rather a floating lattice capable of absorbing seismic intellectual shockwaves.

Sharing this sense of reassurance about human geography with students and newcomers to the field is what this volume is about. Toward that end, the volume introduces human geography by way of extended essays on the discipline's key concepts. The sixteen essays assembled here chronicle, severally

ix

and together, geography's worldview on people and their affiliations with places and environs. Severally, the essays explore a particular concept's intellectual origins, its sinuous development, and its current applications. Following a brief introduction on the virtues of key concepts in human geography, the volume turns to substantive concepts (what we study) in part one and then to methodological concepts (how we study them) in part two. Part one consists of nine essays on the venerable subjects of space, time, nature, culture, landscape, ecology, place and region, boundaries, and innovation diffusion. Part two consists of seven essays on human geography's prevailing methodologies—maps, models and systems, rational economic actors, humanism, structuration, feminism, and postmodernism.

The task of narrowing down our list of concepts to manageable proportions was not an easy one. While we are confident that it offers a fair representation of human geography, we are painfully aware of the volume's omissions and its shortcomings. Doubtless some geographers will be distressed by the omission of one or another of their favorite concepts; in these cases, we urge them to take a closer look at our rationale for selection in the introduction. But in addition, we encourage readers to send us their critiques of and comments on this volume and its contents. We are particularly interested in how the book is received by students. If it enjoys a reasonably favorable response, we intend to revise the individual essays where appropriate and to extend the range of topics covered by commissioning several new essays. In this regard, critical feedback will be essential. It is our hope that something of a dialogue or interactive process between the volume's readers and its authors and editors can be established. Be that as it may, we trust that the essays in this collection will convey a reassuring sense of human geography's depth, scope, dynamism, and worth in otherwise unreassuring times.

Writers accumulate more debts than they are ever able to repay. A kind word or two seem hardly sufficient. For the editors' part, we want to express our gratitude for our authors' jobian patience with this venture. They have responded promptly and efficiently when the need arose. More heroic perhaps were the labors of Ann Whitmer, Elizabeth Vaughan, Maudrie Eldridge, Bobbie Kraft, and Laurie Boudreaux in coordinating and preparing manuscript drafts and of Mary Lee Eggart, Clifford Duplechin, James Kennedy, and Tom Rabenhorst in preparing the final versions of the maps and illustrations. If what they've helped to build does not rank up there with the Empire State Building, it may, one suspects, endure a great deal longer once these words have dried into print. Our thanks to them all.

Introduction

Back to Basics: The Virtues of Key Concepts in Human Geography

Carville Earle, Kent Mathewson, and Martin S. Kenzer

Who would disagree that the social science literature is growing at a phenomenal rate? By any measure it is quickly becoming—if it has not already become—virtually impossible to keep up with the output of any given subfield, let alone an entire discipline. What geographer, for example, can claim specialized knowledge of more than a few subfields of geography, let alone for all of human geography? Matters are much worse for students just entering the profession. They are overwhelmed with myriad citations to sources in disparate journals, which have steadily increased in their own right to accommodate these outpourings of specialized scholarship. Every professor, it seems, directs new students to yet a different set of "relevant" sources. To many students' discomfort, they learn that the "necessary" literature on all but the most esoteric topics is daunting, if not unmasterable, and the literature seems to grow exponentially. New methods of text production, such as word processing and creative software applications, have expanded opportunities for participation, but they have likewise fueled the accelerated pace of academic life. Increasingly, social scientists look outside their specialties to borrow new ideas and concepts from other disciplines. The exhilaration of discovery is tempered by constantly receding horizons and freighted with potential exhaustion. The race to keep up can become—contra Hobbes's famous indictment of primitive existence—a long, often hasty, and dilettantish push to "know it all."

With the future promising more of the same, there comes a time to slow down, to turn away from the exciting research frontiers and look anew at the foundations of a scholarly line of inquiry—in this case, human geography—and to go, as it were, back to basics. Our turn to foundations and basics should not, however, be mistaken for nostalgic reaction or for restoring some status quo ante. That would misread our intentions. Our repeal is prompted rather by our admiration for the remarkable resilience of human geography's key concepts, by their chameleon-like capacity to change with the times, to endure, while remaining slightly out of focus. This capacity of off-focused change is what we call dynamic ambiguity; it is the stuff that makes ordinary concepts interesting and key concepts foundational. More on these matters momentarily.

In order to cut through all of the "relevant" geographical rhetorics and get back to basics, this anthology presents one essay, written especially for this volume, on each of sixteen key concepts in human geography. Although the essays reflect the distinctive expositional styles of their authors, they tend as a group to follow a similar format—outlining, with examples from the geographical literature, what these social science concepts imply and then demonstrating their salience for human geography. Most of the essays adopt a presentational mode that is both historiographic and genetic, one that begins with the origins of a concept, then turns to its changes in response to shifting intellectual and material currents, and concludes by noting current applications and potential extensions. More specifically, the commentaries on origins of concepts typically note the discipline in which the concept arose, the context in which it emerged, and the implicit and explicit assumptions on which it depended. Likewise, the commentaries on change attend to the shifting usages and meanings of a concept through time, to the historical and geographical contexts that produced these changes, and to the scholarly virtues and vices associated with a concept's dynamic ambiguities. The commentaries conclude with a look (based on what exists in the literature today) at future applications and/or revisions in the concept in the social sciences in general and in human geography in particular.

These essays are also bound together by an attentiveness to audience. Each of the essayists has made a special effort to speak with (and not to) students, to introduce them to representative works that pertain to a given concept, and to convey what it is that human geographers do with that concept that sets them apart from other practitioners of social science. The extensive listing of citations alone should serve as a useful guide to the literature for students wishing to know more about a particular concept, about its changes and applications, and about the enterprise of human geography as a whole.

These essays are not written, however, for just any student. What we have in mind is the student on the road to becoming a scholar—someone with a bit of prior training in geography and a bent toward the scholarly turn of mind. Translated into the North American context, this means either a senior-level undergraduate majoring or minoring in geography or a beginning geography graduate student. If others profit from these essays (as certainly the editors have), so much the better, but our first obligation is to those incipient human geographers who are at once prepared for and inclined toward an intellectual journey. This journey will take you from the fact-filled, term-laden world of introductory textbooks (which we certainly do not dismiss) into the slippery and ambiguous conceptual world of scholarship. On this often magical trip you will discover that "all that is solid" can indeed "melt into thin air," that what one believed to be a center filled with secure facts and rock-solid definitions does not hold. As these solidities vaporize and implode, facts and definitions are dissolved into the "temporary verbalizations of concepts," which in the case of "particularly difficult concepts . . . are usually revised repeatedly as knowledge and understanding grows" (Mayr 1982: 45). Concepts and facts are, in one sense, in a world apart. Whereas facts are static, concepts are dynamic; and whereas facts lend themselves to definition, concepts lend themselves more readily to exposition. Because concepts are by nature tentative and provisional, the chapters in this volume are usually in the form of extended and open-ended essays. Closure is not a term that need come to mind in the world of concepts. Conceptual thinking thus represents a different way of thinking or, more precisely, perhaps, a different habit of thought. With concepts frame of mind is everything; it must be—above all else—supple and capable of handling the gymnastics of always "temporary verbalizations" and of making a virtue out of this necessary ambiguity. The irony of concepts is, of course, that the best of them are richly inexhaustible. Understanding these rather magical/magisterial things will, for most, require some suspension of disbelief.

Concepts as Problem and Opportunity

To paraphrase Dickens's epigram on the French Revolution and its times, concepts can be the best of ideas and the worst of ideas. Clearly for students (or for anyone else new to a scholarly discipline), concepts can rank near the bottom of the list. They not only invite misunderstanding and confusion, but are also frustratingly elusive. Just when you think you have a grip on what a concept means, you discover that what you mean, what your professor means, and what the book you are reading means are not quite the same thing. A case in point comes from a recent article on the usage of *equilibrium* in geomorphology (Thorn and Welford 1994). By the time you have finish reading this article, a seemingly straightforward idea has been carved up into five or six different usages—one for mechanics, another for thermodynamics, and so on. To make matters even more complex, each of these meanings of equilibrium has given birth to a whole host of subsidiary concepts—steady state, quasi-equilibrium, dynamic equilibrium, and the like. Although the authors of this particular article make a valiant effort to decide which of these notions is best for geomorphology, one has the sense that the babble of meanings is more nearly a strength than a weakness, more nearly a virtue than a vice. By regarding concepts such as equilibrium as "temporary verbalizations," we acknowledge that our most important concepts are also the most elastic. They are sufficiently supple to withstand repeated revision "as knowledge and understanding grows." To abandon their ambiguities is to risk a blinkered, inelastic, and impoverished view of a dynamic world.

Thinking conceptually may be one of the best ideas for scholarship, but it is hard to sell that notion to beginners who are trying to decipher the meaning of concepts—usually from the ground up. Naturally we believe that these exercises in decoding are worth a bit of effort. The fact of the matter is that scholars are susceptible to constructing partial views of a complex idea or concept and then proclaiming that it constitutes the whole of things; and they too are surprised—and frequently indignant—when they discover that changing times and the growth of knowledge and understanding have converted what they thought was an obvious and eternal definition into a merely ephemeral verbalization.

Intimations of this problem are commonplace in the social sciences. Consider, for example, the recent perambulations in the concept of space—one of human geography's most fundamental ideas. The story, briefly told, begins in the 1960s and 1970s, when a number of human geographers entertained the conceit of having exhausted the ambiguities of space. These geographers were convinced that space consisted of a fixed and immutable grid for the Newtonian play of objects: that it was absolute and enduring, that its geometries (of cartographic objects such as points, lines, and areas) could be measured, and that these geometries could even be divorced from time. Armed with this absolutist conception of space, these geographers proclaimed their role as spatial scientists, as seekers after universal laws of spatial forms (morphology) and spatial relations. All this began to change, however, in the 1980s, owing to an improbable, and often comic, conjuncturing of relativity physics and postmodern relativism. Challenged by science on the one side and humanism on the other, the most basic premises of the spatial scientists began to totter and ultimately collapse. Where they had referenced position in space to a fixed grid, their critics countered that spatial position was invariably contingent on the speed and motion of other objects—or, to put it in postmodern terms, on the relevant spatial and temporal contexts. Critics pointed out that space was relative, not absolute; inseparable from time (contextual), not extricable; and contextually contingent, not universal (see chapter 1 on space in this volume; see also Billinge, Gregory, and Martin 1984; Sack 1980). Although students may be disconcerted and perplexed by this dramatic reversal in the meaning of *space*, they should also note that this reversal has all of the elements of a good mystery. Figuring out how it happened, why it happened, and what it all means makes for a fascinating tale of conceptual development in human geography, not to mention scholarly knowledge in general.

This just-told story of *space* is not unique. It is in fact repeated again and again in the histories of human geography and the social sciences. In the process concepts are refined and enriched by these recurrent mutations of meaning. In that respect their natural histories resemble Michael Crichton's *Andromeda Strain* in which, just as the scientists begin to understand the curvilinear trajectory of mortality caused by an alien organism, the organism mutates into something new and—and this is the point—more challenging. In sum, concepts are endlessly interesting. Their virtue lies in their capacity for change, that is, in their dynamic ambiguity. It is this elasticity that permits (even encourages) new angles of unfocused vision on the world as well as our changing perceptions of it.

The Inequality of Concepts

Not all concepts are created equal. Some of them are richer and more fecund than others, and these are the ones that endure and form the intellectual foundations of systems of thought, be they world views, religions, or disciplines such as human geography. Human geography has a core of two dozen or so key concepts. From these we have selected sixteen to focus on in this book. These, in turn, divide into two groups: the substantive and the methodological. The first of these deal with human geography's subject matter—what it is that we study (hence the term *substantive*). This part of the volume consists of nine extended essays on the concepts of space, time, nature, culture, landscape, ecology, region and place, boundaries, and innovation and diffusion, in that order. Our second set of concepts deals with human geography's methods—how we go about studying human geography's substantive problems (hence the term *methodological*). This part of the volume consists of seven essays on the concepts of maps, models and systems, location theory and rational economic "man," humanism, structuration, feminism, and postmodernism, again in that order.

Taken as a group, we believe that these sixteen essays offer students a fairly comprehensive yet reasonably economical overview of human geography's most basic concepts. In lieu of producing a bigger and much more expensive book, we chose to be selective. To be sure, not every key concept of human geography is represented in the chapters of this book, but most of those not represented by a particular chapter—circulation, migration, or Marxist analysis, for example—are given ample attention within one or more of our sixteen essays. Accordingly, it seems fitting at this point to say a few words about the concepts that we included and those we did not.

Substantive Concepts: The *What* of Human Geography

Human geography probably has a dozen or so key substantive concepts; of these, we selected the nine noted above. Our decisions were based on two criteria: a concept's endurance and its richness. By *endurance*, we simply mean that these concepts are tried and true. In that regard we are fairly confident that the nine concepts we selected in the early 1990s probably would not differ much from the lists selected by geographers in the 1970s or, for that matter, in the 1920s (Bacon 1979; Bacon and Green 1981). While perhaps not literally timeless, these concepts have become so deeply embedded within the discourses of human geography over the past century or so that they are now clearly foundational. By *richness* we mean that these concepts are heavily invested in collateral and subsidiary concepts in human geography and, moreover, that the range of these investments comes close to defining the discipline as a whole. Can one, for example, think of nature without thinking of culture, or of space without thinking of time? Clearly, these paired concepts are invested in one another. When this investiture persists, as it has in human geography, it becomes compounded. These pairs thus form two quads: 1) nature/culture join with ecology/landscape; and 2) space/time join with region-place/boundary. In turn, this investing yields the principal frames of reference—Earth (1) and Map (2)—for all scholarly research in contemporary human geography. Drawing upon one or the other, human geographers have made important practical and theoretical contributions on an enormous range of ecological (Earth) and locational (Map) problems, past and present (Pattison 1964).

This is the edifice of human geography, and it is an impressive one; yet it is also an edifice that is rather deeply divided. The lamentable reality is that most human geographers live out their scholarly lives in just one of these frames of reference, unaware or unappreciative of the debates, perspectives, and scholarly contributions in the other. This is one history that does not need repeating. We see no good reason for students to be enthralled to conceptual constraints imposed by the Map or the Earth frames of reference; rather, we imagine students striving for an integrated and healthy perspective on the whole of human geography. In sum, two frames of reference are better than one. One way of accomplishing this is to give students greater access to the full range (and power) of human-geographical inquiry and expertise. It is for these reasons that we decided to include an essay on a concept—innovation diffusion—that lies at the intersection of human geography's two frames of reference. By virtue of its conjunctive location, innovation diffusion affords an unusually apt illustration of what human geographers can do when (like our essayist, Lakshman Yapa) they invest themselves in inquiries that are at once ecological (Earth) and locational (Map).

The concept of innovation diffusion has, as it were, a foot in both of human geography's camps. For ecologically minded geographers working in the Earth frame of reference, it has played a critical role in geographical inquiries on the neolithic origins of plant and animal domestication and their subsequent dispersals (Sauer 1952; Hugill and Dickson 1988). For their locationally minded colleagues in the Map frame of reference, the concept has advanced understanding of diffusion's spatial patterns and their interactional foundations (Brown 1981; Hägerstrand 1967; Morrill, Gaile, and Thrall 1988). Yapa does his job well by linking the spatial patterns of innovation and diffusion with their ecological conditions (for example, the political economy of agrarian social structures, the constraints of crop and animal production, and the economic biases associated with particular innovations) in the developing world. From this point of view, the shaping of places and landscapes is best understood through the interactions of locational and ecological processes.

Lakshman Yapa's essay serves as a synthesis of sorts for the other eight substantive concepts taken up in part 1 of this volume. His essay reveals, among other things, that human geography reaches its fullest potential when it transcends customary frames of reference. In this quest for transcendence, however, Yapa is hardly alone. As you will see, many of our essayists strive hard to break loose from these constraining frameworks. Crossover is evident in Karl Zimmerer's essay on ecology, which introduces the particularities of space and time; in Andrew Burghardt's essay on boundaries, which reminds us of nature's key role in boundary delimitations; and in Michael Curry's essay on space, which, in noting the varied meanings of that concept, invites attention to the contingencies of human agency and ecological context. The advantage of this strategy—of conceptual cross-investing between one frame of reference and the other—is that it enables our authors to transcend them both and thereby point out new directions for enriching inquiries in human geography.

Methodological Concepts: The *How* of Human Geography

Human geography's substantive concepts, however important, are useless without a modus operandi, that is, without a method (or methods) that puts inquiry in motion. These methodological concepts constitute the core of the second part of this volume. We have selected seven for fuller exposition; these are maps, models and systems, rational economic "man," humanism, structuration, feminism, and postmodernism. We believe these offer a representative survey of human geography's prevailing methodologies. To be sure, our list runs the risk of not fully acknowledging the countermodernist currents embodied in such terms as postpositivism, poststructuralism, post-Marxism, and postcolonialism (Gregory 1994) or in the more theoretically articulated approaches such as behaviorism, critical theory, idealism, logical positivism, phenomenology, realism, structuralism, and so on (Gregory 1978; Johnston 1986, 1991; Unwin 1992). These philosophico-methodological strategies and positions are encountered in various essays, however, especially those on feminism, structuration, and postmodernism.

More critical perhaps is the omission of a chapter on Marxism, and our decision to do so deserves a word or two. We would argue, first, that the contemporary Marxist perspective is shot through the pages in this volume. Marxist (with a small *m*) ideas and discourse have become so fully incorporated within contemporary social thought that we are all marxists to some extent. Consequently, virtually every one of the essays presented here reacts to, elaborates on, or dissents from Marxist methods of analysis and/or Marxist interpretations of history's laws of motion. The subject is surely not slighted. Second, and perhaps more important, doing justice to the intricacies of Marxist methods and the diversity of Marxist interpretations would have entailed an essay longer, perhaps much longer, than the others. To provide an adequate accounting of Marxism's implications for human geography deserves a book-length treatment rather than an essay. Fortunately, part of this account is available in books such as David Harvey's *The Limits of Capital* (1982), Neil Smith's *Uneven Development: Nature, Capital, and the Production of Space* (1984), and Richard Peet's *Global Capitalism: Theories of Social Development* (1991). Beyond the work of geography's Marxist theoreticians there is an immense literature on Marxism itself. Students wanting guidebooks into this literature might well start with baseline readings such as C. Wright Mills's *The Marxists* (1962) and Tom Bottomore's *A Dictionary of Marxist Thought* (1983)—primers that helped inform the current generation of Marxist geographers' initial entries.

So much for what is *not* in part 2; more important are the seven methodological concepts that are. These essays serve as a provisional guide through the often tangled rhetorics of method, philosophy, and epistemology in human geography. The tour begins gently and predictably with an essay on the map—geography's premier research tool. Professor Muehrcke's essay, like the earlier one on diffusion, is appreciative of the map's connective and integrative functions within geography. The map, need we be reminded, is geography's common coin. Whether one regards it as an end in itself—as tends to be the case with geographers in the Map frame of reference—or more nearly as a means to an end—as it tends to be for geographers in the Earth frame of reference, their end being of course the landscape and the perceptions of and the changes in it—the map is our medium of intellectual exchange. In the course of exploring the dynamic and often contested nature of mapping logics, Phillip Muehrcke joins these debates on maps as ends or means, as reality or representations, and points up the paradoxical virtues of cartographic distortion.

The essay on the twin concepts of map and mapping logic is followed first by three essays on older methods in human geography and next by three on newer ones. The older of these methods—systems and models, rational choice, and humanism—we will call modern; two of the newer ones—structuration and feminism—we call transmodern; and the third—postmodernism—speaks for itself. This taxonomy will not do for all purposes, but it serves reasonably well for capturing the historical origins of these methods and their current trajectories.

Our "modern" methods are so-called because they have their origins in the seventeenth and eighteenth centuries with the emergence of modernity ("modern history") in western Europe (Bowen 1981). More immediately, these methods were rooted in European philosophies of science, social science, and the humanities. Each of these provided geography with methods and epistemologies (ways of knowing) that were vital for the discipline's advance (Livingstone 1992). The sciences contributed the ideals of models and systems, the social sciences (particularly political economy and later economics) contributed the doctrines of utilitarianism and rational choice, and the humanities contributed the subjectivist sensibilities associated with humanism. In retrospect scholars usually regard the first two of these as part and parcel of the modernist project. This is because the proponents of science (models and systems) and social science (rational choice) subscribed to the quintessentially modern assumptions of objectivity and measurement, individualist (or atomic) rationality, predictability, and efficiency. Humanism, meanwhile, can be viewed in some lights as countermodern—even antimodern—given its associations with Romantic reactions and critiques of modernist notions such as rationalism and reductive individualism (Ley and Samuels 1978).

The mainstream modernist project has been a durable one, having weathered the dissenting voices of humanists and Marxists and maintained its viability down to the present day. As these critiques suggest, though, the modernist project has rubbed many the wrong way. The hubris of modernist declarations of universal laws, of a human nature that is inherently self-interested, and of a clockworklike view of the world has fostered a great deal of unease, a fair amount of dissatisfaction, and an occasional rebellion (Billinge, Gregory, and Martin 1984). In geography and the social sciences these disaffections appeared in the 1970s, deepened in the 1980s, and have become pervasive in the 1990s. Along the way social scientists experimented with a variety of alternatives to modernism's "foundational" methods and epistemologies. These experiments ran the gamut: some—the postmodern—resulted in a clean break with modernism; others—the transmodern—took a more equivocal stance.

Of these experiments, perhaps the least radical—and therefore the most transmodern—was the structurationist method advanced by Anthony Giddens (1976; 1984; Bryant and Jary 1991). The harsher indictments of structuration as a salvaging operation for the modernist project contain perhaps some small grain of truth. Giddens was, after all, searching for a rapprochement between the social sciences (particularly logical positivism and Marxism) and the humanities (particularly history), between the former's interest in abstract macroscale structures and the latter's interest in concrete microscale human actions (agency). That he found his point of mediation in the betweenness of the mesoscale locale is neither surprising nor without significance for geography. In doing so, Giddens's social theory reinforced human geography's concurrent renewal of interest in place and locality as the via media of social change. For many others, however, Giddens's rescue of the modernist project came too late. This was particularly true among female social scientists who lamented modernism's studied neglect of gender in the past and present. Feminism was their response, voiced, albeit, in tones that were more or less radical. Moderates left open the possibilities of an accommodation with modernism; radicals did not. Moderate feminists thus regarded feminism as a corrective for modernism's most parochial perspective. Radical feminists, by contrast, regarded feminism as a rejection of ideas (modernist) that were irretrievably implicated in an exploitive patriarchal society (see Domosh's chapter on Feminism in this volume). Given this range in opinion on feminist methodology and some uncertainty as to which of these will prevail, the label *transmodern* seems not entirely inapt.

Whatever the outcome of this debate, feminist thought has already had a profound impact on research in human geography. It has contributed to reconceptualizations of substantive concepts such as *nature* and *culture* and methodological concepts such as *rational economic "man."* It has likewise heightened geographical sensibilities to multiple voices, multiple stories, and their gendered tones and constructions. It has also, on occasion, broached the prescriptive possibilities of some stark alternatives to modernist ontologies and epistemologies (Rose 1993).

These alternatives to modernist science, social science, and even humanism lead in a direct, if ironic, path from the anxious world of the transmodern to the secure world of the postmodern (Harvey 1989; Soja 1989). Paradoxically, secure seems the right word for a methodological mode that interrogates as it resists interrogation. From this vantage point postmodernists have set about deconstructing modernist verities and the assumptions upon which they rest. In attacking the foundations of modernist scholarship, postmodernist critiques are almost invariably subversive. They expose the inadequacy of the rhetorical devices that have pinned modernity together. These critiques, in other words, put their accent squarely on the text and its meanings. Texts are to be understood as both pretext and subtext: as the pretexts of the ideological interests that created them and as subtexts of ideological hegemony writ in symbols and signs, in tropes such as metaphors and synecdochies (see Duncan's chapter on Postmodernism in this volume). In this fashion, the text naturalizes as it softens the harsh edges of ideology and hegemonic control; but, for the postmodernist, texts are not texts in the narrow sense. Their messages, in not so many words, are inscribed in the geographical landscapes of the mind and made manifest on the earth's surface (Duncan 1990). It would appear that not a few human geographers are hastening to their deconstruction in these radical projects of reconstruction (Dear 1988).

Deep Structures: A Coda

If by chance the postmodernists are right, a volume focusing on human geography's key concepts would seem as apt as it is timely. Assuredly, concepts are important elements in any text, and, just as assuredly, they do sometimes serve partisan ends, but to stop there would be to miss the larger point. What distinguishes these "temporary verbalizations" is their enduring temporality. Concepts endure because of their capacity for change, for escaping from the strictures of any particular intellectual system or ideological position. This remarkable capacity we have attributed to the dynamic ambiguity of key concepts—the secret of which lies in the extraordinary fecundity (and thus the adaptability) of conceptual connotations.

Proof of these observations is evident, in the first instance, from the persistence of modernist concepts into this age of countermodernisms. This persistence attests to the elasticity of these concepts, to their capacity for radical amendment in the face of withering critique. The strategies of amendation are imaginative indeed; these include, among others, relaxing assumptions, modifying definitions, attaching conditionals, invoking connotations hitherto just out of focus, and so on. However, if these strategies resemble the way that normal science has dealt with evidential anomalies, the resemblances are superficial. Normal science is, as Thomas Kuhn (1962) pointed out, susceptible to revolutionary processes—to what he calls paradigmatic shifts. Concepts, by contrast, are more nearly susceptible to inertial continuity—to what might be called dynamic stasis—or in Bourdieu's (Bourdieu and Wacquant 1992) terms, *habitus*. It is by peeling away new and ever-variant connotations that concepts enable the germs of an idea to endure.

Proof of conceptual endurance comes, in the second instance, from a more ancient genealogy—from the fact that the history of human geography's key concepts really begins long before modernism. We know that Aristotle thought deeply about space and time; that Herodotus did the same for nature and culture, and that the classical Greeks provided us with the conceptual stem of *ecology* (Glacken 1967). In other words, in the dynamic and ambiguous world of concepts, inertia is the driving force of history. The inertial dynamics of concepts, particularly key concepts, confer a peculiar and seldom-noted advantage for scholarly inquiry. These languorous dynamics afford scholars ample time (and thus repeated opportunities) for cross-investments among concepts. These investments lead, eventually and in turn, to conceptual enchainments that constitute our frames of reference (or, if you prefer, schools of thought). Human geography, as noted earlier, has two of these: the first enchains the concepts of space, time, region, place, and boundary to form the Map frame of reference; the second enchains nature, culture, ecology, and landscape to form the Earth frame of reference.

Human geography's next step, however obvious it may be, is hardly inexorable. The investiture of human geography's two principal perspectives will not be an easy task. For some, indeed, it seems like a fool's errand—and not without reason, given the converse scholarly predispositions embedded in these two points of view; yet conceding the truth of these differences need not result in a capitulation to them. To be sure, the divergence in the inclinations of human geography's dual perspectives are formidable, whether one considers means/ends, analysis/interpretation, or scope of inquiry. Students should know (if only for their own safety) and appreciate these differences, namely, that the regional/spatial (Map) perspective is inclined toward the map as an end in itself, toward statistical (and often geometrical) cartographies, and toward distributional processes often several times removed from the earth itself; and that the ecological (Earth) perspective is inclined toward the earth's surface (landscape) as the end in view (maps are means to that end), toward interpretations (often historical, though occasionally behavioral) of the nexus between nature and culture, and toward processes that are more or less anchored on the ground. Given these divergent inclinations within human geography, enchainment would seem unlikely at best and improbable at worst, but it is here that concepts exercise their peculiar advantage. Concepts have the trump of time on their side; speaking metaphorically of course, concepts merely have to await the kinds of cross-investments that are sufficient for the enchainment of human geography's ecological (Earth) and locational (Map) perspectives. The essays in this volume suggest in more than a few places that the moment of investiture may be at hand. Alas, if our prophecy fails, if this Map/Earth synthesis should not come to pass this time around, human geography's key concepts will just continue to hang around until it does. The French have a saying that fits especially well: the more things change, the more things stay the same. Concepts are like that; they are, in the context of human geography, the deepest of our deep structures.

References

Bacon, R. S. 1979. Building a curriculum in introductory human geography through core concepts. *Journal of Geography* 78: 152–56.

Bacon, R. S., and J. E. Green. 1981. Core concepts in introductory physical geography. *Journal of Geography* 80: 104–8.

Billinge, M., D. Gregory, and R. Martin, eds. 1984. *Recollections of a revolution: Geography as spatial science*. London: Macmillan.

Bottomore, T., ed. 1983. *A dictionary of Marxist thought*. Cambridge, Mass.: Harvard University Press.

Bourdieu, P., and L. J. D. Wacquant. 1992. *An invitation to reflexive sociology*. Chicago: University of Chicago Press.

Bowen, M. 1981. *Empiricism and geographical thought: From Francis Bacon to Alexander von Humboldt*. Cambridge: Cambridge University Press.

Brown, L. 1981. *Innovation diffusion: A new perspective*. London: Methuen.

Bryant, C. G. A., and D. Jary, eds. 1991. *Giddens' theory of structuration: A critical appreciation*. London: Routledge.

Dear, M. 1988. The postmodern challenge: Reconstructing human geography. *Transactions of the Institute of British Geographers* N. S. 13: 262–74.

Duncan, J. 1990. *The city as text: The politics of landscape interpretation in the Kandyan Kingdom*. Cambridge: Cambridge University Press.

Giddens, A. 1976. *New rules of sociological method: A positive critique of interpretative sociology.* London: Hutchinson.

———. 1979. *Central problems in social theory.* London: Macmillan.

———. 1984. *The constitution of society: Outline of the theory of structuration.* Cambridge: Polity Press.

Glacken, C. J. 1967. *Traces on the Rhodian shore.* Berkeley: University of California Press.

Gregory, D. 1978. *Ideology, science, and human geography.* New York: St. Martin's Press.

———. 1994. *Geographical imaginations.* Cambridge, Mass.: Basil Blackwell.

Hägerstrand, T. 1967. *Innovation diffusion as a spatial process.* Chicago: University of Chicago Press.

Harvey, D. 1982. *The limits to capital.* Oxford: Basil Blackwell.

———. 1989. *The condition of postmodernity.* Oxford: Basil Blackwell.

Hugill, P., and D. Dickson, eds. 1988. *The transfer and transformation of ideas and material culture.* College Station: Texas A&M University Press.

Johnston, R. J. 1986. *Philosophy and human geography.* London: Edward Arnold.

———. 1991. *Geography and geographers: Anglo-American geography since 1945.* New York: Edward Arnold.

Kuhn, T. S. 1962. *The structure of scientific revolutions.* Chicago: University of Chicago Press.

Ley, D., and M. Samuels, eds. 1978. *Humanistic geography: Prospects and problems.* Chicago: Maaroufa Press.

Livingstone, D. 1992. *The geographical tradition: Episodes in the history of a contested* enterprise. Oxford: Basil Blackwell.

Mayr, E. 1982. *The growth of biological thought.* Cambridge, Mass.: Belknap Press.

Mills, C. W. 1962. *The Marxists.* New York: Dell Publishing.

Morrill, R., G. L. Gaile, and I. G. Thrall. 1988. *Spatial diffusion.* Scientific Geography Series, Vol. 10. Newbury Park, Calif.: Sage.

Pattison, W. D. 1964. The four traditions of geography. *Journal of Geography* 63: 211–16.

Peet, R. 1991. *Global capitalism: Theories of social development.* London: Routledge.

Rose, G. 1993. *Feminism and geography: The limits of geographical knowledge.* Minneapolis: University of Minnesota Press.

Sack, R .D. 1978. *Conceptions of space in social thought.* Minneapolis: University of Minnesota Press.

Sauer, C. O. 1952. *Agricultural origins and dispersals.* New York: American Geographical Society.

Smith, N. 1984. *Uneven development: Nature, capital, and the production of space.* Oxford: Basil Blackwell.

Soja, E. W. 1989. *Postmodern geographies: The reassertion of space in critical social theory.* New York: Verso.

Thorn, C. E., and M. R. Welford. 1994. The equilibrium concept in geomorphology. *Annals of the Association of American Geographers* 84: 666–96.

Unwin, T. 1992. *The place of geography.* London: Longman Scientific & Technical.

Part One

Substance

1

On Space and Spatial Practice in Contemporary Geography

Michael R. Curry

When first confronted with the literature on the nature of space, the new student finds a bewildering set of apparent alternatives. There is real space and perceived space, there is phenomenal space and behavioral space, there is ideal space and material space. Within the confines of this group of broader and contrasting conceptions, there appear to be another set of related contrasts, of place, region, site, location, locale, and situation; hence, we might have a view of the nature of the region within a material, an ideal, or a phenomenal view of space. Complicating the matter further, some students of space have suggested that we need in addition to attend to the language used in discussing space. Is it seen as a container or a network or a grid? The language used, these students assert, reveals deeper commitments to one of the views listed above. Finally, making matters even more complex is the fact that many of those advancing theories today about the nature of space maintain that they are the first to have done so and that previous works either did not exist or were simpleminded excursions in reportage. The matter already seemed difficult, but it now appears worse; we cannot even be sure where the landmarks are.[1]

In several ways, then, the student of the concept of space in geography finds a difficult and confusing situation. We can chalk this confusion up in part to disciplinary politics — one group's dismissal of another may just be a matter of its wish to assert its dominance; but I suggest that there is a second reason for the confusion. Many have not asked, and more find it difficult to answer, a very basic question: Where in the thinking and practicing of geography *might* space be an issue? Instead, they have tended to imagine that the concept of space is important when it comes to the construction of theories and nowhere else.

This view, in turn, has come to be incorporated into the history of the discipline, so that it has become common to imagine that one can understand the ways in which the concept of space has been used in the discipline simply by looking at the theories that geographers have advanced about the nature of space. True, in the last few years some have begun to argue that we need to look beyond explicit theorizations and to the assumptions about space implicit elsewhere within empirical works. This, however, is less of a change than it might first appear, because it still assumes that the place of space in geography is in theory. This, in turn, suggests that before embarking on a research project the geographer needs to make a series of fundamental decisions about which conceptions to adopt.

This appears to leave the geographer with an insurmountable task. How do we choose which of these conceptions and approaches to adopt? How do we argue in favor of this or that conception? How do we do so without implicitly appealing to some set of unexamined spatial notions? Indeed, this way of thinking about the place of space within geography, and within science more generally, appears to leave us quite at sea.

A better approach to understanding the place of space in geography is surely needed, and I suggest that a better approach will be one that attends to the ways in which spatial notions are imbricated in the practices in which geographers engage. In fact, when we recast the matter in this way, the number of options diminishes dramatically; it turns out to be possible to understand the practice of geography as operating within only four families of spatial notions. It turns out, moreover, that these are long-lived notions; the oldest were codified some two thousand years ago; we can see the newest in a recognizable form as far back as two hundred years ago.

I begin by characterizing the ways in which, over the last two thousand years, these alternative conceptions of space have developed within Western thought. Then I turn to the works of geographers, describing the main schools of thought within geography today and characterizing them in terms of the categories they usually use to describe themselves. Finally, I shall show that these schools of thought can better be seen as the embodiments of the spatial conceptions that I earlier identified. Here, though, I suggest that the usual view—that over the course of that period we have seen the adoption of one notion of space and then its rejection and replacement by another—is quite wrong. Rather, I show that we find new conceptions of space developing alongside old ones, and even within the same works. If the old ones lose some theoretical attraction, cease being explicitly appealed to, and are applied within a more narrowly confined set of circumstances, they nonetheless remain important.

On Conceptions of Space

In Western thought there have been really only four main notions of space. Each has gained wide popularity, but each has at the same time been formally codified by a scientist or philosopher. I refer to these notions in terms of the formal codifications, but it is important to see that each has had an existence apart from the work of individual scientists or philosophers. The first, codified by Aristotle, is static, hierarchical, and concrete. It gives greatest attention to a concept of place. The second, which we usually associate with Newton, imagines space as a kind of absolute grid, within which objects are located and events occur. The third, found in Leibniz's work, adopts the scientific outlook of Newton but argues that we need, as Aristotle does, to attend to the relationships among objects and events to the extent that we come to see space as fundamentally relational and defined entirely in terms of those relationships. The last, codified by Kant, turns the tables: where Aristotle and Newton had seen discussions of space as essentially about the world, he argued that we need to see space as a form imposed on the world by humans.

Each of these constitutes a powerful image of space, but, of the three, the Newtonian is the one both most familiar and most often imagined to be accurate and to govern our activities and thoughts. Most people, that is, imagine that after all is said and done they live in a Newtonian world. However, I deny that this is true. In fact, I argue that of the three, the Aristotelian is by far the most important conception of space in everyday life and in the practice of geography. The Leibnizian conception, moreover, while little noticed, is fundamental to thinking within geography and the social sciences. The Newtonian, I grant, is also of fundamental importance, but largely because it is such a powerful *image* and an image that is supported in so many ways. The Kantian, despite its role in cultural studies and its popularity today in the form of the neo-Kantian view that all knowledge is somehow relative to the position of the speaker, exists only against the looming presence of a Newtonian absolutism.

On Aristotle and the Natural Place

When we think of the influence of Greek thinkers on geography, we normally think first of two people—Eratosthenes and Strabo.[2] Eratosthenes (c.273–c.192 BC) is sometimes characterized as the "father of geography," in part because he was the first person to use the term and in part because of his famous attempt to measure the circumference of the earth and thereby take a mathematical and, hence, scientific view of it. George Sarton, for example, has called him — on the basis of this — "one of the greatest geographers of all ages" (Sarton 1959: 102). Strabo (64 BC–AD 20) is widely remembered as the person whose monumental work summarized for the future the geographical knowledge of the time. Even if both Eratosthenes and Strabo were important, however, it is difficult, really, to see their works as essential to, or even connected with, the current practice of geography. Indeed, characterizations like that of Lukermann (1961), to the extent that they show Strabo as developing a view of geography that involved a rich understanding of the interrelatedness of geography, chorography, and topography, demonstrate the extent to which modern-day geographers have failed to appreciate what is important in the work of their predecessors. Would contemporary geography be any different if they had never existed? It is hard to imagine that it would.

By contrast, the views expressed in and first codified by Aristotle (384–322 BC) remain of overwhelming importance today.[3] It would be easy here to misunderstand me. I don't mean to suggest that he was a person of such genius that he invented a philosophical and scientific system that has survived simply through the force of that genius. Rather, I suggest that he was the first writer to notice and elucidate something about the Western way of inhabiting and relating to space. His view has persisted for two reasons: one is that what he noticed was then so important, and the second is that his codification of it — because it was so popular — became deeply ingrained in discourse not only about space and place, but also about the world more generally. Long after his lifetime Aristotle's conception shaped Western discourse about space. When it comes to matters of space, we speak Aristotelian.

Aristotle's physics is based on the belief that what needs to be explained is change, particularly motion (change in location). He assumed that there needed to be a reason or cause for any motion, that motion did not simply occur; but there are really two sorts of motion. On the one hand, there is the motion of the planets and stars, and that motion by all accounts was circular and eternal (in his time and given the instruments available, there was no evidence of changes in such motions). On the other hand, there was the sort of change that we see on the earth, as when I throw a rock in the air and it falls to earth. To Aristotle and many of his contemporaries it seemed as though we actually needed two very different sets of explanations for those two apparently different sets of phenomena. In the celestial realm it appeared as though it was circular motion that needed explanation; in the terrestrial it was linear.

The explanation for the terrestrial is the more important here. It drew on the belief that the world was composed of four substances: earth, water, air, and fire. It did not escape Aristotle's notice that the earth appeared by and large to be composed of earth, that the oceans lay on the earth and were composed of water, that next there was the air, and finally fire. In fact, when left unfettered, earth appeared naturally to fall to earth, water fell to water, air rose to air, and fire continued upward. This change in location, he believed, was what characterized the terrestrial sphere, where what we see is constant degeneration and regeneration. It is here that the notion of place becomes important, because for Aristotle things tend naturally to move toward their own places; indeed, this is the very nature of natural motion.

By contrast, when an object is moved away from its natural place, as when a rock is thrown into the air, what we see is not natural but "violent" motion. When that motion ceases, when its motive force is removed, the rock tends to return to its own natural location. This natural motion tends toward the natural place of things, that is, to their natural sphere. Because earth is the heaviest of the elements, things made of earth tend toward the center of the universe, which, in Aristotle's view, is the center of the earth. For Aristotle objects made of earth fall to the center because it is the center, not because they somehow are attracted by a gravity-like force to the mass already there; indeed, in Aristotle's conception of the world, if the earth were located somewhere else, objects would still fall toward the natural center.

There is a final feature of his physics that is of importance here. His work is overwhelmingly qualitative in thrust. Although Aristotle believed that there is a relationship between the weight of something and the way in which it falls, so that heavier objects fall faster than light ones, there are only a few places—his discussion of the circumference of the earth is a notable one—where he attempts to quantify phenomena. It might be thought that his physics, because it was a qualitative science based on the belief in the natural place of things, has long since been superseded, replaced by something that makes more sense. Before leaping to that conclusion, however, it is important to note that what many today take to be the commonsense view of things, that the universe is a void full of atoms and that space is a featureless grid, was well known to Aristotle. That very view had been developed in some detail by the Greek atomists and eloquently laid out, after Aristotle's time, in Lucretius's (d. 55 BC) *On the Nature of Things*. So Aristotle's failure to adopt this view was not a matter of its not having occurred to him. Rather, it was a result of his belief that such a view could not be developed in a way that saved the phenomena, that accounted for what was obvious to experience. Indeed, current historical work on the development of later alternatives to Aristotle's view suggests that, far from being attempts to develop theories that better fit the phenomena, they often were less, rather than more, successful than their predecessors. Their appeal lay elsewhere.

What does it mean to say that geographers, and people in general, live to-day in an Aristotelian world? There is, of course, the obvious answer: notwith-standing the Copernican revolution, everyday experience still tells us that the earth stands still while the sun, moon, planets, and stars move through the sky in a circular motion. Further, although we are now aware that stars come and go, the heavens appear to change little in comparison with what we see every day on the earth; for most of us the evidence of supernovas comes from the mass media and not from our own experiences. Moreover, the evidence of our senses suggests the truth of the view that water returns to water, earth to earth. Few of us can say that we have experienced the pull of gravity, but most have seen rivers, landslides, or the rise of a bubble through a body of water. Last, and perhaps most important, we live in a hierarchical world where things and people have places where they belong. We are taught early what it means to be out of place.

The Collapse of Hierarchy

Aristotle's view was enormously influential and because of its adoption by the Church remained so well through the Middle Ages.[4] In the seventeenth century it was displaced by a set of views developed by a group, including Descartes, Boyle, Galileo, Newton, and Leibniz, whose works came to estab-lish a radically different understanding of space. Many would argue that these views have totally replaced the earlier view—certainly, when we speak today of space we likely think immediately of Descartes or Newton, or possibly Leibniz—but it should be clear from what I have just said that I believe this not to be the case.

Rather, what has prevailed is a set of *images* of space, images that guide the ways in which people think about space but do not necessarily affect the ways in which they actually organize or act within space. This new image, I sug-gest, has prevailed for two somewhat different reasons. First, it fit well into a technological consciousness that emerged as early as Roman land surveying and military organization and that flourished alongside these conceptions of space (Dilke 1971). Second, and in a sense more important, it provided an im-age of clarity of thought, a vision of such power that in a wide variety of areas, in art, architecture, and politics, as well as science and engineering, it came to be seen as defining the modern age. Its power has been such that it has been able to render almost invisible the omnipresent remnants of the Aristotelian view.

As I suggested earlier, we need to distinguish here between two rather dif-ferent attempts to develop mechanical images of space, one found in Newton and Descartes, the second developed by Leibniz. Newton in the end won out, but not before standing, through an intermediary, in battle with Leibniz. Leibniz's view, though, remains important, both because it provided an alternative to what was to become the orthodox image and because geographers today appeal to it in so many ways.

These notions of space did not emerge fully formed, and, indeed, it is difficult in retrospect to say at what point they fully distinguished themselves from the Aristotelian. For example, if we look back to Euclid, we may be led to believe that we are seeing a view of space that at the very least contains the seeds of the Newtonian. Perhaps more obviously, if we look at Gothic architecture with its extraordinary interplay of lines and spaces and if we compare it to the earlier Romanesque, we may wish to say that the Romanesque is Aristotelian and that the Gothic appears to embody a view of space as a system. Most strikingly, the movement from medieval painting to painting in the Renaissance appears to be an expression of a radically different understanding of space.[5] In medieval painting, although there is clearly a system of perspective involved, the arrangement of the objects and people in space appears to us almost primitive. To the modern eye the size and location of people is especially disconcerting, just because it looks so unreal. In fact, the organization of objects was the expression of a system of order different from ours in two ways. First, social or religious importance was the basis on which the size and location of figures was established. Second, paintings often embodied narrative elements, that is, a painting told a story through the juxtaposition of elements.

After a series of false starts this traditional system received what turned out to be a fatal blow in 1413. In that year Filippo Brunelleschi (c. 1377–1446) displayed a painting based on a mathematical system that placed the eye of the viewer at a single point and through the establishment of a series of lines appeared to place the objects within the painting in such a way that they looked real. It is easy to see this vanishing point perspective in painting and Gothic architecture as embodying new and radically different conceptions of space, but if both pointed in the direction of the modern and more rational view of space, both also viewed space as something created by the juxtaposition of objects within the building or the painting. If in one sense they allowed objects to be let loose within an empty space, in another that space remained confined, to the building or painting itself. In this sense there was little progress here, and what we see is little different from the demonstrations of Euclid, which need involve no space outside of that created within the demonstration itself.

The most important impediment to the move from the Aristotelian view of space, and from isolated systems embodying internal spatial orders to a view wherein space can be seen as an empty grid, was the persistence of the belief in the principle of sufficient reason.[6] This principle, essential to medieval and later religious thought, held that in order for anything to occur, there needed to be a "sufficient reason." So, for example, an object could not move from point X to point Y unless a reason or cause existed, but the suggested abandonment of the notion of natural place seemed to leave no means for explaining why an object might be here rather than there. Because this seemed a clear violation of the principle of sufficient reason, this notion of space was rejected out of hand.

Ironically, perhaps, it was the action of the Church that helped undercut the Aristotelian tradition; indeed, in the Condemnation of 1277—a critique of the views of a set of radical Aristotelians—it was explicitly declared that God *could* create a void, and an infinite one at that. Here, again perhaps ironically, the Church aligned itself with traditional Stoic philosophy, against which Aristotle had argued for the existence of a vacuum. It was not until Descartes (1596–1650) that we begin to find enunciated a view of space that looks modern, and even here the view can be called modern only with substantial qualifications.[7]

In his *Principles of Philosophy* (1644) Descartes argues, "A space, or intrinsic place, does not differ in actuality from the body that occupies it; the difference lies simply in our ordinary ways of thinking . . ." (*Principles* 2: § 10). And "The terms *place* and *space* do not signify something different from the body that is said to be in a place; they merely mean its size, shape, and position relative to other bodies. To determine the position we have to look to some other bodies, regarded as unmoving" (*Principles* 2: § 12). So for him there can be no void, no empty space. Rather, we need to begin with the understanding that all of the characteristics of color, density, and so on that we associate with objects in space are really inessential features and that the only essential feature of objects is their extension, their length, breadth, and height. Once we remove the inessential features, we then see that what is left, extension, is just the same as space. Indeed, space cannot be seen as existing without matter and extension, so space consists simply of the relations among extended objects.

Even so, Descartes believed that space was without limit. "We see, furthermore, that this world—the totality of corporeal substance—has no limits to its extension. Wherever we imagine the boundaries to be, there is always the possibility, not merely of imagining further space indefinitely extended, but also of seeing that this imagination is true to fact—that such space actually exists" (*Principles* 2: § 21). From this it follows that where for Aristotle there had been one physics for the earth and another for the area outside of the moon, for Descartes there is only one. "We can also readily derive the result that celestial and terrestrial matter do not differ; if these were an infinity of worlds, they could not but consist of one and the same kind of matter; and thus there cannot be a plurality of worlds, but only one. . . . Thus it is one and the same matter that exists throughout the universe . . ." (*Principles* 2: § 21–22).

If this view is in some respects familiar, it is in others quite puzzling, especially in its identification of space and matter. It is also one that has more than a few shades of Aristotle, yet behind it we need to see three related features, which were to overwhelm the Aristotelian elements of that work and thereby point to a more modern view. First, in his *Geometry* Descartes developed the connection between algebra and geometry, making possible a move beyond the traditional picture of mathematics. Second, he presented a view wherein mathematics is the model of certainty and, indeed, of all knowledge. Aristotle's physics had been purely qualitative, and in the Middle Ages the Church had actually proscribed the application of mathematics to science; now mathematics became not merely a tool for science, but the very model of science. Finally, Descartes developed a view wherein knowledge developed as a result of "mental vision." Here, echoing Brunelleschi's system of linear perspective, he laid out a way of thinking about the act of acquiring knowledge that made it possible to see the knower as standing outside of any possible situation and viewing it from that detached position.

Newton and Absolute Space

The implications of these views were worked out by Newton (1642–1727) in his *Fundamental Principles of Natural Philosophy* (1686). In the famous "Scholium to the Definitions," he laid them out in the starkest and most straightforward way.

> Absolute space, in its own nature, without relation to anything external, remains always similar and immovable. Relative space is some movable dimension or measure of the absolute spaces. . . . Absolute and relative space are the same figure and magnitude, but they do not always remain numerically the same. For if the earth, for instance, moves, a space of our air, which relatively and in respect of the earth remains always the same, will at one time be one part of the absolute space into which the air passes; at another time it will be another part of the same, and so, absolutely understood, it will be continually changed. (Scholium: § 2)

One consequence is that we need to think of motion in a very different way.

> Absolute motion is the translation of a body from one absolute place into another, and relative motion the translation from one relative place into another. Thus in a ship under sail the relative place of a body is that part of the ship which the body

possesses. . . . Wherefore, if the earth is really at rest, the body, which relatively rests in the ship, will really and absolutely move with the same velocity which the ship has on earth. (Scholium: § 4)

Why do people fail to see that space is absolute?

[B]ecause the parts of space cannot be seen or distinguished from one another by our senses, therefore in their stead we use sensible measures of them. . . . And so, instead of absolute places and motions, we use relative ones, . . . but in philosophical disquisitions, we ought to abstract from our senses and consider things themselves, distinct from what are only sensible measures of them. (Scholium: § 4)

If today we see Newton's work as strictly secular, we need to recall that it in fact has substantial religious overtones. In his "General Scholium" he argued that God "is eternal and infinite, omnipotent and omniscient. . . . He endures forever and is everywhere present. He is omnipresent not *virtually* only but also *substantially*. . . . In him are all things contained and moved, yet neither affects the other; God suffers nothing from the motion of bodies, bodies find no resistance from the omnipresence of God." Yet those overtones have long since faded away, and what has remained is a view of a universe of matter, floating in a space that is infinite, absolute, and eternal. This is an image of extraordinary power. It is an image that seems strikingly clear, certainly subject to quantification, and surely consistent with the requirements of science. Notwithstanding the twentieth century's flirtations, via the popularizations of Einstein's work on space and time, with alternatives, it remains a basic feature of common sense.

Leibniz and Relational Space

But not everyone has been seduced by its power. Indeed, Newton's contemporary, Leibniz (1646–1716), lashed out, arguing that Newton's view of space was literally nonsensical. In a series of letters with Newton's proxy, Samuel Clarke (Alexander 1956), he developed this argument. In a famous passage he noted how people come to believe in space through the concept of motion.

They consider that many things exist at once and they observe in them a certain order of co-existence, according to which the relation of one thing to another is more or less simple. . . . When it happens that one of those co-existent things changes its relation to a multitude of others, which do not change their relation among themselves . . . we then say, it is come into the place of the former; and this change we call a motion in that body. (Leibniz, fifth paper: § 47)

The way in which we understand motion leads to the belief in the existence of absolute space. "And supposing, or feigning, that among those co-existents, there is a sufficient number of them, which have undergone no change; then we may say, that those which have such a relation to those fixed existents, as others had to them before, have now the *same place* which those others had. And that which comprehends all those places, is called *space*" (Leibniz, fifth paper: § 47).

So the belief in the existence of absolute space arises simply by virtue of our noticing that among the objects in the world some appear to move, while some appear not to. To go along with Newton, however, and move from this perception to the conclusion there is something called "absolute space" is to move from the realm of science to that of metaphysics.[8] In order to stay within the bounds of science, he argued, we need to understand that space is nothing more than "something merely relative, as time is; that I hold it to be an order of coexistences, as time is an order of successions" (Leibniz, third paper: § 4). Space, that is—and as according to Descartes—is purely relational; but in contrast to Descartes, Leibniz does not believe that space and matter are identical: space is relational but consists just in those relations and nothing else.

Kant and the Second Copernican Revolution

The dispute between Newton (or his proxy, Clarke) and Leibniz took place between 1715 and 1717, and they seemed to have laid out for the next sixty-five years the main alternatives in discussions about the nature of space. Then, in 1781 Immanuel Kant (1724–1804) published the *Critique of Pure Reason*, a work that fundamentally recast debates about the nature of space.[9] His view is the final of the four alternatives widely subscribed to today.

Kant described himself as having created a "Copernican revolution" in philosophy. Where Copernicus had moved the earth from the center of the universe and replaced it with the sun, Kant had moved the locus of debate about knowledge from the known to the knower. In doing so he recast the question about the nature of space from one about the nature of the world to one about the nature of human knowledge.

His work is notoriously difficult, but, to simplify his argument greatly, he stated that previous accounts of the nature of knowledge—and here he referred to scientific knowledge—could not make sense of that knowledge. In particular, we know that there are certain branches of knowledge, such as mathematics, where we can have certain knowledge, but we never really have a perception of certainty, we never actually see or experience it in the world. From where, then, does it come? His Copernican revolution claimed that the certainty comes from within, that it is built into the way in which we know the world; so, for example, we never actually perceive causes in the world, but we naturally impute causality to the relationships among objects.

If this is true of the imputation of conceptual relationships like causality, it is also true more basically of space and time. In fact, we never actually perceive either. Rather, we perceive a series of instants, or we perceive objects close to or far from one another or objects that seem to occupy volume. He argues in the case of space, however, that if we did not already have built into us in some way the notion of space, the possibility of ordering things in spatial terms, we would be unable to say, "This is next to this." As he put it:

> Space is not an empirical concept which has been derived from outer experiences. For in order that certain sensations be referred to something outside me (that is, to something in another region of space from that in which I find myself), and similarly in order that I may be able to represent them as outside and alongside one another, and accordingly as not only different but in different places, the representation of space must be presupposed. (*Critique of Pure Reason*: A23/B38)

This means that the whole way of discussing space that we find in Aristotle, Newton, and Leibniz needs to be abandoned. It is not only wrong, but also incoherent, because if space is a condition of our understanding the outside world, we can never ask, "What is the world really like spatially?" All of our perceptions of the world are already spatial; we will never be able to get beyond our own perceptions.[10]

Kant himself believed strongly in the truth of Euclid's account of geometry and Newton's account of the physical world—indeed, he believed both to be final and definitive—and yet, by recasting the question of the nature of knowledge in this way he opened the door for a critique of Newton and Euclid and, indeed, for the development in the nineteenth and twentieth centuries of more complex understandings of the nature of space. In fact, it would not be going too far to say that all studies of culture today are a footnote to Kant. Exactly how this happened is not relevant here, but what is is this: during those two centuries, Euclidean geometry, clock time, and Newtonian physics each came to be seen as only one of several possible alternatives. The development of non-Euclidean geometry, for example, suggested that we may perceive space in radically variable ways.

The undercutting of the belief in the universality of traditional absolutist views of space was augmented both by the increasing awareness of alternative cultures and by the romantic reaction in the West to the increasing force of industrialism and urbanism. In this way, by the turn of the twentieth century and by the time that geography began to be constituted as a modern discipline, a set of views that would allow for the belief in real differences in the human occupation of the world and organization of space was solidly in place—but so too were the Newtonian view of space as absolute and the Leibnizian view of space as relational.

Geography in the Twentieth Century

When we look merely at the explicit claims that contemporary geographers make, it is possible to speak—generalizing only a little too rashly—of their understanding of the nature of space and place as having moved within two different, and even separate, streams, streams that diverged perhaps one hundred years ago. For those in the first stream, *place* is a concept about which it is not possible to say anything interesting. Rather, *space* is at the center of attention, and *location* is the concept of preference, where location is seen as a feature of objects or events in *space*. On this view there is something called space, which is typically seen as both real and absolute: a thing's location is simply where it exists within that space. This view has often been cast in terms of a distinction between the characteristics of a site, what a place is like, and its situation, its location in relation to other places or in terms of some abstract grid.

This view has typically been taken to be a commonsensical one, deriving from the Cartesian and Newtonian turns in Western thought. As such it has formed the uncontested groundwork of much thinking in this century about the nature of space and related concepts such as region and place. For example, the first great theoretical tome in modern geography, Hartshorne's 1939 *The Nature of Geography* (see also Hartshorne 1958), argued that the task of geographers was to study the differentiation of phenomena on the surface of the earth. Although Hartshorne devoted much attention to the nature of regions, he took space itself to be unproblematic.

Beginning in the early 1950s, a number of attacks were launched at Hartshorne. His attackers proposed what they took to be a dramatically different view of the discipline, one that would see it as fundamentally the science of space. In doing so they took on the mantle of what is usually termed positivism. Notable among these scholars were Schaefer (1953), Stewart and Warntz (1958), Ullman (1954), Bunge (1973/1962), and the rediscovered Christaller (1966/1933).

There were in several respects important disagreements between Hartshorne and these authors; they argued that geography ought to join the ranks of the sciences, while he demurred. With respect to space, too, there was a certain disagreement: Hartshorne saw space as basically a neutral container, while his opponents gave it greater explanatory efficacy. Notwithstanding this disagreement, though, all of these authors shared the view that space itself is absolute, rigid, and unproblematic.

Alongside this tradition developed a second stream, one that embodied a very different view of the issues of space and place. Developed in France at the turn of the century and then separately in the United States beginning in the 1920s and 1930s, this tradition focused on the ways in which people create cultural areas (Vidal de la Blache 1928/1911; Sauer 1963/1925; Wright 1947, 1966; Brown 1948). Each of these authors argued that different combinations of beliefs and practices lead human groups to occupy and manipulate the earth in different ways. From a set of raw materials with one structure is created a new structure, one in which locations acquire meaning as places and in which human activity is carried on in terms of systems of space.

Although they were interested in the development of places and regions, these authors did not really consider the nature of space itself. Still, because they saw as fundamental to their task the understanding of the human construction of places, their work embodied an attitude toward the nature of both space and places. Many, it should be granted, undoubtedly assumed with the positivists that behind the human constructions of places was a "real," objective space. Nonetheless—and this is the crucial point—they rejected the notion that any absolute or nonhuman space had causal efficacy and hence was worth troubling with.

Through this empirical (albeit in some ways theoretically uninformed) work, Vidal, Sauer, Brown, and Wright laid the groundwork for what was characterized in the early 1970s as a humanistic break with positivist orthodoxy. The earliest figures in this break were Buttimer (1971), Relph (1976), and Tuan (1974a, 1974b, 1977), all of whose works in the initial stages referred in some ways to phenomenology (although it seems fair to say that none took it very seriously). Here Relph argued that there once had been a world of "real" places and that now, under the onslaught of modernism, that world was disappearing and being replaced by one in which people no longer are attached to places. Buttimer followed in this tradition at least to the extent that she focused on human experience. By contrast, here and in later works (1982) Tuan adopted a more synoptic view, one that took as its premise the need to specify the differences among conceptions of space and place and that involved the laying out (nongeographers would say mapping) of the range and types of places that humans construct and associating those places (or those conceptions of space) with various kinds of bases.

None of these authors could be seen today as taking seriously the assertion that they were working within a strictly phenomenological tradition, but there have remained, from time to time, attempts to develop such a tradition in geography. David Seamon (Seamon and Mugerauer 1989) and John Pickles

(1985) have fought this out, with Seamon adopting a soft, furry phenomenology and Pickles taking on the mantle of Husserl's Cartesian, rationalistic phenomenology. Here, occasionally, Bachelard's (1969/1958) phenomenology is mentioned, but these are inevitably just mentions.

As the geography of places developed in the 1970s, positivist geographers were hard at work continuing their attempts to develop a spatial science and applying both mathematical models and statistical devices to the project (see, for example, Gatrell 1983 and Juillard 1972). Elsewhere within the discipline, however, there were changes on two fronts, both related to the issue of space. On one front a group of geographers began to work from a neo-Kantian premise (this was actually news, since most geographers could be seen as pre-Kantian), that people construct their own perceptual worlds. Turning to the issue of space, they argued that people carry "mental maps" of the world around in their heads and that these maps vary from place to place and time to time. There was a real cottage industry of these studies, but most notable were works by Gould (Gould and White 1974) and Downs (1970; Downs and Stea 1973).

Although we might want to see this work as operating within the tradition of cultural anthropology, all of it came directly out of the positivist tradition in psychology. In fact, in an important sense those who worked on mental maps can be seen as having been subcontractors, attempting to replace the inadequate "real" metric space developed by the original large-scale modelers with a more adequate "perceived" space. Notwithstanding the connection to the well-known cartoon version of "The New Yorker's View of the World," this work remained strongly within a positivist and absolutist project, one that argues that behind these mental maps is a real and objective space, accessible to those who have the right tools—reason and the scientific method. This work is still seen, but its initial proponents quickly found the metaphor exhausted and moved on.

The second movement was the attempt to bring a critical, Marxist approach to the discipline. Although for a time there was general use of the term "space economy," (see Harvey 1972 and many others), there was little in this literature in the way of conceptualization of the nature of space. By and large, this work was content to attach a political (and, to a degree, methodological) point of view to standard positivist approaches to space. Typically, arguments in favor of the consideration of places and regions were regarded as fundamentally conservative diversions from the project of developing a more general understanding of the larger space economy.

In the 1980s and early 1990s this simple dichotomy was complicated by several developments with respect to the issues of space and place. These developments have from time to time made it appear that those working within one stream have jumped ship and moved to the other. First, a group sometimes referred to as the new cultural geographers has taken the culturalist/humanist/phenomenological orthodoxy, that both space and place are human constructions (and are conceptually separate), and moved it in a series of directions, both contemporary and historical. Most notable among this group are Cosgrove, Daniels, the Duncans, and Ley (see their contributions in Barnes and Duncan 1992; Duncan and Agnew 1990; and Cosgrove and Daniels 1988; and see below). It is probably fair to say that by now this is a well-developed subdiscipline. Notwithstanding its reliance on the tradition of the study of places within geography, most of its advocates have looked outside the field rather than to their predecessors within the field for intellectual sustenance.

Second, cracks have begun to develop in the Marxist refusal to appeal to other than absolutist views of space. One sign of this is the development of the *locality* movement (see, for example, Cooke 1987a, 1987b; Massey 1985; Lovering 1989; Cox and Mair 1989; and Duncan and Savage 1989), which has developed new and politically progressive regional studies. The localities debate has arisen, in part, as a result of the suggestion that in a global and post-Fordist era we really can make sense of some features of economies at a local level (and that localities in fact retain their importance, rather than becoming less so, or placeless). Still, from the point of view of their approach to space the advocates of localities studies appear not to have broken with their Marxist and positivist predecessors; the locality exists within what is assumed to be an absolute space. Further, and as in the case of the new cultural geography, the localities debate has involved an attempt to reinvent a concept, here the *region*, without reference to its predecessors.

Third, work in geography and gender has begun to become more fully institutionalized (as evidence a new journal on gender and place). Here it is hard to make generalizations about the conceptions of space and place that are involved, other than to say that the work might be seen as integrating elements also found in (but not necessarily derived from) the new cultural geography and various progressive movements. Just a few of these works are Bowlby et al. (1989), Christopherson (1989), Bondi (1990), Foord and Gregson (1986), McDowell (1983; 1988), Mackenzie (1988), and Peake (1985).

Fourth, some geographers have attempted to develop various versions of postmodernism. This has often (as in Dear 1988 and Soja 1989) meant the adoption of an "anything goes" attitude toward space. There have been, of course, a stream of critics, such as Harvey's in his neopositivist *The Condition of Postmodernity* (1989) and the very different pieces by Massey (1991) and myself (1991).

Fifth, these and others have begun to take heart in the interest by nongeographers in issues of space and to argue that this interest is evidence of the coming of age of the discipline. The work of Anthony Giddens (1984) was among the first to be greeted in this way, but so too has that of Foucault (1984/1982 and even his 1986). In part, this has involved a linguistic turn in geography, with much talk of language and metaphor, along with critiques of containerism and the like. More recently, Lefebvre's (1988) *The Production of Space* has been much cited, although it is hard to know its real effects.

Sixth, some geographers have begun to argue against an "absolute" notion of space and in favor of what they term a "relational" view. Because the place tradition sees places as defined often in terms of relations of objects or activities, this move to relational space might in one sense be seen as a move toward convergence. That it is not can perhaps be understood best by considering the extent to which visual metaphors dominate images of relational space while remaining fundamentally at odds with images of place. There is, too, a second point of divergence: whatever their theoretical bent, studies of places tend to reject the desire to be synoptic, while advocates of notions of relational space are operating more often within neopositivist notions of grand theory.

Seventh, the development of computer-based geographic information systems has given a new lease on life to the otherwise moribund absolutist, scientific view of space as a Cartesian grid. Here the ability through computers to manipulate coordinate systems rapidly and easily has allowed geographers to deal with the apparent difficulty—that the world is not Cartesian—that had plagued their predecessors and it has allowed them to do so without abandoning their belief in absolute space.

Finally, there have been a number of recent works about the history of space in social thought, most notably Sack (1980) and Entrikin (1991). These works have attempted to make sense of the arguments between advocates of the study of space and of the study of place.

On Space and Spatial Practice

It might seem difficult to generalize about all of these developments. Indeed, almost all that we might feel safe in saying is that there are a wide range of approaches to space and place within geography and that there is little discussion by one group of the work of others. In fact, many of the moves toward an understanding of the nature of places and regions that have been made by groups previously dismissive of the subject have turned to authority figures outside the discipline, and this appears to make the matter even more complicated.

If we turn, however, to the ways in which conceptions of space are integrated into academic practice, matters are simpler. We find that the many groups mentioned in the previous section have much in common. There is not room here to lay out all of the similarities—and differences; rather, I shall confine myself to pointing to ways in which each of the conceptions of space that I mentioned earlier can be found.

I suggested earlier that most geographers today are Aristotelians. This may have seemed a rash assertion, just because so few today would claim to have intellectual roots extending much beyond Newton, and yet, if we look at the geography of the everyday practice of geographers, it is shot through with Aristotelian assumptions. Most important is that we can see the world in terms of objects and events, each of which having its natural place. If for Aristotle earth, air, fire, and water had a natural place, for the contemporary geographer the list is rather different; women, ethnic groups, economic activity, trees, and rocks all have their own natural places today. Indeed, to be out of place is to be a possible subject of research and to be comfortably where we belong is to be rendered invisible. For example, until very recently geographers assumed that women belonged in the home. As a result, they paid virtually no attention to them. Studies of economics and culture focused on men, and data categories were established in ways that made the activities in which women engaged difficult to see. It was only when on two fronts women became visible— by making it clear that the home was not the only place in which they might fit and by in fact taking up stronger positions outside the home—that geographers began to look more closely at the position of women in society and to notice that they had all along been engaged in important activity.

This example, it should be noted, points to an important feature of the contemporary version of Aristotelianism, that is, that to refer to something as being in its natural place is not simply to make a factual statement, it is also to make an evaluative claim. In contemporary society, to say that something is where it belongs is to say that it ought to be there. Nowhere is this more true than in the thinking of academic geographers about where they themselves belong. If those who characterize themselves as radical have in other ways criticized the academy, they have at the same time claimed—as have women and members of ethnic groups—that they belong there.

In pointing out these features of contemporary geographic practice I am not, I hasten to add, attempting to be critical of those who appeal to these Aristotelian terms. At least, I am not criticizing them insofar as they are ready to notice that is what they are doing. Quite to the contrary, it appears to me that these sorts of appeals are quite inescapable, and so, in pointing to them I am both making a claim about the sorts of things about their own lives and their own world that academics ought to notice and at the same time making a claim about the perspicacity with which Aristotle saw the world.

If we turn to the Newtonian image of space, matters are quite different. We are likely inclined to believe that his image of the world as an object located in a vast and undifferentiated space is the one that we all use, to which we all appeal. The facts, though, are quite otherwise. It may seem baffling that I say this, but if we turn back to the debate between Leibniz and Newton we can see why I do. Recall that Newton argued in favor of the independent and absolute reality of space and that Leibniz countered that the whole notion was incoherent because we could never tell where we really were. Newton's argument, like the arguments of the other absolutists (as in Kant's early work on space), was not that we have evidence that space is absolute and independent, but rather that we must believe that space is absolute and independent. Leibniz's argument is that space is relational because our only way of determining where things are appeals to relations; Newton makes a wholly different argument, that if we do not believe in absolute space we must as a consequence abandon other beliefs and that those other beliefs are not ones we are prepared to abandon.

In fact, then, Newton presents less a falsifiable theory of space than an image of space, and in geography, as elsewhere, it is as an image that space has been important. The image, in effect, provides a backdrop against which those who attempt to develop timeless and universal theories can set their work. In one sense this is a matter of the establishment of what look like grounds for believing that work can be permanent, that the researcher can come back later to what is truly the "same place." There is, however, another and perhaps more vital sense in which the Newtonian image has been important, and that is as a model for the very operation of society. Newton's work was the culmination of what E. J. Dijksterhuis (1961/1950; see also Koyré 1957) has called the "mechanization of the world picture." As such, it provided an image of the ways in which things work and thus, an image of the kinds of explanations that ought to be offered. It has been concluded that these explanations ought to see the world as composed of elements or actions that are interchangeable and that maintain their characteristics when moved to different places.

The influence of this view is obvious. In the classic works on central places, agricultural location, and industrial location the assumption was always that there was some crucial element of the explanation, often utility or buying power, that was absolutely footloose. We see the same view in other, perhaps less obvious, places. Early Marxist works, for example, denied the reality of place and nature but viewed use and exchange value as mobile elements; if their critique of capitalism was that it treated the worker as an atom in Newtonian space, it did so by appealing in its own way to that same image. Finally, contemporary works on spatial perception have tended to adopt a view that is Newtonian in another way. They have couched their analyses of the spatial perceptions of others in terms of a kind of "deviation from the real," where the real is absolute and unchanging—and where the geographer is able for the purpose of analyses to step outside of space.

If the Newtonian view of space has in various ways provided a guiding image for those engaged in geographical work, its very nature—as a view supported by argument rather than evidence—has prevented its use as anything other than an image. In fact, in their everyday work, when geographers are not being Aristotelian, they are unrelentingly Leibnizian. This may seem an odd thing to say. After all, David Harvey, for one, has recently argued that geography made a wrong turn in adopting Newton and ought now to abandon the Newtonian ship and sign on with Leibniz. Once we see the extent of the Leibnizian view, the matter will seem obvious.

If we turn back to Euclid and Brunelleschi, we likely see their work on geometry and linear perspective as presaging the development of the Newtonian view. This, though, is quite wrong. Euclid, for example, attempted to show how certain truths could be deduced from a set of axioms and postulates. In effect, he argued that we could construct the system of geometry simply from them. What is missing here? The rest of the world. In fact, Euclid's geometrical system is completely closed; it exists simply as a system. Much the same can be said of linear perspective in painting. From our point of view it looks as though the Renaissance development of the system of perspective in painting was an attempt to make painting consistent with what later came to be the absolutist, Newtonian view. In fact, though, as in Euclid, the system of a painting is quite closed; it includes only the elements of the painting, along with the viewer. Nothing else matters.

If we turn to geography and to works that look Newtonian, we find much the same thing. The most abstract models are inevitably simply that: models. They consist of elements and relations that are—and, indeed, endeavor to be—utterly self-contained. Today this is perhaps most obvious in the case of geographic information systems; although they appear to be absolutist in intent and although they certainly are in imagery, they are distinctively relational in their understanding of space. When we move beyond the model and theory, matters change very little. Descriptions of the movement of people and goods are couched in terms of locations, but the locations are never absolute; they are always, in turn, characterized in terms of yet other locations in what ultimately becomes a self-enclosed system.

Existing alongside these three notions of space is the fourth, the Kantian. As I suggested earlier, this view directs its attention in a very different way. Where the others saw the question of the nature of space as a question about the nature of the world, for the Kantian the tables are turned, and it becomes a question about the nature of the observer. If for Kant himself this changed little, and Newton was still right, for those who have followed in his footsteps it has been an easy move to the belief that different people live in worlds that are themselves spatially very different.

The Kantian turn in the understanding of space has appeared to be most clearly in evidence in the area of perception studies, in which beginning in the 1970s a group of geographers began to consider the perception of space and of hazards among various groups. Differential perceptions were, of course, central to the work in hazards (Burton and Kates 1964; Kates 1962; Saarinen 1966). In the case of hazards research, however, where the interest was in the perception by residents of flood plains, for example, of the risks of living there, the aim was always to compare the perceived risks with the real risks. To the extent that this notion of the "real" was not problematized by calling into question the objectivity of the researcher, this is not really a Kantian view at all, since it does rest on the belief that there is an identifiable real.

Much the same can be said of most of the work on spatial perception; while it appears to be concerned with space as perceived, there is almost always the underlying assumption that perceived space can be compared with the space that is really out there. There is, of course, another set of works on space and place, that done by people whose concern might best be termed *cultural*. These works (for example, Barnes and Duncan 1992; Cosgrove 1985; Entrikin 1991; Tuan 1982) have tended not to be explicitly reflexive in form but have nonetheless made it clear that the means of conceptual or other ordering of space and place that they describe ought to be seen as applying as much to the author as to the subject. If we thus leave our sights on the general conceptual form of geographical arguments, it turns out to be actually quite difficult to come up with examples of works that see all perceptions of the world as structured by the knowing subject; it is far more common to see it assumed that everyone but ourselves is seeing the world through conceptual blinkers, while we ourselves are the only ones able to see it as it really is.

At the same time, there is a sense in which it is quite common to accept the mental structuring of perceptions of the world, and this is in the matter of the organization of knowledge itself. If we turn back to the recent past, we often find discussions of the organization of science that assert that disciplines are distinguished by their subject matter, so that sociology studies societies, economics studies economies, and geography studies regions. In the last few years, though, this view has come undone, as it has become more and more clear that members of all of the disciplines appear to be studying more or less the same subject matter. In the place of the earlier view one has appeared in which disciplinary divisions are seen as matters of perspective, so that sociologists study the world from the point of view of sociological concepts, geographers through geographical concepts, and so on. To the extent that we do not assume that it is possible to construct a kind of supra-discipline that transcends all of these differences, we are being Kantian in our approach. Indeed, we might be tempted to say that here we are all Kantians, forced to be so by our libraries and publishers.

Conclusion

The concept of space in geography, then, turns out to raise a set of difficult issues. Far from being a matter about which we can adopt a position and from it spin out a coherent and inclusive set of accounts of the world, the issue of space raises problems everywhere. The geographer who wishes to adopt a view of space based on its own obvious merits finds all the ways blocked and is forced to adopt particular notions of space.

These notions are built into our society. They are built into our language and into our means of discussion. They are built into our libraries and into our legal system. They are built into the productive apparatus that we see all around us. Indeed, we are saturated in objects and words that tell us how to think about space and how to talk about it. It is this that makes the question of space so complex. It is not that we are lacking answers, but rather that we are up to our necks in answers. The difficulty is in sorting them out.

I have suggested that there are four different ways of thinking about space. It is now clear that I believe that each of us uses all four. In our everyday lives, discourse, and activity we are all Aristotelians, seeing the world as a place where things belong here and not there, where there are real and palpable hierarchies. In our reflections about space we by and large become Newtonians; we imagine that we exist somewhere within a vast and directionless space, one timeless and utterly unaffected by anything that we do. As we attempt to construct conceptual systems that will comprehend the world, we become Leibnizians, seeing the world in terms of a set of axioms and assumptions that are a world unto themselves. Finally, as we survey the world from our own disciplinary vantage point, seeing that point as one of many, we become Kantians.

If each of us at some point falls into all of these categories, we should not conclude that this must necessarily be so. For some groups, for some societies, one or the other view of space must surely be beyond the pale, an incomprehensible deviation from that which everyone knows and does. Rather, these views of space are supported by a wide range of institutions, by patterns of technological and economic activity—and by the very organization of space that they attempt to explain. If in one sense, then, we may wish to consider the various notions of space as an initial means, or prolegomenon, to the study of geography, they also constitute an important topic of study in their own right.

Notes

This research was carried out, in part, while the author was a resident fellow at the Center for the Critical Analysis of Contemporary Culture at Rutgers University. In addition, it was funded by a grant from the Academic Senate of the University of California, Los Angeles.

1. Note that my discussion here is confined to the issue of *space* and that the concept of *place* is discussed only where place has been viewed as an essential element of spatial theorizing. Those who see place as simply one end of a continuum stretching from the universal to the particular may find this a perplexing approach. Nonetheless, I would argue that the best works on the nature of place (Tuan 1977, 1982; Entrikin 1991) support my view.

2. James and Martin (1981) provide a useful chronology of ancient geography. Bunbury's (1959/1883) is dated but is in a way more useful now for what it tells us about his own era. From within the history of science Sarton's *Introduction to the History of Science* (1959) is the standard work. A more recent and very useful summary of these issues through the end of the Middle Ages is Lindberg's 1992 history. G. E. R. Lloyd's works (1970, 1973, 1979, 1987) are always interesting and provocative. Finally, two useful works more explicitly concerned with physics and astronomy are Crowe (1990) and Pederson (1993).

3. The essential works here are the *Physics* (Physica 1941) and *On the Heavens* (De caelo 1941), both available in many editions. The literature on his scientific work is quite massive; see the bibliography in Pederson (1993).

4. There is a substantial body of work on medieval conceptions of space; Edward Grant's stands out. He has published a long series of articles (1964, 1969, 1976) and books; see especially his 1981 *Much Ado About Nothing: Theories of Space and Vacuum from the Middle Ages to the Scientific Revolution*.

5. The best recent work on this development is Kemp's *The Science of Art: Optical Themes in Western Art from Brunelleschi to Seurat*. Edgerton (1975), Panofsky (1972), and White (1967) provide interesting accounts of the development of pictorial space; Sypher (1955) and Giedieon (1967) argue within the context of art and architecture for the importance of changes in spatial conceptions.

6. See especially Lovejoy (1936); for more recent discussions, all deriving from Lovejoy, see Kane (1976), Knuuttila (1981), Kuntz and Kuntz (1988), and Kuntz (1971).

7. The essential works here are the *Discourse on Method*, *Principles of Philosophy*, *Meditations*, *Optics*, and *Rules for the Direction of Mind*.

8. It is important here to note that although the arguments of Descartes, Newton, and Leibniz can be easily translated into contemporary secular and scientific terms, the work of each was in fact steeped in a concern about the relationship of these issues to religious belief. The Leibniz-Clarke correspondence, for example, begins with Leibniz noting that Newton had called space the sensorium of God; he replies that this is utterly preposterous. Similarly, Leibniz himself argues against the existence of a vacuum on the basis that God would not, and in a sense could not, have created empty space; appealing to what A. O. Lovejoy has called the principle of plentitude, he ar-

gues that God must have created everything that could have been created and that empty space was a denial of God's power. If this set of arguments now seems quaint, Leibniz does refer to a principle of sufficient reason that has been seen in a secular twentieth-century version to have general applicability. As codified in the seventeenth century this principle holds that God must have had sufficient reason for making things one way or another. The consequence, Leibniz argued, was that the idea of absolute and empty space left no reason for an object's being here rather than there, and one was thereby forced to adopt a relational view of space. A twentieth-century version of this, albeit one that has not been applied to the question of space, is the principle of the identity of indiscernibles. It holds that if we have no means of distinguishing between two objects, then there must in fact be only a single object. This view was fundamental to thinking, in the form of the verification principle, in the early twentieth-century logical positivist philosophy of science.

9. Kant had in fact written his inaugural dissertation on space. That work, entitled *On the First Ground of the Distinction of Regions in Space* (1768), has been widely seen as the expression of an earlier and abandoned view of space; scholars have generally divided his work into two periods, with the 1781 publication of the *Critique of Pure Reason* signaling a change of heart. More recent work, though, suggests that with respect to the issue of space there may in fact be more continuity than has been believed (Guyer 1987).

10. There is, of course, another way in which geographers have appealed to Kant. Drawing from his assertion that the world is first organized in terms of space and time and then in terms of concepts, they have suggested that geography and history are the "exceptional" studies of the world, in terms of space and time, and that other sciences, such as physics, operate within the subsequent conceptual realm. We often find this view in discussions that attempt to define geography conceptually. Unfortunately, these works (Hartshorne's discussions of the discipline are an example) typically miss the real significance of Kant's understanding of the nature of space, which is its relationship through neo-Kantianism to the development of the theory of culture.

References

Alexander, H. G., ed. 1956. *The Leibniz-Clarke correspondence, together with extracts from Newton's Principia and Opticks.* New York: Barnes and Noble Imports.

Aristotle. 1941. De caelo. In *The basic works of Aristotle,* ed. Richard McKeon, trans. J. L. Stocks, 398–469. New York: Random House. [Written circa 330 B.C.]

———. 1941. Physica. In *The basic works of Aristotle,* ed. Richard McKeon, trans. R. P. Hardie and R. K. Gaye, 218–397. New York: Random House. [Written 330 B.C.]

Bachelard, Gaston. 1969/1958. *The poetics of space*, trans. Maria Jolas. Boston: Beacon Press.

Barnes, Trevor J., and James S. Duncan, eds. 1992. *Writing worlds: Discourse, text, and metaphor in the representation of landscape.* London: Routledge.

Bondi, Liz. 1990. Feminism, postmodernism, and geography: Space for women? *Antipode* 22 (2): 157–65.

Bowlby, Sophie, et al. 1989. The geography of gender. In *New models in geography*, vol. 2, ed. Richard Peet and Nigel Thrift, 157–75. London: Unwin Hyman.

Brown, Ralph H. 1948. *Historical geography of the United States.* New York: Harcourt, Brace, and World.

Bunbury, E. H. 1959/1883. *A history of ancient geography*, 2 vols. New York: Dover.

Bunge, William. 1973/1962. *Theoretical geography*, 2nd rev. and enlarged ed. Lund, Sweden: C. W. K. Gleerup.

Burton, Ian, and Robert W. Kates. 1964. The perception of natural hazards in resource management. *Natural Resources Journal* 3: 412–41.

Buttimer, Anne. 1971. *Society and milieu in the French geographic tradition.* Chicago: Rand McNally.

Christaller, Walter. 1966/1933. *Central places of southern Germany*, trans. C. Baskin. Englewood Cliffs, N.J.: Prentice-Hall.

Christopherson, Susan. 1989. On being outside "the project." *Antipode* 21 (2): 83–89.

Cooke, Philip. 1987a. Individuals, localities, and postmodernism. *Environment and Planning D: Society and space* 5: 408–12.

———. 1987b. Research policy and review 19: Britain's new spatial paradigm: Technology, locality, and society in transition. *Environment and Planning A* 19: 1289–1301.

Cosgrove, Denis. 1985. *Social formation and symbolic landscape.* Totowa, N.J.: Barnes and Noble.

Cosgrove, Denis, and Stephen Daniels, eds. 1988. *The iconography of landscape: Essays on the symbolic representation, design, and use of past environments.* Cambridge: Cambridge University Press.

Cox, Kevin, and Andrew Mair. 1989. Levels of abstraction in locality studies. *Antipode* 21 (2): 121–32.

Crowe, Michael J. 1990. *Theories of the world from antiquity to the Copernican revolution.* New York: Dover.

Curry, Michael R. 1991. On the construction of post-modern worlds: Language and the strains of modernism. *Annals of the Association of American Geographers* 81: 210–28.

Dear, Michael J. 1988. The postmodern challenge: Reconstructing human geography. *Transactions of the Institute of British Geographers* N. S. 13: 262–74.

Descartes, Rene. 1971/1637. Discourse on the method. In *Descartes' philosophical writings*, ed. G. E. M. Anscombe and Peter Geach, 5–58. Indianapolis: Bobbs-Merrill.

———. 1971/1641. Meditations on first philosophy. In *Descartes' philosophical writings*, ed. G. E. M. Anscombe and Peter Geach, 59–124. Indianapolis: Bobbs-Merrill.

———. 1988/1637. Optics. In *Selected philosophical writings*, trans. John Cottingham, Robert Stoothoff, and Dugald Murdoch, 57–72. Cambridge: Cambridge University Press.

———. 1971/1637. Principles of philosophy. In *Descartes' philosophical writings*, ed. G. E. M. Anscombe, and Peter Geach, 181–238. Indianapolis: Bobbs-Merrill.

———. 1971/1628. Rules for the direction of the mind. In *Descartes' philosophical writings*, ed. G. E. M. Anscombe and Peter Geach, 151–80. Indianapolis: Bobbs-Merrill.

Dijksterhuis, E. J. 1961/1950. *The mechanization of the world picture*, trans. C. Dikshoorn. Oxford: Clarendon Press.

Dilke, O. A. W. 1971. *The Roman land surveyors: An introduction to the* agrimensores. New York: Barnes and Noble.

Downs, Roger. 1970. Geographic space perception: Past approaches and future prospects. *Progress in Geography* 2: 65–108.

Downs, Roger, and David Stea, eds. 1973. *Image and environment.* London: Edward Arnold.

Duncan, James and Nancy Duncan. 1988. (Re)reading the landscape. *Environmental and Planning D: Society and Space* 6: 117–26.

Duncan, James, Nancy Duncan, and John Agnew, eds. 1990. *The power of place.* London: Allen and Unwin.

Duncan, Simon, and Mike Savage. 1989. Space, scale, and locality. *Antipode* 21 (3): 179–206.

Edgerton, Samuel Y. 1975. *The Renaissance rediscovery of linear perspective.* New York: Harper and Row.

Entrikin, J. Nicholas. 1991. *The betweenness of place*. Basingstoke, England: Macmillan.

Foord, Jo, and Nicky Gregson. 1986. Patriarchy: Towards a reconceptualization. *Antipode* 18: 186–211.

Foucault, Michel. 1984/1982. Space, knowledge, and power. In *The Foucault reader*, ed. Paul Rabinow, 239–56. New York: Pantheon.

———. 1986. Of other spaces. *Diacritics* 16: 22–27. Trans. Jay Miskowiec.

Gatrell, Anthony C. 1983. *Distance and space: A geographical perspective*. New York: Oxford University Press.

Giddens, Anthony. 1984. *The constitution of society: Outline of the theory of structuration*. Berkeley: University of California Press.

Giedion, Siegfried. 1967. *Space, time, and architecture: The growth of a new tradition*, 5th ed. Cambridge: Harvard University Press.

Gould, Peter, and R. White. 1974. *Mental maps*. Harmondsworth, England: Penguin.

Grant, Edward. 1964. Motion in the void and the principle of inertia in the middle ages. *Isis* 55: 265–92.

———. 1969. Medieval and seventeenth-century conceptions of an infinite void space beyond the cosmos. *Isis* 60: 39–60.

———. 1976. Place and space in medieval physical thought. In *Motion and time, space and matter: Interrelations in the history of philosophy and science*, ed. Peter K. Machamer and Robert G. Turnbull, 137–67. Columbus, Ohio: Ohio State University Press.

———. 1981. *Much ado about nothing: Theories of space and vacuum from the Middle Ages to the scientific revolution*. New York: Cambridge University Press.

Guyer, Paul. 1987. *Kant and the claims of knowledge*. Cambridge: Cambridge University Press.

Hartshorne, Richard. 1939. *The nature of geography: A critical survey of current thought in light of the past*. Lancaster, Pa.: Association of American Geographers.

———. 1958. The concept of geography as a science of space, from Kant and Humboldt to Hettner. *Annals of the Association of American Geographers* 48: 97–108.

Harvey, David. 1972. *Society, the city, and the space economy of urbanism*. Commission on College Geography Resource Paper, No. 18, Washington D.C.: Association of American Geographers.

————. 1989. *The condition of postmodernity: An enquiry into the origins of cultural change.* New York: Basil Blackwell.

James, Preston, and Geoffrey Martin. 1981. *All possible worlds: A history of geographical ideas,* 2d ed. New York: Wiley.

Juillard, Étienne. 1972/1962. The region: An essay in definition. In *Man, space, and environment: Concepts in contemporary human geography,* ed. Paul English and Robert C. Mayfield, 429–41. New York: Oxford University Press.

Kane, R. H. 1976. Nature, plenitude, and sufficient reason. *American Philosophical Quarterly* 13: 23–31.

Kant, Immanuel. 1965/1781, 1787. *The critique of pure reason,* trans. Norman Kemp Smith. New York: St. Martin's Press.

————. 1929. On the first ground of the distinction of regions in space. In *Kant's inaugural dissertation and early writings on space,* trans. John Handyside, 19–29. Chicago: Open Court.

Kates, Robert W. 1962. *Hazard and choice perception on flood plain management.* Research Paper No. 78. Chicago: University of Chicago, Department of Geography.

Kemp, Martin. 1990. *The science of art: Optical themes in western art from Brunelleschi to Seurat.* New Haven: Yale University Press.

Knuuttila, Simo, ed. 1981. *Reforging the great chain of being: Studies of the history of modal theories,* Dordrecht: D. Reidel.

Koyré, Alexandre. 1957. *From the closed world to the infinite universe.* Baltimore: Johns Hopkins University Press.

Kuntz, Marion Leathers, and Paul G. Kuntz, eds. 1988. *Jacob's ladder: Concepts of hierarchy and the great chain of being,* rev. ed. New York: Peter Lang.

Kuntz, Paul G. 1971. Hierarchy: From Lovejoy's great chain of being to Feibleman's great tree of being. *Studium Generale* 24: 678–87.

Lefebvre, Henri. 1988. *The production of space.* New York: Basil Blackwell.

Leibniz, Gottfried Wilhelm. 1982. *New essays on human understanding,* abridged ed., trans. and ed. Peter Remnant and Jonathan Bennett. Cambridge: Cambridge University Press.

Lindberg, David C. 1992. *The beginnings of Western science: The European scientific tradition in philosophical, religious, and institutional context, 600 B.C. to A.D. 1450.* Chicago: University of Chicago Press.

Lloyd, G. E. R. 1970. *Early Greek science: Thales to Aristotle.* London: Chatto and Windus.

————. 1973. *Greek science after Aristotle.* New York: W. W. Norton.

————. 1979. *Magic, reason, and experience.* Cambridge: Cambridge University Press.

————. 1987. *The revolutions of wisdom: Studies in the claims and practice of ancient Greek science.* Berkeley: University of California Press. [Sather classical lectures, Vol. 52].

Lovering, John. 1989. Postmodernism, Marxism, and locality research: The contribution of critical realism to the debate. *Antipode* 21 (1): 1–12.

Lucretius. 1951. *On the nature of the universe,* trans. R. E. Latham. Harmondsworth, England: Penguin.

Mackenzie, Suzanne. 1988. Building women, building cities: Toward a gender sensitive theory in the environmental disciplines. In *Life spaces,* ed. Caroline Andrew and Beth Moore Milroy, 13–30. Vancouver: University of British Columbia Press.

Massey, Doreen. 1991. Flexible sexism. *Environment and Planning D: Society and Space* 9: 31–57.

McDowell, Linda. 1988. Coming in from the dark: Feminist research in geography. In *Research in human geography: Introductions and investigations,* ed. John Eyles, 155–73. Oxford: Basil Blackwell.

————. 1983. Towards an understanding of the gender division of urban space. *Environment and Planning D: Society and Space* 1: 59–72.

Newton, Isaac. 1953. *Newton's philosophy of nature: Selections from his writings,* ed. H. S. Thayer. New York: Hafner.

Panofsky, Erwin. 1972. *Renaissance and renascences in Western art.* New York: Harper and Row.

Peake, Linda. 1985. Teaching feminist geography: Another perspective. *Journal of Geography in Higher Education* 9: 186–90.

Pederson, Olaf. 1993. *Early physics and astronomy,* rev. ed. Cambridge: Cambridge University Press.

Pickles, John. 1985. *Phenomenology, science, and geography: Spatiality and the human sciences.* Cambridge: Cambridge University Press.

Relph, Edward. 1976. *Place and placelessness.* London: Pion.

Saarinen, Thomas F. 1966. *Perception of the drought hazard on the Great Plains.* Chicago: University of Chicago, Department of Geography.

Sack, Robert D. 1980. *Conceptions of space in social thought: A geographic perspective.* Minneapolis: University of Minnesota Press.

Sarton, George. 1959. Geography and chronology in the third century: Eratosthenes of Cyrene. In A history of science, vol. 2, 99–116. Cambridge: Harvard University Press.

Sauer, Carl O. 1963/1925. Morphology of landscape. In Land and life: A selection from the writings of Carl Ortwin Sauer, ed. John Leighly, 315–50. Berkeley: University of California Press.

Schaefer, F. K. 1953. Exceptionalism in geography: A methodological examination. Annals of the Association of American Geographers 43: 226–49.

Seamon, David and Robert Mugerauer, eds. 1989. Dwelling, place, and environment. New York: Columbia University Press.

Soja, Edward W. 1989. Postmodern geographies: The reassertion of space in critical social theory. London: Verso.

Stewart, John Q. and William Warntz. 1958. Macrogeography and social science. Geographical Review 48: 167–84.

Strabo. 1917. The geography of Strabo, 8 vols., trans. H. L. Jones. London: Heinemann.

Sypher, Wylie. 1955. Four stages of Renaissance style: Transformations in art and literature, 1400–1700. Garden City, New York: Doubleday.

Tuan, Yi Fu. 1974a. Topophilia: A study of environmental perception, attitudes, and values. Englewood Cliffs, N.J.: Prentice Hall.

———. 1974b. Space and place: A humanistic perspective. Progress in Geography 6: 211–52.

———. 1977. Space and place: The perspective of experience. Minneapolis: University of Minnesota Press.

———. 1982. Segmented worlds and self: Group life and individual consciousness. Minneapolis: University of Minnesota Press.

Ullman, Edward L. 1954. Geography as spatial interaction. Annals of the Association of American Geographers 44: 283–84.

Vidal de la Blache, Paul. 1928/1911. The personality of France, trans. H. C. Brentnall. London: Alfred A. Knopf.

White, John. 1967. The birth and rebirth of pictorial space, 2d ed. London: Faber and Faber.

Wright, John K. 1947. Terrae incognitae: The place of the imagination in geography. Annals of the Association of American Geographers 37: 1–15.

———. 1966. Human nature in geography: Fourteen papers, 1925–1965. Cambridge, Massachusetts: Harvard University Press.

2

The Way We Were: Deployments (and Redeployments) of Time in Human Geography

David Hornbeck, Carville Earle, and Christine M. Rodrigue

Time is essential. It organizes and sustains our physical and biological systems. It is a basic human cognitive structure that defines our behavior and our view of our existence. Time is a vehicle that enables group interactions and the creation of society via the synchronization of interactions. Of all the symbolic forms that the human mind has invented, time is the most encompassing and the most deceptive. With time we can create order and even discipline; we can classify, arrange, categorize, and shape the world in which we live (Rifkin 1987: 9). The way we conceive, define, utilize, and implement time shapes much of our daily life. Time is at once limiting and versatile, paradoxical and aggravating. We can ponder what lies ahead, we can scrutinize the past, and we can even detach ourselves from the present, yet we do all this with little understanding of time and its influence on the patterned conduct of our lives (Newton-Smith 1986).

Time is difficult to discuss: it is at once familiarly obvious and inscrutably unknown. As George Kubler observes (1962: 13) in his wise and learned volume on the subject, "time, like mind, is not knowable as such. We know time only indirectly by what happens in it: by observing change and permanence, by marking the succession of events among stable settings, and by noting the contrast of varying rates of change." Time resists simple definition. Our quandary is rather like trying to explain how to ice skate: we know how to do it, but how to say it is another matter. In explaining the process of ice skating, we focus on the mechanics of standing upright on thin metal blades rather than on the sensation of flying over ice. Our explanation is invariably partial. Discussions of time are similarly oblique, intent more on clarifying, defining, and delimiting the subject rather than on the sensation of being in time.

Consider the contrast of time with space. If you are asked to describe an area, you can open an atlas, turn to a map, and discuss the components of the map and their effectiveness in representing the space in question and its contents. If you are asked to describe a period of time, however, your options are limited. You cannot open a comparable atlas of time because time does not lend itself to visualization. The best we can do is turn to those rare diachronic compilations known as timetables or to the discursive texts of world histories.

Unlike a map of an area on earth, time is neither a thing nor an item of experience. When we think of a moment of time, we define it by events that occurred in that moment, and the flow of time is defined, in turn, by the stream of events. We find it difficult to give meaning to time, because time is so very abstract: it cannot be displayed nor can it be studied in any simple and direct fashion (Lucas 1973).

Despite the vagaries attached to time's meaning, this concept permeates all spheres of human geography. Some of geography's most important concepts hinge on time and temporal sequences. Concepts such as cultural hearth, homeland, diffusion, geographical change, and a sense of place are at once spatial and temporal in their cardinal dimensions (Tuan 1977). Moreover, the geographical methods that are used in observing, evaluating, processing, and analyzing geographic data are arranged along time scales that range from seconds (wave velocity) to millennia (livelihood evolution). Time thus provides geographers with units of observation and of analysis (e.g., population density in 1995) and these units permit a description of spatial changes and the processes responsible for them. Seldom, though, is time the central concern of geographical study. In most, if not all, geographical research, time serves as an adjunct to analysis, a metering device, a way of determining the duration and sequencing of environmental or spatial phenomena or processes. In this fashion time serves as a clock or calendar, a metric that enables the analyst to fix spatial events, to measure intervals between them, and to describe their changes from T_1 to T_2 (Thrift 1977: 67). Geographers thus deploy time in ways that are reminiscent of the "chess maps" that plot the sequential moves of opponents in the daily newspapers (Monmonier 1990).

Aside from these metric functions the nature of time has not preoccupied geographers in general or historical geographers in particular. Save for some discussions of geography as a process-oriented discipline, geographers have eschewed debates on the incorporation of time into geographical explanation (Frassen 1985). Even as historians and social theorists have tended to trivialize space as an inert stage for the play of spatial temporal processes of social change (Soja 1989), geographers have tended to marginalize time in their treatments of spatial and ecological dynamics—all this despite time's central role for understanding spaces, places, and patterns of human activity.

So, then, does time move? Is time real or simply an epiphenomenon of the perception of motion or change? Are spans of time measurable? Does it predict? Does it explain? Answers to these and other questions are imperative if geographers are to incorporate time into their explanations of spatial and environmental patterns and relations.

This chapter cannot resolve all of these questions about time; it presents instead some ideas on the ways that geographers might think about a subject that permeates, often unwittingly, our conceptual and philosophical frameworks, our research methods, and our techniques. We thus engage our paradox: whereas time is at the very core of what we do as human geographers, we are on the whole remarkably unreflective about its constructions, uses, and functions.

Space and Time

A reductionist view of time suggests that time can be construed as event sequences, in which case the investigation of time is an empirical matter of reconstructing events and their sequential arrangement. It follows that there can be no time without change; that is to say, the sequence of change in events is the essence of time. If we treat time as a collection of events, no temporal vacuum can exist (Schlesinger 1980). Most geographical research adheres, perhaps unknowingly, to this reductionist view that equates time with change.

The better part of geographical research subscribes implicitly to this reductionist view of time. In regarding time and space as inherent properties of phenomena, geographers have tended to take these properties for granted. From this point of view we assume that everything that exists in space also exists in time, that space and time serve as containers, albeit of various sizes, and that all earthly phenomena may be located in them. An event thus possesses two cardinal coordinate properties: the temporal one of occurrence at a given time and the spatial one of occurrence at a given place (Brentano 1988). It is not surprising, therefore, that most geographers conduct their research on the assumption that space and time are fundamentally similar and that they share common basic properties. In doing so, geographers unwittingly fall victim to what Schlesinger has called the doctrine of the similarity of space and time

(1980). This doctrine holds that there is a direct correspondence between spatial and temporal narratives: to assert the truth or falsity of one statement about space implies the truth or falsity of its temporal counterpart. To manufacture the spatial counterpart for a temporal tale, we need only change each temporal term into a corresponding spatial term (Schlesinger 1980: 10–15).

If this doctrinal view of spatial and temporal similarity always held true, however, some baffling and confusing conclusions would ensue. The fact of the matter is that the concept of time is quite distinct from the concept of space (Lucas 1973: 17). In their properties they differ abruptly. Whereas time is one-dimensional, space is multidimensional; whereas time is ordered and unidirectional (past to future), space is disorderly and multidirectional (Flood and Lockwood 1987). Consider the example of a migration flow from Space A to Space B. This flow in space does not preclude migration from Space B to Space A, nor from any one point to any other in any sequence; yet the migration that begins at Time 1 and ends at Time 2 cannot reverse the clock and move from Time 2 back to Time 1. In the case of sidereal time there is no other azimuthal direction for a temporal event to follow in phenomenal reality (matters are quite different, of course, in the curved space-time of the universe in which, according to the cosmologists, travel forward or backward in time is theoretically possible). Accordingly, the temporal relations of earlier and later, before and after, are logically connected, but in the case of space, no parallel directional relationship exists in two-dimensional space; even notions of near and far do not allow for the infinite range of spatial directions that may be taken. Only by adding a third dimension does space establish a comparable logical connection, and only then provided that the other two coordinates are held constant, for example, above and below at the same latitude and longitude; east and west at the same latitude and elevation; north and south at the same longitude and elevation.

From these examples it should be evident that the doctrine of spatial and temporal similarity is a dubious one, that space and time are different, that time exhibits a unity that space does not possess, and that the spatial characteristics of any given space may be entirely unrelated to those belonging to another space. If disparate spaces are readily imaginable; disparate times are inconceivable. Yet the doctrine of spatial and temporal similarity persists. In seeming opposition to common sense scholars regularly reformulate the empirical evidence so as to achieve consistency between the properties of time and space. Proponents of the doctrine maintain that time and space analogies apply insofar as both statements on time and space are equated with the same properties, that is, time and space must be delimited very specifically, and both must be specified at the same scale (Lucas 1973).

If the debate over space-time equivalence is metaphysical and philosophical, its conclusions sometimes have significant effects on geographical research. If space and time are not equivalent, then geographers will need to pay more attention to how we conduct our research. Conversely, if space and time are equivalent, we will need to devise a more refined understanding of procedures for specification and conditionalization for the simple reason that the doctrine applies only under certain carefully drawn definitions and limits. Some progress along these lines has been made with respect to contextual or relational definitions of space and time, and we shall have more to say on these matters momentarily.

Time and Human Geography

For much of the twentieth century the philosophy and methods of human geography have been dominated by two ahistorical traditions: the regional and the spatial. The regional view, which prevailed between the 1930s and the 1950s, precluded time by definition. Founded on Kant's sharp distinctions between the missions of geography (synthesis in space), history (synthesis in time), and the sciences (systematic analyses of particular phenomena), regional geography or chorology involved describing the areal differentiation of natural and human phenomena and integrating these distributions in ways that delineated distinctive regions (and their characters) on the earth's surface (Hartshorne 1939). This view neither acknowledged nor incorporated time in its agenda in any serious fashion. Time was frozen in the present, which led critics of this static approach to label it as a sort of "*New York Times* geography." During the 1950s human geographers gravitated toward an alternative tradition that was predicated on generalization and lawlike regularities, that is, on science, spatial analysis, and spatial theory, but this new geography, this science of spatial relations, left similarly little room for the inclusion of time in explanatory spatial models. It is probably fair to say that in the 1990s the spatial approach continues as the prevailing ontology of geographical research, albeit in the various guises of behavioralism, Marxism, structurationism, and even postmodernism. Of these spatial variants, only the structurationist and Marxist approaches attach much intellectual utility to time (Pred 1984, Soja 1989, Harvey 1990). By and large, however, human geography's two major traditions—the regional and the spatial—have either ignored or explicitly excluded the role of time in the analysis of geographical processes.

In practice, however, a good many geographers working within the regional and spatial traditions—not to mention almost all geographers working within the Berkeley School's ecological tradition (Leighly 1967)—have defied convention and incorporated time into their research. Proponents of spatial analysis, for example, have occasionally acknowledged that a more complete understanding of spatial structure requires an appreciation and a grasp of the ways that change (over time) occurs. Indeed, in the flush times of the quantitative revolution Curry (1964, 1967) argued that time was a key factor for understanding changes in spatial structure—a thesis that boldly anticipated later appeals by Olson (1969), Berry (1973), Amedeo and Golledge (1975), Harvey (1969, 1973), Thrift (1977), and more recently Scott (1985)—but this rhetoric too often rang hollow. While many geographers acknowledged the critical importance of a temporal component in their programmatic statements, empirical research rarely practiced what these statements had preached.

This half-hearted engagement with time can be explained by the exceedingly circumscribed usages of time in geographical research. These usages have been of three sorts: the technical, the traditional, and the resource oriented—and each is deserving of a few words. First, and perhaps most familiar, is the technical method of incorporating time in geographical analysis. In this usage time is regarded as a metering device (symbolized by the subscript $_t$ in our models) for measuring changes in states. Time's complex and varied connotations are condensed (reified) into a denotative index of chronology. This technical usage of time is associated, of course, with the methodological strategies of science, positivism, reductionism, and, in geography, spatial analysis (Amson 1974). In spatial analysis the usage of time is principally a technical matter in which the analyst measures instants and intervals in a coordinate system (matrix) borrowed directly from the Newtonian and Euclidian branches of the physical sciences. Time serves mainly as an adjunct to standard geographical techniques, as a means for estimating stochastic processes or for forecasting trends in a time-series model (Cliff 1977). Emphasis is placed on time's regularity, consistency, and forward flow (unidirectionality) within a specifically defined and absolute system (grid) of measurement (Hepple 1974). In essence, time serves mainly an instrumental role—a means for computing direction, sequence, and duration, for identifying events in time, and for measuring intervals with great accuracy. In this metrical usage time is more nearly an auxiliary to analysis—a container, as some would have it—than an integral part of it.

The second usage of time, the traditional, is most commonly associated with historical geography and regional geography and their reconstructions of past geographies. In reconstructing these geographies, historical geographers have devised various methodologies that enable them to "see" into the past (Newcomb 1969). Two of their best-known methods involve slicing the past into either horizontal cross sections or longitudinal strands. The cross-sectional method slices the past at times when the regional geography of an area (its character) has crystallized, when the region has reached what might be called a fluorescent moment in its historical development. When a series of these cross-sectional slices is arranged in sequence, the historical geographer secures an animated view of regional change over time—but not, we note, of the processes that cause these changes. This method of animated cross sections is what has become known as the study of sequent occupance (Whittlesey 1929). The second method slices time along its longitudinal or vertical dimension, thereby accenting changes in selected phenomena (themes) over time. Unlike the static cross-sectional approach, the longitudinal approach focuses on processes of change, on times of transition—hence the notion that these two approaches are complementary rather than competitive (Newcomb 1969). These methods notwithstanding, historical geographers have tended to be fairly casual about time in general and dates, years, and periods in particular. Time becomes such an interwoven part of the particular (usually idiographic) analysis that they seldom attempt to clarify its usage or its more general meanings.

Geography's third usage of time regards it as a resource. In this approach, time constitutes the nucleus of what has been called "time geography" (Parkes and Thrift 1980). Derived principally from the work of Torsten Hägerstrand (1975), time geography conceptualizes time as a scarce resource. It bundles human activities into projects that move along time-space paths that are constrained by the prevailing speeds of transport technology. Time geography observes these movements in space-time and attempts to model them (Carlstein 1978). In this regard, time geography's debts to physics are appreciable. Physics' usage of space-time diagrams (defined by the speed of light) and world lines (of objects) have their analogues in time geography's deployment of space-time prisms (defined now by the speed of jet travel) and individual world lines therein (Hägerstrand 1970, Pred 1977, Carlstein 1978, Rucker 1984). While practitioners of time geography do an enviable job of wedding space, place, projects, and time, it is not surprising that this approach with its origins in physics tends to reduce time to its technical and metric elements (Parkes 1977). A refreshing exception to the rule, however, is the work of Allan Pred (1981, 1990). In Pred's rendition of time geography the ebb and flow of daily activities involves more than the physics of movement; it is this ebb and flow that constitutes and reconstitutes spaces into places that are, in his felicitous expression, "ceaselessly becoming." When Pred's seemingly novel analyses are taken to their limit, however, the results amount to little more than the restoration of the traditional historical narrative—albeit in the form of the multiple stories derived from the daily activities of scores of individuals. The sheer weight of Pred's prosopographical project almost invariably crushes generalizations on spatial behavior; we are left with a tangle of idiographic findings on particularity and difference. In all of this, one suspects that Pred's geographical narratives obscure the middle ground between the general and the particular, between science and history—a middle ground that is being cultivated by, among others, Charles Ragin (1987) and his Boolean analyses of event sequences and their patterns.

To summarize, geography relies on three fairly rudimentary uses of time. Generally speaking, traditional historical geography uses time to identify the complex changes taking place in geographical regions, spatial analysis uses time as an abstract technical tool for identifying and modeling particular spatial changes that occur between T_1 and T_n, and time geography regards time as an allocative resource that enables and constrains individual space-time projects (Parkes 1977). It is worth noting that in all of these geographical usages of time, time is portrayed as absolute, as something apart from events, as a Newtonian container in which events transpire. For most geographers, time (and space) exist independently of substance; time tends to be viewed as a fixed moment, a finite duration of occurrence, or a precisely dated interval between events. That is to say that time is almost invariably absolute within a fixed grid; it is less commonly regarded as a relational concept, as a phenomenon that is defined relative to objects moving simultaneously in space-time.

Regardless of how human geography conceptualizes time, two threads run through the several approaches: the first is the commitment to measuring stability (routine) and gauging change (novelty or innovation), the second is the attempt to infer processes of spatial and ecological change. Human geography thus accents a mode of reasoning that we may call causal, that attempts to link time, space, form, and process (Norton 1978). What, in fact, do we know about the relations between time, process, and spatial form? On these matters William Norton (1984: 25) offers a useful point of departure. He highlights the following relations:

(1) Spatial forms are outcomes of processes.
(2) Processes, in turn, may be outcomes of forms; that is, they are circularly causal (a process produces a form that then affects the process).
(3) It follows then that the explanation of a form at T_1 requires reference to the pre-existing form at T_0.
(4) Processes and forms are liable to change through time (this involves, among others, the restoration of equilibrium in a homeostatic system, evolution or devolution via a process of punctuated equilibrium, or irreversible nonlinear transformations of form-process relations).
(5) Processes are scale dependent, and, hence, interpretations of their related forms depend on analyses at the appropriate time-space scales.

(6) A given form may be the consequence of a variety of multiscalar processes; hence, it is not possible to interpret form from a knowledge of one process alone.

(7) A stochastic process may generate more than one form (or in some cases, none at all).

(8) Adjustments in form are not instantaneous responses to processes (responses may lag over some relaxation time, which is benchmarked by the equilibrium state in a given system or more simply by the form at T_1).

(9) Forms are usually the product of multivariate processes that may (we add) operate hierarchically, polyarchically, or anarchically across spatial scales.

Norton goes on to argue that the incorporation of time in geographical analysis involves a minimalist series of queries about events, event sequences, and change:

(1) Delimitation of event sequences: When did the event sequence start and when did it end?

(2) Ordering of events in a sequence: What followed what within the sequence?

(3) Ordering of processes governing the sequence: Why did each event happen when it did within the sequence?

(4) Timing of the event sequences: Why did the sequence of events occur when it did?

(5) Rates of change: How long did it take for completion of the entire sequence of events? Were certain portions of the sequence completed faster or slower than others? Why?

Most human geographers confine their attention to just one or two of these five queries on time. Typically, they identify successive events, measure change between intervals defined by dated events, and position these events on a linear time scale. In other words, change is portrayed and assessed as a narrative of successive events. Human geographers have been less zealous in posing queries on rates, directions, magnitudes, durations, and processes of event sequences (but see Clark 1962, Earle and Cao 1993). More serious than these oversights, however, are the often naive usages of the sequence data that we do collect. Consider the evolutional stage and succession models that so often have confounded geographical understandings of spatial and ecological processes. In these cases the analyst begins by constructing a model of sequential changes of land use or transport using data from one or a few cases;

this model is then extrapolated to other places and times that typically are subject to vastly different conditions. Perhaps the most egregious examples of these models in human geography are the extrapolations of the Burgess concentric-zone model of residential areas in cities and the Taaffe-Morrill-Gould (1963) model of transport expansion in developing countries. When properly conditionalized to relevant times and spaces, these spatial-sequence models have proven to be quite useful; but when—as is more usually the case—they are extrapolated willy-nilly, these models have confused rather than clarified the causal foundations of spatial and ecological processes. Geographers would do well to consider the more sophisticated (and conditionalized) usages of time and event sequences deployed by Skinner (1985) in anthropology, Wallerstein (1974, 1980, 1988) in world-systems analysis, and Abbott (1983, 1988, 1990) and Ragin (1987) in sociology. (Abbott's research is particularly critical of linear models; his work regards outcomes as contingent on the ordering and timing of events. Ragin, meanwhile, deploys inductive Boolean analyses in an attempt to discern the variety of patterns in the event sequences that lead to specific outcomes.)

To the extent that geographers have probed into processes and their causes, they have encountered exceedingly subtle problems of interpretation. At the most rudimentary level of analysis proof of causality entails linking the occurrence of change to an event that is antecedent to the change and that renders its occurrence feasible. The basic premise of this reasoning is that if B happened after A, it may have happened because of A. More rigorously, the logic of causality entails satisfaction of four conditions: 1) temporal order—the effect must occur after the cause; 2) temporal contiguity—the effect normally occurs very soon after the cause, the likelihood of causality varying inversely with their temporal intervals; 3) spatial contiguity—the effect usually occurs very near the cause, the likelihood of causality varying inversely with the distance between the two; and 4) regularity—the effect repeatedly and regularly occurs after the cause (Pazzani 1991, Peuquet 1994). Handled correctly, this mode of temporal reasoning can be very useful in helping to narrow down the potential causes of change; for example, if A occurs before B, we can rule out B as A's cause. Handled badly, however, this sort of reasoning may lead to fundamentally illogical explanations. If B follows A, we cannot infer that B was caused by A. Other factors, C through n, may equally or alternatively account for the outcome of B (Salmon 1963).

To illustrate, it would be ludicrous to claim that the earthquake that occurred immediately after you stomped your foot was the cause of the quake, yet the geographical literature abounds in this form of argument. This fallacy of *post ergo hoc propter hoc* (after this therefore because of this) appears among interpretations claiming, for example, that urbanization is the result of migration (aside from the tautological difficulties of this thesis, might not other demographic, economic, and political processes be responsible for urbanization?); that distance determines consumer shopping behavior (the exceptions that appear in the statistical residuals or errors on that regression line speak for themselves); that farmers plant crops to maximize profits (fraternal members of the order of *Homo oeconomicus* are often disappointed by humanity's economic irrationality); or that the sacrifice of animals by early agriculturalists led to animal domestication (a classic affirmation of the consequent that, on closer review, turns out to have been the antecedent; Rodrigue 1986). These examples contain just enough grains of truth to make them plausible and to inspire the hyperbolic and overreaching generalization. Caution is therefore advised in making too much out of a sequence of events per se.

Causal reasoning thus requires more than event sequences. First, the cause must precede the effect in time (and the closer, the better). Second, the cause and effect must be proximate in space (contiguity). Third, the cause-and-effect sequence must regularly occur under conditions specified by the analyst. In practice, it is difficult to satisfy all of these prerequisites for causal analysis, and the really interesting work has to do with narrowing the scope conditions under which causality is invariable (or highly probable).

The Tacit Logic of Time

One of the qualities of good scholarship is proficiency in telling a good story, a story that has been organized into a narrative framework that makes for interesting and informative reading (Norton 1984). A story, by definition, requires a sense of time, a certain temporal integrity—a beginning, a middle, an end, and a series of transitions in between. A sense of time, however, is not easily acquired, nor is it something that we are accustomed to thinking clearly (or even much) about (Arthur 1968). In this narrative mode the use of time in human geography requires the narrator to do a great deal more than organize events into their "proper" sequence. Narrative, in other words, has certain prerequisites, and these are best approached through indirection, through an examination of the fallacies that arise when these prerequisites are ignored, that is, when scholars deploy what we will call "the tacit logic of time." We identify eight of these fallacies in all: 1) misdating; 2) retrospective theory; 3) "the golden age;" 4) presentism; 5) genesis; 6) "faith in facts" (tory versions of the past); 7) misspecified periodization; and 8) the assumption of infinite possibilities (whig versions of the past).

The Fallacy of Misdating

The first of these fallacies, and perhaps the most common, involves the misdating of events. While dating may seem a trivial problem, a simple mistake in the narrative chronology may have profound consequences. Consider an example that comes from close at home. In an article dealing with Hispanic landownership in California, one of the authors attributed ownership of a land grant to an individual who had not yet been born (Hornbeck 1979). Initially, this error seemed little more than an innocent academic gaffe, but the error was compounded when a subsequent legal brief perpetuated the misdating. Similar errors in chronology occur rather often in studies of pre-literate societies, for example, in reading the archaeological evidence or oral tradition. In these cases the correction of one erroneous date may overturn an entire interpretation of a society.

The Fallacy of Retrospective Theory

A second fallacy involves retrospective reasoning and the "tunnel vision" that comes with it. In this case the analyst interprets the past on the basis of current theories of society and human behavior. Enamored of the universality of his or her theory, the analyst tunnels through time, innocently unaware of the contingencies and the alternatives that were presented to historical actors. In this retrospective version of time the past unfolds inevitably and unproblematically; according to theoretical plan, things look as though they could not have happened otherwise. In this foolproof fashion the analyst imposes contemporary processes on past landscapes in order to document their continuities with present landscapes and processes. Yet this *ex post* imposition so rips history from its context that the people who actually constructed these past landscapes would hardly have recognized the workings of these alleged processes (Pfeiffer 1977: ch. 1). This sort of teleology devalues the past by coupling it so closely with present theory. Moreover, this retrospective mode of analysis largely precludes alternatives, the possibilities of, for example, accident, randomness, nonlinear processes, avenues foreclosed, or, as the historicist would insist, conclusions that are constrained to their relevant epochs or periods.

Examples of the retrospective fallacy are abundant (see Ward 1975), but perhaps the best-known case in human geography is Taaffe, Morrill, and Gould's model of transport evolution in developing countries (1963). These authors derived their generalized transport model from the particulars of West African historical geography; there the transport network evolved through a series of seemingly inexorable stages—from 1) a scattering of coastal ports to 2) differential expansion of one or two ports via linear routes penetrating into the interior to 3) development of smaller nodes on these routes and of feeder lines into them to 4) interconnections among these routes and, finally, to 5) the transport dominance of a single port. Other geographers have applied this retrospective model indiscriminantly to vastly different times and places. In so doing, they have overlooked the obvious fact that these stages more nearly represent certain particular phases (conditions) in the history of European colonization that unfolded between 1830 and 1920. The fact of the matter is that the spatial changes identified by Taaffe, Morrill, and Gould represent quite specific responses to long-wave rhythms in the political economy of the core colonial powers and of their attendant policies; only under these very specific circumstances (conditions) can we regard these transport stages as inevitable and ineluctable. A counterfactual helps to clarify our point. Suppose that West Africa in the 1820s and 1830s had been colonized by mercantilists or imperialists rather than by free-trading merchants; in this case the spatial processes of transport development would have unfolded in quite different ways. Instead of the multiple scattered ports of stage 1, we would find one, or at most a few, dominant ports, and, consequently, in stage 2, we would find only a handful of routes extending into the interior from this small group of ports. Here the usage of retrospective theory idealizes the past to the extent that the patterns under investigation are compelled to fit neatly within our preconceived theoretical schemes. We try, in other words, to fit the square pegs of the empirical past into the smooth circles drawn by retrospective theory.

The Fallacy of the Golden Age

A third fallacy portrays time as prelapsarian. History is anchored ultimately in a world that we have lost, in an earlier "golden age" when life was simpler, purer, more pristine, and more humane; to wit, Pred's (1986) analysis of Swedish enclosure, circa 1790–1840 (see chapter 12). Evident in, among others, the Eden myth, German historicism, Jeffersonian antiurbanism, and Marxist notions on "primitive communism," this sort of nostalgic romanticism tends to misrepresent the past in service of radical reactionary ideologies (on both the left and right) and their critiques of the status quo. In seeking these happier days (status quo ante), these ideologies truncate the full range of human experience that governs the development of spatial and landscape forms and patterns (Shannon 1989: ch. 3). Worse still, these nostalgic glosses on the "golden age" obscure the pains, problems, and tendentiousness in these "kinder" times.

The Fallacy of Presentism

Our fourth temporal fallacy is presentism, which involves using the past as a means for comprehending and clarifying contemporary problems. A case in point comes from the work of the progressive historian-cum-geographer Frederick Jackson Turner. His interpretations of the American past nicely illustrate the strengths and the weaknesses of presentist logic. Turner's thesis of frontier closure in the 1880s enabled him to account for the troubles that confronted American society in the 1890s—Turner's present. By closing the frontier and foreclosing opportunities for social qua geographic mobility for white Americans, Turner was able to account for the hardening of class lines and the ascent of class (labor-capital) conflict that he witnessed in the 1890s. The powerful role that Turner ascribed to the frontier has, however, been called into question by evidence of the frontier's closure as early as the 1840s—a half century ahead of Turnerian schedule (Earle and Cao 1993)—and by critiques of the frontier as concept (Limerick 1987; Meinig 1982). The logic of presentism has also been applied by human geographers who would deny the importance of the past (and of a distinct "historical geography") and who would claim that all geography is historical. Wilbur Zelinsky's (1973) critique of historical geography offers a case in point when he observes that "It is literally impossible to devise any way to slice historic time into neat, separate parcels, so that any basic distinction between contemporary and historical geography (and the geography of the future) in terms of material, methods, or purpose is difficult to defend."

Zelinsky thus argues on behalf of temporal continuity, but his thesis is larger still. He rejects historicism and its contention that the past constitutes a distinctive and valid object of historical-geographic knowledge; more important, he rejects the notion of historical discontinuity, that is, that past periods may be so differentiated by political economy or spirit (Zeitgeist) that they may be understood only in context and on their own terms. In doing so, Zelinsky rejects Marx among others and installs instead a whiggish alternative to historicism. This version of history accents notions of temporal continuity and progress along time's arrow. It obscures qualitative differences between past periods and the present as it reduces time to a metric of essentially equivalent (and undifferentiated) units. For Zelinsky, the present is just like the past, only better, and the future is one of infinite possibility. Zelinsky's whiggish presentism, however, is not precisely identical with Turner's progressivist version of that perspective. Whereas Turner acknowledged critical conjunctures—conjunctures in which social change becomes irreversible, in which society may be changed once and for all—Zelinsky papers over these moments of crisis as unproblematic, as mere epiphenomena on the (liberal) path to the present (and the future).

The Genetic Fallacy

Our fifth temporal fallacy addresses the flip side of presentism. The genetic approach traces the origins of phenomena and their ensuing diffusions, albeit with little regard for their historical contexts. In this case, one event, or set of events, in the past is regarded as more important than all others. The researcher clears away the underbrush to find the singular event—this prime mover—from which all else unfolds. By simplifying the past in this fashion, the analyst runs the risk of obscuring the complexity of history and trivializing the actions, needs, and views of historical actors. Some proponents of critical human geography nibble at the edge of this fallacy when they trace the origins of present-day patterns in the spatial economy via the shaft that leads back from post-Fordism to the oil crisis of 1973 to Fordism and its precursors (Scott 1983, Kern 1983, Storper and Walker 1989). The story looks quite different, however, when analysts work forward in time; in this case, industrialists in the late nineteenth century embarked on mass production not to exploit, among other things, a vulnerable and inexpensive unskilled labor force, but rather to undermine the considerable market power that had accrued to these unskilled laborers in a time of rapid industrial expansion (Earle 1993 and the sources cited therein). Similarly dubious are geographic treatments of innovation diffusion that trace one or another feature of contemporary society to its earliest "hearth" and to the ensuing paths of diffusion. In these cases, the context for and the process of innovation become minor and unproblematic givens; the process of diffusion is largely reduced to matters of proximity and exposure. In these atomistic diffusion models most historical actors are regarded as passive recipients who latch onto innovations devised by "wiser peoples" (Blaut 1977, 1994).

Scholars who conflate present and past in this manner impose a retrospective symmetry on the two. A past that is filled with ambiguity, confusion, and uncertainty is magically transformed into a past that is unambiguously lucid and certain. And all of this is accomplished notwithstanding the fact that our interpretations of the past hang on a mere fraction of the historical record, on a record of experience that has been so fragmented that, like Humpty Dumpty, it cannot be put back together again. Scholars are left with history's legacy of scattered shards, of randomly distributed pieces, that are examined, in turn, for randomly selected scholarly ends (Blumler 1993, Rodrigue 1986). While many of the pieces seem to fit together, we cannot be certain that the story they tell is, in fact, the "right" story. What we do know, however, is that the stories told by the genetic approach are usually wrong (i.e., they are almost invariably partial and out of context).

Faith in Facts

A sixth temporal fallacy is what we call the fallacy of "faith in facts." This approach assumes that all facts are relevant and that all must be gathered because we never know when they will be useful. Practitioners of this approach are known as diggers, as the excavators of the facts that are essential to our understandings of the past. To be sure, facts must be accurately positioned in time and space, and they must be corroborated by other sources or by internal evidence. But to what end? This query gets at the heart of meaning and the difference between the historian and the antiquarian. The historian:

> differs from the antiquarian and the curious searcher much as the composer of new music differs from the concert performer. The historian composes a meaning from tradition, while the antiquarian only re-creates, performs, or re-enacts an obscure portion of past time in already familiar shapes. . . . The historian communicates a pattern which was invisible to his subjects when they lived it, and unknown to his contemporaries before he detected it. (Kubler 1962: 12–13)

Apt in this regard is Tolstoy's venerable division of scholars into foxes and hedgehogs. The fox is a sly creature who constructs clever generalizations out of few key facts. The hedgehog is quite different; it kills its victims by breaking the back of clever generalizations with the embarrassing or anomalous fact. The hedgehog thus keeps faith with the facts of the past (and the present), facts of such enormous complexity and particularity that they defy all but the most narrow of the fox's generalizations. For the hedgehog the only permissible generalization is the narrative chronology, that is, a chronology based on verifiable and verified events (facts). In another venue, of course, this is the tory version of history. In tory ideology (unlike whiggish or radical ones) events are caused by, and are the sole responsibility of, individuals who are motivated by social-psychological circumstances and not by abstract socioeconomic forces. That is why the tory's version of history is so often described (derisively) as "King's and Queen's" history. Geographers have their tory counterparts, of course, and H. C. Darby is our foremost exemplar. Darby's classic volume *The Draining of the Fens* (1940) represents tory historical geography at its best. Anchored in "the great man" school of history, Darby's protagonists consist of a handful of wise, willful, and astute men who initiated (and brought to fruition) one of the most mammoth projects of land reclamation ever undertaken. Although it is fashionable to dismiss tory interpretations of history and the tory's faith in facts, that fashion should be resisted for at least three reasons: first, because all historical interpretations must be able to accommodate the facts assembled by tory hedgehogs; second, because, as clever foxes often remind us, "god resides in the details"; and third, because individual actions (agency) often shape history and historical geography.

The Fallacy of Misspecified Periodization

A seventh temporal fallacy is the problem of misspecified periodization (for a revealing account of periodization's effects on interpretations of process and social change, see Green 1993). This fallacy is commonly encountered in economic geographies that attempt to document the enchainment of a series of specific changes. Consider, for example, American economic geography's fondness for the end of World War II. For these geographers 1945 has become something of a benchmark from which to measure a host of ensuing changes in the American spatial economy. But why 1945? One obvious reason is that this chronological inflection provides perhaps the rosiest view of American economic performance that we can imagine. Contrast this chronology, however, with the chronologies of more radical interpretations of the American past. These are more likely to look to 1929 or 1965 as the critical (downer) points of departure. Historical geographers meanwhile favor 1890 as a dividing line, perhaps because of their familiarity with Turner's thesis of frontier closure. Similarly problematic is the widespread usage by American urban, social, and economic geographers of decennial chronologies that have their origins not in scholarship but rather in the Constitution's call for a census every ten years. To be sure, the usage of these temporal benchmarks is defensible in many cases, but more often than not their selection is arbitrary, unreflective, and problematic (Kubler 1962: 100–103).

A periodization or slicing scheme such as the decennial census may be valid for one problem, but when this temporal sampling is imposed on another problem, difficulties usually arise. Consider an example from periodizations in climatology. When climatologists construct averages of the meteorological conditions over a period of thirty years or more, they do so in order to average out extreme events (in precipitation or temperature, for example); but these averaging methods are less useful if the climatologist is trying to understand the ways in which weather actually works. One reason for this is that a thirty-year climatic series rarely adheres to a normal distribution; in fact, the record consists more nearly of a mixed series of distributions. Consider the probability of a heavy rainfall event. The likelihood that such an event will occur will be much higher under some synoptic conditions than under others (Hirschboeck 1987a, 1987b). For the scholar who is trying to predict flood events (and to minimize their damage) the critical issue is to isolate those synoptic conditions (i.e., some temporal subset of a thirty-year period) in which heavy precipitation events are more likely. Note that this climatological problem entails a radically different usage of time. Instead of using an arbitrarily defined period of thirty years, the analyst differentiates time in accordance with the relevant atmospheric conditions (for the statistical consequences of the nonstationariety of distributions, see Kisiel 1969). The analyst, in other words, converts the absolutes of metric time into the relatives of conditional time. This procedure results in generalized and conditional statements of the following sort: given a synoptic condition of cyclonic advance, the probability of a heavy rainfall event will be high. This procedure is precisely analogous to

Wallerstein's relational division of long waves in the World-System. By distinguishing A and B phases in these half-century waves, Wallerstein is able to conditionalize periods and then to compare social behavior in similar phases over the capitalist epoch (Wallerstein 1974, 1980, 1988; Taylor 1989). Wallerstein's synoptic economic condition of phase A in the long wave is methodologically equivalent therefore to the "synoptic" meteorological condition of, say, an advancing cyclone. In this fashion we escape from the clutches of absolute time and enter into the domain of relativity and relational time.

By partitioning the past into arbitrary temporal divisions, geographers have ignored relativity (i.e., relational time) and thereby subverted the possibilities of temporal generalization and hypothesis testing. Moreover, these arbitrary slicings of the past produce sampling problems of the sort that regularly confront geographers in dealing with spaces. The geographers' choices of a spatial boundary or a spatial scale (the modifiable areal unit problem) (McGrew and Monroe 1993: 222; Openshaw and Taylor 1981) have their analogues in time. Unfortunately, geographers pay far less attention to sampling in time than in space. Consider, for example, the sampling strategy of sequent occupance (Whittlesey 1929). Users of this well-known approach in human geography describe spatial and landscape changes by reconstructing the character of landscapes at specific moments in the past. The problem arises with the way that these analysts slice up time. Proponents of this method adopt a slicing procedure that reveals a series of static landscapes that have reached their apogees, their moments of historical fluorescence. This series of static slices is then put into motion, creating a cinematic portrait of landscape change. This motion, however, is more illusory than real for the simple reason that this sampling procedure obscures transitions and all of the confusions and complexities that attend them. Sequent occupance thus portrays landscape evolution as an inexorable, inevitable, and unproblematic process in which geographies evolve in ways that seem as though they could not have happened otherwise. This is whiggish historical geography with a vengeance—the sort of geography advocated by, among others, Richard Hartshorne (1939) and Wilber Zelinsky (1973). For whigs, history is usually a paen to progress and almost always an abiding expression of faith in time's arrow into the future. When pushed to its logical extremes, whiggery brings us to the brink of "the end of history." This rosy version of past geographies contrasts sharply, of course, with radical or tory versions—versions that fasten their attention on times of transition, albeit accenting the subversions of structural forces in the case of the former and the works of history's "great men" in the case of the latter—which is to say that how we sample in time (times of stasis or transition, for example) is hardly an idle or scholastic exercise; indeed, the times that we pick reveal something of our deepest ideological convictions and not a little of our interpretations that ensue.

The Fallacy of Infinite Possibilities

Our eighth temporal fallacy is perhaps the most subtle and the most pernicious of all. It is what we call the assumption of infinite possibilities. For most of us, the assumption that the future holds unlimited possibilities for novelty and new discoveries is a noncontroversial given. Indeed, this teleological assumption is such an integral part of western culture's view of the world that it underlies nothing less than our theories of the cosmos. As Michael Shallis has observed, the cosmology constructed by physicists in this century:

> tells us little, if anything, about the nature of time, except perhaps that it is a lot stranger than we might think. I do think that it tells us a great deal about ourselves. . . . It tells us of our obsession with technique (we will solve the puzzles that remain if we develop better instruments), about our abstractedness from "normal" human experience, about our inconstancy, our insatiable need for and acceptance of perpetual change, our lack of a base, if you like. . . . It tells us a lot about ourselves and the culture we have built up over the past 300 years or so. . . . If I had to encapsulate what we have learned about time from our cosmology, it would be to say that we appear to have abstracted time, to have lost it or simply that we have passed time by. (Shallis 1986: 78–79)

If the assumption of infinite novelty inheres in our cosmology and our world view, it remains an assumption—albeit one that privileges the future over the past. Suppose, though, that this assumption is wrong, that novelty is finite and that we are approaching its limits. The implications are quite dramatic, as Kubler (1962) makes clear:

> Should the ratio between discovered positions and undiscovered ones in human affairs greatly favor the former, then the relation of the future to the past would alter radically. Instead of regarding the past as a microscopic annex to a future of astronomical magnitudes, we should have to envisage a future with limited room for changes, and these of types to which the past already yields the key. The history of things would then assume an importance now assigned only to the strategy of profitable inventions.

We need not subscribe to the notion of a finite world in order to make the point that our constructions of time reflect the assumptions of our world views. When potentialities are perceived as infinite and virtually unlimited—as in the cosmology of physics or the theories of neoclassical economics—the future matters much more than the past. The hubris entailed by such a world view, however, obscures the utility of the wisdom derived from experience, which perhaps is why we have so utterly failed to appreciate the virtues of ancient arid-land hydraulic systems or of ethnobotanic knowledge formulated by less complex cultures at some "earlier stage" in the evolution of society. Much, of course, is new under the sun, but one suspects that as much that is old (and useful) has been abandoned or discarded or remains as yet undiscovered. Some balance would seem to be in order until such times as the assumption of infinite possibilities is demonstrably proven to be correct.

Some Timely Advice

These eight temporal fallacies by no means exhaust the catalog of possibilities, but they are more than sufficient to reveal the need for geographers to reflect a bit more on their usages of time. Although geography's conventional uses of time—technical, traditional, and as a resource—have served us well up to a point, we suspect that the time has come to entertain new usages, usages that enable us to think about old problems in new ways.

The most obvious lesson to be learned from our gallery of temporal fallacies is that our usages of time are freighted with ideologies, with politics. We see these effects most readily in tory, whig, and radical interpretations of the past. The first of these, the tory conservatives, place their faith in facts (they are hedgehogs, by and large) and in individuals who are culpable for their actions at all times, but most especially in moments of social discontinuity when "great men" (and women) make history. Whiggish liberals, on the other hand, distance themselves from individuals. They see the workings of great forces in an almost providential history that sweeps us into a future of seemingly infinite possibility. If for the tory the past offers vital lessons on individual responsibility (honor, justice, greed, and the like) in those moments of great trial, for the whig the past is merely prologue to an ever-better future. Radicals stand somewhere in between. Like the tories, they accent transitions and discontinuities, but like the whigs, they are preoccupied by structural forces, albeit forces that dance to dialectical rhythms rather than linear ones (e.g., Marx 1974: 97). In their usages of time, in other words, radicals tend toward historicism, whereas whigs and tories tend, respectively, toward linear evolutionism and libertarian individualism.

If geographers are to make effective use of time and the past, we would be advantaged by fuller understandings of the consequences of our ideologies on our interpretations of the past because our ideologies constitute, in a large sense, the metanarrative scaffoldings for our constructions of past, present, and future. We can, of course, reject these foundational metanarratives in favor of postmodernist deconstructions that go so far as to obliterate time and space, not to mention these nineteenth-century ideological constructions; but short of a deconstructionist purge, we may just as well pursue a somewhat more modest strategy, one that effects a shift in the empirical research agenda of social science—a shift from objects to events, from linear associations of variables to the topology of event sequences, and from theories constructed on the assumption that actions are independent of time and space (i.e., universal) to theories that are predicated on the ordering of events in time and space, that is, on a geography of events (see Abbott 1983, 1988, 1990). In doing so, we will have moved full circle back to our queries on narratives and "good" stories that initiated this discussion.

What follows is only a rough sketch of a geography of events (of narrative sequences) and some of the methods that could be useful in these inquiries (see also chapter 11). This geography begins with the assumption that the order of events matters a great deal in shaping locational and ecological actions. This simple assumption constitutes a frontal assault on the alternative (and prevailing) assumptions of social science, namely, of linear reality and its corollary of invariance in time and space (Abbott 1988). More specifically, the linear (or stochastic or variables-based, whichever you prefer) model assumes that objects (e.g., cities) with the same attributes (e.g., city size) will exhibit identical functional relationships with the attributes of a dependent variable (e.g., the strike rates of workers in these cities). It assumes, for example, that two cities of the same size will exhibit identical (or nearly identical) strike rates (Shorter and Tilly 1974, Bennett and Earle 1982); but this assumption defies all that we know from experience. That is to say that the model ignores the cities' histories (and their locations as well). Suppose in the preceding decade, for instance, one of these cities had doubled in size and the other had been halved. Given this historical sequence of events, we would hardly expect these two cities to exhibit the identical strike rates prescribed by the linear model. To be sure, linear analysts might revise their stochastic model to accommodate this simple sequence, but diminishing returns set in when the sequences become more complex, when their time horizons are extended (e.g., a town that grows into a city, shrinks back to a town, and then expands into a metropolitan area), or when complex sequences are enchained, for example, when the sequence of strike events is enchained with the timings and trajectories of unionization, entrepreneurial response, and labor's ensuing gains and losses. The ingenuity of stochastic methodologists notwithstanding, the linear model encounters increasing difficulties in addressing event sequences and enchainments of this sort. Methods such as Box-Jenkins, event-history, and so on essentially compromise the linear model by relaxing its stringent assumptions of variable independence, that is, of time and space invariance. The irony in all of this, of course, is that in the end the user of the linear model invariably returns to storytelling, to the invocation of a narrative that provides a coherent interpretation (story) of the findings derived from a model that is essentially ahistorical—and aspatial (Abbott 1990).

The use of the off-stage narrative is standard practice in social science. Consider its invocation in a recent and very sophisticated statistical analysis of the geography of the Nazi Party vote in Germany during the critical election of 1930 (O'Loughlin et al. 1994). Conducting their study in accordance with the linear model, the authors demonstrate, among other things, the disproportionate support for the Nazi Party by rural Germans in areas of economic duress. In order to make sense of these findings, however—to explain how and why rural Germans behaved in this way—the authors construct a narrative on the following plot line: The Nazi Party's appeal to these beleaguered German farmers rested on Nazi promises to redress their economic plight by installing protectionist trade policies that would maintain agricultural prices. The authors' "story" is at once plausible and inventive. The key variable in their story—the Nazi promise of proagricultural policies—does not appear in the statistical model; nor does the post-hoc narrative tell us anything about the timing of these events, namely, the Nazi's policy declarations. When and where did the Nazis make these promises? How often were they reiterated? Were the Party's promises on the eve of the election in one area as effective as promises made earlier or with more frequency in other areas? The difficulties posed by these queries are compounded, moreover, when the sequencing of Nazi promises is enchained with the sequencing of agrarian economic conditions. Pretty soon the story begins to fall apart, and the linear model stands on the verge of a breakdown.

The alternative, of course, is to abandon the inventive domain of post-hoc narrative in favor of the narrative itself, that is, to abandon the linear, variables-based model and deal directly with the empirical ordering of events, event sequences, and their enchainments. In doing so, we must acknowledge the methodological immaturity of a geography of events, yet, if these methods are neither as formal (sophisticated) nor as fully developed as the methods available for the linear model, the means for dealing with event sequences are not altogether lacking. A geographer of events may resort, for example, to the seriation techniques developed in archaeology, to Markov models, or to Boolean algebra, among other things. To these might be added the arsenal of less formal methods deployed in literary criticism and in history, as well as the emerging body of methods associated with genetic mappings. Whatever the methodological possibilities, though, narrative methods generally subscribe to four key principles: 1) occurrences (not objects) are the units of observation; 2) events (not object attributes) are the units of analysis; 3) event sequences and enchainments (not variables) are the parameters; and 4) the identification of pattern in these narrative sequences (not functional relations) is the analyst's primary aim. For a geography of events, in other words, storytelling is not an afterthought (as in the linear model)—it is, rather, the entire point (Ragin 1987, Abbot 1990).

A geography of events and event sequences may be advanced via alliances with other time-sensitive (and space-sensitive) methods and perspectives. Especially relevant in this regard are the findings of time geography that, when generalized by the methods noted above, will enable the analyst to construct a typology of sequences in the "ceaseless becomings" of a multitude of particular places. Similarly, Braudel's notions on the multiscalar nature of history—of events, conjunctures, and structures—lend themselves to the tests of a geography of events and event sequences (Braudel 1977), as do the comparativist methodologies of Wallerstein (1974, 1980, 1988) and Skinner (1985, 1994), that enable time to be frozen (Wallerstein's A or B phrases in the capitalist epoch or Skinner's notion of "the eve of modernization") in order to compare the attendant differentiations in space and then thawed so as to explore the variability in the sequences that are responsible for the observed spatial structurings of regional systems or world systems. Some mention should also be made of the even more radical conceptualizations of the "new science" that accent event sequences, critical thresholds, and—once these are exceeded—the irreversibility of natural processes. Thus, at the very moment when the topological analysis of event sequences is challenging the relevance of the linear model in the social sciences, the nonlinear dynamics of the new science is challenging the functionalist equilibrium models in the natural sciences. In the latter as in the former, events such as disturbance and perturbation (and their sequences) assume a new and expanded role in shaping the future of natural and social systems (Prigogine and Stengers 1984, Roth 1992).

On the whole, one senses that scholarship—in both the social and natural sciences—has entered into one of these historical moments when the old rules of the game are set aside, when new rules for a new age are coming to the fore. Although the linear model has served us well, that model's shortcomings are increasingly apparent. In one field after another—in history, geography, the social sciences, literature, and the natural sciences—anxieties have arisen with the linear model's stringent (and unrealistic) assumptions of statistical independence and invariance in time and space. These anxieties have led, on the one hand, to a sense of unease with this model and, on the other, to concerted efforts to bring space and time back in, to restore some realism to our understandings of the workings of nature and society. The stakes, of course, are not small. Lest we succeed in these geohistorical reconstructions, an alternative paradigm is eagerly waiting in the wings to deconstruct (usefully) our truly flawed views of the world even as it obliterates (less usefully) the narrative and spatial orderings that were there to be found, had we only looked (Dear 1988; and the critique of Harvey 1990).

Looking Back— and Ahead

Like the narratives discussed here, this chapter consists of a beginning, a middle, and an end. It begins with an abstract and philosophical discussion of time; in the middle presents a fairly concrete appraisal of the ways that geographers have used and misused time (our eight temporal fallacies); and ends with some thoughts on a new paradigm—on a geography of events and event sequences that steers between the Scylla of deconstruction and the Charybdis of a linear model of reality. Along the way we looked at the ways in which time permeates most, if not all, geographical inquiry. We have seen that time is elusive, that attempts to define it devolve into a metaphysical dead end. Perhaps St. Augustine put it best: "What then is time? If nobody asks me: I know, but if I wish to explain it to one that asketh, then I know not" (Augustine 1838: 235). Alas, not much has changed.

Time is too important for geographers to ignore, however. We must address the definition and meaning of time in order to appreciate the historical contexts for contemporary problems; in order to forecast geographical futures and draw on the wisdom and folly of past times; and in order to develop models of the locational and ecological impacts of human activity—models that accommodate the orderings of occurrences, event sequences, and enchainments of event sequences. These and many another usage of time are shot through the literature of human geography. If, on occasion, our usage has been clumsy, we are not on the whole an antihistorical group. Indeed, for most of us, time is an integral if too often implicit part of our analysis. Our instincts are right; all that remains is to develop a fuller appreciation of the varied temporal logics that thread through the scholarly work that we do. Toward that end a geography of events (and the methods appropriate to it—an amalgam of set theory, combinatorics, algebraic topology, seriation, literary criticism, historical analysis, and nonlinear dynamics) has the potential for weaving these threads into a research program that takes seriously the cardinal dimensions of time and space.

References

Abbott, A. 1983. Sequences of social events. *Historical Methods* 16: 129–47.

———. 1988. Transcending general linear reality. *Sociological Theory* 6: 169–86.

———. 1990. Conceptions of time and events in social science methods. *Historical Methods* 23: 140–50.

Amedeo, D., and R. G. Golledge. 1975. *An introduction to scientific reasoning in geography*. New York: John Wiley.

Amson, J. C. 1974. Equilibrium and catastrophic models of urban growth. In *Space-time concepts in urban and regional models*, ed. E. L. Cripps, 108–28. London: Pion.

Arthur, C. J. 1968. On historical understanding. *History and Theory* 7: 203–16.

Augustine. 1838. *The confessions of Saint Augustine*, trans. E. B. Pusey. Mount Vernon, New York: Peter Pauper Press.

Bennett, S., and C. Earle. 1982. The geography of strikes in the United States, 1881–1894. *Journal of Interdisciplinary History* 13: 63–84.

Berry, B. J. L. 1973. A paradigm for modern geography. In *Directions in geography*, ed. R. J. Chorley, 3–21. London: Methuen.

Blaut, J. M. 1994. Invention, diffusion, and the origins of agriculture. Panel presentation at the annual meetings of the Association of American Geographers: special session on the origins of domestication and the Hahn-Sauer-Simoons tradition.

———. 1977. Two views of diffusion. *Annals of the Association of American Geographers* 67: 343–49.

Blumler, M. A. 1993. On the tension between cultural geography and anthropology: Commentary on Rodrigue's "Early animal domestications." *Professional Geographer* 45: 359–63.

Braudel, F. 1977. *Afterthoughts on material civilization and capitalism*, trans. P. Ranum. Baltimore: Johns Hopkins University Press.

Brentano, F. 1988. *Philosophical investigation on space, time, and the continuum*, trans. B. Smith. London: Croom Helm.

Carlstein, T. 1978. Innovation, time allocation, and time-space packing. In *Timing space and spacing time II: Human activity and time geography*, ed. T. Carlstein, D. Parkes, and N. Thrift, 146–61. London: Edward Arnold.

Carlstein, T., D. Parkes, and N. Thrift, eds. 1978. *Timing space and spacing time III: Time and regional dynamics*. New York: John Wiley.

Clark, A. C. 1962. The sheep/swine ratio as a guide to a century's change in the livestock geography of Nova Scotia. *Economic Geography* 38: 38–55.

Cliff, A. D. 1977. Quantitative methods: Time series methods for modelling and forecasting. *Progress in Human Geography* 1: 503–11.

Curry, L. 1964. The random spatial economy: An exploration in settlement theory. *Annals of the Association of American Geographers* 54: 138–46.

Darby, H. C. 1940. *The draining of the Fens*. Cambridge: Cambridge University Press.

Dear, M. 1988. The postmodern challenge: Reconstructing human geography. *Transactions of the Institute of British Geographers* N. S. 13: 262–74.

Doolittle, W. E. 1990. *Canal irrigation in prehistoric Mexico: The sequence of technological change*. Austin: University of Texas Press.

Earle, C. 1993. Divisions of labor: The splintered geography of labor markets and movements in industrializing America, 1790–1930. *International Review of Social History* 38: 5–37.

Earle, C., and C. Cao. 1993. Frontier closure and the involution of American society, 1840–1890. *Journal of the Early Republic* 13: 163–80.

Flood, R., and M. Lockwood. 1987. *The nature of time*. Oxford, England: Basil Blackwell.

Fraassen, B. C. U. 1985. *An introduction to the philosophy of time and space*. New York: Columbia University Press.

Green, W. 1993. *History, historians, and the dynamics of change*. Westport, Conn.: Praeger.

Hägerstrand, T. 1970. What about people in regional science? *Papers of the Regional Science Association* 14: 7–21.

————. 1975. Space, time, and human condition. In *Dynamic allocation of urban space*, ed. A. Karlquist, L. Lundquist, and F. Sinckars, 3–12. Farnborough, England: Saxon House.

Hartshorne, R. 1939. The nature of geography. *Annals of the Association of American Geographers* 29: 173–658.

Harvey, D. 1969. *Explanation in geography*. London: Edward Arnold.

————. 1973. *Social justice and the city*. London: Edward Arnold.

————. 1990. *The condition of postmodernity*. Oxford, England: Basil Blackwell.

Hepple, L. W. 1967. Epistemology, model building, and historical geography. *Geographical Articles* 10: 42–48.

————. 1974. The impact of stochastic process theory upon spatial analysis in human geography. *Progress in Geography* 6: 89–142.

Hirschboeck, K. 1987a. Catastrophic flooding and atmospheric circulation anomalies. In *Catastrophic flooding*, ed. L. Mayer and D. Nash, 23–56. Boston: Allen Unwin.

————. 1987b. Hydroclimatically defined mixed distributions in partial duration flood series. In *Hydrologic frequency modeling*, ed. V. P. Singh, 192–205. Boston: D. Reidel.

Holly, Brian. 1978. The problem of scale in time-space research. In *Timing space and spacing time III: Time and regional dynamics*, ed. T. Carlstein, D. Parkes, and N. Thrift, 5–18. New York: John Wiley.

Hornbeck, D. 1979. The patenting of California's private land claims, 1851–1885. *Geographical Review* 69: 434–48.

Kern, S. 1983. *The culture of time and space.* Cambridge, Mass.: Harvard University Press.

Kisiel, C. 1969. Time series analysis of hydrologic data. *Advances in Hydroscience* 5: 1–119.

Kubler, George. 1962. *The shape of time: Remarks on the history of things.* New Haven: Yale University Press.

Limerick, P. N. 1987. *The legacy of conquest: The unbroken past of the American West.* New York: W. W. Norton.

Leighly, J., ed. 1967. *Land and life: A selection from the writings of Carl Ortwin Sauer.* Berkeley: University of California Press.

Lucas, J. R. 1973. *A treatise on time and space.* London: Methuen.

McGrew, J. C., Jr., and C. B. Monroe. 1993. *An introduction to statistical problem solving in geography.* Dubuque, Iowa: Wm. C. Brown.

Marx, K. 1974. The eighteenth brumaire of Louis Bonaparte. In *Karl Marx and Frederick Engels: Selected works,* 95–180. New York: International Publishers.

Meinig, D. W. 1982. Geographical analysis of imperial expansion. In *Period and place: Research methods in historical geography,* ed. A. R. H. Baker and M. Billinge, 71–78. Cambridge: Cambridge University Press.

Mellaart, J. 1975. *The neolithic of the Near East.* New York: Charles Scribner's Sons.

Newcomb, R. M. 1969. Twelve working approaches to historical geography. *Yearbook of the Association of Pacific Coast Geographers* 31: 27–50.

Newton-Smith, W. H. 1986. Space, time, and space-time: A philosopher's view. In *The nature of time,* ed. R. Flood and M. Lockwood, 22–35. Oxford, England: Basil Blackwell.

Norton, W. 1978. Process and form relationships: Examples from historical geography. *Professional Geographer* 30: 128–34.

———. 1984. *Historical analysis in geography.* London: Longman.

Ogilvie, P. G. 1952. The time elements in geography. *Transactions of the Institute of British Geographers* 18: 1–15.

O'Loughlin, J., C. Flint, and L. Anselin. 1994. The geography of the Nazi vote: Context, confession, and class in the Reichstag election of 1930. *Annals of the Association of American Geographers* 84: 351–80.

Olsson, G. 1969. Central places in the random spatial economy. *Journal of Regional Science* 7: 217–38.

Openshaw, S., and P. J. Taylor. 1981. The modifiable areal unit problem. In *Quantitative geography: A British view*, ed. N. Wrigley and R. J. Bennett, 60–69. Boston: Routledge and Kegan Paul.

Parkes, D. N. 1977. T-P graphs, space-time, and an experimental city: An extension of factorial ecologies. *Geographical Analysis* 8: 277–84.

Parkes, D. N., and N. Thrift. 1980. *Times, spaces, and places: A chronogeographic perspective.* New York: McGraw-Hill.

Pazzani, M. 1991. A computational theory of learning causal relationships. *Cognitive Science* 15: 401–24.

Peuquet, D. J. 1994. It's about time: A conceptual framework for the representation of temporal dynamics in geographic information systems. *Annals of the Association of American Geographers* 84: 441–61.

Pred, A. 1977. The choreography of existence: Comments on Hägerstrand's time geography and its usefulness. *Economic Geography* 53: 207–21.

———. 1981. Social reproduction and the time-geography of everyday life. *Geografiska Annaler* 63B: 5–22.

———. 1986. *Place, practice, and structure: Social and spatial transformation in southern Sweden: 1750–1850.* Totowa, N.J.: Barnes & Noble Books.

———. 1990. *Making histories and constructing human geographies.* Boulder, Colorado: Westview Press.

Prigogine, I., and I. Stengers. 1984. *Order out of chaos: Man's new dialogue with nature.* New York: Bantam Books.

Ragin, C. C. 1987. *The comparative method: Moving beyond qualitative and quantitative strategies.* Berkeley: University of California Press.

Rifkin, J. 1987. *Time wars: The primary conflict in human history.* New York: Simon and Schuster.

Rodrigue, C. M. 1986. An evaluation of ritual sacrifice as an explanation for early animal domestications in the Near East. Doctoral dissertation, Clark University.

Roth, R. 1992. Is history a process? Nonlinearity, revitalization theory, and the central metaphor of social science history. *Social Science History* 16: 197–243.

Rucker, R. 1984. *The fourth dimension: Toward a geometry of higher reality.* Boston: Houghton Mifflin.

Salmon, W. C. 1963. *Logic.* Englewood Cliffs, N. J.: Prentice-Hall.

Schlesinger, George N. 1980. *Aspects of time.* Indianapolis, Ind.: Hackett.

Scott, A. J. 1983. Industrial organization and the logic of intrametropolitan location I: Theoretical considerations. *Economic Geography* 59: 233–50.

————. 1985. Location processes, urbanization, and territorial development: An exploratory essay. *Environment and Planning A* 17: 479–503.

————. 1988. From Fordism to flexible accumulation. *International Journal of Urban and Regional Research* 12: 171–86.

Shallis, M. 1986. Time and cosmology. In *The nature of time*, ed. R. Flood and M. Lockwood, 63–79. Oxford, England: Basil Blackwell.

Shannon, T. R. 1989. *Urban problems in sociological perspective.* Prospect Heights, Ill.: Waveland Press.

Shorter, E., and C. Tilly. 1974. *Strikes in France, 1830–1968.* Cambridge: Cambridge University Press.

Skinner, G. W. 1985. The structure of Chinese history. *Journal of Asian Studies* 44: 271–92.

Soja, E. 1989. *Postmodern geographies.* New York: Verso.

Storper, M., and R. Walker. 1989. *The capitalist imperative: Territory, technology, and industrial growth.* Oxford: Basil Blackwell.

Taaffe, E., R. Morrill, and P. Gould. 1963. Transport expansion in underdeveloped countries: A comparative analysis. *Geographical Review* 53: 503–29.

Taylor, P. 1989. *Political geography: World economy, nation-state, and locality.* London: Longman.

Thrift, N. 1977. Time and theory in human geography I. *Progress in Human Geography* 1: 65–101.

Tuan, Yi-Fu. 1977. *Space and place: The perspective of experience.* London: Edward Arnold.

Wallerstein, I. 1974. *The modern world-system I.* New York: Academic Press.

————. 1980. *The modern world-system II.* New York: Academic Press.

————. 1988. *The modern world-system III.* San Diego, Calif.: Academic Press.

Ward, D. 1975. The debate on alternative approaches in historical geography. *Historical Methods Newsletter* 8: 82–87.

Zelinsky, W. 1973. In pursuit of historical geography and other wild geese. *Historical Geography Newsletter* 3: 1–5.

3

Nature—Mapping the Ghostly Traces of a Concept

Kenneth Robert Olwig

Introduction

What is the relation between the nature of geography as a discipline and the nature that geographers believe ought to be the object of their study? This is a difficult question because the word *nature* is deceptive. To do something naturally is, among other things, to do it without reflecting on it. The natural is naturally taken for granted as in the statement: "Geographers naturally use maps to study the nature of the world." When we make such a statement we are saying that geographers not only use maps as a *matter of course* (without reflecting on it), but also that doing so is so natural for geographers that it would be unnatural for the speaker to have to legitimize his claim. We do not question those things that we all agree are part of the natural course of things. The word *nature* thus is deceptive because its connotations are complex and laden with normative values. The word is loaded and should be mapped with care. The nature that geographers have sought to map as the object of study has meant, in fact, very different things at different times in history. By examining just what it was that geographers thought they studied under the name of nature, it is possible to discover the outlines of a metatheory that geographers took for granted and that in many ways determined the content and character of their discipline.

There is an extra dimension to the problem of the usage of the concept of nature as a geographical concept, and that has to do with the tendency for the term to disappear from geographical discourse in the late twentieth century. This is at least partly because of the criticisms that have been leveled against the concept (and related ideas). Nature was seen as an ambiguous and normative concept, hence it was replaced by supposedly value-neutral concepts such as environment and ecology. Consequently, this analysis of the concept of nature as used in geography must also offer an analysis of the term's abandonment and its relation to the new terms that replaced it. Are they, in fact, euphemisms, which are every bit as embued with social values as the word they replaced? This study, therefore, is not a conventional review of the way different geographers have defined and used a concept; it deals rather with concepts that geographers have taken for granted — and thus failed to define — and with concepts that have changed their identity. We begin therefore with a discussion of the methods for tackling such illusive issues in an analysis of the concept of nature in geography.

Word

Why, we might ask, should a chapter on nature be included in a book about social-science concepts in geography? Indeed, some have argued that nature is such a complex, ambiguous, and value-laden concept that it has no place in a discipline that aspires to be an objective science, and it was for these reasons that the word was virtually erased from geography. I argue, to the contrary, that *nature*, or at least the ghostly trace of nature, is a central and unifying concept in geography and that the connection between the various parts of the discipline is inconceivable without it.

The Nature

We begin at a pivotal time in geography's history, 1938–1939. The young American geographer Richard Hartshorne was in German-speaking Europe at this time, absorbing geographical theory in a part of the world that, since the last decades of the nineteenth century, had become the bastion of academic geography (Elkins 1989: 17–18). His 1939 opus entitled *The Nature of Geography: A Critical Survey of Current Thought in the Light of the Past* (Hartshorne 1961) soon became "*the* text" (Lukermann 1989: 55) or even the "holy text" of the discipline (Smith 1989: 91). His volume "provided a crucial generation of American geographers (the first trained as geographers) with unprecedented self-justification" (Smith 1989: 95). This classic (Entrikin

1989: 1) "of timeless value" appeared at a time when American geography "was a subject grasping for discipline," for "an effective framework for understanding disciplined growth and for explaining that growth to fellow professionals" (de Souza 1989: vii). To put it another way, Hartshorne "defined a paradigmatic position validated historically but also claiming programmatic significance." The volume's significance was not confined to America: it also had "a remarkable effect overseas," where it stimulated "the emerging coherence of world geography as an intellectual discipline" (Stoddart 1989: 163–64). Fifty years after its publication, Hartshorne's book is often referred to simply as *The Nature* (Sack 1989: 41).

The role played by Hartshorne's book was not mere happenstance. Indeed, establishing a mainstream geography was Hartshorne's goal (Lukermann 1989: 57), just as it had previously been the goal for Hartshorne's main German source of inspiration, Alfred Hettner (1859–1941) (Elkins 1989: 20). Both followed in the footsteps of their master, the philosopher Immanuel Kant, who argued that knowledge divides "into definite disciplines even before we obtain the knowledge itself" (quoted in Smith 1989: 98).

The Sound of Silence

The Nature contained a number of curious silences, like the silence of the dog that did not bark in the night in a Sherlock Holmes story. Neil Smith tells us that while Hartshorne was writing "in Vienna immediately following the *Anschluss*," when German geography was becoming implicated in National Socialist ideology, "characteristically, there is little hint of this in the text" (1989: 107). This is curious because German geographical theory dominated Hartshorne's book and the field in general, but rather than discuss the relationships between geographical theory and National Socialist ideology, Hartshorne ignored the issue and geographers avoided a theoretical debate over the book's contents. According to Fred Lukermann, avoidance was a consequence of both the book's massive argumentation "and the interlude of World War II (which) dampened the flames of controversy for a while." As a result, the book had the effect of "literally shutting out other views and other versions of the history of geographic thought until the early fifties" (1989: 55).

One of the ironic casualties in *The Nature* was nature itself, along with the related concept of landscape, which Hartshorne saw as being predicated on the study of a nature/culture dichotomy. If Hartshorne acknowledged landscape as once "the single most important word in geographic language," he also, in Smith's view, "assassinated" the term by branding it of "little or no value as a technical or scientific term." It thereby was "largely excluded from theoretical discourse almost to the present day" (1989: 107). Of nature, or more particularly the nature/culture distinction, Hartshorne could triumphantly report twenty years after the publication of *The Nature* that "nearly all American geographers used this distinction as basic to their thinking in geography. No doubt most of them still do, though it is worthy of note that it is either not included or plays little role in several of the chapters of *American Geography: Inventory and Prospect* of 1954" (Hartshorne 1956: 55).

The word *nature*, along with the nature/culture distinction, steadily disappeared from the texts of mainstream geography, the last vestige of the idea found ironically in the title of the book that had rubbed it out. What remained was space, not empty space, but "the science of space" (Hartshorne 1958). Geographers, particularly those associated with Carl Sauer at the University of California at Berkeley, for whom the concepts of nature and landscape were vital, tended to remain silent. They chose, rather, to let their practice as scholars speak louder than their words (Lukermann 1989: 56). Sauer, according to Lukermann, "responded with some personal bitterness in 1941 but refused to enter into any dialectic with Hartshorne or *The Nature* on substantive issues." The forum for Sauer's "bitterness," a presidential address to the Association of American Geographers, nevertheless provided an inspired argument for the tradition of studying society/environment relations in geography from a historical perspective in which culture, not the environment, is the active agent (Sauer 1969a, orig. 1941). He backed away, however, from the notion of the natural landscape as the medium on which the cultural landscape is created, a notion he had earlier expounded in his influential manifesto "The Morphology of Landscape" (Sauer 1969b, orig. 1925). Sauer concluded that we are "likely to conceal, rather than to answer, the dilemma of area by calling it a natural unit" (Sauer 1969a: 364).

Nature was essentially deleted from the mainstream of geography at a critical juncture in the discipline's history. So how does one write about a concept that has been rubbed out (or "assassinated," in Smith's language)? The answer, as Holmes knew, is elementary—we must attend to the clues given by the dogs that do not bark, by the value-laden word that was erased, and by the ideological implications that are not discussed. A method for detecting such silences and interpreting their meaning is elaborated below.

The Deconstruction of Geography: Discourse, Practice, Institution

The subject of geography can be defined by the self-definition that occurs in discourse, that is, the ongoing process in which geographers meet, confer, and produce texts and thereby create a corpus of work that constructs disciplinary identity — an essence or nature of the subject (Hartshorne 1959, 1961; James 1972). This constructive process determines what is regarded as mainstream, and what is not. *Discourse* refers not to the language expression of an individual in isolation, but rather to the common ground that makes it possible not only to speak, but also to make or write a speech to which others can respond, thereby creating the basis for the extended conversation that is discourse (Ricoeur 1971, 1973). This extended conversation is formalized in the texts of the scholarly discourse that takes place within academic institutions (Lukermann 1964: 167).

In many important respects individual geographers cannot be said to be the authors of their texts; it might be closer to the truth to say that their work is "inscribed in a determined textual system" (Derrida 1976: 159–60; Olsson 1984). The subject that they construct is predetermined to some extent by the premises of a larger discourse, and, hence by factors of which they are not necessarily aware. They may be influenced, for example, by a concept of nature that, although it differs from current usage in their language, is nevertheless latent in the institutionalized structures of their department, university, libraries, course catalogues, textbooks, professional societies, journals, and conferences. To understand, therefore, the role of the concept of nature in geography, it is insufficient to examine the surface of geographical discourse or to read the definitions that geographers have constructed for themselves. It is also necessary to deconstruct what geographers write, to take the writing apart. In the case of the concept of nature, even though the term has largely been rubbed out, the traces and clues that it has left behind may help to clarify the ways in which this concept continues to define the content of geographical texts — despite the best intentions of their authors (Olwig 1989).

One approach to geographical discourse is to look at the discipline not in terms of what geographers talk and write about to each other, but in terms of what geographers do and how it relates to what others do — their practice (Bordieu 1977; Buttimer 1983). It is sometimes said, for example, when frustration over the seeming lack of intellectual unity in the discipline becomes overwhelming, that "geography is what geographers do" or that "if you can map it, it is geography." Geography, this implies, fundamentally involves activities that are mappable — areal planning, landscape analysis, regional description. Mapping has even been claimed to be "the language of geography," and, according to Carl Sauer, the geographer's "most primitive and persistent trait, is liking maps and thinking by means of them" (Sauer 1969c: 389–404). What geographers do, however, is also intimately related to the ways in which the field has become institutionalized. Geography is also an institution, or an amalgam of institutions. Such institutions include academic geography departments, geographical societies, elementary and secondary schools, popular educational magazines and related media, government bodies (e.g., planning agencies and geodetic surveyors) and private industry (e.g., surveyors, environmental consultancy firms). It is legitimate to ask questions of such institutions concerning the relationship between their concept of nature and the social interests that they serve.

These three dimensions, *discourse, practice,* and *institution,* can be viewed together in what might be termed an archaeological (Foucault 1972) context, in which the discipline itself is seen to be a sort of artifactual, institutionalized intellectual construct, situated in given discursive and textual strata, to be explained in terms of its practices and their consequences. It is when geography has been unearthed in this way that it becomes possible to reconstitute it again and see whether the disciplinary site we have excavated bears any useful resemblance to one point of departure—the geography and the seemingly so innocuous concept of nature that we think we know so well in our daily work as students and teachers of the subject.

The Conception of Nature

The definition of the word *nature* fills pages in a standard dictionary such as the *Oxford English Dictionary* (1971); historians of ideas have found sixty-six meanings for the word (Lovejoy and Boas 1935: 447–56). It is no wonder therefore that nature has been termed "perhaps the most complex word in the language" (Williams 1976: 184–89). For this reason a concise etymological definition of the word is given in the appendix, which lists the different definitions of the word in the order of their historical development. To clarify the meaning of nature I at times append to it a number, or numbers, referring to the dictionary definitions of the word intended. I do the same with the related word, *landscape (Oxford English Dictionary* 1971).

The word *nature,* according to the philosopher John Passmore, derives "from the Latin, *nascere,* with such meanings as 'to be born,' 'to come into being.' Its etymology suggests, that is, the embryonic, the potential rather than the actual" (1974: 32). This understanding of the genesis of the term makes sense when seen in the particular context of the organic cosmology of the Greeks in general and Aristotle in particular (Collingwood 1960: 3–4, 80–92; for a definition of *organic,* see Williams 1976: 189–92). In Aristotle's view "all the planets and stars fit snugly together, with intervening atmosphere, as aggregate bodies" (Edgerton 1975: 159). These bodies represent an organically enclosed space such as that possessed by any living organic being, be it a cell or a person. A cosmos constitutes a vast living being, which participates in a creative, birthing growth process in which its potential (as in the case of an embryo or seed) becomes actualized (the mature being or plant). This process of becoming suggests an inner drive, principle, or purpose that motivates the process. Such a notion provides the point of departure for teleological cosmologies that see the universe as being invested with a collective soul and mind and, hence, a purpose. It is in this context that the definition of nature as "the inherent character or basic constitution of a person or thing" (1a) and "a creative and controlling force in the universe" (2a) should be understood.

To be born, something must be conceived through a process that normally involves two poles, the male and the female. In Western culture this became the basis of a cosmology involving a father sky and a mother earth (Merchant 1980: 1–41; Tuan 1974: 129–49). The sky provided, on one hand, the fertilizing rain as well as the rhythmic, geometric movement of the heavenly bodies, which appeared to determine the regular, cyclical periodization of the fertility cycle—whether the periods of the menstruating woman or the seasons of the earth. The earth, on the other hand, brings forth life from the depths of its womb. It is in this generative sense that the definition of nature as "the physical constitution or drives of an organism" (4) derives. This sense is related, in turn, to usages in which nature appears as a euphemism for the sexual drives or more directly denotes semen, the menses, or the female pudendum (OED 1971: "nature" definitions 7, 8). The tendency to identify nature with the female (mother nature), which has its roots in the earliest fertility cults (Duerr 1985: 16–31) and its goddesslike form in medieval allegory (Lovejoy and Boas 1935: 455–56), derives from the fact that it is the woman who gives birth. The male principle, however, also makes a seminal contribution to the process: this explains the notion of an upper celestial nature as a creative force permeating a lower terrestrial nature (Gadol 1969: 93–211). The values placed on this bipolar conception of nature vary, as will be seen, through time.

The generative process that results in birth, as any farmer or parent can testify, is a process fraught with uncertainty and difficulty. The elements must mix and balance in just the right way at just the right time for the earth, or the female creature, to bear. The consequences of infertility can be disastrous. The natural gestation process must follow certain norms to succeed, or unnatural fertility will result. An unnatural society that violates these norms will be visited by famine and depopulation (cf. Kay 1989; Tuan 1971). The concept of nature is thus intimately related to that of the natural, and hence to norms and values. When people act in agreement with their nature (definition 1) and the nature (definition 1) of their surroundings, they act naturally. The Aristotelian cosmology may have been formulated by a philosopher, but it was in fundamental agreement with the experience and values of a society almost totally dependent on agriculture, and, hence, on organic processes, for survival. This was furthermore a society that could conceive of social organization only in terms of familial, or quasi-familial, relations of birth (Merchant 1980: 1–41, 42–68).

Nature and Natural Science

Such sciences as geometry and physics find a natural object of study in the heavenly bodies in the upper nature of the sky, whereas a natural science such as biology clearly finds its subject matter in lower, terrestrial, nature. Those who have defined the modern study of geography, as is the case with so many other disciplines, generally find its roots in the Renaissance, where, as will be seen, it was defined as dealing with both realms. The degree of emphasis attached to nature's cosmic or terrestrial pole is critical, however, in determining the nature of the field. The weighting that the discipline has given one or another aspect of nature during a given epoch in history involves a complex process that engages the discipline's status as a practice, a discourse, and an institution.

The practices that characterize the modern study of geography began in the emerging urban centers of the Italian city-states such as Florence and Venice and in the cities of lowland Europe (modern Holland and Belgium). These practices were tied particularly to the rediscovery of the work of the ancient Greek astronomer and geographer, Claudius Ptolemeus (A.D. 90–168). Ptolemeus was the classical example of a geographer who focused on the cosmic, geometrical aspects of geography in which space was undifferentiated and neutral, to be demarcated by the coordinates of a grid within which things could be located. Ptolemeus states:

> Geography is the representation, by a map, of the portion of the earth known to us, together with its general features. Geography differs from chorography in that chorography concerns itself exclusively with particular regions and describes each separately, representing practically everything of the lands in question, even the smallest details. . . . It is the task of geography on the other hand, to present the known world as one and continuous, to describe its nature and position, and to include only those things that would be contained in more comprehensive and general descriptions. . . . Geography . . . is concerned with quantitative rather than with qualitative matters, since it has regard in every case for the correct proportion of distances. . . . (quoted in Lukermann 1961: 194–210)

This geography saw nature in terms of a systematic space that was infinite, homogeneous, and isotropic (Edgerton 1975: 161). Ptolemeus wrote of a subject that he called geography, and he was renowned for his contributions to cartography, but the Renaissance men who engaged in these activities were not defined as geographers, or even as cartographers, by their contemporaries. They were humanist men of letters with a broad range of interests in subjects that, through their efforts, were then in the process of being defined as arts and sciences in the forms that we recognize today.

A cosmic, Ptolemeic geographic practice served well in an age of discovery and urban economic expansion. It helped make possible the approximation of the dimensions of the globe and the charting of its known and potential regions. Celestial navigation made it possible to locate oneself within the coordinates of an unknown space and to prepare for expected climatic and vegetational patterns — all the sorts of knowledge that are useful for trade and exploration, war, and imperial expansion. By the same token, the ability to survey and map property suited an emerging, commercial, urban society in which land was becoming a commodity to be bought and sold on the market.

The reemergence of Ptolemeus's geography not only suited the practical needs of Renaissance society, it also fit in well with the neo-Platonic philosophy shared by his rediscoverers. Ptolemeic geography suited the Platonic notion that behind the confused, imperfect, shadow world of terrestrial nature was to be found a more perfect rational reality, exemplified by the perfect movement and shape of the heavenly spheres (Merchant 1980: 105–11; Cosgrove 1988: 262–65). The map projection, with its grid coordinated to the cosmos, was the perfect illustration of the idea that there was natural geometric regularity behind the confused phenomena of terrestrial life (Edgerton 1975: 91–123; Gadol 1969: 143–211). It also suited related mystical and cabalistic ideas, which could be wedded to Christianity, and the notion of an invisible heavenly father whose spirit regulates earthly life. For the Renaissance and the Enlightenment the ideal nature was celestial nature, replete with the rational clockwork perfection exhibited by the mechanical movement of the heavenly bodies in which, as Galileo put it, "the book of nature was written in mathematical figures" (Jordanova 1986: 27; Collingwood 1960: 94). As nature became one with reason and the quantifiable laws of natural science, Alexander Pope (as quoted in Williams 1976: 188) could write that:

> *Nature and Nature's laws lay hid in night;*
> *God said, Let Newton be! and all was light!*

As this poet's statement suggests, this conception of nature applied equally well to aesthetics as when Christopher Wren, the Newton of English architecture, wrote "There are two causes of Beauty — natural and customary. Natural is from Geometry, consisting in Uniformity. . . . Geometrical Figures are naturally more beautiful than any other irregular; in this all consent, as to a Law of Nature" (quoted in Miller 1988: 117).

Natural values

The emphasis of the Renaissance and Enlightenment on the higher nature of the cosmos is an expression of the way in which the concept of nature came to be used to express natural ideals. It illustrates a usage of the concept that has led nature to be termed "the chief and most pregnant word in the terminology of normative provinces of thought in the West" (Lovejoy 1927: 444). The map, of course, is an ideal means of representing the way in which a higher rational nature (by invisible means) gives structure and order to the seeming chaos of organic terrestrial nature. The map, in this sense, represents a pregnant conception of nature, both literally and figuratively.

The map, or plan, reduces terrestrial complexity to a series of coordinates, projected and located on a grid defined by celestial coordinates and framed within the flat or planar surface of an isotropic plane. In the hands of an architect it becomes a rational means of representing the forms of a building or city as space. The linear projection drawing, which was developed by many of the same individuals who developed Renaissance cartography and architecture, made it possible to structure pictorial representation in this same way. In all three forms of representation it is the grid that provides the spatial framework for the projection, an invisible, underlying, mathematically rational, geometric spatial structure that allows for a particular projection of, and orientation toward, the irregular organic forms of the terrestrial world (see figure 3.1).

The normative aspect of the concept of nature means that the map and linear perspective drawing function not only as means of representing and structuring the world as we believe we see it, but also as means of projecting on that world our idealized conception of the way things naturally ought to be. We thereby come to represent both the world as we believe we see it and the world as we would like to see it. This quality of maps, in turn, makes them potential tools for consciously or unconsciously changing the world. By using the map and plan to create formal gardens, buildings, or cities that are images of the cosmic utopian perfection envisioned by Plato or the heavenly city of biblical revelation, we can create actual environments that are material manifestations of a natural cosmic ideal (see figure 3.2; Tuan 1971: 24–26). The same rational principles, when applied by a ruler to larger territories, can be used to create administrative areas or regions or to transform the structure of land use (Cosgrove 1984; Harley 1988). *Region*, after all, derives from the Latin word *regere*, which means to rule. Even gardens could be structured in the image of a cosmic nature, with the vegetation clipped in unchanging geometric forms, laid out according to the ruler's line (Löfgren 1989). In this fashion the map became almost literally the territory.

This representation and reshaping of our environs according to the image of the natural principles that (we believe) originally created them can also help foster less tangible changes by legitimating or naturalizing new world views or ideologies. Ideology is a tricky concept in much the same way that nature is. Both refer to conscious, reflected, systematic bodies of ideas and to

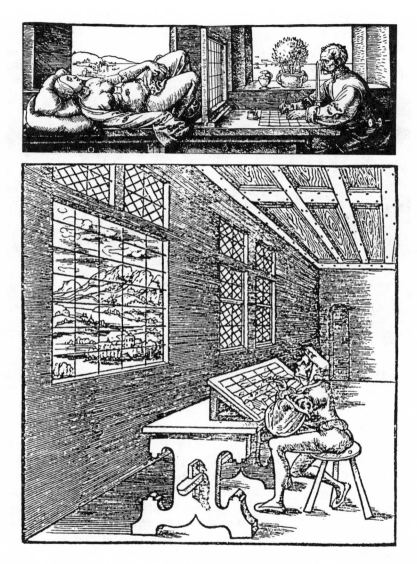

Figure 3.1 Illustrations of the use of the grid in the creation of perspective drawings: "Ur Underweysung der Messung" (top) by Albrecht Dürer, 1525, and "Kurst deg Messens" (bottom) by Johann II of Bavaria and Hieronymus Rodler, 1531. Dürer's artist is "sighting" his perspective with the use of a miniature "monument," much as a surveyor might use an actual monument.

Figure 3.2 Two radically opposed views of nature in the gardens at Chatsworth, England. The foreground shows the remains of geometric formal gardens which were supplemented or replaced in the mid-seventeenth century by landscape gardens in the "natural" style (background) designed by Lancelot "Capability" Brown. Photograph by the author.

unreflected, unconscious, value-laden ideas that are taken for granted as natural—thereby representing a sort of "false consciousness" (Williams 1976: 126–30). In the almost subliminal transition from the first form of ideology to the second, the systematic and reflexive ideas produced in the discourse of science per se come to constitute the unreflected ideology of a period in history. This unreflected ideology, however, also has the effect of favoring certain approaches to science over others—for example, paradigms rooted in the mechanics of physics over those rooted in the organic notions of biology. Cartesianism and Newtonianism belong as much to the Renaissance as Darwinism belongs to the birth of the modern era, both as science (in the first form) and as ideology (in the second).

    Consider, for example, the representations of the city. For feudal society the city as a center of trade and finance represented social forces that were the object of profound mistrust for a society based on natural customary and patriarchic rights and obligations that were tied to the biological inheritance of (rural) land that, in theory, could not be bought or sold. The cadastral map provided a means by which land could be represented as property, a quantifiable parcel that could be valued, subdivided, and sold. It also represented, however, a cosmology that attributed divine qualities to the cartographic principles that reduced the unique organism of the feudal territory to an abstract geometrical space. When such principles become the object of mysticism and religious worship, as they did in the Renaissance, they provide the means by which the city, and the activities identified with it, are naturalized and legitimized as the image of the heavenly city or of the utopian city-states envisioned in classical platonic philosophy (Cosgrove 1984: 92–98; Tuan 1971: 24–26; Sack 1980: 144–64). By the same token, the restructuring of the countryside brought about the intrusion of property rights, and the money economy had the effect of naturalizing new ideologies related to the use and control of land (Merchant 1980: 42–68).

Renaissance Geography

Geography, one might conclude, emerged in the Renaissance as a set of practices that directly or indirectly served concrete social purposes while being tied to an ongoing discourse in areas of endeavor that were themselves in the process of being defined and segmented as disciplines of the arts, architecture, science, and philosophy (Gadol 1969: 157). One of those engaged in this discourse was Bernhardus Varenius (1622–50), a German scholar living in Amsterdam. Varenius defined "the mixt mathematical science" of geography in his treatise *Geographia Generalis* from 1650 (Varenius 1682; James 1972: 124–26). Like other architects of geography as a modern academic discipline, Varenius defined geography in the light of the authority of past masters, including those Renaissance scholars who had illuminated the conception of nature behind geography.

Much as had Ptolemeus, Varenius divided geography into two parts: (1) "general or universal geography" (the subject of his book), which relies on mathematical or astronomical laws to explain phenomena (such as climate) of relevance to the earth in general; and (2) "special or particular geography," which describes areas of the world "having at least a mean magnitude" (chorography) and "any little tract of land, or place" (topography) (Varenius 1682: 2). Varenius clarified the relation between the two as follows:

The *Principles* which *Geography* useth for confirming the truth of her Propositions, are threefold: 1. *Geometrical, Arithmetical,* and *Trigonometrical* Propositions. 2. *Astronomical* Precepts and Theorems; although it may seem like a miracle for the knowledge of the Earth in which we dwell, to use the Celestial Bodies, which are so many thousand miles remote from us. 3. *Experience* for indeed the greatest part of *Geography*, especially that which is Particular, is upheld by the only Experience and Observations of men who have described every Country. (Varenius 1682: 3)

The basic division between general and special geography has persisted to the present time in the distinction between systematic and regional geography. It also played an important role in Hartshorne's thinking, and it is still used, for example, in the cataloging system of the library of the American Geographical Society, which sets the standard for many other libraries.

Though practically oriented pursuits such as cartography had ceased being the amateur pastime of philosophers by the seventeenth century and had become instead a profession of specialists, geography had not yet been institutionalized as an academic profession. It was, however, a respectable intellectual pursuit that engaged thinkers such as Isaac Newton—who edited several editions of Varenius's *Geography Generalis* (Warntz 1989)—and Immanuel Kant (May 1970).

Landscape and Geography

Modern professional geography first began to emerge in the late eighteenth and early nineteenth centuries as part of a generalized romantic reaction to the rational cosmopolitanism and urban orientation of the Enlightenment and the mercantile state. This romantic turn emphasized "The quest for local color; the endeavor to reconstruct in imagination the distinctive inner life of peoples remote in time or space or in cultural condition; the *etalage du moi*; the demand for particularized fidelity in landscape-description, . . . the cultivation of individual, national, and racial peculiarities" (Lovejoy 1973: 292–93). A library could be filled with the books that have been written to explain this change—one of the best being the above referenced work by Lovejoy. My contribution is the more modest one of showing that the seemingly opposite conceptions of nature as celestial and geometrical or terrestrial and organic were, in fact, two sides of the same coin—sides that were integrally related in the process of conception itself and that were effectively represented by the map. What this means, of course, is that we are dealing here less with a radical shift in thought and more nearly with a continuity of thoughts within a larger paradigm.

An important aspect of the shift in sensibility described by Lovejoy was the growing sense of national and regional identity. Here, we see a shift in focus from the abstract, geometrical, undifferentiated space of the cosmos and the city, which was the focus of the mercantilist state, to the particularized, organically enclosed space of the countryside. This shift was also tied to the concept of nature, but this time it was the organic, terrestrial pole that came into focus. Wren's "custom" once again became the natural principle behind social organization, but this time the focus shifted from the customary biological inheritance of the feudal nobility to that of the folk—hence the popularity of the work of scholars such as the German philosopher Johann Gottfried von Herder (1744–1803) and his writings on the folk soul of European nations. The romantic shift was associated with a concept of landscape that, on the one hand, was a product of the Renaissance and, on the other, represented a return to pre-Renaissance values identified with a protolandscape concept.

The Renaissance/Enlightenment concept of landscape was not the product of a mode of discourse identifiable with geography, or even science, but was rather a discourse that derived from art. It sprang, nevertheless, from the same practices that produced the new cartography and the new architecture, and it was intimately related to the development of the modern concept of nature. In classical Greco-Roman society it was commonly believed that civilization was born at the time when people simultaneously domesticated their game (and themselves) and became pastoralists. The word *nat*ion shares the same root with *nat*ure, both referring to the process of being born. The nation, essentially, is made up of the native born, hence the nation is something to which one has a natural birthright. Virgil was the national ideologist of Rome par excellence, and his poetry celebrated the natural virtues of the Greco-Roman shepherd forefathers (who were believed to have hailed originally from a pastoral region of Greece called Arcadia) (Olwig 1984: 1–10).

When painters of the Renaissance and Enlightenment sought to give visual form to natural qualities, particularly as described in the classical poetry of Virgil and others, they applied the techniques of perspective drawing to idealized rural pastoral and bucolic environments, thereby creating an image of natural scenery. The term *scene* itself derives from the visual backdrop that was symbolic of nature (as used in the theater) and that was often seen as a microcosm of the world (Olwig 1993). Not only was Shakespeare's theater called the Globe, but atlases of the globe were called theaters. Thus we find that Jakob Ortelius, Renaissance humanist philosopher and cartographer, calls his pioneering world atlas, *Theatrum Orbis Terrarum*—the theater of the lands of the world. Within the atlas we find maps whose projection and scale bear a close resemblance to landscape painting, and it is therefore not surprising to learn that Ortelius was also a patron for Pieter Brueghel the Elder, one of the first to paint landscapes (Cosgrove 1984: 147–50; Olwig 1987).

These painters were (to use the language of semiotics) using the depicted terrestrial features as a referent, a means of referring symbolically through the sign of the painting to the natural classical values identified with pastoral and bucolic society (see figure 3.3; Olwig 1993). Until this time no one would have called an actual rural environment of this sort "nature." Nature referred, according to Passmore, "to the embryonic, the potential rather than the actual." It is at this time, however, that we find the poet John Dryden writing (in a translation of Virgil from 1697) of "Surveying Nature with too nice a view" (O.E.D. 1971: "nature" definition 13). The rural environment of Virgil's Arcadia was an idealized vision of the natural society, not the actual place, but it was a short step for artists to use actual places as models for their depiction of the natural. It is in this way that nature became synonymous with "natural scenery" (definition 8), and this definition, of course, was also intimately related to definition 7, "man's original condition."

Rural territories were called *landschap* in Dutch, so it was appropriate for the Dutch to call perspective paintings of such scenes "landscape paintings." The seventeenth-century English connoisseurs who purchased these paintings, however, used the term *landschap*, or landscape, to mean a genre of painting, that is, "a picture representing a view of natural inland scenery" or "the art of depicting such scenery," to quote Webster (Webster 1965: "landscape"; see also the appendix to this chapter). In this way the words *nature* and *landscape* became synonymous. The English, however, did not stop at merely painting such environments; they also set about landscaping the rural surroundings of their country seats so that they came to resemble the ideal natural environments depicted in the paintings. Eventually, the term *landscape* was transferred from a mode of painting and shaping our environs to that portion of these environs we would see if they were viewed as we view the world when we make a perspective drawing: "a portion of land that the eye can comprehend in a single view 3. VISTA, PROSPECT" (*Oxford English Dictionary* 1971). The referent used in the representation of nature as landscape thereby became one with the territory. *Nature* as a term referring to the ideal process that generates the things in the material world thus became reified as the things themselves when viewed as scenery (Olwig 1993). This did not mean, however, that these material scenes lost their identification with ideal natural values, but now these values seemed to spring from the material environment itself rather than from the hand of the artist. The landscape garden surrounding the estate thus helped naturalize the power identified with estate ownership (Olwig and Olwig 1979).

Landscape art encouraged the development of a landscape sensibility that eventually inspired travel in search of ideal natural landscapes resembling those of landscape art and gardens. As people reacted against, or sought to escape from, the rigidly regularized landscape created by enclosure and the despoiled surroundings created by industry, they sought a counterpoint in land-

Figure 3.3 Mid sixteenth-century illustrations from Jakob Ortelius's *Theatrum Orbis Terrarum* (top) compared with Pieter Brueghel's sketch "Haymaking." Sources: for the former, Department of Maps, Prints and Photographs, The Royal Library, Copenhagen; for the latter, a sketch commissioned by the author based on the orginial in the National Gallery in Prague.

scapes whose natural virtue was that they were perceived as influenced by contemporary man and his culture. Such people sought, instead, landscapes that still reflected the natural conditions into which the natives of an area were born—and thereby the innate natural (definition 1a) character of humanity (see figure 3.2). This primitivism fostered the notion that nature must somehow be in opposition to the products of (unnatural) human culture, a notion that eventually made it possible to envision a misanthropic natural landscape without humans. The natural values identified with a landscape vary, of course, according to the content and structure of that landscape. There is considerable difference between the values identified with arcadian pastoral landscape, with the agricultural landscape of farmers, and with a wilderness that is uninhabited or inhabited by wild savages (Olwig 1984: 1–9, 23–38; Tuan 1971: 24–26). If the identification of nature with natural values was not lost, it certainly was muddled by this process. Nature was reified and made synonymous with our physical surroundings.

The Nature of Landscape Geography

The transition that occurred in the conception of nature from a vertical relationship between the cosmos and earth to a horizontal conception of nature as landscape (Tuan 1974: 129–36) can be seen in the work of another father figure for modern mainstream geography, Alexander von Humboldt (1769–1859). In the spirit of Varenius, Humboldt's geography required a cosmic understanding of the forces shaping the environment that integrated both the natural and the social sciences—an integration that was evident in the title of his monumental work (1845–62) *Cosmos: A Sketch of a Physical Description of the Universe*. *Landscape* provides an important key for understanding Humboldt's practice of the discipline of geography. The way these two dimensions interrelate is described in his introduction to his *Cosmos*:

> In the uniform plain bounded only by a distant horizon where the lowly heather, the cistus, or waving grasses, deck the soil; on the ocean shore, where waves, softly rippling over the beach, leave a track, green with the weeds of the sea; everywhere, the mind is penetrated by the same sense of the grandeur and vast expanse of nature, revealing to the soul; by a mysterious inspiration, the existence of laws that regulate the forces of the universe. . . .
>   It may seem a rash attempt to endeavour to separate into its different elements, the magic power exercised upon our minds by the physical world, since the character of the landscape, and of every imposing scene in nature, depends so materially upon the mutual relation of the ideas and sentiment simultaneously excited in the mind of the observer.
>   The powerful effect exercised by nature springs, as it were, from the connec-

tion and unity of the impressions and emotions produced; and we can only trace their different sources by analyzing the individuality of objects, and the diversity of forces. (von Humboldt 1849: 3, 5)

Humboldt characteristically brought landscape painters on his expeditions and his geographic writing inspired landscape painters. Nature in the new geography was terrestrial nature, and its object was landscape in the sense of "the landforms of a region in the aggregate." It was also, however, very much the landscape of art imbued with natural arcadian/pastoral aesthetic values (Hard 1965), but it was a new kind of pastoral, not of the impossible, idealized landscapes of the past, but rather of detailed realistic paintings informed by the detailed scientific knowledge of naturalists such as Humboldt. The new arcadianism of geographers and artists alike dealt with real shepherds (and other "natural" peoples) in real places.

A characteristic of the use of the concept of nature is the way it can "slip more or less insensibly from one ethical or esthetic standard to its very antithesis, while nominally professing the same principles" (Lovejoy 1927: 444). In the Renaissance and Enlightenment nature tended to be identified with the rationality of *upper nature*, the geometrical perfection of the cosmos. By the nineteenth century nature had become virtually synonymous with terrestrial landscape scenery. The transition is so insensible that it is hard to pinpoint a rift in the disciplinary discourse of geographers such as Humboldt. The reason is that the practice of geography—the surveying and making of charts and maps—remains at the core of the discipline. The basic cosmology of the map, with its conceptual representation of the intercourse between cosmic and terrestrial nature, remains the same. What has changed is the emphasis placed on the terrestrial as opposed to the celestial pole in this intercourse. It is this shift that brought about the new focus on landscape, on an organic and terrestrial nature. While the basic tools used to create maps and to envision scenes (the method of projection) remained the same, the interpretive emphasis shifted from the mechanical cosmic/geometric frame to the organic terrestrial world.

This shift to an organic conception of nature is evident also in the work of another German founder of modern geography, Karl Ritter (1779–1859). In Ritter's work we see a return to the notion of purposeful nature, or teleology, in which the earth is described as being created by God as a home for humans. When the laws of nature such as those of Charles Darwin's theory of evolution are substituted for Ritter's God, a body of theory tends to develop in which the forces of nature (definitions 1, 2, and 8) embodied in the natural landscape/ environment (and separate from humans) somehow determine the development of the human culture. This sort of environmentalism or environmental determinism culminated in statements to the effect that: "nature's plan is obvious" and humankind's part is to study "the character of the environment . . . so that he can best follow the plan 'determined' by nature" (Griffith Taylor [1880–1963] quoted in Hartshorne 1959: 62). When this plan (or map) is predicated on the precepts of survival of the fittest, we have social Darwinism. Such arguments lend themselves, in turn, to usage outside the bounds of academic discourse in ways that naturalize, and thereby legitimize, social behavior on the grounds that it has been determined by nature. It can be argued, for example, that the competitive, survival-of-the-fittest values of market capitalism are natural or, similarly, that the geopolitics of imperialist expansion are natural because humans, like any other species, will naturally compete for *Lebensraum*.

The organic teleology of German geography facilitated a revival of the Germanic territorial concept of landscape that we saw in the Dutch concept of *landschap* (Hard 1970: 168–241). This change brought the use of the term *landscape* even closer to the value-laden identification of nature with the nation, that is the "natural" natives of an area that had been the point of departure for arcadian/pastoral landscape art. This is so because of the many connotations that the words *land* and *landscape* have in the Germanic languages. The suffix *-scape* is the same as the suffix *-ship* as used in the word *township*, meaning the area belonging to a town. *Land* thus designated, among other things, a territory belonging to a people (or nation) — England was the land of the Angles. We still use the term this way in English when we refer to our country as our "land" ("This land is your land, this land is my land"). At the same time, in the Germanic languages the word *-scape* refers to a shaping process of creation, with analogies to coitus, to carving out something as in the phrase: "the pioneers carved our land out of the virgin wilderness" (O.E.D. 1971: "shape"; Sauer 1969b: 321; Kolodny 1975). Landscapes thus could be regarded as natural, organic regions giving birth, as Oswald Spengler wrote in 1920, to national "cultures that grow with original vigor out of the lap of a maternal natural landscape, to which each is bound in the whole course of its existence" (quoted in Sauer 1969b: 325).

Landscape thus came to be perceived once again as a bounded area of territory much as in the case with the Dutch *landschap*. The term *Landschaft* was often used in German geography in much the same way as *organic, formal,* or *natural* region have been used in English to indicate some form of organic link between the culture of the people living in the area and the physical features of the area (Hartshorne 1961: 256–60, 296–305; Sauer 1969b: 321). In the context of the German nationbuilding during the nineteenth and early twentieth centuries, it is easy to understand how the concepts of landscape and nature, especially when used together, could become extremely volatile, but these concepts need not have ended in an environmentalism that dichotomized nature and humans, with the former determining the latter. Some geographers such as the American George Perkins Marsh (1801–82) saw the relationship between humanity and its environments as one in which humankind, through the development of an intelligence that allowed humanity to physically transform its environment, was able to reflect on and exert influence on the nature of society and its landscape—"whereas (others) think that the earth made man, man in fact made the earth" (quoted in Olwig 1980: 37). The relationship between humanity and nature was not that of two distinct categories, but one involving both physical nature (including the physical nature of people) and the mental nature of humanity, and hence human values. It is this interaction that has had the effect of transforming the relationship of people and their environment through the course of history. Marsh was later to provide a major source of inspiration for the conservation movement and for those geographers who did not join Hartshorne's mainstream. An important example of this kind of geography is the monumental study of human/environment relations, *Man's Role in Changing the Face of the Earth* (Thomas 1956).

Geographical Landscape Discourse

To this day, the concept of nature is synonymous with natural landscape in geographical discourse. Whereas the nature studied by a natural science such as biology or physics might be described as the principles that result in life or matter and movement, the nature of geography is a thing, a natural landscape. Geography, however, and particularly physical geography, does draw on the various natural sciences to explain the physical constitution of the natural landscape. The use of the term *nature* in this context has tended to refer particularly to that aspect of the landscape that has been shaped independently of humanity, yet physical geography, it has been argued, can justify its existence only as part of a larger geographic discipline that seeks understanding of the landscape as a totality shaped by human and physical forces (Sauer 1969b; Hartshorne 1959: 69–80).

Viewed in isolation as scholarly discourse, it is clear that geography has increased our understanding of the physical environment and the ways in which humankind interacts with that environment. It has provided stimulating theories regarding the ways in which the environment has determined or set the parameters for the development of human cultures. It has also helped create an understanding of the ways in which humankind modifies and even destroys the environment. The problem, however, is that geography cannot be viewed exclusively in terms of its scholarly discourses or practices. It also must be viewed in terms of the way in which these discourses and practices become institutionalized and are utilized by society at large.

The Geographical Institution

Although Ritter held a university chair in geography, few of the founders of modern geography had established positions within the university system. Alexander von Humboldt, George Perkins Marsh, and Élisée Reclus (1830–1905) exerted considerable influence without being professional academic geographers; others held chairs in other disciplines. While geography became entrenched in German universities in the late nineteenth century, it was not before the early twentieth century that the university departmental structure that we know today developed in the English-speaking world. The academically institutionalized geography, which serves as the locus for most geographic study today, was the outcome of a long process of institutionalization that had dual beginnings. On the one hand, geography was becoming institutionalized in governmental and industrial practice as a practical science useful in exploration, war, planning, and administration. On the other hand, geography was fostered in programs of popular (informal) and formal geographical education. Indeed, the authors of the great geographical reference works of the nineteenth century—Ritter and Humboldt in Germany and Malte-Brun and Reclus in France—had the idealistic goal of providing informal education for the general population. Institutions such as the Society of Geography, founded in Paris in 1821 by the Dane Conrad Malte-Brun (1775–1826), developed around the publication of these works (Malte-Brun 1834). Long before university departments of geography became common, geography had become a fixed part of the school curriculum in primary and secondary school. The geographical societies that grew up in the latter half of the nineteenth century thus were institutions that served both educational and practical ends, and because geographical information was also useful for the practical tasks of nationbuilding and colonial expansion, these societies were made up of an amalgam of academics, educators, military men, businessmen, and adventurers.

If the institutionalization of geographic methods and information was of practical use for governments and industries, the world view that geography (literally) provided through school texts and popular journals could be equally useful as a means of enlightening people about the world around them. Geography could also be used ideologically, however, in legitimating policy, although geographers did not necessarily serve such purposes consciously. When studying organic processes in terrestrial nature and when seeking to describe how human society relates to those processes, it was inevitable that organic metaphors and analogies would seem useful. This did not necessarily entail, as Sauer points out, the reduction of society to the status of a biological organism (Sauer 1969a: 326). Problems arose, however, when geographers reified such analogies and metaphors (be they organic/biological or spatial/geometrical) by treating them as literal, scientifically unambiguous expressions of objective fact. It is easy to slip from statements that "regions are like organisms" or "cities are like planets that exert a gravitational force, according to their mass, on their surroundings" to statements that "regions are organisms" or "cities exert gravitational force." Unlike physical scientists, human geographers do not study relatively neutral objects such as organisms or planets; geography instead is implicated in and an integral part of the society that is its object of study. This means that geographers must reflect on, and accept responsibility for, the myriad of conscious and unconscious ways that its language and texts will influence, and be influenced by, its object of study. This responsibility cannot be exonerated simply by sidestepping the issue, by cleansing the geographical language of value-laden terms. As long as geography is concerned with a value-laden subject, its terms are similarly laden and suited thereby to ideological use and misuse. This is well illustrated by our present object of study, the concept of nature.

The ideological misuse of geographical concepts became a full-blown problem with the various forms of environmental determinism used by the Germans, among others, in the period preceding World War II. Landscape geography provided fertile soil for the cultivation of ideas such as *Blut und Boden*, with its accent on the natural organic bond between the blood of a people and their soil and its motivation of patriotic identifications with the fatherland; and the concept of *Lebensraum*, with its accent on an organism's demand for space and its legitimation of the annexation of neighboring territories. Because Hartshorne wished to build on the scientific discipline of German geography, he had to find a way of cleansing the discipline of any taint of its ideological misuse without discrediting the German foundations of the discipline as a whole. In doing so, he followed the model of his German academic mentors by appearing to maintain a strict separation between the objective scientific discourse of academic scholarship and the political discourse that had used geographical ideas for ideological purposes. This distinction was particularly important with respect to informal (or popular) education and primary and secondary formal education, both of which were strongly linked to the practice of academic geography. Geography could be kept untainted, therefore, only by appearing to inscribe geographical theoretical debate strictly within the terrain of scholarly scientific discourse. Concepts such as nature and landscape that Hartshorne identified with organic/biological thinking were dismissed as "of little or no value as a technical scientific terms." He sidestepped thereby both the volatile ideological usages that had discredited such terms and geography's traditional role in nonuniversity education. In the words of David Harvey, Hartshorne

> totally rejects aesthetics in geography and reserves its most vitriolic condemnations for the mythologies of landscape geography. Hartshorne, following Hettner, seems to want to expel any opening for the politicizing of academic geography in an era when geography was suffused with politics. . . . The difficulty, of course, is that avoiding the problem does not eliminate it, even in academic geography. (Harvey 1990: 430)

It is a measure of Hartshorne's accomplishment that his strategy managed to discredit the use of organic concepts with roots in the Romantic movement, while leaving untainted the more rationalistic project of the science of space—which was equally susceptible to misuse; thus, fifty years later it could be said that "the legitimacy of Hartshorne's concern with a previous German geography was never in question" (de Sousa 1989: iv).

Postwar Geography and Nature

The concept of nature had become tainted by its use in the context of a nature/culture dichotomy in which nature was seen to have some form of determinant relation to culture—a relation that had to be, and largely was, erased from academic geographic discourse. This does not mean, however, that it was erased from geographers' thinking. Let us reconsider Hartshorne's statement, quoted earlier: "[N]early all American geographers used this distinction as basic to their thinking in geography. No doubt most of them still do, though it is worthy of note that it is either not included or plays little role in several of the chapters of *American Geography: Inventory and Prospect* of 1954" (Hartshorne 1956: 55). He obliquely acknowledges here a distinction between what geographers think and what they write. He marshaled centuries of scholarly geographical discourse in a largely successful effort to exorcise value-laden concepts from the discipline, but even he admitted that despite his best efforts, they remained in the discipline as silent "vestiges" or even as entombed spirits that threatened to rise from the grave no matter how well sealed with intellectual stones (Hartshorne 1961: 257). The problem for him—and for us—is how to confront spirit concepts that, on the surface, have disappeared.

At one point Hartshorne ascribes his own use of the man/nature distinction (despite his intellectual opposition to it) to the fact that it was justifiable on the basis of "current practice." While the term *nature* tended to disappear from postwar geographical discourse, the continued vitality of the man/nature distinction is caused, I believe, by the institutionalized practice of the field, which is why these traces persist. The intellectual traces of the concept of nature—its "ghost"—are to be found everywhere, but because it is a ghost that is rarely visible under its own name, we can only speculate on its identity in geographical discourse.

The institutionalized practice of geography can afford perhaps to fall silent about its fundamental premises because of geography's practical usefulness to society. With the advent of the computer and the satellite, method can be substituted for theory because it is possible for geographers to justify their existence by developing ever more sophisticated methods of doing cartographic and landscape modeling and analysis. The problem is that the reduction of a discipline to a sophisticated tool does not exonerate the discipline from its broader scholarly responsibilities. This means that geography must also take cognizance of the larger ideological and educational implications of its work. Substitution of the vantage point of the airplane or the satellite for the cosmic coordinates of the map does not change the fact that geography plays an important role in shaping people's world view. Whether they wish to recognize it or not, geographers are implicated in larger issues that are reflected in the nature of the landscape. Geography has an obligation as a scholarly discipline to ask, as Harvey does: "Do we teach the static rationality of the Ptolemaic system and insist that geography is nothing more than GIS [geographical information systems], the contemporary version of the Hartshornian rule that if it can be mapped, then it is geography?" (Harvey 1990: 432)

Though some geographers might be accused of pursuing method to the exclusion of theory, others have continued the tradition of theoretical academic discourse. Seen against the background of the historical shifts in the conceptualizations of nature, it is tempting to suggest that geography's massive shift in the late 1950s from the study of man/nature interactions to spatial science represents a reversion to an earlier, cosmic conception of nature. The map remained fundamental in the geographer's own cosmology, but it also came to be seen as an inner, mental construction that informed the behavior of all. This is well illustrated in an epigram at the outset of one of the key textbooks in spatial science, *Spatial Organization: The Geographer's View of the World*: "We make a map of our experience patterns, an inner model of the outer world, and we use this to organize our lives." (Gyorgy Keeps quoted in Abler, Adams, and Gould 1971: 3). Nazism's tainting of the organic, biological analogies of environmental determinism perhaps provided the motivation for this renewed interest in the abstract spatial geometries that underlie the confusion of terrestrial existence. By reducing things to an abstract isotropic plane, confusion was thereby eliminated. In the context of scholarly discourse this approach was useful in a variety of contexts, for example, for planning in the development of locational analysis. In the context of its institutionalized role in society, however, we might suggest that spatial science, in the guise of social physics, also restored geography's earlier role as producer of ideologies that naturalized and legitimized developments within society at large. It thus may stand accused of providing the ideological basis for a new planning technocracy (Mercer 1984).

The reduction of geography to a science of space that rejects the historical study of society/environment relations as manifested in the landscape may well be a response to some of the same mercantile forces that helped motivate the cosmology of Renaissance geography. According to Sauer (1969a: 353–54), the mainstream geography identified with Hartshorne was to some extent a product of the Middle Western environment from which it emanated.

> In the Middle West, original cultural differences faded rapidly in the forging of a commercial civilization based on great natural resources. Perhaps nowhere else and at no other time has a great civilization been shaped so rapidly, so simply, and so directly out of the fat of the land and the riches of the subsoil. Apparently here, if anywhere, the formal logic of costs and returns dominated a rationalized and steadily expanding economic world. . . . Here the growth of centers of heavy industry at points of most economic assembly of raw materials was an almost mathematical demonstration of function of ton-miles, somewhat conventionalized in terms of freight-rate structures. . . . In this brief moment of fulfillment and ease, it seemed that there must be a strict logic of the relationship of site and satisfaction, something approaching the validity of natural order.

A present-day geographer, David Harvey, echoes this point of view in his analysis of the way the economistic mindset inevitably must ignore historical and environmental issues.

> While economists often accept the Keynesian maxim that "in the long run we are all dead" and that the short-run is the only reasonable time horizon over which to operationalize economic and political decisions, environmentalists insist that responsibilities must be judged over an infinite time horizon within which all forms of life (including that of humans) must be preserved. (Harvey 1990: 420)

Much like Sauer, Harvey (1990: 433) also ends by making a plea for a discipline built "around a project that fuses the environmental, the spatial and the social within a sense of the historical geography of space and time."

Environmental Science

Though space became the dominant concept within geography—at the expense of the earlier historical concern with interaction of humankind with nature—the interest in the material world did not die out. It did, however, tend to shift conceptual and institutional ground. What we see emerging from this nexus of interests is a burgeoning new interdisciplinary field—often only loosely related to the mainstream discipline of geography—usually called environmental studies or ecology. Ecology in geography emerges from the same organismic intellectual roots as landscape geography, but in its modern general-systems form it is a denatured geography, divorced from the discourse of values and morality characteristic of its nineteenth-century forerunners (Stoddart 1986: 230–70). The French philosopher Jean Baudrillard writes of this development as follows: "To speak of ecology is to attest to the death and total abstraction of nature. . . . The great signified, the great referent Nature, is dead, replaced by environment, which simultaneously designates and designs its death and the restoration of nature as simulation model (its "reconstitution," as one says of orange juice that has been dehydrated)" (Baudrillard 1981: 202). Nature has died in the sense that it has disappeared from academic discourse, only to be reconstituted as ecosystem under the seemingly neutral term environment.

Environmental studies as a framework for scholarly discourse and academic practice has generated useful concepts, methods, and information. The problem is that the suppression of "the great referent Nature" through its subsumption under apparently neutral concepts such as ecology and environment actually can increase its ideological potency. This happens when values identified with nature become attached to the new terms, which then come to express social values under the guise of an apparently neutral natural science. We thus see that environment is not just a term in academic discourse, but also a movement with unclear values and political content (Douglas and Wildavsky 1982: 126–51; Pepper 1984: 204–14; Tokar 1988). Elements of the German Green political movement, for example, have even been identified with those who promoted notions of landscape used by the National Socialists (Gröning and Bulmahn 1987). The need to protect the environment, furthermore, has been used to justify the preservation of landscapes that, in fact, are the object of concern because of the social values that they embody as an image of the natural (Olwig 1984, 99–202; Heiman 1988, 187–262; 1989). Finally, environmental science, particularly in the guise of ecology, has legitimized the development of new bureaucratic institutions. The fact that such institutions serve useful ends should not blind us to the fact that they can also become ends in themselves (Söderkvist 1986).

The Reconstruction of Nature

Nature has survived as a concept in a number of important countercurrents to mainstream geography. An offshoot of the Berkeley School has produced a

tradition that has focused on the role of historically evolving cultural conceptualizations of our surroundings as a means of comprehending human environmental behavior. Geographers of this persuasion have tended to reflect on
the full historical meaning of the terms they use (rather than leave them unexamined), to redefine them, or to abandon them when their objectivity is
drawn into question. In their hands the value-laden complexities of such
terms as *nature* and *landscape* provide the point of departure for an analysis of
humankind's relation to its environment rather than an argument for their erasure (Glacken 1967; Tuan 1971; Olwig 1984; Lowenthal 1985; Lowenthal
and Penning-Rowsell 1986; Cosgrove and Daniels 1988). In these cases, landscape and nature cease to be objective entities that are simply out there for
study. They are seen not only as material entities, but also as human and cultural intellectual constructs that are manifested through our perceptions and
through the practices whereby we comprehend and transform our surroundings to fit our images of the way we desire the world to be.

If the geographers identifiable with the Berkeley School have tended to focus on conceptual issues, a number of Marxist geographers have tended to focus instead on the way that nature has been produced in relation to the development of society's material basis. In the latter view humanity produces
both the nature that surrounds us and the ideologies that legitimize the ways
that we exploit that nature (Olwig and Olwig 1979; Cosgrove 1984; Smith
1984; Heiman 1988; Fitzsimmons 1985, 1989a, 1989b; Lehtinen 1991).
There are eddies, however, that run between these two countercurrents (evidenced by overlapping citations), because the two approaches are not mutually exclusive.

Conclusion

Seen from a distance, as if our discipline were an archaeological artifact de-
posited as layers of discourse through time, it becomes apparent that geography today is an institutionalized amalgam of bits and pieces of earlier discourses and practices that served various institutional purposes at varying
times. These, in turn, can be seen as fallout from the fission of a once unifying landscape concept. For mainstream geography nature has become encapsulated in, and divided by, the terms *space* and *environment*. Its ghostly
traces, however, can still be detected. Rather than continue to try to exorcise
nature, though, it might be better to engage a concept that is one of the most
vital in our culture and our discipline. Rather than separating the field into
environmental and spatial science, might it not be more fruitful to remarry
geometric abstractions of space with the organic world as experienced by the
human community? Such a marriage might unify geography as an intellec-

tual enterprise that is capable of reflecting on the value-laden complexity of its dual nature.

References

Abler, Ronald, John S. Adams, and Peter Gould. 1971. *Spatial organization: The geographer's view of the world.* Englewood Cliffs, N. J.: Prentice Hall.

Baudrillard, Jean. 1981. *For a critique of the political economy of the sign,* trans. Charles Levin. St. Louis, Mo.: Telos Press.

Bourdieu, Pierre. 1977. *Outline of a theory of practice,* trans. Richard Nice. Cambridge, England: Cambridge University Press.

Buttimer, Ann. 1983. *The practice of geography.* London: Longman.

Collingwood, R. G. 1960. *The idea of nature.* Oxford: Oxford University Press.

Cosgrove, Denis. 1984. *Social formation and symbolic landscape.* London: Croom Helm.

————. 1988. The geometry of landscape: Practical and speculative arts in sixteenth-century Venetian land territories. In *The iconography of landscape,* ed. Denis Cosgrove and Stephen Daniels, 254–76. Cambridge, England: Cambridge University Press.

Cosgrove, Denis, and Stephen Daniels, eds. 1988. *The iconography of landscape.* Cambridge, England: Cambridge University Press.

Douglas, Mary, and Aaron Wildavsky. 1982. *Risk and culture.* Berkeley: University of California Press.

Derrida, Jacques. 1976. *Of grammatology,* trans. G. C. Spivak. Baltimore: Johns Hopkins University Press.

de Souza, Anthony R. 1989. Series editor's preface. In *The nature of geography,* ed. J. Nicholas Entrikin and Stanley D. Brunn, vii. Washington, D.C.: Association of American Geographers.

Duerr, Hans Peter. 1985. *Dreamtime: Concerning the boundary between wilderness and civilization,* trans. Felicitas Goodman. Oxford: Basil Blackwell.

Edgerton, Samuel Y., Jr. 1975. *The renaissance rediscovery of linear perspective.* New York: Basic Books.

Elkins, T. H. 1989. Human and regional geography in the German-speaking lands in the first forty years of the twentieth century. In *The nature of geography,* ed. J. Nicholas Entrikin and Stanley D. Brunn, 17–34. Washington, D.C.: The Association of American Geographers.

Entrikin, J. Nicholas. 1989. Introduction: The nature of geography in perspective. In *The nature of geography*, ed. J. Nicholas Entrikin and Stanley D. Brunn, 1–15. Washington: The Association of American Geographers.

Fitzsimmons, Margaret. 1985. Hidden philosophers: How geographic thought has been limited by its theoretical models. *Geoforum* 16: 139–49.

———. 1989a. The matter of nature. *Antipode* 21: 106–20.

———. 1989b. Guest editorial: Reconstructing nature. *Environment and Planning D: Society and Space* 7: 1–3.

Foucault, Michel. 1972. *The archeology of knowledge*, trans. A. M. Sheridan Smith. New York: Harper Colophon.

Gadol, Joan. 1969. *Leon Battista Alberti*. Chicago: University of Chicago Press.

Glacken, Clarence. 1967. *Traces on the Rhodian shore: Nature and culture in western thought from ancient times to the end of the eighteenth century.* Berkeley: University of California Press.

Gröning, Gert, and Joachim Wolschke-Bulmahn. 1987. Politics, planning, and the protection of nature: Political abuse of early ecological ideas in Germany, 1933–45. *Planning Perspectives* 2: 127–48.

Hard, Gerhard. 1965. Arkadien in Deutschland: Bermerkungen zu einem landschaftlichen Reiz. *Die Erde* 96: 186–97.

———. 1970. *Die "Landschaft" der Sprache und die "Landschaft" der Geographien.* Bonn: Dummlers Verlag.

Harley, J. B. 1988. Maps, knowledge, and power. In *The iconography of landscape*, ed. Denis Cosgrove and Stephen Daniels, 277–312. Cambridge, England: Cambridge University Press.

Hartshorne, Richard. 1958. The concept of geography as a science of space, from Kant and Humboldt to Hettner. *Annals of the Association of American Geographers* 40: 97–108.

———. 1959. *Perspective on the nature of geography.* Chicago: Rand McNally.

———. 1961. (orig. 1939). *The nature of geography.* Lancaster, Pa.: Association of American Geographers.

Harvey, David. 1990. Between space and time: Reflections on the geographical imagination. *Annals of the Association of American Geographers* 80: 418–34.

Heiman, Michael K. 1988. *The quiet evolution: Power, planning, and profits in New York State.* New York: Praeger.

————. 1989. Production confronts consumption: Landscape perception and social conflict in the Hudson Valley. *Environment and Planning D: Society and Space* 7: 165–78.

Horkheimer, Max, and Theodore Adorno. 1972. *The dialectic of enlightenment.* New York: Hawk.

James, Preston E. 1972. *All possible worlds: A history of geographical ideas.* Indianapolis: Bobbs-Merrill.

Jordanova, L. J., ed. 1986. *Languages of nature.* London: Free Association Books.

Kay, Jeanne. 1989. Human dominion over nature in the Hebrew Bible. *Annals of the Association of American Geographers* 79: 214–32.

Kolodny, Annette. 1975. *The lay of the land.* Chapel Hill: University of North Carolina Press.

Lehtinen, Ari Aukusti. 1991. Northern natures. *Fennia* 169: 57–169.

Leighly, John. 1969. Introduction. In *Land and life*, ed. John Leighly, 1–8. Berkeley: University of California Press.

Löfgren, Orvar. 1989. Landscapes and mindscapes. *Folk* 31: 183–208.

Lovejoy, A. O., and George Boas. 1935. *Primitivism and related ideas in antiquity.* Baltimore: The Johns Hopkins University Press.

Lowenthal, David. 1985. *The past is a foreign country.* Cambridge, England: Cambridge University Press.

Lowenthal, David, and E. C. Penning-Rowsell, eds. 1986. *Landscape meanings and values.* London: Allen and Unwin.

Lukermann, Fred. 1961. The concept of location in classical geography. *Annals of the Association of American Geographers* 50: 194–210.

————. 1964. Geography as a formal intellectual discipline and the way in which it contributes to human knowledge. *Canadian Geographer* 8: 167–72.

————. 1989. The nature of geography: *Post Hoc, Ergo Propter Hoc?* In *The nature of geography*, ed. J. Nicholas Entrikin and Stanley D. Brunn, 53–68. Washington, D.C.: The Association of American Geographers.

May, J. A. 1970. *Kant's concept of geography.* University of Toronto Department of Geography *Research Publications*, 4. Toronto: University of Toronto Press.

Malte-Brun, Conrad. 1847. *Précis de la géographie universelle . . .* , 3 vols., trans. J. G. Percival. Boston: Samuel Walker (orig. pub. 1810–29, Paris).

Mercer, David. 1984. Unmasking technocratic geography. In *Recollections of a revolution: Geography as spatial science*, ed. Mark Billinge et al., 153–99. London: Macmillan.

Merchant, Carolyn. 1980. *The death of nature: Women, ecology, and the scientific revolution*. San Francisco: Harper and Row.

Miller, Charles. 1988. *Jefferson and nature: An interpretation*. Baltimore: The Johns Hopkins University Press.

Olsson, Gunnar. 1987. The social space of silence. *Environment and Planning D: Society and Space* 5: 249–62.

Olwig, Karen Fog, and Kenneth R. Olwig. 1979. Underdevelopment and the development of "natural" park ideology. *Antipode* 11: 16–25.

Olwig, Kenneth R. 1980. Historical geography and the science/nature "problematic": The perspective of J. F. Schouw, G. P. Marsh, and E. Reclus. *Journal of Historical Geography* 6: 29–45.

———. 1984. *Nature's ideological landscape*. London: Allan and Unwin.

———. 1987. Art and the art of communicating geographical knowledge: The case of Pieter Brueghel. *Journal of Geography* 86: 47–50.

———. 1989. The childhood deconstruction of nature. *Children's Environments Quarterly* 6: 19–25.

———. 1993. Sexual cosmology: Nation and landscape at the conceptual interstices of nature and culture, or: What does landscape really mean? In *Landscape: Politics and perspectives*, ed. B. Bender, 307–43. Oxford: Berg.

Oxford English Dictionary. 1971. Oxford: Oxford University Press.

Passmore, John. 1974. *Man's responsibility for nature*. New York: Charles Scribner's Sons.

Pepper, David. 1984. *The roots of modern environmentalism*. London: Croom Helm.

Ricoeur, P. 1971. What is a text? Interpretation and explanation. In *Mythic-symbolic language and philosophical anthropology*, ed. D. Rassmussen, 135–50. The Hague: Martinus Nijhoff.

———. 1973. The model of the text: Meaningful action considered as a text. *New Literary History: A Journal of Theory and Interpretation* 5: 91–117.

Sack, Robert D. 1980. *Conceptions of space in social thought: A geographical perspective*. London: Macmillan.

———. 1989. The nature in light of the present. In *The nature of geography*, ed. J. Nicholas Entrikin and Stanley D. Brunn, 141–62. Washington, D.C.: The Association of American Geographers.

Sauer, Carl O. 1969a (orig. 1941). Foreword to historical geography. In *Land and life*, ed. John Leighly, 351–79. Berkeley: University of California Press.

———. 1969b (orig. 1925). The morphology of landscape. In *Land and life*, ed. John Leighly, 315–50. Berkeley: University of California Press.

———. 1969c (orig. 1956). The education of a geographer. In *Land and life*, ed. John Leighly, 389–404. Berkeley: University of California Press.

Smith, Neil. 1984. *Uneven development: Nature, capital, and the production of space*. Oxford: Basil Blackwell.

———. 1989. Geography as museum: Private history and conservative idealism in *The nature of geography*. In *The nature of geography*, ed. J. Nicholas Entrikin and Stanley D. Brunn, 89–120. Washington, D.C.: The Association of American Geographers.

Söderkvist, Thomas. 1986. *The ecologists: From merry naturalists to saviours of the nation*. Stockholm: Almqvist and Wiksell.

Stoddart, David R. 1986. *On geography and its history*. Oxford: Basil Blackwell.

———. 1989. Epilogue: Homage to Richard Hartshorne. In *The nature of geography*, ed. J. Nicholas Entrikin and Stanley D. Brunn, 163–66. Washington, D.C.: Association of American Geographers.

Thomas, William. 1956. *Man's Role in Changing the Face of the Earth*, 2 vols. Chicago: University of Chicago Press.

Tokar, Brian. 1988. Social ecology, deep ecology and the future of green political thought. *The Ecologist* 18: 132–40.

Tuan, Yi-Fu. 1971. *Man and nature*. Commission on College Geography Resource Paper 10. Washington, D.C.: Association of American Geographers.

———. 1974. *Topophilia: A study of environmental perception, attitudes, and values*. Englewood Cliffs, N. J.: Prentice-Hall.

Varenius, Bernhardus. 1682. *Cosmography and geography in two parts*, trans. anon. London: Richard Blome.

von Humboldt, Alexander. 1849–1858. *Cosmos: A sketch of a physical description of the universe*, vol. 1, trans. E. C. Otté. London: Henry G. Bohn.

Warntz, William. 1989. Newton, the Newtonians, and the *Geographia Generalis Varenii*. *Annals of the Association of American Geographers* 79: 165–91.

Webster's Seventh New Collegiate Dictionary. 1963. Springfield, Mass.: Merriam.

Williams, Raymond. 1976. *Keywords: A vocabulary of culture and society*. London: Fontana.

Appendix

Nature *n* (ME, fr. MF, fr. L *natura*, fr. *natus*, pp. of *nasci* to be born—more at NATION)

1a: the inherent character or basic constitution of a person or thing: essence; **b:** DISPOSITION, TEMPERAMENT.

2a: a creative and controlling force in the universe; **b:** an inner force or the sum of such forces in an individual.

3: general character: KIND.

4: the physical constitution or drives of an organism.

5: a spontaneous attitude.

6: the external world in its entirety.

7a: man's original or natural condition; **b:** a simplified mode of life resembling this condition.

8: natural scenery.

Landscape *n, often attrib* (D *landschap*, fr. *land* & *schap* ship)

1a: a picture representing a view of natural inland scenery.

b: the art of depicting such scenery.

2a: the landforms of a region in the aggregate; **b:** a portion of land that the eye can comprehend in a single view.

3: VISTA, PROSPECT.

4

High/Low, Back/Center: Culture's Stages in Human Geography

Kent Mathewson

Within the past century a vast literature has emerged in the humanities and social sciences deploying the term *culture*. Few scholars using the concept of culture have rigorously defined it. Here geographers have been exemplary rather than exceptional. Most users agree that the term resists simple definition. Some hold that culture defies explanation but invites understanding, while for a few it is ineffable. Cultural critic Raymond Williams (1976: 76) feels, "Culture is one of the two or three most complicated words in the English language," surpassed only by *nature* in complexity (see chapter 3). In an earlier study Williams (1958) demonstrated that the term and concept have recoverable histories. He argues that definition is dependent on the variable societal contexts in which the concept of culture has been embedded and periodically reconstituted.

This essay presents a selective sketch of ways in which geographers have thought about and used the concept of culture. Perhaps all too appropriately, the discussion is organized historically, starting with the origins of the term *culture* and moving through the Enlightenment to the Berkeley School, through Carl O. Sauer's thinking on the subject, and beyond. It focuses primarily on the work of cultural geographers. Traditionally, cultural geographers have embraced an historical, even historicist perspective. Some contextual implications of this development are identified herein.

Culture's Origins

The origins of the term *culture*, as with several concepts in this volume, have roots in classical antiquity. Culture, however, unlike nature, place, space, or time, is not grounded in ancient Greek philosophy or geography. The word *culture* and its cognates come from *cultura*, a derivative of *colere*, both from Latin. As Williams (1976: 77) points out, "*colere* had a range of meanings: inhabit, cultivate, protect, honor with worship." From *colonus* (inhabitant) we have received colony and its derivatives. During the 1400s the English language received the word *culture* directly from French. The primary meaning referred to husbandry or the tending of natural growth. From antiquity to the eighteenth century *culture*'s meanings were variously tied to local habitation, worshipful behavior, and, especially, agrarian processes. Resonances of these premodern meanings persist in the ways geographers, particularly cultural geographers, have thought and written about culture.

During the eighteenth century the word *culture* began to assume its modern connotations. The notion of tended growth expanded to include human development, both individual and societal. This was part of the larger shifts in European and North American consciousness that were reflected so clearly in the works of Enlightenment scholars, philosophers, and politicians. The term *civilization* also appeared at this time, first as *culture*'s synonym and occasionally later its antonym (see especially Spengler 1918). Less rigidly, it appears widely as contrastive in scholarship of the past century. The work of German sociologists such as Ferdinand Tönnies and Alfred Weber provide examples (Kroeber and Kluckhohn 1952). From its Enlightenment inceptions to present usage, *civilization* is normally associated with progress, change, and secular processes of human societal development. The civilizational concept is deeply embedded in theories of cultural evolution, generally referring to stages deemed to be advanced (e.g., Childe 1925). In contrast, *culture*'s conceptual trajectory has been neither so linear nor so neat.

Marvin Harris (1968: 10) locates the genesis of the modern culture concept in early Enlightenment thought. He argues that the Enlightenment project was centrally concerned with theorizing culture during the century between John Locke's *An Essay Concerning Human Understanding* ([1690] 1894) and the French Revolution. Locke regarded the human mind at birth as an "empty cabinet": there are no innate ideas. This perspective corroded entrenched political doctrine and religious dogma and encouraged speculations about relationships between environmental conditions and human thought and action.

Contrary to caricatures of the Enlightenment as a uniform reign of reason wherein Newton's physical laws were rotely applied to human history and social organization, the epoch was characterized by diversity of thought as witnessed in national and regional currents within this broad intellectual enterprise. Different disciplines within today's social sciences can point to antecedents among different national currents. For example, political economists look to figures of the Scottish Enlightenment such as Hume and Smith, whereas anthropologists find key precursors among the Scottish moral philosophers and the French *philosophes*. Geographers generally point to their antecedents in the German Enlightenment. (It should be noted, however, that some critics question the notion of a "German Enlightenment," suggesting instead that its regional polities and later the German nation exhibited a succession of "counter-Enlightenment" tendencies and movements, beginning with a precocious Romanticism and culminating in National Socialism.) Immanuel Kant (1724–1804), its foremost philosopher, is often claimed by geographers as one of their own (Martin and James 1993: 109–11; Livingstone 1992: 113–17). Besides his pedagogic service to geography—he taught physical geography at Königsberg for nearly forty years—aspects of his philosophical work have been viewed as formative for geography (Bowen 1981: 206–9; Hartshorne [1939] 1961: 38–39, 1958; May 1970). According to Kroeber and Kluckhohn (1952: 42–43) these did not include, however, contributions to a concept of culture useful to either geographers or anthropologists.

Johann G. von Herder (1744–1803), Kant's student and later critic, offers a richer source of ideas and positions for geographers' concepts of culture. Herder, though mentioned in most histories of geographic thought, is mainly credited as influencing Carl Ritter's teleological outlook (Hartshorne 1961: 54; Martin and James 1993: 129). Characteristically, Glacken (1967: 537–43) gives Herder's views on environmentalism and the earth as the designed abode of humans a careful airing. Livingstone (1992: 122–24) has offered a more up-to-date reading of Herder's relation to (especially cultural) geography. Among other things, he points to Herder's "ethno-geography" and to his insistence that study of culture(s) must proceed from a position of "empathy" and "reconstructive imagination"—not by "rational analysis, general principles, natural laws, or classificatory devices."

An imaginative and reconstructive approach to the impact of Herder's ideas on geography may be found in Speth's (1987) comparison of Herder's and Carl Sauer's historicist world views. Citing Isaiah Berlin's (1976) study of Herder's doctrinal triad, namely, populism, expressionism, and pluralism, Speth describes parallels in Sauer's attitudes and scholarship. That Sauer set much of cultural geography's agenda since the 1920s is not questioned. Though some might contest Mikesell's (1967: 617) view that "the concept of culture is basic to all of human geography," most cultural geographers claim it as central to their approach. Accordingly, both the lineaments and the importance of the culture concept in geography are most clearly evident in the works of cultural geographers. Herder's thought and legacy is an appropriate starting point from which to trace this history.

The Enlightenment Eclipsed

Many claims, some contradictory, have been made for Herder: originator of Romanticism, protoecologist, pioneer of German cultural evolutionism, neologist of the word *nationalism*, and the Enlightenment's prime apostate, to mention a few. He was the first to use the term *culture* in its plural and thus modern anthropological sense. At the time of his *Ideas on the Philosophy of the History of Mankind* ([1784–91] 1803) *culture* and *civilization* were often used interchangeably. He sought an alternative meaning for *culture* freed from the implicit assumptions of progressivist teleology and Eurocentric superiority. It is in this context that his doctrinal triad should be interpreted. Populism concerns the value of belonging to a group or culture, with its political dimension often constituted in oppositional forms evincing a non- or even antipolitical basis. Herder may have coined the term *nationalism*, but he was opposed to the formation of nation-states, classes, races, parties, or any construct that served to oppress the people, or *Volk*. Expressionism refers to the belief that human activity, particularly art, expresses the entire personality of the individual or group. Pluralism celebrates diversity, multiplicity, and the incommensurability of the values of different cultures and societies.

Speth (1987: 31) suggests the concordance between Herder's and Sauer's views in the following list of shared traits: preference for the study of cultural origins and use of the genetic method; reliance on the concepts of development and of organic stages; anthropology as the favored means for understanding human beings and their expressions; true cultural advance as the autochthonous, or indigenous, development of a group in its own habitat; colonial subjugation of native populations as criminal and morally odious; and the desirability of the qualitative approach in morphological studies. Despite Alexander von Humboldt's association with Herder in Weimar's courtly and scholarly circles and the impact of Herder's *Ideas* on both Humboldt and Ritter, it has yet to be demonstrated that Herder's concept of culture found explicit and programmatic expression in the work of modern geography's twin founders (Birkenhauer 1986), or, for that matter, by any subsequent geographer. As Speth (1987) has suggested, though, the connection between Herder and Sauer is one of affinity. Many geographers have accepted a historicist perspective in which the culture concept assumes a central role.

Nineteenth-Century Departures

Culture in word and concept entered the technical vocabulary of German geographers in the second half of the nineteenth century. In Germany Herder's *Cultur*, long since shed of French associations, had become *Kultur*, but the concept lost none of its conceptual complexity. If anything, it had taken on added weight. In anglophone scholarship the concept of culture acquired new meaning through the work of literary critic Matthew Arnold and anthropologist Edward Tylor. In his (1869) *Culture and Anarchy* Arnold claimed culture for the humanities and decried the "mechanical," industrial civilization that Britain was rapidly becoming. Arnold (1971: 44) argued: "Culture . . . [does not have] its origin in curiosity, but . . . in the love of perfection; it is *a study of perfection.*"[1] The culture bearer became the individual rather than the group, and "high" culture's productions the ideal, rather than the genius of the folk as expressed in vernacular workings. In mid-Victorian England this was epitomized by mastery of the "Oxbridge" classical curriculum. Save for some humanistically oriented geographers, working in what might be called geography's own genteel tradition, Arnold's notion of culture is poorly represented in modern geography. Herder's populism and pluralism prevail.

In 1871 Edward Tylor published *Primitive Culture*. The opening sentence stated: "Culture or Civilization, taken in its wide ethnographic sense, is that complex whole which includes knowledge, belief, art, morals, law, custom, and any other capabilities and habits acquired by man as a member of society" (Tylor 1871: 1). For Kroeber and Kluckhohn (1952: 287) this is the point of departure for reconstructing the history of the culture concept in anthropology, but they acknowledged that "the procreation had been German." Stocking (1963), however, argued that Tylor's contribution was not so much foundational as a revision of Arnold's humanistic culture concept, harnessing it to a progressive and positivistic social evolutionism. To locate the nineteenth-century antecedents of the culture concept in geography, we must still identify the Germans as the procreators.

Kroeber and Kluckhohn's (1952) critical review of cultural concepts and definitions has no counterpart in the geographic literature, nor does their bibliography of some two hundred entries contain any references to the work of geographers. The name index of some four hundred persons mentioned in the text includes only a few geographers: Dmitrii Anuchin, Karl Haushofer, and Friedrich Ratzel. The editors (1952: 312) limit Ratzel's contribution, for example, to his "environmental deterministic" departure from the evolutionary approaches of Tylor, Morgan, Maine, and others. A comprehensive and critical study of the German geographical literature, especially in the period from the 1870s to the 1920s, would reveal, I suspect, complex and extensive usage of the term and the concept. Here I can only suggest a few of the directions such an investigation might take.

Humboldt's and Ritter's contributions to the concept of culture and the emergence of cultural geography as a discrete subfield await analysis. At the very least, Ritter contributed indirectly through his student Ernst Kapp

(1808–1896). Credited with coining the term *Cul-turgeographie* (Schick 1982: 118), Kapp perhaps borrowed the idea in the 1840s from Gustave Klemm's (1843) *Allgemeine Kulturgeschichte der Menschheit.* Kroeber and Kluckhohn (1952: 44–46) credit Klemm (1802–1867) variously with being the first to conceptualize culture in its modern usage(s) and influencing anthropologists and other social scientists from Tylor on, but also retaining its Enlightenment connotations. Less sanguinely, Harris (1968: 102–3) considers Klemm an early architect of fin de siècle (and subsequent) schools of racial determinism and the biologizers of history. The question of what impact Klemm had on German geographers after Kapp is yet another topic that is in need of study. Given the explosion of German interest in *Kultur* in all of its variegated dimensions and connotations after about 1870, it would be far too simplistic to assign influence to a single or even to several individuals.

Modern Use of the Culture Concept in Geography

At the outset of this essay reference was made to the "vast literature that has emerged" deploying the concept of culture. Plotting these publications in time and space would probably show that Germany from the 1870s to the 1930s was the most active center of this emergence, but this exercise would not adequately convey the profound significance that the term has had there. Suffice it to say that by 1900 *Kultur* had taken on the collective emotional, intellectual, and aspirational baggage of a German state and society only recently united and self-consciously billowing toward an assumed global superiority. The accumulated "cultural capital" of several centuries of German accomplishments in the arts and sciences underwrote and legitimated these sensibilities.

German geography's role in this florescence was acknowledged by the state (Sandner 1994). Cultural geographers provided state service through their regional inventories of overseas colonies and countries. Cultural geographers also deepened the nation's and Empire's knowledge and pride in imagined collective pasts. Cultural geographers pioneered the study of Germanic settlement history. Complementing the work of folklorists, ethnologists, and prehistorians, cultural geographers mapped the history of the German *Volk*. In short, cultural studies assumed special significance in German geography during this period (the 1870s through the 1930s).

This was less true in other national contexts, though cultural geography has been accorded varying degrees of importance at different times in differing countries. Viewed from its inception to the present, the roots of cultural geography outside of Germany run deepest in the United States and secondarily in Canada and Scandinavia. Under different appellations and forms cultural geography has at times flourished in French and Iberian contexts. Save for a few exceptions (namely, E. E. Evans at Belfast and H. J. Fleure at Aberystwyth) lodged in the odd "Celtic corner," until quite recently it was all but absent in Great Britain.

The significance that geographers and other social scientists have placed on culture varies not only with national context. It has also varied in concert with large-scale historical change. Conceptualizations of culture have experienced fundamental change during the last three decades of each century since the 1600s. Here we are concerned with the two most recent periods. Scholars in many disciplines agree that the economy, society, and culture of the North Atlantic realm underwent profound transformation from about 1870 to the end of the century or thereabouts. Some identify a qualitative change in the realm's political economy: the initial consolidation of capitalism's industrial or monopoly phase (Mandel 1975). Others see the emergence of modernity and the dominance of social and cultural modernism as indicative of this shift (Lears 1981; Kern 1983). Similarly, across a broad spectrum of views there is basic agreement that a transformation of equal magnitude has occurred since the 1970s. In political-economic terms this transition or new stage has been labeled the "postindustrial age," "late capitalism," "global regimes of flexible accumulation," or similar designations depending on one's ideological and/or disciplinary perspective (Bell 1973; Mandel 1975; Harvey 1989). In parallel fashion changes in the social and cultural spheres are described as postmodern (Jameson 1991; Soja 1989; Harvey 1989; see chapter 16). This large-scale tableau provides a useful backdrop for viewing the ways in which geographers of various nationalities have deployed *culture* as a term and concept since the 1870s.

German Impacts on North American Geography

The German role in culture's conceptual construction is drastically compressed. After 1870 it is subordinated to the rise of cultural geography in North America, and that in highly selective ways. Carl O. Sauer (1889–1975) was the key figure in establishing cultural geography in North America. At the outset he was the main conduit of German geographic ideas into American cultural geography (Sauer 1925). From the mid-1920s until his death a half century later he exercised a strong influence over the field through his field work and writings especially through the students he trained (Aschmann 1987; Hooson 1981; Kenzer 1986; Speth 1981). The enterprise he founded and tended (the Berkeley School of cultural-historical geography) includes a large portion of the self-identified cultural geographers in the United States. What then were the elements of German geography's cultural concepts that Sauer introduced into North American geography?

Sauer, during the 1920s especially, drew widely on the work of past and contemporary European geographers. His assimilative approach set him apart from many of his North American colleagues. Those who applied European approaches did so in ways that Sauer often found wanting. In this regard, Ellen Semple's (1911) interpretation of Ratzel's *Anthropogeographie* (1882–91) was based primarily on the first volume, which explored causes of human distribution, in part explained by the effects of the natural environment on individuals and societies. Semple focused on the latter aspect in concert with the popular reception given environmentalism at the turn of the century and beyond. Sauer, on the other hand, sought direction from the second volume of Ratzel's *Anthropogeographie* (1891). It stressed two problems: human distributions on the earth's surface and the relationship with the physical environment and the role of migration in establishing these distributions. Ratzel's methodology included extensive mapping of cultural phenomena such as settlement features and ethnic, national, linguistic, and religious groupings. The implied emphases on cultural chorology, human-land relationships, and diffusion or migration as the agent or mechanism of culture change became central themes in Berkeley School geography. Sauer remained a consistent and persistent critic of "environmentalism" in geography throughout his career.

Sauer and his associates were skeptical of other avowed attempts to study cultures from scientific, causal, or nomothetic approaches. One such attempt was the cultural evolutionism practiced by anthropologists such as Lewis Henry Morgan and Tylor or the sociologist Herbert Spencer. Sauer's predilection was to follow culture historians such as Eduard Hahn rather than the cultural evolutionists (Solot 1986). Peschel's (1876) and Ratzel's (1896) comparative ethnologies contributed to Sauer's project by providing extensive data on culture traits, short of evolutionary schemata. The path that Sauer blazed and most of his students followed was empiricist, historicist, organicist, and populist. He rejected evolutionism's deductive approach, its theoretical and rationalistic emphasis on cause and effect, and its search for cultural universals that fit preconceived stages or cyclical patterns. The founding figure of American anthropology, Franz Boas (1858–1942), had arrived at a similar position a generation earlier, and Sauer came to appreciate the work and perspectives of Boas and the historical particularists through his contacts with Boas's students Alfred Kroeber and Robert Lowie at Berkeley in the 1920s and 1930s (Macpherson 1987).

Another direction that cultural geography might have taken is suggested by Mark Jefferson's (1911, 1929) work on the "culture of nations." A product of Victorian New England with an A.M. degree from Harvard under William Morris Davis, Jefferson was a respected figure in academic geography's first generation. He published widely on an impressive array of topics. Among his interests was devising measures for comparing the world's nations on the basis of cultural achievement. He proposed using four indices: schooling, commerce, railroads, and postal services to arrive at quantitative evaluations. The nations fell into four cultural hierarchic levels; in descending order they were: Teutonic, Mediterranean, Levantine, and Oriental. North European nations and their overseas replications fell into the first category, most Third World nations and colonies into the last. An odd mix of European, Asian, and Latin American nations and colonies are placed in the intermediate categories. His assumptions, methods, and conclusions were inflected with environmental and racial determinism.

Sauer conceptualized culture very differently from Jefferson and like-minded geographers. On epistemological grounds alone he found their positivist approaches and genteel racism repellent. In this regard Sauer's position was similar to Franz Boas's more systematically articulated convictions. Sauer's condemnation of environmentalism and scientific racialism and his distrust of cultural evolutionism's nomothetic and theoretical implications has led to the conclusion that he was non- or even antitheoretical and cared little for methodological prescription. Sauer suggested as much on occasion, but his writings contain pithy asides and clear pronouncements on both theory and practice (e.g., Sauer 1952). A few of his statements on culture and its role in geography demonstrate this. They also serve as touchstones for reviewing the use of the concept of culture by others within the tradition he initiated and inspired.

The Berkeley School Concept of Culture

During the first decade after Sauer received his doctorate at Chicago (1915), he said little or nothing about culture in his published writings, but during this period he had begun to read the work of continental geographers (Martin 1987: ix). In 1925 he published "The Morphology of Landscape." It was among his first methodological papers and is generally considered his most important. It established the bases for cultural geography in North America. What he said about culture was direct: "There is a strictly geographic way of thinking of culture; namely, as the impress of the works of man upon the area." Borrowing from German geographers' distinction between the natural and cultural landscape, Sauer advocated a morphologic approach to the genetic study of landscape as geography's primary objective. This he expressed in diagram and epigram: "The cultural landscape," he wrote, "is fashioned from a natural landscape by a culture group. Culture is the agent, the natural area is the medium, the cultural landscape the result." In later statements he suggested variations on this theme, but in essence it remained for Sauer and many of his followers the main focus of cultural geography.

During the 1930s Sauer's fieldwork and interests began to shift southward from California into the neotropics and ever deeper into the past (Mathewson 1987). The emphasis on morphology and chorology persisted, but the importance he placed on the genetic or historical dimension of cultural studies increased over time. At the onset of the decade Sauer (1931: 622) offered this definition: "Cultural geography is . . . concerned with those works of man that are inscribed into the earth's surface and give it characteristic expression." By 1940 Sauer's (1941) presidential address to the Association of American Geographers offered a more diachronic approach, with explication of cultural processes, growth, and distributions becoming the main objective. He (1941: 24) concluded: ". . . there are no general laws of society, but only cultural ascents. We deal not with Culture, but with cultures, . . . From all the earth in all the time of human existence, we build a retrospective science, . . ."

By the time of this talk Sauer had overseen a dozen dissertations with morphological and/or genetic approaches to both physical and cultural topics. Afterward, he directed another two dozen dissertations on mostly cultural and historical themes, though biogeography and ecology were also represented. In later years Sauer was fond of saying that he "wasted" little effort on methodological discussion after his 1925 statement, yet from time to time he ventured an opinion on the idea of culture in geographical studies. In the "Folkways of Social Science" (1963: 382) he remarked: "We are all trying to know more of the nature of human society. . . . we find that there is a division of interest between 'society' in the singular and in the plural. For the latter we often prefer to use the name 'cultures'. . . . May the experimentally disciplined neo-Spencerian science of society have every success; but let it not cast off those who work in other directions and ways." In his (1952) classic essay on "Agricultural Origins and Dispersals," he evoked biblical scripture: "Man alone ate of the fruit of the Tree of Knowledge and thereby began to acquire and transmit learning, or 'culture.'" In a final seminar at Berkeley in the mid-1960s he further distilled his thoughts on culture: ". . . by cultural [as used in "cultural" geography] we mean something as simple and as comprehensive as a way of life" (Parsons 1987: 154). Through the work, writings, and teaching of his students and their students, and so on into a sixth generation now in some cases, Sauer's basic interest in questions concerning cultural diversity, distributions, and diffusions by and large has been maintained.

If a critical history of cultural geography's first century is ever written, Wagner and Mikesell's (1962) thematic sketch of the field should be a significant marker. Their essay and the volume it introduced took stock, offered exemplars, defined themes, and generally served the interests of "paradigm maintenance." Wagner and Mikesell identified five themes as constituting the core of cultural geography's concerns: 1) culture; 2) culture area; 3) cultural landscape; 4) culture history; and 5) cultural ecology. The volume was welcomed as a major step toward self-definition in a field celebratory of its own eclectic, diffuse tendencies. It also sparked critiques, some immediate, others delayed. Antipodean geographer Harold Brookfield (1964) questioned various implied premises and vigorously disagreed with Wagner and Mikesell's statement, "The cultural geographer is not concerned with explaining the inner workings of culture or with describing fully patterns of human behavior, even when they affect the land, . . ." Brookfield's dissent became one focal point in an emergent and redirected cultural ecological program within geography (Mathewson 1993: 126). Wagner (1974) reassessed the five themes and proposed an emphasis on communication processes and institutions as new directions. Mikesell's (1978) review of the field called for only minor adjustments, while raising counterquestions concerning the efficacy of certain trends within cultural ecology.

Somewhat ironically, Mikesell's (1977, 1978) defense of tradition in the 1970s seemed slightly prophetic by the 1980s. In the last decade geographers have shown a renewed (even revivalist) interest in certain traditional themes and approaches, particularly chorology and regionalism, landscape studies, aspects of culture history, and culture as a category and organizing principle (Price and Lewis 1993). For some, what was merely arcane has become almost avant-garde. For the majority, however, renewed interest in regional geography, for example, carries with it an expectation of reconstruction or reconstitution of chorologic studies through rigorous and critical engagement with social theory and at least potential utility for emancipatory goals (Pudup 1988; Thrift 1994). In the context of these larger reassessments of the concepts of region, landscape, and culture, Wagner and Mikesell's five themes offer an appropriate framework for assessing current developments in cultural geography.

Beyond Sauer's Legacy

There have been some modifications but few abrupt departures or disjunctions within the program Sauer elaborated for cultural geography. For some this is an admirable record of fidelity to first principles; for others it is proof of stasis and a stubborn disregard for contemporaneity. One major modification has come about since the mid-1960s through the influence of ecological anthropology, especially as expressed in the work of cultural ecologists (Mathewson 1994). Other significant departures have occurred since the early 1970s. These are represented by an eclectic interest in the behavioral sciences on the one hand and an engagement with critical social theory on the other (Hugill and Foote 1994). This latter departure has spawned a "new cultural geography," centered in Britain but also expanding in North America and continental Europe. The engagement with social theory has also generated new directions in cultural ecology directed toward and by political-economic studies of Third World societies (see chapter 6). Modifications and departures within cultural geography during the past three decades will be reviewed within the framework of Wagner and Mikesell's five themes.

Culture

As previously suggested, geographers have produced few detailed or sustained discussions of culture as a concept. As in earlier decades, since the 1960s cursory definitions are sometimes offered, but most cultural geographers continue to leave epistemological matters to those willing to pursue them. The lack of interest in theorizing culture contrasts with some sectors and concerns within geography since the 1960s. For example, the so-called quantitative or spatial analytical revolution of the 1950s and 1960s placed a premium on theoretical activity (Harvey 1969; see chapters 11 and 12). The call for a more scientific, analytical, nomothetic, and theoretically based geography presented challenges to those holding and using implicit but largely unexamined notions of culture. Of course, the response varied from mild acceptance to direct disputation or, more commonly, continued disinterest.

From within the precincts of cultural geography, selected practioners have invited fellow enthusiasts to explore more theoretically charged terrains. David Lowenthal's (1961) essay on "Geography, Experience, and Imagination: Toward a Geographical Epistemology" put cultural geography onto less firm ground, but pointed to new possibilities. From the mid-1960s to the present, Yi-Fu Tuan (1974, 1977, 1979, 1982) has explored and elaborated these possibilities with great artistry and insight in numerous books and dozens of articles. From the early 1970s to the present Philip Wagner (1972, 1974, 1975) has elaborated a communicative practice-based cultural geography and commented often on the meanings of culture. These three geographers, all with direct links to the Berkeley School, have drawn extensively on philosophy, psychology, linguistics, literature, and other disciplines previously not well explored by cultural geographers. Writings of others could be cited, and their thoughts recited, but much of the initial work that went beyond anthropology and history in seeking new ways to think about culture was inspired by the above innovators.

Since the 1970s many cultural geographers have become more self-reflexive. Most of their activity is historically focused on particular tenets and tendencies within cultural geography rather than formal analysis and redefinition of the culture concept itself. For example, James Blaut's (1977, 1987) articles on diffusion theory are critical inquiries from a historical materialist/

pragmatist perspective, but they basically reaffirm the Berkeley-Kniffen outlook. His recent book (1993) extends the inquiry with a sustained and full critique of Eurocentric history and geographical diffusionism. James Duncan (1980) reviewed the use of the "superorganic" assumptions in cultural geography, stressing the Berkeley School's adoption of Kroeber's (1917) thesis that culture is a holistic entity with separate ontological status and causative powers operating on an autonomous level beyond, but also subsuming, the thoughts and actions of individuals and groups. Duncan argued that American cultural geographers had largely and uncritically accepted Kroeber's concept of culture's superorganic nature. He considered this an obstacle to the construction of a wider, more critical socio-cultural geography that would experiment with social, pyschological, and political explanations of human interactions with their various environments.

In his study of Sauer's rejection of cultural evolutionism, Solot (1986: 511) questioned the degree to which Sauer and his students explicitly embraced Kroeber's notion of the superorganic. Anthropologist Miles Richardson (1981) also responded to Duncan's charges that traditional cultural geographers have tended to reify culture. Richardson offered a bridging solution. He sketched a concept of culture as "intersubjective reality," drawing on Clifford Geertz's (1973, 1983) interpretative anthropology and sociology's symbolic interactionism. Some interest has been shown in this direction lately. Cultural geography is currently undergoing something of a resurgence as part of the larger turn to cultural studies throughout the social sciences and humanities. Self-reflexive reassessments, celebrations of traditional modes, and self-consciously new approaches in cultural geography are all implicated to varying degrees in what Harvey (1989) terms "the condition of postmodernity."

Culture Area and Culture History

Viewing the four remaining themes, two have spawned little change, while two have been arenas of both modification and departures. Recent studies involving culture areas and culture history generally carry forward earlier emphases and approaches. The concept of culture area or cultural distribution originated in post-1870s American and German ethnographic work as a heuristic device for classifying culture traits and mapping cultural groups. Comfortable with description rather than explanation, the best work of this genre continues to demonstrate artisanal excellence (e.g., Jordan 1982, 1985; Jordan and Kaups 1989). Some modifications might be noted; mapping of perceptual cultural regions is one example (Zelinsky 1980). Potential modifications may include intersections with the current interest in"regional/ locality" studies (Thrift 1990). Cultural chorology, the bedrock of cultural geography and easily accessible to nonspecialists, will probably remain its most effective voice for reaching the larger audience (Hart 1982). Similar comments can be made about culture history. With the new historicism on the rise in the humanities and a poststructuralist, interpretative turn sweeping the social sciences, culture-historical geography, with its traditional emphasis on genetic-contextual explication, should find wider affinities than in the recent past.

Cultural Landscape

At first glance, the theme of cultural landscape does not seem any more likely than that of culture area or culture history to be a site of radical change. The theme remains the rubric under which traditional preferences and approaches continue to be inscribed. Within cultural geography the subtheme of human agency's impact on biophysical environments either still follows or takes its departures from precepts laid down by Sauer and his German counterparts or, more disjunctively, by George Perkins Marsh (Williams 1987). Within the increasingly important field of environmental history, these antecedents are not always acknowledged, but their results are quite familiar (see Cronon 1983, 1991; Worster 1988). Since the late 1970s, however, radically new ways of looking at cultural landscapes have been proposed and produced.

Rowntree and Conkey (1980) helped to initiate study of symbolic action, social processes, and cultural landscape mediations. Cosgrove (1983) proposed restructuring cultural geography along cultural Marxist lines, with Gramsci's (1971) concept of cultural hegemony serving more than heuristical ends. Cosgrove (1984) followed this programmatic piece with a collection of essays on social formations and symbolic landscapes. Cosgrove has joined Jackson (Cosgrove and Jackson 1987) and other geographers on both sides of the Atlantic in laying the foundations for a "new cultural geography." They dedicate part of their work to reconstituting the cultural landscape theme (see also Cosgrove 1985; Cosgrove and Daniels 1988; Duncan 1990; Duncan and Duncan 1988).

Cultural Ecology

From the mid-1960s through the mid-1980s cultural ecology could be identified as cultural geography's most dynamic sector, generating the most theoretically informed literature and differing most consistently with the implicit notions of culture employed by other geographers. The emergence of a social-theoretically oriented "new cultural geography" dilutes this distinctiveness somewhat, but cultural ecology in the 1990s promises to continue to offer alternatives to traditionalist approaches to cultural geography. For background on these departures see Butzer (1989), Denevan (1983), Turner (1989), and Zimmerer (1994 and chapter 6 in this volume). Wagner and Mikesell (1962b: 19) pointed to a key difference in stressing culture history's focus on sequences and cultural ecology's concern with processes of culture change. They also noted cultural ecology's application of the "scientific mode of thinking." At the time of their essay few cultural geographers had used the methods and theories of ecological anthropologists in their work. William Denevan (1966), along with Karl Butzer (1964), was one of the first to explicitly address ecological work then current in anthropology. Denevan and his students, especially Nietschmann (1973), Turner (1974, 1989), Bergman (1980), Mathewson (1984), and Knapp (1991), have continued this interaction with developments in ecological anthropology. At the same time they and many other geographers employing cultural ecological methods maintain links with geography's ecological approaches to the study of cultures (see Butzer 1976, 1989; Porter 1965, 1978).

The main departure within geographical cultural ecology has come with fusions of cultural ecology and political economy. Michael Watts (1983) and his students at Berkeley represent one core of this activity. At the outset of this departure (the late 1970s) culture in its various possible conceptualizations ceased to be a primary focus of this new political-economic cultural ecology. An explanatory priority was placed on structural forces of a political-economic sort over the culturally more contingent and indeterminate factors at work. More recently, however, many of these geographers have shown an interest in reexamining the central role of culture as part of a larger, more critical cultural ecology (Katz and Kirby 1991; Pred and Watts 1992). This is in keeping with the broad changes that have occurred over the past decade throughout large sectors of the social sciences. The broad acceptance and consensus that materialist/rationalist outlooks enjoyed by the late 1970s has been increasingly challenged by relativist and even romantic perspectives (Gregory 1994). Such erstwhile cultural ecologists as Clifford Geertz (1973, 1983) and Marshall Sahlins (1976) have for somewhat more than a decade served as key critics of positions that would preclude interpretative or contextualist approaches to the study of culture and environment.

Conclusions

In a curious way 1989 may be noted as a milestone year in the ongoing discourse about culture and its place in geography. At the level of ever-accelerating academic production and publication two books appeared that were explicitly concerned with cultural geography's past, present, and future (Jackson

1989; Norton 1989). Previous reflections on the nature of cultural geography had been largely limited to articles and commentaries (Sauer 1927, 1931; Dodge 1937; Wagner 1975; Mikesell 1978; Spencer 1978; Duncan 1980; Cosgrove 1983). If book-length methodological attention equals maturity, then it has taken about a century for cultural geography to finally come of age! William Norton's (1989) *Explorations in the Understanding of Landscape: A Cultural Geography* locates the landscape theme at the core of the subdiscipline, while attempting (with reasonable success) to survey the field. Of some five hundred items in the bibliography, about half are by geographers, and about half of these represent the work of cultural geographers. Priority is given to broad strokes rather than in-depth discussion. The presentation is evenhanded; prescriptions and persuasion are muted.

Peter Jackson's (1989) *Maps of Meaning: An Introduction to Cultural Geography* has rather different designs. Jackson is concerned with (re)placing a socio-politically "reconstituted" concept of culture at the core of cultural geography. After a review and critique of "the heritage of cultural geography" (with particular emphasis on the Berkeley School) he explores alternative possibilities, settling on a form of cultural materialism (not to be confused with Marvin Harris's Darwinian-Marxian construct; see Harris 1979). Drawing on Raymond Williams's elaboration of a cultural Marxism and the British cultural studies movement as exemplified in the work of Stuart Hall (Hall et al. 1980) and his associates in the Centre for Contemporary Cultural Studies, Jackson presents a series of examples of how a materialist cultural geography might proceed. The topics of these essays include culture and ideology, popular culture and the politics of class, gender and sexuality, languages of racism, and the politics of language. Jackson argues for a concept of culture freed from its earlier unitary definitions and enabled thereby to recognize the plurality of cultures. In his view, cultures are maps of meaning through which the world is made intelligible. Accordingly, culture in its unitary or universal sense becomes the domain or terrain on which these meanings are received and/or contested. Clearly, Jackson is attempting to map out new meanings for cultural geography as a whole.

In world-historical terms, the year 1989 was more than a milestone. The cultural-political revolutions that swept Eastern Europe and, in part, sparked the implosion of the Soviet political system promise at the very least new grounds for vigorous debate and investigation of the concept(s) of culture in these late-modern times. If the events of the last several years have suggested to some a partial closure of the trajectory begun with the French Revolution in 1789, then to others, especially cultural geographers, these events should suggest a reappraisal and increased attention to the themes of populism, expressionism, and pluralism first sounded by Herder. At the same time, academic debates over the nature of modernity and the grounds for existence of a posterior condition (postmodernity) continue apace (see chapter 16). In fundamental ways the debates over the meaning of postmodernism and related issues are also debates over the concept of culture. Cultural geographers have an opportunity here to become engaged at the sharp edges of scholarly ferment. Not surprisingly, they were slow in accepting this challenge. The initial exceptions were in the area of urban cultural geography, wherein Mona Domosh (1987; 1990) focused on questions of power and architectural style in modern North American cities, and James Duncan (1990) has produced a major departure in cultural landscape studies with his historical-hermeneutic investigation of the politics of landscape interpretation in the Kandyan (Sri Lanka) Kingdom. As demonstrated in Duncan's work, experimentation with methods derived from poststructuralist cultural theory lend themselves not only to studies of cultural landscapes, but also to questions of the geography of modernity and postmodernity.

Given the importance of cultural phenomena in the current conjuncture of global history and the upsurge of cultural studies throughout the humanities and social sciences, cultural geographers are better situated to expand their purview than at any previous time.[2] Whether or not they seize this opportunity will depend in part on their openness to self-reflexive study of their past and on their receptivity to theory to inform their efforts in the future. This is not to say that previous work in geography employing either implicit or explicit concepts of culture have been negligible. The work of Berkeley School cultural geographers and others working from similar vantage points has produced some of geography's most durable (and, one can safely predict) enduring monuments of scholarship. Despite the considerable diversity of talent and topics subsumed in this loosely collective enterprise, with time and distance the monuments, middling works, and even minutiae may begin to take on the aura of the monolithic. As with conceptualizing culture itself, cultural geographers need to continue to ponder, preserve, and promote the plural.

Although Sauer (1925) went on record early as a superorganicist, in his settled ways and later work he was more accurately an organicist. He spoke of the plurality of cultures, especially the premodern ones, and he championed their resistance to dominant power relations. As Philo (1988) pointed out, the lacuna between the new social-theoretical cultural geography and that of the old empirical-historicist may not be all that deep in places (though see Blaut 1993b for a different plotting of these affinities and oppositions). In the spirit of these times it seems more than appropriate that cultural geographers wade in and celebrate each other's differences (Duncan 1994). One result could be the forging of new meanings—perhaps even radically new foundations—of the concept of culture and its place in geography.

Notes

This essay was originally drafted in the summer of 1990, hence the emphasis on the events of the previous fall (1989) as representing a world-historic moment. Developments since then have generally supported this view. At the same time, the cultural turn within the social sciences (and at the edges of some of the physical sciences) has reached a point of considerable returns and now threatens to take center stage — at least for a while. For some scholars with entrenched interests or well-held positions, it may seem a bit like a whirlwind — if not a full-blown tornado — coming from seemingly nowhere, charged with strange energies and an even odder assortment of enthusiasms, poised to uproot and overturn a wide range of prior certitudes and practices, but, like so many of our present postings, this too may be mostly an academic media event. Its course is hardly predictable: it may yield useful recombinations and disciplinary fusings, or it may scatter portions of paradigms and epistemic fragments across wider spaces than ever before. Most likely, both will occur, but geographers with an appreciation of culture's conceptual moorings and past tacks and turns should be well equipped to navigate in these new surroundings.

I would like to thank Philip Wagner for his generous and helpful advice on matters prosaic as well as conceptual, and Kathy for listening to talk of portions in progress.

1. There is a growing literature on the culture concept within cultural geography and debates over where cultural geography is heading. A sampling of these sources not cited elsewhere in this essay includes: Cosgrove 1989, 1992; Gregory and Ley 1988; Jackson 1980; Kofman 1988; Ley 1985; McDowell 1994; Rowntree 1988; Rowntree, Foote, and Domosh 1989.

2. During the past five years the surge of debate and publication within human geography on postmodernism and related topics has continued apace (Dear 1994). Increasingly, attention is being directed toward culture as a focus of contemporary research along with its salience in everyday life and current realities. The scope of this interest is far too wide and deep to survey here. Examples of newer positions, approaches, and strategies include postcolonial, subaltern, and identity studies; the cultural/social construction of race, gender, sexuality, and nature; contextualism, deconstructionism and intertextuality; and cartographies of cultural/symbolic capital and corporeality. Clearly geographers' exploratory opportunities are far from being a thing of the past.

Some idea of current thinking along lines of particular interest to geographers can be gleaned from the following volumes: Agnew and Duncan 1989; Anderson and Gale 1992; Barnes and Duncan 1992; Clifford and Marcus 1986; Duncan and Ley 1993; Godlewska and Smith 1993; Gregory 1994; Haraway 1989; Harvey 1989; Hooson 1995; Jameson 1991; Keith and Pile 1993; Kobayashi and Mackenzie 1989; Philo 1991; Pred 1990; Said 1993; Shurmer-Smith and Hannam 1994; and Spivak 1988. Some might even glimpse in these and related readings (mostly presented in edited volumes and often set in a rather tight intrareferential field) the outlines, if not the foundations, of a new or counter canon in formation. Within this construction cultural questions appear variously as appliqué and ornament, framing and fenestral, even mortar and block, but clearly they are an integral part of what is being created.

References

Agnew, John A., and James S. Duncan. 1989. *The power of place: Bringing together geographical and sociological imaginations.* New York: Unwin Hyman.

Anderson, Kay, and Fay Gale, eds. 1992. *Inventing places: Studies in cultural geography.* New York: Halstead Press.

Anonymous. 1910. Herder, Johann Gottfried von (1744–1803). *The Encyclopedia Britannica.* 13th ed., 347–49.

Arnold, Matthew. (1869) 1971. *Culture and anarchy.* Cambridge: Cambridge University Press.

Aschmann, Homer. 1987. Carl Sauer, a self-directed career. In *Carl O. Sauer: A tribute,* ed. M. S. Kenzer, 137–43. Corvallis, Oreg.: Oregon State University Press.

Bagby, Philip. 1959. *Culture and history: Prolegomena to the comparative study of civilizations.* Berkeley: University of California Press.

Barnes, Trevor J., and James S. 1992. *Writing worlds: Discourse, text, and metaphor in the representation of landscape.* London: Routledge.

Bell, Daniel. 1973. *The coming of postindustrial society.* New York: Basic Books.

Bergman, Roland W. 1980. *Amazon economics: The simplicity of Shipibo wealth.* Dellplain Latin American Studies, No. 6, Ann Arbor, Mich.: University Microfilms.

Berlin, Isaiah. 1976. *Vico and Herder: Two studies in the history of ideas.* New York: Viking Press.

Birkenhauer, J. A. C. 1986. Johann Gottfried Herder, In *Geographers: Bibliographical studies,* ed. T. W. Freeman, vol. 10, 77–84. New York: Mansell Publishing Ltd.

Blaut, James M. 1977. Two views of diffusion. *Annals of the Association of American Geographers* 67: 343–49.

———. 1987. Diffusionism: A uniformitarian critique. *Annals of the Association of American Geographers* 77: 30–47.

———. 1993a. *The colonizer's model of the world: Geographical diffusionism and Eurocentric history.* New York: Guilford Press.

———. 1993b. Mind and matter in cultural geography. In *Culture, form, and place: Essays in cultural and historical geography,* ed. K. Mathewson. *Geoscience and Man* 32: 345–56.

116   Kent Mathewson

Bowen, Margarita. 1981. *Empiricism and geographical thought: From Francis Bacon to Alexander von Humboldt*. Cambridge: Cambridge University Press.

Brookfield, Harold C. 1964. Questions on the human frontiers of geography. *Economic Geography* 40: 283–303.

Butzer, Karl W. 1964. *Environment and archeology: An introduction to Pleistocene geography*. Chicago: Aldine.

———. 1976. *Early hydraulic agriculture in Egypt: A study in cultural ecology*. Chicago: University of Chicago Press.

———. 1989. Cultural ecology. In *Geography in America*, ed. G. L. Gaile and C. J. Willmott, 192–208. Columbus: Merrill Publishing Co.

———. 1990. The realm of cultural-human ecology: Adaptation and change in historical perspective. In *The earth as transformed by human action: Global and regional changes in the biosphere over the past 300 years*, ed. B. L. Turner II et al., 685–701. Cambridge: Cambridge University Press.

Carroll, Joseph. 1982. *The cultural theory of Matthew Arnold*. Berkeley: University of California Press.

Childe, V. Gordon. 1925. *The dawn of western civilization*. New York: Knopf.

Clifford, James, and George E. Marcus. 1986. *Writing cultures: The poetics and politics of culture*. Berkeley: University of California Press.

Cosgrove, Denis E. 1983. Towards a radical cultural geography. *Antipode* 15: 1–11.

———. 1984. *Social formation and symbolic landscape*. London: Croom Helm.

———. 1985. Prospect, perspective, and the evolution of the landscape idea. *Transactions of the Institute of British Geographers*. N. S. 10: 45–62.

———. 1989. A terrain of metaphor: Cultural geography 1988–1989. *Progress in Human Geography* 13: 566–77.

———. 1992. Orders and a new world: Cultural geography 1990–91. *Progress in Human Geography* 16: 272–80.

Cosgrove, Denis E., and Peter Jackson. 1987. New directions in cultural geography. *Area* 19: 95–101.

Cosgrove, Denis E., and Stephen J. Daniels, eds. 1988. *The iconography of landscape: Essays on the symbolic representation, design and use of past environments*. Cambridge: Cambridge University Press.

Cronon, William. 1983. *Changes in the land: Indians, colonists, and the ecology of New England*. New York: Hill and Wang.

————. 1991. *Nature's metropolis: Chicago and the great west.* New York: W. W. Norton.

Curry, Michael. 1985. Review of *Local knowledge: Further essays in interpretive anthropology,* by Clifford Geertz. *Annals of the Association of American Geographers* 75: 291–93.

Dear, Michael. 1994. Postmodern human geography: A preliminary appraisal. *Erdkunde* 48: 2–13.

Denevan, William M. 1966. A cultural-ecological view of the former aboriginal settlement in the Amazon Basin. *Professional Geographer* 18: 346–51.

————. 1983. Adaptation, variation, and cultural geography. *Professional Geographer* 35: 399–407.

Dickinson, Robert E. 1969. *The makers of modern geography.* New York: Fredrick H. Praeger.

Dodge, Stanley D. 1937. Round table on problems in cultural geography. *Annals of the Association of American Geographers* 27: 155–77.

Domosh, Mona. 1987. Imaging New York's first skyscrapers. *Journal of Historical Geography* 13: 233–48.

————. 1989. New York's first skyscrapers: Conflict in the design of the American commercial landscape. *Landscape* 30: 34–38.

Duncan, James S. 1980. The superorganic in American cultural geography. *Annals of the Association of American Geographers* 70: 184–98.

————. 1990. *The city as text: The politics of landscape interpretation in the Kandyan Kingdom.* Cambridge: Cambridge University Press.

————. 1994. After the Civil War: Reconstructing cultural geography as heterotopia. In *Re-reading cultural geography,* ed. K. E. Foote, P. J. Hugill, K. Mathewson, and J. M. Smith, 401–08. Austin: University of Texas Press.

Duncan, James S., and Nancy Duncan. 1988. (Re)reading the landscape. *Environment and Planning D: Society and Space* 6: 117–26.

Duncan, James S., and David Ley, eds. 1993. *Place/culture/representation.* New York: Routledge.

Ellen, Roy. 1988. Persistence and change in the relationship between anthropology and human geography. *Progress in Human Geography* 12: 229–62.

Geertz, Clifford. 1973. *The interpretation of cultures.* New York: Basic Books.

————. 1983. *Local knowledge: Further essays in interpretive anthropology.* New York: Basic Books.

Glacken, Clarence J. 1967. *Traces on the Rhodian Shore: Nature and culture in western thought from ancient time to the end of the eighteenth century.* Berkeley: University of California Press.

Godlewska, Anne, and Neil Smith, eds., 1993. *Geography and empire.* Oxford: Blackwell.

Gramsci, Antonio. 1971. *Prison notebooks: Selections.* New York: International.

Gregory, Derek. 1994. *Geographical imaginations.* Oxford: Blackwell.

Gregory, Derek, and David Ley. 1988. Culture's geographies. *Environment and Planning D: Society and Space* 6: 115–16.

Hall, Stuart, et al., ed. 1980. *Culture, media, language.* London: Hutchison/Centre for Contemporary Culture Studies.

Haraway, Donna. 1989. *Primate visions: Gender, race, and nature in the world of modern science.* New York: Routledge.

Harris, Marvin. 1968. *The rise of anthropological theory: A history of theories of culture.* New York: T. Y. Cromwell.

———. 1979. *Cultural materialism: The struggle for a science of culture.* New York: Random House.

Hart, John Fraser. 1982. The highest form of the geographer's art. *Annals of the Association of American Geographers* 72: 1–29.

Hartshorne, Richard. 1958. The concept of geography as a science of space, from Kant and Humboldt to Hettner. *Annals of the Association of American Geographers* 48: 97–108.

———. 1961 [1939]. *The nature of geography.* Lancaster, Pennsylvania: The Association of American Geographers.

Harvey, David. 1969. *Explanation in geography.* London: Edward Arnold.

———. 1989. *The condition of postmodernity: An enquiry into the origins of culture change.* Oxford: Basil Blackwell.

Herder, Johann G. von. 1803 (1784–1791). *Outlines of a philosophy of the history of man.* T. Churchill, trans. London, Luke.

Hooson, David. 1981. Carl O. Sauer. In *The origins of academic geography in the United States,* ed. B. W. Blouet, 165–74. Hamden, Conn.: Archon Books.

———, ed. 1994. *Geography and national identity.* Oxford: Blackwell.

Hugill, Peter J., and Kenneth E. Foote. 1994. Re-reading cultural geography. In *Re-reading cultural geography,* ed. K. E. Foote, P. J. Hugill, K. Mathewson, and J. M. Smith, 1–23. Austin: University of Texas Press.

Jackson, Peter. 1980. A plea for cultural geography. *Area* 12: 110–13.

———. 1989. *Maps of meaning: An introduction to culture geography.* London: Unwin Hyman.

Jameson, Fredric. 1991. *Postmodernism, or the culture of late capitalism.* London: Verso.

Jefferson, Mark. 1911. The culture of nations. *Bulletin of the American Geographical Society* 18: 241–65.

———. 1929. The geographic distribution of inventiveness. *Geographical Review* 19: 649–61.

Jordan, Terry G. 1982. *Texas graveyards: A cultural legacy.* Austin: University of Texas Press.

———. 1985. *American log buildings: An Old World heritage.* Chapel Hill: University of North Carolina Press.

Jordan, Terry G., and Matti Kaups. 1989. *The American backwoods frontier: An ethnic and ecological interpretation.* Baltimore: Johns Hopkins University Press.

Kaplan, David, and Robert A. Manners. 1972. *Culture theory.* Englewood Cliffs, N. J.: Prentice-Hall.

Katz, Cindi, and Andrew Kirby. 1991. In the nature of things: The environment and everyday life. *Transactions of the Institute of British Geographers.* N. S. 16: 259–71.

Kenzer, Martin S., ed. 1987. *Carl O. Sauer: A tribute.* Corvallis, Oreg.: Oregon State University Press.

Kern, Stephen. 1983. *The culture of time and space: 1880–1918.* Cambridge: Harvard University Press.

Keith, Michael, and Steve Pile, eds. 1993. *Place and the politics of identity.* New York: Routledge.

Klemm, Gustave. 1843. *Allgemeine Cul-turgeschichte der Menschheit.* Leipzig: Leubner.

Knapp, Gregory W. 1991. *Andean ecology: Adaptative dynamics in Ecuador.* Boulder: Westview Press.

Kobayashi, Audrey, and Suzanne Mackenzie, eds. 1989. *Remaking human geography.* Boston: Unwin Hyman.

Kofman, Elenor. 1988. Is there a cultural geography beyond the fragments? *Area* 20: 85–87.

Kroeber, Alfred L. 1917. The superorganic. *American Anthropologist* 19: 163–213.

Kroeber, Alfred L., and Clyde Kluckhohn. 1952. *Culture: A critical review of concepts and definitions.* New York: Vintage Books.

Lears, T. J. Jackson. 1981. *No place of grace: Antimodernism and the transformation of American culture, 1880–1920.* New York: Pantheon.

Ley, David. 1985. Cultural/humanistic geography. *Environment and Planning D: Society and Space* 9: 415–23.

Livingstone, David N. 1992. *The geographical tradition: Episodes in the history of a contested enterprise.* Oxford: Blackwell.

Locke, John. 1894 [1690]. *An essay concerning human understanding.* Oxford: Clarendon Press.

Lowenthal, David. 1961. Geography, experience, and imagination: Toward a geographical epistemology. *Annals of the Association of American Geographers* 51: 241–60.

Macpherson, Anne. 1987. Preparing for the national stage: Carl Sauer's first ten years at Berkeley. In *Carl O. Sauer: A tribute,* ed. M. S. Kenzer, 69–89. Corvallis: Oregon State University Press.

Mandel, Ernest. 1975. *Late capitalism.* London: New Left Books.

Manuel, Frank E., and Fritzie P. Manuel. 1979. *Utopian thought in the western world.* Oxford: Basil Blackwell.

Martin, Geoffrey J. 1987. Foreword. In *Carl O. Sauer: A tribute,* ed. M. S. Kenzer, ix–xvi. Corvallis: Oreg. State University Press.

Martin, Geoffrey J., and Preston E. James. 1993. *All possible worlds: A history of geographical ideas,* 3d ed. New York: John Wiley & Sons.

Mathewson, Kent. 1984. *Irrigation horticulture in highland Guatemala: The tablón system of Panajachel.* Boulder, Colo.: Westview Press.

————. 1987. Sauer south by southwest: Antimodernism and the austral impulse. In *Carl O. Sauer: A tribute,* ed. M. S. Kenzer, 90–111. Corvallis, Oreg.: Oregon State University Press.

————. 1993. Human geography in the American tropics: A forty-year review. *Singapore Journal of Tropical Geography,* 14: 123–56.

————. 1994. Introduction: How the world works. In *Re-reading Cultural Geography,* ed. K. E. Foote, P. J. Hugill, K. Mathewson, and J. M. Smith, 167–72. Austin: University of Texas Press.

May, Joseph A. 1970. *Kant's concept of geography and its relation to recent geographical thought.* Toronto: University of Toronto, Department of Geography, Research Paper No. 4.

McDowell, Linda. 1994. The transformation of cultural geography. In *Human geography: Society, space, and social science*, ed. D. Gregory, R. Martin, G. Smith. 146–73. Minneapolis: University of Minnesota Press.

Mikesell, Marvin. 1967. Geographic perspectives in anthropology. *Annals of the Association of American Geographers* 57: 617–34.

———. 1977. Cultural geography. *Progress in Human Geography*. 1: 460–64.

———. 1978. Tradition and innovation in cultural geography. *Annals of the Association of American Geographers* 68: 1–16.

Nietschmann, Bernard Q. 1973. *Between land and water: The subsistence ecology of the Miskito Indians, eastern Nicaragua*. New York: Academic Press.

Norton, William. 1989. *Explorations in the understanding of landscape: A cultural geography*. New York: Greenwood Press.

Parsons, James J. 1987. Now this matter of cultural geography: Notes from Carl O. Sauer's last seminar at Berkeley. In *Carl O. Sauer: A tribute*, ed. M. S. Kenzer, 153–163. Corvallis, Oreg.: Oregon State University Press.

Peschel, Oscar. 1876. *The races of man*. London: H. S. King.

Philo, Chris. 1988. New directions in cultural geography: A conference of the Social Geography Study Group of the Institute of British Geographers, University College London, 1–3 September 1987. *Journal of Historical Geography* 14: 178–81.

———, comp. 1991. *New words, new worlds: Reconceptualising social and cultural geography*. Lampeter: Social and Cultural Study Group of the Institute of British Geographers.

Platt, Robert S. 1962. The rise of cultural geography in America. In *Readings in cultural geography*, ed. P. L. Wagner and M. Mikesell. 35–43. Chicago: University of Chicago Press.

Porter, Philip W. 1965. Environmental potentials and economic opportunities: A background for cultural adaptation. *American Anthropologist* 67: 409–20.

———. 1978. Geography as human ecology. *American Behavioral Scientist* 22: 15–39.

———. 1982. The kinship of anthropology and geography. In *Crisis in anthropology*, ed. E. A. Hoebel et al., 223–43. New York: Garland.

Pred, Allan. 1990. *Lost words and lost worlds: Modernity and the language of everyday life in late nineteenth-century Stockholm*. Cambridge: Cambridge University Press.

Pred, Allen, and Michael Watts. 1992. *Reworking modernity: Capitalism and symbolic discontent.* New Brunswick, N. J.: Rutgers University Press.

Price, Edward. 1968. Cultural geography. *International encyclopedia of the social sciences,* vol. 6, 129–34. New York: Macmillan & Free Press.

Price, Marie, and Martin Lewis. 1993. The reinvention of cultural geography. *Annals of the Association of American Geographers* 83: 1–17.

Pudup, Mary Beth. 1988. Arguments within regional geography. *Progress in Human Geography* 12: 369–90.

Ratzel, Friedrich. 1882–91. *Anthropogeographie,* vol. 1, *Grundzüge der Anwendung der Erdkunde auf die Geschichte;* vol. 2, *Die geographische Verbreitung des Menschen.* Stuttgart: J. Engelhorn.

———. 1896. *The history of mankind.* London: Macmillan.

Richardson, Miles. 1981. Commentary on the superorganic in American cultural geography. *Annals of the Association of American Geographers* 71: 284–87.

Rowntree, Lester B. 1988. Orthodoxy and new directions: Cultural/humanistic geography. *Progress in Human Geography* 12: 575–86.

Rowntree, Lester B., and Margaret W. Conkey. 1980. Symbolism and the cultural landscape. *Annals of the Association of American Geographers* 70: 459–574.

Rowntree, Lester B., Kenneth E. Foote, and Mona Domosh. 1989. Cultural geography. In *Geography in America,* ed. G. Gaile and C. Willmott, 209–17. Columbus, Ohio: Merrill.

Sahlins, Marshall. 1976. *Culture and practical reason.* Chicago: University of Chicago Press.

Said, Edward. 1992. *Culture and imperialism.* New York: Columbia University Press.

Sandner, Gerhard. 1994. In search of identity: German nationalism and geography, 1871–1910. In *Geography and national identity,* ed. D. Hooson, 71–91. Oxford: Blackwell.

Sauer, Carl O. 1915. The geography of the Ozark Highland of Missouri. Ph.D. dissertation, Department of Geography, University of Chicago, Chicago.

———. 1920. *The geography of the Ozark Highland of Missouri.* Chicago: University of Chicago Press.

———. 1925. The morphology of landscape. *University of California Publications in Geography,* 2: 19–54.

————. 1927. Recent developments in cultural geography. In *Recent developments in the social sciences*, ed. E. C. Hayes, 154–212. Philadelphia: J. B. Lippincott.

————. 1931. Geography, cultural. *Encyclopedia of the social sciences* 6: 621, 624. New York: Macmillan Co.

————. 1941. Foreword to historical geography. *Annals of the Association of American Geographers* 11: 1–24.

————. 1952. *Agricultural origins and dispersals*. New York: The American Geographical Society.

————. 1963 [1952]. Folkways of social science. In *Land and life: A selection of the writings of Carl Ortwin Sauer*, ed. J. Leighly, 380–88. Berkeley: University of California Press.

Schlick, Manfred J. 1982. Otto Schluter 1872–1959. *Geographers: Biobibliographical studies* 6: 115–22. London: Mansell.

Schneider, Louis, and Charles M. Bonjean, eds. 1973. *The idea of culture in the social sciences*. New York: Cambridge University Press.

Semple, Ellen C. 1911. *Influences of geographic environment on the basis of Ratzel's system of anthropo-geography*. New York: Henry Holt.

Shurmer-Smith, Pamela, and Kevin Hannam. 1994. *Worlds of desire, realms of power: A cultural geography*. New York: Edward Arnold.

Singer, Milton. 1968. The concept of culture. *International encyclopedia of the social sciences* 3: 527–43. New York: Macmillan and Free Press.

Solot, Michael. 1986. Carl Sauer and cultural evolution. *Annals of the Association of American Geographers* 76: 508–20.

Sopher, David E. 1973. Place and location: Notes on the spatial patterning of culture. In *The idea of culture in the social sciences*, ed. L. Schneider and C. M. Bonjean, 101–17. New York: Cambridge University Press.

Spencer, Joseph E. 1976. What's in a name?—The Berkeley School. *Historical Geography Newsletter* 6: 7–11.

Spengler, Oswald. 1926–1928 [1918]. *The decline of the west*, 2 vols. New York: Alfred Knopf.

Speth, William W. 1981. Berkeley geography, 1923–1933. In *The origins of academic geography in the United States*, ed B. W. Blouet, 221–44. Hamden, Conn.: Archon Books.

————. 1987. Historicism: The disciplinary world view of Carl O. Sauer. In *Carl O. Sauer: A tribute*, ed. M. S. Kenzer, 11–39. Corvallis, Oreg.: Oregon State University Press.

124   Kent Mathewson

Spivak, Gayatri C. 1988. *In other worlds: Essays in cultural politics.* London: Routledge.

Stocking, George W., Jr. 1963. Matthew Arnold, E. B. Taylor, and the uses of invention. *American Anthropologist* 65: 783–99.

———. 1966. Franz Boas and the culture concept in historical perspective. *American Anthropologist* 68: 867–82.

Thrift, Nigel. 1990. For a new regional geography 1. *Progress in Human Geography* 14: 272–79.

———. 1994. Taking aim at the heart of the region. In *Human Geography: Society, space, and social science,* ed. D. Gregory, R. Martin, and G. Smith, 200–31. Minneapolis: University of Minnesota Press.

Tuan, Yi-Fu. 1974. *Topophilia: A study of environmental perception, attitudes, and values.* New York: Prentice-Hall.

———. 1977. *Space and place: the perspective of experience.* Minneapolis: University of Minnesota Press.

———. 1979. *Landscapes of fear.* New York: Pantheon.

———. 1982. *Segmented worlds and self: Group life and self-consciousness.* Minneapolis: University of Minnesota Press.

Turner, B. L., II. 1984. *Once beneath the forest: Prehistoric terracing in the Río Bec region of the Maya lowlands.* Dellplain Latin American Studies, No. 13. Boulder, Colo.: Westview Press.

———. 1989. The specialist-synthesis approach to the revival of geography: The case for cultural ecology. *Annals of the Association of American Geographers* 79: 88–100.

Tylor, Edward B. 1871. *Primitive culture: Researches into the development of mythology, philosophy, religion, language, art, and custom.* London: J. Murray.

Wagner, Philip L. 1972. *Environments and peoples.* Englewood Cliffs, N. J.: Prentice-Hall.

———. 1974. Cultural landscapes and regions: Aspects of communication. In *Man and cultural heritage: Geoscience and Man,* vol. 5, ed. H. J. Walker and W. G. Haag, 133–42. Baton Rouge: School of Geoscience, Louisiana State University.

———. 1975. The themes of cultural geography rethought. *Yearbook: Association of Pacific Coast Geographers* 37: 7–14.

Wagner, Philip L., and Marvin W. Mikesell, eds. 1962a. *Readings in cultural geography.* Chicago: University of Chicago Press.

————. 1962b. General introduction: The themes of cultural geography. In *Readings in cultural geography*, ed. P. L. Wagner and M. W. Mikesell, 1–24. Chicago: University of Chicago Press.

Watts, Michael. 1983. *Silent violence: Food, famine, and peasantry in northern Nigeria*. Berkeley: University of California Press.

White, Leslie A. 1959. The concept of culture. *American Anthropologist* 61: 227–51.

Williams, Michael, 1987. Sauer and "Man's Role in Changing the Face of the Earth." *Geographical Review* 77: 218–31.

Williams, Raymond. 1958. *Culture and society, 1780–1950*. New York: Columbia University Press.

————. 1976. *Keywords: A vocabulary of culture and society*. New York: Oxford University Press.

Worster, Donald, ed. 1988. *The ends of the earth: Perspectives on modern environmental history*. New York: Cambridge University Press.

Zimmerer, Karl S. 1994. Human ecology and the "new ecology": The prospect and promise of integration. *Annals of the Association of American Geographers* 84: 108–25.

Zelinsky, Wilbur. 1973. *The cultural geography of the United States*. Englewood Cliffs, N. J.: Prentice-Hall.

————. 1980. North America's vernacular regions. *Annals of the Association of American Geographers* 70: 1–16.

5

The Cultural Landscape Concept in American Human Geography

Lester B. Rowntree

While the concept of the cultural landscape[1] is frequently used in human geography, the term is an ambiguous one that carries a variety of meanings. This etymological elusiveness is both liability and asset; to some, the notion of cultural landscape is an appropriate bridge between space and society, culture and environment, while to others this definitional fluidity weakens the concept and disqualifies it from serious analytic usage. Carl O. Sauer promoted the concept of cultural landscape as an essential focus of human geography in the 1920s, yet Richard Hartshorne, in his subsequent critique of the field, found the concept flaccid and unacceptable. This "assassination" of landscape (Smith 1989: 107) furthered the polarization of academic geography into two traditions, or cultures, that at times have been mutually exclusive. The first tradition draws heavily on historicism, interpretation, and humanism, while the other is more closely allied with empiricism and logical positivism. Historically, the notion of cultural landscape has been more closely connected to the first tradition and overlapped only rarely with the positivist research agenda.

Landscape studies today are still primarily associated with humanistic inquiry; however, this distinction is less important as epistemological boundaries become blurred in the movement away from methodological dogma. As a result, the concept of cultural landscape plays a prominent role in a diverse array of geographic research, some of which is linked closely to traditional research questions, while another domain—commonly called *new directions*—

claims a new degree of analytic power by drawing on contemporary social theory. If true, then cultural landscape will play a central role in a reinvigorated human geography of the 1990s (Cosgrove 1989, Cosgrove and Jackson 1987, Kobayashi 1989). Evaluating this claim assumes some understanding of how landscape studies have been done in the past.

In this chapter I trace the intellectual heritage of the cultural landscape concept in American human geography by looking, first, at the etymological roots and definitional ambiguities of the term. This sets the scene for an examination of Sauer's landscape agenda and helps to explain Hartshorne's critical reaction. That section concludes with an assessment of Sauer's legacy for landscape studies. The postwar period is treated next, for which two foundational themes—landscape as material culture and landscapes of the mind—are discussed. Following this historical overview, the chapter concludes with a discussion and examples of the varied usage of landscape in contemporary human geography. In that section landscape studies are placed within a heuristic framework that compares the similarities and differences between traditional work and research associated with new directions in human geography.

The purpose of this chapter is to provide readers with a sense of the intellectual heritage of a central term and concept in human geography and to provide enough material (content and bibliography) for thoughtful self-exploration of the varied domains of landscape research. Thus equipped, geographers can clarify their own thinking and feelings about this often-used yet sometimes elusive concept.

Defining Landscape

Etymological Roots: Region and Scenery

The definition of *cultural landscape* offers a point of departure: What does it mean? How did the meaning originate? Is there agreement on its use? How is the term applied? This exercise is particularly germane because *landscape* has dichotomous roots that impart an ambiguity that has fueled debate and dissatisfaction with the concept. The first of these roots is the Old English notion of landscape as a district owned by a lord or an area inhabited by a particular group of people; the second derives from late sixteenth-century Dutch landscape painters, who emphasized the visual or aesthetic traits of a place. Historically, the first definition of landscape as area or region prevailed in American geography until the 1930s, when increasing attention was paid to the cultural expression of human settlement. This, obviously, entailed description and analysis of the visual dimension (for definitional and etymological elaboration, see Billinge 1981; Cosgrove 1984, 1985; J. B. Jackson 1986; and Mikesell 1968). Some geographers have trouble with a perceived contradiction or intellectual tension between the notion of area, which they assume can be analyzed objectively, and the visual, which to them involves human sentiment and subjectivity. As a result, those with a rigid notion of geography as a spatial science find the landscape concept unacceptably contaminated by its association with subjective social complexities.

Definitional Ambiguity

Instead of a simplistic and mutually exclusive "region-or-scenery" opposition, most researchers today blend these different etymological ingredients so that space, environmental modification, and human values are all touched on. This produces a wide variety of research emphases, perspectives, and results within both human and physical geography. To some, a cultural landscape is simply an environment modified by human action and the research emphasis, then, is to document empirically the consequences or process of that interaction, be it subtle or overt. The landscape thus is treated as an apparently objective by-product or artifact of human habits and habitation. This is fairly close to Sauer's early intentions (see below) and is still common today, particularly in Europe. Simmons (1988), for example, ponders the impact of prehistoric humans on the physical environment outside his study window in Britain to ascertain how baseline "natural" landscapes have been changed by humans; similarly, a recent collection of articles (Birks et al. 1988) documents ecological changes resultant from historical habitation and agriculture in northern Europe. While both Simmons and Birks use *cultural landscape* in their titles, notions of subjectivity, scenery, and interactivity between people and environment (beyond our immediate subsistence and habitation needs) are not explicit concerns in their research. The term refers instead only to an altered nature.

More common than this narrow ecological use of *landscape* is a broad, sometimes all-encompassing conceptualization that implies a larger degree of subjective interaction between humans and their surroundings. For example, Christopher Salter defines the cultural landscape as "that segment of earth space which lies between the viewer's eye and his or her horizon" (1978: 71). This perspective encourages a variety of interests and themes accenting the arrangement of material forms in the landscape and, often of equal importance, human responses to them. The products of this broad approach are ubiquitous in the geographic literature and Peirce Lewis (1983) provides an excellent review. Even within this definitional spectrum, however, there can be found important conceptual distinctions that draw on landscape's diverse etymological roots. For example, J. B. Jackson, a seminal figure in landscape studies, elegantly revives the Old English meaning of the concept to reinforce his long-term commitment to the vernacular landscape that is lived in (not looked at) by common people (1986: 65–76). Throughout his eclectic assortment of writings (see Zube 1970), Jackson maintains a clear focus on the inhabited and occupied populist landscape.

Jackson's view contrasts with Denis Cosgrove's critical emphasis on the historical dimensions of landscape as an elitist "way of seeing, a composition and structuring of the world so that it may be appropriated . . . through the composition of space according to the certainties of geometry" (1985: 55). For Cosgrove, *landscape* is primarily a social construct of control and appropriation linked to elitist ideologies. For example, he uses the metaphor of theater to describe the interaction of peoples, environment, power, and landscape-as-scenery in Renaissance Venice, implying that the city was "stage-managed" to reinforce the power structure's visibility and, consequently, its authority (Cosgrove 1990).

From this etymological introduction, two points are important: first, the duality of the term *landscape*. By drawing on two distinct linguistic and cultural traditions and conveying two kinds of messages (space and scenery), landscape poses a problem for a rigid conceptualization of geography as a spatial science. This point is developed in the next section. Second, this dichotomy may be responsible for the fact there is no precise definition of *cultural landscape*. Instead, there is a certain definitional ambiguity that allows varied uses and research emphases. If this is bothersome for some, it provides creative license for others to explore the complicated interface between humans and our varied environments.

Carl Sauer and the Cultural Landscape

Conventional wisdom posits that Carl O. Sauer led American human geography from the cul-de-sac of environmental determinism by promoting cultural landscape study as the essential task of geography and by creating a distinct Berkeley School of landscape geography, which constituted a contrasting pole to Midwestern spatial science geography. Though these differences are now ameliorated, the primary legacy of Sauer and Berkeley is inextricably linked to landscape. This wisdom, though containing some truth, exaggerates a more complicated intellectual history and demands refinement.

First, while Sauer was of considerable importance in codifying an intellectual response to determinism and while his 1925 essay "The Morphology of Landscape" was an early vehicle for articulating a more robust human geography, his impact on American geography transcends the notion of landscape. Second, though the landscape concept was often central to Sauer's methodology, it was not always the dominant method. The salient characteristics of Sauer and the Berkeley School are more readily defined by other traits such as interdisciplinary contact with anthropology, regional interests in Latin America, historical ecological inquiry, and the emphasis on human agency's effects on the Earth (Butzer 1989: 35; Parsons 1979; Price and Lewis 1993). Third, while there are notable Berkeley scholars closely associated with landscape studies (Fred Kniffen, James Parsons, Wilbur Zelinsky, and Christopher Salter are examples), there are others who are not (William Denevan and Richard Peet come to mind). More important, numerous American geographers prominently connected with landscape studies have no formal associations with Berkeley (Peirce Lewis, Donald Meinig, John Fraser Hart, and John Jakle are illustrations). The point, then, is simple: while Sauer was instrumental in folding the European concept of cultural landscape into American human geography and while he and his students have had considerable influence on American geography, their legacy goes beyond landscape. To think of landscape and the Berkeley School as synonymous is errant for several reasons, not the least of which is that it overlooks the considerable influence of non-Berkeley geographers on landscape research.

More germane here is Sauer's historical use of landscape and its premature rejection by Hartshorne and others from the mainstream of geographic thought.

"The Morphology of Landscape," 1925

Because Sauer's 1925 essay "The Morphology of Landscape" is treated in detail elsewhere, I offer only an overview here (see, for example, Entrikin 1984, Kenzer 1987, Mikesell 1968, Solot 1986). The intellectual foundation for Sauer's notion of landscape came from European geography's emphasis on humans—working through the medium of culture—as active agents of environmental transformation. This contrasted with environmental determinism's conceptualization of humans as passive actors. To escape determinism, Sauer argued that geography must claim a body of objective phenomena as its own; landscape, which was "an area, made up of a distinct association of forms, both physical and cultural" (Sauer in Leighly 1963: 321), was that realm. Landscapes could be studied inductively as spatial facts (contrasted with history's time facts), explicated, and then compared to other landscapes so that each might be placed in a system or taxonomic scheme.[2]

Though Sauer's "Morphology" influenced American geography by reinforcing the drift away from environmental determinism and by integrating
more methodologically advanced European thought into the discipline, this
redefinition of geography as the study of landscape morphology proved to have
serious practical and methodological problems. Indeed, some were so troublesome that Sauer either refined or repudiated them in later work (Mikesell
1968: 577; also, see Sauer 1941, 1956). Perhaps most vexing was his notion
that each landscape study should begin with an undisturbed or natural landscape that served as a baseline or reference mark for subsequent change. Although this stumbling block stimulated critical thought on the profound and
sometimes subtle expression of aboriginal environmental modification—for
example, the impact of prehistoric burning on allegedly natural vegetation
(Aschmann 1959)—the method was problematic for others. Hartshorne, for
example, dismissed the notion of a natural landscape as "a theoretical conception that not only does not exist in reality, but never did exist" (1961: 173).

Hartshorne's Critique of Landscape

That was only a minor point in Hartshorne's general critique of Sauer's
agenda. Smith opines that Hartshorne's argument against landscape—his "assassination"—was successful enough to convince succeeding generations of
geographers that the concept had "little or no value as a technical or scientific
term," with the result that landscape has been largely excluded from serious
theoretical discourse until recently (Smith 1989: 107). Hartshorne argued that
the term *landscape* is too ambiguous to provide a logical foundation for geographic inquiry. Moreover, the term is redundant with *area*, which adequately
expresses the spatial concept in English. Last, because landscape refers only
to the surface of the land, it is literally a superficial phenomenon, and a field
of science that concentrated on landscape would itself be superficial
(Hartshorne 1961: 165).

For Hartshorne, landscape was an untidy and chaotic concept that contaminated the Kantian logic of objective space (as in area and region) with the
subjectivity of aesthetics and human values. This a priori muddling of space
and society, Hartshorne opined, had contributed to the debacle of environmental determinism, and this was anathematical to his search for the separation and logical classification of different phenomena (Smith 1989: 109).
Only with this objective schema could geography proceed as a spatial science.

Sauer apparently felt no compulsion to defend landscape against
Hartshorne's charges. In the first place Sauer had moved beyond the narrow
methodology of "Morphology" so that landscape was now only one of many
facets of geographical inquiry. In the second, he was much more disturbed by

Hartshorne's critique of temporal depth in geographic method, of origins and diffusion research questions, and of physical geography. It was to allay criticism of these ideas, and not to defend landscape, that Sauer directed his rebuttal in his 1940 Association of American Geographers presidential address, "Foreword to Historical Geography" (Sauer 1941).

Nevertheless, Sauer's longstanding interest in the ecological consequences of human settlement ensured a central role for the cultural landscape as a means of assessing environmental transformation. This view was codified by his considerable influence on the shape and content of the landmark conference, "Man's Role in Changing the Face of the Earth," held in 1955 (Thomas 1956). According to Williams (1987), Sauer was adamant about stiffening the conference with diachronic and empirical depth to counter what he considered the reductionist, futurist, and prescriptive tendencies of 1950s social scientists, and the cultural landscape concept was used in compelling fashion for describing historical environmental impacts (see, for example, Sauer's "The Agency of Man on the Earth" in Thomas 1956: 49–69).

Sauer's Landscape Legacy

In summary, Sauer's 1925 essay "The Morphology of Landscape" was instrumental in moving American human geography beyond environmental determinism in favor of an emphasis on humans as active agents in environmental change and, equally important, of an articulation of explicit and rigorous method. Initially, Sauer posited that landscape study was the essential task of geography, but within a decade he had expanded his view so that landscape was just one of various conceptual tools in a humanistic cultural ecology that focused on explaining an array of historical problems from the origin and diffusion of agriculture and subsistence strategies to human impact on the environment (Leighly 1987, Mathewson 1987, Turner 1987).

Hartshorne reacted strongly to Sauer's 1925 landscape agenda by calling into question the term's vitality and applicability to scientific geography because of the subjective implications of studying "scenery." Many American geographers accepted this critique and, as a result, the term *cultural landscape* became suspect among those involved with the postwar quantitative and theoretical revolution. However, the concept remained in use by those researchers documenting human impact on the environment, a methodology reinforced by the 1955 "Man's Role" conference, and, it might be added, by usage outside of geography. By the late 1960s, though, partially in reaction to methodological excesses and arrogance by the "geography-as-spatial-science" school, a humanistic geography arose that resurrected the cultural landscape concept as a major vehicle for analyzing the ties between culture and environment. Though there were some linkages with Sauer's agenda, there were probably more differences than similarities, as noted below.

Postwar Foundations: Landscape, Material Culture, and Social Meaning

The decades following World War II are usually described as a time of change and intellectual clarification as Anglo-American human geography moved beyond the pragmatism demanded by the 1930s and 1940s. These currents are discussed fully elsewhere (see, for example, Johnston 1986, 1987). For the purpose of discussing the intellectual evolution of the landscape concept, we can work with the simplified dichotomy of two epistemological approaches: the first of these, which was reinforced by similar trends in allied social sciences such as economics and sociology, drew heavily on new forms of data quantification within the guidelines of logical positivism; the second and contrasting school, characterized by historical and interpretative methods, emerged by the 1970s as a full-blown humanistic geography. Landscape was central to the intellectual maturing of this latter endeavor because it provided an explicit vehicle for description and analysis of the interaction between humans and their culturally constructed environment.

For the sake of discussion, we can decipher two main ways in which landscape was used by this emerging humanistic geography during the period 1950 to 1970. The first emphasized the visible and material details of landscape, while the second stressed the cultural perception and visual preferences—the sentiment and emotion, some would say—of our surroundings. In the first approach landscapes were conceptualized as tangible expressions of material culture, with descriptive weight placed on documenting environmental arrangements such as house types, field patterns, and fence arrangements; these artifacts could then be placed within a larger cultural context to yield insights into social processes such as the diffusion of technologies or ideas or distinct cultural groupings. This focus differed considerably from the perception studies in which the goal was understanding how people cognized and responded to their environment.

Although many landscape studies were written during this period by diverse authors, this intellectual richness cannot be addressed in this short chapter. I focus instead on only those themes and individuals that seem foundational for the emergence of contemporary landscape research. Because there are other ways to conceptualize this important period in human geography, and even more ways to organize the development of landscape studies, readers are also advised to consult Meinig (1979) and Lewis (1983), since their perspectives and overviews contain material not discussed here.

J. B. Jackson: The Vernacular Voice of Landscape Studies

We cannot understand the concept of cultural landscape without acknowledging the immense influence of J. B. (John Brinckerhoff) Jackson. Since the 1950s his message has been clear: look at the common, vernacular American landscape. This call was somewhat unique at the time, for, unlike Sauer, Jackson was not particularly concerned with ecological consequences. Instead, his agenda was (and still is) understanding how common people shape their lived-in surroundings. While Jackson's interests developed apart from academic geography and anthropology, they paralleled and interacted with research by cultural materialists—those who look to everyday vernacular items for insight into cultural patterns and processes. Examples are Fred Kniffen's classic studies of house types (1936, 1965) or the works of folklorist Henry Glassie (1975) and the historical archaeologist James Deetz (1977).

The podia for Jackson's ideas were several—the magazine *Landscape*, which he founded in 1951 and edited until 1969; teaching positions at Berkeley and Harvard (in landscape architecture, not geography); considerable writings (see, for example, Jackson 1972, 1980, 1984; and Zube 1970); and his warm and affectionate interaction with students of landscape from various disciplines (Prentice 1981).

Although Jackson's ideas are best grasped, as Lewis says, through his writings in *Landscape*, volumes 1 through 19 (Lewis 1983: 248), good overviews appear in Lewis's article (1983) and the more extended essay by Meinig (1979: 210–44). In this essay on landscape teachers, Meinig captures the seven philosophical touchstones of Jackson's work.

1. The idea of landscape is anchored in human life; we study landscape not as an artifact or work of art, but for insight into the creator or artist.
2. Landscape is a unity, a wholeness, an integration of community and environment. The separation and dichotomy of human and nature is "a 19th century aberration and in time it will pass."
3. Landscapes are living, therefore judgments of landscape quality should assess it "as a place for living and working."
4. The individual dwelling is the elementary unit in the landscape, and other elements are related to it functionally and historically.
5. Understanding the landscape requires primary attention to the prosaic environments of the workaday world, the vernacular.
6. All landscapes are symbolic in that they represent striving to achieve a spiritual goal of making the earth over in the image of some heaven.
7. Landscapes are constantly changing; there is no such thing as a static human landscape. (Meinig 1979: 228–29)

If these touchstones of Jackson's philosophy seem to be a reasonable agenda for contemporary humanistic landscape studies, they are probably more congenial now within the context of paradigmatic revision and intellectual fluidity than they were during the era of methodological rigidity, when Jackson began his writings. These earlier tensions produced an uneasy encounter with academic geography. Although he originally subtitled *Landscape* "the magazine of human geography," Jackson later dropped the subtitle without editorial comment; moreover, none of his academic appointments were in geography departments.

Though Jackson in many ways legitimated a humanistic interpretation of landscape, his magazine was discounted by many university tenure committees because it conscientiously eschewed footnotes and other trappings of professional writing and because it was edited in a way that made it accessible for the intelligent layperson rather than academics. Style, grace, and interpretive insight prevailed over method and theory. Others complain that Jackson's writings (and the articles in *Landscape*) are too individualistic and interpretive; critics charge that these mental gymnastics are unverifiable, irreproducible, and unlinked to theory and prediction. Jackson's work has also been criticized as not problem oriented, as unfashionably tolerant of visually offensive landscapes or environmental degradation, and as too rarely judgmental or prescriptive. Instead, given Jackson's defense of the common person's right to shape landscapes as they wish, unregulated and removed from zoning or architectural controls, we might suspect that he would be flattered by some of these criticisms.

While it is premature to attempt a final assessment of J. B. Jackson's influence on landscape studies in America because he remains a viable contributor to the field, several points are offered in summary. First, his writings have inspired a generation of scholars and students interested in the vernacular landscape of common Americans; these writings constitute a model for the study and exposition of this landscape. Second, his influence is probably greater outside of geography than within. Design professionals particularly respect Jackson's work. Third, with two former students now teaching the classes he initiated at Berkeley and Harvard, landscape studies enjoy a distinct degree of visibility and legitimization. Fourth (as mentioned earlier), his interpretive, humanistic landscape study is much more fashionable now than it was earlier because it complements recent emphases on recovering meaning from material culture, on locality and the emotion of places, and on the exquisite richness of individual and small-group experience. Though Jackson chose not to overlay his writing with theory,[3] contemporary researchers must acknowledge that he was instrumental in building a creditable foundation for this realm of inquiry.

Landscapes of the Mind: Perception and Meaning

Another foundation for landscape studies emerged in the postwar decades; it placed the emphasis on how people and groups perceive and feel about their environments. Though Jackson was interested in these questions, they were raised to explicit levels by landscape studies in the 1960s. These were shaped by two currents; one was primarily intuitive and interpretive, the other empirical and behavioral.

The interpretive vein of landscape perception can be traced to John Kirkland Wright, who was associated with the American Geographical Society (AGS) from 1920 to 1956 as librarian, research editor, and, ultimately, director. His 1946 Association of American Geographers' presidential address, "*Terrae Incognitae*: The Place of Imagination in Geography" (Wright 1947), was the groundwork for what became the environmental perception subfield of geography (see Lowenthal 1969, Lowenthal and Bowden 1976). If Wright planted the seed, his long-time colleague at the AGS, David Lowenthal, tilled and harvested these fields. In several noteworthy articles during the 1960s he demonstrated how eclectic sources provide insights into our visual biases and "landscape tastes" (Lowenthal 1961, 1968; Lowenthal and Prince 1964, 1965) and how these tastes resonate through a culture and interact with other social values. In so doing, Lowenthal was able to generate descriptive taxonomies that linked perception and visual biases to other cultural patterns. English landscapes, for example, reflected that society's proclivity for the bucolic, picturesque, and tidy and their rejection of the present, sensual, and functional (Lowenthal and Prince 1965). These contrasted with the landscape of the American countryside with its "casual chaos," its "cult of bigness," and its tolerance of present-day ugliness in pursuit of a supposedly glorious future (Lowenthal 1968).

While these works stimulated and inspired others to retrieve "landscapes of the mind" (Tuan 1974, 1976), they also produced a certain unease in the positivistic context of the 1960s. Inferences and conclusions were personal and intuitive rather than overt and replicable, products of a subjectivity foreign to science, or so critics would charge. Lowenthal's preference for secondary and proxy sources such as literature and newspaper commentary—utterings of an elite literati, not the common person—gave his works a certain anecdotal tone that became the accepted model and style for a subsequent generation of humanistic landscape interpretations. For many, however, these articles also constituted a refreshing alternative to the methodological rigor and quantitative tyranny of the theoretical revolution. If these works reaffirmed the positivist's commitment to a "scientific" spatial geography by confirming their worst fears, they also provided sound academic footing and authority to an emerging humanistic geography that probed into the sentiment and meaning underlying landscape.

A bridge of sorts between these two camps could be found in the behavioral approach to landscape studies that emerged in the 1960s. This research used interviews, surveys, and questionnaires to produce generalizations about landscape cognition. Because these methods produced data that could be processed quantitatively, perception studies were closer in spirit to mainstream positivist geography and must be set apart from the humanistic inquiries of Jackson, Wright, Lowenthal, and Tuan.

The geographical roots for these behavioral studies are found in natural hazard research that was driven by needs to understand how humans perceived environmental hazards such as flood and drought. This agenda was set by Gilbert White, first at the University of Chicago and later at Colorado, and by his students, for example, Robert Kates on the perception of floodplain hazards (1962) and Tom Saarinen on the perception of Great Plains drought hazards (1966; for a review of the natural hazards literature, see Mitchell 1984, 1989) who produced valuable behavioral landscape research.

Impetus for the study of perceived urban landscapes came from the planner Kevin Lynch. In his classic work *Image of the City* (1960) Lynch drew on interviews and questionnaires to determine how city dwellers used visual landmarks to organize their mental maps of a place. This information provided insight about a city's "legibility"; the assumption was that design professions could then use this material to promote specific planning solutions for enhancing urban quality. Whether these data were ever used in that way is unclear, but there is no question that important information was generated, most notably that social and ethnic groups within the city perceived the urban landscape in vastly different ways (see, for example, City of Los Angeles, 1971). This linkage between social groups, their perception of the environment, and, by extension, their mobility and behavior became a fundamental concern of subsequent behavioral landscape studies (for reviews of this extensive literature, see Aitken, Cutter, Foote, and Sell 1989; and Sell, Taylor, and Zube 1984).

In summary, the postwar decades are usually thought of as a time when methodological rigor, associated with the quantitative and theoretical revolution, reigned; but this was also a decade when prominent and foundational currents of landscape studies became increasingly visible; these, we could say, set the stage for contemporary usage of the cultural landscape concept in American human geography. Momentum from the "Man's Role" conference and volume along with Sauer's influence on the discipline helped sustain use of the concept as a vehicle for human modification of environments, a theme that persists in various expressions both inside and outside of geography. J. B. Jackson's voice on vernacular landscapes was heard through *Landscape* magazine and his classes at Berkeley and Harvard, while Lowenthal's series of influential articles in mainstream geographic journals demonstrated how information from eclectic sources could supply insight on social and cultural biases in landscape perceptions. These two voices were instrumental in adding landscape to the emerging agenda of humanistic geography, which henceforth included the study of the interactions between peoples, environment, and society with an interpretive methodology. Empirical, behavioral landscape perception studies meanwhile moved closer to the positivistic paradigm; natural-hazard research and urban planning studies there drew on method and theory from an incipient environmental psychology to produce yet another distinct subfield within human geography.

Contemporary Landscape Studies

Toward an Organizational Scheme

Having traced the roots of the landscape legacy in American human geography through the twentieth century, we turn now to contemporary landscape studies, but first some organizational matters must be discussed. The first problem is the overwhelming number of articles that use the notion and concept of landscape. They are far too numerous for a complete and comprehensive review; I instead present examples that are chosen to illustrate selected themes.

The second issue is an appropriate organizational scheme. What kind of taxonomy will show both similarities and differences in this vast landscape literature? Arranging them into conventional epistemological categories has some advantages (Rowntree 1987,1988), yet on closer and more critical examination we find that most landscape research transcends methodological boundaries by drawing liberally from different domains. For example, a landscape study might draw on empirical description, subject it to humanistic arrangement and interpretation, and then attempt some generalizations shaped by structuralist theory. While critics use this as evidence that landscape is too ambiguous a concept for serious analytic consideration, its proponents argue the opposite—that its strength lies in its applicability and complementarity to different research frameworks.

Given that epistemological distinctions are becoming increasingly blurred as geography moves away from the methodological dogma of the past, there is no compelling reason to force landscape studies into these conventional categories. More meaningful is a heuristic framework illustrating how the cultural landscape concept is used to shape geographic research: What kinds of questions are asked, and how is landscape applied in answering those questions?

New Directions in Landscape Study

This brings us to the matter of new directions in landscape study. Because human geographers are currently rethinking many of their fundamental concepts, methods, and theories, the cultural landscape notion is also under scrutiny. Critics charge that traditional landscape research is too idiosyncratic, atheoretical, politically conservative, and reliant on outmoded conceptualizations of culture and society (Cosgrove and Jackson 1987; P. Jackson 1980, 1989; Kobayashi 1989). This questioning from the new-directions people, interestingly enough, is the only sustained critique of the landscape concept since Hartshorne, but, unlike Hartshorne, they are unwilling to dismiss the conceptual vitality of landscape in spite of these shortcomings. On the contrary, they see landscape as playing a central role in a new and reinvigorated human geography, provided the concept is informed by contemporary social theory (P. Jackson 1989, Kobayashi 1989).

What does that mean? Although there are different agendas linking landscape to social theory, the following points seem to be held in common:

- a reformulation of the concept of culture emphasizing human action over passivity. Culture is thought of as a process and expression of negotiated, even contestatory, personal and group interactions, hence it is constantly changing and contingent on context. This contrasts with a traditional superorganic conceptualization.[4]
- an emphasis on the symbolic, as well as on the behavioral interaction or recurrence between humans and their environment that attempts to reconcile the tensions between individual action and cultural structures.
- a problematization of social categories, such as gender, ethnicity, class, and race and examination of the ways landscape is implicated in the construction and maintenance of these categories.
- the centrality of symbolic expression in the landscape and metaphorical conceptualizations of human-environment interaction as "text," "theater," "carnival," and "spectacle" to emphasize the arrangement and manipulation of environments by power structures (Ley and Olds 1988).
- an awareness of the power of language by subjecting landscape narratives (and authors) to critical reflection and self-conscious interpretation that reveals ideological bias (Duncan 1990, King 1990).
- explicit or implicit connections to theoretical frameworks, such as neo-Marxism, post-structuralism, and postmodernism (Dear 1988, Mills 1988).[5]

In the organizational scheme below, both traditional and new-direction landscape studies are intermingled; in this I offer hints of the new without granting it special status or privilege. When illustrating these new emphases, linkages are drawn also to earlier landscape research that developed similar themes. This is done intentionally so that readers can ponder the uniqueness and analytic efficacy of newer work in context with the full landscape legacy in American human geography.

Landscape as Ecological Artifact

As noted earlier in this chapter, Carl Sauer saw the landscape as a primary source of information on human transformation of the Earth; researchers continue to ask similar questions today in which landscape constitutes the ultimate authority on and evidence for environmental change and disturbance. Following Sauer, many of these studies emphasize change to vegetation because of human influences.[6] A recent example is Conrad Bahre's study, *A Legacy of Change: Historic Human Impact on Vegetation of the Arizona Borderlands* (1991), in which he challenges conventional wisdom that vegetation change resulted from climatic change and posits instead that cattle grazing, fuel-wood cutting, and wildfire suppression are the causes of landscape change. A common form of evidence in these landscape studies is repeat photography, where present-day photos are compared with historical scenes that document vegetation change. Another example of this method is Veblen and Lorenz's study (1991) of landscape and ecological change in Colorado's Front Range.

Because of the ascendency of specialized proxy information—such as palynology—for environmental change, there is an increasingly interdisciplinary scientific tone to research conducted often within a structured, positivistic framework (see, for example, Birks et al. 1988, B. Roberts 1987, N. Roberts 1989, Simmons 1988). Hard data and rigorous testing have moved this traditional form of landscape study into the contemporary arena of global environmental problems (Kates 1987) where physical geographers and cultural ecologists interact with other disciplines in compiling documentation of large-scale environmental change, much in the spirit of the 1956 "Man's Role in Changing the Face of the Earth" conference. The most prominent recent example is the "Earth as Transformed by Human Action" conference organized by Clark University in 1989 (see Turner et al. 1990).

Outside of geography, environmental historians use landscape as the organizing theme for work generated primarily from archival sources. William Cronon's *Changes in the Land* (1983), a study of human impact on the ecology of New England, is exemplary. In his bibliographic essay Cronon directs readers to the works of Sauer (1983: 217) and links the emerging field of ecological history with traditional landscape study. Carolyn Merchant's *Ecological Revolutions* (1989) puts New England's environmental transformation into the context of larger social currents such as gender and science politics. While the documentation of landscape change remains resolute, the abstract causes of those changes is the primary focus of her work.

Landscape as Evidence for Origins and Diffusion

The landscape also contains and corroborates historical information on the development and spread of human technologies and subsistence strategies that have had lasting effects on global environments. In these works, as with Sauer's paradigmatic study on agricultural origins (Sauer 1952), the landscape is primarily a backdrop for developments inferred or deduced from other sources. The landscape, then, is modified as a result of these changing subsistence strategies; however, the nature of that environmental transformation is secondary to the emphasis placed on the spatial and temporal spread of cultural assemblages. Two studies by Butzer illustrate this theme: one (1985) examines the diffusion of early irrigation techniques in Spain, and the other (1988) traces the historical antecedents for livestock strategies that were transferred from the Old World to the New.

A subset of this category traces the origin and diffusion of overtly material traits, for example, Kniffen's classic work on the diffusion of folk housing (1965) or, more recently, Jordan's tracking of log buildings (1985). Diffusion methodology is also used to trace the abstract values and sentiment behind the material and visible landscape, as in Hugill's study (1986) documenting the spread of English landscape biases into the United States. In a work illustrating the marrying of a new emphases on power structure and social categories with traditional research questions, Hugill argues that these can be linked to changing conditions of class, labor, and social control.

Landscape as Material Culture

Very closely related to the previous category, and yet with less evidence on the spatial dynamics of origin and diffusion, are those studies that look to the landscape for visual or material information on human occupation and settlement—an approach Lewis calls using the landscape as "cultural spoor" (1975). Fundamental emphasis is given to the "look of the land" (Hart 1975): barn types, fence architecture, field patterns, the arrangement of outbuildings—all of these occupy the attention of material culturalists.

While this interest brings geographers together with other disciplines, such as folklore (Glassie 1975; Schlereth 1983, 1985a, 1985b), historical architecture (Stilgoe 1982; Upton and Vlach 1986), and certain kinds of historical archeology (Leone 1986; Rubertone 1989), the ultimate use of this material culture information often differs. While geographers may study the visual landscape as an end in itself or as a means of reinforcing notions of origin and diffusion, those researchers closer to anthropology often use material culture (including the landscape) to draw more detailed conclusions about social values, the creation and maintenance of social activities, group boundaries, and subsistence strategies.

Urban Landscapes

Because of the kinds of research questions asked by traditional landscape analysis, rural environments were the preferred locale until the rise of urban geography in the 1960s (and the urban crisis of that decade) forced increasing attention on cityscapes. This hesitancy to examine urban landscapes was odd, given European geography's traditional emphasis on townscape and urban morphological analysis (Conzen 1979, Vance 1977), yet these inhibitions have given way today. Befitting the complexity of urban environments, a range of research questions is being asked of cityscapes. To illustrate, Clay (1980) uses the metropolitan landscape to access information about recent land use change, while Arreola (1984, 1988), working at the neighborhood and household level, draws on visual and material culture for insight into ethnic constructions of space and place.

Many of the new-direction landscape studies focus on urban and suburban environments, often framed by postmodern theory. Two examples are Paul Knox's recent study of Washington, D.C. (1991), which explains the "restless urban landscape" as a product of commodity aesthetics and patterns of consumption among a "new bourgeoisie," and Jeffrey Hopkins' study of the West Edmonton (Canada) mall as a landscape of "myth and elsewhereness" (1990). Both articles articulate the interconnectivity between late capitalist ideologies and landscape.

Art, Literature, and Landscape Meaning

Long central to the humanistic enterprise of uncovering human experience and meaning has been the perspective that much can be learned by the way people depict the landscape in their art, be it written, drawn, or in other media. This perspective makes the assumption that these artistic renderings feed back into society by elevating and privileging certain scenes or ways of looking at the environment that often become symbolic of larger cultural constellations, for example, the American sense of historical eclecticism (Lowenthal 1968) or the English proclivity toward cultural connoisseurship of certain views and perspectives (see, for example, Cosgrove 1984, 1985). Obviously, research of this kind emphasizes the aesthetic or scenic component of landscape's heritage, but this pursuit is not unique to geography; it is also found in various humanistic endeavors such as art history and folklore. This literature is too vast to mention here; the reader is advised instead to consider geographic approaches to this topic via articles such as Rees (1977), Salter (1978), Sandberg and Marsh (1988), Sopher (1986), and an important volume by Norwood and Monk (1987), *The Desert is No Lady: Southwestern Landscapes in Women's Writing and Art.*

This last-mentioned work is particularly important because it attempts to redress the hegemony of a male point of view in humanistic geography. Put differently, the male experience, be it through art, literature, or diaries and journals, has been privileged and taken to be the common human experience; men—the assumption went—speak for all culture. Obviously, this view is invalid, yet only recently and in only a few articles do we hear female voices about landscape (see also Monk 1984). This project, of course, is framed within the larger issues of a feminist geography (Gruntfest 1989; also see chapter 15).

Landscape as Visual Resource

Also tied closely to the etymological root that connects landscape to aesthetics is the domain of research that treats the landscape as a visual resource. This perspective, both inside and outside of geography, pushes beyond mere scenic appreciation of landscape, because it is driven often by a legislative mandate of control, regulation, and protection (Groth 1990: ix). This movement is founded on the assumption that visual quality is an integral part of a larger environmental quality; visual blight, for example, is analogous to air and water pollution and can be mitigated (if not exorcised) by direct legislative action. There are strong connections between the geographers' traditional interest in art and landscape and their participation in the study of visual resources (see Kennedy, Sell, and Zube 1988).

Despite this longstanding involvement with visual resources, geographers seem less willing than design professionals to move their landscape analyses into the realm of prescriptive measures through legislated aesthetic controls. Compare, for example, the works of landscape architects (Litton 1990) with geographers (Jakle 1987, Relph 1981) and note the difference in applied orientation.

The Landscape as Ideology

Landscapes are studied for what they reveal about ideologies—the ideas and objectives that act as political and social guidelines for a national culture. Lowenthal and Prince's pioneer work (discussed earlier), for example, coupled ideas about English national character with landscape expressions (1964, 1965), and many urban geographers were inspired by Mumford's (1960) analysis of the historical city as an ideological stage or playing field for promoting the visibility and power of the elite.

This theme continues today, often associated with the critical perspectives of neo-Marxism and postmodernism, in which national culture is intertwined with the economic goals of late capitalism to produce such distinctive landscapes as franchised strips (MacDonald 1985), suburban malls (Hopkins 1990), high-tech corridors, gentrified neighborhoods, and preserved historical buildings and neighborhoods (Knox 1991).

For historical landscapes an important source of stimulation comes from the allied field of historical archaeology, where researchers test archival material against an excavated empirical record to tease out discontinuities between the two that reveal ideological manipulation of the landscape (Bender 1992, Kelso and Most 1990, Leone 1986, Rubertone 1989, Wylie 1985).

Landscape's Role in the Production and Maintenance of Social Categories

The cultural landscape is conceptualized as a repository of information about social behavior (Wagner 1972, 1974), a visual expression, we might say, of the cues and clues that guide society. While earlier studies tended to use this assumption in subtle ways, contemporary social theory, with its emphasis on abusive expressions of power, has increasingly problematicized this notion over the last decade. The social sciences now probe more deeply into the mechanisms through which society constructs and maintains discriminatory, racist, and sexist social categories; landscape, territory, and space have been implicated in those processes as individuals and institutions shape and control the environment to produce and reinforce power relations (Wolch and Dear 1989: 5–6). Anderson (1987), for example, shows how racial definitions were structured through the interaction between Vancouver's Chinatown landscape, social structure, and political practice, and the Duncans (1984) reveal how conspicuous consumption is embodied in suburban landscapes so as to construct and reinforce class and status categories. Finally, Peter Jackson (1989), drawing on the growing interdisciplinary field of cultural studies, has suggested ways of integrating these perspectives in his book *Maps of Meaning* (1989).

The Landscape as Text, Symbols, and Signs

Landscapes have long been treated metaphorically as texts that were authored and, hence, could be read by insightful observers. This metaphor is evidenced in the titles of professional works on landscape reading (Clay 1980, Lewis 1979, Meinig 1979, Watts 1975), landscape authors (Samuels 1979), and landscape signatures (Salter 1971, 1978). More recently, this traditional conceptualization has been enriched by scholarship from other disciplines on the symbolic interaction between environments and humans. Daniels and Cosgrove (1988), for example, look to iconography as a vehicle for landscape analysis, while others draw on the interdisciplinary study of semiotics (Duncan 1987, Foote 1985, Hopkins 1990, Preziosi 1986), which conceptualizes landscape into sign and symbol systems.

Contemporary social theory interacts with critical literary analysis (Eagleton 1983) to form a new foundation for the metaphorical treatment of landscape as text (Duncan and Duncan 1988), where the interaction process between reader and text becomes as important as the material objects themselves. The best current example of this is James Duncan's *The City as Text: the Politics of Landscape Interpretation in the Kandyan Kingdom* (1990). However, Peet's (1993) review of this work should also be read.

Summary and Conclusion

The concept of the cultural landscape has been part of American human geography since the 1920s, when Sauer promoted landscape study as a method to undercut environmental determinism. Although landscape has been primarily linked to postwar humanistic geography, there is a resurgence of interest today in the concept—both inside and outside of geography.

In part, this interest exploits the definitional fluidity of the term; *landscape* is all things to all people. There is no concise definition. Instead, researchers fold together ingredients from the dichotomous etymological roots that draw on different linguistic traditions. One researcher, drawing primarily from historical Dutch usage, emphasizes the visual dimension of landscape, while another draws more heavily on English and German connotations of region or area. Though these definitional distinctions remain important to some— and were fundamental to Hartshorne's critique of Sauer's 1920s agenda—the primary appeal of the term *landscape* today is to imply the formal and functional totality of diffuse and separate parts. It is used to link, for example, the various components of a historical rural settlement system—house, barn, outbuildings, parcel size and shape, and so on—as well as those of a contemporary urban scene. Whereas physical geographers may apply the term to capture interaction between various environmental factors, such as vegetation, climate, and humans, others place the emphasis on the social perception and response to environments, the cognition, feelings, and behavior associated with places.

Hartshorne found *landscape* too ambiguous a term for serious analytic usage in the spatial science he envisioned. As a result, the concept was initially associated with Sauer and his followers and their concerns with human ecological modification. With the emergence of humanistic geography in the 1960s and 1970s cultural landscape study expanded dramatically. One expression was connected with the study of vernacular material culture, best exemplified by the work of J. B. Jackson. Another was in the humanistic project of examining environmental perception and sentiment—Wright, Lowenthal, and Tuan were instrumental in promoting this agenda. Subsequently, a behavioral component was added that drew on an emerging field of environmental psychology and that bridged humanistic and positivist methodologies.

Today, the use of *landscape* is so diverse that it crosses traditional epistemological categories. While critics charge that the concept is still too ambiguous and weak for serious consideration, others see this conceptual fluidity as appropriate and complementary to a revisionist human geography. Along with these proponents of new directions, with their emphasis on the linkage of landscape and contemporary social theory, is the use of *landscape* in a wide range of research frameworks including ecological analysis, origins and diffusion, material culture studies, urban analysis, depiction of environment in art and literature, and visual resources and planning. Illustrations of these, along with a discussion of new directions in landscape study, are discussed earlier in this chapter.

Cultural landscape will remain a fundamental concept in human geography more because of its momentum than because of its conceptual clarity. *Landscape's* definitional or methodological shortcomings notwithstanding, the term has been used too long and in too many ways to be radically revised. Furthermore, a receptive lay audience awaits our writings about *landscape* because it strikes intuitive chords about the visual and material environment. A seductive ambiguity provides hospitable refuge for all; *landscape*, it seems, embraces whatever we ask from our curiosity about human-environment interactions. This conceptual conviviality is at once an asset and a liability.

Notes

1. The terms *landscape* and *cultural landscape* are central to many fields other than geography. Readers should be sensitive to the interactivity and cross-fertilization that

fuels the concept's vitality. For example, the use of *landscape* in literature has long inspired humanistic geographers to lucid descriptions of places and regions. In another domain, the biological sciences use *landscape* to analyze nested ecosystems at the regional scale. This landscape ecology is discussed further in note 6 below. Interdisciplinary usage of *landscape* may be found in such journals as *Landscape, Landscape Research, Landscape Journal, Landscape Ecology,* and *Place.*

2. Probably the best example of what Sauer intended was Jan Broek's prototypal study, *The Santa Clara Valley, California: A Study in Landscape Changes* (1932). This was Broek's doctoral dissertation for the University of Utrecht (Netherlands) and was researched and largely written when he was a visiting scholar at Berkeley. Thus Sauer's influence is strong.

3. Paul Groth, who inherited Jackson's landscape class at the University of California-Berkeley, made some interesting remarks at a recent conference about Jackson's intersection with contemporary social theory. When Jackson passed on his original lecture notes, Groth found copious and detailed margin notes linking the lecture content to such social theorists as Giddens and Foucault. Groth concludes that Jackson was extremely well read on these matters, yet chose not to make overt connections between this emerging body of theory and his own musings on landscape.

4. Duncan (1980) charges that a superorganic conceptualization of culture—which holds that culture simply "happens," then follows its own course, and that individuals are merely passive culture bearers—has dominated American cultural geography since the 1920s because of Sauer's acceptance of this view. By implication, landscape studies replicated this template. Whether or not this constitutes a fatal flaw is a matter of opinion—Duncan implies widespread dissatisfaction with this totalizing view of culture among the social sciences. To counter this, he emphasizes recentering individuals and groups within an active framework emphasizing the social construction of culture.

5. Many of these issues are discussed elsewhere in this book; the reader may want to consult the relevant chapters to place these revisionist ideas in their appropriate contexts.

6. This emphasis on vegetation is also found in the landscape ecology of the new biological sciences, in which plant life is thought of as the "green glue" holding together the rest of the landscape (Bridgewater 1988: 485). The landscape scale in these works is favored because it allows the nesting of ecosystems into a hierarchy of spatial units for the purpose of studying energy fluxes and systemic perturbations. Readers should be aware of the growing literature in landscape ecology (see, for example, Foreman and Noble 1986, Naveh and Lieberman 1984).

References

Aitken, Stuart C., Susan Cutter, Kenneth E. Foote, and James L. Sell. 1989. Environmental perception and behavioral geography. In *Geography in America,* ed. G. Gaile and C. Willmott, 218–38. Columbus: Merrill.

Anderson, K. J. 1987. The idea of Chinatown: The power of place and institutional practice in the making of a racial category. *Annals of the Association of American Geographers* 77: 580–98.

Arreola, Daniel. 1984. Mexican American exterior murals. *Geographical Review* 74: 409–24.

———. 1988. Mexican American housescapes. *Geographical Review* 78: 299–315.

Aschmann, Homer. 1959. The evolution of a wild landscape and its persistence in southern California. *Annals of the Association of American Geographers* 49 (Supplement): 34–46.

Bahre, Conrad J. 1991. *A legacy of change: Historic human impact on vegetation in the Arizona borderlands.* Tucson: The University of Arizona Press.

Bender, Barbara. 1992. Theorizing landscapes, and the prehistoric landscapes of Stonehenge. *Man* 27: 735–55.

Billinge, Mark D. 1981. Cultural landscape. In *The dictionary of human geography*, ed. R. J. Johnston, 67–68. Oxford: Basil Blackwell.

Birks, Hilary H., H. J. B. Birks, Peter Emil Kaland, and Dagfinn Moe. 1988. *The cultural landscape — Past, present and future.* Cambridge: Cambridge University Press.

Bridgewater, P. B. 1988. Biodiversity and landscape. *Earth-Science Reviews* 25: 486–91.

Broek, Jan O. M. 1932. *The Santa Clara Valley, California: A study in landscape changes.* Utrecht: N.V.A. Oosthoek's Uitgevers.

Butzer, Karl W. 1988. Cattle and sheep from old to new Spain: Historical antecedents. *Annals of the Association of American Geographers* 78: 29–56.

———. 1989. Hartshorne, Hettner, and the nature of geography. In *Reflections on Richard Hartshorne's the Nature of Geography.* ed. J. N. Entrikin and S. Brunn, 35–52. Washington, D.C.: Association of American Geographers.

Butzer, Karl W. et al. 1985. Irrigation agrosystems in eastern Spain: Roman or Islamic origins? *Annals of the Association of American Geographers* 75: 479–509.

City of Los Angeles. 1971. *The visual environment of Los Angeles.* Los Angeles: Department of City Planning.

Clay, Grady. 1980. *Close-up: How to read the American city.* Chicago: University of Chicago Press.

Conzen, Michael. 1979. Analytical approaches to the urban landscape. In *Dimensions of human geography: Essays on some familiar and neglected themes*, ed. K. Butzer, 128–65. Chicago: University of Chicago, Department of Geography Research Paper, No. 186.

Cosgrove, Denis E. 1984. *Social formation and symbolic landscape.* London: Croom Helm.

————. 1985. Prospect, perspective and the evolution of the landscape idea. *Transactions of the Institute of British Geographers* N. S. 10: 45–62.

————. 1989. A terrain of metaphor: Cultural geography, 1988–89. *Progress in Human Geography* 13: 566–75.

————. 1990. Spectacle and society: Landscape as theater in pre-modern and post-modern cities. In *Vision, culture, and landscape,* ed. P. Groth, 221–39. Berkeley: University of California, Department of Landscape Architecture.

Cosgrove, Denis E., and Peter Jackson. 1987. New directions in cultural geography. *Area* 19: 95–101.

Cronon, William. 1983. *Changes in the land: Indians, colonists, and the ecology of New England.* New York: Hill and Wang.

Crouch, David. 1989. The allotment, landscape and locality: Ways of seeing landscape and culture. *Area* 21: 261–67.

Daniels, Stephen, and Denis Cosgrove. 1988. Introduction: Iconography and landscape. In *The iconography of landscape: Essays on the symbolic representation, design, and use of past environments,* ed. D. Cosgrove and S. Daniels, 1–10. Cambridge: Cambridge University Press.

Darby, H. C. 1951. The changing English landscape. *The Geographical Journal* 17: 377–94.

Dear, Michael. 1988. The postmodern challenge: Reconstructing human geography. *Transactions, Institute of British Geographers* N. S. 13: 262–74.

Deetz, James. 1977. *In small things forgotten: The archaeology of early American life.* Garden City, N.Y.: Anchor Books.

Domosh, Mona. 1990. Shaping the commercial city: The retail districts of nineteenth-century New York and Boston. *Annals of the Association of American Geographers* 80: 268–84.

Duncan, James S. 1980. The superorganic in American cultural geography. *Annals of the Association of American Geographers* 70: 181–98.

————. 1987. Review of urban imagery: Urban semiotics. *Urban Geography* 8: 473–83.

————. 1990. *The city as text: The politics of landscape interpretation in the Kandyan Kingdom.* Cambridge: Cambridge University Press.

Duncan, James S., and Nancy G. Duncan. 1984. A cultural analysis of urban residential landscapes in North America: The case of the Anglophile elite. In *The city in cultural context*, ed. J. A. Agnew, J. Mercer, and D. E. Sopher, 255–76. Boston: Allen and Unwin.

————. 1988. [Re]reading the landscape. *Environment and Planning D: Society and Space* 6: 117–26.

Eagleton, Terry. 1983. *Literary theory: An introduction*. Minneapolis: University of Minnesota Press.

Entrikin, J. Nicholas. 1976. Contemporary humanism in geography. *Annals of the Association of American Geographers* 66: 615–32.

————. 1984. Carl Sauer, philosopher in spite of himself. *Geographical Review* 74: 387–407.

Foote, Kenneth E. 1985. Space, territory, and landscape: The borderlands of geography and semiotics. *Recherches Semiotiques/Semiotic Inquiry* 5: 158–75.

Foreman, R. T., and I. R. Noble, eds. 1989. *Landscape ecology*. New York: John Wiley.

Glassie, Henry. 1975. *Folk housing in middle Virginia: A structural analysis of historic artifacts*. Knoxville, Tenn.: University of Tennessee Press.

Groth, Paul. 1990. Dividing lines and meeting grounds in cultural landscape interpretation. In *Vision, culture, and landscape*, ed. P. Groth, vii–x. Berkeley: University of California, Department of Landscape Architecture.

Gruntfest, Eve. 1989. Geographic perspectives on women. In *Geography in America*, ed. G. L. Gaile and C. J. Willmott, 673–83. Columbus: Merrill.

Hart, John Fraser. 1975. *The look of the land*. Englewood Cliffs, N. J.: Prentice-Hall.

Hartshorne, Richard. 1939. *The nature of geography: A critical survey of current thought in the light of the past*. Lancaster, Pa.: Association of American Geographers.

————. 1959. *Perspective on the nature of geography*. Monograph Series, No. 1. Chicago: Rand McNally and Association of American Geographers.

Holdsworth, Deryck W. 1990. The landscape and the archives: Texts for the analysis of the built environment. In *Vision, culture, and landscape*, ed. P. Groth, 187–204. Berkeley: University of California, Department of Landscape Architecture.

Hopkins, Jeffrey S. 1990. West Edmonton Mall: Landscape of myths and elsewhereness. *The Canadian Geographer* 34: 2–17.

Hoskins, William. 1955. *Making of the English landscape*. London: Hodder and Stoughton.

Hugill, Peter. 1986. English landscape tastes in the United States. *Geographical Review* 76: 408–23.

Jackson, J. B. 1972. *American space: The centennial years, 1865–1876*. New York: W. W. Norton.

————. 1979. Landscape as theatre. *Landscape* 23: 3–7.

————. 1980. *The necessity for ruins, and other topics*. Amherst: University of Massachusetts Press.

————. 1984. *Discovering the vernacular landscape*. New Haven: Yale University Press.

————. 1986. The vernacular landscape. In *Landscape meanings and values*, ed. E. C. Penning-Rowsell and D. Lowenthal, 65–81. London: Allen and Unwin.

Jackson, Peter A. 1980. A plea for cultural geography. *Area* 12: 110–13.

————. 1989. *Maps of meaning: An introduction to cultural geography*. London: Unwin Hyman.

Jakle, John A. 1987. *The visual elements of landscape*. Amherst: University of Massachusetts Press.

Johnston, Ronald J. 1987. *Geography and geographers: Anglo-American human geography since 1945*. London: Edward Arnold.

————. 1986. *Philosophy and human geography*, 2nd ed. London: Edward Arnold.

Jordan, Terry G. 1985. *American log buildings: An Old World heritage*. Chapel Hill: University of North Carolina Press.

Kates, Robert W. 1962. *Hazard and choice perception in flood plain management*. Chicago: University of Chicago, Department of Geography Research Papers, No. 78.

————. 1987. The human environment: The road not taken, the road still beckoning. *Annals of the Association of American Geographers* 77: 525–34.

Kelso, William and Rachel Most. eds. 1990. *Earth patterns: Essays in landscape archaeology*. Charlottesville: The University Press of Virginia.

Kennedy, Christina B., James L. Sell, and Ervin H. Zube. 1988. Landscape aesthetics and geography. *Environmental Review* 12: 31–55.

Kenzer, Martin S. 1987. *Carl O. Sauer: A tribute*. Corvallis, Oreg.: Oregon State University Press.

King, Anthony. 1990. The politics of vision. In *Vision, culture, and landscape*, ed. P. Groth, 171–86. Berkeley: University of California, Department of Landscape Architecture.

Kniffen, Fred B. 1936. Louisiana house types. *Annals of the Association of American Geographers* 26: 173–93.

———. 1965. Folk-housing: Key to diffusion. *Annals of the Association of American Geographers* 55: 549–77.

Knox, Paul L. 1991. The restless urban landscape: Economic and sociocultural change and the transformation of metropolitan Washington, D.C. *Annals of the Association of American Geographers* 81: 181–209.

Kobayashi, Audrey L. 1989. A critique of dialectical landscape. In *Remaking human geography*, ed. A. L. Kobayashi and S. Mackenzie, 164–83. Boston: Unwin Hyman.

Leighly, John. 1963. *Land and life: A selection from the writings of Carl Orwin Sauer.* Berkeley: University of California Press.

———. 1987. Ecology as metaphor: Carl Sauer and human ecology. *Professional Geographer* 39: 405–12.

Leone, Mark. 1986. Symbolic, structural and critical archaeology. In *American archaeology, past and present*, ed. David Meltzer, Don Fowler, and Jeremy Sabloff, 415–38. Washington: Smithsonian Institute Press.

Lewis, Peirce. 1975. Common houses, cultural spoor. *Landscape* 19: 1–22.

———. 1979. Axioms for reading the landscape. In *The interpretation of ordinary landscapes*, ed. D. W. Meinig, 195–244. New York: Oxford University Press.

———. 1983. Learning from looking: Geographic and other writing about the American cultural landscape. *American Quarterly* 35: 242–61.

Ley, David. 1987. Styles of the times: Liberal and neoconservative landscapes in inner Vancouver, 1968–86. *Journal of Historical Geography* 13: 40–56.

Ley, David, and K. Olds. 1988. Landscape as spectacle: World's fairs and the culture of heroic consumption. *Environment and Planning D: Society and Space* 6: 191–212.

Litton, Jr., R. Burton. 1990. The visual landscape resource idea. In *Vision, culture, and landscape*, ed. P. Groth, 101–30. Berkeley: University of California Department of Landscape Architecture.

Lowenthal, David. 1961. Geography, experience, and imagination: Towards a geographical epistemology. *Annals of the Association of American Geographers* 51: 214–60.

————. 1968. The American scene. *Geographical Review* 58: 61–88.

————. 1969. John Kirkland Wright: 1891–1969. *Geographical Review* 59: 598–604.

Lowenthal, David, and Martyn J. Bowden. 1976. *Geographies of the mind: Essays in historical geosophy in honor of John Kirkland Wright.* New York: Oxford University Press.

Lowenthal, David, and Hugh C. Prince. 1964. The English landscape. *Geographical Review* 54: 309–46.

————. 1965. English landscape tastes. *Geographical Review* 55: 186–222.

Lynch, Kevin. 1960. *The image of the city.* Cambridge: MIT Press.

MacDonald, Kent. 1985. The commercial strip: From main street to television road. *Landscape* 28: 12–19.

Mathewson, Kent. 1987. Humane ecologist: Carl Sauer as metaphor. *Professional Geographer* 39: 412–13.

Meinig, Donald. 1979. *The interpretation of ordinary landscapes: Geographical essays.* New York: Oxford University Press.

————. 1979. Reading the landscape: An appreciation of W. G. Hoskins and J. B. Jackson. In *Interpretation of ordinary landscapes,* ed. D. Meinig, 195–244. New York: Oxford University Press.

Merchant, Carolyn. 1989. *Ecological revolutions: Nature, gender, science in New England.* Chapel Hill: University of North Carolina Press.

Mikesell, Marvin W. 1968. Landscape. In *International encyclopedia of the social sciences,* vol. 8, 575–80. New York: Macmillan and Free Press.

Mills, C. A. 1988. Life on the upslopes: The postmodern landscape of gentrification. *Environment and Planning D: Society and Space* 6: 169–89.

Mitchell, James K. 1984. Hazard perception studies: Convergent concerns and divergent approaches during the past decade. In *Environmental perception and behavior: An inventory and prospect,* ed. Thomas F. Saarinen, David Seamon, and James Sell, 35–59. Chicago: University of Chicago, Department of Geography Research Papers.

————. 1989. Hazards research. In *Geography in America,* ed. G. L. Gaile and C. J. Willmott, 410–24. Columbus: Merrill.

Monk, Janice. 1984. Approaches to the study of women and landscape. *Environmental Review* 8: 23–33.

Mumford, Lewis. 1960. *The city in history.* New York: Harcourt Brace Jovanovich.

Nairn, Ian. 1965. *The American landscape: A critical view.* New York: Random House.

Naveh, Zev, and Arthur S. Lieberman. 1984. *Landscape ecology: Theory and application.* New York: Springer-Verlag.

Nelson, Howard J. 1959. The spread of an artificial landscape over southern California. *Annals of the Association of American Geographers* 49 (Supplement): 80–99.

Norton, William. 1987. Humans, land, and landscape: A proposal for cultural geography. *The Canadian Geographer* 31: 21–33.

———. 1989. *Explorations in the understanding of landscape: A cultural geography.* New York: Greenwood Press.

Norwood, V., and J. Monk. 1987. *The desert is no lady: Southwestern landscapes in women's writing and art.* New Haven: Yale University Press.

Parsons, James J. 1979. The later Sauer years. *Annals of the Association of American Geographers* 69: 9–15.

———. 1986. A geographer looks at the San Joaquin Valley. *Geographical Review* 76: 371–89.

Peet, Richard. 1993. Review of James S. Duncan, The city as text: The politics of landscape interpretation in the Kandyan Kingdom. *Annals of the Association of American Geographers* 83: 184–87.

Penning-Rowsell, E., and David Lowenthal. 1986. *Landscape meanings and values.* London: Allen and Unwin.

———. 1986. Themes, speculations and an agenda for landscape research. In *Landscape meanings and values,* ed. E. C. Penning-Rowsell and D. Lowenthal, 114–28. London: Allen and Unwin.

Porter, Philip W. 1978. Geography as human ecology: A decade of progress in a quarter of a century. *American Behavioral Scientist* 22: 15–39.

———. 1988. Sauer, archives, and recollections. *Professional Geographer* 40: 337–39.

Prentice, Helaine Kaplan. 1981. John Brinckerhoff Jackson. *Landscape Architecture* 71: 740–45.

Preziosi, Donald. 1986. Reckoning with the world: Figure, text, and trace in the built environment. *American Journal of Semiotics* 4: 1–15.

Price, Marie, and Martin Lewis. 1993. Reinventing cultural geography. *Annals of the Association of American Geographers* 83: 1–17.

Rees, Ronald. 1977. Landscape in art. In *Dimensions of human geography: Essays on some familiar and neglected themes,* ed. K. Butzer, 48–68. Chicago: University of Chicago, Department of Geography Research Papers, No. 186.

Relph, Edward. 1981. *Rational landscapes and humanistic geography.* London: Croom Helm.

Roberts, B. K. 1987. Landscape archaeology. In *Landscape and culture: Geographical and archaeological perspectives*, ed. J. M. Wagstaff, 77–95. Oxford: Basil Blackwell.

Roberts, Neil. 1989. *The Holocene: An environmental history*. Oxford: Basil Blackwell.

Rowntree, Lester B. 1987. Cultural/humanistic geography. *Progress in Human Geography* 11: 558–64.

———. 1988. Orthodoxy and new directions: Cultural/humanistic geography. *Progress in Human Geography* 12: 575–86.

Rowntree, Lester B., and Margaret W. Conkey. 1980. Symbolism and the cultural landscape. *Annals of the Association of American Geographers* 70: 459–74.

Rowntree, Lester B., Kenneth E. Foote, and Mona Domosh. 1989. Cultural geography. In *Geography in America*, ed. G. L. Gaile and C. J. Willmott, 209–17. Columbus: Merrill.

Rubertone, Patricia E. 1989. Landscape as artifact: Comments on "The archaeological use of landscape treatment in social, economic, and ideological analysis." *Historical Archaeology* 23: 50–54.

Saarinen, Thomas F. 1966. *Perception of drought hazard on the Great Plains.* Chicago: University of Chicago, Department of Geography Research Papers.

Saarinen, Thomas F., David Seamon, and James L. Sell. 1984. *Environmental perception and behavior: An inventory and prospect.* Chicago: University of Chicago Press.

Salter, Christopher L. 1971. *The cultural landscape.* Belmont, Calif.: Duxbury Press.

———. 1978. Signatures and settlings: One approach to landscape in literature. In *Dimensions of human geography: Essays on some familiar and neglected themes.* ed. K. Butzer, 69–83. Chicago: University of Chicago, Department of Geography Research Papers.

Samuels, Marwyn S. 1979. The biography of landscape. In *The interpretation of ordinary landscapes*, ed. D. W. Meinig, 51–88. New York: Oxford University Press.

Sandberg, L. A., and J. S. Marsh. 1988. Focus: Literary landscapes—geography and literature. *The Canadian Geographer* 32: 266–76.

Sauer, Carl O. 1925. The morphology of landscape. *University of California Publications in Geography*, 19–54. Berkeley: University of California Press.

————. 1931. Cultural geography. In *Encyclopedia of the social sciences*, ed. Edwin Seligman, vol. 6, 621–23. New York: Macmillan.

————. 1941. Foreword to historical geography. *Annals of the Association of American Geographers* 31: 1–24.

————. 1952. *Agricultural origins and dispersals*. New York: American Geographical Society.

————. 1956a. The education of a geographer. *Annals of the Association of American Geographers* 46: 287–99.

————. 1956b. The agency of man on the earth. In *Man's role in changing the face of the earth*, ed. William L. Thomas, 49–69. Chicago: University of Chicago Press.

Schlereth, Thomas J. 1983. Material culture studies and social history research. *Journal of Social History* 16: 111–43.

————. 1985a. *U.S. 40: A Roadscape of the American experience*. Indianapolis: Indiana Historical Society.

————. 1985b. *Material culture: A research guide*. Lawrence, Kans.: University Press of Kansas.

Sell, James L. 1980. Environmental perception. *Progress in Human Geography* 4: 525–48.

Sell, James L., J. G. Taylor, and E. H. Zube. 1984. Toward a theoretical framework for landscape perception. In *Environmental perception and behavior: An inventory and prospect*, ed. T. F. Saarinen, D. Seamon, and J. L. Sell, 61–83. Chicago: University of Chicago Press.

Simmons, I. G. 1988. The earliest cultural landscapes of England. *Environmental Review* 12: 105–16.

Smith, Neil. 1989. Geography as museum: Private history and conservative idealism in *The Nature of Geography*. In *Reflections on Richard Hartshorne's The Nature of Geography*, ed. J. N. Entrikin and S. D. Brunn, 89–120. Washington, D.C.: Association of American Geographers.

Solot, Michael. 1986. Carl Sauer and cultural evolution. *Annals of the Association of American Geographers* 76: 508–20.

Sopher, David E. 1986. Place and landscape in Indian tradition. *Landscape* 29: 1–9.

Speth, William W. 1977. Carl Ortwin Sauer on destructive exploitation. *Biological Conservation* 11: 145–60.

Stilgoe, John. 1982. *Common landscape of America: 1580–1845*. New Haven: Yale University Press.

Storper, Michael. 1985. The spatial and temporal constitution of social action: A critical reading of Giddens. *Environment and Planning D: Society and Space* 3: 407–24.

Thomas, William L., ed. 1956. *Man's role in changing the face of the earth,* 2 vols. Chicago: University of Chicago Press.

Tuan, Yi-Fu. 1974. *Topophilia: A study of environmental perception, attitudes, and values.* Englewood Cliffs, N. J.: Prentice-Hall.

———. 1976. Humanistic geography. *Annals of the Association of American Geographers* 66: 266–76.

Turner, II, B. L. 1987. Comments on Leighly. *Professional Geographer.* 39: 415–16.

Turner, II, B. L. et al., eds. 1990. *The earth as transformed by human action: Global and regional changes in the biosphere over the past 300 years.* Cambridge: Cambridge University Press.

Upton, Dell, and John Michael Vlach., eds. 1986. *Common places: Readings in American vernacular architecture.* Athens: University of Georgia Press.

Vance, James. 1977. *This scene of man: The role and structure of the city in the geography of western civilization.* New York: Harper's College Press.

Veblen, Thomas, and Diane Lorenz. 1991. *The Colorado front range: A century of ecological change.* Salt Lake City: University of Utah Press.

Wagner, Philip L. 1972. *Environments and people.* Englewood Cliffs, N. J.: Prentice-Hall.

———. 1974. Cultural landscapes and regions: Aspects of communications. *Geosciences and Man* 5: 133–42.

Wagner, Philip L., and Marvin W. Mikesell, eds. 1962. *Readings in cultural geography.* Chicago: University of Chicago Press.

Wallach, Bret. 1979. The potato landscape: Aroostook County, Maine. *Landscape* 23: 15–22.

Watts, May Theilgaard. 1975. *Reading the landscape of America,* 2d ed. New York: Collier (orig. pub. 1957).

Williams, Michael. 1987. Sauer and "Man's Role in Changing the Face of the Earth" *Geographical Review* 77: 218–31.

Wolch, Jennifer, and Michael Dear. 1989. *The power of geography: How territory shapes social life.* Boston: Unwin Hyman.

Wright, John Kirkland. 1947. Terrae incognitae: The place of imagination in geography. *Annals of the Association of American Geographers* 37: 1–15.

Wylie, Alison. 1985. Putting Shakertown back together: Critical theory in archaeology. *Journal of Anthropological Archaeology* 4: 133–147.

Zube, Ervin., ed. 1970. *Landscapes: The writings of J. B. Jackson.* Amherst: University of Massachusetts Press.

Zube, Ervin, J. L. Sell, and J. G. Taylor. 1982. Landscape perception: Research, application, and theory. *Landscape Planning* 9: 1–33.

6

Ecology as Cornerstone and Chimera in Human Geography

Karl S. Zimmerer

Ecological concepts rooted deeply in human geography are at once persistently foundational and yet doggedly problematic in their application. The brief definition of scientific ecology—"the interrelations among organisms and the environment"—belies a surprising diversity of concepts in this discipline. Tracing and distinguishing the varied concepts of scientific ecology currently in use requires uncovering how they gained visibility in the academic landscapes of Western Europe and North America beginning in the late 1800s (Bramwell 1989, Goodland 1975, Worster 1977). Though their modern history originated with the discipline of biology, which established the first scientific meanings of ecology, these early ideas soon became paired with views of human groupings that were emerging in the nascent social sciences and the field of geography in particular.

Shortly after the turn of the twentieth century, the modern field of geography preceded its social scientific counterparts in an embrace of the ecological partner, thus setting out to enlarge its scientific inquiry within the wide-ranging "interrelations among organisms and the environment." At stake was no less than the formidable challenge of joining the analysis of humans and nature. As human geography announced the incorporation of ecology as early as 1907 (Goode 1907), many similarities could be identified that matched the ecological perspectives on humans with then-current views of plants and animals. Human geography thus began its rewarding prospecting of ecological concepts in biological science, a legacy whose modern origins I consider in the introductory section, "The History of Early Scientific Ecology," of this chapter.

Traditions of ecological thought in human geography have displayed a notable currency throughout the present century, but the stock of ecological knowledge tended in the common soil of geography eventually bore separate approaches as human geographers branched out in their choice of ecological concepts and topics. On the basis of these criteria we can distinguish five main ecological approaches in human geography: 1) human ecology (including the natural hazards approach); 2) cultural-historical ecology (derived from the Sauerian school); 3) systems ecology (a subset of human ecology as defined here); 4) adaptive dynamics ecology (sometimes referred to as cultural ecology); and 5) political ecology.

The individual sections of this chapter discuss the history, conceptual cornerstones, and integration of each approach. Terms and operational definitions for the five approaches would likely differ if my classification were to prioritize other criteria such as the institutional categories exemplified by the broad-based Cultural Ecology Specialty Group of the Association of American Geographers (Butzer 1989, Turner 1989). I choose instead to weight most heavily the scholarly products of each approach. My assessment is undertaken by crafting a historical perspective beginning with the earliest subfield, that of human ecology, and leading to the most recent offshoot, that of political ecology. The historical emphasis helps to delineate both exchanges and similarities as well as differences among approaches and with cognate disciplines such as biology, ecology, sociology, and anthropology (Ellen 1988, Entrikin 1980).

By dealing broadly with ecological concepts in each approach, this essay serves to complement a number of specialized reviews on cultural and human ecology (Butzer 1989; Denevan 1983; Grossman 1977, 1981; Kates 1987; Knapp 1985; Porter 1978; Turner 1989), political ecology (Black 1990, Blaikie and Brookfield 1987, Bryant 1992, Zimmerer 1991a), and the new biological ecology (Zimmerer 1991b, 1994a). Because the approaches drawn here bring ecological concepts into broad intellectual frameworks, the term *ecological geography* overstates the centrality of ecology in many cases; instead, the description *ecological approach* better expresses the moderate degree of actual debt. Like other assessments of the history and character of wide-ranging geographical ideas, my account cannot cluster authors into coordinate-like categories with an unassailable precision, a constraint compounded by shifts in the viewpoints of some key geographers. Nevertheless, I find that by focusing primarily on these persons' scholarship a number of major distinctions can be readily drawn among the five ecological approaches.

Of course various aspects of ecological concepts themselves might be weighed for the purpose of distinguishing the chief traditions developed in human geography. We should be mindful that the term *ecology* has elucidated at least three distinct aspects of organism-environment relations, that is, scientific interpretations, general interpretations that harness the idea of interrelatedness, and ethical concerns. In this essay I direct attention mainly toward the first aspect, that dealing with scientific interpretations, and toward the ethical concerns of ecology as a secondary theme. In turn, I distinguish a pair of subthemes within the scientific-style usages of ecology: human relations to biophysical environments and nonhuman organisms in relation to those environments. Once aware of these two distinct areas where ecological concepts are applied, we are better able to draw out and appreciate the salient features of the five main approaches (Zimmerer 1994a).

A final introductory note accents the dissimilar settings selected for study in each analytical approach. As discussed at length below, several approaches, namely cultural-historical ecology, systems ecology, and adaptive dynamics ecology, emphasize small-scale, non-Western societies.[1] The peasant and indigenous settings studied in these three traditions offer a stark contrast to the industrialized Western societies of developed countries and advance a powerful environmentalist critique of them, albeit one that is implicit. At the same time, the environmental concerns of communities in the United States, Britain, and Canada were not enlisted as study topics. By contrast, emphasis within the human ecology approach has provided technical expertise in the service of planning institutions and training for cadres of future governmental workers. Finally, the newness of political ecology precludes a firm characterization in this respect, though it appears to show a mix of regional settings.

The History of Early Scientific Ecology

The ecological concepts that geographers first adopted from biology had their own origins in interdisciplinary formulations. In 1866 Ernst Haeckel (1834–1919), a zoologist at the University of Jena, Germany, coined *ecology* to denote "management of [nature's] household" (Goodland 1975). The common linguistic root of the new term *ecology* and the older *economics* ("discourse of the household") revealed their mutual reference to the concept of *household*, which at the time was thought to be the basic unit of the monetary economy. Haeckel's choice of this term can be traced, in turn, to his belief, and that of other early ecologists, that the biological world shared fundamental modes of organization with the human economy (Worster 1977). Living organisms were believed to be united in an all-encompassing "economy of nature," a holistic union inspired by natural history advances and the synthetic, comprehensive taxonomy of Charles Linnaeus (1707–1778), published in his 1735 *The System of Nature*.

Historical circumstances of Western Europe in the nineteenth century reinforced this shared etymology of *ecology* and *economy* (Bramwell 1989, Worster 1977). A transforming social reality of urban growth and industrialization riven with class differentiation and ethically dubious colonialism helped upset customary traditions of economic and political thought. Sensing harsh social circumstances and the need to regulate them, political economists had forged models of a smoothly functioning human order that attained equilibrium through the compensating effects of competition and specialized cooperation. Biological scientists put forth remarkably similar formulations in the nascent ecology; the red-in-tooth-and-claw impulses of an equilibrium-seeking economy of nature were supposed to be mitigated as well as regulated by specialized cooperation. Belief in this cooperation was held strongly enough that Haeckel and others shunned one axiom of Darwinian evolution, that of competitive exclusion. Rather than fully adopt Darwin's paradigm of evolution based on natural selection, these early ecologists seized the metaphor of organisms coexisting in a "tree of life"—a symbol that originated in the Romantic movement and its critique of the social and intellectual conventions contained in older Classicism.

Haeckel and the other early ecologists withdrew from the defining dualisms framed in classical thought—particularly man and nature—as well as certain unwelcome prospects of the rapid and sometimes tumultuous modernization of life in the nineteenth century. Their ecological tenets sought to forge an amalgam of interacting elements that could be unified in a new crucible that eclipsed the older dualistic traditions. In a general sense the ecologists and many of their followers sought to mold a new order that would offset the unsettling social and economic reality of their time. These philosophical foundations of ecological thought were influenced by the somewhat holistic ideas then circulating widely in Germany and northern Europe (Bramwell 1989). According to ecology's founders, their new field thus wed man and nature in an allegedly holistic union, one that offered sharp contrast to both the classical view and the nature-as-resource perspective of Europe's expansive economies.

At that time, too, a fledgling cohort of scientific ecologists launched their efforts to ascertain the regulating mechanisms of nature's economy. They granted attention especially to the functional relations that were supposed to connect organisms in stable patterns of specialized cooperation. Biological webs of life were seen to channel the flow of matter and species in both space and time, much as the economy directed the movement of goods, labor, and money, the latter of course being commonly referred to as another type of species. Danish botanist Eugenius Waring and Germans Andreas Schimper and Oscar Drude directed experimental research and field studies on the compatibility and cooperation of coexisting plant species through symbiosis. Waring also erected a model of succession for the temporal replacement of species groups. Across the Atlantic the American plant ecologists Henry Cowles and Frederick Clements pursued further the temporal patterning of groups of plant species, which came to be known as *communities* on the basis of field investigations along Lake Michigan and in the Nebraska prairie. By the close of the nineteenth century the intellectual worth of biological ecology was attracting attention from the modernizing accounts of the social sciences, especially human geography.

Human Ecology

The term *human ecology* was coined in 1907 by J. P. Goode, then chair of the newly founded Department of Geography at the University of Chicago (Martin 1987; see also Leighly 1987). Influenced by the well-known Frederick Clements and other faculty in botany and zoology, Goode defined human ecology as "the geographic conditions of human culture." The ambitious scope of this term resembled the plant and animal geography claimed by biological ecology. A little later, the term *human ecology* was proposed to anchor human geography even more decisively, as Yale geographer Ellsworth Huntington addressed the budding Ecological Society of America in 1916. Defining geography itself as human ecology, Huntington also cast geography as the analogue of biological ecology. This viewpoint—albeit an altered version—became enshrined in Harlan Barrows's 1922 presidential address to the Association of American Geographers, which proclaimed the idea of "geography as human ecology" (Barrows 1923). According to Barrows, a human ecological geography pursued the "mutual relations between man and his natural environment" (Barrows 1923: 3). Such relations entailed "man's adjustment to the environment" through economic and political organization in general and land use in particular. Barrows's idea of human relations to nature thus delivered an explicit corrective to Huntington's environmental determinism.

During the decades following Barrows's proclamation, human ecology gained salience and stature as an important approach, although its first institutional residence was in sociology rather than in geography (Entrikin 1970). Sociological interest in human ecology flourished at the University of Chicago, where an ecologically oriented group of sociologists—known eventually as the Chicago school of urban ecology—pioneered the ecological analysis of urban societies (see Entrikin 1980, Schnore 1961). Adopting the tenets of biological ecology, and especially the familiar axiom of specialized cooperation, the Chicago sociologists held that the "ecological conception of society is that of a society created by competitive cooperation" (Park and Burgess 1922: 558). Fruitfully extending analogies with plant ecology, the group of Robert Park, Ernest Burgess, and their students pondered urban patterns of succession and natural areas that they took to undergird the spatial organization of ethnic and socioeconomic groups in cities. These ecological concepts generated the groundwork for models of concentric zones in urban land use that later stimulated research by an early wave of quantitative geographers.

The study of human ecology that became rooted in Chicago's Department of Geography differed, however, from that of its sociological neighbor insofar as the geographers treated the environment as physical rather than solely spatial. Barrows and his students brought their attention to bear on environmental calamities that precipitated costly economic damage and that dislocated people and their communities, perhaps even wielding the threat of social unrest. The Chicago geographers especially studied the effects of river flooding and the planning of flood control. Throughout his career Barrows assumed various government posts on such projects. This emphasis led to the self-conscious metamorphosis of Barrows's human ecology into natural hazards research when Gilbert White, a student of Barrows, filed his 1945 dissertation on *Human Adjustment to Floods* (Burton, Kates, and White 1978, White 1945). White's landmark work presaged the future scope of natural hazards research, for it delimited eight "adjustments to floods": land elevation, flood abatement, flood protection, emergency measures, structural adjustments, land use, public relief, and insurance (White 1945: 128–204). Natural hazards research achieved a highly visible profile through the endeavors of Ian Burton and Robert Kates, students of White, who similarly specialized in flood effects and management. Burton and Kates also rooted their study of natural hazards firmly in the human ecological concept of the organism ("man") adjusting to the environment ("extreme geophysical events") (Burton, Kates, and White 1978, xii and *passim*; see also Burton, Kates, and White 1968 and Burton and Hewitt 1974).

Before the mid-1960s, geographers applying the human ecology approach to natural hazards concentrated largely on advising governments in the United States and Canada about limiting the loss of human lives, the property damage, and revenues caused by flooding. In 1967 the research program of natural hazards was extended to settings "beyond those that had thus far been covered in North America" with the support of developing-country governments and international organizations (White 1974: 4). While broadening the spectrum of calamities and cultures under consideration, human ecology research abroad retained its conceptual orientation and standard methodologies. Perceptions and decisions of individual actors and the consequences of their behavior in terms of government planning still occupied the core of this approach (Burton, Kates, and White 1978). Questionnaires and sentence-completion tests furnished primary methodologies (White 1974).

To date, the natural hazards approach of human ecology minted by Barrows and White remains a mainstream tradition. Some of its earlier traits, however, especially its ecological conception of society and politics of management, have suffered incisive and sometimes harsh criticism. Its preoccupation with the decision making of persons dwelling in hazard-prone areas — an outlook shared with, if not derived from, the organism-environment concept of biological ecology — was faulted for overlooking the potential role of socioeconomic factors. According to critics, individual persons tended to be viewed in isolation from their historically forged social circumstances (Hewitt 1983; see also Watts 1983a). Natural hazards research also was criticized because "it serves to conceal both a particular *metaphysic of enquiry* and *politics of management*" (original emphasis; Hewitt 1983: 29; Waddell 1977). "Politics of management" in this case referred to a support of government policies that often did not promote the democratic participation or political empowerment of local residents while paradoxically benefiting them at the moment (Hewitt 1983, Waddell 1977; see also Emel and Peet 1989, Harvey 1974). Such criticisms have led to recent studies that stress the historical and social contexts of environmental risks. A study of drought impact on Mexican farmers, for instance, finds that response to this hazard varies among individual cultivators according to their economic resources (Liverman 1990).

Cultural-Historical Ecology

Ecological concepts played a quite distinct role in the cultural-historical ecology formulated by Carl Sauer and followed by numerous human geographers whom I refer to as the Sauerians. Defining the use of the concept *ecology* by Sauer and the Sauerians is nonetheless difficult, for they conspicuously avoided the terms *ecology, cultural ecology,* and *human ecology* (Leighly 1987). Indeed, ecological concepts were deemed ill-suited in accounts of human practices of all sorts, explanations that the Sauerians imputed to culture and history. Even the biota was thought, in the last instance, beyond the explanatory scope of conventional ecology, at least when a prolonged historical dimension held sway. Sauer penned his personal preference and prejudice in the introduction to *Agricultural Origins and Dispersals:* "I prefer natural history with its sense of real, non-duplicated time and place to ecology" (1952: 2).

Despite the lack of an acknowledged debt, ecological concepts have indeed informed the Sauerians in their examination of cultural landscapes, the guiding problematic etched in Sauer's "Morphology of Landscape" (Sauer 1925). Because ecological reasoning enabled the Sauerians to appraise the historical impact of human activities on cultural landscapes, their approach warrants the term *cultural-historical ecology*. This guiding interest in human-modified environments fed the empirical wellspring of cultural-historical ecology, which asked not only whether certain habitats had been modified by humans, but also what the nature of these alterations had been. Only with the use of ecological concepts could the Sauerians ferret out the alterations of natural landscapes into cultural ones caused by the economies, settlement patterns, and technologies of human inhabitants.

Most frequently, it was vegetation that presented the Sauerians with the material for exploring the cultural landscape.[2] The contribution of George Perkins Marsh, the nineteenth-century statesman and author of *Man and Nature* whom Sauer lauded as precursor and exemplar of his approach, had already demonstrated the fruitfulness of focusing on the anthropogenic shaping of plant cover. Vegetation study by the Sauerians stipulated a grasp of the distributional qualities of individual species and plant assemblages with respect to physical factors (soils, climate, landforms) and human activities (for example, fire, agriculture, livestock grazing, mining, and collecting for food, shelter, or other purposes). Where environments displayed a human imprint, the Sauerians selectively borrowed ecological concepts in order to gauge the scale, frequency, and magnitude of human activities. Cultural-historical ecology has commonly been marshaled in the study of environments subject to burning, grazing, and deforestation, though potentially it is applicable to more varied settings.

Frequently, the landscape impacts of indigenous peoples during the pre-European period formed a focus for cultural-historical ecology. The anthropogenic creation of grasslands and pine savannas comprised a signature subject (Denevan 1992). Interest in this topic followed Sauer's influential 1950 paper on "Grassland Climax, Fire, and Man," which postulated that the long-term history of human-set fires had spread tropical grasslands into areas that did not match so-called savanna climates (Sauer 1950). Among the vegetation types other than grassland explored in terms of human impacts, pine forests in particular drew attention. The pine forests and grasslands in Central America were examined in a series of field studies by James Parsons (1953), Carl Johannessen (1954–56), and William Denevan (1957). These studies concluded that intentional burning by indigenous people during the pre-European period had likely carpeted the region with large grasslands, pine-studded savannas, and open pine woodlands and that such impacts metamorphosed again following European settlement, indigenous depopulation, and colonial regimes of land use (Denevan 1961, Johannessen 1963, Parsons 1955).

A cardinal principle of cultural-historical ecology was the complete distinction drawn between the ecological analysis of human-modified environments on one hand and explanation for the origin of human activities on the other. As approached by the Sauerians, each category of inquiry retained analytical independence, albeit with the two entwining. Leighly has commented on Sauer's rationale for separating the two categories: "To him (Sauer), most human actions are expressions of culture, an attribute that other organisms do not possess. The relations between human groups and their environments thus differ qualitatively from those of other species" (1987: 406). Here the Sauerians veered most sharply from the tradition of Barrows, White, and other geographers working in human ecology. In fact, Sauer's quite different use of ecological concepts supplied one fulcrum on which he consciously pivoted his geography away from the Chicago viewpoint. Moreover, because the Sauerians did not adopt theories of society or sociocultural change, the forces driving human-induced modification of the environment seldom merited scrutiny. When more or less pressed to pass a verdict on the cause of accelerating environmental modification at the renowned symposium on "Man's Role in Changing the Face of the Earth" (chaired and contributed to by Sauer; see Thomas 1956, Leighly 1987, Williams 1987), various geographers of the cultural-historical bent blamed modernization—the behemoth of technology, industry, population growth, and new attitudes and values—that besieged both the environment and earlier lifeways.

Ethical aspects of ecology were clearly at play in cultural-historical ecology, with Sauer convinced that "humanity has a moral responsibility towards its environment" (Leighly 1987: 406). At his opening address to the "Man's Role" symposium Sauer decried the recent acceleration of resource exploitation and degradation and revealed his search for "an ethic and aesthetic under which man, practicing the qualities of prudence and moderation, may indeed pass on to posterity a good Earth" (Sauer 1956: 68; see also Williams 1987). This emphasis on ethics mixed with aesthetics, their unwavering commitment to explanations based on cultural-historical process, and their home bases in universities rather than in governmental posts led the Sauerians to exercise a different sense of ecological ethics than their human ecology counterparts.

Cultural-historical ecology can be compared briefly with a pair of different approaches bearing similar names. Cultural ecology of a geographical type—geographical-cultural ecology—was stamped by Philip Wagner and Marvin Mikesell as "an application of the scientific mode of thinking [that] concerns the *process* implied in a sequence of events" (emphasis in the original; Wagner and Mikesell 1961: 19). The two Berkeley-trained geographers held that

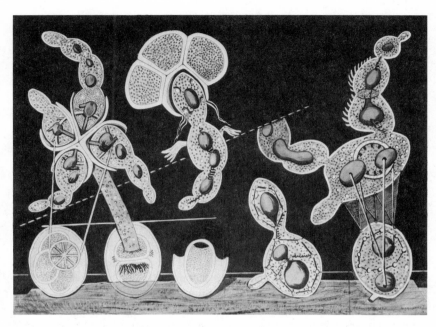

Figure 6.1 Max Ernst's painting of 1920–1921 entitled "The gramineous bicycle garnished with bells the dappled fire damps and the echinoderms bending the spine to look for caresses" (anatomical chart altered with gouache). Ernst's surreal depiction of plants and animals reflects one of the major rifts in ecological ideas in human geography during the twentieth century. The unresolved tension between metaphors of nature as animated—apparent in Ernst's playful rendering of a grass, an herb, and a crustacean—are shared with Sauerian "cultural-historical ecology" and adaptive dynamics ecology insofar as environments embody a living memory of the cultural landscape and its modification. Views of nature as mechanical—the machines and grid lines in Ernst's painting—have flourished in human ecology and systems ecology which have found environments subject to engineering solutions and concepts. Reprinted with permission of The Museum of Modern Art, New York.

the ecological processes of their approach consisted of those that were active in shaping human landscapes. Geographical cultural ecology was therefore similar to the cultural-historical ecology described above, although the former highlighted the processual aspect of landscape change rather than its artifactual content. The geographical-cultural ecology proposed by Wagner and Mikesell was not widely adopted, however, and even their own works may be seen as part of Sauerian cultural-historical ecology (Wagner 1961, Mikesell 1961).

Another cultural ecology grew outside geography and differed conspicuously from the one proposed by the two geographers. Founded by anthropologist Julian Steward, this cultural ecology earmarked an environmentalist theory of culture change that was based on the adaptation of cultural forms and social organization to a culture core, described as those "features which are most closely related to subsistence activities and economic arrangements" (Steward 1955: 37). A handful of human geographers applied anthropological cultural ecology to the study of pre-European contexts (e.g., Aschmann 1959, Butzer 1976, Denevan 1966). Butzer borrowed from Steward's approach in interpreting his landmark findings on irrigation history in Egypt in which he assigned social organization as a dependent variable while environment, technology, and population were taken to be independent variables (1976: iv).

Ecological concepts applied to the main branch of cultural-historical ecology have not been targeted by its principal critics. Instead, most criticism and, for that matter, defense of this approach have taken issue with the human and social dimension of Sauerian geography (e.g., Brookfield 1964, Duncan 1980, Price and Lewis 1993). Two criticisms of Sauerian geography by Brookfield in particular prompted the pioneering of subsequent approaches: first, inattention to social organization and to the inner workings of culture and, second, lack of detailed field study in local communities (Brookfield 1964).

Systems Ecology

The advent of a systems ecology approach among human geographers in the 1960s flagged a turn more toward the human ecology inaugurated by Barrows than Sauerian cultural-historical ecology. Systems ecology generated enthusiasm because of its prospect of an advanced and holistic scientific method that appealed greatly to many specialists in human ecology and natural hazards. Kates (1971), for instance, heralded General Systems Theory (and systems ecology) as the key to rebuilding natural hazards inquiry. The new systems ecology promised to make more penetrating the study of human-environment relations at the local scale, a miniaturizing of the field of study advocated in the criticism of cultural-historical ecology (Brookfield 1964). Carried by post-World War II innovations in computing, cybernetics, communication theory, and systems engineering, Systems Theory's incorporation into human geography seemed to require only a compatible biological model, and this was provided by the existing concept of the ecosystem.

The ecosystem concept was defined in 1935 by British plant ecologist Sir Arthur Tansley as a means of synthesizing the interactions among organisms and their surrounding biophysical environment. The application of systems theory to ecosystems, and eventually to human geography, however, also rested on subsequent advances in ecosystem science and especially the universal-style synthesis of ecological principles by leaders such as Eugene Odum (Odum 1952; 1953). Yet, rather than Odum or other ecosystem ecologists active during the 1950s and early 1960s, it was Raymond Fosberg—a zoologist, biogeographer, and South Pacific expert—who seems to have most influenced adoption of the ecosystem concept in physical as well as human geography. An ecosystem, Fosberg (1963: 2) penned in an often-quoted passage, comprised "a functioning, interacting system composed of one or more living organisms and their effective environment, both physical and biological."

The integrative and holistic aspects of the ecosystem concept magnetized many geographers by its potential bridging of the poles of biophysical environments at one end of the analysis with humans and their activities at the other (the "human component," as it was often called). General Systems Theory served as the main artifice for this framework. Introduced to geomorphology by Richard Chorley (1962), General Systems Theory was transposed shortly thereafter to human ecosystems, thus christening the systems ecology approach in human geography. Brookfield's 1964 article, mentioned above for its influential critique of cultural-historical ecology, argued programmatically that human geography should become "the study of the human ecosystem." The agenda-setting Brookfield avowed that the ecosystem approach would enable geography to become "more syncretic than other sciences." His clarion call was echoed enthusiastically by Stoddart (1965) in a proposal that General Systems Theory serve as the linking function for all geography.

Though geographers championed systems theory and its promise for human geography, anthropologists authored the first studies. Clifford Geertz's (1966) renowned *Agricultural Involution* contrasted the human-ecosystem properties of swidden and rice-paddy agriculture in Indonesia. An equal or greater intellectual clamor in that heyday of system ecology emanated from *Pigs for the Ancestors*, by anthropologist Roy Rappaport (1968), in which certain religious rituals of the Tsembaga people in the Central Highlands of Papua New Guinea were found to regulate environmental relations and ensure an "undegraded environment." Whereas Geertz's' study, however, was noteworthy for dealing with cultural, political, and economic history—albeit without relying on systems ecology in this historical inquiry—Rappaport's stirring study delivered a mostly synchronic, ahistorical perspective (Rappaport 1968). The latter study managed to unloose a torrent of criticism, but not without also touching off a small wave of human-geographic systems ecology.

Geographer Bernard Nietschmann (1973) brandished the systems-ecology approach in appraising food procurement among the Miskito people on the eastern coast of Nicaragua. His *Between Land and Water* begins thus: "By studying the ecology of subsistence within an ecological matrix, some of the functional relationships which couple and regulate man-environment interchanges may be identified and measured." Nietschmann assessed these functional relations through detailed budgets of resource expenditures (labor, land, money) on food procurement. While he surmised that loss over time of local economic autonomy undermined resource-based livelihoods among the Miskito, Nietschmann's historical analysis stood apart from the application of systems ecology, much as Geertz's application had. Butzer (1980: 517) selected a systems ecology lens to view "civilizations as ecosystems that emerge in response to sets of ecological opportunities, that is econiches, to be exploited." He applied this ecological vantage point as far as assigning ecosystem principles of the trophic pyramid to social hierarchies and interpreting human demographic history on the basis of adaptation (ecological fitness).

Systems ecology in human geography lauded General Systems Theory as the unprecedented prospect for a holistic union of organism and environment, similar to, but more sophisticated than, that of earlier human and biological ecology. General Systems Theory posited that human-environment systems act like equilibrium-maintaining engineering devices known as servomechanisms (see Nietschmann [1973: 6] on the merits of the gyroscope as the appropriate metaphor). Systems ecologists defined human-environment couplings in the form of related and often self-regulating variables whereby "change in the value of a variable initiates a process that either limits further change or returns the value to a former level (negative feedback)" (Rappaport 1968: 9). Relationships among variables functioned to maintain equilibrium through either limited random variation ("homeostatic equilibrium") or regular fluctuations ("dynamic equilibrium"). The functioning of environmental variables, in turn, created structural attributes such as niche, adaptation, carrying capacity, succession, and trophic level which could be applied to biological as well as to human ecosystems.

System ecology's depictions of sound, if not exemplary, environmental management by peasants and indigenous peoples frequently aired an ethical meaning of ecology. In a few cases such critiques were explicit; assessment of comparative energy costs in peasant-indigenous versus industrial agriculture, for instance, was used to argue persuasively for the former's advantages in terms of efficiency (Rappaport 1971). In many cases an ethical meaning of ecology remained only implicit in systems ecology. By conveying the environmental soundness and rationality of land use practices by peasant and indigenous peoples, the studies implicitly critiqued their home communities (Brush 1977, Nietschmann 1973).

The use of General Systems Theory to interpret human-environment relations rested, however, on a perilous foundation in its assumption of functional, equilibrium-maintaining processes, as critics have pointed out (Ellen 1982, Friedman 1974, Orlove 1980, Vayda and McKay 1975, Watts 1983a). A model based on such processes could not satisfactorily explain why environmental change occurs, even if it sparked hope with its potential to address how such changes happen. Not surprisingly, therefore, the application of systems ecology often conformed to an ahistorical analysis, its principles quantifying certain functions and clarifying how they work but without elucidating their genesis. By the early 1990s the systems ecology tide had ebbed as a result of this weakness and the troubling recognition of limitations in the purely ecosystemic view of biophysical environments (Winterhalder 1984).

Adaptive Dynamics Ecology

A new-found focus on the practices and decisions of individual actors marked the turn toward an approach referred to as adaptive dynamics ecology (Knapp 1984, 1992). Tracking the conceptual directions mapped out by anthropologist John Bennett (1969, 1976) and prior work in human geography (Denevan 1983; Denevan and Schwerin 1978; Waddell 1972, 1977), the adaptive dynamics approach accents those coping behaviors used to engineer the nature of environments—particularly decision making, problem solving, and technological innovation. As adaptive dynamics ecology has gained a foothold during the past decade, it has enhanced our sensitivity to ethnographic method and individual behavior beyond the coarser calculus carried out in human ecology and cultural-historical ecology.

The central questions in adaptive dynamics ecology have been how individuals decide about environment-related activities (adaptive strategies) and how, summed across a human population, repeated individual choices lead to patterns of environmental modification (adaptive processes). Numerous human geographers opting for this approach have adopted a suite of ecological concepts to detail those biophysical properties that enabled or constrained options available to decisionmakers. Climate, soils, and vegetation frequently figured among the chief parameters. A core of adaptive dynamics research has addressed the use of labor, knowledge, techniques, and technology by farmers and herders to modify environmental resources for crop and animal production.

Two broad topics have attracted great interest in adaptive dynamics ecology: first, the discovery and investigation of agricultural landforms, especially wetland raised fields, tilled in the Americas prior to the period of European rule and, second, the present-day adaptations of land use among peasant and indigenous farmers. Initially, the discoveries of raised fields had drawn the observant notice of cultural-historical ecology; pioneering studies of raised fields outlined morphological features (such as size, shape, and patterning) and their geographic distribution, with remarkable discoveries shortly dotting the Latin American landscape in particular (Parsons and Denevan 1967). A perspective akin to cultural-historical ecology also guided the interpretation of a contemporary system of raised-field farming in highland Guatemala (Mathewson 1984). At about the same time other perspectives were brought to bear on the general topic: Turner's (1983) study of pre-Hispanic terracing in Mexico, for instance, adopted elements of the systems ecology approach as evidenced in its application of carrying capacity.

A few of the adaptive dynamics studies take us directly to the farm practices of contemporary peasants and indigenous people while, at the same time, reflecting on pre-European intensive agriculture. The collaborative study of Denevan with anthropologist Karl Schwerin, for instance, featured adaptations in present-day wetland agriculture of the Karinya people in the Venezuelan Llanos, "the only surviving instance of aboriginal drained-field cultivation in tropical South America" (Denevan and Schwerin 1978). Adaptation, as they saw it, comprised the responses of farmers to environmental, technological, social, and demographic conditions, and in the last instance the measure of such adaptations was survival. On another front, in highland Ecuador, the adaptive dynamics of present-day field and farming systems helped elucidate food production strategies there under pre-European Andean civilizations (Knapp 1984, 1991). Other adaptive dynamics research, however, has chosen contemporary adaptations as its sole subject matter. Waddell innovated an early study of this type, integrating it with a natural hazards perspective, in his work with the indigenous Fringe Enga cultivators in Papua New Guinea, who devise multiple coping strategies to minimize crop losses caused by recurrent frost (Waddell 1972, 1977).

Geographical studies in adaptive dynamics ecology have staked their claims to the rational-actor model of neoclassical economic theory and principles of Darwinian natural selection. These theoretical foundations indicate a deliberate effort to succeed where systems ecology had failed, namely, in accounts of historical change.[3] For example, adaptive dynamics ecology has built on the rational-actor and Darwinian selection models to explain changes in food-producing strategies. As summed up by Denevan, the "question of why a tool, idea, or behavioral pattern is applied in a particular ecological situation, place, or point in time" could be answered if, among other correctives, "geographers become more sensitive to small-scale variation as a key to understanding changing cultural adaptation in response to a changing human or physical environment" (Denevan 1983: 399, 400). Use of neoclassical economic theory and natural-selection principles from Darwinian evolutionary theory in adaptive dynamics research has been reviewed insightfully by anthropologists Raymond Hames and William Vickers (1983). Their comparison of the two theoretical frameworks describes both methodological similarities (e.g., linear programming) and theoretical contrasts (adaptation as the attainment of culturally defined goals versus reproductive success or foraging efficiency).

An ethical sense of ecology has been implicit in the adaptive dynamics approach, which has often uncovered the sound environmental logic of land use, and especially farming, by peasant and indigenous peoples. Recent research in adaptive dynamics ecology investigates not only the plight of environmental deterioration, but also the prospects for sustainable land use (Browder 1989; Doolittle 1989; Treacy 1989, 1994). Productive and environmentally sound adaptations worked out in raised fields, crop terraces, local soil management, and crop biodiversity offer such prospects. The collection of papers in *Fragile Lands of Latin America* attests to this newly explicit attention to conservation combined with development (Browder 1989). Still, the adaptive dynamics approach has not thus far pursued many projects in Western, urbanized, and industrialized settings (*cf.* Bennett 1969).

One chief criticism of adaptive dynamics ecology dwells on the idea of adaptation, which is central to its view of human-environment relations. Critics question the extent to which environment-related behaviors are governed solely by this purpose. Social relations, it has been argued, mediate much environmental modification, and thus the intent to modify environments often does not bear the whole explanation for behavior. Eric Wolf (1982: 78), for instance, reasoned concisely that: "Between people and resources stand the strategic relationships governing the mode of allocating social labor to nature." Wolf and others have asserted that the emphasis of adaptive dynamics on individual decision makers does not satisfactorily illuminate social processes of cooperation, conflict, and contradiction through which arise many practices important for environmental modification (Love 1983, Orlove 1980, Watts 1983a, Wolf 1982).

Political Ecology

The political ecology approach in human geography was defined by Piers Blaikie and Harold Brookfield (1987: 17) as: "[combining] the concerns of ecology and a broadly defined political economy. Together this encompasses the constantly shifting dialectic between society and land-based resources, and also within classes and groups within society itself." Blaikie and Brookfield's statement built on mounting interest in similar ecological orientations. Perhaps the first to use the term *political ecology* was anthropologist Eric Wolf (1972) in reviewing a 1972 symposium entitled "Ownership and Political Ecology" which dealt with the ecological anthropology of the Alps. Wolf contended that ecological explanation of current land use ought to consider the interaction of local peoples with larger-scale political and economic forces. During the 1970s and the early 1980s various anthropologists and sociologists sought to expand Wolf's viewpoint and apply it to settings such as the Peruvian highlands (e.g., Guillet 1981). The term *political ecology* also became attached to several perspectives that addressed issues involving politics, political organization, and the environment (Cockburn and Ridgeway 1979, Jordan and Rowntree 1982).

In human geography the political ecology approach gained further definition through Piers Blaikie's *The Political Economy of Soil Erosion in Developing Countries* (Blaikie 1985). Blaikie outlined a dynamic access model to explain the environment-related decisions and practices of land users. This model constructs a bottom-up analysis from individuals to larger social aggregates, at each scale examining the social relations that shape opportunities and constraints for land users. Blaikie's approach resembles the "progressive contextualization" framework usefully soldered by anthropologist Andrew Vayda (1983), as well as other ensuing models (Schmink and Wood 1987, Sheridan 1988). Empirical studies of political ecology, similar to Blaikie's work in Nepal, have underscored the role of access to resources, as this circumstance is molded by property rights, state power, commercial pressures, and ideology (e.g., Watts 1983b, Sheridan 1988).

Forerunners of the political ecology approach in human geography included a pair of studies with significant ecological emphasis (Grossman 1984, Hecht 1985). In *Peasants, Subsistence Ecology, and Development in the Highlands of Papua New Guinea*, Grossman (1984) gauged the ecology of recent changes of vegetative cover occurring in overgrazed cattle pastures set up by an ill-conceived government project. By showing the impact of vegetative change on worsened soil erosion, he stressed not only environmental degradation, but also the social impact of locally uneven development that favored the livestock-raising tribal "Big Men." Similar emphasis on soil degradation, cattle raising, and socially uneven development policy coalesced in Hecht's studies of the Brazilian Amazon (e.g., Hecht 1985, Hecht and Cockburn 1989). In her 1985 paper Hecht determined the deterioration of nutrient status and soil structure that resulted from deforestation followed by pasture formation and cattle grazing, plain proof of soil worsening that refuted the government's then-current claims of pasture improvement.

Political ecology has adopted a dual set of epistemologies: on one hand it has used ecological concepts to understand the environmental impacts of human activities, while on the other hand the human organization of those activities, their dynamics, and their origins have been primarily the prerogative of the political economy perspective. The latter seeks to understand "a social economy, or way of life" in which are embedded the social relations of production and exchange. With regard to the aforementioned use of ecological concepts, several have figured prominently in political ecology: 1) environmental impact is gauged via biological ecology measures such as degradation, resilience, and sensitivity (or susceptibility) (Blaikie and Brookfield 1987); 2) the decision making of individuals, framed in a "responses in context" model, forms a necessary (but not sufficient) focus for explaining land use (Bassett 1989, Blaikie and Brookfield 1987); and 3) an ethical ecology committed to conserving the environments needed for the livelihoods of local inhabitants is tied to broader political issues of human rights and democratic models of economic development (Hecht and Cockburn 1989, Zimmerer 1993).

Worthy of note are the core analyses of social organization, spatial scale, and the relations between social organization and land use, all characteristic of political ecology, that seek to redress the perceived shortcomings of a variety of ecological approaches. In the case of the social realm, inquiry often settles on power and its impact on the allocation of labor, land, and capital resources among land users. Scale issues are frequently forefronted as political ecology geographers plot out—typically in qualitative terms—the spatial prospects of relevant social processes that typically reach beyond the local community to encompass regional and sometimes national and international scales. Households frequently form the socioeconomic and political locus of decision making about land use, and the Blaikie and Brookfield model anchors the "chain of explanation" that links land use and environment-related behavior to the forces at work in these persons' socioeconomic and political surroundings.

Political ecology appears poised to draw on a variety of insights from human geography and related disciplines. Several approaches dealing with the environmental consequences of economic organization potentially offer useful concepts. Innovation diffusion, staple theory, and environmental history are three such fields. Geographers Lakshman Yapa (1977, 1979) and Carville Earle (1988), for instance, have shown the social and environmental repercussions of the diffusion of agricultural innovations in a variety of settings. Earle ties the spatial and temporal rhythms of innovation diffusion to large-scale economic patterns explicated by economic cycles and the staple theory of economic geographer Harold Innis (1956). Sociologist Stephen Bunker (1989) draws on Innis's staple theory to examine the economic and social patterning of environmental change in the Brazilian Amazon. Finally, the fledgling field of environmental history not only appears remarkably similar to political ecology in its core subject matter, but it also opens new insights into richly textured treatments of environment-related social organization (e.g., Carney 1993, Cronon 1983, Worster 1988; on connections to historical geography see also Darby 1956, Evans 1956). In any case, political ecology must integrate a historical perspective in overcoming the reductionist and philosophically unsound propositions that at times have undermined ecological study in human geography.

To be sure, political ecology promises new insights, though its maturing project is a work in progress still subject to sizable doses of revisionist critique and much-needed refinement. One difficulty noted nearly at the outset was the seeming rift that distanced the systemic examination of political-economic context on one hand from the decision making of individuals acting within this context on the other. This troublesome gap between subject and surrounding was spread by the awkward insertion of a model akin to that of "responses in context" or the "actor-in-context" (Johnston 1986). Individual persons and households, though, take part in determining their local contexts, a truth dawning again on much social science. The dialectical concept of structuration can redress this artificial gap, as demonstrated in a study of the recent development of wetland, drained-field agriculture in highland Peru (Zimmerer 1991a, 1994b; see also Black 1990). In the Peruvian case indigenous peasants gained from a number of social practices and resistance ideologies—formed during a long history of opposition toward rural elites—that helped them extract production benefits from a reformist national government in the 1970s. Contextual circumstances that enabled the agricultural transformation of wetland environments were, therefore, partly products of individuals' local actions. Notwithstanding these modest advances in political ecology, the subfield must be seen still as consolidated only in part. By way of conclusion we might note that its future contribution could show a considerable success if the nature of environmental modification is more fully and recursively integrated with theories of regional development and underdevelopment, because most political ecology has conceived the environment solely as a receptor of modification.

Discussion: The Genres of Geographical Ecology

Distinguishing and depicting the various genres of our geographical ecologies enables us to grasp how ecological concepts of human-environment relations have been used to frame quite diverse images of humans, other organisms, and surrounding biophysical environments. Inspired by nineteenth-century Monism, a number of ecologically oriented approaches in human geography have sought to render ecology-inspired depictions of "the interrelations among organisms [including humans] and the environment" on a single canvas subject to a single epistemological perspective. Human ecology and systems ecology, and to a lesser degree adaptive dynamics ecology, each strove to cast human-environment relations within a unified field of concepts. For those three approaches ecological ideas born in the biological sciences could furnish an adequate framework for environment-related human behavior. Ecological concepts thus offered these branches of geography a recurring chimera of unity in which physical and human geography might be welded into a seamless, holistic discipline. Bolstered claims to scientific rigor and intellectual legitimacy have been no less important stimuli for the frequent engagement with ecological concepts in these approaches.

Cultural-historical ecology and political ecology, by contrast, have demanded the analytical separation of the environment (and the nature of its modification) from human behavior and society. In both approaches ecological concepts are reserved for the consideration of environmental factors but not human-environment relations per se, but cultural-historical ecology and political ecology differ greatly in their treatment of human behavior, society, and culture. Cultural-historical ecology follows Sauer in self-consciously rejecting theories that claimed to explicate human behavior and thought, instead relying on history as the principal mode of advancing understanding. Political ecology has steered a quite different and more critical course through the lens of social theory. This latter approach remains vaguely defined in several respects, as numerous topics and conceptual problems await examination. For instance, highly publicized dilemmas such as deforestation and soil degradation have overshadowed subjects such as industrial pollution.

Another challenge to political ecology lies in the integration of concepts from biological ecology that can contribute to accurate assessments of environmental modification and prospects for conservation. Practitioners of biological ecology are newly interested in the nature of human-modified environments (Zimmerer 1994a). The growing fields of landscape ecology and agroecology, for instance, have begun to innovate and aggregate, as well as apply, concepts and methodologies that are well suited to ecological research in human geography. Their intensifying focus on environmental modification, moreover, accompanies a resurgent interest in time, space, and the prevalence of nonequilibrium states in nature. Integrating concepts from this recent ecological theory can be expected to benefit greatly the explanatory capacity of political ecology. We can also hope for this integration both to invigorate the intradisciplinary discourse between human and physical geography and to renew a vital history of transdisciplinary exchanges.

Notes

I owe debts of gratitude to Bruce Winterhalder, Tom Bassett, Gregory Knapp, Lawrence Grossman, Kent Mathewson, James Parsons, and Michael Watts for discussions that date back to the drafting of this chapter in 1989. Meetings with David Campbell, Nancy Peluso, Dianne Rocheleau, Paul Richards, and Ted Whitesell at the 1994 Political Ecology Workshop at Michigan State University further inspired my thinking on this chapter's topic, though its main contents were long since in place. Carville Earle, Kent Mathewson, and William M. Denevan offered many helpful comments on the manuscript. These debts do not diminish my full responsibility.

1. This same orientation has also marked ecological approaches in anthropology that frequently furnished the chief cognate discipline for geographers in these three ecological approaches.

2. Though some pursued landscape topics in soils and geomorphology, and the latter was, of course, one of Sauer's principal interests at first, these have remained a secondary emphasis in the Sauerian project.

3. The shift from systems ecology to adaptive dynamics reflected two realizations: that the ecosystem concept was flawed and that, in any case, neither it nor General Systems Theory were actually theories, but instead only concepts that "isolate and systematically define relationships or processes felt to be especially worthy of analytic attention" (Winterhalder 1984: 303).

References

Aschmann, H. 1959. The Central Desert of Baja California: Demography and ecology. *IberoAmericana* 42. Berkeley: University of California Press.

Baker, W. L. 1989. Landscape ecology and nature reserve design in the Boundary Waters Canoe Area, Minnesota. *Ecology* 70: 23–35.

Barrows, H. H. 1923. Geography as human ecology. *Annals of the Association of American Geographers* 13: 1–14.

Bassett, T. J. 1988. The political ecology of peasant-herder conflicts in the Northern Ivory Coast. *Annals of the Association of American Geographers* 78: 453–72.

Bennett, J. W. 1969. *Northern plainsmen: Adaptive strategy and agrarian life.* Chicago: Aldine.

————. 1976. *The ecological transition: Cultural anthropology and human adaptation.* New York: Pergamon.

Black, R. 1990. Regional political ecology in theory and practice: A case study from northern Portugal. *Transactions of the Institute of British Geographers* N. S. 15: 35–47.

Blaikie, P. M. 1985. *The political economy of soil erosion in developing countries.* London: Longman Scientific.

Blaikie, P. M., and H. C. Brookfield, eds. 1987. *Land degradation and society.* London: Methuen.

Bramwell, A. 1989. *Ecology in the 20th century: A history.* New Haven: Yale University Press.

Brookfield, H. C. 1964. Questions on the human frontiers of geography. *Economic Geography* 40: 283–303.

Browder, J. O., ed. 1989. *Fragile lands of Latin America: Strategies for sustainable development.* Boulder, Colo.: Westview.

Brush, S. B. 1977. *Mountain, field, and family: The economy and human ecology of an Andean valley.* Philadelphia: University of Pennsylvania.

Bryant, R. L. 1992. Political ecology: An emerging research agenda in Third World studies. *Political Geography* 11: 1–36.

Bunker, S. G. 1989. Staples, links, and poles in the construction of regional development theories. *Sociological Forum* 4: 589–610.

Burton, I., R. W. Kates, and G. F. White. 1968. The human ecology of extreme geophysical events. Department of Geography, University of Toronto, Working Paper No.1.

————. 1978. *The environment as hazard.* New York: Oxford University Press.

Burton, I., and K. Hewitt. 1974. Ecological dimensions of environmental hazards. In *Human ecology,* ed. Frederick Sargent II, 25–84. New York: American Elsevier Publishing Company.

Butzer, K. W. 1976. *Early hydraulic civilization in Egypt: A study in cultural ecology.* Chicago: The University of Chicago.

————. 1980. Civilization: Organism or systems? *American Scientist* 68: 517–23.

————. 1989. Cultural ecology. In *Geography in America,* ed. G. L. Gaile and C. J. Willmott, 192–208. Columbus: Merrill.

Carney, J. A. 1993. From hands to tutors: African expertise in the South Carolina rice economy. *Agricultural History* 67: 1–30.

Chorley, R. J. 1962. Geomorphology and General Systems Theory. United States Geological Survey, *Professional Paper* No. 500–B.

Cockburn, A., and J. Ridgeway, eds. 1979. *Political ecology*. New York: Times Books.

Cronon, W. 1983. *Changes in the land: Indians, colonists, and the ecology of New England*. New York: Hill and Wang.

Darby, C. H. 1956. The clearing of the woodland in Europe. In *Man's role in changing the face of the earth*. ed. W. L. Thomas Jr., vol. 1, 183–216. Chicago: University of Chicago Press.

Denevan, W. M. 1961. The upland pine forests of Nicaragua: A study in cultural plant geography. *University of California Publications in Geography* 12: 251–320.

———. 1983. Adaptation, variation, and cultural geography. *Professional Geographer* 35: 399–407.

———. 1992. The pristine myth: The landscape of the Americas in 1492. *Annals of the Association of American Geographers*. 82(3) Supplement: 369–385.

Denevan, W. M., and K. H. Schwerin. 1978. Adaptive strategies in Karinya subsistence, Venezuelan Llanos. *Antropológica* 50: 3–91.

Doolittle, W. E. 1989. Arroyos and the development of agriculture in northern Mexico. In *Fragile lands of Latin America*, ed. J. O. Browder, 251–69. Boulder, Colo.: Westview Press.

Duncan, J. S. 1980. The superorganic in American cultural geography. *Annals of the Association of American Geographers* 70: 181–98.

Earle, C. 1988. The myth of the Southern soil miner: Macrohistory, agricultural innovation, and environmental change. In *The ends of the earth*, ed. D. Worster, 175–210. Cambridge: Cambridge University Press.

Ellen, R. 1982. *Environment, subsistence, and system: The ecology of small-scale social formations*. Cambridge: Cambridge University Press.

———. 1988. Persistence and change in the relationship between anthropology and human geography. *Progress in Human Geography* 12: 229–62.

Emel, J., and R. Peet. 1989. Resource management and natural hazards. In *New models in geography: The political economy perspective*, vol. 1, ed. R. Peet and N. Thrift, 49–76. London: Unwin Hyman.

Entrikin, J. N. 1980. Robert Park's human ecology and human geography. *Annals of the Association of American Geographers* 70: 43–58.

Evans, E. E. 1956. The ecology of peasant life in western Europe. In *Man's role in changing the face of the earth*. ed. W. L. Thomas Jr., vol. 1, 217–39. Chicago: University of Chicago Press.

Forman, R. T. T., and M. Godron. 1986. *Landscape ecology*. New York: John Wiley and Sons.

Fosberg, F. R. 1963. The island ecosystem. In *Man's place in the island ecosystem*, ed. F. R. Fosberg, 1–6. Honolulu: Bishop Museum.

Friedman, J. 1974. Marxism, structuralism and vulgar materialism. *Man* 9: 444–69.

Geertz, C. 1966. *Agricultural involution: The process of ecological change in Indonesia*. Berkeley: University of California Press.

Goodland, R. 1975. History of "ecology." *Science* 188:313.

Grossman, L. S. 1977. Man-environment relationships in anthropology and geography. *Annals of the Association of American Geographers* 67: 126–44.

———. 1981. The cultural ecology of economic development. *Annals of the Association of American Geographers* 71: 220–36.

———. 1984. *Peasants, subsistence ecology, and development in the Highlands of Papua New Guinea*. Princeton: Princeton University Press.

Guillet, D. 1981. Agrarian ecology and peasant production in the Central Andes. *Mountain Research and Development* 1: 19–28.

Hames, R. B., and W. T. Vickers. 1983. Introduction. In *Adaptive responses of native Amazonians*, ed. R. B. Hames and W. T. Vickers, 1–28. New York: Academic Press.

Harvey, D. 1974. Population, resources, and the ideology of science. *Economic Geography* 50: 256–77.

Hecht, S. 1975. Environment, development, and politics: Capital accumulation and the livestock sector in Eastern Amazonia. *World Development* 13: 663–84.

Hecht, S., and A. Cockburn. 1989. *The fate of the forest: Developers, destroyers, and defenders of the Amazon*. London: Verso.

Hewitt, K. 1983. The idea of calamity in a technocratic age. In *Interpretations of calamity*, ed. K. Hewitt, 3–32. Boston: Allen and Unwin.

Innis, H. A. 1956. *Essays in Canadian economic history*. Toronto: University of Toronto Press.

Johannessen, C. L. 1963. Savannas of interior Honduras. *Ibero-Americana* 46. Los Angeles: University of California.

Johnston, R. J. 1986. *On human geography*. Oxford: Basil Blackwell.

Jordan, T. G., and L. Rowntree, eds. 1982. *The human mosaic*. New York: Harper and Row.

Kates, R. 1971. Natural hazard in human ecological perspective: Hypotheses and models. *Economic Geography* 47: 438–51.

—————. 1987. The human environment: The road not taken, the road still beckoning. *Annals of the Association of American Geographers* 77: 525–34.

Knapp, G. W. 1984. Soil, slope, and water in the Equatorial Andes: A study of prehistoric agricultural adaptation. Ph.D dissertation, University of Wisconsin, Department of Geography.

—————. 1985. Cultural ecology. In *A geographical bibliography for American libraries*, ed. C. D. Harris, 130–34. Washington, D. C.: Association of American Geographers and National Geographic Society.

—————. 1991. *Andean ecology: Adaptive dynamics in Ecuador*. Boulder, Colo.: Westview Press.

Leighly, J. 1987. Ecology as metaphor: Carl Sauer and human ecology. *Professional Geographer* 39: 405–12.

Liverman, D. M. 1990. Drought impacts in Mexico: Climate, agriculture, technology, and land tenure in Sonora and Puebla. *Annals of the Association of American Geographers* 80: 49–72.

Love, T. 1983. To what are humans adapting? *Reviews in Anthropology* 10: 1–8.

Marsh, G. P. 1965 (1864). *Man and nature, or, physical geography as modified by human action*. Cambridge, Mass.: The Belknap Press of Harvard University Press.

Martin, G. J. 1987. The ecologic tradition in American geography 1895–1925. *Canadian Geographer* 31: 74–77.

Mathewson, K. 1984. *Irrigation horticulture in highland Guatemala: The tablón system of Panajachel*. Boulder, Colo.: Westview Press.

Mikesell, M. W. 1961. Northern Morocco: A cultural geography. *University of California Publications in Geography* 14: 1–136.

Nietschmann, B. Q. 1973. *Between land and water: The subsistence ecology of the Miskito Indians, eastern Nicaragua*. New York: Seminar Press.

Odum, E. P. 1952. Relationships between structure and function in the ecosystem. *Japanese Journal of Ecology* 12: 108–18.

—————. 1953. *Ecology*. Modern Biology Series. New York: Holt, Rinehart and Winston.

Orlove, B. S. 1980. Ecological anthropology. *Annual Review of Anthropology* 9: 235–73.

Park, R. and E. Burgess. 1922. *Introduction to the science of sociology*. Chicago: University of Chicago Press.

Parsons, J. J. 1955. The Miskito pine savanna of Nicaragua and Honduras. *Annals of the Association of American Geographers* 45: 36–63.

—————. 1971. Ecological problems and approaches in Latin American geography. In *Geographic research on Latin America, Benchmark 1970,* ed. B. Lentnek, R. L. Carmin, and T. L. Martinson, 13–32. Muncie, Ind.: Ball State University.

Parsons, J. J., and W. M. Denevan. 1967. Pre-Columbian ridged fields. *Scientific American* 217: 92–101.

Peet, R., and N. Thrift, eds. 1989. *New models in geography: The political-economy perspective.* 2 vols. London: Unwin Hyman.

Price, M., and M. Lewis. 1993. The reinvention of traditional cultural geography. *Annals of the Association of American Geographers* 83: 1–17.

Porter, P. W. 1978. Geography as human ecology. *American Behavioral Scientist* 22: 15–39.

Rappaport, R. A. 1968. *Pigs for the ancestors: Ritual in the ecology of a New Guinea people.* New Haven: Yale University Press.

———. 1971. The flow of energy in an agricultural society. *Scientific American* 225: 116–32.

Richards, P. 1985. *Indigenous agricultural revolution: Ecology and food production in West Africa.* London: Unwin Hyman.

Roughgarden, J., R. M. May, and S. A. Levin, eds. 1989. *Perspectives in Ecological Theory.* Princeton, N. J.: Princeton University Press.

Sauer, C. O. 1925. The morphology of landscape. *University of California Publications in Geography* 2: 19–53.

———. 1950. Grassland climax, fire, and man. *Journal of Range Management* 3: 16–21.

———. 1952. *Agricultural origins and dispersals.* Bowman Memorial Lectures, Series 2. New York: American Geographical Society.

———. 1956. The agency of man on the earth. In *Man's role in changing the face of the earth,* ed. W. L. Thomas Jr., 49–69. Chicago: University of Chicago Press.

Schmink, M., and C. H. Wood. 1987. The "political ecology" of Amazonia. In *Lands at Risk in the Third World: Local level perspectives,* ed. P. D. Little and M. H. Horowitz, 38–57. Boulder, Colo.: Westview Press.

Schnore, L. 1961. Geography and human ecology. *Economic Geography* 37: 207–17.

Sheridan, T. E. 1988. *Where the dove calls: The political ecology of a peasant corporate community in northwestern Mexico.* Tucson: University of Arizona Press.

Stoddart, D. R. 1965. Geography and the ecological approach: The ecosystem as a geographic principle and method. *Geography* 50: 242–51.

Tansley, A. G. 1935. The use and abuse of vegetation concepts and terms. *Journal of Ecology* 2: 194–202.

Thomas, W. L. Jr., ed. 1956. *Man's role in changing the face of the earth.* Chicago: University of Chicago Press.

Treacy, J. M. 1989. Agricultural terraces in Peru's Colca valley: Promises and problems of an ancient technology. In *Fragile lands of Latin America*, ed. J. O. Brower, 209–29. Boulder, Colo.: Westview Press.

———. 1994. Teaching water: Hydraulic management and terracing in Coporaque, the Colca valley, Peru. In *Irrigation at high altitudes: The social organization of water control systems in the Andes*, ed W. P. Mitchell and D. Guillet, 99–114. Washington, D.C.: The Society for Latin American Anthropology.

Turner, B. L. II. 1983. *Once beneath the forest: Prehistoric terracing in the Río Bec region of the Maya lowlands.* Boulder, Colo.: Westview Press.

———. 1989. The specialist-synthesis approach to the revival of geography: The case of cultural ecology. *Annals of the Association of American Geographers* 79: 88–100.

Vayda, A. P. 1983. Progressive contextualization: Methods for research in human ecology. *Human Ecology* 11: 265–81.

Vayda, A. P., and B. J. McKay. 1975. New directions in ecology and ecological anthropology. *Annual Review of Anthropology* 4: 293–306.

Waddell, E. 1972. *The mound builders: Agricultural practices, environment, and society in the Central Highlands of New Guinea.* Seattle: University of Washington Press.

———. 1975. How the Enga cope with frost: Responses to climatic perturbations in the central highlands of New Guinea. *Human Ecology* 3: 249–73.

———. 1977. The hazards of scientism: A review article. *Human Ecology* 5: 69–76.

Wagner, P. L. 1958. Nicoya: A cultural geography. *University of California Publications in Geography*, vol. 12: 195–250.

Wagner, P. L., and M. W. Mikesell. 1962. The themes of cultural geography. In *Readings in Cultural Geography*, ed. P. L. Wagner and M. W. Mikesell, 1–24. Chicago: University of Chicago Press.

Watts, M. 1983a. On the poverty of theory: Natural hazards research in context. In *Interpretations of calamity*, ed. K. Hewitt, 231–262. Boston: Allen and Unwin.

———. 1983b. *Silent violence: Food, famine, and peasantry in northern Nigeria.* Berkeley: University of California Press.

White, G. F. 1945. *Human adjustment to floods*. Chicago: University of Chicago, Department of Geography Research Paper No. 29.

————, ed. 1974. *Natural hazards: Local, national, global*. New York: Oxford University Press.

Williams, M. 1987. Sauer and "Man's Role in Changing the Face of the Earth." *Geographical Review* 77: 219–31.

Winterhalder, B. 1984. Reconsidering the ecosystem concept. *Reviews in Anthropology* 11: 310–13.

Wolf, E. R. 1972. Ownership and political ecology. *Anthropological Quarterly* 45: 201–205.

————. 1982. *Europe and the people without history*. Berkeley: University of California.

Worster, D. 1977. *Nature's economy: The roots of ecology*. San Francisco: Sierra Club Books.

————, ed. 1988. *The ends of the earth: Perspectives on modern environmental history*. Cambridge: Cambridge University Press.

Yapa, L. 1977. The green revolution: A diffusion model. *Annals of the Association of American Geographers* 67: 350–59.

————. 1979. Ecopolitical economy of the green revolution. *Professional Geographer* 31: 371–76.

Zimmerer, K. S. 1991a. Wetland production and smallholder persistence: Agricultural change in a highland Peruvian region. *Annals of the Association of American Geographers* 81: 443–63.

————. 1991b. The regional biogeography of native potato cultivars in highland Peru. *Journal of Biogeography* 18: 165–78.

————. 1993. Soil erosion and labor shortages in the Andes with special reference to highland Bolivia, 1950–1991: Implications for "conservation-with-development." *World Development* 21: 1659–75.

————. 1994a. Human geography and the "new ecology": The prospect and promise of integration. *Annals of the Association of American Geographers* 84: 108–25.

————. 1994b. Transforming Colquepata wetlands: Landscapes of knowledge and practice in Andean agriculture. In *Irrigation at high altitudes: The social organization of water control systems in the Andes*, ed. W. P. Mitchell and D. Guillet, 115–40. Washington, D.C.: The Society for Latin American Anthropology.

7

Ramifications of Region and Senses of Place

Jonathan M. Smith

Region and *place* are multifarious concepts; each can be used in several senses and at many levels of theoretical sophistication. *Place* in particular is a word of many senses, and *region* is not barren of metaphorical offspring. Such multiple senses of meaning can be likened to ramifying branches thrown out by a tree. Writing of such ramifications, Lewis notes that "historical circumstances often make one of them dominant during a particular period," and, therefore, "whenever we meet the word, our natural impulse will be to give it that sense" (Lewis 1967: 12, 13). Professional circumstances engender similar prejudice. In this essay I review a selected range of senses of region and place in the hope that this will tame the geographer's natural impulse to in every instance impute to *region* and *place* the geographer's senses of these words. I have not rendered the entire tree, only some of the principal limbs.

Place and *region* are in their most general sense concepts used to describe certain aspects of spatiality. *Place* denotes the fact that every physical body must occupy a position and in so doing preclude the occupation of that position by some other body. A *region* is a subdivision of something larger, more extensive. These general senses we may regard as the trunks of our conceptual trees; clearly, each is of ample circumference and capable of sprouting many branches. In both cases one of these will almost certainly be a geographic branch, since geography is concerned with positions in, and subdivisions of, an extensive portion of reality, but we cannot study the geographic branch in isolation, since all branches sway together.

189

A concept is a general idea that is used to understand a category of physical, psychic, imaginary, or supernatural phenomena. To have a concept is to understand a category: to understand what it includes and excludes and to understand the nature of the included items so as to relate to them in an appropriate manner. I have a concept of dogs, for instance, that is assembled from chance experiences and hearsay. This concept permits me to discriminate between dogs and cats and even between dogs and coyotes. Concepts, though, are not only for classification; they also advise those who hold them of an appropriate deportment. My concept of dogs is that some are friendly and others are vicious, and it advises me to approach an unfamiliar dog warily. People who utterly ignore, heedlessly embrace, or instantly flee a strange dog have, to my mind, a very poor concept of dogs. It is a poor concept because it advises an inappropriate deportment and causes those people to suffer surprising, painful, or arduous experiences that a superior concept would have spared them.

This is no less true for specialized concepts such as *region* and *place*. A geographer demonstrates understanding of these concepts by using them in a fashion deemed correct by some relevant audience. Poor concepts of region and place are those that lead the geographer to commit semantic blunders and misapprehensions, errors that call his or her scholarly competence into question; good concepts are those that avoid these embarrassments and earn the geographer a reputation for understanding. Good concepts of region and place are not, however, definite concepts, because region and place, like dogs, come in many shapes, sizes, and dispositions. Good concepts are flexible, ambiguous, suitable to any occasion, and fit for any eventuality.

What follows is a series of seven sections, each devoted to the use of the concepts of region and place in a particular book. Only three of these sections cover books by geographers, because I wish to tame the geographer's natural impulse to assume the geographic senses of *region* and *place* and to see these senses as independent of all the others. In most cases I have avoided works that offer a formal definition of either word, and I have emphasized instances of casual usage, because I believe authors write most honestly and lucidly in the passages they feel no one will notice.

Place and Region

Place is an old word, used in English before 1200, and derived from French, Latin, and Greek roots that mean a spot, broad street, or courtyard. It largely supplanted the Old English words *stow* and *stede* (Bosworth and Toller 1898).

The first of these, which sometimes indicated a holy place, remains with us in words such as *stowaway* or in place names such as Stow on the Wold ("place on the high ground cleared of forest"); the second survives in words such as *instead* or *farmstead* or in place names such as Hamstead ("home place") (Ekwall 1960).

Physical theories of place have suffered from a certain ambivalence over the precise meaning of the term. On the one hand, place is taken to refer to position (Greek *thesis*); on the other, it is taken to refer to the surface of a containing body in contact with a contained body (Greek *topos*). The first sense of place as position is sometimes called *formal place* or *rational place*, and it is described using a fixed system of coordinates. St. Thomas Aquinas, for instance, described rational place as a position at a certain distance from the earth's immovable center in the direction of some point on the immovable empyrean sphere (Duhem 1985). Sir Isaac Newton described the same concept as "absolute place," an immovable position in absolute space (Koyré 1957). The geographer's concept of absolute location apparently sprang from this branch.

Aristotle is credited with the second definition of *place*, material place, which he defined as the boundary of the containing body in contact with the contained body. The concept is certainly older. Because it presents place as a sort of cavity in which a body is lodged, material place is similar to environment. Indeed, medieval writers frequently referred to the containing body as an ambient body. A material place is a dwelling place, a home, or a housing. It is this sense of place, as we will see, that allowed later writers to use the word *niche* to denote the concept Charles Darwin denoted as *place*. Because material place embraces a body, it is possible to speak of a place "knowing" an occupant. In Job 7:10, for instance, we read: "He shall return no more to his house, neither shall his place know him any more." This sense of *place* is evident into the nineteenth century. In *Wuthering Heights* (1847), for instance, the punishment proposed as proper to the unpardonable sin of tedium is to pull the speaker down and "crush him to atoms, that the place which knows him may know him no more" (Brontë 1992: 41). The geographer's concept of sense of place apparently sprang from this branch.

Region is also an old word, used in English before 1300 and derived from French and Latin roots that mean a ruler and, by extension, the boundaries that rulers draw and the tracts of land or sky that boundaries enclose. In the eighteenth century there seems to have been some agreement that a geographical region was the territory of a people. In John Kersey's *Dictionarum Anglo-Britanicum* (1708) it is written that "in geography" a region is "a large extent of land, inhabited by many people of the same nation" (Kersey 1969;

see also Buchanan 1967). From this it appears that the formal region of contemporary geography originated as a means to understand ethnic territories before these became coterminous with the state. In an age of maritime exploration and imperialism it is not surprising to find that region also indicated a certain extent of coastline.

Region was also used to describe delineated portions of the heavens, the atmosphere, or the body. Kersey lists each of these senses, which we might call the cosmologic, atmospheric, and anatomic senses of region (Kersey 1969). The first of these is based on the Ptolemaic model of the cosmos, which Kersey describes as consisting of an "Elementary Region," a "Planetary Region," and an "Ethereal or Celestial Region." In the nineteenth century we find the novelist Nathaniel Hawthorne using *region* in this sense. For instance, the evil and earthly Professor Westerwelt of *The Blithesdale Romance* is described as cognizant of "whatever happened, in regions near or remote. The boundaries of his power were defined by the verge of the pit of Tartarus, on the one hand, and the third sphere of the celestial world, on the other" (Hawthorne 1964: 188). Hell is frequently alluded to as a region, as in *Fanshawe*, where Edward Walcott awakes, only to wonder whether "he was now in those regions" to which death in a duel would condemn him (Hawthorne 1964: 408). In *The Scarlet Letter* there is uncertainty whether Roger Chillingworth's inspiration for revenge is "celestial, or from what other region," and many of his fellow citizens suppose that the fire in his lab was brought "from the lower regions, and . . . fed with infernal fuel" (Hawthorne 1962: 140, 127). Similar allusions are made to the region of heaven, which Hawthorne variously describes as "the better regions," "the regions of the blest," "an upper region," or "a higher or purer region" (Hawthorne 1965: 245; 1962: 143; 1968: 164, 269).

The vertical arrangement of regions is repeated in Kersey's division of the atmosphere into an upper region, which vaults the highest mountains; a middle region, which extends from the mountaintops to the lower air; and the lower region, "that Part of the Air which we live in, and which is bounded by the Reflection of the sunbeams." As we will see, Ellen Churchill Semple uses *region* in this sense. Kersey suggests that this same vertical arrangement can be extended to the human body but does not develop the point. By the end of the eighteenth century the term *region* had acquired the sense of "a part of the body, within" (Sheridan 1967). Once again we find this sense alive in the writings of Nathaniel Hawthorne, who described the "lower region of his face," "the region round his heart," "the gastric region," and "the region of the thorax" (Hawthorne 1965: 116, 204, 268, 272).

The concept of material place, and the use of the term *region* to describe a symbolic or psychological order, opens the way for the use of these words as terms of evaluation. Place is not simply a location, but a condition; it is granted not on the basis of contingencies, but on the basis of right or justice; it is adhered to not for matters of convenience, but out of a sense of obligation. As Hawthorne expresses it in *The Scarlet Letter*, there can be "a kindred" relation between a place and its occupant, as when "long connection of a family with one spot, as its place of birth and burial, creates a kindred between the human being and the locality, quite independent of any charm in the scenery or moral circumstances that surround him" (Hawthorne 1962: 11). Likewise, region is not only a subdivision of space, but is also an aspect of existence or an attitude of mind. Hawthorne describes the pensive mind as "deep in its own region" and empathy as transportation "into the regions of another's mind" (Hawthorne 1962: 239, 248). Hester Prynne's stigma, the scarlet letter, prohibits entry to conventional society but serves as "a passport to regions where other women dared not tread" (Hawthorne 1962: 199). Sorrow is "a far-off region," a "dim region," "a remote and inaccessible region," "the unwholesome region of remorse" (Hawthorne 1968: 64, 66, 205, 273).

Place and Justice in the Authorized Version of the Bible

The ramified senses of *place* are well developed in the Authorized Version of the Bible, which was published by special command of King James I in 1611 and which has subsequently left a deep impression on the phraseology, diction, and cadences of English (Lowes 1936). *Region* on the other hand is almost entirely restricted to its geographical sense, as a district or vicinity or as the territory of a king or people. *Place* is frequently used in a similar, strictly geographical sense to describe a position, city, or country; however, there is also a very clear tendency to use *place* to indicate the concept of proper place. This is the sense identified by Trusler in his dictionary of 1766, where he writes that the difference between the verbs place and put is that place has the more limited sense, "meaning to put, orderly, and, in a proper place" (Trusler 1970: 178).

The concept of proper place rests, it seems, on three ideas: that place is home, that this home is adequate or inadequate to its occupant's needs, and that this place should be suitable to its occupant's rank. These ideas are applied not only to humans but are extended to all things, "all his works in all places of his dominion" (Psalms 103:22). Underlying this idea is a concept of cosmic, geographic, social, and moral order based on stability, the adherence of persons, peoples, things, and intangibles to their proper places. The corollary of this is that eviction, exile, and wandering without habitation indicate a deterioration of order, as does the removal of things or intangibles from the place proper to them or the introduction of things or intangibles into improper places. Such dislocations are a mark of human sin and the divine wrath it provokes. The anger of God thus "shaketh the earth out of her place"; infuriated, he "will shake the heavens, and the earth shall remove out of her place." (Job 9:6; Isaiah 13:13). Not only the earth is shaken out of its place; being out of place is pervasive throughout creation. This is true even of intangibles. "And moreover I saw under the sun the place of judgement, that wickedness was there; and the place of righteousness, that iniquity was there" (Ecclesiastes 3:16).

The theme of eviction is, of course, central to the human condition as this is described in the Bible, since expulsion from the garden begins human history. The importance of place, the pain of its loss, and the yearning to return is further enhanced by the theme of exile, a legacy of the Israelites' geographic position between the empires of Egypt and Babylon. Generations raised on the Bible must have absorbed this sense of proper place and of the happiness of those who knew and occupied the place that was proper to them; but they were also told that they were exiles, lost and ignorant of their proper place. Knowledge of place was the province of God, as he makes clear in the questions with which he taunted Job. "Where is the way where light dwelleth," God asks, "and as for darkness, where is the place thereof that thou shouldst take it to the bound thereof, and that thou shouldst know the paths to the house thereof" (Job 38:19–20).

To be deprived of or removed from place is to disappear or be destroyed. The unfaithful friends of Job, for instance, like a stream in summer's heat "are consumed out of their place," and mortal man is like the flower that dies "and the place thereof shall know it no more" (Job 6:17; Psalms 103:16). In Nebuchadnezzar's dream the monarch image of gold, silver, brass, iron, and clay is smashed, but to convey its utter annihilation it is said that the fragments were blown away and "no place was found for them" (Daniel 2:35). A similar phrase describes John's dream of the annihilation of creation on the day of judgment, when the earth and heavens flew from the face of God "and there was no place found for them" (Revelations 20:11).

Whatever the cosmic significance of place, the Bible suggests that place should be understood as adequate or inadequate to the needs of its occupants. This is based on the sense of place as room or room in which to live. It was in this sense that Isaiah enjoined Israel to "enlarge the place of thy tent" (Isaiah 54:2), that Jeremiah warned of the hecatomb that would require burials in Tophet "til there be no place" (Jeremiah 19:11), and that Zechariah foresaw the gathering of the Israelites back to the land of Gilead and Lebanon, til "place shall not be found for them" (Zechariah 10:10). Because place is understood as room, a difficult or unenviable place is described as cramped or narrow. The sons of the prophets, for instance, complained to Elisha that "the place where we dwell with thee is too strait for us" (II Kings 6:1), and Elihu advised Job that, as God delivers the poor, "even so would he have removed thee out of the strait into a broad place" (Job 36:16). In the Psalms the Lord delivers the faithful "into a large place" (Psalms 18:19). Standing behind this is the unmistakable presence of agricultural land, the abundance or paucity of which figures so largely in the sum of human happiness.

Place is also rank, or position in the social order. In Luke, for instance, the wedding guest who has taken a seat at the table above that suited to his station is ordered to "give this man place" when a more worthy guest arrives (Luke 14:9). The archaic phrase *give place* means to step aside and yield to better claims. It is an expression of justice, as when the water at the bottom of the sea gives place to a sunken stone. The opposite of this is to deny the justice of rival claims, to stand one's ground, or, in Anglo-Saxon, to stand steady or steadfast. Paul thus writes of the false brethren "to whom we gave place by subjection, no, not for an hour," and he enjoins the Ephesians "neither give place to the devil" (Galatians 2.5; Ephesians 4.26). To give place means simply to yield, and one can yield to either right or might, as is evidenced by the gallant and grim senses of the word *surrender*. This is seldom apparent to the victors, who see in conquest eloquent testimony to right. Such would seem to be Adam Smith's meaning when he writes that the natives of North America "give place to the new settlers" (Smith 1976: 564, 567).

Region and Place in the Manifold Geography of John Milton

It is widely believed that in former times humans thought that the earth was flat. There is little evidence that this was so and much that it was not so, but the belief persists; it is too important an item of evidence in the case for progress and the superiority of all things modern to be discarded. Belief in a flat earth is one sure mark of a backwards ignoramus, recognition that it is round is a badge of citizenship in the modern world; and yet, in at least one sense, no human geography has been flatter than our own, our interest being limited to the exceedingly thin, or, we might say, flat, rind of the biosphere (Hartshorne 1959: 22–25). This flattened geography is nowhere more evident than in our use of the terms *region* and *place*, whose only conceivable arrangement is horizontal.

The world was in the past a thicker place; regions were indeed stacked one on top of the next, and serious questions were asked about the tops and bottoms of regions. Since it was widely appreciated that the earth, and indeed the entire universe, was spherical, it was readily understood that the bottoms of regions were always convex and the tops of regions were always concave. The most important boundary of this sort, as Aristotle argued, was marked by the orbit of the moon. Above this were the heavens, the region of regularity and permanence, below this the sublunar regions of earth and sky, the region of imperfect regularity and change. In the late fifties B.C., Cicero described the view from the topmost region:

> Do you not see what regions you have entered! Observe: everything is constructed in nine spheres or globes. The outermost is celestial . . . upon it are affixed those everlasting journeys of the revolving stars, and subject to it are the seven spheres which ply their paths in motions reverse and contrary to those of the sky. . . . Below this body the sun . . . holds sway in the mid-region. . . . On the lowest sphere rides the moon, and everything below is subject to death and decay save the souls bestowed on the race of mankind. (quoted in Vives 1989: 75–77)

This model of the cosmos informed most imaginative efforts to represent the universe at least to the seventeenth century (Lewis 1964), and it is fundamental to John Milton's epic, *Paradise Lost* (1667), a poem particularly rich in geographical imagery. Milton did, of course, conceive of regions and places in the geographer's senses because "the subject of geography was full of appeal to his curiosity and imagination" (Hanford 1929: 101). This is clear in *A Brief History of Muscovia* (1642), which is really a geography of "the most northern Region of Europe reputed civil," in *The History of Britain* (1670), and throughout his polemical writings (Milton 1971, vol. 8: 475). Milton was, however, never slow to represent psychological states or moral conditions as regions or places. In *Areopagitica* (1644), for instance, he defends a free press by arguing that virtue is impossible without a knowledge of vice and that uncensored texts permit us to "with lesse danger scout into regions of sin and falsity" (Milton 1971, vol. 2: 517).

Milton's concept of place is more complicated, since he seems to have believed that every thing, every creature, and every person has a proper place, a place appropriate to its nature. Milton thus writes of "the place of evil, Hell" (*Paradise Lost*, hereafter *P.L.* vi: 276). Should their nature change, so would their place. He thus speaks of Lucifer's insurrectionists, "whom their place knows here [in heaven] no more" (*P.L.* vii: 144). Place is, in fact, for Milton a fundamental feature of creation, which, along with time and dimension, serves to distinguish it from primordial chaos. Standing at the gates of Hell, surveying the womb and grave of nature, Satan sees:

> *the hoary deep, a dark*
> *Illimitable ocean, without bound,*
> *Without dimension; where length breadth and highth*
> *And time, and place, are lost; where eldest* Night

And Chaos, *Ancestors of Nature*, hold
Eternal anarchy. (P.L. ii: 891–94)

The act and the fact of creation are for Milton matters of putting things in place; thus, when God calls confusion to order, each star "had his place appointed" (*P.L.* iii: 720). Creation caused a rushing of the elements to their proper places. "Then founded, then conglob'd," he writes, "like things to like; the rest to several place/disparted" (*P.L.* vii: 240), and some lines later God commands "be gathered now ye Waters under Heav'n/ Into one place" (*P.L.* vii: 284). The concept of proper place also had a social aspect, as in "the place" established by God for Adam over Eve (*P.L.* x: 148). Place is important for Milton because it is the expression of justice in creation, of the moral order that is counterpart to physical and temporal order. We learn of Hell: "Such place eternal justice had prepared/For those rebellious" (*P.L.* i: 70).

Place is problematic when applied to Adam and Eve. Their proper place was, evidently, Eden, "this happy place," as Uriel says, "this delicious place"; but the Fall changed their nature, and properly "a place/ Before his [Adam's] eyes appear'd, sad, noisome, dark" (*P.L.* iv: 562, 729; xi: 477). This "dark region," as Milton elsewhere described it, is proper to human minds in a state of rebellion. It is thus foretold that the garden will be swept away by the Flood, "to teach thee that God attributes to place/ No sanctity, if none be thither brought/ by men" (*P.L.* xi: 836). As Satan observes in a famous line, "the mind is its own place" (*P.L.* i: 254).

Milton's concept of region is not consistent, and it seems at times to mean little more than a portion of creation. Hell is in some passages a region, as when Satan asks: "Is this the Region, this the Soil, the Clime. . . . That we must change for Heav'n"; but he later discovers in it a more complex geography of "many a Region dolorous" (*P.L.* i: 242; ii: 619). Beyond the gates of Hell lies an "unknown Region" that is similarly susceptible to subdivision (*P.L.* ii: 443). It includes the "eternal regions" of heaven and the multiple regions of the void, "Regions," as the Archangel Raphael describes them, "to which/ All thy Dominion, *Adam*, is no more/ Than this Garden is to all the Earth" (*P.L.* iii: 349; v: 749–51). The earth, too, has its regions, primary among them Eden, "the World's first Region" (*P.L.* iii: 562).

In Milton's cosmology the creation has dimension, or space, as one of its three defining characteristic; regions are subdivisions of this space; but his regions are in some passages very like his places, in that they are the proper abode of certain things and an unfit home to others. Hell thus is described as "Regions of sorrow, doleful shades, where peace/ And rest can never dwell" (i: 65–66), while the "fields and regions" of the sun "Breathe forth Elixir pure" (iii: 606, 607). The mind itself is a region, hospitable to some thoughts and hostile to others, as Adam and Eve discover when they are evicted from Eden, "Thir [sic] inward State of Mind, calm Region once/ And full of Peace, now tost and turbulent" (ix: 1125).

Adam Smith and the Marketplace

Adam Smith did not think of himself as a geographer, and he made no explicit mention of geography in his most renown work, An Inquiry into the Nature and Causes of the Wealth of Nations (1776). It is, nevertheless, a book whose theory is profoundly geographical, and it is today, perhaps, more salient to an understanding of modern geographies than it is to an understanding of modern economies. It is widely recognized that nothing has more deeply altered the meaning of place than the emergence of the capitalist world system, and thus it is appropriate to inquire into the meaning of place for that system's great advocate and architect. Smith's specific contribution is to reduce all places to marketplaces and to visualize geography as little more than a rugged terrain of fluctuating prices for labor, stock (capital), and rent.

It is well known that Adam Smith was a proponent of laissez-faire capitalism who denounced any interference in the free operation of the market and criticized the policy of Europe for "not leaving things at perfect liberty" (Smith 1976: 135). He argued that the factors that yield the necessities of life would be brought to market if only urban corporations and nation-states would remove impediments to their movement. Another way to state this is to say that residents of a place, be it a city or a nation, must renounce any prerogative to the wealth (objects and instruments of value) of that place in order to ensure their own prosperity. It is as inefficient to grant residents any special claim on a place as it is for a place to make any special claims on its residents. Since Smith wrote his treatise prior to the achievement of significant productivity gains through mechanization, factory organization, or the removal of physical obstacles to overland transportation, this elimination of legal obstacles to trade was, perhaps, the only viable strategy to enhance productivity.

The foundation of Smith's theory of wealth is, of course, the division of labor, a systematic specialization of tasks that results in enhanced collective output; the only limit on the minuteness of the tasks into which the fabrication of a product may be divided, and consequently on the improvements to productivity that might be enjoyed, is the extent of the market open to "any particular place" (Smith 1976: 680). As the range of a place widens, the skills of its individual inhabitants narrow. This insight leads Smith to anticipate central-place theory and note that, as market size increases and the division of labor is elaborated, different types of places come into being. In making this argument he is suggesting that we understand any particular place in austerely abstract terms, as a distinct ensemble of investment and employment opportunities. The porter must, for example, seek out the great town, for he can "find employment and subsistence in no other place" (Smith 1976: 31).

A great part of Smith's book is devoted to a discussion of price, but since price is always understood as a function of the time and place of sale, it might be said that this is in large part a discussion of place. Indeed, the entire discussion of price is punctuated with the phrase "in the same time and place." Smith thus argues that "at the same time and place" the real price of a commodity (its equivalent in goods and services) is in exact proportion to the nominal price of that same commodity (its equivalent in money). As a consequence, profits accrue only to those merchants who sell what they have purchased at a different time (speculation) or in a different place (trade) (Smith 1976: 63). Similarly, the cost of labor, stock, and rent will together set the natural price of a commodity "at the time and place" it is made, while factors of supply and demand will set the market price at the time and place it is sold (Smith 1976: 72).

Having established the benefits to productivity that accrue to places to which a large market is open and the benefits to prices that accrue to places open to many markets, Smith is in a position to argue for the free circulation of labor, capital, and commodities. As he says in a more specific context of silver and gold, they should move "from the places where they are cheap, to those where they are dear, from the places where they exceed, to those where they fall short of . . . effectual demand" (Smith 1976: 435). He repeatedly criticizes restrictions on the movement of "labor and stock, both from employment to employment, and from place to place" (Smith 1976, 135). The geography he describes is, in fact, geography as it is perceived by a merchant who, "it has been said very properly, is not necessarily the citizen of any particular country" because "it is in great measure indifferent to him from what place he carries on his trade. . . . " (Smith 1976: 426). Although Smith notes that "a man is of all sorts of luggage the most difficult to be transported," he appears to look forward to a day when everyone has learned to understand place in this cosmopolitan sense (Smith 1976: 93). Too bad, to take a line from Milton's *History of Britain*, that "they who through weakness of Sex or Age, or love of the place went not along, perish'd by the Enemie (Milton 1971: 78).

Charles Darwin and the Fitting Place

If Adam Smith reduced place to price, Charles Darwin reduced place to food. Place was for him a place at nature's table, which any given species was more or less fit to occupy. He is remembered for proposing that evolution is governed by the survival of the fittest (although the phrase is Spencer's); however, the meaning of that memorable phrase has been, I believe, obscured by confusion over the meaning of the word *fit*. Darwin's *fit* is the fit of a gem to its setting, not the *fit* of the fitness center or the exercise enthusiast. Fitness for Darwin is fitness to place, and it has much more to do with being well adapted than it does with being well exercised. It is for this reason that he writes that "each being assuredly is well fitted for its place in nature"; it is for this reason that a seed that falls on a spot optimal for germination falls, according to Darwin, in a "fitting place" (Barrett and Freeman 1987: 179, 66).

The central mechanism of evolution proposed by Darwin is natural selection, which is a process that results from the struggle and competition for places. "All organic beings are striving," he writes, "to seize on each place in the economy of nature," and every species "is constantly suffering enormous destruction . . . from enemies or from competitors for the same place and food" (Barrett and Freeman 1987: 102, 69). Contests occur over "any unoccupied or ill-occupied place in nature," which is to say "some place" that is "not so perfectly occupied as it might be," and the progress of natural selection is largely determined by "the nature of the places which are either unoccupied or not perfectly occupied by other beings" (Barrett and Freeman 1987: 472, 102, 119). These deadly contests occur most frequently between species that "fill nearly the same place in the economy of nature," those "fitting nearly the same place in the natural economy of the land" (Barrett and Freeman 1987: 76, 173).

There is in Darwin a sort of justice in the assignment of places, an affirmation that natural selection at least temporarily grants each species the place it deserves, the place that is fitting. It is certainly far removed from the moral selection of "eternal justice" that we find in the King James Bible and *Paradise Lost*, but the concept of place is not fundamentally different. *Place* clearly carries connotations of propriety, suitability, and appropriateness.

Ellen Churchill Semple and Homologous Regions

In Semple's *Influences of Geographical Environment* (1911) the concept of region is imperfectly developed, and the concept of place, although in some ways implicit, is not overtly employed. Given Darwin's looming presence in the book this omission may appear strange; however, Semple (following Ratzel) reinterprets Darwin and changes the competition for place into a competition for space. "The struggle for existence means a struggle for space," she writes, and her book describes historical movement as a manifestation of "the struggle for space in which humanity has forever been engaged" (Semple 1911: 170, 188).

Semple's concept of region is not readily apparent, in part because it is developed in widely scattered passages. It is further obscured by her use of several related words—*lands, districts, tracts, zones* and *belts*—that may or may not be intended as exact synonyms. Finally, *region* itself is for her a flexible word that in some places signifies a mere portion of terrestrial reality and in others denotes a theoretical entity. Despite this inconsistency and the fact that Semple nowhere imposes on herself the lexical constraint of a definition, the concept of region is fundamental to her work. Region combines the idea of "territory," "mere area," or the spaces over which humanity has immemorially struggled, with the contents of these territories, areas, and spaces, with the "specific geographic conditions," environment, milieu, or geographical factor (Semple 1911: 51). This is consistent with Darwin's usage, as when he argues that a species differentiates by becoming "adapted to the conditions of life in its own region" (Barrett and Freeman 1987: 173). Regions are geographically localized conditions of life, whether these be hard, as in a region of "hopeless sterility," or congenial, as in a "fruitful region" (Semple 1911: 54, 500).

Anthropogeography studies "existence in various regions of terrestrial space," writes Semple: "given a region, what is its living envelope, asks anthropogeography" (Semple 1911: 10, 79). More specifically, anthropogeography proposed to identify types of regions, each corresponding to a type of condition and each supporting a type of existence or "living envelope." Semple described these typical regions as homologous regions. "The continents show . . . homologous regions of lowlands, uplands, plateaus and mountains, each district sustaining definite relations to the natural terrace above or below it, and displaying a history corresponding to that of its counterpart in some distant part of the world, due to similar relations" (Semple 1911: 475).

As this passage makes clear, "anthropogeography has to do primarily with the forms and relief of the land"; its regions are those of the geomorphologist (Semple 1911: 473). This is evident in several of the chapter headings— "Coast Peoples," "The Anthropology of Rivers," "Island Peoples," "Plains, Steppes and Deserts"—which are in fact the names of homologous regions, and it accounts for Semple's otherwise bizarre preoccupation with mountain, Alpine, and highland regions. The Netherlands are a "region," apparently, because their levels of "water-soaked alluvium" are geomorphologically distinct from the surrounding "solid ground of older and higher land" (Semple 1911: 245). Of course not all the earth is made up of "natural regions with sharply defined boundaries, like islands and oases," but this does not deter the anthropogeographer since "even the slightest surface irregularities . . . can draw faint dividing lines among the population" (Semple 1911: 67, 480).

Semple also describes "the great climatic regions of the earth." She refers repeatedly to the undistinguished careers of the "hottest regions" and writes of "arctic and sub-arctic regions inimical to all historical development" (Semple 1911: 661, 263). Of course she also describes the "regions of better climate" that have so often tempted barbarian invasion, the "temperate regions" so remarkable for the "unflinching industry" of their inhabitants (Semple 1911: 190, 630).

Semple employs the term *region* to describe altitudinal zonation as well, a usage approved, as we have seen, by Kersey in 1708. With this in mind she writes of "the hotter regions of the plains" and of Switzerland where "half of the country lies above the region where agriculture is possible" (Semple 1911: 489, 564). Altitudinal zonation particularly interests Semple because the presence of several environments within a small compass perfectly exemplifies her theory that areas with "an abundance of . . . naturally defined regions . . . serve as cradles of civilization" (Semple 1911: 394).

Mountain regions, coastal regions, and steppe regions are examples of what we might call formally homologous regions. Semple presents a second sort, which we might call functionally homologous regions. She describes the former as "habitat," "specific geographic location," or "natural location," that is, approximations of the concept of site; the latter she describes as "mediate" or "vicinal" location, that is, approximations of the concept of situation. "A people has, therefore, a twofold location, an immediate one, based upon their actual territory, and a mediate or vicinal one, growing out of its relations to the countries nearest them" (Semple 1911: 132).

Of the functionally homologous regions perhaps the most interesting is the "transit region," those inhospitable or uninhabitable expanses of upland, desert, or sea where humans move but do not settle (Semple 1911: 529, 541, 542). All such regions give rise to homologous populations, a class of "professional carriers," and homologous places, "the typical outfitting point such as springs up on the margin of any pure transit region" (Semple 1911: 531, 550). Transit regions assume importance when they are situated between "complementary trade regions," most notably when one of these is located in the tropical and the other in the temperate zone (Semple 1911: 616, 554). Vicinal location also gives rise to "border regions," the insecure sphere of a people's territory that is subject to incursion, conquest, and colonization by neighboring peoples (Semple 1911: 78). Like transit regions, these foster homologous populations "differentiated from the core or central group through assimilation to a new group which meets and blends with it along the frontier" (Semple 1911: 117).

A central theme in Semple is that "the struggle for land means a struggle also for the best land, which therefore falls to the share of the strongest peoples" (note the loss of the Darwinian sense of fitness) (Semple 1911: 113). This leads her to develop two concepts of functionally homologous regions: the "region of migration" and the "region of retreat." Examples of the former are accessible, fertile, salubrious, and otherwise desirable: they are the prizes of the struggle for the best land. Semple is, however, far more interested in the latter, where there is "close in-breeding" rather than a "mingling of peoples," because, for her, it is isolation and not interaction that accounts for cultural variety (Semple 1911: 115, 45). The geographic conditions of a mountain region, for instance, "strong in their power to isolate, create the conditions for inevitable variation" (Semple 1911: 596). Regions of retreat are the last resort of "weaklings" and "displaced peoples" who seek "to place between themselves and their pursuers a barrier of sea or desert or mountains" (Semple 1911: 113, 403, 94). Isolated and impoverished, they become "regions of retardation," inhabited by "'retarded provisional peoples'" who eke out an existence and await "the expansion of European peoples over the retarded regions of the world" (Semple 1911: 530, 177, 120).

Clearly, Semple sees the concept of region primarily as a geographical aspect of the concept of race. Following Tylor, she argues that "certain races belong to certain regions" and "every geographical region of strongly marked character . . . attracts certain racial or economic elements, and repels others" (Semple 1911: 391, 160–61). A coast region, for instance, "is a peculiar habitat"; it belongs to a coast people, a homologous type characterized by "ethnic amalgamation" and transcultural inventions such as a lingua franca (Semple 1911: 271, 303). The peoples of mountain regions are also homologous. Independent, with a "repugnance to central authority," they are "isolated peoples to whom both the idea and the technique of combined movement were foreign" (Semple 1911: 595, 495). Frugal by necessity and frequently pressed beyond parsimony to exodus, whether as emigrants or mercenaries, or to thievery and brigandage, mountain folk are for Semple particularly illustrative of the connection between a homologous region and its "living envelope."

Richard Hartshorne and the Integration of Total Reality

In the middle decades of the twentieth century many geographers sought to define and clarify the concept of region, their hope being that the region, understood as "a unitary concrete object existing in reality," would provide geography with a definite object of study and ensure the field's status as a "systematic science" (Hartshorne 1959: 31). These hopes were, as Richard Hartshorne puts it, "short-lived." One result of this activity was that geographers began to "use the term 'region' for a number of different concepts"

(Hartshorne 1959: 129). Semantic confusion was worsened by recognition of certain weaknesses in these concepts. Even their defenders acknowledged them poorly suited to hypothesis building, prediction, and verification and recognized that those who took the region for their object of study might well entertain a "fear of loosing scholarly caste" (Finch 1939: 6).

Richard Hartshorne's explications of the regional concept are widely regarded as the most thorough and rigorous in the English language (Entrikin and Brunn 1989). I focus here on his *Perspective on the Nature of Geography* (1959), his mature reflection on *The Nature of Geography* (1939), and the controversy it helped incite. Of the books reviewed here this is the only methodological work. Unlike the authors discussed above, Hartshorne approaches the concept of region self-consciously, aware that he is being watched. I deviate from the rule of preferring casual to self-conscious usage in this case because such self-conscious usage of terms has become such a conspicuous feature of late twentieth-century geographic discourse.

Hartshorne's understanding of region is rooted in the conviction, derived from Hettner and more distantly from Ritter's notion of *Zusammenhang*, that geography exists to study the integration of "total reality" (Hartshorne 1959: 33). Unlike Semple, who, following Davis, limits her inquiry to the integration of organic and inorganic elements, Hartshorne argues that geography "studies phenomena of unlimited variety in interrelationships of the greatest variety" (Hartshorne 1959: 34). Geographers are free to study "integrations of inorganic and organic elements as well as social ones," so it is proper that they investigate "all kinds of things in all kinds of combinations" (Hartshorne 1959: 125, 160). He does, however, impose his own restriction on this otherwise daunting mandate. He limits the concern of the field to the integrations "which vary from place to place" (Hartshorne 1959: 74).

Hartshorne's central interest is, in fact, in places, not regions; following Vidal de la Blache he regarded geography as, essentially, "the study of places" (Hartshorne 1959: 116, 157). Places are integrated, internally and externally, and geography, the study of "integration in terms of place," attends both "to the integration of phenomenon in place and to the integration of areas" (Hartshorne 1959: 36, 114). Internal integration of phenomena is responsible for the "character of places," external integration for the "interconnection of places" (Hartshorne 1959: 137).

The basic unit of analysis for Hartshorne is the element complex, "an elementary integration of two or more dissimilar elements closely dependent on each other" (Hartshorne 1959: 123). He offers as an example the Corn Belt farm as "an integration of types of landholding, fields, barns, machine cultivation, and particular crop and livestock combinations . . . in close relations with other conditions of soil, relief and climate" (Hartshorne 1959: 125).

Despite the idiosyncrasies of individuals and cultural groups, he regards these as generic concepts. Once several element complexes have been identified, it is necessary, Hartshorne writes, to attempt their combination "in a complex, though necessarily looser, integration of a higher order" (Hartshorne 1959: 126). These partial integrations are known as a segment (Hartshorne 1959: 74, 116). "A complex of loosely interrelated segments" together constitute "a region within which the over-all integration varies less than it does over the entire area" (Hartshorne 1959: 114, 127).

Hartshorne is careful to emphasize that geographers study integration, not regions; regions are merely "creations of the student's mind," convenient spatial representations of "the integration under study" (Hartshorne 1959: 160, 129). Most regions are, in fact, no more than "the areal expression of a logical generalization of process relationships" (Hartshorne 1959: 133). These logical generalizations take two forms. They may identify "significant similarities in the character of places" and group these similar places in uniform or formal regions defined by "homogeneity of character," or they may identify the "location-relationship of reciprocal connections among places" and combine these connected places in functional regions defined by "degree of interconnection" (Hartshorne 1959: 130).

These concepts must not, however, "be confused with what we commonly call regional geography," that is the study of "an area that is in some particular way distinctive from other areas" (Hartshorne 1959: 129, 145). Regional geography studies distinctive areas rather than particular integrations that vary from place to place, but it is no less dependent on the concept of integration. Regional studies in fact "analyze the most complex integrations" and "the maximum complex of interrelations" to provide "an integration . . . of the structural patterns presented by separate topical studies" (Hartshorne 1959: 139, 127). Such regions are generalizations based on judgment rather than logic, and delimitation of these "divisions of area which are neither formal or functional regions" will require "a large number of compromises," since they are derived using "no technical concept" (Hartshorne 1959: 141–42).

Disintegration and the Distinctive Socio-Spatial Formation

Geographers continue to use the concepts of region and place in spite of the fact that they have "occupied an ambiguous position in the conceptual landscape of twentieth-century social science" (Entrikin 1991: 27). Johnston, for instance, has endorsed the concept of place and a regional perspective as a unifying theme for a fracturing field, and the new manual of national geography standards insists that the concepts of region and place are fundamental to the "geographically informed person" (Johnston 1991; National Geography Standards Project 1994). Agnew has argued that "the concept of place," understood as "the physical and social contexts for action," is necessary to any understanding of "space and society as inextricably intertwined" (Agnew 1993: 261).

In order to gain some sense of the concepts as they have been recently employed, this section will consider two books: Massey's *Spatial Divisions of Labor* (1984) and Gregory and Urry's edited anthology *Social Relations and Spatial Structures* (1985). Massey's book embodies many of the important conceptual changes of recent decades, while essays selected from the anthology permit amplification and corroboration of these changes. The use of two books in this section also serves to recognize important changes in the way that concepts are formed and used in geography. Casual usage such as Semple's is for the most part gone, replaced almost entirely by a self-conscious technical vocabulary. Gone too is the calm, deliberate, and authoritative tone of Hartshorne; in its place we find a committee of individuals whose conceptual accord is always partial and provisional.

Today's authors may decline to speak with one voice on many matters, but they are united in their insistence that their usages of the terms *region* and *place* must not be confused with the usages of the past. Theirs is not, by their own account, a cowardly "retreat 'back to basics,'" but rather a bold advance "at the conceptual vanguard of the discipline's contribution to the social sciences" (Pudup 1988: 369). "Places and regions . . . are the essence of traditional geographic inquiry," admits Pred, but, "until recently, they have been conceptualized as little more than frozen scenes for human activity" (Pred 1985: 337). Cooke simply scraps all existing versions of "the vexed concept of region" and begins "moving toward a working definition of the category 'region,'" taking the unlikely figure of Antonio Gramsci as his guide (Cooke 1985: 213, 214).

Changes in the real world provide much of the impetus for changes in the concept of region. Of particular importance is the fundamental restructuring of the global economy that began in the years just after publication of Hartshorne's *Perspective on the Nature of Geography* (1959) and which, over the course of the ensuing quarter century, largely dismantled the metropolitan regions that the concept of functional region was invented to describe (Hartshorne 1959: 134). Urry, for instance, discards the concept of region because it supposes "coherent regional economies," which no longer exist (Urry 1985: 34). The economies of former regional centers have, by his account, disintegrated, both internally and externally, as economies of agglomeration have weakened and output has shifted from the regional to the global market. Although "regional spaces" may, in Harvey's description, "hang together as some kind of structured coherence within a totality," revolutions in transportation and communication technologies have rendered their boundaries "highly porous and unstable" and made "interregional interdependence more significant than a regionally defined coherence" (Harvey 1985: 146, 147). The "structured regional coherence" of the integrated regions of the past was, it now appears, nothing more than a transitory manifestation of particular "technologically-determined spatial constraints" (Harvey 1985: 150).

" 'Regions,' " Massey writes, "are constantly reproduced in shifting form" as a result of "the spatial reorganization that is an important aspect of industrial reorganization" (Massey 1984: 195, 196). Existing regional concepts are increasingly inadequate as, in Harvey's words, "patterns of regional coherence are thrown into disarray" (Harvey 1985: 157). Formal regions, or "the concentration of particular regions . . . in the production of particular goods, became less marked," Massey writes, as decentralization of production and its "division between regions" allowed each divisible stage in the production process to respond to its own "specific location factors" (Massey 1984: 1, 79). Similarly, the concept of functional region has lost much of its utility with the rise of "large multi-plant enterprises" in which any local branch "may well serve the whole national or international market, and not just a region" (Urry 1985: 34). The rise of "multi-plant, multiregional and multinational companies" has, in short, served to superannuate traditional concepts of region (Massey 1984: 79).

This new economy has not, however, eliminated the need for a concept of region in its most basic sense, as a subdivision of something larger and more extensive. This basic sense is evident in Massey's definition of a region as "any sub-national area of any size" or in Giddens's claim that "regionalization encloses zones of time-space" (Massey 1984: 11; Giddens 1985: 277). What is new is the emphasis on the fact that "individual regions play different 'roles' within the overall system," that these roles "combine certain aspects of the technical division of labor with spatial differentiation in the workforce," and that this spatialization of capitalist class relations has yielded a "geography of dominance and subordination" (Massey 1984: 107, 88, 99).

The key issue here is "the removal from some regions, and the concentration in others, of the more powerful, conceptual, and strategic levels of control over production" (Massey 1984: 112). What emerges is a "dual economy" in which a central or metropolitan region, which contains the bulk of managerial jobs, controls "a peripheral region" (Urry 1985: 34). Massey describes the latter as a "non-headquarters region in which certain parts of the functions of economic ownership and possession are missing" (Massey 1984: 101). This yields the conclusion that regions vary according to "the class characteristics of management" and that their boundaries are, in Cooke's words, "coterminous with the limits of dominant class practices" (Massey 1984: 110; Cooke 1985: 213). We thus reach a central thesis of all this work, namely, that social structure yields spatial structure (and, for some authors, temporal structure) and that the regional concept is the geographer's way of approaching a "socio-spatial formation" (Cooke 1985: 222).

The concept of place is important to this geographical theory because it permits "understanding of general trends with a recognition, alongside and within that, of very great diversity" (Massey 1984: 120). Places are accumulations of "layers, of the successive imposition over the years of new rounds of investment," and they have grown unique as "the product of many determinations" (Massey 1984: 117–18, 120; see James 1952: 222). Although "we talk of peripheral regions," we must therefore recognize that "they are all very different" because they are "products of long and varied histories" (Massey 1984: 117). So might we say that we talk of the working class, but members of it are all very different because they are products of long and varied biographies. Stated with utmost simplicity, in fact, the scheme here is this: social structure is equivalent to spatial structure, region is equivalent to class, and place is equivalent to personality.

The Value of Ambiguity

I began this essay with the claim that region and place are multifarious concepts, and I built this essay's body out of samples of some of the several senses and many levels of theoretical sophistication with which they can be used. I conclude with the claim that multifarious concepts are essentially ambiguous and that their ambiguity is what makes them useful and attractive.

Any definite sense of a concept is like a branch of a tree, discrete and yet connected to the other senses by a common trunk; thus, place as physical position and place as mental condition are both offshoots of an indistinct and perhaps undefinable trunk concept of place. Ordinarily, the relatedness of definite senses is not apparent because individual instances of usage are insulated by their context. If I say I am in the market for a house in the region of $100,000, for instance, a listener is unlikely to suppose that $100,000 is the name of a place near which I wish to reside. Stripping away context, as I have done in the preceding pages, removes this insulation and forces us to consider concepts such as region and place not in this sense or that sense, but in this sense and that sense. It forces us to recognize their ambiguity.

This idea runs contrary to the normal tendency in academic discourse, which is to seek certainty, to refine and clarify concepts, and to replace the ambiguous with the definite. I have moved in the opposite direction because

I believe there is something to be gained from ambiguity. For example, when Robert Frost writes, "we make ourselves a place apart," place is ambiguous (Frost 1969: 19). He may mean that we make ourselves into such a place or that we have made such a place for ourselves. Actually, I suppose he means both, and a good deal else as well. What should follow from this is an understanding that the concept of place, like any multifarious concept, is not reducible to one of its definite senses and that we best understand any one of its definite senses when we bear all the others in mind. Not all concepts possess these ambiguities, but those that lack them do not, in my experience, reward the reflective geographer.

Notes

I would like to thank Professor D. C. Smith for his assistance with a portion of this paper.

References

Agnew, J. 1993. Representing space: Space, scale, and culture in social science. In *Place/culture/representation*, ed. J. Duncan and D. Ley, 251–71. London: Routledge.

Barrett, P. H., and R. B. Freeman, eds. 1987. *The works of Charles Darwin, vol. 15: On the origin of species*. New York: New York University Press.

Brontë, E. 1992. *Wuthering heights: A novel*, ed. Linda H. Peterson. Boston: St. Martin's Press.

Bosworth, J. and T. N. Toller. 1898. *An Anglo Saxon dictionary*. Oxford: Oxford University Press.

Buchanan, J. 1967. *Linguae britannicae vera pronunciato* [1757]. Menston, England: The Scholar Press.

Cooke, P. 1985. Class practices as regional markers: A contribution to labour geography. In *Social relations and spatial structures*, ed. D. Gregory and J. Urry, 211–41. New York: St. Martin's Press.

Duhem, P. 1985. *Medieval cosmology: Theories of infinity, place, time, void, and the plurality of worlds*, ed. and trans. R. Ariew. Chicago: University of Chicago Press.

Ekwall, E. 1960. *The concise Oxford dictionary of English place-names*. Oxford: Clarendon Press.

210   Jonathan M. Smith

Entrikin, J. N. 1991. *The betweeness of place: Towards a geography of modernity.* Baltimore: Johns Hopkins University Press.

Entrikin, J. N., and S. D. Brunn. eds. 1989. *Reflections on Richard Hartshorne's The Nature of Geography.* Washington, D.C.: Association of American Geographers.

Finch, V. C. 1939. Geographical science and social philosophy. *Annals of the Association of American Geographers* 29: 1–28.

Frost, R. 1969. *The Poetry of Robert Frost,* ed. E. C. Lathem. New York: Holt, Rinehart and Winston.

Hanford, J. H. 1929. *A Milton handbook.* New York: F. S. Crofts.

Hartshorne, R. 1939. *The nature of geography.* Lancaster, Pa.: Association of American Geographers.

———. 1959. *Perspective on the nature of geography.* Chicago: Rand McNally.

Harvey, D. 1985. The geopolitics of capitalism. In *Social relations and spatial structures,* ed. D. Gregory and J. Urry, 128–63. New York: St. Martin's Press.

Hawthorne, N. 1962. *The centenary edition of the works of Nathaniel Hawthorne,* ed. W. Charvat, vol. 1: *The scarlet letter.* Columbus: Ohio State University Press.

———. 1964. *The centenary edition of the works of Nathaniel Hawthorne,* ed. W. Charvat, vol. 3: *The Blithedale romance and Fanshawe.* Columbus: Ohio State University Press.

———. 1965. *The centenary edition of the works of Nathaniel Hawthorne,* ed. W. Charvat, vol. 2: *The house of seven gables.* Columbus: Ohio State University Press.

———. 1968. *The centenary edition of the works of Nathaniel Hawthorne,* ed. W. Charvat, vol. 4: *The marble faun: or, the romance of Monte Beni.* Columbus: Ohio State University Press.

James, P. 1952. Toward a further understanding of the regional concept. *Annals of the Association of American Geographers* 42: 195–222.

Johnston, R. J. 1991. *A question of place: Exploring the practice of human geography.* Oxford: Blackwell Publishers.

Kersey, J. 1969 (1708). *Dictionarium anglo-britannicum.* Menston, England: The Scholar Press.

Koyré, A. *From the closed world to the infinite universe.* Baltimore: Johns Hopkins University Press.

Lewis, C. S. 1964. *The discarded image: An introduction to medieval and renaissance literature.* Cambridge: Cambridge University Press.

————. 1967. *Studies in words*, 2d ed. Cambridge: Cambridge University Press.

Lowes, J. L. 1936. *Essays in appreciation*. Boston: Houghton Mifflin.

Massey, D. 1984. *Spatial divisions of labor: Social structures and the geography of production*. New York: Methuen.

Milton, J. 1971. *The complete prose works of John Milton*, vol. 2, ed. F. Fogle. New Haven: Yale University Press.

————. 1971. *The complete prose works of John Milton*, vol. 8, ed. F. Fogle. New Haven: Yale University Press.

National Geography Standards Project. 1994. *Geography for life: National geography standards, 1994*. Washington D.C.: National Geographic Society.

Pred, A. 1985. The social becomes the spatial, the spatial becomes the social: Enclosures, social change and the becoming of places in Skåne. In *Social relations and spatial structures*, ed. D. Gregory and J. Urry, 337–65. New York: St. Martin's Press.

Pudup, M. B. 1988. Arguments within regional geography. *Progress in Human Geography* 12: 369–90.

Semple, E. C. 1911. *Influences of geographic environment: On the basis of Ratzel's system of anthropogeography*. New York: Henry Holt.

Sheridan, T. 1967 (1780). *A general dictionary of the English language*. Menston, England: The Scholar Press.

Smith, A. 1976. *An inquiry into the nature and causes of the wealth of nations*, ed. R. H. Campbell, A. S. Skinner and W. B. Todd. 2 vols. Oxford: Clarendon Press.

Trusler, J. 1970 (1766). *The difference between words esteemed synonymous*. Menston, England: The Scholar Press.

Urry, J. 1985. Social relations, space, and time. In *Social relations and spatial structures*, ed. D. Gregory and J. Urry, 20–48. New York: St. Martin's Press.

Vives, J. L. 1989. *Somnium et vigilia in somnium scipoinis* [Commentary on the *Dream of Scipio*], ed. E. V. George. Greenwood, S. C.: Attic Press.

8

Boundaries: Setting Limits to Political Areas

Andrew F. Burghardt

Boundaries are much more than lines on a map; they are functional, cultural features planted on a physical landscape, vitally related to their bordering regions.
—Stephen Jones.

Boundaries have existed in most parts of the world for thousands of years, yet the analysis of their locations and functions has developed only within the last few centuries, principally in Europe. Perhaps because of their Greek and Roman heritage, Europeans tried to impose order and precision on all aspects of their lives, including the delimitation of political areas. The technology to do this had existed in the ancient world but, as far as we know, was never exercised on a broad scale. Following their post-1492 conquest of the world, Europeans were able to impose their territorial concepts on the non-European world, yet even within Europe, boundary concepts, as we now know them, did not appear before the development of the modern centralized state. A new ideology, nationalism, worked toward the matching of "nations" to specific territories; this led to deep emotional attachments to boundary locations. The totalitarian trends of the twentieth century led in turn to a strengthening of the uses (functions) of boundaries.

The earliest complete listings we have of the location of boundaries are those in the Bible (Numbers 34). The Israelites were told what the bounds of their Promised Land were to be. Since this land was to be occupied by the en-

213

tire people—the nation we would now say—and was not seen as the holdings of individual rulers, this division of territory anticipated much of the boundary making of the past four centuries.

Three aspects of this delimitation are of special interest to us. First was the acceptance of a huge physical feature as an ultimate boundary. The "Great Sea" (the Mediterranean) was seen as the obvious western boundary of The Promised Land, much as the oceans, the North Sea, the Sahara, and other broad empty areas were assumed to mark outer limits at a later date. The second aspect was the use made of other physical features, especially of rivers. The line formed by the Jordan River and the Dead Sea was declared to be the eastern boundary, while the "river of Egypt," a large wadi at the northern end of the Sinai, was to mark the southwestern end (figure 8.1). Rivers, creeks, and wadis served the purposes well in that they were linear, relatively narrow, and unmistakable in the landscape. The northeastern corner of the new national territory was placed at Mount Hor (Hermon?), north of the headwaters of the Jordan. The third aspect was the lack of continuity of the outer boundary. Only the eastern and western limits were unbroken, because the sea and river that determined them continued along their full length. The path of the

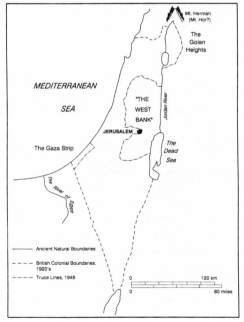

Figure 8.1 The boundaries of Israel, ancient and modern.

southern limit from the Dead Sea to "the river of Egypt" was not fully specified, since no usable clear physical feature existed in the area. Because of the lack of permanent settlements in this desert zone, the imprecision of the boundary location was not of great importance. David's campaigns against the desert raiders indicates that this was in fact a fluctuating boundary. At the northern end, however, where a similar imprecision occurred between Mount Hor and the Mediterranean Sea, the population density was considerably higher, and the boundary did not pass in a direct line to The Great Sea. Precise demarcation in such an area had to wait for the formation of divides between settlements and, of course, differences in political power.

The Bible also lists the subdivision of the Promised Land into tribal areas (Joshua 13:19). In this case physical features, particularly stream courses, often were not available. In such cases the boundaries between the tribal territories were given in terms of the preexisting settlements ("cities"). Presumably, these internal boundaries would have been set between the areas occupied by the settlements on opposite sides of the lines.

These approaches to the establishment of boundaries have remained vital through the millennia since their first development. What has changed with time has been principally their clarification, classification, and explanation. Undoubtedly other peoples developed similar methods of perceiving terrain and determining limits. One of the more interesting variations in the ancient world was the creation of physical barriers where suitable ones did not exist. The Great Wall of China and the Roman walls in northern Britain and along the drainage divide of the Rhine and the Danube are the best examples.

Through the thirteen centuries between the collapse of the western Roman Empire and the rise of the nation-state, boundaries as such received relatively little attention. Within a territorial system based on feudal holdings boundaries were seen mainly as the edges of the holdings and not as important features in themselves. Small states grew by gathering up holdings, and wars were fought for the most part over rights of ownership to previously defined parcels of land.

These counties, free cities, duchies, principalities, and kingdoms had to have limits, however. In addition there were a few major boundaries such as those between kingdoms (e.g., Hungary, Bohemia, and Poland; England and Scotland) that required precise delimitations. Wherever possible, these boundaries made use of streams that happened to be in the area concerned and that flowed in the right direction. Any rivulet would do: several stretches of the "Thousand Year Boundary" between Hungary and Austria made use of creeks that can be straddled without getting one's feet wet. Even when the boundary was placed along a mountain chain, the exact location of the line tended to be on a water course wherever a road crossed the boundary.

The reasons for this have been stated above. In the absence of adequate sur-veying medieval rulers, like the Israelites before them, took advantage of the precision, linearity, and visibility of stream courses and the defense possi-bilities of the ravines or swamps that often accompanied them. Certain rivers came to be recognized as "natural" subdividers of territory; the opponents of King Henry IV of England used the Severn and the Trent as the limits of the areas they expected to receive. Where streams were not available, bound-aries were often placed in the middle of wooded areas, preferably those that lay along uplands. If a stretch between stream-following segments was relatively short, the precise location of the boundary came to be along the divide of the land holdings of the villages or manors on opposite side. A century ago the Austrian geographer, Robert Sieger, coined the term *Zusam-menwachsgrenze*—a growing-together-boundary—for these gradual adjust-ments through the ages.

Once these boundaries had been determined, they rarely changed because the territorial holdings were moved back and forth as units; thus it was that Eu-rope consisted of a patchwork of holdings with few large, compact countries.

Boundaries became important in themselves with the expansion of Euro-peans overseas. In claiming territories in other parts of the world, Europeans for the most part ignored the organizational areas of the native peoples and imposed their own boundaries (*colonial boundaries*) to serve as divides be-tween areas allotted to groups of traders or settlers. In the eyes of the Euro-peans there were few preexisting local boundaries. Also, the European mon-archs or their deputies knew little of the topography of the areas to be handed out. In North America a few of the larger rivers that flowed into the Atlantic were known at first and could be used as boundary features. Among these were the Delaware and the Potomac. Other rivers, however, were entry corridors into the continent and became axes of settlement; thus the rivers of Maine, the Hudson, the James, and even Chesapeake Bay were not used as boundary lines. Instead, the Europeans invented the *geometric boundary*, which ad-mirably served the purpose of dividing up an unknown continent (figure 8.2). From a distance, and in almost complete ignorance of the details of the ter-rain, rulers could allot segments of the land to different claimants.

Geometric boundaries most commonly followed lines that ran directly north-south or east-west, since these were by far the easiest to survey. Although more difficult to trace, diagonals were also used, as between the two Caroli-nas and along the eastern boundaries of New York. Even an arc was used to determine the boundary between Delaware and Pennsylvania. Although a measure of expediency, the geometric boundary remained popular even after a fuller knowledge of the continent had been gained. An east-west line was surveyed by Mason and Dixon to separate Maryland and Pennsylvania, and a

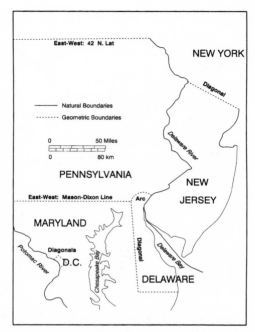

Figure 8.2 Colonial boundaries in the northeastern United States. The figure illustrates the juxtaposition of natural and geometric boundaries.

host of geometric lines was used to divide up the two-thirds of the United States west of the Mississippi and the half of Canada west of Lake Superior. In the nineteenth century the geometric was again employed on a wide scale by Europeans, this time in Africa. Even as late as 1920, Great Britain and France divided up the northern reaches of the Arabian Peninsula on the basis of geometric lines.

The disadvantages of the geometric have been long understood. It ignores terrain, travel difficulties, and cultural or marketing areas. For example, the Peace River agricultural region of northeastern British Columbia is separated by the Rockies from the rest of its province and by the provincial boundary from the main part of the region in Alberta (figure 8.3). A high mountain range runs right through the middle of Colorado. This does not appear to be a serious matter, however, as long as the units are not independent countries. If Pennsylvania and Maryland or Maine and New Hampshire had been fully independent states, it is questionable whether the boundaries between them would have remained as they are.

Whereas the geometric boundary may be thought of as the boundary par

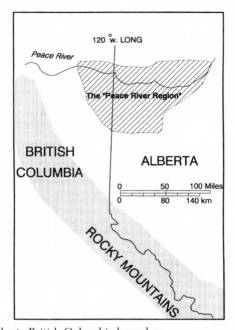

Figure 8.3 The Alberta-British Columbia boundary.

excellence of imperialism, the natural boundary may be considered to have been the boundary of science, replete with a healthy dose of determinism. As Pounds (1954) has demonstrated, the idea of natural boundaries developed and flourished in France. This was partly because France possessed boundaries closely tied to major physical features: the North Sea, the English Channel, the Atlantic, the Pyrenees, the Mediterranean, the Alps, and the Jura.

The belief in natural boundaries rested on two philosophical positions. First, every country was perceived to have limits prescribed to it by nature and the right to reach those limits. Perhaps inevitably, those limits were often seen to extend beyond the existing boundaries of that state. Second, these preordained limits, set as they were on physical ("natural") features, could be easily determined by looking at the landscape. In the case of France all the boundaries were natural except for the stretch between the Rhine River and the North Sea (figure 8.4). The French, therefore, proclaimed their right to expand to their natural boundary, that is, to the mouth of the Rhine River. Of course, that meant the absorption of all of Belgium and Luxembourg, the southern third of the Netherlands, and the Cologne area of Germany; but to the French this was clearly less important than having *la belle France* attain the boundary that holy mother nature had predetermined for her.

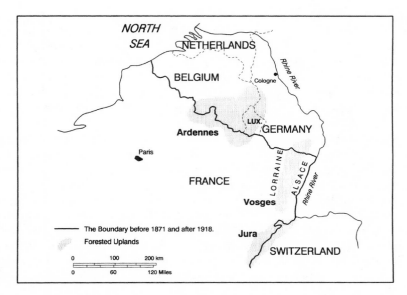

Figure 8.4 The northeastern boundaries of France.

The problems with this concept are obvious. First of all it is a license for aggression. France did, in fact, absorb all the area west of the Rhine during the Napoleonic years, and it occupied the Rhine's German portions (loosely called the Rhineland) after the First World War. Second is the difficulty of determining just which natural features are to be the natural boundaries. For the French it was the Rhine River, largely because all their maps depicted it as a heavy blue line. For the Germans, on the other hand, it was in the Vosges and the Ardennes hill lands west of the Rhine.

Many large rivers or mountain crests do carry boundaries, but more do not. The broad St. Lawrence is not even a provincial boundary in Canada. (Perhaps the United States could claim it as the natural northern boundary of New England!) The biggest river of Central Europe, the Danube, is not even a provincial boundary in Austria. The huge rivers of Siberia, the Nile, and the Niger are not boundaries for most of their length. The Rockies form a natural boundary only between parts of Idaho and Montana, and British Columbia and Alberta; elsewhere, they run right through the middle of states. In fact, a physical feature will be used for a boundary only if it is located where a boundary is needed and only if it runs in the desired direction. Because the word *natural* is so loaded with the sense of rights, and hence the possibilities of self-righteous aggression, scholars and diplomats have attempted to substitute alternative terms such as *physiographic* or *geomorphic* to indicate boundaries that coincide with landform features. Despite the dangers involved in the use of the concept, it must be admitted that boundaries are strengthened and made more visible and more acceptable by their coincidence with physical features. There is more of a sense of crossing an international boundary at the Detroit and Niagara Rivers than there is in driving along flat country between two customs posts. Names such as Trans-Euphrates, or Trans-Leitha (Hungary) and Cis-Leitha (Austria) remind us of the importance of rivers in defining boundaries.

In the nineteenth century European intellectuals became fascinated by the existence of *nations*, that is, of groups of people who shared the same traditions, histories, and culture. Language was seen as the principal determinant of nationhood. Since the nation was the most important social unit, the belief arose that the boundaries of the state should coincide with the limits of the nation. Despite the fact that few states are true nation-states, the idea of the nation-state as the political norm was born. The boundary concept that emerged was usually called the national boundary, or the nationalistic or ethnic or anthropogeographic boundary. It was felt that the ideal boundary was one that would separate peoples who spoke different languages and who thus belonged to different nations.

The first major clear-cut application of this principle was the treaty that ended the Franco-Prussian War in 1871. Germany obtained from France most of Alsace and the northern third of Lorraine because those areas were German speaking (figure 8.4). The boundary was placed on the divide between German and French speakers. (This did not prevent the French from devoting all their efforts to a return of these territories and hence a move back to their natural boundary along the Rhine River.) It was during and after World War I, however, that this boundary concept became dominant, at least in dealing with the territory of the defeated powers. Austria-Hungary in particular was divided into a multitude of successor states on the basis of nationalities (language groups). The concept was so strongly held that Denmark, which had not even been in the war, received a slice of territory from Germany. In a number of disputed areas plebiscites were held to try to determine the national preferences of the local populations.

Unfortunately, the concept of national boundary also had its difficulties when applied in the real world. For one thing, ethnic divides were not clean (figure 8.5). Many of the villages in the frontier zones had mixed populations. Further, national sentiments tended to be far stronger among the urban than among the rural populations. In addition, the victorious powers chose to ignore the strict application of the ethnic concept when other considerations seemed to be in their favor. By the ethnic principle Alsace and the northern third of Lorraine should have remained with Germany, but the French were

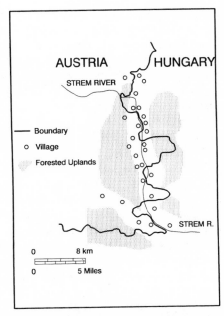

Figure 8.5 A "national" (ethnic) boundary: The division of the Strem Valley, 1922.

adamant in their demands for their return; besides, France had suffered griev-
ously in the war and Germany had lost.

Despite its inherent problems this concept remained popular until the end
of the Second World War. Indeed just prior to the start of World War II, Hitler
used the argument that all the German peoples should be in one country as
justification for annexing Austria and stripping Czechoslovakia of its German-
speaking border zones. It was probably Hitler's use of this idea that led to its
demise. After 1944 the countries that had lost land to Germany because of the
application of this idea responded by driving out the Germans resident in their
lands. They thus achieved a new form of the nation-state—one based on the
expulsion of peoples who did not belong to the dominant group, a practice
currently being followed in the Balkans. Formerly referred to as *population
transfer* or *exchange*, it is now termed, euphemistically, *ethnic cleansing*.

Still, the concept that boundaries should follow ethnic lines is popular with
groups wishing to become independent. Perhaps the most notable recent examples have been the Tamils in Sri Lanka and the Basques in Spain. At base,
this concept maintains that the land should belong to the resident people—
notably the rural people—and that boundaries should be run between groups,
irrespective of natural or economic features of the landscape.

Boundaries that existed for long periods of time, either in the present or in the past, are commonly called historic boundaries. Unfortunately, nations remember only too well their past historic boundaries, and much blood has been shed by attempts to regain those limits.

Because the boundaries of a state are the edges that face actual or potential enemies, state concerns for security have often dictated that those edges be strong. The defense boundary, accordingly, is one that is militarily strong (for example, along a mountain range) or helps in some other way to protect the vital areas of the country. The Israeli movement of the de facto boundary up over the Golan Heights in 1967 is of this type.

The period 1917–1923 witnessed more international boundary changes than any similar period in history. For the next three decades boundaries were discussed frequently. Isaiah Bowman (1921), probably the most prominent geographer of his time, wrote an influential book, *The New World*, which dealt with the massive changes of territory in Europe. Subsequently, S. W. Boggs (1940) and Stephen Jones (1945) contributed books on boundaries. Richard Hartshorne (1935) introduced German concepts on boundaries into the American geographic literature. Henceforth, geographers made clear distinctions among terms that had served almost as synonyms. The *boundary* is the sharp, thin line, almost always legally defined, that separates two political units. A *border* is not necessarily a line, but rather a zone adjacent to a boundary. Except in French, a *frontier* is a broader belt yet, and can exist between two nations even where no boundary exists. A frontier also has a military aspect, while the other terms usually do not. Outside of political geography, *frontier* can also mean an area open to settlement, beyond the limits of occupied areas.

In an attempt to establish a scientific classification of boundaries, terms were borrowed from physical geography. The approach was chronological in that boundaries were viewed in their relationship to the timing of settlement. A boundary established before settlement was termed *antecedent*. Sometimes the word *pioneer* was used to denote an extreme case. Since there were very few, if any, parts of the world's land surface that did not have some form of human use, *antecedent* really meant before European settlement. Native tribal areas were usually ignored.

A boundary that was drawn after the settlement of an area was called *subsequent*. If the new boundary cut through a fully developed human landscape with its networks of interconnections, it was said to be *superimposed*. This last term became quite popular, perhaps because so many of the post-1918 boundaries cut through crowded landscapes. Drawn along ethnic divides, these new lines tended to ignore marketing areas and transport systems and thus inevitably played havoc with established interrelationships.

A boundary that was so solidly established and accepted that it was regarded as an inevitable part of the landscape was said to be *incised* or *entrenched*. This was not in the ground itself, but rather in the minds of the peoples on both sides of the line. The boundary between the United States and Canada, although seemingly illogical at times, is never questioned in its details by either side. Lastly, *relic* boundary constituted a former boundary that visibly persisted in the landscape because of cultural differences between its two sides.

The process of establishing a boundary was said to consist of four steps. In the first, allocation, the territory was divided in general terms. This was usually accomplished by national leaders or their deputies, who determined the boundary's overall course. Next came delimitation, which established the precise location of the new boundary. This was usually done by a team going into the field and determining exactly where the line should run through every meter of its course. The third step, demarcation, involved the physical construction of the boundary in the landscape: setting up the boundary markers, customs posts, border guard towers, or even concrete and barbed wire walls and fences. Finally, with the boundary clearly in place, came administration, as the countries on either side of the boundary imposed on it the functions they wished the border to serve.

During World War II the Western Allies agreed that all the European boundaries were to revert to the locations that held before 1938. The only changes occurred to the east, where the Soviet Union moved boundaries to suit its territorial ambitions. The new line between Poland and the USSR was a national boundary that divided Poles on one side from Ukrainians and White Russians on the other. The western boundary of Poland was moved to the natural boundary formed by the Oder and Neisse Rivers. The Soviets also moved their boundary with Romania from the Dniester to the Pruth River (two natural boundaries), and in the Far East the Soviet Union took over the Kurile Islands from Japan and thus moved the boundary from one strait to another.

Since World War II, a number of boundaries have been added or changed. In 1948 the legal boundary of the new state of Israel (according to the United Nations resolutions) was set along the truce line that separated the two opposing armies (Israeli and Arab) at the close of their war. In 1967 the Israelis moved the boundary to the natural and historic line along the Jordan River, but this has never been accepted by the United Nations; that is, it is a de facto boundary, but not de jura. In southern Asia the British colony of India was subdivided into India and the new state of Pakistan on an ethnic principle, only here not on the criterion of language but rather on religion. The boundary caused great difficulties; its demarcation and the subsequent disputes led to several wars and the establishment of East Pakistan as yet another country,

Bangladesh. Within Kashmir the boundary marked the truce line between the two armies at the end of the first war between them. In Korea the initial boundary between North and South Korea was along a geometric line (the 38th parallel), but after a long and bloody war it was shifted to yet another truce line. The boundary between North and South Vietnam also ran along a straight-lined geometric boundary.

Except for the boundary changes in Asia, there have been few international boundary changes since 1945. (To be sure, many nations in Africa and Asia secured their independence, but their colonial boundaries remain largely intact.) The general opinion in the world today is clearly against any attempts to change them. This conservative attitude has been clearly expressed in the United Nations charter as well as in the Helsinki Declaration. The feeling is that the older boundary concepts were used as excuses for aggression and that the only way to ensure international peace is to outlaw attempts to change the locations of boundaries. This does not mean, of course, that people will not try to change them (as they have in Eritrea and are attempting to do in the southern Sudan), but certainly the dominant international community is strongly in favor of the status quo, no matter how unjust it may seem in individual cases.

The breakup of the former Yugoslavia and Soviet Union has thus presented the international community with a dilemma. The first reaction was to try to maintain the territorial status quo in Yugoslavia, but as the secessions led to bloody conflict, the aim of the United Nations became an attempt to stop the fighting. In the ensuing civil war the Croats, Bosnians, and Slovenes all claimed their preexisting historic boundaries, many of which were natural in that they followed rivers or ridges. The Serbs, on the other hand, fought for the creation of new national or ethnic boundaries that would include areas of Croatia and Bosnia populated by Serbs (with other groups driven out). Similar conflicts between overlapping historic and national boundary claims broke out in some of the former republics of the Soviet Union.

Recent "fine tuning" of boundary placements has occurred principally within water. Small streams generally have not been a problem since their widths and economic potentialities are small and insignificant, respectively. In larger rivers, however, the placement of the line becomes a matter of some importance. In these cases the boundary can be placed along one bank, in the exact middle, or in the middle of the principal navigational channel (the *thalweg*), or in the middle of the widest channel. Where there are islands, for example, the Thousand Islands in the St. Lawrence River, each must be allotted to one side or the other. Special problems arise when the river is to be dammed for power or navigational purposes. In the case of lakes the median line halfway between the two sides is generally favored, although this has at times been generalized into straight-line segments between median points. In bays, seas, oceanic channels, and the like, the median line has been applied most often, but boundary makers have also relied on channels, offshore islands or banks, and the general trend of the coastline direction.

Unfortunately, river courses, channels, and coastlines are constantly changing, despite dredging and the construction of levees and dikes. The Mississippi River, for example, has been notorious for its swings back and forth through the centuries. However, once a boundary on the Mississippi has been legally established, it remains in its precise location despite changes in the river or channel. We thus find bits of the state of Arkansas on the other side of the river in what should be the state of Mississippi, and vice versa. These meanderings may cause great inconvenience, especially in supplying services such as education, but the boundary remains as it was unless the states concerned can agree to change the line to fit the new location of the river. This rarely happens, because one side must always give up more than it receives.

Perhaps the most important boundary questions in the future will concern the oceans. How far out from the continents are the boundaries to be drawn? What levels of sovereignty and jurisdiction will apply? In these cases international agreement is hard to achieve because the countries facing the oceans wish to extend their limits outward, while the landlocked states are opposed to these extensions. Moreover, wealthy trading nations tend to prefer freedom of the seas, whereas poorer nations wish to control as much of the ocean as they can.

Students of ocean boundaries agree that the innermost line is the baseline—the line from which all outward distances are measured. The baseline smooths out the coastline by connecting the headlands, capes, and islands; the smaller inlets and bays are treated as if they were dry land. Traditionally, the boundary beyond the baseline was the three-mile limit where a country's sovereignty ended—for the reason that three miles was how far a cannonball fired from the shore could reach about the year 1800. Despite major improvements in artillery power, this limit remained in force until after World War II, and it still marks the outer edge of the territorial waters—the zone of undisputed total sovereignty.

In recent decades a number of other ocean boundaries have been proposed or proclaimed by individual countries. The most commonly accepted line now is the twelve-mile limit. Theoretically, a country may not exercise total sovereignty out to twelve miles, but for all practical purposes most countries do. Well beyond this is the two-hundred mile limit, which is used to mark the outer edge of fishing, resource development, and pollution control. Increasingly, the two-hundred limit is coming to be the real outermost boundary, despite a lack of international agreement.

Complicating matters even more is the continental shelf, which is considered to be the underwater continuation of the dry land part of the country. Here the limits depend on the depth of the water above the shelf. Initially, the limit was set at one-hundred fathoms or six-hundred feet. This was later changed to its metric equivalent of two-hundred meters. There is, however, a great temptation for nations to drill for oil or mine the seabed when shelf depth exceeds two-hundred meters, but is still within the two-hundred mile limit. Of course when a deposit straddles the line, countries are tempted to follow it out or down beyond the limits.

Finally, beyond these limits lies the open sea, where the traditional policy of freedom of the seas still applies. Even here, however, proposals have been drawn up for carving up the oceans into zones of jurisdiction on the basis of the median-line principle. Because of its two-ocean frontage and its possession of the Aleutians and Hawaii, the United States would gain control of a major portion of the earth's ocean surface. Needless to say, the many countries not bordering on oceans are strongly opposed to any further extensions of national boundaries out into the oceans.

Boundaries may be said to have three principal purposes: to bound, to separate, and to enclose. *To bound* means to set limits to the areas under the administration of some level of government and to hold rights to the revenues gained from those areas. Since every square millimeter of land must be allotted to some jurisdiction, the boundaries become hairline precise in allocating terrain to one side or the other. The boundary can thus be seen as a plane of no thickness intersecting the surface of the earth and reaching downward to the center of the earth and indefinitely upward out into space.

In practice, the reach upward extends only as far as the range of modern satellites and spacecraft. For a time it seemed that the outward reach was only defined by the distance that a country could extend its power into space, but that assumption was proved wrong when the United States' ability to overfly all countries ended with the Soviet Union shooting down a U2 spy plane. Since then a modus vivendi has been reached that, in practice even if not in law, allots airplane space above a country to that country, while assigning the outer space beyond that to an international sphere. For now at least, a kind of freedom of the seas exists in outer space.

The second principal function of a boundary is to separate one unit from another. The boundary becomes the edge along which a country can exercise its rights to exclude people, goods, diseases, and ideas from its lands. Tariffs and import restrictions are examples of the exercise of these rights; so too is the Great Wall of China—the largest and most famous attempt to enforce this function—and the defense boundary so sought after in the last century.

The boundary is also used to enclose, that is, to keep people, goods, finances, and even technological ideas within the country. The most famous examples of this function made tangible are the Berlin Wall and the heavily armed fence, the Iron Curtain, running through East Central Europe. These material enclosures forcibly kept people and money within the state. Export restrictions, though a less dramatic example, serve the same function with respect to goods. Within the enclosed unit the imposition of one sytem of education and of state-controlled news may serve to create a unified ideology.

Boundaries vary greatly in terms of the rigor with which these functions are applied. We speak of open or closed boundaries, of boundaries that are permeable or impermeable, of those that are weak and those that are strong. The boundary between Belgium and the Netherlands can be called open, or permeable, or weak in that there are few customs posts and almost no restrictions on the movement of persons, goods, or ideas. For the non-native there is no sense of crossing a boundary; yet while the separating and enclosing functions are almost absent, the bounding of administrative and jurisdictional units, with all that that means in terms of laws, courts, taxes, and services, remains fully intact. In contrast, the old Iron Curtain was closed, impermeable, and strong. Of these two extremes the great multinational corporations prefer the former. They wish to avoid the separating and enclosing functions as much as possible; in fact, they would prefer to have no constraints at all on international traffic. The elimination of those two functions would give the corporations the ability to take full advantage of differences in taxing policies, local regulations, and comparative advantage more generally.

Two effects follow from the application of these boundary functions: barrier and perception. The barrier effect is a result of the separating and enclosing functions. Its impact is heightened by the fact that an international boundary can generally be crossed only at certain points. Traffic must go to a relatively few border crossings, which act as narrow funnels. Anyone who has tried to cross a boundary when a smuggling search is on will know what a constriction on movement these border posts can be. Boundaries as barriers thus affect the volume of international interactions (usually by reducing it).

The placement of the boundary also skews our perception of relative space as several Canadian examples make clear. To anyone in southern Ontario, Winnipeg feels much closer than Memphis, Tennessee, yet Memphis is actually closer. On the provincial level Kenora in the westernmost part of Ontario seems much closer to someone in southern Ontario than Saint John, New Brunswick, on the Atlantic. In fact, Saint John is closer in miles. In the first case, both Winnipeg and southern Ontario are in Canada; Memphis is not. In the second case, Kenora is in the same province, Ontario, whereas Saint John is not. The moral is simple: we construct space in terms of the units we are in, and those spaces are formed by the boundaries around them.

With the external boundaries of states relatively secure (except as otherwise noted earlier), attention has shifted to boundaries within countries, those that mark off the lower levels of government. In the past, railroads and factory complexes often avoided annexation in order to remain outside of urban units with their high tax rates. Similarly, prestige suburbs were established to ensure the existence of desired social standards within small areas. Their high tax bases allowed them to provide excellent services, especially in education, whereas the old central cities were left with poorer tax bases, but higher demands for welfare, maintenance, and policing. In judging these boundary changes scholars and planners use criteria such as efficiency, effectiveness, social justice, and bureaucratic constraints. Governmental areas have been analyzed in terms of their size, shape, and fiscal capacity. In all of these cases the focus of the analysis has not been on the boundary, as such, but rather on the area included within the boundary. None of these recent studies has concerned itself with the precise location of the lines or the effects their location may have on the people living alongside them.

We thus find ourselves back in the feudal condition as far as the study of boundaries is concerned. Boundary lines are seen as the edges of the areas to be dealt with and not as important features in their own right. Pieces of territory may be moved around, but attention is riveted on the content of the parcels and not on the exact location of the lines that determine their size; yet anyone who has lived alongside a boundary will know that major differences can exist on the two sides of the line, and the line itself can be a strong factor in the movements and life-styles of the people. On the local level, fire protection, schooling, road maintenance, and the like are all affected by the locations of boundaries.

Relatively few boundary changes have occurred within countries during the last half of the twentieth century. Federal structures virtually guarantee the continued, unchanged existence of the component provinces, even if they are as small as Delaware, Prince Edward Island, or Tasmania. Local boundaries have remained remarkably unchanged within the United States, despite the explosive growth of urban complexes. The proliferation of suburbs has been made possible by great improvements in transportation, the scattering of local business centers, and the ability of the suburbs to supply and finance the required services. Cities such as Los Angeles, Pittsburgh, and Chicago are constrained within boundaries that appear to be totally illogical and inefficient.

However, other Western countries have eliminated hundreds of intraurban boundaries through enforced amalgamation of metropolitan areas. The extreme conservatism in local boundary making within the United States is in contrast with the new dynamism in other countries, based on the desire for increased efficiency. Even in Great Britain, Germany, Canada, and other countries, though, the new urban boundaries are generally based on previously existing limits, so that few truly new boundaries are drawn.

Boundary studies have progressed in a cycle—from a long time of little attention to one of intense scrutiny during a period of great flux to a present of relative inattention. Our current disinterest could change dramatically, however, if the present world order should disintegrate (as it appears to have in the Balkans and the Caucasus). In that case, we may be sure that the location and functions of boundaries would again become matters of great interest and importance, not least for geographers since the drawing of boundaries has proven to be one skill almost unique to their craft. While other disciplinary specialties may make greater claims to understanding the political, economic, or sociological characteristics of areas, the placement of the boundary remains within the expertise of geographers. No other discipline seems able to weigh all the factors involved in the delimitation and the functioning of boundaries, whether on the local or the international level. The drawing of efficient and just boundaries thus represents one of the greatest contributions that geographers can make to society.

References

Boggs, S. Whittemore. 1940. *International boundaries.* New York: Columbia University Press.

Bowman, Isaiah. 1921. *The New World: Problems in political geography.* Yonkers-on-Hudson, N.Y.: World Book Company.

Burghardt, Andrew F. 1962. *Borderland: A historical and geographical study of Burgenland, Austria.* Madison, Wis.: University of Wisconsin Press, 71–80, 189–206.

Glassner, Martin I., and Harm J. de Blij. 1980. *Systematic political geography,* 3d ed. New York: John Wiley and Sons, 72–73, 82–93, 168–93.

Hartshorne, Richard. 1935. Recent developments in political geography. *American Political Science Review* 29:748–804, 943–66.

Hasson, Shlomo, and Eran Razin. 1990. What is hidden behind a municipal boundary conflict? *Political Geography Quarterly* 9: 267–83.

Johnston, Douglas M., and Phillip M. Saunders. 1988. *Ocean boundary making: Regional issues and developments.* Kingston, Ontario: McGill-Queens University Press.

Jones, Stephen B. 1945. *Boundary-making.* Washington, D.C.: Carnegie Endowment for International Peace.

————. 1959. Boundary concepts in the setting of space and time. *Annals of the Association of American Geographers* 49: 241–55.

Kristof, Ladis K. D. 1959. The nature of frontiers and boundaries. *Annals of the Association of American Geographers* 49: 269–82.

Nelson, H. J. 1983. *The Los Angeles metropolis*. Dubuque, Iowa: Kendall-Hall, 301–17.

Norris, Robert E., and L. Lloyd Haring. 1980. *Political geography*. Columbus, Ohio: C. E. Merrill, 123–37.

Pounds, Norman J. G. 1954. France and 'Les limites naturelles' from the seventeenth to the twentieth centuries. *Annals of the Association of American Geographers* 44: 51–62.

Prescott, J. R. V. 1978. *Boundaries and frontiers*. London: Croom Helm.

9

Innovation Diffusion and Paradigms of Development

Lakshman Yapa

The term *innovation* refers to a thing that is new. It may " . . . encompass a new product, a new technique, a new practice or a new idea. . . an item classified as an innovation might be intrinsically new or it might be new to the setting in which we find it" (Brown 1981: 1–2). The spatial diffusion of an innovation refers to the spread of a new item over a large area through time, starting from a few locations (Morrill, Gaile, and Thrall 1988: 7).

There is a close connection between economic development and the adoption of innovations. While development means a great variety of things to different people, most observers agree that in order for a country to develop there should be changes in what and how things are produced. Widespread changes in the material production forces of the economy are brought about through the development, introduction, diffusion, and adoption of innovations. The term *production forces* is used here in a sense similar to that employed by Marx to refer to the means of production: machinery, raw materials, energy, and labor power.

Innovation diffusion was a popular topic of research and study in the geographic literature of the 1960s and 1970s. Even today introductory textbooks on college geography contain a chapter devoted to the topic of diffusion. In the last decade, however, diffusion as a research topic went into a state of decline, the sense of which was well captured in the titles of two critical essays: "Suspended Animation: The Stasis of Diffusion Theory," written by Gregory in 1985, and "The Theory of the Spatial Diffusion of Innovations: A Spacious

Cul-de-sac," written by Blaikie in 1978. The principal criticism of diffusion studies that emerged in the 1980s was their preoccupation with spatial form and their neglect of social content and context (Blaut 1977, 1987; Yapa 1980), a preoccupation that characterized much wider areas of geography at this time (see Harvey 1973; Peet 1977; Slater 1977b; Johnston 1986). The neglect of social theory and the consequent decline of diffusion studies was unfortunate, because the subject of innovations remains, and will remain, critically important for the economic development of the Third World.

In this paper I make a case for a revival of interest in the geographic study of innovation diffusion because of its importance to issues of poverty in the Third World. The first section offers a brief review of the geographic literature on diffusion and development and an assessment of the waning interest in diffusion studies. The second section presents a social theory of innovation centered around the concepts of the nexus of production relations and biased innovations. The third section reviews the employment of innovation diffusion within three major paradigms of economic development: neoclassical economics, radical political economy, and sustainable development. And the fourth section reiterates the usefulness of the nexus of production relations and biased innovations as a framework for a social theory of innovation relevant to economic development.

Traditions of Diffusion Research in Geography

The spatial diffusion of innovations has attracted the interest of a variety of geographers, including historical, cultural, social, economic, quantitative and theoretical.[1] Of these, the work relevant to issues of economic development can be grouped into four major research traditions: cultural geography; location theory; market and infrastructure; and Third World development.

Cultural Geography

In *Readings in Cultural Geography* (1962) the editors, Wagner and Mikesell, devoted a fourth of the anthology to the theme "Cultural Origins and Dispersals," or what later came to be known as spatial diffusion. This section contained two well-known essays on diffusion — Hägerstrand's "The Propagation of Innovation Waves" and Stanislawski's "The Origin and Spread of the Grid Pattern Town" — that foreshadowed two types of diffusion studies, the former representing location theory; the latter, cultural geography. Hägerstrand's work on innovation waves and location theory was the precursor of a tradition of research that came to dominate the wider field of geography in later years.

Most studies of diffusion in geography usually begin with a brief reference acknowledging the work of cultural geographers, particularly Sauer's *Agricultural Origins and Dispersal* (1952), and quickly move on to the themes engaged by Hägerstrand: simulation, modeling, hierarchical effects, and so on.[2] Despite the marginality accorded to Sauer's work, it is my belief that his work offers seminal and important insights for the discourse on diffusion and development. The massive ecological destruction wrought by modern industry and agriculture that Sauer deplored have now emerged as major issues in international development. If our aim is to assure sustainable development in the future through ecologically sound innovations, then the issues raised by Sauer in "Theme of Plant and Animal Destruction in Economic History" (Sauer 1963b) and in "The Agency of Man on the Earth" (Sauer 1956) must become an important part of a new social theory of diffusion. Although Jackson (1989: 10–23) has taken Sauer to task for the negative impact on American cultural geography of his enormously influential essay "The Morphology of Landscape" (Sauer 1963a), an essay that persuaded cultural geographers to focus excessively on the material elements of the landscape, I wish to call attention to a more neglected aspect of Sauer's work in which he anticipated the destruction that attended modern agriculture, industry, and urbanization and the need for understanding indigenous systems of production (Sauer 1952a). The significance of these themes to contemporary problems promises a vital role for cultural geography in writing a new social theory of innovation diffusion for economic development. I shall return to this theme in the section on sustainable development.

A most interesting contribution to the social theory of innovations is the work of Earle (1988) relating agricultural innovations to the Kondratieff cycles (or long waves) using examples from the agricultural history of the American South. He argues that the notion of the Southern farmer engaging in ecologically ruinous agricultural practices over a period of two hundred years is not an accurate picture of what happened. The true story is complicated by interactions between the movements of the macrohistorical economic cycles and the course of innovation diffusion. Periods of economic depression and hardship lead to creativity, experimentation, and innovation. Periods of prosperity lead to new kinds of innovation, higher rates of profits, rapid growth, overexpansion, and, often, economic decline and ecological degradation. Earle (1988) cites two examples of this hypothesis. The Chesapeake tobacco economy entered bad times in the decade of 1680, with tobacco prices hitting rock bottom. In a classic illustration of local innovation and diffusion, Chesapeake planters responded by introducing a complex system that combined shifting cultivation (or land rotation), slave labor, and diversified crops (tobacco, corn, beans, peas and small grain). The new system was profitable and

ecologically sound. A hundred years later this system came under severe criticism as being primitive, and diversified cropping was replaced by modern
high farming systems which had devastating environmental consequences in
soil erosion, soil exhaustion, and farm abandonment. The second example
comes from the cotton economy of the South (1840–1890). Following the invention of the cotton gin, there was a rapid overexpansion of cotton cultivation in the South, which led to the massive collapse of cotton prices in the
1830s. Economically broken farmers began to replace the destructive mono-
culture with diversified complex systems of crop rotation that included cotton,
corn, leguminous crops, and the raising of pigs. In the late nineteenth
century, under pressure from market economics and advocates of scientific
farming, cotton planters abandoned the diversified system in favor of higher
profits from cotton specialization and intensive fertilizer application. The depression years of 1890 were also times of serious environmental degradation
in the cotton plantations. Earle's work as a cultural/historical geographer combines economic history, agricultural science, and ecology in a single framework that anticipates the concept of the nexus of production relations that I
use in this paper.

Location Theory

Location theory recognizes two types of diffusion called relocation diffusion
and expansion diffusion, after a typology introduced by Brown (1968: 4–12).
A relocation-type diffusion is one in which some members of the population
change their locations from time T to T + 1, as in the movement of migrants
among cities. An expansion-type diffusion is one which new members are
added to the population between times T and T + 1 as in the case of the adoption and spread on an innovation (figure 9.1). It is not clear why the distinction between these two types of diffusion is made and why it persists in the literature (Gould 1969: 4; Haggett 1983: 306; Morrill, Gaile, and Thrall 1988:
12). Structurally, migration and diffusion of innovations are very different
processes. Migration involves the movement of people from one location to
another; one place loses while another gains. The process of the diffusion of
an innovation is quite different, because the adoption of an innovation in one
place does not prevent its adoption elsewhere. To clarify, consider the divergent roles of intervening places (or what is called the rule of intervening opportunities) in these two processes. In migration, the probability of a person
moving from A to B during a given time period decreases as the number of intervening opportunities increase, because the migrant may choose to settle in
one of the intervening places. In diffusion the role of intervening places is re-
versed. An innovation that has been adopted in place A is more likely to be

Relocation - Type Diffusion

Time T   Time T+1

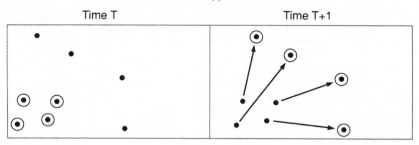

Expansion - Type Diffusion

Time T   Time T+1

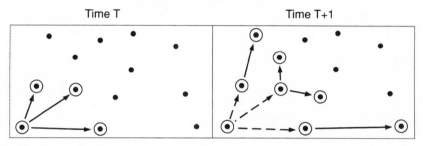

● Indicates a potential location of the diffusing phenomenon

◉ Indicates an actual location of the diffusing phenomenon during the time indicated

●——▶● Indicates that during the indicated time a stimulus passed from the node at the origin end of the arrow to the node at the destination end and resulted in location of the diffusing phenomenon at the destination node

●— ▸● Indicates that the stimulus represented in ●——▶● passed during a time period previous to the one indicated

Figure 9.1 Two types of diffusion: relocation (top panel) and expansion (bottom panel). Source: Brown 1968. Reprinted with permission of Lawrence Brown.

adopted in neighboring place B if the number of intervening places increases, because there is a greater probability of information moving from A to B. Moreover, the diffusion of an innovation is a process of growth to which items are added over time, whereas migration is a process of locational rearrangement. Regarding the two processes as diffusion merely because they both show some kind of movement serves no useful purpose.

A useful way to describe a topic such as diffusion is to see how popular textbooks in geography have treated this subject. Consider Haggett's *Geogra-*

phy—A Modern Synthesis (1983), which devotes an entire chapter to spatial diffusion. He begins the chapter with two stories: the diffusion of cholera from the island of Celebes in Indonesia in the early 1960s and the spread of hot pants in the West in the early 1970s. He continues:

> Things as different as influenza epidemics and oral contraceptives, bank rate charges and computer data banks, Dutch Elm diseases and fire ants have one thing in common. They originate in a few places and later spread over a much wider part of the world. Why are geographers interested in such diverse things? Principally because their spread provides valuable clues to how information is exchanged between regions. Where are the centers of diffusion—and why? At what rates do diffusion waves travel, and along what channels? Why do some waves die out rapidly and others persist? (Haggett 1983: 303–4)

Haggett also tells us why such knowledge can be helpful to planners. Again in his words:

> If we wish to speed up the diffusion of certain cultural elements, like the adoption of family-planning methods, a knowledge of precisely how waves of change pass through a regional system may be of help. If we wish to halt or reduce the spread of other cultural patterns like drug abuse . . . this knowledge may be helpful there, too. (Haggett 1983: 304)

The quotes from Haggett are particularly interesting because they reveal both the strengths and weaknesses of the locational approach to diffusion. This research is exciting because it offers the hope of discovering isomorphic models for the spread of such disparate items as computer data banks, hot pants, contraceptives, and fire ants; but similar claims for this research first appeared almost twenty-five years ago. In the ensuing years little useful knowledge has emerged from the much-repeated observations that these different phenomena are isomorphic, that they originate in a few places and later spread to other places. An example may clarify the gap between the practice and the promise of diffusion. For many years the government of India spent large amounts of money and carried on a very intensive campaign to spread the use of birth-control measures among its people. To my knowledge family planning authorities in India have had little help from diffusion models of "waves of change passing through regional systems." One may learn a great deal more about population planning from Mamdani's book, *Myth of Population Control* (1972). His interviews with people who had rejected the use of contraceptives distributed in Punjab by the Indian government and the Rockefeller Foundation are revealing. Their reasons for refusing to use contraceptives had to do with personal preferences, their social practices of family life, and the circumstances of life in rural northern India. I learned more about family planning in northern India of this period from Mamdani's narrative than I did from countless simulations I have run using spatial models of diffusion.

The rosy view of diffusion models nonetheless endures in the latest geographical review of diffusion, a volume entitled *Spatial Diffusion* (Morrill, Gaile, and Thrall 1988), one of a series of monographs called the "Scientific Geography Series." The authors repeat the excessive claims made in the past for spatial diffusion. Chapter 1 contains seven examples of spatial diffusion: 1) the distribution of ash fall from the 1980 eruption of Mount Saint Helens; 2) the spread of influenza; 3) the diffusion of a new word or phrase; 4) the purchase of personal microcomputers; 5) the spread of retail outlets belonging to a particular commercial franchise; 6) the expansion of an ethnic ghetto in an urban neighborhood; and 7) the spread of the built-up area at the edge of a city. They envision the possibility of a spatial theory of diffusion that explains these disparate phenomena because they all have a common thread. The fact that we have not been able to deliver on such claims after twenty-five years of research should cause us to reflect on the inadequacy of reasoning based on the similarity of geometric form. Although Gregory (1985) and Blaut (1977) make this point forcefully in their earlier critiques of spatial diffusion theory, neither is cited in the bibliography of *Spatial Diffusion* (Morrill, Gaile, and Thrall 1988).

At the heart of the location theory approach to diffusion is the work of Hägerstrand and his book on innovation diffusion published in Swedish in 1953. In 1967 it was translated into English by Allan Pred under the title *Innovation Diffusion as a Spatial Process*. Hägerstrand exerted much influence on geographers, particularly on those who applied diffusion models to development. I shall review Hägerstrand's work under three headings: empirical context, spatial theory of diffusion, and modeling methods.

Empirical context: Hägerstrand wanted to understand how innovations spread. To this end he studied the spread of a series of innovations in an agricultural community of the Kinda-Ydre districts of southern Östergtöland in south Sweden. These included the spread of the adoption of grazing improvement subsidies, bovine TB control, and soil mapping of the farms (figure 9.2). Hägerstrand's work reveals a masterful attention to empirical detail in the description of the study area and in the selection of diffusion indicators. For years his work inspired many younger geographers as a model that balanced a desire for theory and a care for empirical detail. As Pred has noted: "One could . . . argue that the book [*Innovation Diffusion as a Spatial Process*] is more important as a defensive bulwark against those who would deny the utility of empirical microanalysis in the construction of theory" (Hägerstrand 1967: 307).

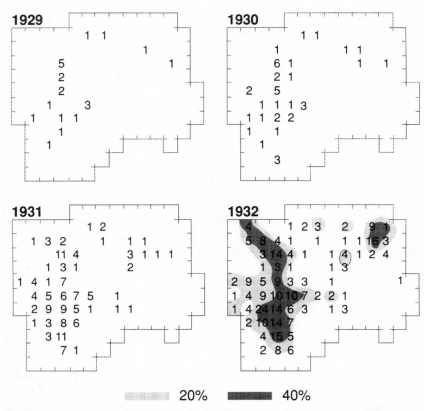

Figure 9.2 The observed spread of subsidies for improved pasture on small farms between 1929 and 1932 in Kinda-Ydre district of southern Östergötland in south Sweden. The cells are 5 km on a side, and the figures within the cells report the absolute
number of adopters from the start of the process to the end of the given years. The frequency of potential adopters is relatively uniform across the study area. The isolines on
the 1932 map depict the adopters as a proportion of potential adopters in the various
cells. Source: Hägerstrand 1968: 376. Reprinted by permission of Prentice-Hall, Inc.

Spatial theory of diffusion: Hägerstrand's primary concern was with the gen-
eralizability of his findings and with understanding diffusion as a spatial
process. Frequently, he stated that he was not concerned with the analysis of
a specific area nor with particular innovations. He referred to innovations as
"indicators" (Hägerstrand 1967: 1, 11, and 14). The spatial theory he discovered was that innovation spreads in a community through a network of face-
to-face interpersonal communication such that the likelihood of an adoption
at a given site is higher when it is close to a site of previous adoption, a sort of

"neighborhood effect." He also observed the influence of the urban hierarchy on the course of a diffusion when adoptions may by-pass neighboring places and short-circuit directly to the more important places at a greater distance. Hägerstrand's work deeply influenced subsequent emphases on the role of information in the diffusion of an innovation.[3]

Although Hägerstrand cautioned that his illustrative innovations had been deliberately chosen so as to clarify the spatial process at work, his younger disciples fixed on his seemingly exclusive focus on information. Hägerstrand has written that he consciously avoided those indicators "where it was obvious that economic or technical factors could impede their development" (1967: 11). For example, in explaining the adoption of grazing subsidies in southern Sweden, he said that the indicator was chosen because the subsidy was limited to a relatively homogeneous class of farmers, which essentially freed him "from the difficult task of bringing large interpersonal economic differences into play when interpreting the diffusion process" (1967: 70). Scholars who applied diffusion to development ignored this advice, however. This was a crucial mistake, because interpersonal economic differences and class play important roles in determining who does and who does not adopt agricultural innovations in the rural areas of the Third World—a point that has been stressed repeatedly by several observers (Blaut 1977; Griffin 1974; Havens and Flinn 1975; and Yapa and Mayfield 1978).

Modeling methods: Hägerstrand's modeling was part of a larger movement in quantitative geography and spatial theory that had been inspired by Christaller, Von Thünen, Weber, Lösch, and Isard. Hägerstrand's impact in the 1960s was in no small measure due to his methods, namely, modeling of diffusion as a stochastic process using Monte Carlo methods to simulate the spread of an innovation. I shall not describe his technique since it has been told and retold in hundreds of previous articles, monographs, and books, but I do feel compelled to share my reaction to it as a young graduate student at Syracuse University. I recall my fascination at seeing animated line printer computer maps moving from one frame to another as the Monte Carlo model simulated the "chancy life-like" spread of an innovation. As the maps moved from one time frame to another (time T_1, T_2, and so on) I sensed at once that I was dealing with something dynamic and that as a social scientist I might be able to perform a controlled experiment.[4] Time has tempered my enthusiasm, however. It is clear now that the stochastic element of Hägerstrand's Monte Carlo simulation of diffusion was more apparent than real. A few years later I noticed that the number of adoptions in each cell was actually being generated from a simple binomial distribution. Instead of drawing random numbers from a Monte Carlo distribution, it would have been easier to calculate the expected value of the number of adoptions by multiplying the probability of adoptions at any time T_i by the number of potential adopters remaining in the cell (Yapa 1975, 1976). My point here is that Monte Carlo methods conveyed the impression that the underlying process was complex and that this was the best available methodology to model the dynamic process. Actually, the transformation from one map of adoptions to another was being driven by simple binomial probabilities. Our imagination had been so completely captured by dizzying thoughts of modeling complexity and the excitement of Monte Carlo methods that we refused to look carefully at the process and at what was going on in the model itself. Another plausible explanation for our fixation with this model lies in the academic socialization we all underwent in our search for spatial order. As Szymanski and Agnew have shown through numerous examples in their book *Order and Skepticism* (1981), geographers have selectively seized on those examples that confirmed a sense of spatial order, regardless of how untypical or isolated they may be.

Hägerstrand viewed time and space as providing a backdrop for a series of events, namely, the pairwise contacts and adoptions, that were strung out along a one-dimensional time line and located in a two-dimensional space. In the Hägerstrand models of diffusion context is absent—time has no sense of history and space has no sense of place. Gregory (1985: 303) comments on this by drawing a useful distinction between time and history: "dependencies which are contained in such simulations are purely formal characteristics of a statistical series; they have nothing to do with any substantive theory of historical structuration."

Hägerstrand's modeling methods impacted his conceptualization of the diffusion process. He offered no serious discussion of the structure of social relations and systems of social practices through which innovations filter, nor of the consequences of the adoption of an innovation (Gregory 1985: 304). Doing so would have required greater attention to the innovation and to the circumstances surrounding the development of that innovation. To Hägerstrand, the innovation held little interest except as an indicator. As Gregory (1985: 304) argues, the consideration of the innovation is limited to the chorological—a sequence of distributional changes that are severed from the production and reproduction of social structures and systems. "In place of these multidimensional social processes, Hägerstrand substitutes the geometry of locational structure as simultaneously a space of description and of explanation." Actually, Gregory's characterization of diffusion can be generalized to the vast majority of work that passed under the rubric of spatial theory. In my assessment, as well as in Blaut's (1977) and Blaikie's (1978), it was the absence of social theory more than anything else that led to the demise of the spatial theory of innovation diffusion.

Market and Infrastructure Perspective

Brown (1981) has called the location theory approach to diffusion the "adoption perspective" because of its focus on adoption and demand aspects of diffusion. According to Brown, the adoption perspective implicitly assumes that all people have an equal opportunity to adopt, and hence the focus is on individual characteristics as an explanation for the timing of adoption (Brown 1981). In his book *Innovation Diffusion: A New Perspective* Brown introduces a new approach:

> The market and infrastructure perspective takes the stance that the opportunity to adopt is egregiously and in many cases purposely unequal. Accordingly, focus is upon the process by which innovations and the conditions for adoption are made available to individuals or households, that is the supply side of diffusion. At the base of this perspective . . . is the conviction that individual behavior does not represent free will so much as the choices within a constraint set and that it is government and private institutions which establish and control the constraints. . . . We can account for a great deal of variance in many social science phenomena by looking at institutional, rather than individual behavior. (Brown 1981: 7)

Brown conceptualizes the market and infrastructure perspective as a process that involves three activities or stages: the initial activity is the establishment of the diffusion agencies (or outlets) through which the innovation will be distributed; the second activity is the implementation of a strategy by each outlet to induce adoptions in its service area; and the third activity is the adoption of the innovation by individuals, the focus of most previous research, including that of Hägerstrand.

The market and infrastructure perspective is indeed very useful for development planning in poor countries because of its obvious relevance to things such as extension, sales and service of agricultural machinery, and the granting of rural credit. Brown claims that the development perspective is a logical extension to the market and infrastructure approach to diffusion because the latter "calls attention to the importance of access to resources and public infrastructure in innovation diffusion" (1981: 9–10). His claim is somewhat exaggerated, because what has come to be known as the development perspective covers many other topics, including the radical critique of diffusion theory (Blaut 1977, 1987; Blaikie 1978; Yapa 1981). The radical work focuses on constraints to access of resources arising from the context of underlying social structures, both domestic and international. Consider, for example, the spread of the green revolution in South Asia. Despite an adequate marketing system for fertilizer, pesticides, new hybrid seeds, irrigation pumps, and agricultural machinery in many regions (Brown's infrastructure), the pattern of adoption of innovations was socially uneven because not all potential adopters could afford to purchase inputs (Yapa and Mayfield 1978; Pearse 1975).

Development Perspective

In his book *Innovation Diffusion: A New Perspective* Brown spoke of the development perspective as a third approach in diffusion studies. Geographers' contributions here are of three kinds: spatial diffusion of modernization; market and infrastructure; and nondiffusion of innovations. Since these issues are considered in the subsequent section on paradigms of development, I shall not discuss them here in great detail.

Examples of the spatial diffusion of modernization are Gould's study in Tanzania (1970) and Soja's study in Kenya (1968).[5] These studies reflect the influence of two trends. The first is the theory of modernization emanating from sociology, anthropology, and political science in the 1960s and 1970s, especially the writings of Deutsch (1969), Dalton (1971), Pye (1963), Schramm (1964), Rogers (1969), Rostow (1960), and numerous others. The second is Hägerstrand's notion of innovation diffusion. Gould (1970) argues that the expansion of modernization measured by such things as the degree of urbanization, miles of railroads, and number of hospitals, schools, and markets should be viewed as a process of spatial diffusion. The infrastructural variables grouped into composite indices were mapped to yield statistical surfaces of modernization.

An example of the application of Brown's market and infrastructure approach to development is Garst's (1974) study of agricultural innovation among the Gusii people in the Kisii district of Kenya. Garst traces the diffusion of a series of innovations: coffee, pyrethrum, tea, passion fruit, hybrid maize, and high-grade cattle. In contrast to receptivity and information processes emphasized by Hägerstrand, the Gusii study confirmed Brown's view of the importance of infrastructure in the adoption of innovations.

The nondiffusion approach developed by Yapa (1977; 1979) and Blaut (1977; 1987) argues that diffusion of innovations in social spaces is characterized by class competition and differential access to productive resources. Mapping the spatial diffusion of an innovation in such spaces can mislead by concealing the fact that some potential adopters do not adopt because they simply cannot afford to do so. When a diffusion takes place at one level (class) of society, there is another active process of nondiffusion taking place at another level of the same society.

I shall return to this discussion after sketching a social theory for critically examining diffusion studies.

A Social Theory of Innovation Diffusion

To examine the role of diffusion theory in development studies, I begin by developing a framework of social theory around the concepts, the *nexus of production relations* and *biased innovations*. In this scheme the innovation and its attributes move to the center of the analysis in order to observe the evolution of production forces as part of the intricate web that forms the relations of production.

Nexus of Production Relations

The nexus of production relations refers to the bundle of relations associated with production and the mutual interactions among them. For purposes of this argument that bundle consists of five types of production relations: technical, social, ecological, cultural, and academic (figure 9.3). I have borrowed the term *production relations* and the dialectical mode of reasoning it implies from Marx. I have, however, extended the meaning of *production relations* beyond the social and tried to avoid the problems of the Marxian scheme of associating social relations with economic base, and matters of culture, knowledge, and ideology with superstructure. I explore the dialectical interactions among production relations without a priori theorizing about which among them is more determinate.

Technical relations of production refer to a concept that is similar but not identical to Marx's notion of forces of production, by which he meant the raw materials, resources, labor, and technology used in production. The term *technical relations* calls attention to the fact that the attributes of production forces are not independent of the larger context in which production occurs. Technical relations are determined by and, in turn, determine the form of other relations of production. Production forces are seldom neutral because they

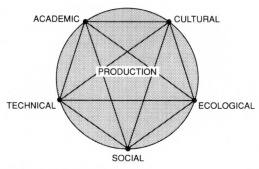

Figure 9.3 The nexus of production relations.

evolve through a process of biased innovations (Griffin 1974; Yapa and May-field 1978). When technical change is biased toward one factor of production or another the innovation is said to carry a factor bias. The introduction of bi-ased innovations, often planned, is one of the primary mechanisms by which existing social relations are reproduced. Griffin (1974) uses the concept of capital bias in innovation in describing the uneven social adoption of hybrid seeds of the Green Revolution in South Asia.

The expression *social relations of production* is employed here in a manner similar to its use in Marxian economics. It refers to the characteristics of the ownership of the means of production, the manner in which the means of pro-duction are utilized, and the rules for the social distribution of the final prod-uct. Technical and social relations of production interact in reciprocal ways. Social relations utilize innovations to develop particular technical relations that reinforce and reproduce existing social relations. Similarly, attributes of production forces limit and constrain forms of social relations. Technical and social relations, in turn, interact with ecological, cultural, and academic rela-tions of production.

Production may be usefully viewed as the social creation of use values from material through the application of information, energy, and labor. Produc-tion requires not only matter and energy, but also a repository for waste heat and material, which sets in motion a myriad of interactions with the biophys-ical environment—*the ecological relations of production*. Since production is embedded in nature, it is subject to the laws of ecology as expressed in the thermodynamics of matter and energy; the workings of the great chemical cy-cles on earth; and the biology of plants and animals. The environmental lit-erature is replete with examples of the impact of production forces on the ecosystem, air, water, land, and all forms of life. Conversely, these ecological changes also impact social relations of production, a theme developed in the influential international report *Our Common Future* (WCED 1987). Indeed, some of the major contradictions in advanced industrial economies are of eco-logical origin. The imperatives of growth are essentially incompatible with the existence of real limits to that growth posed by depleting resources and the planet's capacity to absorb wastes. Examples abound as accelerated produc-tion destroys the very base that sustains production and continued accumula-tion (O'Connor 1988).

Cultural relations of production refer to the mutual interactions between culture and economy. The culture of human groups represents a shared set of meanings, beliefs, values, and symbols. As an example, consider the impact of capitalist economics on the creation of values. Capitalists view workers not only as a supply of labor, but also as a source of demand for their product. The continued prosperity of capitalists depends on the rate of extraction of surplus value as well as on the rate of consumption of the workers. The rate and magnitude of consumption is maintained through well-known mechanisms eloquently described in Galbraith's classic *The Affluent Society* (1958) and in Packard's *The Hidden Persuaders* (1958). Expansion of demand for consumer goods is accomplished in part by the conscious creation of values, attitudes, and beliefs that are conducive to consumption. Through a cultural process known as consumerist socialization, the composition of a market basket of consumer goods has come to dominate how individuals are defined, their sense of self-worth and even of their dignity.[6] As Illich (1978: 4–53) has observed, in the last hundred years capitalist culture has molded patent solutions to our basic human needs and transformed these needs into a demand for manufactured products. Consumerist socialization is but one example; other manifestations of cultural relations include the roles of gender, family, and ethnicity in production.

Academic relations of production are of two broad types. One is related to research, innovation, and development of the productive forces (technical relations). This type has received much attention in the United States because of the impact of private industry and the military on the research agenda of the universities (Hightower 1973; Van den Bosch 1978; Dickson 1984). The other type of academic relations is less well known, its effects are more subtle, and it springs from our social theories of production. Paradigms of production can be distinguished by the categories, models, language, and habits of thought (epistemology) they employ. Concepts such as *overpopulation, resources, progressive farmers,* and *surplus value* reveal as much about specific academic paradigms as they do about production.

Consider the concept of overpopulation as an example. In neoclassical economics, *overpopulation* means that there are too many people in relation to a given resource base. When the population of an agrarian economy increases, more and more labor is applied to a fixed quantity of land, thus causing the onset of diminishing marginal returns to labor. Since the amount of land is fixed, the marginal returns to labor, at a certain point will equal zero, and beyond that point is the region of surplus labor, and hence of overpopulation. This argument, which appears in all standard textbooks on economics, is grounded in the economists' belief that land is a fixed factor of production. This assumption does not arise from absolute, immutable facts of geography nor from the abstract ratio of land to labor. On the contrary, surveys show that many overpopulated poor countries of the world are overpopulated simply because land ownership is concentrated in the hands of a few (Griffin 1976; Ahmed 1987; Eckholm 1979). When large areas of land are used for the cultivation of export-oriented commercial crops, the absence of land for the cultivation of food crops for people's subsistence arises from a socially induced scarcity. In this case the presumed fixed nature of land is an artifact of land tenure and patterns of landuse that in turn are determined by the social relations of private ownership. It is not possible to discuss overpopulation in the abstract without also referring to land systems and the manner in which land has been used. The notion of overpopulation thus arises in the context of an academic science that refuses to engage or question the rationality of the manner of utilization of land. A complete argument on the nature of the population problem would require a discussion of the meaning and origin of the concept of resources as well as of the problems of rapid growth of population, tasks that would take us beyond the scope of this paper. My point is simply that the way we think about development and the academic categories and models that we use are grounded in specific paradigms of production, and these academic relations of production affect the development and diffusion of innovations.

This leads to my principal hypothesis: production weaves technology, society, culture, ecology, and knowledge into a tight structure that I call the nexus of production relations (figure 9.3). Since innovations constitute the leading edge in the development of production forces, a social theory of innovations needs to be grounded in the context of production, that is, in the nexus of production relations.

Biased Innovations

The concepts of biased innovation and nexus of production relations should lie at the core of a social theory of innovation diffusion. It is odd that theories of spatial diffusion heretofore have paid little attention to the attributes of innovations. As the leading edge in development, innovations often foreshadow the form of the production forces to come. These attributes are not intrinsic to the innovations; rather, they are defined and emerge in the context of a nexus of production. Innovations are seldom neutral, and their biases reflect the context of production relations in which innovations are developed, adopted, and used.

Production relations are closely related through dialectical interactions that act and react constantly to maintain dynamic historical processes of innovation, noninnovation, adoption, and nonadoption. What appears to be technical from one angle or at one point in time becomes academic or social from another angle or at a different point in time, or what is academic is actually social or cultural. The discussion of innovation bias in the ensuing paragraphs contains some repetition, which I have consciously retained because I do not wish to convey the impression that production relations are sharp, analytical categories. They are constructs intended to facilitate a discussion, and are not freestanding entities amenable to precise definition.

The idea of biased innovations has been developed by several writers (Griffin 1974; Yapa 1977; Ellis 1988: 210–217). Consider a production function with an isoquant where two producers attain their equilibrium with different ratios of factor proportions (points A and B on isoquant Q1 in figure 9.4). Such a situation occurs in fragmented factor markets where producers face price discrimination in access to inputs (Ellis 1988: 201–206). An innovation is said to have taken place if a new technique produces the same output at a lower level of input (isoquant Q2 in figure 9.4). The innovation is said to be superior and neutral when it has moved the isoquant toward the origin parallel to the original one at Q1. The two producers will move to the new isoquant while maintaining the same factor proportions. A situation that pushes an isoquant away from the origin is said to be inferior (Q3 of figure 9.4).

Technical Bias

In technical change that is neutral, the ratio of inputs— say labor to capital—remains the same at given factor prices, but technical change is seldom neutral to factors. When technical change is biased in favor of one or more inputs over another, then we say the innovation carries a factor bias. The isoquants in biased innovation, instead of moving parallel to themselves, swivel steeply toward one factor (figure 9.5). The producer equilibrium will move from point B on Q1 to B' on Q2 for the same factor price ratio. As the figure shows, this innovation uses less labor and more capital.

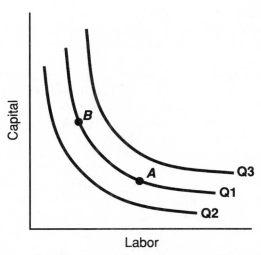

Figure 9.4 Factors of production and the representation of innovation.

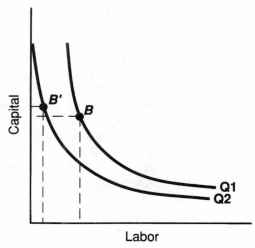

Figure 9.5   Representing factor bias in innovations.

Social Bias

When social access to factors of production are unequal, technical bias acquires a social bias (Yapa 1981). The prices of land and credit in South Asia provide numerous examples of social differentials in real factor prices (Griffin 1974; Ellis 1988; Hartman and Boyce 1988). The adoption of biased innovations no doubt impacts the social relations of production, but it must be remembered that by working through the process of research and development, social relations also determine the nature of the innovation process. The way in which social relations develop production forces and reproduce existing relations is well illustrated by the history of the diffusion of the Green Revolution in Mexico.

The story of high-yielding seeds, though often told, merits repeating. The story goes back at least to 1934, when Lazaro Cardenas, a general with rural origins, was elected president of Mexico. He instituted a series of sweeping land reforms in an effort to strengthen peasant cooperatives while at the same time initiating in the Mexican ministry of agriculture a program of research for the improvement of rain-fed crops grown by peasants, particularly corn and beans. Cardenas's other activities, however, which included the nationalization of foreign-owned railroads and oil interests, caused alarm both in Mexico and in the United States. By 1942 those opposed to his agrarian reforms moved back into power after the election of Avila Camacho as president. In 1943, the Camacho administration invited the Rockefeller Foundation to participate in a new program of agricultural research that discarded previous programs oriented toward nonirrigated, rain-fed subsistence agriculture and peasants. As public policy shifted from cooperative agriculture to rapid industrialization and the strengthening of private commercial farming, a new technology of high-yielding hybrid seeds responsive to material inputs was born. Proponents of the policy believed that the food surplus from commercial farming would feed the new industrial labor of Mexico and that agriculture in turn would provide markets for fertilizer, chemical pesticides, irrigation pumps, and agricultural machinery. The emphasis on high-yielding seeds thus grew out of a research program committed to the development of capital intensive commercial agriculture.

A social theory of innovation offers a reinterpretation of this classic story. The physical attributes of high-yielding seeds are really technical relations of production that reflect the academic relations directing the research, and they in turn mirror the economic power structure prevailing in Mexico in the 1940s. The relationship between the attributes of high-yielding seeds and social relations of production was reciprocal. During the presidencies of Avila Camacho (1941–1946) and Miguel Aleman (1947–1952) power elites determined the priorities in agricultural research. Certain segments of the society, namely landlords with access to large landholdings in northwest Mexico in the province of Sonora, took advantage of a technology that required irrigated land, facilities for irrigation, access to credit, and heavy material inputs, that is, capital. The Green Revolution, as this program came to be known, did much for agribusiness manufacturers of pumps, machines, fertilizer, and pesticides but little for the nutrition and welfare of Mexican peasants (Hewitt de Alcantara 1976).

Other examples of social bias come from industrial firms that resort to innovation to discourage competition through ever-higher levels of capital investment in mechanization, automation, and robotics. These firms know that the value of invested capital cannot be recuperated when technology is easily copied. This is a reason why the development of appropriate technology for the Third World cannot be left to oligopolistic international capital; it will raise the capital cost of innovation to the point that it cannot be easily copied and adapted for widespread use in poor countries.

Ecological Bias

Insofar as an innovation impacts the environment, we may also speak of its ecological bias. Innovations can be evaluated according to the type and amount of energy required, the amount and nature of waste heat and material generated, the amount of nonrenewable resources required, and the degree to which ecological systems are disrupted. When energy physicist Lovins

(1977) speaks of soft and hard energy paths, he is referring to the notion of ecological bias in innovation. Soft technologies, according to Lovins, are flexible, resilient, sustainable, and ecologically benign.

The concept of ecological bias in innovation is important for two reasons. The first comes from the need to develop innovations that are sustainable and ecologically benign. The second is related to the possibility of developing innovations that require little capital and material and that maximize the capture of use values created by nature. Advocates for the use of soft technology in poor countries envision a process of innovation that is socially biased toward the needs of the poor—peasant farmers, landless laborers, urban unemployed, and those marginalized in the informal economies of Third World cities. Such innovations capture use values created by nature and are difficult for the propertied classes to monopolize (McRobie 1981; Schumacher 1973). The large amount of literature on appropriate technology demonstrates the technical feasibility of developing such innovations (Darrow and Saxenian 1986).

To illustrate the notion of ecological bias, I return to the Green Revolution. Wherever high-yielding seeds were adopted, the following effects ensued: the contamination of groundwater from pesticides and fertilizer, elimination of nontarget populations from chemical poisoning, deterioration in soil structure and increase in soil erosion resulting from the increased use of chemical fertilizer and reduction in the use of organic matter, the elimination of practices such as crop rotation and the growing of leguminous crops, and the loss of biological diversity in plants resulting from the cultivation of genetically uniform plants. The loss of genetic variety in plant material is a less visible but nonetheless most serious consequence of the spread of high-yielding varieties. Whereas the traditional varieties of wheat, rice, corn, and potatoes have great genetic diversity because they have adapted over thousands of years to small geographic variations in soil, slope, and moisture, the crops of the Green Revolution were genetically uniform, bred selectively for high yields at the expense of other characteristics (Mooney 1979). Some scientists view the loss of genetic diversity in crops and animals with great alarm because it threatens the long-term food security of the planet (Ehrlich, Ehrlich, and Holdren 1977: 344). In the short term it poses a threat to the livelihood of poor farmers in the Third World, who rely on the genetic diversity of plants as a major resource for coping with plant diseases, climatic fluctuations, and geographic variations in site.

Cultural Bias

The notion of innovation bias also extends to the realm of culture. The connection between receptivity to certain kinds of innovations and products and value systems of people is obvious. Earlier I referred to a concept called consumerist socialization, which affects the values of people in market societies. A Third World example of the impact of advertising, image-making, values, and cultural bias is the story of the spread of infant formula to poverty-stricken mothers. Formula was developed in a modern, industrial culture where mothers work for long hours away from home, where household incomes are ample to purchase the product, and where water and sanitary conditions are adequate to safeguard the prepared formula from bacterial contamination. For many years a few infant formula manufacturing companies carried out a major advertising campaign to condition values and persuade Third World mothers that bottle feeding was better because that was what "modern moms" did. The tragic consequences of this innovation has now been widely publicized (Dobbing 1988).

To illustrate another aspect of the concept of cultural bias in innovation, consider the sociological model that defines two categories of culture—modern and traditional. Writers such as Rogers (1969), Dalton (1971), and Rostow (1960) define *traditional* to mean backward societies that were slow to innovate or undertake change. This conceptualization devalues traditional societies. In contrast, I use the term to mean a community where the conduct of activity and the transfer of knowledge is based on experiences transmitted from one generation to another (Wilken 1987). The process of knowledge transfer in traditional cultures is informal and oral. This is perhaps one reason why traditional societies are perceived as being noninnovative. Another reason is that innovations are often subtle and cost little. In his uniformitarian critique of diffusionism, Blaut (1987) offers an excellent discussion of how and why we perceive traditional cultures to be noninnovative. He notes that the spread of European colonialism and culture was seen as scientifically correct and morally justifiable because the landscapes and cultures into which these things were inserted were seen, in one sense or another, as empty. Support for such views come to us from the recent literature on traditional agricultural technology (Altieri and Anderson 1986). Based on surveys of traditional farming conducted in several sites from southern Mexico and Middle America, Wilken observes:

> I did not survey much of the region, and, even in the limited study areas, I suspect I missed more than I found. The reasons lie in both the practices and the observer. Traditional technology is closely attuned to local environmental and social conditions and varies, sometimes dramatically, from one area to another. A single valley may shelter management techniques unknown elsewhere. In addition, traditional management forms are small and unobtrusive, seldom evidenced by specialized tools or impressive structures. The outside observer, accustomed to agroecosystem manipulations on a grand scale, can easily miss the

significance of a row of stones on a hillside or a shading branch over a seed bed.
(Wilken 1987: 8–9)

Wilken goes on to describe traditional resource management techniques in
energy supply, soil classification, and the management of soil, water, slope,
and space. An important point of Wilken's study is that traditional tools and
techniques are not easily duplicated because most of the traditional technology requires understanding local conditions and ways of managing resources
by using local energy and materials. Harrison (1987) in his book *The Greening of Africa* reports on a wide array of indigenous, traditional techniques for
soil conservation, water use, and agroforestry that have been very successful in
local areas but often are unknown to people in neighboring valleys. He calls
for the diffusion of a new Green Revolution in Africa that incorporates these
traditional practices—an idea reiterated by Richards (1985) in his book on
West African agriculture, *The Indigenous Agricultural Revolution*. My point is
that the modern literature on diffusion in the Third World profoundly misrepresented and misinterpreted traditional societies as backward and noninnovative. This cultural bias, abetted in part by academics, affected public policy and the course and consequences of diffusion.

Academic Bias

Academic bias in innovation arises from two sources that correspond to the
two kinds of academic relations of production. First is the academic bias in
the development of technology. A concrete example is the disproportionate
funding for development of chemical pesticides as compared to biological or
cultural methods of pest control. The late Van den Bosch (1978), a noted entomologist, in his book *The Pesticide Conspiracy* described the resistance and
harassment encountered at his university during his study of the hazards of
chemical pest control and the development of ecologically benign low-cost alternatives. Biological methods represent little cost to the user, although their
research can be expensive, and yet little funding has been channeled into this
area. According to entomologist Paul Debach, the funding for research in biological methods is small because these methods do not generate profits compared to chemical methods (cited in Nebel 1981: 428–29).

The second aspect of academic bias in innovation is less obvious and has to
do with the impact of prevailing social theory on the development, promotion,
diffusion, and adoption of innovations. Recall my reference to the distinctions
between modern and traditional society used by such writers as Rostow (1960)
and Rogers (1969). According to Rogers, a traditional society is characterized
by its lack of innovativeness. He argues that Third World peasants generally

do not react to new ideas with a positive attitude. By contrast, modern societies are innovative and responsive to change. Rogers's conception of society has clear implications for the nature and diffusion of innovations: innovations originate in modern societies; innovations by definition are good because they are associated with modernity; innovations spread from modern to traditional societies; traditional societies need to change and they need to be modernized; and the task of modernization will be accomplished through the adoption of innovations, among other things. Students of modernization theory should not look to traditional society for innovation; moreover, it is inconceivable that a modern society would adopt an innovation developed in a traditional society. To conclude the point, it is impossible to understand the meaning of *innovation* in modernization theory unless it is viewed in the context of the static definition of traditional society (Rogers 1969; Pye 1963; Gould 1969).

My second example of academic bias is the diffusion of birth control in South Asia and the authoritative influence it acquired in prevailing theories of population. I earlier referred to the academic theory of the economic origin of overpopulation. That theory holds that poverty in the Third World is caused by the presence of large numbers (overpopulation), the continued rapid growth of these numbers, and a shortage of capital, technology, land, and resources in general. This view of the population and poverty problem conferred a new urgency to the program for the diffusion of birth control techniques. In the foreword to Ehrlich's (1971) famous book *The Population Bomb* appears the following line: "The roots of the new brutality . . . are in the lack of population control. There is, we must hope and predict, a chance to exert control in time." By constructing the problem in this manner population theorists foreclosed the possibility of a broad spectrum of solutions to the problem. Doubtless such views influenced the vigor and pace of the Indian government's pursuit of family planning programs in the 1970s. These programs focused on the control of reproduction through technical means that were, according to Indian news reports, sometimes high-handed and coercive—forced mass sterilizations, for example. The point is that the specific interpretation of the problem (academic relations) determined the solution and the manner in which the family planning and birth-control campaign was conducted. The campaign's emphasis on birth control as the innovation for diffusion, its organization, the money provided for it by the government, and the tactics employed in the diffusion of birth control cannot be understood apart from the demographic social theory that defined India's problem of poverty as one of overpopulation.

India's problems of poverty and population were hardly so simple. As noted earlier, the shortage of land in the Third World is a socially induced relation that has to do with the concentration of land ownership and the allocation of land to export crops for foreign markets instead of growing food crops for domestic consumption. Also, the concept of resources that is prevalent in poor countries is one that has come to them from modern industrial societies. The now copious literature on appropriate technology helps to redefine our view of resources. According to this new thinking, resources exist in places and are embodied in regional complexes made up of several elements: topography, climate, drainage, plants, animals, land tenure, language, culture, and local knowledge of people. In this sense, resources are place specific; it is meaningless to talk of the absence of resources in the abstract. If overpopulation is caused by a lack of resources, then the discussion of resource scarcity must be grounded in the place specifics of regional geography. In this version of social theory the problem of overpopulation becomes more complex; it is constructed differently. Our solutions, and the ensuing campaigns of diffusion, will differ radically from what we have seen in South Asia. My argument should not be misconstrued. The rapid rate of population growth is a problem in some places, but the solutions to that problem should begin by understanding why families feel the need for many children.

Innovation Bias and the Two Faces of Production

Production is conventionally defined as the creation of use values. When production forces are stagnant and underdeveloped, the economy lacks basic goods or use values; hence, the expansion of production and the diffusion of innovations constitute the main vehicles of economic development and the solutions to poverty. Production, however, is Janus-faced. Under certain circumstances it at once creates and destroys use values. Given the two faces of production, poverty often arises out of this creative/destructive dialectic of production. The concept of innovation bias can be used to clarify this dual aspect of production forces.

We have already cited several examples of the destructive power of production. Recall the case of high-yielding seeds. Their adoption was attended by the introduction of commercial pesticides and chemical fertilizer, which led to a concurrent discontinuance of traditional methods of biological and cultural pest control, crop rotation, and the use of organic material to enhance soil quality. The diffusion of high-yielding varieties also reduced and suppressed the role of beneficial natural and biological interactions in the agricultural system. The spread of high-yielding varieties in South Asia in a Hägerstrand innovation wave thus was accompanied by a corresponding, albeit lagged, wave of destruction that reduced genetic diversity, discounted biological and cultural resources, devalued local knowledge, degraded the environment, and fostered poverty through socially induced scarcity.

The history of production is a complex dialectical whole; it cannot be reduced to separate histories of technology, political economy, and ecology. Dismembering production in this fashion conceals the dual nature of modern production and diffusion, the dialectic of creation/destruction. It is mistaken to think of the ecological and social crises of Third World poverty as external problems that have specific solutions. On the contrary, ecological degradation and poverty are normal, routine, everyday manifestations of production itself and hence form internal relations of production. We can discern these relationships by examining the biases of innovation and production forces.

In summary, what do we mean when we speak of the diffusion of an innovation? When we map the adoption of high-yielding seeds? These maps reveal the areal spread of some but not all aspects of the attributes of production forces. They obscure the consequences, the bundle of interacting, reinforcing, and contradictory effects embedded in the nexus of production relations. We ignore these effects because our epistemology of diffusion is hopelessly trapped in the visible cartography of maps and the reductionist logic of diffusion studies.

Views of Innovation in Development Theory

This section examines the views of innovation embodied in the three major paradigms of economic development from the perspective of the nexus of production relations. The three paradigms of development are the school of neoclassical economics, Marxian political economy, and sustainable development.

Neoclassical Economics

Neoclassical economists view Third World countries as structurally dualistic economies—one sector is modern and dynamic, and the other is traditional, static, and slow to change. In this view the low state of development of productive forces in the traditional sector is caused by the lack of savings, investment, capital, infrastructure, and the persistence of rapid rates of population growth. This structural imbalance can be corrected by the transfer of capital and know-how from rich countries to poor and internally from dynamic sectors to static ones. The orthodox view holds that the objective of development is the attainment of levels of industrialization and high mass consumption comparable to those of developed market economies in the West. Success is measured by the growth in a nation's per capita income.

The Green Revolution of high-yielding seeds is a good example of the use of the diffusionist paradigm by neoclassical economists. These seeds were developed at the international research centers such as CIMMYT, the International Center for the Improvement of Maize and Wheat in Mexico, and IRRI, the International Rice Research Institute in the Philippines. The diffusion of the seeds was supported through two networks, the first consisting of agricultural extension agents that provide information and advice, and the second consisting of marketing and distribution outlets (Brown's marketing and infrastructure). The basic strategy was to induce an increase in the rate of seed adoption in the hope that diffusion would increase food production. The logic was as follows: food production was low because of poor technology and production forces; thus the solution involved the spread and adoption of improved production forces (diffusion of new seeds and the purchase of inputs). This example typifies the diffusionist approach of the neoclassical paradigm. If the principal problem with Third World agriculture is poor production, then the solution is to transfer new technology, in this case hybrid seeds and the inputs to use them, to the traditional sector. In the language employed in this paper, the attributes of the new seeds are technical relations that reflect social structures, academic research priorities, social science models of non-innovating traditional societies, ecological conditions, and value systems; hence, it is the nexus of production relations which determine the form of diffusion and its consequences. By focusing on only the technical aspects of seed diffusion, neoclassical analysis ignores the larger context in which diffusion takes place. This is not merely an academic argument of wishing to add more independent variables to the problem. The context, that is, the nexus of production relations, changes our perception of what these seeds mean and do.

Radical Political Economy

A second approach to development is radical political economy. This paradigm regards social relations of production as the key to development and underdevelopment. The argument runs as follows: the distribution of poverty in the world reflects the evolution of the global system of capital that fostered development in Europe and North America (the core) and underdevelopment in South America, Africa, and Asia (the periphery). The colonial powers introduced productive forces in the colonies in order to meet their domestic needs for raw materials, markets, industry, and food needs of laborers. In the colonies food production competed for land with commercial export crops. Taxes on peasants induced them to earn money by laboring for owners of mines and plantations. Colonial authorities discouraged native industry as the British did in the case of Indian textiles. Railroads and other infrastructure, built in a dendritic pattern, drained the surplus from the interior to coastal ports and thence overseas (Stavrionos 1981; Magdoff 1978; Frank 1970). This process of surplus extraction took place with the active collaboration of a small class of local elites, Baran's "comprador bourgeoisie" (1957: 205–18). Not even the liquidation of colonial empires has ended the process of surplus extraction, which continues to impoverish the peasants, the landless, the urban poor, and the unemployed (Hayter 1981). The circuits of surplus extraction persist through the efforts of local elites and multinational business aided by: 1) deteriorating terms of trade for export commodities (Emmanuel 1972); 2) repatriation of profits by foreign enterprises; 3) transfer pricing (Barnett and Muller 1974); 4) overseas capital flight; 5) military purchases; 6) charges for debt servicing (George 1988); and 7) use of land, infrastructure, research, and other resources for the promotion of export crops instead of food production (Lappe and Collins 1977).

The principal contribution of radical political economy is the recognition that social relations of production are central to the creation of development and underdevelopment in the global system of capital. Frank (1970) characterizes this situation as "the development of underdevelopment," a process that can be understood only by a detailed examination of the history of the utilization of the economic surplus appropriated from various regions. Such views have several implications for our discussion on innovation diffusion. It was radical political economists who first pointed out the shallowness of the location-theoretic neoclassical views of diffusion. These views, they argued, misrepresented colonial society as static and traditional, when in fact it was really a dynamic manifestation of the arrested state of development of production forces under capitalist relations of production (Slater 1973; 1977a). The corollary of this critique, the nondiffusion of innovations, was developed by Blaut (1977) and Yapa (1977). This argument holds that privileged access to resources in the Third World determines who adopts innovation and who does not. Diffusion occurs at one level of society while nonadoption occurs at another level. Nonadoption is permanent, but it is not to be equated with a passive state caused by ignorance or apathy. It is an active state related to the economic and class institutions of the society.

Efforts to incorporate social relations of production into diffusion processes have enhanced our understanding of the limitations of conventional models. Indeed, the concept of the nexus of production relations owes much to Marx's dialectical conception of social relations. When the concept of production relations is extended beyond the social, however, the radical conception of innovation diffusion becomes clearer and its drawbacks more evident.

First, radical political economy has not developed a critical theory of the qualitative attributes of production forces. The refusal of political economy to accord theoretical significance to these qualitative attributes may be because of the intellectual legacy of classical Marxism and its uncritical enthusiasm for the quantitative development of production forces. *The Communist Manifesto* contains several eloquent passages praising the progressive role of the bourgeoisie in unleashing the power of industry, agriculture, transport, and communication. The feudal relations of property disappeared, Marx explained, because they stood in the way of further development of production forces. Similarly, capitalism would one day come to act as a fetter on the economy, and it too would burst asunder and be swept away by the forward march of production forces and history. Marx notwithstanding, there is reason to speculate that capitalist relations will be changed not by the forward march of production forces but rather by the ecological contradictions inherent in that forward march. Qualitative attributes of production forces thus are key concerns for diffusion and development theory. The widespread environmental destruction and the urgent need to develop alternative technologies insist on this perspective.

Second, radical political economy has not explored the impact of production forces on social relations and the potential role of technology in changing social relations. Bookchin (1986), Illich (1973), and Gorz (1980) have all commented at great length on these issues. To quote Gorz:

> The techniques on which the economic system is based are not neutral. In fact, they reflect and determine the relations of the producers to their product, of the workers to their work, of the individual to the group and the society, of people to their environment. Technology is the matrix in which the distribution of power, the social relations of production, and the hierarchical division of labor are embedded. The inversion of tools is a fundamental condition of the transformation of society. . . . Socialism is no better than capitalism if it makes use of the same tools. The total domination of nature inevitably entails a domination of people by the techniques of domination. (Gorz 1980: 20)

Third is the neglect of ecological issues. Today, some of the major contradictions in the advanced industrial economies are ecological in origin (O'Connor 1988). The basic incompatibility in the imperatives of growth on the one hand and the existence of limits to growth and on the planet's capacity to absorb wastes on the other are increasingly evident. Examples of accelerated production destroying the productive base that sustains production are all too frequent (Ehrlich, Ehrlich, and Holdren 1977: 621–94). The ecological relations of production thus are important for a discussion of diffusion and development, not least because nature creates value. Consider these examples from the extractive and agricultural sectors of the economy. In extractive economies the inputs of capital and labor are low relative to the value of commodities such as petroleum, minerals, and lumber from natural forests (Bunker 1984; Hecht 1988). Since lumber exports acquire much of their value from the mineral wealth of the soils of natural forests, the trade in lumber between regions has ecological as well as economic characteristics. In the case of agriculture consider the production of X bushels of corn requiring Y kilograms of chemical fertilizer. Suppose that the required quantities of nitrogenous fertilizer are obtained by using cultural and biological technologies such as crop rotation and interplanting with legumes (Miller 1988: 203–6). Further suppose that these methods created a value of nitrogen equal to or greater than that provided by chemicals. We can then argue that a part of the new value was created by nature. There is a growing literature related to this argument, particularly in the area of sustainable agriculture.[7] In a wider sense advocates of AT (appropriate technologies) have claimed that low-cost, affordable technologies already exist for capturing use value created by nature in the area of food production, nutrition, health, and construction. Regrettably, this literature on alternative technology in economic development has been virtually ignored in the radical literature in geography.[8]

There are two kinds of Marxist theories to explain underdevelopment: world-systems theory and orthodox Marxist theory. In world-systems theory underdevelopment and poverty are explained as the normal way capitalism manifests itself in the periphery of the world-system; this view holds that development could not be achieved within the capitalist framework of the world economy (Frank 1970; Wallerstein 1987; Baran 1957). Orthodox Marxists who have adopted a line of reasoning more consistent with classical Marxism contest the claims of the world-systems theorists; they argue that underdevelopment represents a failure of capitalism to get established in parts of the Third World (Warren 1983). From the perspective developed in this paper the difference in the claims of the classical Marxists and world- systems theorists is not very fundamental. In both these viewpoints underdevelopment in the Third World receives its defining character from a reflection of development in the First World. In this sense the varieties of Marxist theories are similar to neoclassical economics in their definition of underdevelopment, and in a normative sense they all agree on the desirability of development and the forward march of progress. Marxism, despite its brilliant unraveling of bourgeoisie ideology and its science, carries the burden of its own unexamined epistemic roots in European industrial culture.

The implications of the radical paradigm for innovation diffusion are obvious: development requires the diffusion and adoption of modern industrial and agricultural production forces as developed in the West; the transition from poverty to development requires the socialist transformation of production relations, but the nature of technology and type of production forces used are not problematic issues. Depending on our philosophical perspective, whether neoclassical or radical, development amounts to transforming a traditional society or a mode of peripheral capitalism. In either case, the lot of the poor of the Third World allegedly will be improved through the diffusion of modern industrial and agricultural science, and by the universal notions of progress.

Sustainable Development

Today a third paradigm called sustainable development has arisen, although it is not clear to what extent it constitutes an alternative to neoclassical economics and radical political economy. This paradigm sprang out of the realization that present patterns of economic growth cannot be sustained in the long run because they pose serious threats to the environment. A recent influential statement on sustainable development, the report of the U.N. World Commission on Environment and Development (WCED 1987) titled *Our Common Future*, describes sustainable development as an effort to meet the needs of the present without compromising our ability to meet future needs. The following excerpt summarizes the Commission's argument:

> The problems of poverty and underdevelopment cannot be solved unless we have a new era of growth in which developing countries play a stronger role and reap greater benefits. . . . The world's decisionmakers are beginning to understand that it is impossible to separate economic development from environmental issues. Poverty is both a cause and effect of global environmental problems. Sustainable development is best understood as a process of change in which the use of resources, the direction of investments, the orientation of technological development, and institutional change all enhance the potential to meet human needs both today and tomorrow. (Lebel and Kane 1989: 2–3)

Our Common Future emphasizes what I have called the ecological relations of production. Proponents of sustainable development advocate the use of appropriate technology, recommend the use of local resources, and counsel us to pay greater heed to "nonexpert" local knowledge. What view of innovations is most compatible with the paradigm of sustainable development? The Commission takes up this question in a section titled "The Diffusion of Environmentally Sound Technologies": "The promotion of sustainable development will require an organized effort to develop and diffuse new technologies, such as for agricultural production, renewable energy systems and pollution control" (WCED 1987: 87). The real implications of this and many other statements in the report are not clear. A possible explanation of the problem is that the Commission tries to address three issues without exploring their mutual contradictions—the need for economic growth, the need to protect the environment, and the need to eradicate poverty. The report makes the astonishing claim that sustainable development provides a framework for accomplishing all three objectives. It is difficult to imagine an innovation theory that is compatible with the goals of sustainable development as stated in *Our Common Future*. I shall explain some of the difficulties by returning to the concept of the nexus of production relations.

Our Common Future, based as it is on ahistorical accounts of environmental degradation, conveys the impression that these mistakes are attributable to past excesses, irrationality, and lack of ecological information. This is true in many cases, but it is not a satisfactory explanation in many other instances. Consider the following examples: continual underfunding of U.S. research into methods of organic farming despite a well-documented history of problems associated with high-energy factory farming three decades after Carson's *Silent Spring* (1962); continued underfunding of research on alternatives to chemical control of crop diseases; and the generous funding of research on high-yielding varieties of cereals despite knowledge of their genetic vulnerability to disease. Although *Our Common Future* commendably promotes the diffusion of environmentally sound technologies, success will require searching analyses of academic relations of production and why such technologies have not been forthcoming.

Second, *Our Common Future* argues that poverty is both a cause and effect of global environmental problems; accordingly, it calls for a new era of economic growth that would eradicate poverty. These arguments are troublesome because they are not compatible with the data they present. According to statistics cited by the Commission, we now have a $13 trillion world economy. Industrial production has grown more than fiftyfold over the past century and four-fifths of this growth has occurred since 1950 (WCED 1987: 31), that is, since the independence of former colonies; yet, in 1980, 340 million people in 87 developing counties were not getting enough calories to prevent stunted growth and serious health risk (WCED 1987: 29). If economic growth of these magnitudes is accompanied by widespread hunger, what conceivable grounds are there for assuming that new economic growth will make a difference? Ironically, the current annual increases in industrial production are so large that amounts of environmental destruction that used to take decades are now squeezed into one year. When past economic growth has brought so much environmental destruction and so little improvement for the poor, what is the logic of calling for a new era of economic growth? Sustainable development for the eradication of poverty needs a theory of innovation that takes into account the mutual interdependencies of production relations along the lines indicated in this paper. In the absence of policy that would follow from such an analysis, *Our Common Future* amounts to a blueprint of good intentions with little prospect of being effective.

Questions of sustainable development give a new urgency to the role of cultural geography in the emerging debates. Although many cultural geographers have turned their back to the themes that Sauer (1956) articulated in his "The Agency of Man on the Earth," it is worth recalling his strictures on modernity. In the final section of that paper, Sauer wrote a brilliant critique of modern economic growth that anticipated many of the issues being debated today. I quote from several passages:

> Progress is the common watchword of our age, its motor innovating techniques, its objective the ever expanding "dynamic economy," with ever increasing input of energy. Capacity to produce and capacity to consume are the twin spirals of the new age which is to have no end . . . our principal problem now is to accelerate obsolescence.
>
> The current agricultural surpluses are not proof that food production has ceased to be a problem. . . . Our output has been secured at unconsidered cost and risks by the objective of immediate profit, which has replaced the older attitudes of living with the land. This change got under way especially as motors replaced draft animals. Land formerly used for oats and feed crops became available to grow more corn, soybeans, cotton, and other crops largely sold and shipped. The traditional corn-oats-clover rotation, protective of the surface and maintaining nitrogen balance, began to break down. . . . Soil-depleting and soil-exposing crops were given strong impetus in the shift to mechanized farming. (Sauer 1956: 66)

Sauer also commented on the transfer of this technology overseas—the diffusion of modern agriculture. "Our programs of agricultural aid pay little attention to native ways and products. Instead of going out to learn what their experiences and preferences are, we go forth to introduce our ways and consider backward what is not our pattern" (Sauer 1956: 68).

Sauer's critique of modern economic growth and his counsel to learn from the study of indigenous systems are recurrent themes in the contemporary dialogue on development (Wilken 1987; Harrison 1987; Richards 1985; Jackson, Berry, and Colman 1984). A proper response requires fruitful collaboration between political economy and cultural ecology to produce a new social theory of innovation.

Conclusion

Studies in spatial diffusion of innovations, after enjoying much popularity in geography during the 1960s and 1970s, fell into a state of neglect in the middle 1980s. Some observers such as Gregory believe that the diminished influence of diffusion theory came about because of its lack of attention to social theory. The theme of diffusion also suffered setbacks from the radical critique of economic modernization. This turn of events was unfortunate because the topic of innovation diffusion remains central to issues of poverty, development, and ecology. Innovations represent the forward edge of changes in production forces that will reduce poverty or deepen it, that will conserve nature or degrade it. What sort of social theory is most appropriate for innovations and their diffusion in the context of development?

I have drawn on the concepts of the nexus of production relations and biased innovation in developing a social theory of diffusion relevant to economic development and evaluating the views of innovation diffusion in the development paradigms. In the past, geographers, economists, and Marxist economists paid little attention to the attributes of the innovation—mistakenly, I believe. The attributes of an innovation are not merely intrinsic properties; they are relations of production whose character imparts a bias to the innovation. As with the example of high-yielding seeds, an innovation has technical, social, ecological, cultural, and academic relations that are seamlessly interwoven with each other. When a geographer maps the spatial diffusion of an innovation, what usually results is a map of only the surface material form of the innovation; but what actually spreads from one place to another is a nexus of production relations and associated innovation bias. Understanding that nexus, I believe, reveals the meaning of innovation for poverty, ecology, and development.

Notes

I wish to thank Glenda Laws and Carville Earle for helpful comments on this chapter.

1. Excellent reviews are Gould (1969); de Souza and Porter (1974); Blaut (1977); Agnew (1980); Brown (1981); and Morrill, Gaile, and Thrall (1988).

2. A significant exception to this tendency is the writing of Blaut (1977: 348) where he referred to Kniffen's work in the following words, "Conceptual diffusion theory owes as much to the work of Fred B. Kniffen as formal theory does to that of Hägerstrand."

3. Of course there were other sources of influence feeding into the location theory tradition of diffusion research. These included the work of the sociologist Katz (1955) and his coworkers on the role of interpersonal communication in consumer decisions, the work of rural sociologists such as Rogers (1969) and Lionberger (1960) in farm innovations and extension, and the work of communication theorists such as Schramm (1964) and Pye (1963).

4. More than twenty-two years ago, those were heady times in graduate school. Gerald Karaska, the current editor of *Economic Geography*, then an assistant professor of geography at Syracuse, told us that we were "young turks" ushering in the new quan-

titative revolution. Inspired by Hägerstrand, Isard, Chorley, Haggett, and Bertalanffy, a few graduate students led by Thomas Wilbanks and Richard Szymanski got together with Gerald Karaska to form a systems group to explore the relevance of General Systems Theory for geography.

5. Although I read Gould and Soja on modernization in a very critical way, in all fairness to the authors it must be noted that these studies were done more than twenty-five years ago in the context of a very different intellectual milieu. Gould, who has continued to make contributions to the diffusion literature from time to time, is currently working on the application of spatial modeling techniques to the spread of AIDS (Gould 1991). This work needs urgent application to the study of the spread of AIDS in the Third World, particularly in Africa. Soja (1980) in the last few years has pioneered the production of a Marxian theory for spatial analysis—the study of the so-ciospatial dialectic.

6. This aspect of capitalism, culture, and consumption continues to be neglected in Marxist scholarship. On this point, see Bell's (1990) review of Marxist geographic scholarship contained in *New Models in Geography: The Political-Economy Perspective*, edited by Peet and Thrift (1989).

7. A special issue of the *American Journal of Alternative Agriculture*, vol. 2, no. 4 (1987), carried several articles on the role of ecology and information in low-input agriculture.

8. The lengthy two-volume work *New Models in Geography*, edited by Peet and Thrift, generally ignores this theme, although the essay by O'Riordon makes a passing ref-erence to the role of ecology and appropriate technology in the eradication of poverty.

References

Agnew, J. P., ed. 1980. *Innovation research and public policy*. Syracuse: Department of Geography, Syracuse University.

Ahmed, S. 1987. Landlessness in rural Asia: An overview. *Land reform: Land settlement and cooperatives*, 133– 51. Rome: FAO.

Altieri, M. A. and M. K. Anderson. 1986. An ecological basis for the development of alternative agricultural systems for small farmers in the Third World. *American Journal of Alternative Agriculture* 1: 30–38.

Baran, P. 1957. *The political economy of growth*. New York: Monthly Review Press.

Barnet, R., and R. Muller. 1974. *The power of multinational corporations*. New York: Simon and Schuster.

Bell, T. L. 1990. Political economy's response to positivism. *Geographical Review* 80: 308–315.

Blaikie, P. 1978. The theory of spatial diffusion of innovations: A spacious cul-de-sac. *Progress in Human Geography* 2: 268–95.

Blaut, J. M. 1977. Two views of diffusion. *Annals of the Association of American Geographers* 67: 343–49.

———. 1987. Diffusionism: A uniformitarian critique. *Annals of the Association of American Geographers* 77: 30–47.

Bookchin, M. 1986. *The modern crisis.* Philadelphia: New Society Publications.

Brown, L.A. 1968. *Diffusion processes and location: A conceptual framework and bibliography.* Philadelphia: Regional Science Research Institute.

———. 1981. *Innovation diffusion: A new perspective.* New York: Methuen.

Bunker, S. 1984. Modes of extraction, unequal exchange, and the progressive underdevelopment of an extreme periphery: The Brazilian Amazon, 1600–1980. *American Journal of Sociology.* 89: 1017–64.

Carson, R. 1962. *The silent spring.* Boston: Houghton Mifflin.

Dahlberg, K. A. 1979. *Beyond the green revolution: The ecology and politics of global agricultural development.* New York: Plenum.

Dalton, G. 1971. *Economic anthropology and development: Essays on tribal and peasant economies.* New York: Basic Books.

Darrow, K., and M. Saxenian. 1986. *Appropriate Technology Sourcebook.* Washington, D.C.: VITA.

de Souza, A. R. and P. W. Porter. 1974. *The underdevelopment and modernization of the Third World.* Washington, D.C.: Association of American Geographers.

Deutsch, K. W. 1969. *Nationalism and social communication.* New York: Knopf.

Dickson, D. 1984. *New politics of science.* New York: Pantheon.

Dobbing, J., ed. 1988. *Infant feeding: Anatomy of a controversy.* New York: Springer-Verlag.

Earle, C. 1988. The Myth of the Southern soil miner: Macrohistory, agricultural innovation, and environmental change. In *The ends of the earth: Perspectives on modern environmental history,* ed. D. Worster: 175–210. Cambridge: Cambridge University Press.

Eckholm, E. 1979. *The dispossessed of the earth: Land reform and sustainable development.* Washington, D.C.: Worldwatch Institute.

Ehrlich, P. R. 1971. *The population bomb.* New York: Ballantine.

Ehrlich, P. R., A. H. Ehrlich, and J. P. Holdren. 1977. *Ecoscience: Population, resources, environment.* San Francisco: W. H. Freeman.

Ellis, F. 1988. *Peasant economies: Farm households and agrarian economies.* Cambridge: Cambridge University Press.

Emmanuel, A. 1972. *Unequal exchange.* New York: Monthly Review Press.

Frank, A. G. 1970. *Latin America: Underdevelopment or revolution.* New York: Monthly Review Press.

Galbraith, J. K. 1958. *The affluent society.* New York: New American Library.

Garst, R. D. 1974. Innovation diffusion among the Gusii of Kenya. *Economic Geography.* 50: 300–12.

George, S. 1988. *A fate worse than debt: The world financial crisis and the poor.* New York: Grove Press.

Glaeser, B. 1987. *The Green Revolution revisited.* London: Allen & Unwin.

Gorz, A. 1980. *Ecology as politics.* Boston: South End Press.

Gould, P. R. 1969. *Spatial diffusion.* Washington, D.C.: Annals of the Association of American Geographers, Resource Paper Series.

————. 1970. Tanzania 1920–63: The spatial impress of the modernization process. *Journal of Modern African Studies.* 2:149–70.

————. 1991. Modeling the geographic spread of AIDS for educational intervention. In *AIDS and the social sciences,* ed. R. Ulack and W. F. Skinner, 30–44. Lexington: University of Kentucky Press.

Gregory, D. 1985. Suspended animation: The stasis of diffusion theory. In *Social relations and spatial structures,* ed. D. Gregory and J. Urry, 296–336. London: Macmillan.

Griffin, K. 1974. *The political economy of agrarian change: An essay on the Green Revolution.* Cambridge, Mass.: Harvard University Press.

Griffin, K. 1976. *Land concentration and rural poverty.* New York: Holmes & Meier.

Hägerstrand, T. 1967. *Innovation diffusion as a spatial process.* Chicago: University of Chicago Press.

————. 1968. A Monte Carlo approach to diffusion. In *Spatial analysis: A reader in statistical geography,* ed. B. J. L. Berry and D. F. Marble, 368–84. EnglewoodCliffs, N. J.: Prentice-Hall.

Haggett, P. 1983. *Geography: A modern synthesis.* New York: Harper & Row.

Harrison, P. 1987. *The greening of Africa.* New York: Viking Penguin.

Hartman, B., and J. K. Joyce. 1983. *A quiet violence: View from a Bangladesh village.* San Francisco: Institute for Food and Development Policy.

Harvey, D. 1973. *Social justice and the city.* Baltimore: Johns Hopkins University Press.

Havens, A. E. and W. L. Flinn. 1975. Green Revolution technology and community development. *Economic Development and Cultural Change* 23: 469–81.

Hayter, T. 1981. *The creation of world poverty.* London: Pluto Press.

Hecht, S. B. 1988. The subsidy from nature: Shifting cultivation, successional palm forests, and rural development. *Human Organization* 47: 25–35.

Hewitt de Alcantara, C. 1976. *Modernizing Mexican agriculture: Socioeconomic implications of technical change, 1940–1970.* Geneva: United Nations Research Institute for Social Development.

Hightower, J. 1973. *Hard tomatoes, hard times: The failure of the land grant college complex.* Cambridge, Mass.: Schenkman Publishing.

Illich, I. 1973. *Tools of conviviality.* New York: Harper & Row.

———. 1978. *Toward a history of needs.* Berkeley: Heyday Books.

Jackson, P. 1989. *Maps of meaning: An introduction to cultural geography.* London: Unwin Hyman.

Jackson, W., W. Berry, and B. Colman, eds. 1984. *Meeting the expectations of the land: Essays in sustainable agriculture and stewardship.* San Francisco: North Point Press.

Johnston, R. J. 1986. *On human geography.* Oxford: Basil Blackwell.

Katz, E., and P. F. Lazarsfeld. 1955. *Personal influence: The part played by people in the flow of mass communications.* New York: The Free Press of Glencoe.

Label, G. C., and H. Kane. 1989. *Sustainable development: A guide to our common future.* Washington, D.C.: The Global Tomorrow Coalition.

Lappe, F. M. and J. Collins. 1977. *Food first: Beyond the myth of scarcity.* New York: Ballantine Books.

Leighly, J. ed. 1963. *Land and life: A selection from the writings of Carl Ortwin Sauer.* Berkeley: University of California Press.

Lionberger, H. 1960. *Adoption of new ideas and practices.* Ames, Iowa: Iowa State University Press.

Lovins, A. B. 1977. *Soft energy paths.* New York: Harper & Row.

McRobie, G. 1981. *Small is possible.* New York: Harper & Row.

Magdoff, H. 1978. *Imperialism: From the colonial age to the present.* New York: Monthly Review Press.

Mamdani, M. 1972. *The myth of population control: Family, caste, and class in an Indian village.* New York: Monthly Review Press.

Miller, G. T. 1988. *Living in the environment*. Belmont, Calif.: Wadsworth.

Mooney, P. R. 1979. *Seeds of the earth: A public or private resource?* San Francisco: Institute for Food and Development Policy.

Morrill, R., G. L. Gaile, and G. I. Thrall. 1988. *Spatial diffusion*. Scientific geography series, vol. 10. Beverly Hills: SAGE Publications.

Nebel, B. J. 1981. *Environmental science*. Englewood Cliffs, N. J.: Prentice-Hall.

O' Connor, J. 1988. Capitalism, nature, socialism: A theoretical introduction. *Capitalism, nature, socialism* 1: 11–38

Packard, V. 1958. *The hidden persuaders*. New York: Diamond Publishing Co.

Pearse, A. 1975. *Global II project on the social and economic implications of the introduction of new varieties of foodgrains, Parts 1–4*. Geneva: United Nations Research Institute for Social Development.

Peet, R. 1977. *Radical geography: Alternative viewpoints on contemporary social issues*. Chicago: Maaroufa Press.

Peet, R., and N. Thrift. 1989. *New models in geography: The political–economy perspective*. London: Unwin Hyman.

Pye, L.W. ed. 1963. *Communication and political development*. Princeton: Princeton University Press.

Richards, P. 1985. *Indigenous agricultural revolution: Ecology and food production in West Africa*. London: Hutchinson.

Rogers, E. M. 1969. *Modernization among peasants: The impact of communication*. New York: Holt, Rinehart & Winston.

Rostow, W. W. 1960. *The stages of economic growth: A non-communist manifesto*. Cambridge: Cambridge University Press.

Sauer, C. O. 1952. *Agricultural origins and dispersals*. New York: American Geographical Society.

————. 1956. The agency of man on the earth. In *Mans's role in changing the face of the earth*, vol. 1, ed. W. L. Thomas, 49–69. Chicago: University of Chicago Press.

————. 1963a. The morphology of landscape. In *Land and life*, ed. J. Leighly, 315–50. Berkeley: University of California Press (orig. pub. 1925).

————. 1963b. Theme of plant and animal destruction in economic history. In *Land and life*, ed. J. Leighly, 145–54. Berkeley: Univeristy of California Press (orig. Pub. 1938).

Schramm, W. 1964. *Mass media and national development: The role of information in the developing countries*. Stanford: Stanford University Press.

Schumacher, E. F. 1973. *Small is beautiful: Economics as if people mattered.* New York: Harper & Row.

Slater, D. 1973. Geography and underdevelopment 1. *Antipode* 5: 21–53.

———. 1977a. Geography and underdevelopment 2. *Antipode* 9:1–31.

———. 1977b. The poverty of modern geographical enquiry. In *Radical geography: Alternative viewpoints on contemporary social issues,* ed. R. Peet, 40–57. Chicago: Maaroufa Press.

Soja, E. 1968. *The geography of modernization in Kenya.* Syracuse: Syracuse University Press.

———. 1980. The socio-spatial dialectic. *Annals of the Association of American Geographers* 70: 207–25.

Stavrianos, L. S. 1981. *Global rift: The Third World comes of age.* New York : William Morrow.

Szymanski, R., and J. A. Agnew. 1981. *Order and skepticism: Human geography and the dialectic of science.* Washington, D.C.: Association of American Geographers.

Thomas, W. L., ed. 1956. *Mans's role in changing the face of the earth.* Chicago: University of Chicago Press.

Van den Bosch, R. 1978. *The pesticide conspiracy.* Garden City: Doubleday.

Wagner, P. L. and M. W. Mikesell, eds. 1962. *Readings in cultural geography.* Chicago: University of Chicago Press.

Wallerstein, I. 1987. *The capitalist world economy.* Cambridge: Cambridge University Press.

Warren, B. 1983. The postwar economic experience of the Third World. In *The political economy of development and underdevelopment,* ed. C. K. Wilber, 109–33. New York: Random House.

World Commission on Environment and Development (WCED). 1987. *Our common future.* Oxford: Oxford University Press.

Wilken, G. C. 1987. *Good farmers: Traditional agricultural resource management in Mexico and Central America.* Berkeley: University of California Press.

Yapa, L. 1975. Analytical alternatives to the Monte Carlo simulation of spatial diffusion. *Annals of the Association of American Geographers* 65: 163–76.

———. 1976. On the statistical significance of the observed map in spatial diffusion. *Geographical Analysis* 8: 255–68.

———. 1977. The Green Revolution: A diffusion model. *Annals of the Association of American Geographers* 67: 350–59.

270   Lakshman Yapa

————. 1979. Ecopolitical economy of the Green Revolution. *Professional Geographer* 31: 371–76.

————. 1980. Diffusion, development, and ecopolitical economy. In *Innovation Research and Public Policy*, ed. J. P. Agnew, 101–41. Syracuse: Department of Geography, Syracuse University.

————. 1981. Ecopolitical economy of agricultural innovations. In *Agriculture, rural energy, and development*, ed. R. S. Ganapathy, 118–37. Ann Arbor: Graduate School of Business Administration, University of Michigan.

Yapa, L., and P. Mayfield. 1978. Non-adoption of innovations: Evidence from discriminant analysis. *Economic Geography* 54: 145–56.

Part Two

Method

10

From Reality to Map

Phillip C. Muehrcke

Most people seem to find maps easy to accept at face value. For these individuals the map is an illustration, a representation of the environment in graphic miniature. If asked to explain their ready acceptance of maps, they usually point to the obvious similarity between the visual appearance of maps and the geographical setting that they describe. Visualization so true to apparent form is believable.

Even professional geographers are prone to embrace this notion of verisimilitude, of "map as illustration," uncritically. If the map is thought of merely as a technical representation, then it follows that cartographers are at best skilled technicians and cartography is at worst devoid of serious intellectual content. For proponents of this naive view cartographic education is merely a matter of training or skill building in the craft. Individuals who subscribe to this line of thought tend to avoid cartographic instruction, with the result that a large portion of geography faculty and students are cartographically illiterate. When departments adopt this attitude, they tend to treat cartography as tangential rather than integral in their curricula. Maps, however, have far too much to offer geographers to be left to professional cartographers.

The superficial acceptance of maps may seem justified, but this impression is misleading. By placing emphasis on the execution of mapping technology, we ignore the fact that mapping is a form of geographical thought inextricably linked to human thought in general (Muehrcke 1981). Maps, like the statistical and mathematical tools employed by geographers, are human creations that are deeply rooted in our cognitive processes. If we want to under-

273

stand maps, we must look at people and their thoughts. My explanation for the credibility of maps is that they closely reflect the way people think and communicate.

In this chapter we explore the conceptual link between reality and maps. We begin by considering the physiological and psychological roots of the map concept, stressing the importance of the ideas of categories and symbols. In the next section we weigh the abstract nature of symbols in the context of environmental representation (or mapping). Here we are introduced to the inevitability and power of cartographic distortion. Because distortion in mapping is inevitable and useful, we next explore the issue of map accuracy, concluding that truthfulness in mapping is related to mapping effect, which is determined by mapping logic. We see that new forms of mapping logic have emerged periodically through the centuries, providing us today with diverse options for cartographic representation. There is content as well as method in mapping, of course, so we next consider the importance of environmental knowledge to the success of cartographic representation. We end with a reminder of the creative power of controlled distortion, which is the essence and purpose of mapping in the first place. A successful map is one expressive enough to trigger thought processes that evoke information only suggested by the cartographic facade.

Roots of the Map Concept

In order to understand the basis of mapping we must look first at how we come to know and represent the environment. People apparently came on the notion of thinking abstractly some thirty thousand years ago. A variety of artifacts of that period indicate experimentation with symbolism, of letting something stand for something else (Davis 1986; White 1989). The vehicles that we use for knowledge representation (natural languages, mathematics, graphics) share and build on this separation of symbol from reality.

Symbols have many useful applications in thought, communication, and mobility. Among the most useful is that symbols detach what is represented from the constraints of physical reality. Symbols lift the burden of our sensory world that is context bound in space and time. They let us shift spatiotemporal position. Through symbols we can visualize environments that are distant as well as immediate, past as well as future. In other words, symbols encourage our imagination. They free us to ask "What if . . . ?" irrespective of time, space, or the state of our physical reality. The insight we derive from symbolic abstraction often goes unappreciated, however.

This brings us to the symbolic concepts of geographical maps. Maps provide visual responses to geographical queries. If we are interested in politics, we can map the political boundaries of the United States in planimetric form, where we assume an infinity of vertical vantage points. Similarly, in the case of weather phenomena, we can map the weather pattern over the United States as it would look from a vantage point twenty thousand miles above the Equator at 90 degrees west longitude. Although neither map is the United States, the lack of fidelity serves the useful purpose of giving concrete form to otherwise abstract concepts.

Environmental Knowing

The concept of mapping is tied closely to the way we come to know our surroundings. At best we are highly selective in this endeavor. In gathering raw perceptual data our sensory organs function within rather narrow physiological limits. These sensory data are then filtered through our cognitive system to create feature-oriented information. In the case of our visual sense we learn to see in a way peculiar to humans. We speak of roads, rivers, and mountains as if they are discrete, clearly defined entities (Jackendoff 1983). We even speak of invisible entities, such as soil, vegetation, or climate zones. This is done so unconsciously that we often fail to realize that these labels refer to environmental concepts of our own making (Rosch et. al. 1976; Rosch and Lloyd 1978; Lakeoff 1987). In a properly nurturing setting we may transform information into environmental knowledge and knowledge into wisdom that we call understanding. The important thing here is that, when we speak of environmental knowing, we are referring to a process that has several rather distinct stages, one of the most important of which is visualization.

If we focus on the role of visualization in knowing, it is apparent we can take several approaches. We can process sensory data all at once with emphasis on holism; we can organize sensory data into features that can be considered separately; or we can alternate between holistic and analytical styles of data processing. There is even some evidence that our brain is structured so that these holistic and analytical styles are lateralized in our two cerebral hemispheres (Springer and Deutsch 1985). There is also evidence of independence in the way that the brain processes visual sense data pertaining to shape, color, and spatial organization/movement/location (Livingstone 1988). The feature (shape) signal appears to be stronger than the attribute (color) signal.

Because of this, the fact that traditional maps emphasize edges is unlikely to be mere coincidence. It more likely means that these maps reflect a basic aspect of human cognition or, at the least, a learned trait in western cultures (Vernon 1973; McKim 1972). We do know that we learn to view our surroundings in stereotypes rather than to see in the raw form of sensory data (Edwards 1986). Perception, in other words, is active, not passive, which explains why several people looking at the same scene see different things.

Nature of Environment

This raises the issue of the nature of reality. It seems obvious that the only reality we can discuss is the one we contrive with the aid of thought and communication. To use these tools is to deal in abstractions; thus, the environment we discuss is one of categories, labels, or stereotypes. Because maps are eminently spatial in nature, from a mapping standpoint the geometrical characteristics of environmental abstractions are of primary interest here.

Our ultimate aim is to explore the relation between maps and categories we impose on the environment. To accomplish this goal, it would be helpful to have an exhaustive taxonomy of environmental features that could then be compared to available mapping techniques. With this in mind, let me offer the following scheme (Muehrcke 1992). Discrete features such as buildings and bridges probably constitute the most obvious and uncontroversial category. When several discrete objects of the same type form a unit, we recognize a second category of discontinuous but coherent features. A university with its many buildings falls into this class. When separate areal units exhaustively cover space, we have what can be called a continuous mosaic distribution. This third class of environmental features includes, for example, political partitioning and thematic zonation (climates, soils, etc.). In this threefold taxonomy of features the edges of objects may vary from sharply defined to transitional. The more fuzzy the boundary of a feature, the more conceptual is its object definition; thus, the category *forest* differs markedly from the category *road* in its clarity around the edges of the object.

Continuous distributions do not have to be characterized by type or attribute differences between units, of course. Magnitude differences may also distinguish one place from another. When intensity of some phenomenon varies from place to place, we can describe the feature as a mathematical or statistical surface. Such a surface may be stepped, as in the case of tax rates from state to state. In this case uniformity exists within unit boundaries and discontinuities occur in the surface along unit boundaries. Stepped statistical surfaces are typically of human origin.

In the natural environment, by contrast, a magnitude surface most commonly varies smoothly from place to place, as in the case of an undulating terrain surface or an air-quality surface. Notice the wide range in our conceptualization of surfaces. At one extreme we have tangible distributions such as the landform, where values exist everywhere. At the other extreme we have derived distributions such as population density, where the surface value does not actually exist at any point but refers to a neighborhood aggregation.

This scheme for categorizing environmental features is itself an abstraction, of course, but it can prove insightful in evaluating the geographical fidelity of mapping methods. Before doing so, however, we must consider what form abstraction takes when applied to maps.

Cartographic Abstraction

Our ability to abstract, when applied to the task of mapping, entails the concepts of selection, classification, simplification, exaggeration, and symbolization. The power of cartographic abstraction comes from the combined effect of these processes (Tobler 1979b). The degree of separation between reality and map is a matter of degree (figure 10.1). In theory this abstraction gradient is boundless, as suggested by Bunge's (1966) use of the term *metacartography*. In practice, however, maps have been restricted to the depiction of environmental variables in three-dimensional Euclidean space. Representations of space inversions such as time-distance or value-by-area transformations are usually treated as a novel category of maplike objects called *cartograms*.

The nearly limitless possibilities for cartographic abstraction means that truth in mapping is rarely obvious. For that matter, what is truth in mapping? Truth in mapping at the least must be judged in the context of the constraints on map design. These include the scale and purpose of the map, the nature of geographical reality and available data, the technical limits of production/reproduction, the intended map audience, and the conditions (lighting, motion, time, viewing distance, etc.) under which maps are used. Clearly, the evaluator of the truth status of a map has considerable latitude. Truth or fidelity is not the issue, however. Because all maps by nature are abstractions and, therefore, distortions, what we should be focusing on is mapping effects.

The irony of cartography is that it often promotes understanding through deliberate distortion. Cartographic distortion enables us to visualize things about the environment that otherwise would be physically impossible — seeing the whole earth simultaneously, for instance, or seeing the distribution of climate zones across the continent. We can map the world on a postage stamp or depict our neighborhood on a wall-size mural. The key is to match the map user's purpose with the appropriate level of cartographic abstraction. Because there are no absolutes, the neighborhood map is no more or less truthful than the world map. To think of maps as mere technical representations of the environment to be judged solely in terms of positional accuracy misses the point.

Figure 10.1 Photo map and line map representation.

Indeed, the origins of maps owe more to concept than technique, and it is these conceptual roots that provide the basis of mapping logic (Peuquet 1988).

Clearly, there are two dimensions to cartographic abstraction. What is represented constitutes the map content, whereas how the content is shown defines the mapping logic. The logic of the mapping strategy and the nature of the information mapped interact to form the character of the representation. To grasp the conceptual foundations of mapping, then, we need to reflect on both the logic and the content of cartographic abstraction.

Mapping Logic

The concept of mapping traces directly to our ability to think abstractly. Although our literature is full of comments suggesting that maps came first and environmental concepts such as distribution and climate zone followed, the reverse is more likely the case. Maps first and foremost provide visualizations of human conceptions of the environment (Muehrcke 1990). It is the conceptions that get mapped, and, as human conceptions change through the centuries, so too does the logic embedded in maps. A few examples of the dynamics of mapping logic may prove illustrative.

Focus on Object Location

The earliest maps emphasized the locations of objects such as rivers, lakes, mountains, trails, and so on. These representations are commonly called reference or general-purpose maps. Tangible, static features are given primary emphasis. Discrete symbols (point, line, area) predominate, even when features naturally have fuzzy edges. The symbols representing these features become progressively more generalized as map scale decreases. This class of maps is conceptually simple, but even these simple maps have proven useful down to the present. The U.S. National Map Accuracy Standards, for example, continue to be applied to well-defined features of the type shown on reference maps.

Focus on Space

In the 1700s maps focusing on the spatial variation of phenomena such as vegetation or soils gained prominence (Robinson 1982). These thematic maps introduced a second form of cartographic logic. The emphasis was on spatial distribution of some environmental phenomenon, not on the location of individual features. A great deal of cartographic license may be exercised in depicting the spatial variation of geographical phenomena, especially if the distribution must first be derived from several factors, as is the case for climate or

soils. Clearly, the matching of map symbol with geographic feature is impre-
cise, which may explain why no formal map accuracy standards address thematic mapping. In general, thematic maps are inherently more conceptual
than are reference maps.

Focus on Numerical Distributions

With the advent of statistical surface mapping in the 1800s, several new
forms of mapping logic emerged. In cases in which the distribution exhibited
values at all locations, such as with temperature or precipitation, there is no
practical way of measuring all possible values. Instead, a limited sample of values must be selected to represent the whole, and spatial prediction (interpola-
tion/extrapolation) techniques must be used to fill in the map between the scattered sample points. For instance, the official weather map for the United
States presents a continuous picture of the phenomenon, yet it is based on data
gathered at only a few hundred recording stations (figure 10.2). The fidelity of
the map thus varies directly with the representiveness of the sample data (a matter of sample size and scatter) and the sophistication of the prediction method
and inversely with the complexity of the geographical distribution. For this type
of map there are few rules and no formal standards of accuracy.

When data represent regional aggregations of discrete entities, as might be
reported in census results, a different mapping logic prevails. These value-by-
area data may be depicted as a stepped distribution, assuming homogeneity
within data-gathering zones and breaks in the distribution at zone borders. Because geographical distributions are rarely stepped in reality, this mapping
logic can be quite deceptive. The way the shape, size, and orientation of data-
collection units interacts with the data distribution may mask rather than reveal the geographical character of the setting; moreover, as the units of aggregation increase in size, spatial detail in the map representation decreases.

An alternative to a stepped-surface representation is to assign data aggregates to region centroids (center of the areal unit or the center of unit population) and then use these centroid values to interpolate a smooth statistical
surface. This mapping logic gets around the artificial assumption of homogeneous regions with all distribution variation occurring at unit boundaries, but
it introduces other assumptions about the surface. More specifically, the cartographer must select a centroid as well as an interpolation model. These factors, as well as the size, shape, and orientation of census regions and the nature of the underlying geographical distribution, all pose fidelity problems. In
other words, the cartographer is damned if he does and damned if he doesn't.
Each mapping logic thus has advantages and disadvantages and, therefore,
must be chosen or rejected on the basis of the mapping effect desired.

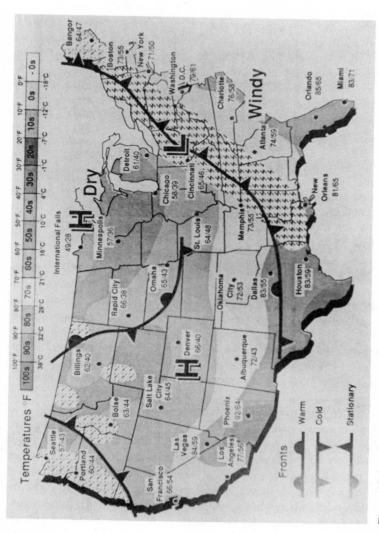

Figure 10.2 Distribution map.

One way around some of these problems involves use of gridded or cell-based data zones (Tobler 1979a, 1967). The motivation for this form of mapping logic derives from several sources. One motivation is the desire to eliminate the variability that results when geographers use different sample scatters or when data-collection regions have different sizes, shapes, and orientations. A second motivation is the aim to take advantage of modern technology for gathering and processing data. Electronic scanners used in remote sensing provide data in cell-based matrix form. Digital computers and statistical/mathematical methods are also designed to handle matrix information efficiently. The advantages of using gridded data notwithstanding, the method imposes an artificial and unnatural structure on the landscape—an imposition that is only partially rectified by decreasing cell size.

Forming Multivariate Composites

The oldest tradition in mapping used separate symbols to depict different environmental variables. If, however, our interest is in the relation between several variables, we are forced to compare visually the separately mapped distributions. This task becomes more difficult, of course, as the number of variables increases.

The typical topographic map series produced by many national mapping agencies uses superimposed symbols to represent several aspects of the environment at once thereby broadening the potential user audience (figure 10.3). Notice that these maps combine mapping traditions and logic in a single depiction. Roads, landforms, and vegetation vary markedly conceptually, and also differ in the logic underlying their cartographic representation; thus, effective use of a topographic map raises issues that go far beyond those associated with the perceptual task of comparing symbols for the separate environmental features.

An alternative logic to the common symbol-superimposition strategy is to combine the several variables into an index and map them as a single or composite variable. This composite variable is purely conceptual in origin bcause it cannot be measured directly in the environment. It is, in other words, an expression of our conceptual model of the environment. Topics treated in cartographic modeling include preference (places rated), sustainability, trafficability, susceptibility, and suitability (figure 10.4). In each case the index depends on three factors: the choice of variables, the weights assigned to these variables, and the link (additive, multiplicative, etc.) between the weighted variables (Hopkins 1977). If maps based on these indices are unsatisfactory, the model can be modulated so that it conforms with conceptual expectations.

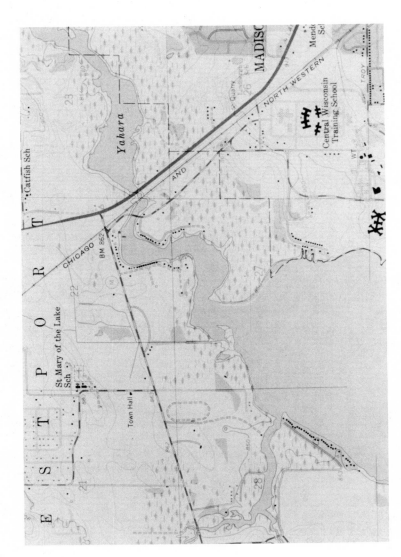

Figure 10.3 Topographic map.

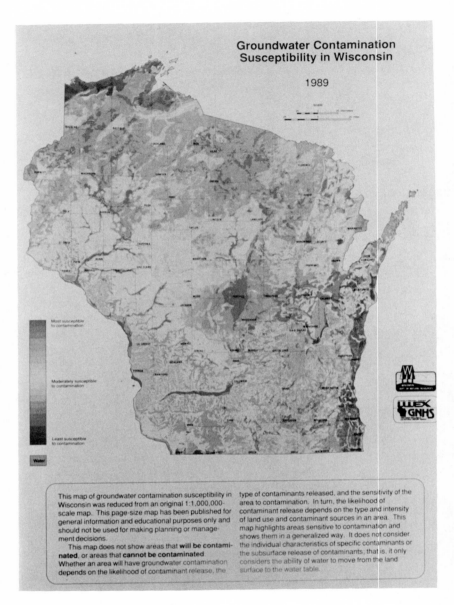

Figure 10.4 Composite variable map.

Treatment of Time

When we think of maps, time does not usually spring to mind. In fact, maps traditionally have emphasized spatial matters while purporting to holding time constant. Although this synchronic logic may seem reasonable, it is wise to remember that thinking simply about something as complex as the environment leaves us with only a simplistic view. We must conclude that representing a dynamic environment with static maps leads inevitably to a degraded impression. Furthermore, if our interests are in change or process, we must try to put several of these freeze-frame maps into mental motion. This is frequently difficult and almost always ineffective.

Fortunately, modern technology offers new opportunities for incorporating time into maps. For instance, animations of sequences of weather satellite images are now common in television weather reporting. Watching the swirling progress of a hurricane system across the Caribbean is much more dramatic than seeing frozen time slices of the same event. In cases in which the temporal dimension is critical to understanding environmental phenomena, the logic of animation is welcome.

Dynamic mapping need not be restricted to the animation of past or present environments. Environmental simulations, for example, enable us to visualize what would happen to the environment if certain assumptions were changed. Modern display devices, driven by powerful computers, convey an unnerving sense of realism to these simulations, but, just as with composite variable mapping, it is worth remembering that what we see in a map simulation is a conceptual environment of our own making. Concept, not reality, is the driving force.

These examples of mapping logic are hardly exhaustive, yet they suffice to make my central point—the critical role of the concept behind the map of the environment. We should be mindful that there is no such thing as *the* map of reality. It may be more appropriate to speak of *a* map of reality since any given map is only one of many possible representations.

Map Content

Although our discussion of mapping logic has focused on the map as a vehicle of thought and communication, it would be a mistake to overlook the information that maps convey; that is to say that maps contain substantive content. They are not neutral or hollow information channels. Quite the opposite is true, because these concrete, opaque forms of representation have impacts on content. We must recognize these impacts if we are to unlock the information encoded in maps.

It has been said of statistical methods that effective use depends on knowing a great deal in advance about the data being analyzed. The same is true of maps. The more a person knows about the geographic phenomena being mapped, the greater the insights that can be gained by mapping. This proposition separates those who would see cartography as a science devoid of environmental content (Morrison 1978) from those who see it as inextricably geographic. Soviet cartographers in particular reacted strongly against the science of cartography literature when it was published (Salichtchev 1973).

Proponents of the science of cartography attempted to separate the disciplines of cartography and geography. Little came of their effort, thanks in large part to the rapid shift of attention in the 1980s from cartography to the notion of geographical information systems (Chrisman et al. 1989). In any event, talk of cartographic secession was misdirected. Effective use of the cartographic language requires more, not less, integration between mapping and geography.

To make good maps and to use them effectively requires a grasp of geography that is commensurate with our understanding of mapping logic. Cartographers must be aware of the complex processes that guide the workings of the environment and cognizant that the division of these processes into physical and human forces is merely an analytic artifice for understanding the environmental whole. Similarly, the partitioning of the physical environment into hydrosphere, lithosphere, atmosphere, and biosphere subsystems, or the human environment into technological, political, economic, social, and political spheres, is merely a matter of convenience. Reducing the complexity of the environment for purposes of analysis does not simplify the environment. Indeed, analytic simplification can make understanding more difficult because our ultimate interest is in the interaction of physical and human subsystems in shaping the environmental condition. Successful mapping and map use depends on understanding this environmental whole (Muehrcke 1992). This dictum applies in the case of geographical information systems as well as in traditional cartographic representation.

Geographical literacy is the linchpin that joins cartographic information with environmental knowledge. Although anyone can learn map information, the capacity to create useful knowledge from this information depends on environmental understanding. The cartographic medium and the geographical content thus are inextricable.

Creative Power of Abstraction

We have seen that representation entails abstraction and, thus, distortion. Conversely, it is distortion that makes representation possible. The power of representation lies in controlling this distortion to serve special purposes. In this context we see that controlled distortion is the essence of mapping. Indeed, in the preceding discussion we saw that mapping logic is based on the proposition that maps invariably distort time, space, and the phenomena represented. This distortion should be a matter of concern for anyone wanting to use maps as surrogates for the environment in critical decision-making contexts.

For maps to be successful they must be just expressive enough to trigger the desired response. Too little distortion is just as detrimental to effective mapping as too much.

Expressive Adequacy of Maps

If we are to have confidence in using maps, we need to know how adequately they express the essence of the mapped environment. Although distortions that potentially degrade cartographic representation can be reduced through the clever choice of projection geometry or the use of multitemporal perspectives and multivariate symbols, these artifices also increase the map's information load. In other words, the price of reducing cartographic distortion is increased conceptual complexity. Because conceptually sophisticated maps may appear perceptually similar to simpler map representations, maps based on complex data manipulations can be deceptive. These conceptually intense maps subtly shift the burden of deriving meaningful knowledge from the map designer to the map interpreter. If the interpreter lacks a sufficient conceptual foundation of environmental and mapping knowledge, these maps will fail in their role as thought and communication tools. The point is that the greater the conceptual sophistication of maps, the greater the degree of geographical and cartographic literacy needed to use them effectively.

Modern electronic technology is enhancing the expressiveness of maps in several important ways. Animation, for example, adds an explicit time dimension to maps that can be helpful when a user attempts to follow environmental trends. When high-quality display screens are driven by powerful computers equipped with sophisticated software and detailed databases, the maps are so believable that the industry refers to them using the term *photorealism*. When provision is made for the viewer to interact with the image through an intuitive user-computer interface, the result is called *artificial* or *virtual reality*. The expressiveness of these interactive maps can be astonishing. In fact, the immense potential of these cartographic simulations promises new explorations into "What if . . .?" environmental scenarios.

Neorealist cartography notwithstanding, technology cannot yet recreate environmental reality. When the environmental context of sight, sound, touch, taste, smell, and size is taken away for purposes of representation, the mood disappears. If mood is critical in determining an appropriate response to the environment, the disengagement inherent in representational decontextualization constitutes a serious problem. In this case, and others, the map concept by itself may be an inadequate means of knowing the environment.

Maps as Imagination Triggers

Words, numbers, and graphics are each inadequate to the task of capturing the graininess of detail and complex interrelations of our surroundings. Even when we integrate these thought and communication vehicles as fully as possible, the result still falls far short of the ideal. Because maps combine words, numbers, and graphics into a single hybrid representation, no matter how expressive they might be they are always a pale and thin reflection of the environment represented. The old adage that "the map is not the territory" continues in force. Regarding a map as territory is justified only when its aesthetic qualities are the sole matter of interest. but only when maps are viewed as art can they legitimately be accepted at face value. Otherwise, maps must be treated as abstractions.

Cartographic abstraction has advantages and disadvantages. On the positive side mapping is contingent on our willingness to distort reality according to accepted cartographic principles. This distortion makes it possible to free ourselves from the severe constraints imposed by physical reality. Decision making that is broad in scope and of long term often hinges on a suppression of the emotion and immediacy of our physical existence—yet sustainability of our life on earth often demands just that. By getting outside ourselves, by taking an abstract cartographic perspective, we may be able to see beyond the here and now. This bigger picture of reality can be a useful context from which to make difficult decisions that affect the broader good of people and their environment.

If we are to appreciate the advantages of cartographic abstraction, we must also recognize the pitfalls. Maps have significant potential for abuse (Muehrcke 1992). Abuse commonly occurs when the abstraction is confounded with reality. Committing this error can lead to human suffering, environmental degradation, and propagandizing.

Abuse of the mapping concept also occurs when reality is regarded in maplike terms, for example, when someone exclaims that "it looks just like a map." A reality-as-map perspective is quite natural, of course, because our willingness to view the environment as a collection of features and edges is what led to the map concept in the first place, but this natural tendency toward maplike thinking does not negate the fact that to conceptualize the environment in the selective and skeletal terms typical of mapping is to overlook the richness of our surroundings.

Environmental wisdom requires going beyond the information given on maps and invoking the powers of imagination. The map achieves its highest purpose when it triggers our imagination about the environment. The map triggers or stimulates linkages between this abstraction and our vast personal storehouse of knowledge. When the map triggers efficiently and when the user is appreciative of environmental complexity, we speak of the user "getting lost in the map." The visualization we gain through maps thus serves as a powerful device for setting our minds into motion.

Conclusion

We have seen that minimalist map representation is a powerful conceptual artiface with roots in the way we come to know our surroundings. The conceptual foundation of cartography was elucidated in this chapter by exploring relationships between how we think about and how we represent our surroundings. We saw that mapping is a form of abstraction with diverse logical ends and, as such, involves distortion; but by distorting our representations to achieve special creative effects, we can often gain more than we lose. A map that evokes the desired response is successful, regardless of its degree of abstractness. Fidelity to reality is of secondary importance at best and may actually be confusing and detrimental.

The aim in cartographic representation is allegedly to simplify our surroundings to their most basic structure and form with respect to a given perspective. To argue, as some prominent geographers have (Goodchild 1988), that our map symbology is a consequence of representation optimized for drafting tools seems to miss the crucial point of cartographic representation. Sticks were lying around for many generations before someone had the insight to pick one up and draw the first simple map. The act of picking up this map-drawing tool thus represents a far greater leap in conception than in technology.

In spite of statements in the literature to the contrary, making maps look more realistic may cause them to be conceptually counterintuitive. More detailed maps may actually communicate less in many situations than more abstract ones. What this means is that we should not expect modern electronic technology to cause the disappearance of familiar map abstractions built on point, line, and areal symbols. The map idea, not mapping technology, is the driving force.

Maps express the way we think about our surroundings. They are less a depiction of reality than a representation of our concepts of reality. The map is not something to be attained as an end in itself, but is rather a means for enriching and enhancing our perspective on geographical knowledge. Sociocultural and technological changes lead to changes in map content, map production, and map uses. Recently, for example, the ascent of an ecological/systems/process view of the environment on the one hand and of powerful electronic technologies (computers, satellites, telecommunications) on the other have had dramatic impacts on mapping. Maps have become more dynamic (animations), speculative (simulations), timely (Doppler radar) and conceptually more sophisticated (susceptibility, sustainability, trafficability, suitability, potential). Simultaneously, they have become less concrete (physical/tangible) and more ephemeral. Focus thus has shifted from the map as an end (object) to the map as a means to an end (environmental decision making/problem solving).

Because our mapping tools set limits on what we can know, the recent changes in mapping open new opportunities for environmental understanding that, in turn, have the power to enhance thought, communication, and mobility. It is important, however, to remember that the mapping logic that underlies much geographical thinking is dynamic; as with other human devices, it changes as we change. Because mapping is limited only by the bounds of our imagination, maps will continue to influence the way geographers think and do their work—provided that geographers make an effort to understand what it means to map. For many geographers this will require a shift in emphasis from technical limitations to conceptual possibilities.

References

Bunge, W. 1966. *Theoretical geography*. Lund, Sweden: Gleerup.

Chrisman, N. R., D. J. Cowen, P. F. Fisher, M. F. Goodchild, and D. M. Mark. 1989. Geographic Information Systems. In *Geography in America*, ed. G. L. Gaile and C. J. Willmott, 776–96. Columbus, Ohio: Merrill.

Davis, W. 1986. The origins of image making. *Current Anthropology* 27: 193–216.

Edwards, B. 1986. *Drawing on the artist within*. New York: Simon and Schuster.

Goodchild, M. F. 1988. Stepping over the line: Technological constraints and the new cartography. *The American Cartographer* 15: 311–19.

Guelke, L. 1976. Cartographic communication and geographic understanding. *The Canadian Cartographer* 13: 107–22.

Hopkins, L. D. 1977. Methods of generating land suitability maps: A comparative evaluation. *Journal of American Institute of Planners*. 43: 386–98.

Jackendoff, R. 1983. *Semantics and cognition*. Cambridge, Mass.: MIT Press.

Lakeoff, G. 1987. *Women, fire, and dangerous things: What categories reveal about the human mind*. Chicago: University of Chicago Press.

Livingstone, M. S. 1988. Art, illusion, and the visual system. *Scientific American* 260: 78–85.

McKim, R. H. 1972. *Experiences in visual thinking*. Monterey, Calif.: Brooks/Cole.

Morrison, J. L. 1978. Towards a functional definition of the science of cartography with emphasis on map reading. *The American Cartographer* 5: 97–110.

Muehrcke, P. C. 1981. Whatever happened to geographic cartography? *Professional Geographer* 33: 397–405.

————. 1992. *Map use: Reading, analysis and interpretation*, 3d ed. Madison, Wis.: JP Publications.

————. 1990. Cartography and geographic information systems. *Cartography and Geographic Information Systems* 17: 7–15.

Peuquet, D. J. 1988. Representations of geographic space: Toward a conceptual synthesis. *Annals of the Association of American Geographers* 78: 375–94.

————. 1994. It's about time: A conceptual framework for the representation of temporal dynamics in geographic information systems. *Annals of the Association of American Geographers* 84: 441–61.

Robin, H. 1992. *The scientific image from cave to computer*. New York: Harry N. Abrams.

Robinson, A. H. 1982. *Early thematic mapping in the history of cartography*. Chicago: University of Chicago Press.

Rosch, E., C. B. Mervis, W. D. Gray, D. M. Johnson, and P. Boyesbra. 1976. Basic objects in natural categories. *Cognitive Psychology* 8: 382–439.

Rosch, E., and B. B. Lloyd, eds. 1978. *Cognition and categorization*. New York: Halstead.

Salichtchev, K. A. 1973. Some reflections on the subject and method of cartography after the Sixth International Cartographic Conference. *The Canadian Cartographer* 10: 106–11.

Springer, S. P., and G. Deutsch. 1985. *Left brain, right brain*. New York: Freeman.

Tobler, W. R. 1967. Of maps and matrices. *Journal of Regional Science* 7: 275–80.

————. 1979a. Cellular geography. In *Philosophy in Geography*, ed. S. Gale and G. Olsson; 379–86. Dordrecht, Holland: Reidel.

————. 1979b. A transformational view of cartography. *The American Cartographer* 6: 101–6.

Thompson, B., and B. Thompson. 1991. Overturning the category bucket. *Byte* 16: 249–56.

Vernon, J. 1973. *The garden and the map.* Urbana, Ill.: University of Illinois Press.

White, R. 1989. Visual thinking in the ice age. *Scientific American* 261: 92–99.

11

Formal and Narrative Models and Their Value as Instruments of Understanding

John U. Marshall

Reality is complex. Our responses to this complexity are of two basic kinds: holistic and analytical. A holistic response is an intuitive reaction or feeling. It involves no conscious deployment of our conceptual or logical abilities and is, in essence, an esthetic experience. An analytical response, in contrast, is an act of intellectual dissection. It occurs only when we make a deliberate attempt to specify the functionally significant parts of a whole, to identify structural interrelationships, and to isolate causes and effects. When we respond holistically, we take life as it comes. When we respond analytically we take life apart, breaking down the ever-present complexity in an effort to expose underlying patterns and mechanisms. In the day-to-day conduct of our activities, whether academic or otherwise, interplay between holistic and analytical responses is constant and, I believe, unavoidable because it is genetically programmed. Together, the two approaches constitute our path to understanding.

Systems and models are major components of the analytical approach. A *system* is a segment of reality that is conceptually distinct and thus capable of being treated as a more or less self-contained entity for the purpose of detailed study. (Incidentally, reality as a whole can be viewed as a system; but this limiting case, in which whole and part are identical, has no analytical importance.) A *model* is a simplified representation of some particular type of system, a representation in which certain features are thrown into sharp relief while other features are temporarily suppressed. In short, to model is to simplify. The basic purpose of modelbuilding is to draw attention to features that are believed to be essential for an adequate description of the type of system in question. Models can also be helpful in the construction of satisfactory explanations. The manner in which models are related to the construction of explanations will be examined toward the end of this essay. Here at the outset, however, we need a little historical background—and a concrete example to serve as a basis for further discussion.

Some History—and a Word of Caution

What was the earliest geographical model? We cannot answer with certainty, but a leading contender for this honor must surely be the ancient Greek concept of the *klimata* (figure 11.1). The *klimata*, from which the modern English word "climate" is derived, were a series of five latitudinal zones—one torrid, two temperate, and two frigid—that encircled the earth and reflected not only the prevailing Hellenistic faith in the symmetry of Nature, but also the belief that human life was possible only where zonal (i.e., climatic) conditions were neither too hot nor too cold (Bunbury 1959, 1: 125, 397, 625–26; Martin and James 1993: 28).

Notwithstanding its antiquity, the concept of the *klimata* displays all the features now regarded as the hallmarks of a satisfactory model. First, it represents a conceptually distinct system that is of interest to the geographer: namely, climate—or, more narrowly, the temperature of the air.

Second, the model presents reality in a simplified form. The zones in the model are mutually exclusive and rigidly defined, but the real world displays numerous anomalies, such as the fact that daytime temperatures in the Sahara are frequently higher than those in the forested lands closer to the equator or the fact that winters on Vancouver Island are not nearly as cold as those of places lying farther south but in the interior of the continent. The model, in short, presents a generalized picture of the system it represents.

Third, despite the simplification, the world of the model is nevertheless a reasonable facsimile of the world we actually inhabit. The model is generalized, but not utterly unrealistic. After all, the tropical zone, taken as a whole, is in fact uncomfortably hot (though not, as many of the ancients believed, uninhabitable), and the polar regions are in fact uncomfortably cold. In other words, when used predictively, the model provides answers that are empirically true, at least as a first approximation. It should not be inferred, however, that models therefore represent laws of nature in a deterministic sense. We will return to the important issue of determinism later in this section.

The fourth feature worthy of note is that the model, at least implicitly, points toward an explanation for a particular class of empirical observations.

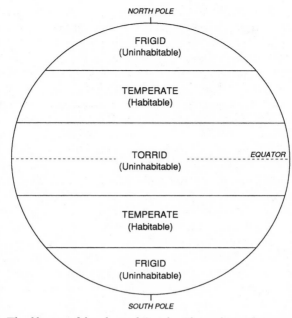

Figure 11.1 The *klimata* of the classical Greeks: The archetypal geographical model. The Greeks lived in the northern temperate zone. Assuming a symmetrical world, they believed that a southern temperate zone existed and was habitable. It could not be visited, however, because one could not survive passage through the torrid zone in attempting to reach it. Some later versions of this model incorporated more than five zones, but the basic symmetry remained.

In the case of the *klimata* the relevant underlying question is as follows: How can we explain the geographical distribution of the human population? (Alternatively: Why does average population density vary systematically with changes in latitude? Various wordings are possible.) The *klimata* model suggests an answer to this question in terms of a causal connection between climatic conditions and the broad pattern of human settlement across the face of the earth: population density is a function of habitability, which in turn is largely governed by climate.

To recapitulate, four general characteristics of a satisfactory model are as follows: 1) it represents a clearly defined system; 2) it depicts this system in a simplified form; 3) it nevertheless yields predictions that, in broad terms, are empirically true; and 4) it provides, or at least suggests, an explanation for a particular class of empirical observations. These four characteristics may be accepted as diagnostic features of a successful model. The quality of performance under each of these four headings varies from model to model, however, and it must therefore be recognized that different degrees of overall success are possible. Some models, in short, are more satisfactory than others.

There is a fifth characteristic of the *klimata* model that I have not yet mentioned: namely, the fact that the simplified structure presented in the model displays mathematical regularity. The *klimata* are arranged symmetrically on the globe, with the equator bisecting the torrid zone and the north and south poles lying at the centers of the frigid zones. Should we regard mathematical regularity as a fifth diagnostic characteristic of a satisfactory model? Broadly speaking, the answer is yes. There is, however, an important group of models to which this fifth criterion does not apply: namely, narrative models that summarize the stages of development of some particular region or class of earth-surface phenomena. Because they are episodic in form, stage models do not possess the potential for mathematical expression that is normally present when one examines either the spatial arrangement of phenomena at a fixed point in time or changes created in the landscape by processes that can be viewed as being continuous rather than episodic (e.g., river erosion or population growth). In what follows, stage models are treated as a distinct, non-mathematical category.

The example of the *klimata* is interesting because it shows that model-based thinking was not unknown in the ancient world. It must be acknowledged, however, that modelbuilding played an extremely small role in geography before the middle of the twentieth century. In fact, the emergence of a conscious, explicit, and widespread interest in models among human geographers coincided with the rapid and unprecedented increase in the use of statistical techniques that took place during geography's quantitative revolution—that is, the quarter-century of methodological transformation ushered in by the famous (or, depending on your sympathies, infamous) call to arms published by F. K. Schaefer in 1953 (Schaefer 1953, Taylor 1976, Martin 1989). Without doing too much injustice to what was actually a very complex period in the history of our discipline, it may be stated that the quantitative revolution was partly a reaction against the prevailing preoccupation with stylized regional description and partly an attempt to make geography less idiographic and more theoretical (Johnston 1987: 47–54).

The quantitative revolution was also a time when many human geographers, though often only implicitly, took the position that our intellectual needs would best be served by embracing the philosophy of logical positivism (Harvey 1969; Amedeo and Golledge 1975; Livingstone 1992: 316–28). For present purposes we need to consider briefly two specific features of positivist ideology: namely, its explicit commitment to determinism and the closely related belief that the ultimate goal of all research, in the social as well as the natural sciences, should be the discovery and verification of universal laws.

To mention determinism and universal laws is to open a veritable Pandora's box of fascinating and unresolved problems, most of which, for lack of space, I shall simply have to ignore. Most readers will be aware, however, that geographers flirted with one particular species of determinism—namely, environmental, or geographical, determinism—during the early decades of the twentieth century, and most will also know that this approach was eventually deemed unacceptable by leading scholars in the field. Such, at least, is the standard version of our history. It can be argued, in point of fact, that very few geographers—possibly no more than five or six—ever espoused determinism in an unadulterated form. Rather, what hostile observers chose to see as determinism was really nothing more than a figure of speech, or a sort of poetic license (Sprout and Sprout 1965: 48–70). Nevertheless, the orthodox view is that many geographers of the early twentieth century were indeed determinists. Later, it came to be held that this adherence to determinism was misguided; by about midcentury, deterministic thinking had fallen out of favor. Students entering geography during the 1950s—myself among them—were taught that environmental determinism had been an error of earlier generations and that it should be avoided at all costs. Paradoxically, however, the opponents of environmental determinism generally raised no objections against the positivistic leanings that could be discerned in the quantitative revolution. With the advantage of hindsight, it seems fair to say that most geographers of the 1950s and 1960s were unaware that positivism requires the acceptance of a deterministic point of view.

We have noted that an interest in models and an interest in positivism arose within geography at essentially the same time. Given this simultaneity, the following train of thought springs readily to mind. Models are a manifestation of positivism; positivism is another name for determinism; and determinism has been judged philosophically unacceptable. Therefore, models are a Bad Thing.

At first glance this appears to be a convincing argument against the use of models. The argument contains a fallacy, however. The key point is that the employment of models does not necessitate the acceptance of positivist ideology. Reduced to essentials, a positivist is one who believes that all events are governed by immutable natural laws. A builder of models, in contrast, is one who seeks a parsimonious description of a particular empirical situation. Because many models involve some degree of mathematical regularity, the builders and users of models are usually persons who are reasonably good at mathematics and who enjoy working with numerical information. It does not follow, however, that such persons must believe that all events are governed by universal laws. If you do happen to believe that everything is governed by universal natural laws, you will doubtless try to express these laws in mathematical terms, but the mere use of mathematical reasoning, whether in modelbuilding or in statistical analysis, does not logically entail that you must believe in the existence of universal laws (Marshall 1982: 122–37).

This, then, is the word of caution referred to in the title of this section: users of models are not necessarily positivists. The point needs emphasis because there has been a tendency in recent years for the distinction between positivism and modelbuilding to be ignored. The difference, though, is quite clear and simple. Models are investigative tools that are intended to illuminate their subject matter by means of abstraction and simplification. Positivism is a metaphysical position embodying the belief that all events are governed by universal laws. The two belong to quite separate planes of experience.

It may be pointed out, for the sake of completeness, that the truth or falsity of determinism cannot be decided by empirical demonstration. By and large, determinism is currently out of fashion in the social sciences; but to say that an idea is out of fashion is not to say that it has been observationally disproved. In fact, the whole of our experience, including our belief in freedom of the will, is perfectly consistent with the truth of the determinist thesis. Everything that has ever happened to date, and everything that will ever happen in the future, down to the smallest detail, might well have been preordained in the original Big Bang—if that, indeed, is how it all began. Perhaps we will never know, but we should not chastise users of models even if they do claim to believe in determinism—for predestination could be true after all.

A Survey of Geography's Major Models

The models used by geographers can be classified in more than one way. One approach is to classify models according to their subject matter—agriculture, manufacturing, the structure of cities, and so forth (Chorley and Haggett 1967). This approach, however, tends to divert attention away from the conceptual characteristics of the models themselves. With the aim of emphasizing the latter I have adopted a simple threefold classification based on the dominant mode in which each model is normally expressed. The first two categories involve geometric and algebraic representations, respectively; together these two categories may be identified as *formal* models. The third category—here termed *narrative* models—involves models that are purely verbal in character. This category is reserved for stage models of historical development.

Geometry: Models of Locational Pattern

The Spatial Hierarchy of Towns

The most fully developed models of locational pattern—and, in the eyes of many, the most significant models in human geography—are Christaller's models of the spatial structure of systems of central places (Christaller 1966). The term *central place* refers to an urban center's role as a provider of consumer goods and services to persons residing outside its own borders. Almost all urban centers are central places in greater or lesser degree, but central-place activity is by no means the only economic function that towns perform. Indeed, it is vital to recognize that Christaller's models were never intended to be all-encompassing models of urban systems. They exclude—and the exclusion is deliberate—all activities not directly concerned with the provision of consumer goods and services to external customers. Most notably, they exclude manufacturing. Essentially, central-place models are models of the retailing sector of the economy. It must be kept in mind, however, that the role of marketplace for consumer goods and services is the most widespread and fundamental function that urban centers perform throughout the world as a whole. Although central-place models are not all-inclusive, then, they focus on the particular type of activity that plays the leading role in molding the spatial structure of most regional and national urban networks (figure 11.2).

I will not attempt, in an essay of this length, to describe central-place models in detail. This has been done elsewhere (King 1984; Berry et al. 1988: 49–69; Marshall 1989: 139–77). It is instructive, however, to draw attention to a few contextual points. First, there is the question of the empirical stimulus. The basic purpose behind these models is to find satisfactory explanations for two familiar features of real-world urban systems: the fact that small towns are more numerous than large ones and the fact that towns larger than any given threshold of population size are, in general, uniformly spaced. The point to be emphasized is that the models were not developed as a purely theoretical exercise or as a means of indulging their creator's interest in geometry. They were part of an attack on specific empirical problems (Christaller 1972).

But second, although the models were initially stimulated by real-world observations and are therefore empirical and inductive, they are also the result of a theoretical argument, that is, a deductive chain of reasoning put forward as a tentative explanation of the original empirical observations. The theoretical argument, in turn, rests on a set of assumptions (e.g., the assumption of an isotropic plain), each of which represents some aspect of reality in a simplified form. If the assumptions are taken as given, the models emerge as logically consistent answers to the following question: What would be the spatial structure of an urban system under the ideal conditions described by the set

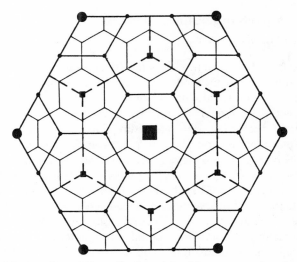

Figure 11.2 The simplest of Christaller's models of the arrangement of central places and their market areas under ideal conditions. In this model, known as the "marketing model," the market areas increase in area by a factor of three as one moves upward through the levels of the urban hierarchy. The diagram shows four levels of centers and market areas, distinguished by means of different point and line symbols. Additional levels are possible and the pattern may be extended indefinitely in all directions.

of assumptions? Christaller gave three distinct answers, differing slightly in details, but all three requiring that the urban system take the form of a spatial hierarchy. (The three answers are the marketing, traffic, and administration models; their differences are not important in the present context.) Low-order centers serve small market areas that are nested within the larger market areas of higher-order centers. Several distinct levels of centers, interrelated in this manner, emerge. Low-order centers are numerous because their market areas are small. High-order centers serve large areas and are correspondingly fewer in number and farther apart. Centers functioning on or above any particular level within the hierarchy serve market areas of broadly uniform size and therefore are evenly spaced. The number, size, and spacing of urban centers are thus seen to be consequences of the efficiency inherent in a hierarchical organization of retail provision.

   Third, central-place models do not on their own provide a complete explanation of real urban systems. Each model presents an arrangement of towns that is geometrically precise, but this high degree of regularity is derived, of course, from the simplicity of the underlying assumptions. To the extent that the real world fails to match these assumptions, the real urban pattern will differ from that of the model. A full explanation therefore consists, conceptually, of two parts: 1) an application of the appropriate model, followed by 2) an appreciation of the effects of factors not incorporated in the associated theoretical argument. In central-place studies the additional factors normally include physiographic heterogeneity (in effect, we acknowledge that the region is not a perfectly isotropic plain) and the presence of non-central activities, notably manufacturing, in some or all of the towns.

Christaller's ideas have been challenged by an alternative model put forward by Lösch (1954: 101–37). It has been shown, however, that Lösch's model is inferior to the models developed by Christaller. The theoretical argument that accompanies Lösch's model possesses the same degree of internal logical consistency as the argument presented by Christaller, but Lösch's initial assumptions are less realistic than those of Christaller, and the fit between model and reality is closer for Christaller than for Lösch (Marshall 1989: 261–76). The comparison of Lösch with Christaller draws attention to the fact that a model's value should not be judged solely by the internal logical coherence of the theory on which it rests. The realism of the underlying assumptions and the empirical verisimilitude of the model must also be taken into account.

Concentric Zones

A second important family of models concerned with locational pattern consists of what may be termed *concentric zone* models. Historically the earliest member of this family was Von Thünen's model of the structure of agricultural land use around a centrally located market town (see chapter 12). Von Thünen lived during the early nineteenth century in northern Germany, where he owned and operated a large rural estate. The essence of his contribution was to demonstrate theoretically that agricultural land use around a central market town would normally vary according to distance from the market, even if conditions of relief, soil, rainfall, and other physical factors were everywhere the same (figure 11.3). (It is interesting to note that Von Thünen, like Christaller a century later, used the concept of the isotropic plain as a means of neutralizing natural environmental conditions. Christaller, incidentally, was aware of Von Thünen's work.)

For each agricultural product the cost per hectare of growing and marketing the product can be divided into two components: fixed cost and variable cost. The fixed cost includes the cost of seed, farm implements, labor, and any other inputs required at the actual site of production. (These elements of cost might, of course, vary through time; but Von Thünen's analysis is static, i.e., it is concerned only with the pattern of land use at some particular point in

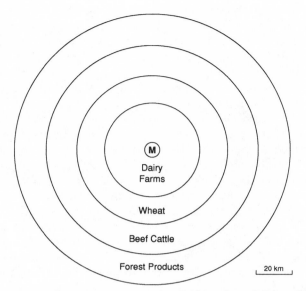

Figure 11.3 An example of Von Thünen's rings. Physical conditions are assumed to be uniform. At any given distance from the market town M, the profitability of each type of land use depends upon its particular combination of production and transport costs per hectare. Assuming profit-maximizing behavior, the resulting map of land uses takes the form of concentric rings. Note that the specific products shown here are hypothetical. The essence of the model is the regular pattern of concentric zones.

time.) The variable cost in turn is the cost of transporting the final product to the central market town. The cost of transportation increases—not necessarily in a linear fashion—with increasing distance between the farm and the market; hence the profitability of each product declines with increasing distance from the market. The numerical (dollar value) details of this relationship vary from product to product. Assuming that farmers seek to maximize profits (or that landlords seek to maximize rents, which amounts to the same thing), it follows that the type of farming practiced at any particular distance from the market will be the type that yields the greatest profit per hectare. The geographical result is a series of concentric rings of different land uses centered on the market town (Von Thünen 1966; Found 1971: 57–82; Chisholm 1979: 13–32).

Since Von Thünen wrote, models incorporating concentric rings have turned up in a variety of other contexts and at widely differing scales, sometimes with and sometimes without echoes of the narrowly economic argument that sustained the original agricultural application. One example, originating in sociology but much used by geographers, is the Burgess model of concentric zones of land use within an idealized North American metropolis (Burgess 1925; Yeates 1990: 110–11). Another, carrying the ideas of Burgess outward into the countryside, is Russwurm's model of the spatial structure of the typical metropolis's tributary area: the urban fringe lies immediately adjacent to the built-up area of the city, followed by the urban shadow and finally the zone of long-range commuting (Russwurm 1977). Very different in scale is the intriguing zones-and-strata model devised by Taylor to explain the persistence of early somatic (i.e., racial) features and primitive cultural traits in remote regions of the globe. In this model, which is partly a model of process as well as a model of pattern, it is assumed that innovations, both biological and cultural, move radially outward from their place of origin with the passage of time. Newer forms are continually added in the source area and move outward in their turn, replacing older features. The result is a concentric zonation of forms in which the most recently evolved characteristics are found at the center, the oldest on the periphery. Older forms can also be retrieved archaeologically from vertically ordered strata within the area of origin (Taylor 1938: 327–28; 1946: 43–50). This model is not without its problems, notably Taylor's evident belief that significant innovations have originated almost exclusively in the region extending from Western Europe to the Middle East. Nevertheless, the zones-and-strata model deserves recognition as a bold attempt to summarize important aspects of biological and cultural distributions at the global scale.

Mention must also be made of models in which a specified territory is divided into a core and a periphery (or a heartland and a hinterland, or a center and a margin). Core-and-periphery models are mainly concerned with areal differences in employment structure and levels of economic welfare. The area designated as the core displays the following five characteristics: 1) it is relatively small when compared with the total size of the territory under consideration; 2) it is relatively densely populated; 3) it contains a disproportionately large share of all employment in the manufacturing sector, particularly in the metal-working, machinery, and electronics industries; 4) it contains virtually all head-office employment serving the entire territory and virtually all major sources of venture capital and therefore contains the lion's share of all decision-making power; and 5) it has a higher average standard of living than the area designated as the periphery, though it should be noted that in certain respects such as environmental amenities and the general pace of life, the periphery may be preferable to the core.

The published literature on the core-and-periphery concept is large. Among the most influential contributions may be the works of Myrdal (1957), Ullman (1958), Hirschman (1958), and Friedmann (1966, 1972). One of the points to emerge from this literature is that the core-and-periphery model is in effect the simplest spatial expression of the more general concept of regional economic disparity (Sant 1974; Brown and Burrows 1977; Phillips 1982). In contrast to the simplicity of the model the observed spatial pattern of economic welfare may be quite irregular, and the so-called core may even be geographically fragmented. For example, in a recent study of Spain, Ferrer and his colleagues defined the national core as a set of three separate areas: a) greater Madrid; b) a strip of territory along the northern coast from Oviedo to Pamplona; and c) a strip along the Mediterranean coast from the French border southward as far as Murcia. The remainder of the national territory, including the whole interior of Spain except for greater Madrid, is designated as the periphery (Ferrer et al. 1989: 31–34). Here we have a situation in which the core is not only fragmented but also positioned chiefly on the outer margins of the national territory: that is, geometrically speaking, the core is largely on the periphery. Spain is, perhaps, an unusual case; but Ferrer's study is useful in demonstrating that core-and-periphery need not be expressed in the ideal inner and outer geometry that the model suggests.

The general concept of core-and-periphery lends itself readily to applications at different scales. At the subnational scale a single metropolis (e.g., Minneapolis-St. Paul) can be regarded as a core while its surrounding sphere of influence (e.g., the Upper Midwest) is treated as the periphery (Borchert 1987). At the national scale, in contrast, it is common to define the core as a region rather than a single city: ordinarily, the national core is identified with the principal manufacturing belt (or belts). Familiar examples include the northeastern manufacturing belt of the United States (Marshall 1989: 82–89) and the Windsor-Quebec axis in Canada (Yeates 1975, 1985; McCann 1982). Finally, the core-and-periphery model can also be applied at the intercontinental scale. For example, under the label "heartland-hinterland paradigm" one group of geographers has used the distinction between core (i.e., industrialized) and peripheral (i.e., agrarian) countries as their basic organizational principle in a successful textbook on world economic geography (Berry, Conkling, and Ray 1976). Also on the global scale the sociologist Wallerstein has employed a four-chambered version of the same model (consisting of core, semiperiphery, periphery, and external arena) as the framework for his multivolume economic history of the world since the sixteenth century (Wallerstein 1974–1989; see also Shannon 1989 and Blaut 1993), and the geographer Meinig, building in part on earlier work by Ward, has used the core-and-periphery model to good effect in clarifying the relationships between European mother countries and their American offshoots during the period ending in 1800 (Ward 1971: 11–49; Meinig 1986: *passim*, but especially 258–67).

Other Geometric Models

Models of the central-place hierarchy and models expressed in terms of concentric zones account for most of the models that may conveniently be grouped under the general heading of geometry. Two additional items also call for brief mention. The first is the sector or pie-slice model devised by Hoyt to describe spatial variation in socioeconomic status within cities (Hoyt 1939; Yeates 1990: 111–12). At first glance the Hoyt model appears to contradict the Burgess model of concentric zones mentioned above. The resolution of this difficulty is a topic for the next section. The second item is the family of probability models that have been applied to the analysis of point distributions with a view to determining whether the points in question are distributed in a clustered, uniform, or random manner. Though once quite popular, these models are used infrequently in human geography at the present time. They have been reviewed by Rogers (1974), Thomas (1977), and Getis and Boots (1978).

Algebra: Models of Functional Relationships

Models of functional relationships are members of the set of statistical techniques known collectively as the general linear model (Neter and Wasserman 1974, Johnston 1978). It is obviously impracticable in a short treatment to attempt to describe these techniques in detail. That is a job for courses in statistics. It is possible, however, without using much mathematics, to draw attention to salient features of the anatomy of these models and to show in a general way how they achieve their objectives. In what follows I rely on verbal exposition as much as possible. Mathematical symbolism is held to an absolute minimum.

Bivariate Regression and Correlation

Suppose that we are studying the variability of wheat yields across a large agricultural region. To make matters as concrete as possible, let us assume (without loss of generality, as mathematicians say) that our region is divided into fifty administrative units, which we will call counties, and that our basic information consists of the yield of wheat in each county, measured in bushels per hectare. We thus have a set of fifty observations of the variable that is defined as wheat yield in bushels per hectare. These data might refer to a single year, or they might be averages calculated over a period of several years. In the present context this is not important as long as any other variables that enter our study refer to the same time frame.

It might occur to us — perhaps as a result of mapping the basic data or because we have talked with some of the farmers — that the observed variation in wheat yields could be related to differences from county to county in average daily temperature during the growing season, so we assemble the necessary climatic data and proceed to draw a graph. The vertical axis of this graph shows wheat yields; the horizontal, average daily temperature. Each county is represented on the graph by a dot located at the appropriate coordinates. Let us assume that the graph reveals a positive association between the two variables: the higher the temperature, the higher the yield (figure 11.4).

Using the standard technique of least-squares regression, we can model the general relationship between the variables as a best-fitting straight line. In the bivariate case (i.e., when there are only two variables under consideration) the equation of this line takes the following form:

$$\hat{Y} = b_0 + b_1 X. \tag{1}$$

In this equation the symbol $\hat{Y}$ (pronounced "wye hat") refers to the dependent variable, that is, the variable whose pattern of variation we seek to explain. In the present example $\hat{Y}$ refers to wheat yield. The hat on the symbol denotes the fact that $\hat{Y}$ is not an observed value but an estimated value. It is the value of the dependent variable that is predicted by the best-fitting equation, given a particular value of X.

The symbol X refers to the independent variable—in this case, temperature. The independent variable, also known as the explanatory variable, is one that we think might be causally related to the behavior of the dependent (or response) variable. In effect, therefore, the regression equation represents a causal hypothesis. We will say more about causality in a moment.

The symbols b_0 and b_1 are the parameters of the equation: b_0 is the intercept and b_1 is the slope of the regression line. For a fixed set of data the values of these parameters are constant. We might obtain different values, though, if we repeated our study for a different set of counties. The word *parameter* is often used loosely in everyday speech to refer to relevant conditions in a particular situation, but its meaning in statistical modelbuilding is very precise and definite: it is a numerical quantity whose value remains constant for a given set of data but might change if the set of data is altered.

Associated with every regression equation is a quantity known as the coefficient of correlation. Normally denoted by r, the coefficient of correlation measures the strength of the relationship between the variables. The value of r lies between -1 and $+1$. A value of $+1$ identifies a perfect positive correlation: as the independent variable increases in value, the dependent variable also increases, and the regression equation predicts the values of the dependent variable without error. Conversely, a perfect negative correlation produces a value of -1 for r. A value of zero signifies that the two variables are completely unrelated.

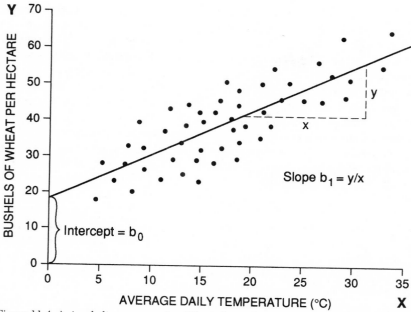

Figure 11.4 A simple linear regression. The independent variable is denoted by X and the dependent variable by Y. In this example the correlation between X and Y is positive. Each dot represents a different county (the data are hypothetical). The position of the best-fitting regression line is determined by the method of least squares.

We are now ready to take up the important issue of causality. Textbooks in statistics are careful to mention that a strong correlation (whether positive or negative) between two variables does not constitute incontrovertible proof that the variables are, in reality, causally connected. In our set of fifty counties, for example, it might be the case, simply by coincidence, that wheat yields are strongly correlated with Little League batting averages, but few people would want to claim that differences in wheat yields are caused by variations in children's baseball skills. The high absolute value of *r* in this instance would be an example of what is called a nonsense correlation. The textbooks, of course, are quite correct on this point. Correlation does not prove causality. But then, if *prove* means *demonstrate empirically*, neither does anything else. Causality is a relationship that cannot be directly observed, let alone measured. What we observe are simply events or occurrences, not causal connections. Causality, in short, is a nonempirical concept. As I have noted elsewhere, "causality is not a species of 'data' but an explanatory framework imposed upon the data by the observer" (Marshall 1985: 121).

Causality is an element of our theories, not of our empirical observations. When I introduced average daily temperature as the independent variable in the example of the wheat yields, I doubt if any reader was greatly surprised. Why so? Because theoretically it seems possible that yields could be affected by temperature. If I had introduced Little League batting averages instead of a climatic factor, the reaction would have been very different. This serves to emphasize the fact that the selection of independent variables is primarily a theoretical rather than an observational activity. (I say "primarily" because our ability to suggest sensible independent variables clearly depends on our repertoire of previous but similar experiences, from which we argue by analogy.) In order to justify the inclusion of any particular independent variable we must be able to point to a plausible causal mechanism. The independent variable, in short, must appear to be theoretically capable of influencing the behavior of the dependent variable. The ensuing regression and correlation analysis then becomes, in effect, an empirical test of a hypothesis about causal connections, a hypothesis derived from a theory that embodies causal mechanisms. If we obtain a strong correlation, we feel encouraged because the empirical evidence is consistent with the claim that our theory is correct. If the correlation is weak, we infer that the independent variable was chosen unwisely. Back to the drawingboard! This, in a nutshell, is the manner in which much of our research proceeds.

While still at the level of bivariate relationships, epitomized by equation (1), we may note two particular applications in which geographers have shown special interest. The first concerns variation in the density of population within the residential areas of large cities. If the central business district—an essentially nonresidential area—is excluded from the analysis, it is generally found that population density in the cities of industrialized countries declines in a regular fashion with increasing distance outward from the city center. (Actually, the "empty heart" can be included, but this calls for a more complex model.) The relationship between distance and density is not linear, however, but exponential. The equation has the following form:

$$d_x = ae^{-bx}, \qquad (2)$$

where d_x is the density of population at distance x from the city center, a and b are parameters, and e is the base of natural logarithms (a mathematical constant whose value is approximately 2.71828). By taking logarithms this exponential equation can be linearized:

$$log_e d_x = log_e a - bx, \qquad (3)$$

Equation (3) has the same basic form as equation (1) and can be calibrated by ordinary least-squares regression. This model has been applied, with various modifications and refinements, to the study of urban population densities in many parts of the world (Berry and Horton 1970: 276–305; Yeates 1990: 136–43).

Equation (3) is a special case of equation (1) in the sense that the independent element—distance—is an intrinsically geographical variable. The dependent element—density of population—declines in value as the distance from a specified point of origin increases. Because the relationship is inverse, the term *distance decay* is used to describe the behavior of the dependent variable.

The second noteworthy application is the urban rank-size rule. In many countries and large regions, the sizes of urban centers can be described with reasonable accuracy by an equation of the following form:

$$logP_n = a - b.logn, \qquad (4)$$

where P_n is a city's population, a and b are parameters, and n is rank, according to population size, within the urban system in question. This model has a pedigree that extends back to the early years of the twentieth century (Auerbach 1913; Marshall 1989: 326–39). It has recently been shown, however, that some urban systems are described more accurately by an alternative model in which the population of each city from rank 2 onward is a constant proportion of the average size of all larger cities combined:

$$P_{n+1} = (S_n/n) [(1 - G)/(1 + G)], \qquad (5)$$

where P_{n+1} is a city's population; n is rank; S_n is the combined population of all cities from rank 1 to rank n, inclusive; and G is a constant for the system in question—actually a form of the Gini index of concentration (Marshall 1993). The determination of the relative merits of equations (4) and (5) is an important topic for current research on the frequency distribution of city size.

Multiple Regression

A logical extension of the bivariate models exemplified above is the consideration of functional relationships that involve more than one independent variable. This extension, known as multiple regression, is one of the most powerful tools available to the quantitative model builder. The general form of the resulting equation is as follows:

$$\hat{Y} = b_0 + b_1X_1 + b_2X_2 + b_3X_3 + \ldots + b_kX_k, \qquad (6)$$

Properly manipulated, the coefficients in such an equation can reveal the relative importance of the various independent variables $(X_1, X_2, \ldots, X_k)$ in accounting for the behavior of the response variable. Care must be taken, however, to ensure that the independent variables in multiple regression are indeed independent of one another, that is, they should be mutually uncorrelated.

The techniques of simple and multiple regression are by no means unique to geography. In fact, they were first developed in other disciplines, notably psychology, and have entered geography only within the past thirty years, but applications of these standard models may fairly be said to be geographical in content if the data refer to geographical areas such as states, counties, or census tracts. Among important early applications of multiple regression in human geography we may note the works of Thomas (1960) on population growth within Chicago, King (1961) on the spacing of urban centers in various parts of the United States, and Yeates (1965) on Chicago land values. Other applications have recently been reviewed by Cadwallader (1986).

One particular set of applications deserves special mention: namely, studies in which the dependent variable is a measure of spatial interaction, such as telephone messages, airline passenger movement, or migration. The basic conceptual framework in such cases is the gravity model, so named because it was derived by analogy with Sir Isaac Newton's famous inverse square law concerning the force of gravity in the physical universe. The gravity model postulates that the volume of flow between two interacting locations is directly proportional to the "masses" of the locations (generally measured by population size) and inversely proportional to the distance across which the interaction takes place. (Note that the gravity model thus incorporates the idea of distance decay.) When applied to a system composed of numerous interacting localities, this model is seen to be a special case of multiple regression: the dependent variable is the magnitudes of the flows and the independent variables are the masses and the distances. With various modifications, the gravity model has been applied successfully to a wide variety of situations in which the structure of interaction across space is a central concern (Olsson 1965; Lowe and Moryadas 1975: 176–97; Thomas and Huggett 1980: 132–68; Gould 1985: 57–88).

Factor Analysis

The techniques of simple and multiple regression are appropriate for studies in which one particular variable — the dependent variable — is given privileged status as the variable whose spatial structure we seek to explain. It is sometimes the case, however, that we do not wish to single out any particular variable in this way; rather, we wish to place all variables on an equal footing and study the extent to which they are interrelated. In such cases we are interested in relationships of interdependency rather than dependency. Our objective is not to explain the behavior of a single variable in terms of cause and effect, but to address the question of whether a large number of seemingly different variables can be summarized effectively by a small number of more or less independent dimensions or factors. Such factors represent, in effect, the deep structure of the original set of variables.

We can accomplish a reduction of this sort by employing one or another member of the family of techniques known as factor analysis (Johnston 1978; Manly 1986). Typically, a factor analysis of a set of data containing several dozen variables results in a set of five or six basic factors that account for at least half of the total variability present in the original data. Great descriptive economy is thus achieved. Each factor can be given a name based on the variables with which it is most strongly correlated. The factors can then be mapped in order to yield insight into the latent spatial structure of the original set of data.

In the previous section we noted an apparent contradiction between the models of urban structure proposed by Burgess (concentric zones) and by Hoyt (sectors). Factor analysis lies at the heart of the resolution of this conflict. If we apply factor analysis to a large number of socioeconomic variables that refer to urban census tracts, the two most important factors that emerge are normally identifiable as economic status and family status. The former is associated chiefly with household income, level of education, and type of occupation; the latter, with age structure, marital status, and the presence or absence of nonfamily households. In addition, economic status typically appears on a map as distinct sectors, whereas family status appears as concentric zones. In effect, therefore, the Burgess and Hoyt models are both valid, but they refer to different dimensions of socioeconomic structure. This demonstration of the complementarity of the Burgess and Hoyt models has been one of the leading accomplishments of urban geography in recent years (Berry 1965; Murdie 1969; Jones and Eyles 1977: 112–20; Yeates 1990: 156–61).

Hägerstrand Models

The models described above are concerned primarily with static relationships and not with the dynamics of change: they are models of pattern rather than process. In general, so far as processes of change are concerned, human geographers have either avoided modelbuilding entirely or else have resorted to models that are purely verbal in character. Models of this latter type are discussed in the next section. There exists, however, one important group of models that are simultaneously process oriented, quantitative, and inherently geographical: namely, models of spatial diffusion.

As it happens, diffusion is the subject of a separate contribution to this volume, and therefore I will not discuss models of diffusion here (see chapter 9). No review of models in geography can be complete, however, without at least mentioning the name of Hägerstrand, whose ground-breaking research on the spread of innovations in Sweden inspired a significant number of later studies and still ranks today as one of the most original contributions in the entire literature of geography (Hägerstrand 1952, 1967a, 1967b). Among later works inspired wholly or partly by Hägerstrand's research, those of Bowden (1965), Morrill (1965), Robson (1973), and Pred and Törnqvist (1973) are especially noteworthy.

Narrative Models: Stages of Historical Development

Stage models, as they are commonly known, are created by imposing an arbitrary yet meaningful episodic structure on what is, in reality, a continuous process of change. In effect, stage models attempt to capture the dynamics of a particular class of phenomena by identifying a series of evolutionary periods through which the phenomena have passed on their way to attaining their present form. Each stage is separated from its predecessor by the emergence of a significant new trend within the overall process of development. In a sense, stage models are Darwinian: the system under investigation displays a succession of adaptations to changes in the relevant external conditions. Each major adaptation signals the onset of a new stage in evolution.

Many studies in historical geography have used stage models on an ad hoc basis, either as an organizational framework or as a means of summarizing the results of the investigation. (For example, "In conclusion, the region is seen to have passed through three stages of development.") In a few cases, however, models have appeared that are distinguished by an exceptionally wide range of applicability. Among the best known may be the model proposed by Taaffe, Morrill, and Gould (1963) to explain the evolution of transportation networks in underdeveloped countries (see chapter 2), Borchert's model of the evolution of American metropolitan centers (Borchert 1967), and Muller's model of stages of development in frontier regions, as exemplified by the Ohio Valley (Muller 1976, 1977).

Arguably the most influential of all such models, at least for studies of North America, has been the mercantile model devised by Vance (1970: 148–59). Conceptually, this model is closely related to the so-called staple theory of economic development constructed by Canadian economic historians such as Innis (1954, 1956) and Watkins (1963). Vance's inquiry, however, was not addressed to economic development as a general, nonspatial process, but rather to the specific forces that have molded the evolution of the spatial structure of the urban system of North America. The mercantile model is composed of five stages, as follows:

(1) Exploration
(2) Harvesting of naturally occurring resources

(3) Emergence of farm-based staple production
(4) Establishment of interior (i.e., trans-Appalachian) depot centers
(5) Economic maturity and central-place in-filling

The basic premise of the model is that the spatial structure of the North American urban system is fundamentally a reflection of the establishment of overseas commercial outposts by European powers, chiefly England and France. The emphasis, in other words, is on the role of urban centers as control points for the development of long-distance trade in staple commodities. Initially, Europeans sought knowledge of the economic potential of the new land (stage 1). Trade began almost immediately, at first in naturally occurring resources such as codfish, furs, and timber (stage 2) and later in farm-based staples such as grain, salted pork, tobacco, indigo, and cotton (stage 3). As the demand for these products in Europe increased, and as more settlers arrived in North America, mercantile interests reached farther westward in an effort to maintain a steady flow of trade (stage 4). Later still, a healthy domestic manufacturing sector emerged (economic maturity) and many small central places arose to serve the rural areas that lay between the major routes of staple trade (stage 5). Within each region, however, the initial impetus for urban development was provided by the establishment of one or more control points in the expanding system of long-distance commodity movement. Concentrations of manufacturing and a fully articulated network of central places were later developments.

The interpretation of the historical record that is inherent in this model embodies the explicitly geographical idea that the skeleton of the urban system is a combination of points and lines: the points are the mercantile cities and the lines are the principal routes of long-distance trade. This skeleton is exogenously determined, since the key decisions that bring it into existence are made outside the system, in Europe. Once in place, the skeleton of points and lines acts as a sort of master plan to which other components of the evolving urban system are obliged to conform. As the principal creative force establishing the basic spatial structure of the system, long-distance trade thus takes precedence, both historically and functionally, over manufacturing and central-place activity.

We began our survey of geographical models with Christaller's simplified portrayal of the central-place hierarchy. In an important sense we have come full circle, for Vance's mercantile model supplies the dynamic element that is absent from the static Christallerian models of hierarchical structure (Marshall 1989: 284–85). Each major urban foundation in the New World, Vance argues, is first and foremost a response to the needs of long-distance trade, but it is only natural that agricultural pioneers in the immediate vicinity will require consumer goods and services, and hence the mercantile cities take on, essentially from the first day of their existence, a central-place role. Although these centers are initially small, each of them is the largest node in its own district, and therefore the mercantile cities become the highest order places in the central-place network. From the beginning, in other words, there exists a geographical concordance between the mercantile and central-place systems: prominence as a central place is contingent on initial establishment as a significant mercantile node. Like the models of Burgess and Hoyt, those of Vance and Christaller are additive and mutually reinforcing, thereby enhancing our understanding of the structure and evolution of the North American system of cities.

Models, Systems, and Explanations

As noted earlier, every model represents an attempt to summarize the essential properties of some particular system—that is, a segment of reality that has captured our interest and is therefore isolated by intellectual fiat for the purpose of close investigation. Systems that differ in terms of their subject matter may nevertheless be amenable to representation by models that are identical in form. For example, both the daily flux of commuters within a metropolitan area and the annual movement of migrants across an entire country can be analyzed by means of the gravity model, expressed as a problem in multiple regression. This type of similarity, in which two or more models are different in content but identical in form, is known as *isomorphism*.

During the 1950s recognition of the existence of isomorphisms prompted several scholars to pursue the idea that it might be possible to subsume all fields of science, social as well as natural, under a single, integrated set of all-purpose equations. This idea formed the basis of General Systems Theory (Von Bertalanffy 1951; Boulding 1956). Although greeted with interest at the time, General Systems Theory did not live up to its early promise (Chisholm 1967). One of the chief difficulties is that similarity of form does not necessarily entail similarity of process. Accordingly, a general systems perspective might be helpful at the descriptive level but has little to offer when it comes to formulating explanations. Another important point is that isomorphisms are largely an outcome of the fact that we are constrained, in all our investigations, by the structure of our language, including our mathematical conventions. Of necessity, therefore, we approach different subjects with similar tools, and it is not surprising that we sometimes end up describing different phenomena in similar ways.

This is not to say, of course, that there is no value in the basic concept of a system as a distinctive component of our experience, nor is it to deny that reasoning by analogy can be a fruitful approach to a new topic. These common-sense principles, however, are hardly an adequate basis for the creation of an all-encompassing superscience. With the advantage of hindsight it is not difficult to understand why General Systems Theory failed to attract a wide following.

It remains for us to consider the relationship between models and explanations. Putting the matter in the most general terms, a satisfactory explanation is a statement, or set of statements, that reduces puzzlement (Passmore 1962). Philosophers identify several types of explanation—genetic, functional, deductive-nomological, and so forth—but the reduction of puzzlement is the fundamental element in all these types. Whenever a satisfactory explanation is given, we feel that things have become more intelligible and that our subject matter is less mysterious than before. Of course, the giving of an explanation can create fresh puzzles that call for additional explanations. The process of inquiry comes to an end only when no one feels inclined to ask any more questions—at least for the time being.

The explanatory power of a model depends on its plausibility, which depends in turn on the theory on which the model is based. *Theory* is used here in the general sense of an extended argument grounded in specific assumptions and leading to conclusions that are falsifiable in principle, that is, they are capable of being disconfirmed by empirical evidence (Popper 1972). The testable conclusions of any such theory constitute a model. If the assumptions from which the theory is launched are realistic (and this, too, can be empirically tested) and if the theoretical argument is logically rigorous, then the resulting model has a high degree of plausibility; however, if the assumptions are unrealistic and the argument is tenuous or unclear, the model's plausibility is low.

A model of high plausibility may justifiably be used as a partial explanation of the real situation to which it refers. The completion of the explanation then requires that reasons be found to account for real-world deviations from the predictions of the model. This two-stage form of explanation is characteristic of the model-based approach to understanding. The model provides, in effect, half of the necessary insight, and the other half involves particularized explanations for observations that do not conform to the pattern embodied in the model.

Conclusion

The attainment of understanding rests on a constant interplay between theory and observation. Models play a vital role in this process because they stand squarely at the crossroads where theory and observation intersect. On the one hand, models are empirical: they are created by inductive generalization in an attempt to simplify a mass of particular observations. On the other hand, models are theoretical: they are the end products of abstract arguments put forward as tentative explanations. Successful models emerge when inductive generalization and theoretical argument converge to a common result. A satisfactory model does not merely have relevance to the investigation currently in hand; it also has heuristic value in telling us what to expect, or at least what to watch out for, on future occasions. Viewed thus as instruments of discovery, models are an indispensable component of the equipment we bring to bear on the problem of explaining our world. As the old saying goes, models are like army boots: they do not always provide a perfect fit, but they have been known to cover a lot of ground.

References

Amedeo, D., and R. G. Golledge. 1975. *An introduction to scientific reasoning in geography.* New York: Wiley.

Auerbach, F. 1913. Das Gesetz der Bevölkerungskonzentration. *Petermanns Geographische Mitteilungen* 59/1: 74–76.

Berry, B. J. L. 1965. Internal structure of the city. *Law and Contemporary Problems* 30: 111–19.

Berry, B. J. L., and F. E. Horton, eds. 1970. *Geographic perspectives on urban systems.* Englewood Cliffs, N. J.: Prentice-Hall.

Berry, B. J. L., E. C. Conkling, and D. M. Ray. 1976. *The geography of economic systems.* Englewood Cliffs, N. J.: Prentice-Hall.

Berry, B J. L, et al. 1988. *Market centers and retail location: Theory and applications.* Englewood Cliffs, N. J.: Prentice-Hall.

Blaut, J. M. 1993. *The colonizer's model of the world: Geographical diffusionism and Eurocentric history.* New York: Guilford Press.

Borchert, J. R. 1967. American metropolitan evolution. *Geographical Review* 57: 301–32.

———. 1987. *America's northern heartland: An economic and historical geography of the Upper Midwest.* Minneapolis: University of Minnesota Press.

Boulding, K. E. 1956. General Systems Theory: The skeleton of science. *Management Science* 2: 197–208.

Bowden, L. W. 1965. *Diffusion of the decision to irrigate: Simulation of the spread of a new resource management practice in the Colorado Northern High Plains.* Research Paper No. 97. Chicago: Department of Geography, University of Chicago.

Brown, A. J., and E. M. Burrows. 1977. *Regional economic problems: Comparative experiences of some market economies.* London: George Allen and Unwin.

Bunbury, E. H. 1959. A *history of ancient geography among the Greeks and Romans from the earliest ages till the fall of the Roman Empire,* 2 vols. New York: Dover (orig. pub. 1883).

Burgess, E. W. 1925. The growth of the city: An introduction to a research project. In *The city,* ed. R. E. Park, E. W. Burgess, and R. D. McKenzie, 47–62. Chicago: University of Chicago Press.

Cadwallader, M. 1986. Structural equation models in human geography. *Progress in Human Geography* 10: 24–47.

Chisholm, M. 1967. General Systems Theory and geography. *Transactions of the Institute of British Geographers* 42: 45–52.

———. 1979. *Rural settlement and land use: An essay in location,* 3d ed. London: Hutchinson.

Chorley, R. J., and P. Haggett. eds. 1967. *Models in geography.* London: Methuen.

Christaller, W. 1966. *Central places in southern Germany,* trans. C. W. Baskin. Englewood Cliffs, N. J.: Prentice-Hall. (orig. pub. 1933).

———. 1972. How I discovered the theory of central places: A report about the origin of central places. In *Man, space, and environment: Concepts in contemporary human geography,* ed. P. W. English and R. C. Mayfield, 601–10. New York: Oxford University Press.

Ferrer, M., et al. 1989. Recent evolution of the Spanish settlement system. In *The changing geography of urban systems: Perspectives on the developed and developing worlds,* ed. L. S. Bourne et al., 21–37. Pamplona, Spain: Department of Human Geography, Universidad de Navarra.

Found, W. C. 1971. A *theoretical approach to rural land-use patterns.* Toronto: Macmillan.

Friedmann, J. 1966. *Regional development policy: A case study of Venezuela.* Cambridge: MIT Press.

———. 1972. A general theory of polarized development. In *Growth centers in regional economic development,* ed. N. M. Hansen, 82–107. New York: Free Press.

Getis, A., and B. Boots. 1978. *Models of spatial processes: An approach to the study of point, line and area patterns.* Cambridge Geographical Studies No. 8. Cambridge: Cambridge University Press.

Gould, P. 1985. *The geographer at work.* London: Routledge and Kegan Paul.

Hägerstrand, T. 1952. *The propagation of innovation waves.* Lund Studies in Geography, Series B, No. 4. Lund, Sweden: Department of Geography, Royal University of Lund.

————. 1967a. *Innovation diffusion as a spatial process*, trans. A. Pred with the assistance of G. Haag. Chicago: University of Chicago Press (orig. pub. 1953).

————. 1967b. On Monte Carlo simulation of diffusion. In *Quantitative geography: Part 1: Economic and cultural topics*, ed. W. L. Garrison and D. F. Marble, 1–32. Northwestern University Studies in Geography No. 13. Evanston, Ill.: Department of Geography, Northwestern University.

Harvey, D. 1969. *Explanation in geography.* London: Arnold.

Hirschman, A. O. 1958. *The strategy of economic development.* New Haven: Yale University Press.

Hoyt, H. 1939. *The structure and growth of residential neighborhoods in American cities.* Washington, D.C.: Federal Housing Administration.

Innis, H. A. 1954. *The cod fisheries: The history of an international economy*, revised ed. Toronto: University of Toronto Press.

————. 1956. *The fur trade in Canada: An introduction to Canadian economic history*, revised ed. Toronto: University of Toronto Press.

Johnston, R. J. 1978. *Multivariate statistical analysis in geography: A primer on the general linear model.* London: Longman.

————. 1987. *Geography and geographers: Anglo-American human geography since 1945*, 3d ed. London: Arnold.

Jones, E., and J. Eyles. 1977. *An introduction to social geography.* Oxford: Oxford University Press.

King, L. J. 1961. A multivariate analysis of the spacing of urban settlements in the United States. *Annals of the Association of American Geographers* 51: 222–33.

————. 1984. *Central-place theory.* Scientific Geography Series, Vol. 1. Beverly Hills: Sage.

Livingstone, D. N. 1992. *The geographical tradition: Episodes in the history of a contested enterprise.* Oxford: Blackwell.

Lösch, A. 1954. *The economics of location*, trans. W. H. Woglom with the assistance of W. F. Stolper. New Haven: Yale University Press (orig. pub. 1944).

Lowe, J. C., and S. Moryadas. 1975. *The geography of movement.* Boston: Houghton Mifflin.

Manly, B. F. J. 1986. *Multivariate statistical methods: A primer.* London: Chapman and Hall.

Marshall, J. U. 1982. Geography and critical rationalism. In *Rethinking geographical inquiry*, ed. J. D. Wood, 75–171. Geographical Monographs No. 11. North York, Ontario: Department of Geography, Atkinson College, York University.

———. 1985. Geography as a scientific enterprise. In *The future of geography*, ed. R. J. Johnston, 113–28. London: Methuen.

———. 1989. *The structure of urban systems*. Toronto: University of Toronto Press.

———. 1993. Toward an umland-based model of city sizes. In *Canada: Geographical interpretations: Essays in honour of John* Warkentin, ed. J. R. Gibson, 231–54. Geographical Monographs No. 22. North York, Ontario: Department of Geography, Atkinson College, York University.

Martin, G. J. 1989. The Nature of Geography and the Schaefer-Hartshorne debate. In *Reflections on Richard Hartshorne's The Nature of Geography*, ed. J. N. Entrikin and S. D. Brunn, 69–90. Washington, D.C.: Association of American Geographers.

Martin, G. J., and P. E. James. 1993. *All possible worlds: A history of geographical ideas*, 3d. ed. New York: Wiley.

McCann, L. D., ed. 1982. *Heartland and hinterland: A geography of Canada*. Scarborough, Ontario: Prentice-Hall.

Meinig, D. W. 1986. *The shaping of America: A geographical perspective on 500 years of history, Vol. 1: Atlantic America, 1492–1800*. New Haven: Yale University Press.

Morrill, R. L. 1965. *Migration and the spread and growth of urban settlement*. Lund Studies in Geography, Series B, No. 26. Lund, Sweden: Gleerup.

Muller, E. K. 1976. Selective urban growth in the Middle Ohio Valley, 1800–1860. *Geographical Review* 66: 178–99.

———. 1977. Regional urbanization and the selective growth of towns in North American regions. *Journal of Historical Geography* 3: 21–39.

Murdie, R. A. 1969. *Factorial ecology of metropolitan Toronto, 1951–1961: An essay on the social geography of the city*. Research Paper No. 116. Chicago: Department of Geography, University of Chicago.

Myrdal, G. 1957. *Economic theory and underdeveloped regions*. London: Duckworth.

Neter, J., and W. Wasserman. 1974. *Applied linear statistical models: Regression, analysis of variance, and experimental designs*. Homewood, Ill.: Richard D. Irwin.

Olsson, G. 1965. *Distance and human interaction: A review and bibliography*.

Bibliography Series No. 2. Philadelphia: Regional Science Research Institute.

Passmore, J. 1962. Explanation in everyday life, in science, and in history. *History and Theory* 2: 105–23.

Phillips, P. 1982. *Regional disparities.* Toronto: Lorimer.

Popper, K. R. 1972. *Objective knowledge: An evolutionary approach.* Oxford: Clarendon Press.

Pred, A. R., and G. E. Törnqvist. 1973. *Systems of cities and information flows: Two essays,* Lund Studies in Geography, Series B, No. 38. Lund, Sweden: Gleerup.

Robson, B. T. 1973. *Urban growth: An approach.* London: Methuen.

Rogers, A. 1974. *Statistical analysis of spatial dispersion: The quadrat method.* London: Pion.

Russwurm, L. H. 1977. *The surroundings of our cities: Problems and planning implications of urban fringe landscapes.* Ottawa: Community Planning Press.

Sant, M. E. C. 1974. *Regional disparities.* Basingstoke, England: Macmillan.

Schaefer, F. K. 1953. Exceptionalism in geography: A methodological examination. *Annals of the Association of American Geographers* 43: 226–49.

Shannon, T. R. 1989. *An introduction to the world-system perspective.* Boulder: Westview Press.

Sprout, H., and M. Sprout. 1965. *The ecological perspective on human affairs, with special reference to international politics.* Princeton: Princeton University Press.

Taaffe, E. J., R. L. Morrill., and P. R. Gould. 1963. Transport expansion in underdeveloped countries: A comparative analysis. *Geographical Review* 53: 503–29.

Taylor, G. 1938. Correlations and culture: A study in technique. *Scottish Geographical Magazine* 54: 321–44.

―――. 1946. *Environment, race and migration: Fundamentals of human distribution, with special sections on racial classification, and settlement in Canada and Australia,* 2d ed. Toronto: University of Toronto Press.

Taylor, P. J. 1976. An interpretation of the quantification debate in British geography. *Transactions of the Institute of British Geographers,* N. S. 1: 129–42.

Thomas, E. N. 1960. Areal associations between population growth and selected factors in the Chicago urbanized area. *Economic Geography* 36: 158–70.

Thomas, R. W. 1977. *An introduction to quadrat analysis.* Concepts and Techniques in Modern Geography No. 12. Norwich, England: Geo Abstracts.

Thomas, R. W., and R. J. Huggett. 1980. *Modeling in geography: A mathematical approach.* Totowa, N. J.: Barnes and Noble.

Ullman, E. L. 1958. Regional development and the geography of concentration. *Papers and Proceedings of the Regional Science Association* 4: 179–98.

Vance, J. E., Jr. 1970. *The merchant's world: The geography of wholesaling.* Englewood Cliffs, N. J.: Prentice-Hall.

Von Bertalanffy, L. 1951. General Systems Theory: A new approach to the unity of science. *Human Biology* 23: 303–61.

Von Thünen, J. H. 1966. *Von Thünen's isolated state,* trans. C. M. Wartenberg, ed. P. Hall. Oxford: Pergamon Press (orig. pub. 1826).

Wallerstein, I. M. 1974–1989. *The modern world-system,* Volumes 1–3. New York and San Diego: Academic Press.

Ward, D. 1971. *Cities and immigrants: A geography of change in nineteenth-century America.* New York: Oxford University Press.

Watkins, M. H. 1963. A staple theory of economic growth. *Canadian Journal of Economics and Political Science* 29: 141–58.

Yeates, M. H. 1965. Some factors affecting the spatial distribution of Chicago land values, 1910–1960. *Economic Geography* 41: 57–70.

———. 1975. *Main street: Windsor to Quebec City.* Toronto: Macmillan.

———. 1985. The core/periphery model and urban development in central Canada. *Urban Geography* 6: 101–21.

———. 1990. *The North American city,* 4th ed. New York: Harper & Row.

12

The Model of Rational Economic Man and Its Alternatives: A Brief for Intermittent Rationality

Carville Earle

The construct of *economic man*—the notion that humankind is a rational, maximizing animal—constitutes one of the underpinnings of theoretical models in economic geography in general and locational analyses of agricultural, industrial, and urban land uses in particular. It also happens to be one of social science's most controversial concepts, one that cuts to the core of our most private definitions of humanity and human nature. When deployed in the study of society, the model of economic man almost invariably ignites controversy in academic discourse, converting what had been polite academic discussion into polemic debate and dispassionate analysis into fractious contention. Why should this be so? What is it about this seemingly innocent notion—that human beings rationally calculate their interests and then act on them—that enrages otherwise civil scholars, that divides them into armed philosophical camps (Machlup 1978a, 1978b; Johnston 1981)? This essay explores these questions as they bear on discourse in human geography and its controversial applications of a model of economic man. The discussion proceeds in four parts: 1) the definition and origins of economic man within mainstream economics; 2) the applications of this construct in economic geography; 3) the conventional critique of its assumptions; and 4) a resolution of this intellectual clash via a more dynamic and problematic model of human behavior properly specified in time and in space—a model of intermittent rationality. Our review begins with the origins of *homo economicus* in nineteenth-century economics and philosophy.

Definitions and Origins

There is an old joke about economists that gets to the heart of the concept of economic man. The joke begins with three scholars marooned on a desert island with nothing to eat but a can of baked beans. The humanist begs his colleagues to pray for rain so that food might grow; the physicist urges them to immerse the can of beans in the ocean so that the salt water will rust the can and crack it open; and the economist, as economists are wont to do, declaims sardonically, "assume a can opener." The concept of economic man is like that. It assumes a great deal: that men (and women) are logical, that they are rational, that they maximize their economic interests, and that they have full and complete (perfect) information; but, unlike the assuming economist in our joke, the assumptions in the model of economic man have had, and continue to have, marvelous utility for the social sciences as well as for economics.

The notion of economic man as a formal academic construct seems to date from the marginalist revolution in economics in the last half of the nineteenth century.[1] Preferring a theoretical as opposed to an institutionalist, historicist framework for the emergent discipline of economics, neoclassical economists recognized the utility of creating a mythical rational actor, a *Homo economicus*, who allocated scarce resources purely on the basis of rational calculation. This mythical economic man they endowed with a large kitbag of economic skills. In his possession were perfect information on all facets of the economy, a capacity for anticipating and tabulating every conceivable benefit and cost, and a set of marginalist principles for economic maximization (Seligman 1962; Hogarth and Reder 1986; Blaug 1980; Georgescu-Roegen 1968, 1973). These assumptions, though dismissed as heroic and presumptuous by Thorstein Veblen and kindred social critics, served the useful purposes of simplifying the complexity of economic decision making, benchmarking rational economic behavior against which the real world might be compared, and laying the theoretical foundation for the microeconomics of the firm. Judging by the spectacular success of economics in ensuing years, the effort expended in the creation of this heuristic caricature of economic man seems to have been, whatever its shortcomings, worth the candle (Hogarth and Reder 1986).

Like all good caricatures, economic man succeeded because it possessed a certain verisimilitude—it revealed just enough of the truth to be taken seriously; indeed, a good case can be made for an unusually close correspondence between the marginalists' caricature and the real world behavior of entrepreneurs in the industrial world of the late nineteenth century—when capitalism was in full sway and telegraph and telephone delivered economic information in ways that, though not perfect, must have seemed so by the standards of communication of the time. Merchants and farmers, industrialists and financiers all seemed to behave in reasonable accordance with the model of rational economic man—they received market information almost instantaneously; they were numerate and literate, enabling them to calculate the relevant benefits and costs; they had a clear-cut preference for profit maximization; and they benefited immensely from doing so, which is to say that at the moment of its creation the model of economic man may not have been altogether overdrawn.[2]

The notion of economic man was not all sweetness and light, however. The caricature got caught up in the polemic policy debates and sectarian politics that were rife in the late nineteenth century. The concept of economic man was used and abused for parochial political ends. Conservatives on the one hand mixed a dose of the new economics with some "survival-of-the-fittest" economic Darwinism and transmuted the heuristic model of rational economic man into a normative statement of how human beings ought to behave in the marketplace. In the popular conservative mind economic man henceforth represented not merely a caricature of the real world, but the idealized norm for all social behavior. Radicals, on the other hand, saw in economic man a convenient strawman for their critique of capitalism's worst excesses. They poured their venom on a model of man that wickedly, in their view, glorified self-interest and damned altruism and the public interest.[3] Whether justly or not, the theory premised on economic man had been pushed onto the slippery slope that separates analytical science and conservative political ideology. Mainstream economics remains on that slope even today, hence its perennial subjection to critique by those who prefer alternative models of human nature and behavioral motivation and/or different models of ideology and political economy.

The construct of economic man was born in ideological controversy, and in large measure that was its birthright. Sired by controversial hedonistic and utilitarian philosophies, economic man came to be seen by its critics as an extension of these philosophies, as a paen to a psychology of self-interest, quests for pleasure over pain, and decisions based on rational calculation of personal consequences. For the enemies of these ancient philosophies, marginalist economic man seemed merely a more formal exposition of doctrines of questionable merit, an academic apologia for doctrines which blithely ignored models of humanity premised on virtue, altruism, or collective welfare (Georgescu-Roeger 1968, 1973; Chalk 1964).

Modern economists, to their credit, have worked hard at getting off the slippery slope that leads toward ideology. In collaboration with psychologists and theoreticians of rational choice, they refined the construct of economic man, reexamined its primitive assumptions, and explored the fit between the caricature and the real world. In consequence, mainstream economic theory has subtly shifted its ground from a normative caricature of economic man toward a more perceptual and probabilistic rendition of what individuals actually do when making economic decisions. Whereas earlier economists made predictions "of the aggregate behavior of individuals based on the assumption that individuals are, by and large, 'reasonable,'" modern theoreticians allow that "reasonableness" itself varies from one individual to another and that, even when people do behave in economically rational ways, their actions are often clouded by perceptions of what they believe to be the economic facts rather than the objective facts themselves (this, of course, is the justly famous notion of rational expectations) (Marschak 1968).

These refinements in contemporary microeconomic theory have caused the discipline of economics to tack between two not altogether complementary points of view: one, the descriptive, seeks a sweeping revision in our dated caricature of economic man; and two, the prescriptive, envisions a modest revision that preserves the primordial caricature while blurring slightly its omniscient perception of economic realities (rational expectations) (Marschak 1968).

Descriptive theorists—the more revisionist of the two groups—regard the proposition of economic man as empirically problematic. They ask: is there a good match between the caricature of economic man and actors in the real world? Is our behavior, individually and collectively, economically rational? In what degree? The answers thus far have been mixed. Economic rationality seems to be a capacity that varies widely within and across societies and cultures. Take the case of rational maximization, a skill that is contingent on the capacity for rank ordering our preferences (the notion of transitivity). Experiments with this crucial aspect of rationality reveal sizable variations in this capacity. Business executives on the one hand did quite well in these experiments. They achieved a logically transitive rank ordering of their preferences in all but four percent of the cases, which suggests a keen ability for maximizing behavior. Student subjects on the other hand had a more difficult time with rank ordering, violating the rule of transitivity in some twenty-seven percent of the cases. They were much less sophisticated in their capacity for maximizing behavior (MacCrimmon 1965; May 1954).

The moral is that economic man seems to offer a faithful caricature for many, though by no means all, economic actors. It offers a good match for the behavior of the business executive who, given choices among profits, sales, power, and status, rationally prefers (hypothetically) profits to sales, sales to power, and power to status. The model makes a bad fit, though, in the case of the logically confused individual who prefers profits to sales, sales to power, and power to profits. In this case, rational maximizing behavior (and the model of economic man) is precluded by an inability to impose a transitive ordering on our preferences.

These experiments do not tell us why economic rationality varies from one person to another. Is the variance the result of selection or learning? Or both? Are business executives more rational because their jobs select for these capacities or because business experience has taught them to act in that fashion (or both)? For the student of political economy, the answers to these vexing questions are vitally important for the future of capitalist society: if selective forces are primary, capitalist society must look forward to a persistent class structuring; if, however, learning is primary, capitalism offers at least the opportunity for socioeconomic mobility. Marx, of course, focuses on these contradictions between capitalism's relentless imposition of rational values and its incapacity for overcoming initial inequalities among persons and wealth. Given their uncertainties as to the causes of these variations in rational economic behavior, descriptive theorists caution against an overly zealous application of the model of economic man.

Prescriptive theory, in contrast, focuses on the rule rather than the exceptions, that is, on the many individuals who behave as reasonable economic men. The new version of economic man differs from the original, however, in that he is somewhat less omniscient about market conditions and somewhat more given to bouts of uncertainty and probabilistic calculation. He has been, as it were, humanized. The consistent individual, according to this view, behaves as though she assigns personal probabilities to events, attaches numerical utilities to the results of her actions, and chooses the action with the highest expected utility (various essays in Hogarth and Reder 1986; on Bayesian analysis based on probabilistic assessments of this sort, see Skyrms 1990; Hudson 1989). Translated into ordinary language, this means that economic man still possesses the critical capacity for rational maximization—to assign numerical values to her utilities and to choose what is in her self-interest. He is, however, less confident about foreseeing the future. His information may be faulty, his perception somewhat askew. He acts on his rational expectations of what will probably come true rather than what in fact becomes true. All of this assumes, of course, that risks can be assessed with reasonable probabilities. Although some critics have dismissed rational expectations as little more than an after-the-fact rationalizing of reality and model, a fairer assessment might be that it reveals a certain humility among prescriptive theorists impressed as much perhaps by the exquisite behavioral variability discerned by their counterparts in descriptive microeconomic theory as by the improvements in the power of their theories.[4]

Whatever its shortcomings—and they are many—the economist's model of rational economic man has contributed mightily to the remarkable advance in the study of society. Social science, for example, has been the beneficiary of an especially persuasive interpretation of economic behavior in developed economies during the capitalist epoch—and in some cases, in developing economies (e.g., the notion of the rational peasant). Collateral theories of modern politics, social systems, organizational behavior, and location have been enriched by the application of rational assumptions and decision logic (Becker 1976, 1981; Opp 1989; Olson 1965; Dunn 1954; Gordon 1983). Finally, the profession of economics itself has so sharpened its theoretical repertoire that it has been assured a position of preeminence within the social sciences and in the study of humankind. Perhaps the best testimony to this caricature's achievement, however, is that it is hard to imagine the contemporary world of scholarship without it.

The Model of Economic Man Enters Human Geography

Anglo-American economic geography experienced something of a transformation in the halcyon days following World War II, and perhaps rightly so. A new generation of geographers, having mastered the demons of tyranny and depression, wanted nothing so much as a restoration of reason and rationality, and in their quest for this more reasonable world of boundless peace and limitless prosperity, what better model for them to turn to than the economist's model of rational economic man? With no small irony, these students of reason launched a vigorous and sustained attack on an older economic geography premised on the study of particular commodities and case study methods. Following some nasty infighting during the 1950s and 1960s, the rebel paradigm of neoclassical location theory, rational economic man, and quantitative methodology emerged triumphant in economic geography. Despite internal and external critique during the past two decades, it persists as the mainstream view of the geography of economic activity (Chorley and Haggett 1968; McNee 1959; Chisholm 1966; Johnston 1986. For critiques of the mainstream, see Harvey 1973; Shepphard and Barnes 1990; Storper and Walker 1989).

The new economic geography was inspired by three bodies of neoclassical location theory (agricultural, industrial, and urban) formulated during the period of most vigorous capitalist expansion—1800 to 1930. The order of their emergence reflects the unfolding logic of capitalism itself. First came the theory of agricultural land use formulated by the Prussian landowner, Johann Heinrich von Thünen at the beginning of the nineteenth century. It was followed nearly a century later by Alfred Weber's theory of industrial location and a few years after that by Walter Christaller's theory of central places. Each of these theories premised their explanations of the spatial distribution of land use on a more or less explicit model of rational economic behavior. The case of agriculture location theory serves as a useful illustration of the applications of that model.[5]

In his theory of agricultural location Thünen made a series of simplifying assumptions about economic behavior in order to explain the roughly concentric zonations of agrarian land use. He first created an ideal-typical geographical landscape—what he called the isolated state. Located on a perfectly flat plain (isotropic surface), this state consisted of a central market city surrounded by an extensive agricultural hinterland. He further assumed that the farmers in his isolated state were rational economic men in that they sought to maximize their rents (or, in today's terminology, their rates of return); possessed complete information about market prices and production and transportation costs; and were numerate accountants capable of calculating comparative rates of return on multiple commodities. In Thünen's world farmers compared commodity rates of return with respect to distance from the market and produced the commodity that yielded the greatest return. Following this logic, maximizing farmers in each zone produced the crop with the highest return for its zone as shown graphically in figure 12.1. Agricultural land use thus varied in concentric fashion with distance from the city. The highest returns accrued to those who farmed nearest the city, the lowest to those on the edge of the isolated state. Land values in turn reflected these spatial variations in productivity (rate of return or what Thünen called rent), because farms nearer the city were required to use land more intensively than those at a distance (Grotewold 1959; Chisholm 1962; Dunn 1954).

Although Thünen's model of the isolated state has received a great deal of criticism, the difference between his real and imagined worlds were remarkably few. In some sense his Prussian world offered the ideal laboratory for deploying the model of rational economic man. In that world decisions on agrarian land use were almost entirely in the hands of a few well-educated and highly rational grain barons, men who, in addition to controlling vast estates, controlled also the mass of the population—indeed, not until 1807 did the King of Prussia embark on peasant emancipation. Prussian agricultural geography, in other words, was not cluttered up by small farmers who might disrupt neat concentric patterns by making irrational agrarian choices (Carsten 1954; Taylor 1946; Rosenberg 1958). That the rational model of man seems to work best when unfettered by widespread freedom of choice should serve as a cautionary statement about the model's scope conditions.

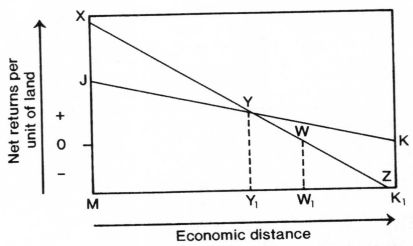

Economic distance

Figure 12.1 The relationship of net returns (per unit of land on two crops or land-use combinations) and the costs of transport (economic costs). In this case, rational farmers produce crop Y when located nearer the market M, that is, between M and Y_1; and they produce crop W at distances between locations Y_1 and W_1. Beyond W_1, net returns are negative. Source: Pred 1967:69. Reprinted with the permission of Lund Studies in Geography, Department of Geography, The Royal University of Lund, Sweden.

The latter concerns have been addressed by Allan Pred (1967, I: 67–81), who has suggested the need for accommodating economic irrationalities within neoclassical location theories. Departures from rational economic behavior are more likely as the number of agrarian producers expands. Consequently, Thünen's neatly circumscribed zones of land use are blurred by variability among individual farmers in, inter alia, their receipt and perception of prices and costs, their capacity to calculate comparative rates of return, and their individual preferences and utility rankings (whether some prefer simply to go fishing or to ensure subsistence first). Pred notes that variability effects are particularly noticeable on the margin of Thünen zones, where refined discriminations are required, but the blurring is equally evident in the core of these zones, as students of crop combinations in the United States will readily attest (figure 12.2).

These revisionary criticisms notwithstanding, the neoclassical theory of agricultural location is still the best theory we have for explaining agricultural land-use patterns. It has been deployed enlighteningly in explaining spatial variations in land-use intensity and crops at the scale of the farm (Chisholm 1962), the region (Lemon 1972), the nation (Peet 1970), and the world (Schlebecker 1960). It has been effectively applied in the past (Thünen 1875;

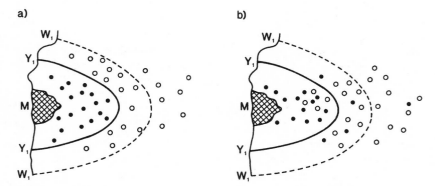

Figure 12.2 Models of land-use zonation in theory and practice. Figure 12.2a depicts the sharply differentiated land-use zones predicted by land-use theory and its assumptions of rational economic choice and profit maximization. Figure 12.2b depicts the messier transition of land-use zones evident in the real world in which decision makers are constrained by the information available to them and their ability to use it. Source: Pred 1967: 73. Reprinted with the permission of Lund Studies in Geography, Department of Geography, The Royal University of Lund, Sweden.

Lemon 1972) and the present (Dunn 1954), at home and abroad, around Addis Abbaba (Horvath 1969), and among the hunting and gathering Bushmen of southern Africa (Lee 1969).

Because these conclusions about the utility and shortcomings of the model of economic man also apply to the neoclassical geographical theories of industrial location and central place, it would be pointless to rehearse them for these economic sectors. Suffice it to say that those who would attempt to dislodge this admittedly narrow and parochial view of human nature have their work cut out for them.

The Conventional Critique of the Model of Economic Man

Criticism of the model of economic man in the disciplines of geography and economics may be divided into three schools of opinion. In descending order of sympathy, they are the descriptive-behavioral, the epistemological, and the contextual.

The descriptive-behavioral school offers perhaps the most congenial critique of the model of rational economic man. Based in psychology and descriptive economics, these critics express reservations about the absolutism of the model of economic man. Their critique focuses not so much on the postulate of self-interested behavior, which, generally speaking, they share, as on economics' unrealistically strong claims for rationality—what Simon has referred to as the .9944 model of economic man (by which he meant a nearly perfect 100 percent; Simon 1986). A battery of evidence from case studies and laboratory experiments has eroded the empirical foundation of these claims.[6] From the extensive catalogue of often counterintuitive behavioral deviations from the model of economic man, I offer here a partial listing:

1) Information access varies with respect to one's position in a network of economic communications.

2) Information perception and processing vary among individuals (e.g., individuals overlook or are ignorant of alternative choices), thus affecting the probability assignments attached to future events.

3) The capacity for probabilistic estimation of event occurrence varies with experience, learning, and a sufficiently large sample size for calculating the odds.

4) The capacity for maximization (as noted earlier) varies because many individuals seem incapable of rank ordering all of their preferences—and hence are unable to make an unequivocal choice of the criterion to be maximized.

5) Among those with maximizing capacities, the criterion for maximization may vary widely (e.g., profits or sales).

6) Numerical capacities for the arcane task of equating marginal prices and costs vary widely, and hence some economic actors are privileged over others.

7) Individual utility functions vary because self-interest may be maximized over the short or long run or because benefits and costs may be logarithmic rather than linear (e.g., salaries in many large corporations tend to increase with the cube root of firm size rather than in linear fashion).

8) In the branching decision tree, anterior decisions influence subsequent decisions (also known variously as the principle of limited possibilities, path dependence, the scrabble principle, or the path not taken), for example, sunk capital may preclude present investments with higher rates of return.[7]

These findings, and others like them, have fostered the formulation of more realistic models of economic man, models that match more closely behavioral assumptions and experimental and observational evidence. Economic geography, in turn, has been informed by and has contributed to these revisions. In an early analysis of the irrationalities of locational decision making, Julian Wolpert drew heavily on Herbert Simon's model of bounded rationality and satisficing behavior—the notion that entrepreneurs may settle for suboptimal rates of return in order to achieve other goals (Wolpert 1964), for example, the payment of wages in excess of marginal product for the purpose of thwarting unionization. More recently, Allan Pred's revision of location theory has interwoven two strands of the behavioral critique (see figure 12.3). He pointed out in the first instance that perceptual intersubjectivity produced deviations from the normative expectations of neoclassical location theory and in the second instance that access to perfect information is occluded by the time-distance and spatial barriers between information source and actor and by uncertainties regarding future events (the lack of an empirical basis for probabilistic estimation) (Pred 1967, 1).

Economic geographers have explored other constraints on rational economic action. These include, for example, the choice of suboptimal industrial locations as a consequence of subjective preferences—the owner's desire that the firm should be near her home—or the corporate conviction that, insofar as an economically feasible window of territorial opportunity allows, manufacturing plants should be located so as to minimize labor unrest and unionization (i.e., in rural areas in right-to-work states). In these new versions of location theory, rational economic man endures, albeit his actions are more constrained and his preferences are somewhat more variable (Massey and Meegan 1985; Pred 1967, 1: 5–15, 30–64, 81–97; Hamilton 1968).

The behavioral critique has a sharper edge, however. Herbert Simon (1986) has pointed out that the model of economic man has insufficient predictive capacity in the absence of auxiliary assumptions about the relevant parameters for rational choice. These amount to add-ins. The calculus of the rational maximizer, according to Simon, must add in assumptions on, inter alia, prices, costs, and interest rates, none of which are specified by the model. Parameter estimation in turn requires additional theoretical assumptions regarding the determinants of these parameters (slopes of the supply and demand curves, the nature of markets, and so on). Since these matters are vexing even to professionally trained economists, is it appropriate for our models to impute precise sets of probabilities or rational expectations to entrepreneurs and firms?

The danger in spinning out this web of assumptions, as Simon warns, is that it obscures the real world confronted by economic actors. In his critique of modern economics John Kenneth Galbraith (1971) makes the point bluntly when he dismisses neoclassical economics as an anachronism, as a nineteenth-century doctrine inappropriate to an understanding of the dynamics of the new industrial state. Les King (1976) has made a similar observation with respect to geographical location theory that, contrary to the evidence that policy parameters have displaced economic ones, persists in the belief that econ-

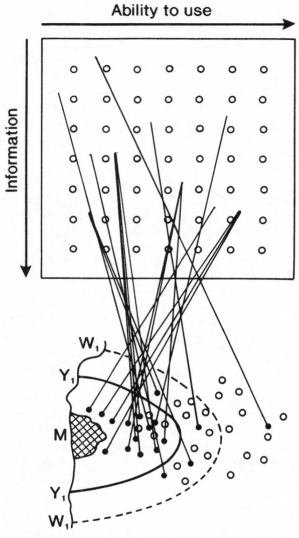

Figure 12.3 Linking Pred's behavioral matrix and the real-world land-use transition (see also figure 12.2b). Note that the number of rows and columns in Pred's behavioral matrix may be expanded or contracted depending on the varied types of information that are relevant for agrarian decisions. Source: Pred 1967: 76. Reprinted with the permission of Lund Studies in Geography, Department of Geography, The Royal University of Lund, Sweden.

omy is the paramount determinant of land-use decisions. While neither Galbraith nor King would deny the continuing behavioral significance of rationality and self-interest, each insists that the parameters that define the market are increasingly the products of state policy, interest groups, and power rather than of pure economy. To take just one example, American farmers, though highly rational, are responding to prices and costs that have little to do with market forces; more precisely, the parameters that define their choices are the artifacts of price supports, land withdrawal schemes, and the effects of nonmarket policies on interest rates. Farmers in the new industrial state have been compelled to make a radical change in their auxiliary assumptions, which now are embedded as much in policy making and political economy as in supply and demand, and because our capacity to predict policy parameters is not very good (recall the Stockman days, when policymakers suddenly decreased the debt-equity ratio on farm loans and a spate of foreclosures ensued), we cannot in turn expect rationality in farm expectations when policy shifts are themselves irrational (McDonald 1974; Galambos 1982).

By exposing the shaky empirical foundations of the model of rational economic man, the behavioral critique has undermined the model's epistemological justifications as well. The epistemological critique, as summarized by Barnes, points out

> the contradiction between the claims to knowledge that *homo economicus* makes, and the lack of a convincing theory of knowledge that can support such a claim. Specifically, it is argued that on grounds of logical consistency each of the four common epistemological justifications [empiricism, instrumentalism, a priorism, ideal typicalism] which have historically been put forward by economists fail to provide a deeper grounding for *homo economicus*. The consequence is that one is left with no firm bedrock on which to claim *homo economicus* represents a foolproof method. (Barnes 1988: 483; 1987)

The epistemological critique highlights the numerous discrepancies between epistemological claims and observational outcomes. In Barnes's view the several justifications of economic man are doubtful. Empirical justifications are clouded by the findings of the descriptive-behavioral school; Friedman's instrumentalism—the notion that the construct provides predictive power—is clouded by predictions which are 1) often inaccurate or weak, 2) dependent on a web of additional assumptions, or 3) derivable from other premises and assumptions; a priorism—the claim that constructs such as economic man rest on a few intuitively obvious and introspectively derived truths—is clouded by humanity's demonstrable variability in thought, motive, and action; and ideal typicalism is clouded by the empirical distance separating the heuristic model from economic action in the real world. The epistemological critique thus concludes that the claims for the model of economic man are overstated and that alternative philosophies of human nature may rival, and in some cases surpass, the power of its interpretive insights (Barnes 1988, 1989).[8]

These alternative epistemologies, grounded in context, relativism, and historicism, constitute the third and last of the conventional critiques of economic man. They reject as reductionist the notion that economic behavior is governed by certain universal and intuitively obvious rules of conduct. Contextualists maintain that the human economic experience in all its richness and variety is to be understood rather through the study of particular contexts, of the jostling and commingling of human agency and structures in particular times and places, of what Abrahms has called the process of structuring—the ceaseless production and reproduction of society by the determinative and contingent encounters between individuals and social, economic, and ecological forces (structures) (Abrahms 1982; Barnes 1989).

Contextual interpretations are, by definition, historicist and relativist in epistemology, but these labels obscure the variety in contextual points of view—a range that stretches from the structural emphasis of Marxism at one extreme to the liberated agency of phenomenology (or perhaps deconstructionism) at the other. Realist and structurationist epistemologies stand somewhere near the middle of the range. This discussion confines attention to just one of these contextual epistemologies, structurationism, because it stands near the midpoint in the contextual continuum, speaks perhaps most directly to the issues of locational theory, and is one with which I am most familiar (see various essays in Gregory and Urry 1985 and chapter 14 in this volume).

Structurationist interpretation reveals an economic landscape vastly more complex and problematic than conventional location theory. Allan Pred's (1986) study of agrarian transformation in southern Sweden circa 1790 to 1850 offers a case in point. Breaking sharply with neoclassical theory, Pred explores the dramatic impact of political economy on agrarian systems. His detailed reconstruction documents the breakup (-down?) of a corporate peasant society in southern Sweden and its reconstitution into a society of capitalist family farms following a series of state-imposed enclosures. In doing so, Pred effectively challenges the universality of rational economic man, blurs beyond recognition Thünen's neat concentric rings, and undermines neoclassical models that divorce economic action from social and political context.

Pred challenges the universality principle on the very outset. By fixing his sights on an epochal historical transformation—from the corporate and collective norms of peasant villagers to the capitalist ones of isolated and atomistic family farmers—he implicitly rejects the generality of the neoclassicist's model of rational economic man. Prior to 1800, as Pred recounts, solidarity among the peasants in these fat grain lands derived from corporatist rather than rationalist (self-interested) mentalities. Corporate village councils, acting in accordance with the interests of the commonweal, made the essential agrarian decisions in this landscape of peasant communal villages, open fields, and diversified subsistence crop production. Although individual farmers owned scattered holdings among the open fields, it was council members who determined agrarian resource allocation: they determined when, where, and how much to plant and harvest and who should be deployed in labor during the annual round. These corporatist Swedish peasants, then, were hardly the rational economic actors posited by neoclassical economic theory.

By the same token, their landscape did not, of course, resemble the neatly compartmentalized series of concentric crop zones predicted by neoclassical theory—which is Pred's second point. Peasant corporatism and Durkheimian mechanical solidarity perpetuated a rather different segmental landscape, one that consisted of a honeycomb of nearly identical spatial units and that stood in stark contrast with the sprawling concentric zones being carved out at that very moment and just a few hundred miles away by Thünen's rational Prussian landlords.

State-coerced enclosure changed everything, however—which is Pred's third point. By demonstrating the suddenness with which a shift in political economy could transform corporatist peasants into rationalist, market-oriented family farmers, Pred underscores his neoclassical critique which is that economy, far from being a pure and abstract entity, is deeply embedded in society and polity. Discerning these interconnections is not easy, especially when analyses focus on societies in stasis; but when things begin to change, when societies experience transformation, as southern Sweden did in the early nineteenth century, the intricate mesh of tendrils running between economy, society, and polity are clearly revealed.[9]

Some romantic overstatement of this transformation notwithstanding, Pred commendably traces the social and spatial consequences of enclosure. He points out the hierarchy of tensions that accompanied the rearrangement of southern Swedish society—how market-oriented farmers were compelled to depend on distant urban merchants who, if not as grasping as Pred makes them seem, were not always to be trusted; how the wives of farmers and farm laborers surrendered independence to the increasingly paternalist domination of the male heads of households; and how council members and clerics in the old peasant villages succumbed at once to the augmented power of distant markets and local farm paternalism. Pred's conclusion: southern Sweden paid a steep price for state enclosure and market rationality, and it is easy to forget how steep it was if inquiry confines itself merely to a static portrait of the economy long after the transformation has taken place. Only by freezing history is it possible to regard the rational economic mentality of farmers as a timeless attribute of a human nature disembodied from politics, society, and ecology.

Ironically, Pred's story is not news for anyone who is slightly acquainted with early modern European historical geography. Precisely these kinds of transformations and societal consequences have been traced for years by historians concerned with the transition from feudalism to capitalism. Regrettably, social scientists have paid little heed to the historians' masterful reconstructions of, for example, English enclosure in the sixteenth century; indeed, it is this epochal transformation from a precapitalist mentality to a rational capitalist one that transfixed Marx and that underlined his historicist conclusion that *homo economicus* was indeed an ephemeral, albeit durable, product of history. Discerning the laws of history so as to assist in the reshaping of the capitalist mentality was, of course, his principal project (for starters, see Tawney 1967; Thirsk 1967; Ashton and Philpin 1987).

The contextual critiques of rational economic man thus have come full circle back to history and historical geography, and in doing so they enter the contested terrain of the philosophy of history. Is rational economic man, as Marx maintained, the momentary product of a historical epoch? Or is "he," as idealist historians have at times averred, merely a chimera in the restless imagination of mankind? Or can we have it both ways? Can our model of human nature accommodate at once freedom and necessity, "great men" and social forces, ideology and materialism—which leads me to my rather unconventional critique of the neoclassical model of economic man (Guelke 1982).

A Dynamic Model of Human Nature: An Unconventional Critique of Economic Man

Models of human nature are Olympian in their condescension toward the complexity of human behavior. They tend to portray human nature as all one thing or all the other, as consistently rational or consistently irrational (or, better perhaps, nonrational). I want to suggest in the final section of this essay that both sides may be right, that the impasse created by these disjunctive and conflicting models of human nature is reconcilable. Human nature, I will argue, deserves (indeed requires) a model that is more dynamic, that accommodates the remarkable variabilities in human behavior captured in previous models of human nature. The model that I propose, however provisionally, is premised on the assumption that human nature in capitalist societies is intermittently rational (or irrational, as the case may be) in time and in space.[10]

The American experience offers numerous examples of intermittent rationality. Take, for example, Arthur Schlesinger, Jr.'s compelling interpretation of American history, that it cycles every twenty-five to thirty years or so between private and public interests. In the small, Schlesinger is arguing that American political behavior has alternated between public commitment and the pursuit of private gain, between altruism and self-interest. A decade of public political activism in the 1960s, for example, is succeeded by a decade of greed in the 1980s. In the large, Schlesinger's interpretation constitutes a refreshingly novel perspective on the variability of human nature in the American past. In some times and places the caricature of individuals as rational economic actors is apt; in others it falls far from the mark and we would do better to look toward more particularistic models of human nature (Schlesinger 1986). Theories of human behavior that ignore the valvelike openings and closings of economic rationality capture but a portion of human behavior and social change.

Schlesinger's cycles of public and private interests offer a point of departure for a more refined and problematic model of human nature. His interpretation, though it captures the essence of behavioral variabilities in American history, does not account for their rhythmic recurrence. How is it, for example, that public interests are ascendant in such fundamentally divergent times as the 1930s and the 1960s—the former a time of social malaise and protracted depression, the latter of supreme confidence and seemingly boundless prosperity? Similarly, Schlesinger's cyclical interpretation is confined to politics; it overlooks corresponding changes in American society and economy. The cycling of human nature in the American past would thus seem to be rather more complex than Schlesinger's interpretation allows.

Some of the shortcomings of Schlesinger's interpretation can be overcome by regarding his political cycle as a cycle within a longer and more encompassing macrohistorical rhythm—what I call the periodic structure of the American past.[11] American history in this view consists of eight historical periods, each of a half century, more or less, stretching between 1630 and 1990. Each period thus encompasses two Schlesingerian cycles, that is, two public-interest phases and two phases of private interests. In addition, my interpretation of intermittent rationality extends beyond politics to embrace corresponding cycles in society and economy. That interpretation is predicated on three provisional propositions about American macrohistory. These are, in desperately compressed summary:

Proposition 1: American history exhibits a periodic structure of a half century, more or less. That structure is defined by the historical period, a half-century conjuncture of policy cycles, religious revitalization and revivals, long waves in the economy, and the logistic diffusion of fundamental innovations. It divides American history into eight periods which begin in the 1630s, 1680s, 1740s, 1780s, 1830s, 1880s, 1930s, and 1970s.

Proposition 2: (the most relevant for intermittent rationality) Each forty-five to sixty-year historical period divides into six sequential phases: 1) crisis (severe and protracted economic depression); 2) creativity (the search for social, political, and economic innovations that may resolve crisis, e.g., state enclosure in southern Sweden); 3) conflict (the outbreak of international war, either large or small, early or deferred); 4) diffusion (the spread of innovations and an acceleration of economic growth); 5) dissent (internal contention over civil issues in the midst of the period, e.g., colonial rights, 1770s; slavery, 1850s; labor, 1910s; and minorities, 1960s); and 6) decline (deceleration of economic growth and increased tension over issues of income and wealth distribution) (see figure 12.4). Owing to the intermittence of rationality, our capacity to predict human behavior varies dramatically across these phases. In some phases, most notably those of creativity and dissent (Schlesinger's public interests), behavior is wildly unpredictable, while in others (diffusion and decline, Schlesinger's private interests), behavior is on the whole accurately captured by rational actor models.

Proposition 3: The periodic structure of American history is propelled by recurrent processes of agrarian innovation and logistic diffusion. Following a phase of experimentation (creativity), a few fundamental innovations are elected for diffusion during the ensuing half-century. These innovations sustain economic growth for three to four decades, at which time the innovation saturates the potential market, productivity gains are wrung out, output exceeds demand, and prices fall, culminating in economic decline and then crisis. Crisis in turn sets in motion a search for new innovations, and the cycle begins anew in the ensuing half-century period.[12]

These propositions on the periodic structure of American history permit a closer examination of the variability of human nature in the American case. As noted above, when Americans have sought solutions to economic crisis or have engaged in widespread civil dissent, their behavior has been prompted by political and social forces as well as economic ones, and their actions have been guided by criteria other than rationality. In the analysis of behavior in these phases the model of rational economic man does not do well. Conversely, when the economy expands (as it does, more or less rapidly during the phases of diffusion and decline), *Homo economicus* provides a faithful caricature of American behavior. All of this gives an ironic twist to interpretations of past behavior, namely that rational actor models are least effective during phases of dramatic social change—the very phases that, of course, have preoccupied historians and humanists.

The phase of creativity offers an apt illustration of this interpretive division between social science and humanism. During these times of experimentation—so flatteringly described by Schumpeter's heroic entrepreneurs—ration-

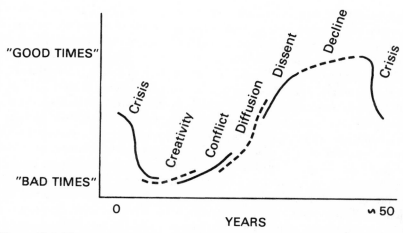

Figure 12.4 The six phases in a typical period of American history. Periods average fifty years, more or less, with a range of forty-five to sixty years. Rational economic behavior is most likely in the phases of diffusion and decline and least likely in the phases of crisis, creativity, and dissent. Source: Earle 1992.

al models of human nature are superseded by other factors: class, ethnicity, religion, ideology, individual and social psychologies, ideas, and so on. Faced with a bleak present and an uncertain future, society's various levels, from the household to the state, and spheres, from political economy to religion, engage in a frantic search for solutions to economic and social crisis. American behavior in the 1840s reveals the stunning range of experimentation and its unpredictability. Religious and ethnic groups, for example, sought their solution for crisis through escape to frontier refuges. In exiting from the mainstream they were motivated more by the ethnocultural considerations of persecution and millennial perfection than by narrowly rational economic desiderata (Earle 1977, 1992; Meinig 1965; McLoughlin 1978). Others sought solutions at home, through reform and revision of existing agrarian systems. Southern planters, for example, experimented with a variety of agrarian innovations that included, among others, interstate conventions aimed at controlling the supply of cotton, economic development through diversification, emigration to fresh lands, increased usage of guano, and a crop rotation of cotton, corn, and cowpeas—the last of which effected a quiet transformation in southern agrarian systems.

The critical point for our purposes is that none of these experiments was privileged, none had a claim on being the best strategy for ending crisis; nor did there exist a probabilistic basis on which to make a rational assessment of the superiority of one innovation over another. Accordingly, the triumph of one of these experiments (crop rotation) over others depended more on the irrational factors of family, faith, and class and the contentious application of rhetoric, politics, ideology, and the like.[13]

The strength of these irrational forces in the phase of creativity is confirmed, albeit unwittingly, in the massive literature on innovation diffusion. That literature innocently divides innovators into two basic types: the deliberate and thoroughly respectable member of the middle or elite classes and the wild-eyed, crackpot eccentric. These pejorative characterizations, unbeknownst to diffusion scholars, reveal more about the class bias of their informants than about innovators per se. Elites—the informants who typically provide the fullest accounts—quite naturally described their innovations in the most favorable light. Elite and middle-class innovators are caricatured as responsible, scientifically informed, and judicious; folk and lower-class innovators, meanwhile, are dismissed as irresponsible, ignorant, and bizarre. Even objective scholars, it seems, may be caught up in the contention and controversy over innovation,[14] and rightly so, perhaps, because a great deal is at stake. The innovation that triumphs has enormous ramifications for the prosperity and welfare of society in the ensuing half-century. When elite innovations prevail, costs of entry are typically higher, innovation diffusion is disproportionately concentrated among middle- and upper-class agrarians, and society becomes increasingly inegalitarian as diffusion progresses. American history provides the classic example of biased innovation—the case of the introduction of mass slavery in the colonial South between 1680 and 1740. In a mere sixty years that innovation transformed an egalitarian, socially mobile society into a highly stratified one in which half of the white households possessed neither land nor slaves (Earle 1988; Main 1982; Kulikof 1986; see also chapter 9).[15]

The kinds of fundamental agrarian innovation described here, the ones that begin in the phase of creativity and subsequently transform regional economies and societies, have their origins in nonrational economic processes. Their success depends on agrarian persuasion, on the mobilization of knowledge, argumentation (though not always reasonable), rhetoric, and politics in the interests of class. Only when an innovation has taken hold, when a reasonably large number have adopted it, is this contentious model of human nature displaced by one of rational calculation.

As for the model of economic rationality, it does not begin to apply in American history until the diffusion phase. At that point, ten to fifteen years into a historical period, the statistics of innovation diffusion favor a shift from nonrational to rational sources of innovation legitimation. As the proportion of adopters approaches ten percent of the potential pool, the adopters constitute a sufficiently large and representative sample to permit a probabilistic basis for rational assessments of an innovation's profitability in the short run. Over the next thirty-five to forty years, the model of economic rationality offers useful insights on decision making during the course of long-wave economic growth. Rates of return are carefully calculated, opportunity costs are fully assessed, and Thünen's model of agrarian land use (as well as Weber's of industrial location and Christaller's of central places) performs efficiently. The riotous behavioral variance characteristic of preceding phases narrows sharply toward the rational norm during the phases of diffusion and decline—much to the joy of social scientists and to the dismay of social critics. Whereas the former deploy the assorted models of rational behavior; the latter lament the ascendance of a "a nation of sheep," "lonely crowds," the atomization of behavior, and the sterility of "happy days."[16]

Rationality's hegemony is never fully secure, however. Midway into every period in American history, the routine of business as usual is disrupted by the explosion of civil dissent (and on two occasions, internal war). A small but expanding band of dissenters commit their energies, and in some cases their lives, to securing the civil rights of individuals, regions, and nations—of colonial legislatures in the 1720s, of Americans in the 1770s, of sections in the 1810s, of slaves and free men in the 1850s, of labor in the 1910s, and of minorities in the 1950s and 1960s. In these times the narrow calculus of marginalist economics is erased by the high drama of political and ideological contention. That is not to say that economic motivation disappears from the scene; quite the contrary, because much of the debate over civil rights has to do with defining the limits of rational calculation—that is, of the paradigmatic political economy. Furthermore, the geography of dissension is typically rooted in the regional disequilibrations that have resulted from rapid economic growth, but while economic forces may help to initiate the phase of dissent, they are insufficient to account for the swift extension of protest to the nation at large.[17]

A case in point is Boston's role as vanguard of the American Revolution in the 1760s and 1770s. At a time when other colonies and ports were experiencing the boundless prosperity of a "golden age of colonial culture," Boston's distinctive foreland economy was taxed disproportionately by British neomercantilists. For a city that depended almost exclusively on the wholesaling and re-export trade, the taxation policies of the British seemed biased and punitive. While we might argue that the revolutionary response of Bostonians was grounded in rational calculation—a matter of economic survival—that was not the case for their prosperous colonial neighbors along the Atlantic seaboard. The latter, after all, had little to gain from revolution — as indicated by their half-hearted response to the early taxes levied by the British. Bostonians thus were required to mobilize a larger base of dissent, which they accomplished through ideology, rhetoric, committee organization, and revolutionary action and British overreaction. In little more than a decade their revolutionary strategies had expanded the arena of dissent from a small coastal enclave in Massachusetts to virtually every one of the colonies on the Atlantic coast (Earle 1992: chapter 4).

In 1770 no one in his or her right mind would have given even money that the Bostonians could have effected a revolution against the greatest power in the world, but they defied the odds, and history lurched abruptly in new directions. Models of economic rationality simply cannot explain one of the greatest transformations in American, indeed world, history. The American Revolution changed everything. Abroad, the revolutionary spirit that had somehow triumphed in the United States was widely emulated, first in France and later in Latin America. At home, the American way of life was redefined. In short order land was made available west of the Appalachians, infant industries were protected, and internal improvements were initiated. While Americans soon after the Revolution would resume their calculating ways, their horizon of opportunities and constraints (what Simon would call the "add-ins") was forever changed.

The phase of dissent thus constitutes an attempt to circumscribe the limits of rationality. It has at various times precluded British sovereignty, slavery, labor exploitation, and minority discrimination. It has accomplished these ends through means that are usually nonrational and almost always unpredictable—through protest, internal war, and ensuing constitutional amendment.

The macrohistory of the American past amply illustrates the intermittence of rational behavior in a capitalist society. In this, the premier case of capitalism, behavior has alternated regularly and recurrently between the two poles of rationality and private interest (in the phases of diffusion and decline) on the one end and irrationality and public interest (in the phases of creativity and dissent), on the other. All things being equal, Americans have probably spent more time in phases that have been committed to rationality over irrationality, to private interests over public ones, but in the study of history and social change, all phases are not equal. The phases responsible for the decisive changes in American history—those that contribute new and fundamental innovations or circumscribe the application of economic rationality—involve a messier motivational mixture that is part politics and ideology, part rhetoric and ethics, part class and ethnoculture, and part human agency and organizational structure. These, of course, are the times of great men (and women) and movements whose charismatic behavior and spontaneity mock our paltry attempts at prediction based on rational models of human nature.

Although rational models of human nature have achieved an unusually high level of prestige among scholars, their success is not entirely warranted.

Much of it has been based on the misleading quantitative fact that in the course of capitalist history the number of years of rational economic behavior exceeds the number in which nonrational behavior prevails. As noted previously (and as the various catastrophe theories that now abound reaffirm), however, the critical changes in the structure of a society often occur in a span of a few weeks, months, or years. Consider for a moment the extraordinary changes engineered in the world scene by Mikhail Gorbachev. Almost over night, and against all odds, things were accomplished that only months before were inconceivable; but then, of course, capitalist history had entered into the phase of creativity, a phase when all bets are off, when great men and women displace atomized lonely crowds, and when social science theories of chaos, catastrophe, and random walks mask our ignorance of the way in which history and geography are transformed. The Berlin Wall has come down, and, for the moment at any rate, the most reasonable explanations for this strange geographical event are probably lodged in alternative philosophies of human nature—in narrative, phenomenology, idealism, and psychology. In due course, though, the exhilarating unpredictability of these times will give way to the prosaic routine of calculation and then, unless I miss my guess, to the high drama of civil dissent a decade or so into the third millennium. Such is, and has been, our intermittent fate in the periodic structure of American geographical history.[18] Understanding our fate, not to mention changing its course, would seem to require a commensurately supple model of humankind.

Notes

1. Perhaps the earliest formulation of the concept appears in John Stuart Mill's 1836 essay "On the Definition of Political Economy."

[W]hat is now commonly understood by the term "Political Economy" makes entire abstraction of every other human passion or motive; except those which may be regarded as perpetually antagonizing principles to the desire of wealth, namely, aversion to labour, and desire of the present enjoyment of costly indulgences. . . . Political Economy considers mankind as occupied solely in acquiring and consuming wealth; and aims at showing what is the course of action into which mankind . . . would be impelled, if that motive . . . were absolute ruler of all their actions. . . .The science . . . proceeds . . . under the supposition that man is a being who is determined, by the necessity of his nature, to prefer a greater portion of wealth to a smaller in all cases, without any other exception than that constituted by the two counter-motives already specified. Not that any political economist was ever so absurd as to suppose that mankind are really thus constituted, but because this is the mode in which science must necessarily proceed (Mill 1967: 321–22; also Bell 1981).

2. The special pertinence of the concept of economic man for nineteenth-century behavior is a recurrent, if implicit, theme in John Kenneth Galbraith's *The New Industrial State* (1971).

3. The concept of economic man was invariably caught up in the polemic debate over economic policy in the late nineteenth century. Representative of the critics are H. C. Carey's *Principles of Social Science* (1858) and Thorstein Veblen's *The Place of Science in Modern Civilization* (1919). It is somewhat ironic that the foundations of neoclassical economics—marginalist analysis, competition, and free trade—were being laid precisely when national policy was shifting toward protectionism abroad and the elite distribution of resources at home. On the changing contours of the American political economy, see Lowi 1972 and McCormick 1979.

4. Among descriptive theorists, see especially the models of bounded rationality and satisficing put forth in Herbert Simon's *Models of Man* (1957) and his "Rationality in Psychology and Economics" (1986); on rational expectations, see Cyert and De-Groot (1974) and Willes (1981).

5. The classic texts are Johann Heinrich von Thünen, *Von Thünen's isolated state* (1966; orig. pub. 1826); Alfred Weber, *Theory of the location of industry* (1920; orig. pub. 1909); and Walter Christaller, *Central Places in Southern Germany* (1966; orig. pub. 1933).

6. Simon's seminal volume, *Models of Man* (1957), set in motion a wide-ranging critique of the postulates of economic rationality, pointing out that economic behavior is at times nonmaximizing (satisficing), is frequently plagued by uncertainty, is usually probabilistic, and is almost always bounded by auxiliary assumptions about society and psychology. See, for example, the various essays in Hogarth and Reder (1986). Historians and social psychologists have extended this critique, the former privileging the "cake of custom" and the latter the role of relevant social networks, influentials, and reference groups. See, respectively, Hobsbawm (1964) and Archibald (1978).

7. The skepticism of descriptive theorists toward economic rationality traces its origins to Simon's *Models of Man* as well as to Frank H. Knight's *Risk, Uncertainty, and Profit* (1921), among others. See also the essays in Bell and Kristol (1981) and, for economic geography, Pred (1967).

8. Barnes's dismissal of neoclassical economics and Marxian essentialism may be precipitous. Is it wise to discard models that, in times and places, have proven their capacity for illuminating human behavior? The issue is not to purge these explanations, but rather to specify precisely when and where they apply—and when and where they do not.

9. Although Pred's philosophy has shifted dramatically over the past twenty years, his structurationist perspectives on the impacts of Swedish enclosure are remarkably similar to his positivist notion of disequilibration through "parametric shock" noted in his *Behavior and Location* (1967, part 2: 69–91).

10. Structurationists have been edging toward this conclusion for some time, but the absence of a macrohistorical and a macrogeographical perspective has prevented them from specifying the locations where and the dates when behavioral variability

around the norm will be large or small. This imprecision in specification is particularly evident in various essays by Derek Gregory. See, for example, his rather casual treatment of historical time in his essay "Suspended Animation: The Stasis of Diffusion Theory" (1985) and of space (the reification of Manchester) in his "Contours of Crisis? Sketches for a Geography of Class Struggle in the Early Industrial Revolution in England" (1984).

11. I have dealt with these matters at length in an extended essay entitled "The Periodic Structure of the American Past: Rhythms, Phases, and Geographic Conditions" (1992).

12. The argument derives in part from Joseph Schumpeter's *Business Cycles* (1939). The massive literature on diffusion notwithstanding, diffusion scholars heretofore have tended to overlook the temporal associations of agrarian innovation, historical periods, long waves, policy cycles, and religious awakenings and revivals because their conceptualization of time is generically abstract rather than historically specific. The boldest statement of diffusionists is the suggestion that we might explore the relations between logistic diffusion and long waves (Parkes and Thrift 1980: 415).

13. Pred (1967, 2: 69–91) and Gregory (1985), though nibbling at the edges of these points, tend to overlook the contentiousness of the struggle over innovation and the sizable stakes that are involved. On the politics and the welfare economics of agrarian innovation, see Earle (1988), Yapa (1982), and chapter 9 in this volume.

14. On types of innovators, see Brown (1981) and Pred (1967, 2: 69–91). When we conceptualize these distinctions among innovators as a function of class, for example, ordinary folk versus elites, we strike more nearly at the heart of the scholarly debate that divides the diffusionists of the Kniffen school from those of the Hägerstrand school of thought.

15. More generally, on the welfare implications of agrarian innovation, see Lakshman Yapa on "Innovation Bias, Appropriate Technology, and Basic Goods" (1982).

16. See the lamentations of social critics over the sterility and atomization (the essence of rational choice) of American society and culture during the 1950s, for example, Vance Packard's *The Status Seekers* (1959) and David Riesman's *The Lonely Crowd* (1950). For their counterpart for the 1970s, see Christopher Lasch's *The Culture of Narcissism* (1978).

17. For indirect confirmation, see Schlesinger (1986) and Harold Kerbo's "Movements of Crisis and Movements of Affluence" (1982). Perhaps in these times the rationality of economics is replaced by an as-yet unexplored rationality associated with participation, self-realization, and altruism; or as one Lincoln Brigade veteran of the Spanish Civil War put it: "Struggle is the elixir of life, the tonic of life. I mean, if you're not struggling you are dead" (quoted in Powers 1994). See the provocative thoughts of Paul Gomberg on "Marxism and Rationality" (1989), Robert H. Frank's *Passions Within Reason: The Strategic Role of the Emotions* (1988) and, more recently, Randall Collins's "Emotional Energy as the Common Denominator of Rational Action" (1993).

18. I suspect that proper specification of events in time and space—and the application of the proper method and philosophy in situations thusly specified—will resolve many, if not all, of the historiographic controversies between freedom and determin-

ism, mind and matter, agency and structure, and altruism and self-interest. All of this, of course, requires a refined sense of the structuring of regional and temporal systems in the manner of G. William Skinner's provocative essay on "The Structure of Chinese History" (1985).

References

Abrahms, Philip. 1986. *Historical sociology*. Ithaca, N. Y.: Cornell University Press.

Archibald, W. Peter. 1978. *Social psychology as political economy*. Toronto: McGraw-Hill Ryerson.

Arrow, Kenneth. 1986. Rationality of self and others in an economic system. In *Rational choice: The contrasts between economics and psychology*, ed. Robin Hogarth and Melvin W. Reder, 201–15. Chicago: University of Chicago Press.

Ashton, J. H., and C. H. E. Philpin, eds. 1987. *The Brenner debate: Agrarian class structure and economic development in preindustrial Europe*. Cambridge: Cambridge University Press.

Barnes, Trevor J. 1987. Homo economicus, physical metaphors, and universal models in economic geography. *Canadian Geographer* 31: 299–308.

———. 1988. Rationality and relativism in economic geography: An interpretive review of the Homo economicus assumption. *Progress in Human Geography* 12: 473–96.

———. 1989. Place, space, and theories of value: Contextualism and essentialism in economic geography. *Transactions of the Institute of British Geographers* N. S. 14: 299–316.

Becker, Gary S. 1976. *The economic approach to human behavior*. Chicago: University of Chicago Press.

———. 1981. *A treatise on the family*. Cambridge: Harvard University Press.

Bell, Daniel. 1981. Models and reality in economic discourse. In *The crisis in economic theory*, ed. Daniel Bell and Irving Kristol, 46–80. New York: Basic Books.

Blaug, Mark. 1980. *The methodology of economics: Or how economists explain*. Cambridge: Cambridge University Press.

Brown, Lawrence. 1981. *Innovation diffusion: A new perspective*. London: Methuen.

Carey, H. C. 1858. *Principles of social science*. Philadelphia: J. B. Lippincott.

Carsten, F. L. 1954. *The origins of Prussia.* London: Oxford University Press.

Chalk, Albert F. 1964. Economic man. In *A dictionary of the social sciences*, ed. J. Gould and W. L. Kolb, 223–25. New York: Free Press.

Chisholm, Michael. 1962. *Rural settlement and land use.* London: Hutchinson.

Chorley, Richard J., and Peter Haggett, 1968. *Socioeconomic models in geography.* London: Methuen.

Christaller, Walter. 1966. *Central places in southern Germany*, trans. C. W. Baskin. Englewood Cliffs, N. J.: Prentice-Hall (orig. pub. 1933).

Collins, Randall. 1993. Emotional energy as the common denominator of rational action. *Rationality and Society* 5: 203–30.

Cyert, R. M. and M. H. DeGroot, 1974. Rational expectations and Bayesian analysis. *Journal of Political Economy* 82: 521–36.

Dunn, Edgar S. 1954. *The location of agricultural production.* Gainesville: University of Florida Press.

Earle, Carville. 1977. The first English towns of North America. *Geographical Review* 67: 34–50.

———. 1988. The myth of the southern soil miner: Macrohistory, agricultural innovation, and environmental change. In *The ends of the earth: Perspectives on modern environmental history*, ed. Donald Worster, 175–210. Cambridge: Cambridge University Press.

———. 1992. *Geographical inquiry and American historical problems.* Stanford, Calif.: Stanford University Press.

Ferber, Marianne A., and Julie A. Nelson, eds. 1993. *Beyond economic man: Feminist theory and economics.* Chicago: University of Chicago Press.

Frank, Robert H. 1988. *Passions within reason: The strategic rule of the emotions.* New York: W. W. Norton.

Galbraith, John K. 1971. *The new industrial state*, 2d ed. rev. New York: New American Library.

Galambos, Louis. 1982. *America at middle age: A new history of the United States.* New York: New Press.

Georgescu-Roegen, N. 1968. Utility. In *International encyclopedia of the social sciences*, ed. David Sills, 16: 236–67. New York: Macmillan and the Free Press.

———. 1973. Utility and value in economic thought. In *Dictionary of the history of ideas*, ed. P. Weiner, 450–59. New York: Scribner's.

Gomberg, Paul. 1989. Marxism and rationality. *American Philosophical Quarterly* 26: 52–62.

Gordon, David, ed. 1983. *Conversations with economists: New classical economists and their opponents speak out on the current controversy in macroeconomics.* Savage, Md.: Rowman & Littlefield.

Gregory, Derek. 1984. Contours of crisis? Sketches for a geography of class struggle in the early industrial revolution in England. In *Historical geography: Interpretative essays,* ed. Alan R. H. Baker and Derek Gregory, 68–117. Cambridge: Cambridge University Press.

————. 1985. Suspended animation: The stasis of diffusion theory. In *Social relations and spatial structures,* ed. Derek Gregory and John Urry, 296–336. New York: St. Martin's Press.

Gregory, Derek and John Urry, eds. 1985. *Social relations and spatial structures.* New York: St. Martin's Press.

Grotewold, Andreas. 1959. Von Thünen in retrospect. *Economic Geography* 35: 346–55.

Guelke, Leonard. 1982. *Historical understanding in geography: An idealist approach.* Cambridge: Cambridge University Press.

Hamilton, F. E. Ian. 1968. Models of industrial location. In *Socioeconomic methods in geography,* ed. Richard J. Chorley and Peter Haggett, 360–424. London: Methuen.

Harvey, David. 1973. *Social justice and the city.* London: Edward Arnold.

von Hayek, Friedrich A. 1968. Economic thought: The Austrian school. In *International encyclopedia of the social sciences,* ed. David Sills, 4: 458–62. New York: Macmillan and the Free Press.

Hobsbawm, E. J. 1964. *Labouring men: Studies in the history of labour.* London: Heidenfeld and Nicolson.

Hogarth, Robin, and Melvin W. Reder, eds. 1986. *Rational choice: The contrast between economics and psychology.* Chicago: University of Chicago Press.

Horvath, Ronald. 1969. Von Thünen's isolated state and the area around Addis Ababa, Ethiopia. *Annals of the Association of American Geographers* 59: 308–23.

Hudson, James L. 1989. Subjectivization in ethics. *American Philosophical Quarterly* 26: 221–29.

Johnston, Ron J., ed. 1981. Economic man. In *Dictionary of human geography,* 96. New York: Free Press.

————. 1986. *Philosophy and human geography: An introduction to contemporary approaches,* 2d ed. London: Edward Arnold.

Kerbo, Harold. 1982. Movements of crisis and movements of affluence. *Journal of Conflict Resolution* 26: 645–63.

King, Les J. 1976. Alternatives to positive economic geography. *Annals of the Association of American Geographers* 66: 293–308.

Knight, Frank H. 1921. *Risk, uncertainty, and profit.* Boston: Houghton Mifflin.

Kulikoff, Allan. 1986. *Tobacco and slaves: The development of southern cultures in the Chesapeake, 1680–1800.* Chapel Hill: University of North Carolina Press.

Lasch, Christopher. 1978. *The culture of narcissism: American life in an age of diminishing expectations.* New York: W. W. Norton.

Lee, Richard B. 1969. !Kung bushman subsistence: An input-output analysis. In *Environment and cultural behavior,* ed. Andrew P. Vayda, 47–79. Garden City, N. Y.: Natural History Press.

Lemon, James T. 1972. *The best poor man's country: A geographical study of early southeastern Pennsylvania.* Baltimore: The John Hopkins University Press.

Lowi, Theodore J. 1972. Four systems of policy, politics, and choice. *Public Administration Review,* July/August 1972: 298–310.

McCormick, Richard L. 1979. The party period and public policy: An explanatory hypothesis. *Journal of Interdisciplinary History* 66: 279–98.

MacCrimmon, K. R. 1965. An experimental study of the decision-making behavior of business executives. Ph.D. dissertation, University of California at Los Angeles.

McDonald, Forrest. 1974. *The phaeton ride: The crisis of American success.* Garden City, N. Y.: Doubleday.

Machlup, Fritz. 1978a. Homo economicus and his classmates. In *Methodology of economics and other social sciences,* 267–81. London: Academic Press.

———. 1978b. The universal bogeyman. In *Methodology of economics and other social sciences,* 283–301. London: Academic Press.

MacLoughlin, William G. 1978. *Revivals, awakenings, and reform: An essay on religion and social change, 1607–1977.* Chicago: University of Chicago Press.

McNee, Robert B. 1959. The changing relationships of economics and economic geography. *Economic Geography* 35: 189–98.

Main, Gloria L. 1982. *Tobacco colony: Life in early colonial Maryland, 1650–1720.* Princeton: Princeton University Press.

Marschak, Jacob C. 1968. Decision-making: Economic aspects. In *International encyclopedia of the social sciences*, ed. David Sills, 42–55. New York: Macmillan and the Free Press.

Massey, Doreen, and Richard Meegan, 1985. *Politics and method: Contrasting studies in industrial geography*. London: Methuen.

May, Kenneth O. 1954. Intransitivity, utility, and the aggregation of preference patterns. *Econometrica* 22: 1–13.

Meinig, Donald W. 1965. The Mormon culture region: Strategies and patterns in the geography of the American West, 1847–1964. *Annals of the Association of American Geographers* 55: 191–220.

Mill, John Stuart. 1967. *Collected works, essays on society and economy*, ed. J. M. Robson, vol. 4. Toronto: University of Toronto Press.

Olson, Marcus. 1965. *The logic of collective action: Public goods and the theory of groups*. Cambridge: Harvard University Press.

Opp, Karl-Dieter. 1989. *The rationality of political protest: A comparative analysis of rational choice theory*. Boulder: Westview Press.

Parkes, Don, and Nigel Thrift. 1980. *Times, spaces, and places: A chronogeographic perspective*. Chichester, England: John Wiley.

Peet, Richard. 1970. Von Thünen theory and the dynamics of agricultural expansion. *Explorations in Economic History* 8: 181–201.

Powers, Richard Grid. 1994. The real Robert Jordans: An unsentimental review of the Americans who fought in the Spanish Civil War. *New York Times Book Review*, 7 August: 12.

Pred, Allan. 1967. *Behavior and location: Foundations for a geographic and dynamic location theory*, 2 parts. Lund, Sweden: C. W. K. Gleerup.

Riesman, David. 1950. *The lonely crowd: A study of the changing American character*. New Haven, Conn.: Yale University Press.

Rosenberg, Hans. 1958. *Bureaucracy, aristocracy and autocracy: The Prussian experience, 1660–1815*. Cambridge: Harvard University Press.

Schlebacher, John T. 1960. The world metropolis and the history of American agriculture. *Journal of Economic History* 20: 187–208.

Schumpeter, Joseph. 1939. *Business cycles*, 2 vols. New York: McGraw-Hill.

Seligman, Ben B. 1962. *Main currents in modern economics: Economic thought since 1870*. New York: Free Press.

Shepphard, Eric, and Trevor J. Barnes. 1990. *The capitalist space economy: Geographical analysis after Ricardo, Marx, and Sraffa*. London: Unwin Hyman.

Simon, Herbert. 1957. *Models of man.* New York: John Wiley.

———. 1986. Rationality in psychology and economics. In *Rational choice: The contrasts between economics and psychology,* ed. Robin Hogarth and Melvin W. Reder, 25–40. Chicago: University of Chicago Press.

Skinner, G. William. 1985. The structure of Chinese history. *Journal of Asian Studies* 44: 271–92.

Skyrms, Brian. 1990. *The dynamics of rational deliberation.* Cambridge: Harvard University Press.

Slote, Michael. 1989. *Beyond optimizing: A study of rational choice.* Cambridge: Harvard University Press.

Stigler, George. 1950. The development of utility theory. *Journal of Political Economy* 58: 307–27, 373–96.

Storper, Michael, and Richard Walker. 1989. *The capitalist imperative: Territory, technology, and industrial growth.* New York: Basil Blackwell.

Tawney, R. H. 1967. *The agrarian problem in the sixteenth century.* New York: Harper & Row.

Taylor, A. J. P. 1946. *The course of German history: A survey of the development of Germany since 1815.* New York: Coward-McCann.

Thirsk, Joan, ed. 1967. *The agrarian history of England and Wales, Volume IV, 1500–1640.* Cambridge: Cambridge University Press.

von Thünen, Johann Heinrich. 1966. *Von Thünen's isolated state,* trans. C. M. Wartanberg, ed. P. Hall. Oxford: Pergamon Press (orig. pub. 1826).

Veblen, Thorstein. 1919. *The place of science in modern civilization.* New York: Viking Press.

Weber, Alfred. 1909. *Theory of the location of industry,* ed. C. J. Friedrich. Chicago: University of Chicago Press (orig. pub. 1909).

Willes, Mark H. 1981. Rational expectations as a counterrevolution. In *The crisis in economic theory,* ed. Daniel Bell and Irving Kristol, 521–36. New York: Basic Books.

Wolpert, Julian. 1964. The decision process in spatial context. *Annals of the Association of American Geographers* 54: 537–58.

Yapa, Lakshman. 1982. Innovation bias, appropriate technology, and basic goods. *Journal of Asian and African Studies* 18: 32–44.

13

Humanism: Wisdom of the Heart and Mind

Edmunds V. Bunkše

Humanity is yet to fully realize,
What a single word has wreaked. *
    Ojārs Vācietis, *Ex Libris* (1988)

O, they were hot for the world they
lived in, these Maya, hot to get it
down the way it was—the way it
is, my fellow citizens.
    Charles Olson, "Human Universe" (1967)

The meaning of life depends
on ourselves.
    Werner Heisenberg, "Discussions about Language" (1933)

Humanism in Its Historic Context

Modern humanism is traced back to the Italian Renaissance, from which it emerged. What is understood by *humanism* today, however, is not quite the same as it was during the Renaissance, or before that, in classical antiquity. Like many other *-isms, humanism* today stands for a nebulous, far flung, and

---

*All translations are by the author.

ambiguous (Lamont 1982: 29) way of seeing and relating to the world. Claims have been made that there is no core to humanist philosophy. Popular views on humanism are characterized by the belief in rational, scientific thought that unlocks nature's secrets and informs human decisions and actions in the world. Many regard humanism as a type of religion. It is, as Christopher Lasch describes it, "a materialistic conception of reality" (1984: 87). It has become a dominating force in the history and geography of the modern world.

This kind of humanism, also known as scientific, rational, or positivistic humanism (Ehrenfeld 1978; Relph 1981; Kohàk 1984: 118), is but a narrow strand in a broader humanist weave that emerged during the Italian Renaissance—a weave that was unraveled by the division of art and science into separate modes of interpreting the world (Snow 1978; that division is not as absolute as Snow made it out to be). Originally, humanism included both the "hypothetico-deductive reasoning" of Galilean and Newtonian science "as well as art and the celebration of the human person as microcosm of the universe" (Buttimer 1988).

The roots of humanism are found in ancient Greek impulses. Of all that the Greeks bequeathed to Western culture and the world, nothing is more significant than the legacy encapsulated in the unique notion that "man is the measure of all things." To modern ears, this Protagoran maxim sounds chauvinistic and hopelessly anthropocentric, but it represents, for better or for worse, a body of thought that for the Greeks included such ideas as the separation of humans from the divine and the beastly; the idea that "man attain the excellence that he is capable of"; as well as a tragic conception of life on this earth (Hadas 1960: 13). André Malraux dramatizes this legacy, as distinct from common Oriental world views, in the epistolary novel, *The Temptation of the West* (1961: 32–33). A Chinese traveler tells of his experience in Athens, where:

> a bust of a young man, eyes open, suddenly confronted me, like an allegory of Greek genius, with this penetrating intimation: measure all things by the duration and intensity of a *single* human life. To my Asiatic consciousness, all of Greece's genius rests on that single concept and on the sensibility derived from it. Therein resides an act of faith. Greeks saw man set aside from the world, as the Christian sees him bound to God, as we see him bound to the world. . . . The Greeks thought of man as an individual, a being who is born and dies. . . . For the [Oriental] awareness, or what I should call the sensation, of being a particle of the universe, they substituted the awareness of being a living organism, complete, discrete, on a friendly earth, where the only impassioned images were those of men and the sea.

The Greek cultural legacy to humanism cannot, of course, be summarized in such monistic fashion, nor can it be said unequivocally that the Orient did not know human-centered tendencies (in the opinion of the Indian author Narayan, "It is personality alone that remains unchanging and makes sense in any age or idiom, whether the setting is 3000 B.C. or 2000 A.D." [Moynahan 1990]). And yet it is not too much of an oversimplification to assert that this most audacious and original invention of the Greeks, the human-centered universe, is inextricably linked to such other original inventions as the idea of a citizen, of participatory democracy and the institutions that went with it or, for that matter, that eventually led to the modern concern for human rights.

Humanism as a concept is derived from the above sensibility and from the ancient Greek admonition, engraved at Delphi, "Know thyself!" What we, however, understand by the term *humanism* and what other eras have understood by it has profoundly changed. The thinkers of each era select from the past what most resonates with their own situation in the world.

Humanism in the Contemporary World

Giustiniani (1985) writes that the term *humanism* is derived from the Greek *hōmo*, which became *hōmanus* in Latin. These words stood for human nature "which encompassed very different powers and faculties . . . : intelligence, passions, instincts." To these usages was added the suffix *ismus*, which in effect made an already equivocal concept many more times so. "Thus the meaning of 'humanism', has so many shades that to analyze all of them seems hardly feasible." It is, as Giustiniani (1985: 167–95) puts it, a perpetual *signum contradictionis* (sign of contradiction). This is so because the center of attention, the human being, or, specifically, human nature, remains a most difficult and elusive phenomenon, manifesting itself as both a material and immaterial entity. Suffice it to say that in the original Latin *humanus* had two specific meanings, denoting both a humane and a learned person. The origins of these meanings are attributed by Cicero to Isocrates and perhaps also to Aristippus, but whoever the originator, in modern usage *humane* is the principal association with the term; the idea of being learned has disappeared (Giustiniani 1985: 168–69).

The loss of erudition from the modern conception of humanism illustrates the fact that choices have been made as to what historic aspects of humanism to select as important. In our era the tendency has been, not surprisingly, to single out those founders of humanism who were preoccupied with systems. We thus honor the "grand master of system, the father of scholasticism—Aristotle," as well as that "other great systematician, Plato" (Maurina 1950: 59–60). That was not the case during the Renaissance, when humanism was reborn. Plato and Aristotle were not especially admired because they were identified with the system then under attack, the system of other-worldly religious ideas that had ruled over the medieval world. During the Renaissance "first place was accorded to the human being and not to an idea . . . not to life of holy happiness in the heavens, but to full-blooded life on earth" (Maurina 1950: 61). Renaissance scholars admired Plutarch, the moralist and biographer, and Diogenes Laertius, the collector of anecdotes (Maurina 1950: 60). In short, the story and the sharing of experiences in the world was important. We hear echoes of the Renaissance transformation today as we seek to extricate ourselves from the meaningless triteness of postmodernism; and as human beings are increasingly circumscribed by technical and bureaucratic systems, the story of human experience in the world once again assumes importance (see, for example, Lopez's [1981, 1986] "Winter Count" and *Arctic Dreams*, but especially Kearney [1988] *The Wake of Imagination*). In fact, as we shall see later, the story may be the only way out from the deeply dehumanizing effects of postmodern culture.

The humanism that unfolded during the Italian Renaissance includes the following characteristics:

1) the reemergence of worldliness—of interest in life on this earth and a celebration of living in the here and now
2) the idea that humans are free and willful agents of their own natures, their place in nature, and their destiny
3) the notion of civil duties and responsibilities
4) the idea of the essential nobility of the human spirit, capable of breaking away from "need and gratification . . . with the vision of the good, the true, the beautiful" (Kohák 1984: 116)
5) rediscovery of the classical world as the precedent for humanism
6) scholarship devoted to honoring and illuminating the creations of the classical world as well as to using them as models for the rebirth of humanism
7) a specific ideal of humanistic education, including the study of the classics, rhetoric, oratory, poetry, and skepticism toward all doctrines

The so-called scientific or rational humanism arose from the above set of ideas. As such, it represents a less catholic approach to the phenomenal world than during the Renaissance. The treatise on scientific method by René Descartes (1960 [1637]) was the major instrument of that development, although according to Isaiah Berlin, Vico in 1625 had already defined the schism between art and science (1980: 108–10). Kant also "helped steer Western thought along the solipsistic lines of the Copernican revolution, reducing reality in itself to unknowability and turning the task of knowledge from seeing and listening—clear vision and faithful articulation—to one of designing constructs" (Kohák 1984: 116). Reason was singled out as the leading characteristic of humanism by the philosophers of the Enlightenment to become the foundation for modern scientific humanism. It is obviously quite different from the humanism of the Italian Renaissance, that regarded "clear vision and faithful articulation" as central to humanism.

As art and science became polarized during the nineteenth century, the humanism associated with learning and with sharing insights and experiences has come to be identified with what Susan Sontag (1982b: 294) refers to as the literary-artistic culture of our era. This humanism inspired Vico (1948 [1625]) to assert the importance of communicating meaning as the basis of humanity; Montaigne to write his famous defense of cannibalism (1910: 189–18 [1588]); Voltaire to deflate the myth of a perfect creation in *Candide* (1930 [1759]); George Orwell (1949) to expose the horrors of unbridled scientific rationalism in *1984*; Camus (1955), in *The Myth of Sisyphus*, to articulate the idea of the absurd, not as a nihilistic submission to fate, but as an affirmation of humanness. Many contemporary artistic creations are informed by this humanism: the poems of Neruda and Milosz calling humans back to their human roots; the writings of Atwood and Lopez calling for a nonanthropocentric vision of nature; and the films of Ingmar Bergman and Federico Fellini illuminating dilemmas of modern existence. It is a humanism that holds "a sensitive regard for each man [and woman] as his [or her] own end and for man as responsible for man" (H. J. Blackham 1973: 36), with a clarity of sensuous and intellectual vision.

Literary-Artistic Humanism and the Environment

Literary-artistic humanism exists in the shadow of its scientific or rational counterpart, that dominates the arenas of social, economic, and political power (including power over nature). The former is more a humanism of thought than action, found in literary, artistic, and critical domains. In that sense it is a relatively private and unobtrusive humanism—at times a wise humanism, surfacing here and there as a concern for the human being as an end in its own right and not as a component of systems (Ortega y Gasset 1957, Moravia 1966). It often stands in opposition to actions taken under the aegis of rational humanism in the political world and in landscapes—but more as a voice of criticism rather than power in the material world.

In the making and controlling of environments, ecologically oriented ideals have achieved at least visibility and a certain amount of lip service, if not much actual material success (pollution control legislation is a notable exception).

Literary-artistic humanism is cultivated in one's garden, as Voltaire would have it.

As noble as that sentiment might be, unfortunately, it symbolizes a sad truth of the modern world: the often radical qualitative differences between public and private landscapes. While one's "garden," that is, the private landscape, is cultivated (the dormitory room, apartment, house—indeed, in some instances, even a garden) and may embody evolving humane ideals, with very few exceptions the public landscape is the result of abstract economic, political, and social forces. Unfortunately, many private landscapes also bear the marks of these forces, the result of political control or mass-culture marketing. It is often an efficient and utilitarian landscape and represents the tenets of scientific or rational humanism. As such, it is a dehumanized environment because it does not reflect deep-seated affective concerns. Cultivation in the sense of a growing entity is not characteristic of it, only construction, upkeep, or maintenance. Airports, schools, and office towers are the most notorious examples of it. Indicative of this situation is the well-known fact that talented architects of the public landscape often inhabit domiciles that bear little stylistic relationship to what they are required to create in their work places. The most radical expression of the difference between public and private landscapes that I have witnessed exists in Latvia, especially in the massive Soviet-imposed residential apartment blocks of Rīga. The mindless sameness and bleakness of these blocks bears no relationship to the often elegant if minuscule interiors of private apartments, where modern design is combined with traditional and even ecological themes.

To bring dehumanized public landscapes into closer accord with more humane private interior ones entails addressing fundamental aspects of sociopolitical structures. Before that can occur, literary-artistic humanism has to be recognized as having at least as much to contribute to the shaping of public landscapes as its scientific counterpart (as I have argued elsewhere, 1990). This can be done only if it becomes a part of public debate. The task is not easy. Achieving the current, nearly worldwide popularity of the so-called ecological consciousness took well over a hundred years and countless articulations of all types (if George Perkins Marsh's 1864 treatise on the subject is taken as an important starting point). To develop a parallel literary-artistic consciousness vis-á-vis cultural landscapes will be equally daunting.

The importance of literary-artistic humanism (I shall simply refer to it as humanism, or else note otherwise) resides in the fact that it examines and illuminates precisely those values that concern thoughtful people in the closing years of the twentieth century, that is, questions of ontology, significance, and the human condition in general (Meinig 1983; Bunkśe 1990). Both factual reality and transcendence are addressed by it; thus, while poetry may be generally regarded as raising reality to the level of art through imagination, "one of the cardinal functions of poetry is to show [to] the other side [i.e., rationalism] the wonders of everyday life; not poetic irreality but the prodigious reality of the world" (Paz 1975: 51).

Imagination

The key element of humanism is imagination—it is the source of creativity and artistic wisdom: "If existentialism yields a timeless mood and mysticism yields a timeless psychology, then humanism yields a timeless imagination, a universal sensibility" (Arisian 1973).

It is imagination that provides the foundation for humanist (of all persuasions) confidence in the human ability to control our own destiny. In the modern era, however, imagination has come to be identified largely with the arts and not with the sciences, that, not surprisingly, tend to frown on the flights of fancy to which an unbridled imagination is prone.

Imagination is of course fundamental to both art and science, but it is not understood very well by science, if at all (but see Bronowski 1978; Blakeslee 1993). In literature and the arts it is a common subject for discussion and examination, but more so in terms of its creations than as a major characteristic of the human species. Given their scientific inclinations, geographers have not concerned themselves overly much with imagination, even though it is difficult to think of any cultural landscape (or for that matter, relationships with nature) apart from the role that imagination has played in shaping it (in that respect, J. K. Wright's 1966 essay on imagination is a remarkable document; see also Lowenthal and Prince 1976). The workings of imagination are implicit in the geographer's examinations of the subtle and elusive aspects of human sense of place, but along with other environmentally oriented professionals geographers have preferred to study perception, cognition, the structure of language, communication, and even the brain itself. These aspects of the human being represent mechanistic and secondary characteristics of the primary role that imagination plays in defining and shaping human actions in nature (Bronowski 1978; Davenport 1981) and as a key element of human consciousness (Bronowski 1978: 18). It was imagination that enabled humans to conceive of themselves as microcosmic counterparts of the cosmos, for the Dogon to create circular villages, or for Brasília to take its particular shape in the middle of a great human emptiness.

Imagination represents the unique human ability to step outside the immediate context of life, to, as it were, absent ourselves from the here and now and to enter into other realities or to create entirely new realities. This may take various forms (Cobb 1977; Rugg 1963; Warnock 1976; Sartre 1950; Bronowski 1976; Blakeslee 1993). Imagination is part of our daily lives. We constantly project ourselves beyond our immediate sensory material contexts into other material contexts, past, present, or future. More significant for cultural change (and therefore for the confidence to create human destiny, especially among rational-scientific humanists) is the ability of the imagination to come up with new relationships in the material world and to develop new aesthetic and ethical dimensions of behavior and being (as did Humboldt, who, when confronted by the seemingly chaotic tropical rainforests of Latin America, applied the idea of unity to the variety and diversity of nature). In this regard, though, the most striking aspect of the imagination is its largely mysterious ability to imagine worlds and ways of being beyond the sensory realm—an ability shared, among others, by children, geniuses (individuals who never abandoned childhood, according to Cobb 1977), and poets. (I have always been fascinated by the fact that Democritus and Lucretius were able to conceptualize atoms and space within matter long before the physics for such an interpretation had been developed.)

Individual Human Natures, Universal Resonances

We do not need to reveal ourselves to others, but only to those we
love. For then we are no longer revealing ourselves to seem but in
order to give.
    A. Camus, *Notebooks 1935–1942* (1963)

The problem with accepting the imaginative works of humanists into the practice of geography (and, ultimately, their materialization in human environments) as valid and important sources of truth and insight is that geographers perceive them to represent individual, idiosyncratic subjectivities, lacking in universal significance and theory-building possibilities. That is undeniably so if the Cartesian test for truth is applied. It is not so if the test is that which humanists themselves apply to their works—that of resonant and intersubjective communication. This becomes clear if the implicit assumptions within the humanist enterprise are examined, namely, the origin and nature of humanist knowledge.

In terms of origins, the human being itself is the source of humanist knowledge, not an other-worldly power beyond the realm of human experience nor a worldly power devoid of direct connection to the human being (which is, at least in theory, the working methodological assumption on which law-seeking science is founded). The nature of humanist knowledge is transcendental to the degree that it communicates the human condition from one place, generation, or era to another. In this sense scientific and technical knowledge may also be transcendental if it communicates something of the human condition. Democritus's and Lucretius's imagining of the atom speaks eloquently of human wonder about this world, as does Einstein's theory of relativity, but unless there is an account of the existential context within which these discoveries occurred, the transcendental quality of the communication will be muted.

Humanist knowledge is derived and created from personal experience, intellect, inspiration, and imagination, as well as from secondary sources (not least of which might be scientific)—in short, from a whole variety of origins. There is no prescribed method, no dogma to follow. As in Renaissance humanism, the only commitment in humanist truth is "to a method of free inquiry and to the use of critical intelligence" (Kurtz 1973: 182). A "mature humanist wisdom, accordingly, would allow many flowers to bloom, many paths to be taken." (Kurtz 1973: 183) From this it follows that the nature of humanist knowledge is neither "prescriptive nor unprescriptive," but open-ended (Blackham 1973: 36). The point to underscore is that knowledge is derived from the interaction of human nature with the world.

Communicating human experience thus assumes paramount importance, not necessarily because it constitutes the culturally created storehouse of wisdom (which it certainly is), but because through communication across generations it conveys the thoughts and experiences of other minds in other times and places. In this regard we are reminded of the story of the day that the post brought Rousseau's *Émile* to Kant. Kant is said to have become so agitated by Rousseau's brilliant "discovery" that on that one day he gave up his daily walk (Cassirer 1945: 1). The story illuminates the kind of communion among humanists initiated by the Renaissance. After all, the primary reason for the fascination with classical antiquity during the Renaissance was to get in touch with people who had, as it were, been there before (and who were obviously brilliant).

It is hard for us, living in the postmodern era, to appreciate the Renaissance ideal of intellectual exchange. Communication has become an ahistoric and mechanistic commodity among commodities (Kearney 1988). Conditioned by images and abstractions of reality (such as sound bites), the postmodern mind cannot fully apprehend the magic of the moment when Renaissance humanists discovered kindred spirits across the gulf of centuries in Classical architecture, art, poetry, prose, philosophy, and drama. Reading the letters of Pliny was like conversing with him in person. (It is still possible to capture that charm in reading Lucretius or Marcus Aurelius.) Human beings learned about the fate of others in situations similar to theirs, which enabled them to better confront their own fates and, indeed, to transcend fate and to become free and independent entities in the world.

The transcendence of humanist communication is crucial to the whole tradition of humanism, yet in modern existential and other writings it is virtually ignored (see, however, Malraux, 1968; Lowenthal and Prince 1976; Pocock 1981: 15–16).

A sense of transcendental communication through the work a person left behind became important as Westerners developed increasing independence from deterministic structures (teleologic, environmental, biologic) and began to assume responsibility for their own fate—a trend that began in ancient Greece with challenges to the authority of gods and patriarchs (Tuan 1982: 154–55). With secularization, humanistic thought, as expressed especially in literary and artistic creations, took on a life of its own that reached beyond the temporal boundaries of a single lifetime. Cassirer explains it as the subjectivity of a life objectified in the "symbolic forms that are created by the individual—language, poetry, plastic art, and religion" (Cassirer 1974: 215). A certain illusion of immortality is attained if a person's work survives beyond mortal life in this world. At least in part, transcendent artistic qualities of the work itself assures its survival, even when it is as bluntly realistic as the Confessions of Jean Jacques Rousseau, The Possessed by Dostoevsky (Malraux 1968: 4), or The Magic Lantern (1989) by Ingmar Bergman. In an artistic truth it is not "a question of conveying a particular knowledge of man" (Malraux 1968: 3–4), but rather, as in the Confessions of Rousseau, of placing life on the plane of art. As André Malraux (1968: 4) writes, "This metamorphosis of a fate undergone into a fate transcended is one of the most profound that man can create." Baudelaire, the first modern poet, was well aware of the transcendent qualities of art when he said that art saved him from "the terrors of the Pit" (Schorske 1966: 111). Recently, in a public statement, Milan Kundera sought to give back to literature the role that it has lost during the meaningless eclecticism of the postmodern era, namely, of illuminating life's mundane truths in artistic terms.

Transcendental communication is of course at the core of humanism, whereby transcendence is found principally within the realm of human experience, not in a sacred or moral order outside the human being, in the cosmos. It is the human being who gives meaning to the world, who invents, as it were, self and world. In that sense it is severely limited, because it is "wholly contained in temporality" and lacks a significant spatial dimension, as Kohák characterizes it (as I understand it, Kohák [1984: 119] means by this a sacred order of nature). Limited though humanism may be for its lack of a spatial dimension (although it can be argued that the sense of vastness in large cities and in nature provides that dimension), it has nonetheless given rise to major creative outbursts of the human imagination in the twentieth century.

The transcendental qualities of humanist creations are not passive, though they may appear so when they lie unexamined on forgotten shelves in dark corners of attics. They merely await the engagement with a sympathetic reader or observer to initiate humanist communication. Thus engaged, they may inform a consciousness or inspire and motivate new creations. Imagination can be kindled as much by falsehood as by truth, or by right as well as wrong insights (there is, of course, no guarantee that evil resonances would not occur, as happened with Ezra Pound's enthusiastic support for fascism. In free societies, however, critical examination may counter such tendencies before they do much harm.) The engagement initiates a resonant, intersubjective transformation of cultural mores. Work inspired by a communion with human minds of earlier eras may result in syncretic creations that illuminate past and present human situations and the human condition in general. Modern art of all kinds has thrived on resonances with the minds of the pre-Socratics in particular (Davenport 1981), as well as with those of the prehistoric past. Such resonances with the past influenced Robert Graves and Ezra Pound. Charles Olson, Robinson Jeffers, and Gary Snyder resonated with native Americans. Picasso and Braque created perhaps the most inspiring syncretic journeys into the distant, atavistic past. These journeys enabled their creators to illuminate certain essential aspects of our humanity that would have been difficult, if not impossible, to access through the linear logic of the archeologist or even the historian.

Resonant communion with prehistory is not always confined to the relatively private worlds of humanists. The recent Latvian struggle against Soviet-imposed oppression was supported in part by a deep sense of an ancient past in which Latvian culture evolved in close interaction with earth and sea. To a considerable extent, that sense has been defined by art, especially by folk poetry and by contemporary writers. In this regard the powerful syncretic images of modern and paleolithic life in the poems of Jānis Peters are particularly notable (1989) — images that not only sustain morale in an uneven struggle, but that help to define the future political and cultural landscapes of Latvia (it is not entirely coincidental that Peters represented Latvian interests in 1990 and 1991 negotiations with Moscow).

Much of this is obvious when stated and is evident throughout humanistic thought. There is the longstanding tradition of referential quotations, raised perhaps to unequaled perfection in Montaigne's essays. In the seventeenth century Giambattista Vico (1948 [1625]) sharpened the distinction between knowing nature and knowing the minds of human beings in their creations. Because God made nature, nature could never be fully intelligible to humankind (or, as the evolutionary psychologist would say, evolution did not prepare the mind to fully comprehend human consciousness); however, the minds of humans are accessible through their works because humans made them. As humans share basic emotions and intellect, the values, fears, and intentions of one age are intelligible to another. Vico claimed that the minds of early peoples can be understood by direct consciousness and awareness of their signs, symbols, and words (Berlin 1980: 96). When Herder (1807) revolutionized the study of history to include ordinary folk in ordinary landscapes and to use their folklore as a source of their history and of their minds in history, he was merely expanding the idea of temporal transcendence of human creations to the so-called folk or little tradition. That his theories of folklore and folk culture were later used for nasty nationalistic ends does not diminish their intrinsic worth in opening the way for contact with the minds of earlier generations including women and ordinary people.

In effect, the degree to which the humanistic tradition speaks or communicates to others across space and time, from one culture to another, one era to another, determines the truth of humanistic knowledge that individuals create. When gauged against the rigor of science, this proposition is highly subjective. The point is, however, that it is precisely such comparisons that have rendered humanistic knowledge soft and therefore contributed to its largely ineffective role in our culture in general and in geography in particular. It will become hard knowledge only if judged on its own terms—in other words, *not according to an absolutist but a relativistic yardstick.* (Humanists should probably bear the brunt of the blame for this condition, having either withdrawn from the worldly arena where military-industrial and business complexes rule or engaged in unconvincing discourses dressed in scientific garb, as in the case of postmodernist literary criticism, particularly deconstruction.)

A Hierarchy of Truths

If I have tried to define something, it is . . . simply the common
existence of history and of man, everyday life with the most possible
light thrown upon it, the dogged struggle against one's own
degradation and that of others.
     Camus, "The Artist and His Time" (1955)

To address the issue of hard and soft knowledge it is necessary to establish the validity of artistic subjectivity—especially of ambiguity and syncretism—as a source of truth. This involves addressing the hierarchical idea of truth by which the arts are presumed a priori to be inferior to science. The issue becomes moot if the relativistic world view of humanism is accepted in lieu of scientific absolutism.

The hierarchical idea of truth—the notion that knowledge ranges from least to most truthful, from least to most reliable—is a tradition that extends back to Plato. Plato articulated this hierarchy by distinguishing between knowing the world through the senses and knowing it through the mind; between individual subjectivity and the objectivity of universal values and facts. In its essence it is the difference between subjectivity and reason. Subjective imagination, the major source of myths and the arts (including architecture), is the most unreliable, while reason, particularly mathematical reason, establishes absolute truths (Murdoch 1977: 2–3). In Plato's scheme art is unreliable, even dangerous. "All things . . . are produced either by nature, by fortune, or by art; the greatest and most beautiful by the one or the other of the former, the least and the most imperfect by the last" (Montaigne 1910, 2: 198). Poetry is the most light-headed of the arts because it comes from divine inspiration (from *entheos*, "the god within"; Dubos 1972: 4). The poet is regarded as possessed, even mad. The propensity of artists to imitate one another only compounds the unreliability of art (Murdoch 1977: 2–5). Moreover, reality as portrayed by the poet is inferior to that of the artisan and craftsman who create in the context of a workaday world (Frye 1983: 79). "Most devaluations of poetry ever since [Plato], whether Platonic, Puritan, Marxist or Philistine, have been attached to some version of a work ethic, which makes it a secondary or leisure-time activity" (Frye 1983: 79).

We might expect that Plato's epistemological hierarchy of truth was toppled with the development of relativism, especially the relativism of cultural values that came into being with Montaigne's essay on cannibalism (Montaigne 1910: 189–218), and by subsequent humanistic writings (especially ethnographic and anthropologic). Today there certainly is more acceptance of "lesser" truths, including myth, folklore, and poetry. There is, however, the tendency to rationalize them, to look for underlying facts, functions, and structures (Bascom 1965). We assume that a myth, a folk song, or a poem must have at least a kernel of truth in order to be believable. Such an assumption may be entirely justified for a myth to be believable, but there is a tendency to emphasize the kernel of truth and to dismiss the rest. The events in Homer's Iliad are thus presumed to have occurred at specific sites. A folk song about the Battle of New Orleans is thought to represent historic facts (Hoffman 1952). A piece of folk meteorology is expected to have an actual empirical observation behind it. Observe, however, that in assessing art, science is the yardstick—attempts are made to determine the actual geography of the *Iliad*, find the historic facts of the Battle of New Orleans, and ascertain the scientific accuracy of folk meteorology. Plato's hierarchy of knowledge remains essentially intact in the distinctions between soft and hard knowledge. Even the relatively softer notions of rational elucidation or *Verstehen*, though not as hard-edged an approach to truth as *Wissen*, retain an absolutist cast. The fact is that hardness—an interesting metaphoric usage in its own right—is assumed axiomatically to be the most desirable quality of knowledge.

To be sure, not everyone subscribes to this view of truth. The relativism of truth, of facts, especially those having to do with values and perspectives on the world and the human conditions in it, is fundamental to a substantial segment of modern humanism (Goodman 1978: 20–21), at least on the part of artists, if not always of critics. Indeed, ambiguity and syncretism are key features of the artistic imagination. As such, these perceptions stand in sharp contrast to the scientific search for unambiguous laws of nature (or, at the very least, for consensual objectivity).

A recurrent theme in modern art is the frustration that artists feel when confronted with criticism and interpretation framed within the parameters of science or the marketplace. Such approaches tend to regard art in ancillary terms or purposes and not for its own sake or for the sake of the general public (admittedly, there is much art that is not particularly accessible). As a rule, scientific scholars or researchers do not penetrate a work of art to ascertain its essential being (although deconstructionists would probably disagree). Science dissects and interprets art, uses it as data toward some end other than a deepening of our awareness of its being. (In that regard, Umberto Eco's (1990) *The Limits of Interpretation* is a significant, if still largely academic, reminder that interpretation should have more respect for the reader than for the exercise of interpretation.) Indeed, scientific criticism frequently renders a work more opaque, more forbidding, and, in effect, more academic, that is, divorced from existence. Artists will either refuse to enter into the game, or they will mock its artificiality. As Susan Sontag protests (1982a: 7–8), "the world, our world, is impoverished enough. Away with all duplicates of it, until we again experience more immediately what we have." For Sontag, scientific (she really means academic) interpretation poisons human sensibilities, just as the fumes of automobiles and industry poison urban air. "In a culture whose already classical dilemma is the hypertrophy of the intellect at the expense of energy and sensual capacity, interpretation is the revenge of the intellect upon art" (Sontag 1982a: 7–8). The intellect, by squeezing out the maximum content from a work of art, effectively prevents direct human experience of it (or as Bachelard [1964] argues over and over again, interpretation hardens a poetic image so that it becomes lifeless in the reader's mind and prevents the imagination from expanding on it). To render a work of art lifeless is to diminish the function of modern art (all art), because art today is "a new kind of instrument, an instrument for modifying consciousness and organizing new modes of sensibility" (Sontag 1982b: 296). The role of the student of art, of the critic—of the humanistic geographer—should be to make works of art and human experience more rather than less real (Sontag 1982a: 14), to deepen the experience of a work of art by making accessible whatever modes of sensibility might be embodied in it, to not turn it into dry academic chaff but instead to reveal its sensuous or spiritual character. "In place of a hermeneutics we need an erotics of art" (Sontag 1982a: 14). Sontag's plea for the sensuous may be a bit hyperbolic, but it emphasizes the same earthy characteristics of life celebrated by the humanists of the Italian Renaissance. It is a call to admit into intellectual and human life the senses and, above all, the subjective imagination; or as Henry Miller (1941) would put it, to admit the "wisdom of the heart."

How might this be done? Given the overbearing dominance of scientific and pragmatic reason, we probably should not attempt to effect a marriage between subjectivity and reason, art and science. The result would be an unequal partnership, a disproportion of weight. In our value system nuances of meaning, the subtle shading of a *Gestalt*, the evocation of an epiphany unfortunately do not have the same weight as facts and nomothetic constructions. Even when the two domains receive more or less equal treatment, as they did in certain segments of Humboldt's work, the results are often cumbersome, with metaphor getting in the way of scientific fact (Bunkśe 1981, 1990). Exceptions do exist, including general works on art and science in the hands of a talented and skilled writer such as Barry Holstun Lopez (1986) or in a lifeworld situation, such as that which John Western (1986) encountered in apartheid South Africa, wherein he was able to combine the objective structural (political-social-economic) context with individual subjectivities. The point is that at this particular time the dominance of science (and technology) in our societies is somewhat like that of religion in Galileo's day. As Galileo had to separate his science from religion in order to do proper science, we have to separate our critical faculties from science in order to do proper humanism. This does not in any way suggest a negation of science (just as Galileo did not negate the importance of religion, in the name of which he was persecuted anyway). It does seem to be the only practical means to begin raising humanism to a more important role in the world.

Humanistic geographers have largely resisted a full acceptance of literary and artistic truths about the phenomenal world (Bunkśe 1990). Perhaps the most telling in this regard is R. J. Johnston's summary of the humanist movement in geography. As Johnston writes (1987: 242), humanists "have argued for a *different conception of science* [emphasis added], one that focuses on subjectivity. Such a science is clearly incommensurable with positivistic spatial science." Note that it is science that is the alternative to positivistic spatial science and not the humanities (or literary-artistic humanism). In effect, this means a continuation of the limitations that the scientific method imposes on any piece of work that deals with subjectivity (see Bunkśe 1990).

There are, however, a number of significant exceptions to this general resistance to literary and artistic sources of geographical insight (e.g., A. Buttimer [1974, 1976, 1981, 1983a, 1983b, 1993], C. G. Glacken [1965, 1966, 1967, 1970a, 1970b], D. Ley and M. Samuels [1978], D. Lowenthal [1961, 1985], Lowenthal and Prince [1976], Lowenthal and Bowden [1976], D. W. Meinig [1971, 1979, 1983], K. Olwig [1984], D. C. D. Pocock [1981, 1988], R. Rees [1982a, 1982b], Y. F. Tuan [1971, 1976a, 1976b, 1978, 1982, 1986], Bunkše [1994], and others.) The decades of the 1960s and 1970s were the most inspired for humanistic approaches in geography, but by the early 1980s widespread interest had waned (Buttimer 1993). This had to do, in part, with attacks on general (scientific-rational) humanism by ecologically oriented individuals (Ehrefield 1978, Relph 1981) and in part by questions that were raised about its merits as an approach to geographic issues. Entrikin's contention that a humanistic approach amounts to a type of criticism (Entrikin 1976) probably did much to dissuade many geographers from literary-artistic directions (but see Lowenthal 1985, Buttimer 1993, and Relph 1993, and the collection of essays edited by R. B. P. Singh 1994).

The recourse is to become more relativistic in understanding the intrinsic value of art and science, subjectivity and reason, and of the kinds of truths each has to offer. Nelson Goodman (1978: 20) has phrased this well: " . . . our passion for *one* world is satisfied at different times and for different purposes, in *many* different ways." In a certain sense such relativism requires one to approximate the ancient, pre-Socratic Greek acceptance of both religious and scientific knowledge, where the "world of gods . . . [was] a sensuous correlate of the aspects of intellectual knowledge" (Worringer 1957: 22).

This may not be as onerous as it sounds. It requires recognition that there are different kinds of truth, with each having its own set of criteria or test of validity. It further requires that the criteria for one set of truths be not applied to another, that is, the truth of a religious belief, a myth, or an imaginative, artistic insight, image, or orientation should not be tested by Cartesian-inspired methodologies. Following the classic humanist requirement for communication, the efficacy with which a particular literary-artistic truth resonates among humans becomes the critical test of its validity. It goes without saying that the danger of socially malignant truths will be always there, but in enlightened societies with free discourse such malignancies can be exposed—unless humanists themselves become so confident of the positive course of their civilization and its values that they cease to be vigilant—as Ortega y Gasset (1957) warned. In short, the humanist must embrace a truly relativistic view of how the phenomenal world is known. In a world where a mechanistic vision of the universe is the dominant paradigm and there is a yearning for absolute order and control (see, for example, Bloom 1987), this is not the easiest of undertakings.

Literary-Artistic Humanism in the Postmodern Era

"There is only one wise religion: to pray
to the sun and to the sun in humans."
Zenta Maurina, *Tragiskais Skaistums*
(Tragic Beauty) (1950)

It can be argued that to bring humanism into the world of affairs is but a quixotic exercise, that it cannot compete against the hegemony of science and technology (Root-Bernstein 1984) and that it has little relevance in the modern world. (If I were a realist I would probably take heed of R. J. Johnston's (1987: 242) analysis of the failure of humanistic paradigms to command center stage among geographers.) George Steiner (1971), a major literary scholar, has in fact argued that literary humanism and multifaceted notions of relativity belong to the past; that the die has been cast, irrevocably, in favor of science, and that ours is an age of "binary dialectics" (1971). Steiner (1971: 139) asks, albeit with thinly disguised irony, "Where is the actual program for a mode of human perception freed from the 'fetishism of abstract truth'?" Steiner's (1971: 139) view becomes seemingly impregnable when he argues it from the standpoint of environmental determinism:

> The pursuit of the facts, of which the sciences merely provide the most visible, organized instance, is no contingent error embarked upon by Western man at some moment of elitist or bourgeois rapacity. . . . Given an adequate climatic and nutritive milieu, it was bound to evolve and to augment by a constant feedback of new energy. The partial absence of this questioning compulsion from less-developed, dormant races and civilizations does not represent a free choice or feat of innocence. It represents, as Montesquieu knew, the force of adverse ecological and genetic circumstance.

Steiner (1971: 140) concludes that "We cannot turn back. We cannot choose the dreams of unknowing."

Steiner's pessimism about the inevitable fate of the Western human being may be overdrawn, but it is difficult to argue against his fatalism concerning the lack of a program in humanism. It is even more difficult to contradict his assessment of the weakness of humanistic culture in the marketplace of brains and in the general decline of the arts, especially verbal ones, as conveyors of cultural values (Steiner 1971: 125). Moreover, literary-artistic culture is by definition more internal than external—it aims at the cultivation of an internal state of being, as opposed to scientific culture, "which aims at accumulation and externalization" (Sontag 1982b: 294). It may indeed be futile to ask geographers to cultivate our ties to the external world, to places and landscapes, by humanistic means.

Nevertheless, Steiner's fatalism is unacceptable, if for no other reason than because so much of modern humanism in arts and letters is a cry against the destructive side of science and technology and against the kind of rational or scientific humanism that employs binary opposition, especially for values of good and evil, as a formula of truth. Historically, the truths of black and white, without the nuances of gray in between, have contributed to the dehumanization of human beings and their conditions of life. Absolutist truth is an unacceptable truth in both the interpretation of what human nature is all about and in the making of modern environments to suit that purported nature. In planning habitats for living, science and technology simplify human nature (Bunkśe 1979: 393–94). This has meant the spiritual impoverishment of modern life. A human being is more than a bundle of binary oppositions; she or he does not always crave an absolute social, spatial, or universal order. A human being can accept and even thrive on the ambiguities of humanist relativism. Indeed as the sciences dealing with human issues partake of the relativity of quantum physics (Wheeler 1982) and chaos research, it seems possible that humanist relativism will also have its day and that art and science may become unified; but until such time we should probably accept art and science as disparate yet complementary means of knowing nature and human nature.

Beyond Postmodernism

The arguments in favor of humanism may amount to no more than pointless idealism in light of current postmodern technological and artistic realities. According to Richard Kearney (1988) and others (Hassan 1971, Benjamin 1968, Newman 1985), modern technology, especially in the mass reproduction of images, may be destroying the confidence and the power of human imagination to define self and world. In other words, the very promise of humanism, that the human being is the maker of self and habitat, may be a hollow one in the postmodern era.

Kearney (1988: 2–3) contends that ours has become a "civilization of the image," dominated not by the inventiveness of individual imaginations but by a faceless, authorless, placeless, and ahistoric mass image industry, the industry of image reproduction: multichannel satellite TV, video recorders, computer screens and printouts, facsimile machines, artwork reproduction processes, and the like. Images thus produced mediate our perceptions and interpretations of the world around us, including that of nature, as well as of our inner, psychic world (witness the manipulation of sexual impulses by soap operas). In the postmodern era an important shift in perception has occurred in our world view in that the image has replaced reality or, as Kearney puts it, "reality has become a pale reflection of the image." Fact and fiction, the real and the imaginary, an original and its reproduction are almost impossible to distinguish. So too the difference between "high" and "low," individual and mass cultures has been reduced to almost zero. All of these postmodern conditions challenge the humanist idea of the human being as a source of meaning in the world or, more specifically, that an individual imagination can give authentic expression to an individual subjectivity at a particular point in time and space. The imagination has thus lost its special humanist status because the originality of a particular image and, by extension, of any humanist creation, is now in doubt. "There is a growing conviction that the images we possess," writes Kearney, "are reproduced copies of images already there before us. The image which *is* has *already been*." It is therefore not surprising that a postmodern artist such as Warhol "does not claim to express anything because he does not have anything to express," resulting in art that has as its paradigm the "incessant play between inter-reflecting mirrors. . . . But the mirror of the postmodern paradigm reflects neither the outer world of nature nor the inner world of subjectivity; it reflects only itself—a mirror within a mirror within a mirror. . . ." (Kearney 1988: 4–5).

By contrast, the humanist tradition had confidence in the creative powers of the imagination—confidence that reaches back to the myth of Prometheus and to the Biblical Adam; to the early Renaissance of Pico dela Mirandola; to the Enlightenment; but especially to the modern era of the willful and self-responsible worldly individual, as defined by Nietzsche (1971 [1883–1891]), which culminated in the brash assertions of the Futuristas (Apollonio 1973) and in the thoughtful explorations of creativity, control, and responsibility by such existentialists as Malraux, Camus, and Sartre, as well as Ortega y Gasset, Saint-Exupéry, and the phenomenologist Bachelard. (I am obviously not considering the darker side of Adam or Nietzsche, mainly because we can, after all, choose, as did Camus, to admire "the invincible sun within" ourselves.)

I have to agree with Kearney that in postmodern, also deconstructionist, terms we are indeed witnessing the "wake of imagination" and, by extension, of humanism (Kearney 1988). In a certain sense the death of humanism as a whole is not a bad thing, especially if this means scrapping the idea of progress and indiscriminate anthropocentrism, in the name of which we have sacrificed nature and perhaps also human nature; but in realistic terms it would be a wake only for literary-artistic humanism, because it is difficult to see a redirection of the scientific or rational humanism that provides the theoretical underpinnings for the technologic and materialistic culture that increasingly dominates the earth and the human being. Moreover, with the loss of literary-artistic humanism as a perspective, we would lose the power of criticism over the forces of dehumanization, as well as the ability to imagine alternatives to the status quo.

Kearney's analysis, however, supports my own concern for developing literary-artistic humanism in geography as a means of generating and cultivating humane and spiritual values in our ties with environments (Kearney 1988: 359–97; Bunkše 1990). He too refuses to accept a cognitive model (i.e., of postmodernism) that ignores spiritual values and at best ascribes a passive observer role vis-à-vis history to the creative subject that once was the humanist. He refuses to accept the notion that to think through postmodernism will result only in "being condemned to the postmodern disease of endless circularity." He is especially concerned that the "death of imagination also implies the death of a philosophy of *truth* (along with the corresponding notions of interpretation, meaning, reference, narrative, history and value)." He argues that even if there are no "epistemological limits" to the postmodern deconstruction of imagination, there are ethical limits, because, sooner or later, our sense of values is challenged by images from the world so odious (as the famous Vietnam War photograph of a naked, severely burned girl running down a village road) as to force us to make a stand, which in effect calls on the imagination to, as it were, sort things out. To be sure, in the new context of postmodernism the imagination will no longer be neutral as it was for the rational or scientific humanist. It will be an ethical-poetic imagination that neither ignores the indifference of postmodernism nor returns to a humanist anthropocentrism. Rather, it will focus on two aspects: 1) the needs of the other, meaning anything other than the subject (e.g., another human being or group, or a plant or animal) that demands an ethical decision from the subject; and 2) the exploration of alternate social systems in ethical-poetic terms.

The exploration of alternate social systems is a familiar theme in utopian writings, often with autocratic overtones. Here nothing more is implied than exploration of alternative lives and landscapes in ethical-poetic contexts. The needs of the other is a perspective that we have tended to leave to professionals in the humanities and the arts, that is, we have accorded it a secondary role, but environmental relationships entail people and ethics and therefore also for:

> the other to be heard, and to be respected in his/her otherness, [which] is irreducible to the parodic play of empty imitations. It breaks through the horizontal surface of mirror-images and, outfacing the void, reintroduces a dimension of depth. The face of the other resists assimilation to the dehumanizing processes of commodity fetishism. Contesting the cult of imitation without origin, it presents us with an image which does indeed relate to something: the ethical existence of the other as *an other*—the inalienable right to be recognized as a particular person whose very *otherness* refuses to be reduced to a mimicry of *sameness*. Beyond the mask there is a face. Beyond the anonymous system, however all-en-

compassing it may appear, there is always what Emmanuel Levinas has termed, the resistant ethical relation of the "face to face." (1968, in Kearney 1988: 361–62)

It is easy to avoid ethical issues engendered by face-to-face encounters when, as a field of learning, geography claims to be a spatial science, but not when our work ceases to be purely academic and enters the stream of history, that is, of human actions in the environment. We cannot then dismiss as an ethical issue the effects on the other of our pure (often Platonic) forms.

For Kearney the way out of the postmodern dilemma of surfaces and mirrors is the story or, in a more specific sense, the history of imagination, as long as we are prepared to listen to the lessons in the story. The lessons are that individual imagination responds to the demands of an other existing beyond the self, that the responsibility for "invention, decision and action" is always present, and that, in the current image civilization, people can come into contact with each other in spite of the threat to our sense of reality by images as surrogate realities. Most important is a historic imagination that interprets stories or cultural narratives, not with the goal of creating one grand, totalized narrative or a narrative in a final, frozen form (as is the case with a model or a blueprint for utopia), but a diversity of ever-evolving narratives that would help us envision what came before postmodernism and what might come after it, not in a utopian sense but in a sense that a future is possible after the perceived timelessness of the postmodern present (Kearney 1988: 386–96).

That, then, is one story of humanism — a brief one of a long struggle to make sense of human nature, that "second nature in the world of nature," as Cicero would have it.

Notes

I wish to express my gratitude to Lisa Davis, George Henderson, and Anne Buttimer.

References

Apollonio, U., ed. 1970. *Futurist manifestos.* New York: Viking Press.

Arisian, K. 1973. Ethics and humanist imagination. In *The humanist alternative: Some definitions of humanism,* ed. P. Kurtz, 169–72. Buffalo, N. Y.: Prometheus Books.

Bachelard, G. 1964. *The poetics of space.* Boston: Beacon Press.

Bascom, W. 1965. Four functions of folklore. In *The study of folklore,* ed. A. Dundes, 279–98. Englewood Cliffs, N. J.: Prentice-Hall.

Benjamin, W. 1968. The work of art in the age of mechanical reproduction. In *Illuminations*, ed. H. Arendt, 219–53. N. Y.: Harcourt, Brace & World.

Bergman, I. 1989. *The magic lantern*. London: Penguin.

Berlin, I. 1980. *Against the current: Essays in the history of ideas*. New York: Viking Press.

Blackham, H. J. 1973. A definition of humanism. In *The humanist alternative: Some definitions of humanism*, ed. P. Kurtz, 35–37. Buffalo, N, Y.: Prometheus Books.

Blakeslee, S. 1993. Seeing and imagining: Clues to the workings of the mind's eye. *New York Times*, 31 August 1993: C1, C7.

Bloom, A. 1987. *The closing of the American mind: Education and the crisis of reason*. New York: Simon and Schuster.

Bronowski, J. 1978. *The origins of knowledge and imagination*. New Haven: Yale University Press.

Bunkše, E. V. 1979. The role of a humane environment in Soviet urban planning. *Geographical Review* 69: 379–94.

———. 1981. Humboldt and an aesthetic tradition in geography. *Geographical Review* 71: 127–46.

———. 1990. Saint-Exupéry's geography lesson: Art and science in the creation and cultivation of landscape values. *Annals of the Association of American Geographers* 80: 96–108.

———. 1994. The emerging postindustrial landscape as exile and its possible consequences for sense of place. In *The spirit and power of place: Human environment and sacrality*, ed. R. P. B. Singh, 63–74. Varanasi, India: National Geographic Society of India.

Buttimer, A. 1974. *Values in geography*. Commission of College Geography, Resource Paper 24. Washington, D.C.: Association of American Geographers.

———. 1976. Grasping the dynamism of lifeworld. *Annals of the Association of American Geographers* 66: 277–92.

———. 1981. On people, paradigms, and "progress" in geography. In *Geography, ideology, and social concern*, ed. D. R. Stoddart, 81–98. Totowa, N. J.: Barnes and Noble.

———. 1983a. *The practice of geography*. London: Longman.

———. 1983b. *Creativity and context: A seminar report*. Lund, Sweden: The Royal University of Lund.

———. 1988. Personal communication.

————. 1993. *Geography and the human spirit*. Baltimore and London: Johns Hopkins University Press.

Camus, A. 1955. *The myth of Sysiphus and other essays*. New York: Random House.

————. 1963. *Notebooks 1935–1942*. New York: The Modern Library.

Cassirer, E. 1945. *Rousseau, Kant, Goethe*. Princeton: Princeton University Press.

————. 1974. *The logic of the humanities*. New Haven: Yale University Press.

Cobb, E. 1977. *The ecology of imagination in childhood*. London: Routledge and Kegan Paul.

Davenport, G. 1981. *The geography of the imagination*. San Francisco: North Point Press.

Descartes, R. 1960. *Discourse on method*. Baltimore: Penguin Books.

Dubos, R. 1972. *A god within*. New York: Charles Scribner's Sons.

Eco, U. 1990. *The limits of interpretation*. Bloomington, Ind.: Indiana University Press.

Ehrenfeld, D. 1978. *The arrogance of humanism*. New York: Oxford University Press.

Entrikin, N. 1976. Contemporary humanism in geography. *Annals of the Association of American Geographers* 66: 615–32.

Frye, N. 1983. *The critical path; An essay on the social context of literary criticism*. Brighton, Sussex: Harvester Press.

Giustiniani, V. R. 1985. Homo, humans, and the meaning of humanism. *The Journal of the History of Ideas*. 46: 167–95.

Glacken, C. J. 1965. This growing second world within the world of nature. In *Man's place in the island ecosystem: A symposium*, ed. F. R. Fosberg, 75–100. Honolulu: Bishop Museum Press.

————. 1966. Reflections on the man-nature theme as a subject for study. In *Future environments of North America*, ed. F. F. Darling and J. P. Milton, 355–71. Garden City, N. Y.: Natural History Press.

————. 1967. *Traces on the Rhodian shore*. Berkeley: University of California Press.

————. 1970a. Man against nature: An outmoded concept. In *The environmental crisis: Man's struggle to live with himself*, ed. H. W. Helfrich, Jr., 127–42. New Haven: Yale University Press.

————. 1970b. Man's place in nature in recent Western thought. In *This little planet*, ed. M. Hamilton, 163–201. New York: Charles Scribner's Sons.

Goodman, N. 1978. *Ways of worldmaking.* Indianapolis: Hackett Publishing Company.

Hadas, M. 1960. *Humanism: The Greek ideal and its survival.* New York: Harper.

Hassan, I. 1971. *The dismemberment of Orpheus: Toward a postmodern literature.* New York: Oxford University Press.

Heisenberg, W. 1971. Discussions about language. In *Physics and beyond,* ed. R. N. Anshen, 125–40. New York: Harper & Row.

Herder, J. G. von. 1807. *Stimmen der Völker in Liedern.* Tübingen: J. G. Gotta.

Hoffman, D. G. 1952. Historic truth and ballad truth: Two versions of the capture of New Orleans. *Journal of American Folklore,* 65: 295–303.

Johnston, R. J. 1987. *Geography and geographers: Anglo-American human geography since 1945.* London: Edward Arnold.

Kearney, R. 1988. *The wake of imagination: Toward a postmodern culture.* Minneapolis: University of Minnesota Press.

Kohák, E. 1984. *The embers and the stars.* Chicago: University of Chicago Press.

Kurtz, P. 1973. Epilogue: Is everyone a humanist? In *The humanist alternative: Some definitions of humanism,* ed. P. Kurtz, 173–86. Buffalo, N. Y.: Prometheus Press.

Lamont, C. 1982. *The philosophy of humanism.* New York: Frederick Ungar.

Lasch, C. 1984. *The minimal self: Psychic survival in troubled times.* New York: W. W. Norton.

Ley, D. and M. Samuels, eds. 1978. *Humanistic geography.* Chicago: Maaroufa Press.

Lopez, B. 1981. *Winter count.* New York: Charles Scribner's Sons.

———. 1986. *Arctic dreams: Imagination and desire in a northern landscape.* New York: Charles Scribner's Sons.

Lowenthal, D. 1961. Geography, experience, and imagination: Towards a geographical epistemology. *Annals of the Association of American Geographers* 51: 241–60.

———. 1985. *The past is a foreign country.* Cambridge: Cambridge University Press.

Lowenthal, D., and M. Bowden, eds. 1976. *Geographies of the mind: Essays in historic geosophy.* New York: Oxford University Press.

Lowenthal, D., and H. C. Prince. 1976. Transcendental experience. In *Ex-*

periencing the environment, ed. S. P. Wapner, S. B. Cohen, and B. Kaplan, 117–31. New York: Plenum Press.

Malraux, A. 1968. *Anti-memoirs*. New York: Holt, Rinehart and Winston.

Marsh, G. P. 1965. *Man and nature*, ed. D. Lowenthal. Cambridge, Mass.: John Harvard Library.

Maurina, Z. 1950. *Renesanse un mēs* (Renaissance and we). In *Tragiskais skaistums* (Tragic beauty), A. Maurina, 59–72. Chicago: Alfreds Kalnajs.

Meinig, D. W. 1971. Environmental appreciation: Localities as humane art. *Western Humanities Review* 25: 1–11.

———, ed. 1979. *The interpretations of ordinary landscapes*. New York: Oxford University Press.

———. 1983. Geography as an art. *Transactions of the Institute of British Geographers* N. S. 8: 314–28.

Miller, H. 1941. *The wisdom of the heart*. Norfolk, Conn.: New Directions Books.

Montaigne, M. de. 1910 [1588]. *The works of Michel de Montaigne*, 2 vols. New York: Edwin C. Hill.

Moravia, A. 1966. *Man as an end: A defense of humanism*. New York: Farrar, Straus and Giroux.

Moynahan, J. 1990. India of the imagination. *New York Times Book Review.* 15 July: 8.

Murdoch, I. 1977. *The fire and the sun: Why Plato banished the artists*. Oxford: Oxford University Press.

Newman, C. 1985. *The post-modern aura: The act of fiction in an age of inflation*. Evanston, Ill.: Northwestern University Press.

Nietzsche, F. 1971. *Also sprach Zarathustra*. Bern: Herbert Lang.

Norris, M. 1985. *Beasts of the modern imagination: Darwin, Nietsche, Kafka, Ernst, and Lawrence*. Baltimore: Johns Hopkins University Press.

Olson, C. 1967. Human universe. In *Human universe and other essays*, ed. D. Allen, 3–15. New York: Grove Press.

Olwig, K. 1984. *Nature's ideological landscape*. London: George Allen & Unwin.

Ortega y Gasset, J. 1957. *Man and people*. New York: W. W. Norton.

Orwell, G. 1949. *1984*. New York: Harcourt, Brace.

Paz, O. 1974. *Children of the mire: Modern poetry from Romanticism to the Avant-Garde*. Cambridge, Mass.: Harvard University Press.

Peters, Jānis. 1989. *Svētā mierā, sāpēs mūzīgās* (In holy peace, in eternal pain). Rīga: Liesma.

Pocock, D. C. D., ed. 1981. *Humanistic geography and literature: Essays on the experience of place.* London: Croom Helm.

———. 1988. Geography and literature. *Progress in Human Geography* 12: 87–102.

Rees, R. 1982a. In a strange land . . . : Homesick pioneers on the Canadian prairie. *Landscape* 26: 1–9.

———. 1982b. Constable, Turner, and views of nature in the nineteenth century. *Geographical Review* 72: 253–69.

Relph, T. 1981. *Rational landscapes and humanistic geography.* London: Croom Helm.

———. 1993. Responsive methods, geographical imagination and the study of landscapes. In *Remaking human geography,* ed. A. Kobayashi and S. Mackenzie, 149–63. Boston: Unwin Hyman.

Root-Bernstein, R. S. 1984. Creative process as a unifying theme of human cultures. *Daedalus* 113: 197–219.

Sartre, J. P. 1978. *The psychology of imagination.* London: Methuen.

Schorske, C. E. 1966. The idea of the city in European thought: Voltaire to Spengler. In *The historian and the city,* ed. O. Handlin and J. Burchard, 95–114. Cambridge, Mass.: MIT Press.

Singh, R. P. B., ed. 1994. *The spirit and power of place: Human environment and sacrality.* Varanas, India: National Geographic Society of India.

Snow, C. P. 1978. *The two cultures and a second look.* Cambridge: Cambridge University Press.

Sontag, S. 1982a. Against interpretation. In *Against interpretation,* S. Sontag, 3–14. New York: Farrar, Straus and Giroux.

———. 1982b. One culture and the new sensibility. In *Against interpretation,* S. Sontag, 293–304. New York: Farrar, Straus and Giroux.

Steiner, G. 1971. *In Bluebeard's castle: Some notes towards the redefinition of culture.* New Haven: Yale University Press.

Tuan, Y. F. 1971. Geography, phenomenology, and the study of human nature. *Canadian Geographer* 15: 181–92.

———. 1976a. Literature, experience, and environmental knowing. In *Environmental knowing: Theories, research, and methods,* ed. G. T. Moore and R. G. Golledge, 206–72. Stroudsburg, Pa.: Dowden, Hutchinson, and Ross.

————. 1976b. Humanistic geography. *Annals of the Association of American Geographers* 66: 266–76.

————. 1978. Literature and geography: Implications for geographical research. In *Humanistic geography*, ed. D. Ley and M. Samuels, 194–206. Chicago: Maaroufa Press.

————. 1982. *Segmented worlds and self: Group life and individual consciousness*. Minneapolis: University of Minnesota Press.

————. 1986. *The good life*. Madison, Wis. and London: University of Wisconsin Press.

Vācietis, O. 1988. *Ex Libris*. Rīga: Liesma.

Vico, G. 1948. *The new science of Giambattista Vico*. Ithaca, N. Y.: Cornell University Press.

Voltaire. F.-M. A. 1930. *Candide* [1759]. New York: Random House.

Warnock, M. 1976. *Imagination*. London: Faber & Faber.

Western, J. 1986. The authorship of places: Reflections on fieldwork in South Africa. In *Syracuse Scholar* 7: 4–17.

Wheeler, J. A. 1982. Bohr, Einstein, and the strange lesson of the quantum. In *Mind in nature*, ed. R. Q. Elvee, 1–30. San Francisco: Harper and Row.

Worringer, W. 1957. *Form in gothic*. New York: Schocken Books.

Wright, J. K. 1966. Terrae incognitae: The place of the imagination in geography. In *Human nature in geography*, ed. J. K. Wright, 68–88. Cambridge, Mass.: Harvard University Press.

14

Structure and Agency: Contested Concepts in Human Geography

Vera Chouinard

Debates about the relative significance and respective roles of human agency and social organization or structures in determining the course of societal change are as old as philosophy and science themselves. To inquire into the conditions that make human knowledge possible is to confront difficult questions about freedom and social constraints and about the extent to which human reasoning and comprehension are shaped either by individuals or by prevailing societal norms and power structures. The structure-agency debate, as it has been termed in recent years, also cuts across disciplinary boundaries and research programs; it surfaces in work on the philosophical underpinnings and societal applications of the natural and social sciences and in research throughout the social sciences, ranging across philosophical, theoretical, and methodological positions as diverse as behavioralism, humanism, structural-functionalism, feminism, Marxism, and postmodernism.

Nature and the Significance of the Structure-Agency Debate

Clearly, the concepts of structure and agency have a longstanding and central significance in scientific inquiry and a multiplicity of research origins. In this essay I focus on relatively recent attempts to develop critical social theories of structure and agency and to apply these concepts in explanations of social practices, struggles, and societal change. I emphasize, in particular, debates in critical social geography, where assessments of the relative merits of Marxist, post-Marxist, and postmodern perspectives have hinged on the structure-agency question. To help put these debates in context, the remainder of this section outlines the significance of the concepts of structure and agency for geographic research specifically and the social sciences generally. The second section explores the various conceptions of structure and agency employed in critical social theory in general and geography in particular. The third section assesses contemporary approaches to the structure-agency question in geographic research. I argue that very significant advances have been made in conceptualizing and demonstrating the complex linkages between structure, agency and societal change. There remains, however, a pressing need for further conceptual and empirical work on the precise ways in which social structures shape human action and on how people's practices help to perpetuate or challenge those structures. Recent Marxist and feminist work on the uneven development of class and gender relations and on the implications of these relations for social action and identities indicates promising ways of addressing these challenges in geographic research.

The concepts of structure and agency refer, respectively, to the basic organizational features of particular societies and people's capacities to act within this social context. Marxist geographers, for example, define social structure in terms of how the production of goods and services is organized in particular class societies. Social divisions in control over the resources needed to produce food, shelter, and other commodities give rise to class differences in economic and political power (e.g., to the control of industrial resources and wealth by the capitalist class and to working-class dependence on industrial employment under capitalism). Human agency is seen as being shaped by both social structure and conditions of daily life. People's capacities to act as agents of social change are limited in important ways by their position within the class structure. For instance, members of the working class must depend on the wages gained from employment in capitalist industries to meet basic household needs for food, shelter, and clothing because they lack the resources, such as investment capital and machinery, needed for independent production or self-employment; however, working-class capacities to effect social change are also influenced by conditions of daily life. Experiences of effective worker opposition to low-wage rates and hazardous working conditions in local industries, for example, can increase working people's capacities to contest capitalist control of the workplace by improving organizing skills and political morale (Edel 1981 provides a useful discussion of Marxist approaches to urban change; for discussions of recent geographic research, see Peet and Thrift, eds., 1989; Wolch and Dear, eds., 1989).

As the preceding example indicates, the concepts of structure and agency derive from specific theories of the dynamics of societal change; theories that include propositions about how organizational features of societies enable or constrain people's capacities to effect change and how people's practices in turn help to reinforce or challenge prevailing social relations or structures. The concepts of structure and agency are thus clearly of crucial importance for explanation in the social sciences because they help us to better understand the nature and use of power in society and the ways in which different social groups attempt to negotiate and challenge prevailing power relations.

In geography, recent debate over the structure-agency question has been sparked by discussion of the relative merits and limitations of Marxist and other critical theories of social change (see Peet and Thrift [1989] for an account of debates in the political economy literature). The past decade, in particular, has been a period of critical reappraisal of developments in Marxist geography and intense and lively debates about the contributions of feminist, humanist, and other critical perspectives to rethinking approaches to geographic research (Kobayashi and MacKenzie, eds., 1989; Peet and Thrift, eds., 1989; Wolch and Dear, eds., 1989; Saunders and Williams 1986, 1987; Harvey 1987; Smith 1987; Sayer 1987; Graham 1988; Dear 1988; Gregory and Walford, eds., 1989; Chouinard 1990a). A central theme in these debates has been the need for broader, more flexible conceptions of the social relations that constitute the structure of society and thereby help to empower and disempower specific groups within society (e.g., recognition that relations of gender, race, and ethnicity are as fundamental as class relations to the reproduction of power in contemporary societies). A related theme has been the need for more sophisticated conceptions of the nature and determinants of human agency: of the importance of subjective experiences in enhancing or limiting people's capacities for social action and of the power of discourses to invoke or silence particular voices and forms of knowledge.

Approaches to Conceptualizing Structure and Agency

Over the past two decades the structure-agency question has been at the heart of debates about critical social theory and methods in the social sciences.[1] As a result, many different and exciting conceptions of structure and agency are available for researchers to draw on. I concentrate in this section on those conceptions that have assumed central importance in geographic research since the 1970s. Geographers have, of course, been grappling with problems of structure and agency in various ways throughout the history of the discipline — debates about environmental determinism are a case in point (see James and Martin 1981) — but it has only been in recent years, as geographers have drawn on critical social theory, that the role of structure and agency in social change has become a pivotal issue in debates about geographic inquiry. My discussion therefore focuses on a crucial chapter in the development of geographic theories of structure and agency. Although important theoretical contributions outside the geographic literature are referenced, I make no attempt here to offer a comprehensive survey of developments in critical social theory. My discussion begins with early Marxist perspectives in the geographic literature. It then turns to humanist, feminist, and other critical perspectives and their role in encouraging a rethinking of Marxist conceptions of structure and agency in human geography, and concludes with a discussion of contemporary approaches to conceptualizing structure and agency in critical social geography.

Early Marxist Perspectives on Structure and Agency

The 1960s and 1970s saw the revival and rapid development of a Western Marxist tradition of research in the social sciences (see Anderson 1980, 1983). In geography a growing demand for social relevance in research and dissatisfaction with existing behavioral and neoclassical economic models of urban and regional change combined to encourage new interest in anarchist and Marxist social theories (see Peet 1977; Peet and Lyons 1981; Peet and Thrift 1989). Marxist geography laid the foundations for recent structure-agency debates by challenging prevailing assumptions of individual choice and consumer sovereignty and insisting that people's decisions and actions were highly constrained by their class position and role within the accumulation process. Harvey's (1973) *Social Justice and the City* provided a forceful critique of existing conceptions of urban and regional development and became symbolic of radical geographers' efforts to build a new tradition of geographic inquiry. Harvey (1973) explicitly rejected liberal conceptions of urban poverty and change as the outcomes of market decisions and policy failures and advanced in their place a Marxist conception of urban change as a process based on fundamental class inequalities in urban society and driven by the accumulation of wealth (or "social surplus") and the exploitation of subordinate classes by members of the ruling class. A key message of this early work was that human capacities for social action and change are shaped in very significant ways by people's positions within prevailing class relations or power structures; in other words, agency cannot be understood in isolation from class divisions in economic, political, and cultural power.

In retrospect, it is clear that some of this early research tended toward structural determinism, or structuralism, as it is sometimes called. That is to say, these scholars emphasized the causal significance of structural forces (e.g., contradictions or disruptions in the capital accumulation process) at the relative expense of human agency in their explanations of urban and regional change. Harvey (1973), for example, placed considerable emphasis on the notion that structures have their own internal logic or "transformation rules" (see also Peet and Thrift 1989). Phenomena such as housing submarkets and gentrification were sometimes depicted as being primarily the outcome of the exercise of class power through major institutions such as banks and development corporations; the role of class struggle, political experiences, and social practices received relatively little attention (Harvey and Chatterjee 1974; Smith 1979).

It is important to keep in mind, however, that to some extent the apparent structuralism of early Marxist conceptions of structure and agency in geography was a matter of emphasis rather than theorization. As Peet and Thrift (1989) point out, geographers did not embrace the extreme structuralism of the French Althusserian school (epitomized in the conception of human agents as the "bearers of structures") (see Althusser and Balibar 1970; Anderson 1980, 1983), nor were they content with conceptions of urban and regional processes that neglected human experiences and action. Paris (1974: 7), for example, stressed the importance of close attention to social struggles in radical analyses of urban change: "What, then, are the particular social processes affecting urban change, and how may we best conceptualize the social organization of urban structure? The first point to stress is that of the *differences* between cities in various social and political situations. We must also emphasize the importance of considering the role of *organized* collectivities of actors seeking to achieve shared and conflicting goals." Questions about political advocacy and the role of geographers and social scientists as advocates were also central to early work in radical geography (see for example, Breitbart 1972). Harvey (1978) argued that changes in the built environment of cities were as much a result of struggles over a whole way of life (between workers and capitalists) as of the process of accumulating wealth or capital from investment in urban property and redevelopment.

Rethinking the Structure-Agency Question

By the late 1970s debates about Western Marxist conceptions of structure and agency were intensifying within the social sciences. The decade had seen major advances in Marxist conceptions of the links between structure and agency, including detailed work on cultural forces shaping experiences of capitalist societies, in-depth historical analyses of the concrete development of class relations and working-class experiences in particular localities, and close investigation of the role of class divisions and conflict in struggles over state development (Anderson 1980, 1983; Williams 1973, 1980; Foster 1977; Jessop 1982; Poulantzas 1978; Esping-Anderson et al. 1976; Wright 1979). As Anderson (1980, 1983) demonstrates, these advances were made possible by the development of new Western Marxist traditions of inquiry in the 1960s and 1970s, traditions that built on both humanistic and structuralist reinterpretations of classical Marxist texts (such as *Capital* and the *Grundrisse*), the work of the Frankfurt School and Gramsci, and ground-breaking research by a new generation of left-wing scholars in the West. This innovative research included E. P. Thompson's (1969) monumental *Making of the English Working Class*—a study that celebrated working people's experiences of and struggles over the transition to industrial capitalism in Britain and that continues to inspire social historians today. It also included Althusser's painstaking efforts to develop the philosophical, methodological, and conceptual tools that might enable Western Marxism to steer a middle course between the radical, descriptive humanism espoused by analysts such as Thompson and the social determinism of Eastern interpretations of Marxism (see Althusser and Balibar 1970; Althusser 1969, 1971; and Anderson 1980, 1983). Students of the French Althusserian school, such as Poulantzas and Castells, in turn, made major contributions to efforts to develop more convincing, rigorous, and theoretically informed Marxist explanations of such phenomena as changes in the class composition of advanced societies, state intervention in urban and regional development, and changes in the form and functions of cities (Poulantzas 1974, 1976, 1978; Castells 1979).

E. P. Thompson's (1978) passionate polemic against Althusser's structural Marxism, "The Poverty of Theory or an Orrery of Errors," helped to force concerns about structural determinism and the perceived marginalization of human experiences and action as forces of social change in structural explanations to the forefront of academic debate. Unfortunately, as Anderson (1980) has demonstrated, Thompson's polemic was seriously misleading: not only did it fail to convey the significance given to human agency in structural Marxist theory (e.g., the centrality of questions about how people come to identify in practice with ideologies of the ruling class), but it was silent on key issues in conceptualizing the linkages between structure and agency (such as the role of class alliances and state intervention in shaping social experiences, practices, and struggles). This meant, in turn, that Thompson's proposals for more humanistic Marxist explanations of social change were at times based on little more than an emotional appeal to "resist theory." This polarization of debate was unfortunate because many of these issues had been addressed (albeit imperfectly) by researchers influenced by the French structuralist school. Nonetheless, the debates of the 1970s intensified efforts to develop more sophisticated Marxist conceptions of the role of human agency in social change—conceptions that treated both human experiences and actions and societal structure as mutual determinants of social outcomes. These efforts had contributed to significant advances in conceptualizing linkages between agency and structure in Marxist geography specifically and in the social sciences generally by the early 1980s. There was increased attention, for example, to how people's relations with state agencies and bureaucrats and their political organizing strategies helped to shape their responses to such aspects of urban change as downtown renewal and the ghettoization of service-dependent populations (see Fincher 1981; Dear and Scott, eds., 1981). Dear (1981), for instance, argued that the social and spatial exclusion of the mentally ill in urban areas was perpetuated in part through hierarchial relations of authority between clients and state bureaucrats. Fincher's (1981) study of urban renewal in Boston demonstrated how a complex set of implementation strategies was used by state agencies in order to defuse and deflect public opposition to redevelopment and to create a profitable urban environment for corporate capital.

Despite these advances, humanist geographers began to voice dissatisfaction with Marxist conceptions of structure and agency. Central to this early humanist critique was the (incorrect) notion that the structural tradition of Western Marxist inquiry was so firmly entrenched and pervasive in Marxist geographic research that advances in conceptualizing and explaining the role of human agency in urban and regional change were precluded by this grand "metatheoretical" tradition (Eyles 1981; Duncan and Ley 1982). Duncan and Ley's (1982) characterization of Marxist geographic research as irredeemably flawed by structural determinism initiated an intense debate between Marxist and other critical social geographers over the structure-agency question (see Chouinard and Fincher 1983; Walker and Greenburg 1982a, 1982b). This debate continues today and has been broadened and enriched by the contributions of feminist geographers and proponents of structuration theory and postmodernism. Before turning to these developments, however, I want to focus on how the humanist critique encouraged a rethinking of the structure-agency question.

Although the early humanist critique failed to appreciate significant advances in Marxist conceptions of structure and agency and the modest extent of structural Marxism's influence in geography, it served as an important catalyst for improvements in conceptions of structure and agency in Marxist geography and encouraged geographers to explore the merits of critical social theories such as structuration (Giddens 1981, 1984). In particular, the humanist critique reemphasized the need for more sophisticated conceptions of the forces shaping people's subjective experiences, of the role of these experiences in shaping people's practices and struggles, and of the significance of subjective knowledge in scientific accounts of social change—all of which remain significant themes in political economy research in geography during the 1990s (see Thrift and Peet, eds., 1989). The humanist critique also helped pave the way toward discussions of a common ground between humanistic and other critical traditions in human geography. Humanistic research methods in socialist-feminist investigations, for example, have documented the ways in which gender relations shape women's capacities to cope with industrial change and have accented the importance of narrative (as distinct from analysis) in political-economic accounts of regional change (Kobayashi and Mackenzie, eds., 1989; Sayer 1989a, 1989b).

The search for more flexible, less deterministic conceptions of structure and agency encouraged some scholars to consider Giddens's theory of structuration as a possible complement or alternative to Marxist perspectives. Giddens envisages structuration theory as a comprehensive alternative to Marxist social theory; arguing that it avoids structural determinism through constant emphasis on the interplay of structure and agency, offers a broader conception of social power as the outcome of struggle over allocative and authoritative resources (i.e., material wealth and decision-making power, respectively), and recognizes the significance of spatial organization in the structuration of social relations (Giddens 1981, 1984). Critics point out that the virtues of Giddens's proposed theory over Marxist alternatives may be more apparent than real. Not only does Giddens's theory fail to make a convincing case for key theoretical propositions, such as the alleged dominance of authoritative power in noncapitalist societies (Wright 1983), but in many respects it serves more as a general checklist of forces to be considered in analysis rather than as a substantive conceptualization of the processes of social change (Fincher 1987; Gregson 1986).

Whatever its substantive limitations, structuration theory has influenced the course of debate about the roles of structure and agency in critical social geography. This influence consists not so much of direct, empirical applications of Giddens's theory in geographic analysis (but see Pred 1983, 1984a, 1984b; Dear and Moos 1986; Moos and Dear 1986; Warf 1990) as of extensions to and enrichment of critical theories of the political economy of urban and regional change (Thrift 1983; Gregson 1987; Walker 1989; Thrift and Peet 1989).

Structuration theory has helped highlight, for example, the need for closer attention to how social meanings are signified (represented) and conveyed and to how particular social practices and relations are legitimated. Gregory (1989: 375) points out that Giddens's conceptualization of "time-space distanciation" tends to emphasize the role of structures of domination in the allocation of social resources at the relative expense of signification and legitimation—processes that Giddens argues to be of equivalent importance in understanding the contradictions or tensions between the immobility of spatial structures and their capacity to stretch across time and space. Structuration theory has also reinforced longstanding claims, by Harvey (1973, 1982, 1989) and Soja (1980, 1989) in particular, that the spatiality of social life plays a central role in determining how structure and agency combine to alter class societies. Through its emphasis on structuration processes it has encouraged recursive rather than linear conceptions of the relation of structure and agency, that is, conceptions of duality (or mutual constitution) rather than of dualism (or linear causation) (Gregory 1989: 354).

The humanist critique and structuration theory, by challenging Marxists and other social geographers to refine their conceptions of structure and agency, have helped geographers to improve their explanations of the role of structure and agency in social change. Feminist research, however, has gone a step further. By rocking the foundations of critical conceptions of human agency and oppression, feminist theory has enriched the conceptual and methodological tools of geographers and other social scientists and brought new insights about the ways in which human agency challenges and perpetuates existing power structures. Feminist research and debate expanded rapidly in the social sciences during the 1980s. This work included challenges to prevailing (male-dominated) conceptions of objectivity and rationality in scientific practice, to critical social theories that ignored or marginalized gender relations as axes of social power and oppression, and to modes of theorizing that perpetuated conceptual dichotomies or dualisms that masked the social forces giving rise to the oppression and silencing of women (e.g., public-private, subject-object, production-reproduction) (Miles and Finn, eds., 1989; Harding, ed. 1987; Mackinnon 1989; Bowlby, Lewis, McDowell, and Foord 1989). In geography, existing conceptions of structure and agency, including Marxist approaches, have been most directly and forcefully challenged from socialist-feminist perspectives (e.g., McDowell 1983; Massey 1983; but see Foord and Gregson 1986; McDowell 1986; and Johnson 1987 for arguments that hint in passing at the influence of radical feminism and Bondi 1990a, 1990b, and Massey 1991 for arguments influenced by postmodern feminist thought). Through exciting and innovative studies this research has demonstrated that the reproduction of class inequalities and power in capitalist cities and regions cannot be understood in isolation from gendered social divisions and forms of oppression (Nelson 1986; McDowell 1983; Bowlby 1984; Massey 1983, 1984; Peake 1988; Fincher 1989). Nelson (1986), for instance, shows how the suburbanization of back offices in the San Francisco Bay region has been intimately linked to a corporate search for a relatively immobile, white, well-educated but docile female labor force—a labor force concentrated in suburban rather than central city locations. Massey (1983, 1984) shows some of the ways in which both gender and class relations have been transformed through industrial restructuring in Britain: the decline of traditional industry in the coal-mining regions, for example, has meant not only changes in class relations and conflict (e.g., increased control of local industries by capital external to the region and decline in traditional, male-dominated unions), but also a transformation in male and female roles in the workplace and households as male unemployment has risen and women have been employed in new, branch-plant operations. This research has also shown that the social construction and experience of gender is of fundamental importance to processes of urban and regional change: determining among other things the roles that women may play in industrial and domestic labor processes and women's capacities to effectively contest conditions of everyday life in the workplace and community (Mackenzie 1988, 1989; Bondi and Peake 1988; Peake 1990; Rose 1989; Kofman and Peake 1990). Rose (1989), for example, indicates how the gentrification of three Montreal neighborhoods is linked to the expansion of professional jobs within the service sector, rising female employment in professional occupations, and the needs of nontraditional households (such as those headed by female professionals) for central residential locations (e.g., to facilitate access to specialized services such as daycare).

It is important to emphasize that the feminist contribution to rethinking the structure-agency question in critical social geography has gone well beyond empirical demonstration of the difference that gender makes (e.g., the differences between male and female travel behavior and needs) to make major advances in conceptualizing urban and regional development as gendered processes (see also McDowell 1989; Mackenzie 1988; and Bowlby, Lewis, McDowell, and Foord 1989). Gender relations are conceptualized as as integral to the reproduction of social power and oppression within the home, workplace, and residence community as are class relations. Both gender and class formation (i.e., the concrete development of specific gender and class relations) are seen as playing central roles in shaping people's experiences of class societies and their capacities to effect social change (McDowell 1986; Mackenzie 1988; Moss 1993; Fincher 1991, 1993). Socialist-feminist research thus has broadened critical conceptions of social structure by treating gender and class as fundamental elements in the organization and dynamics of industrial and so-called post-industrial societies. Simultaneously, the feminist critique has encouraged Marxist and other critical theorists to adopt more nuanced conceptions of human agency, which accommodate the role of gender inequalities in shaping people's capacities to act and, in a normative sense, challenge the class and patriarchal power structures of contemporary societies. Whether this encouragement will translate into major changes in critical social geography remains to be seen, because, as Bondi (1990b) and Massey (1991) note, much of the literature continues to suffer from sexism in conceptual approaches and research design.

Of all the recent contributions to rethinking the structure-agency question in critical social geography, those offered from a postmodernist perspective are perhaps the most difficult to characterize and assess. This reflects, on the one hand, the recency of this perspective's introduction into the geographic literature (dating from the late 1980s) and, on the other, the ambiguities in understanding structure and agency that are central to the postmodernist project. By distancing critical analysis from the modernist fascination with rationality, logic, and totalizing explanation, postmodernists celebrate uncertainty, indeterminacy, pluralism, and particularity as keys to the critical understanding of social life. Gregory (1989b: 348–49) summarizes the postmodernist challenge:

> [P]ostmodernism can be seen to mark an unprecedented crisis of intellectual activity within the contemporary crisis of modernity. The debate then has the liveliest of implications for the project of a critical human geography (and critical theory more generally) because it raises acute questions about the very possibility of critique itself. More directly, is there anything which entitles us to redeem the Enlightenment project and reaffirm our faith in rationality? to think of human history as an epic of progress? to be optimistic about the advance of science and the improvement of the human condition? Or are the resources of modernity so exhausted that we feel only incredulity toward those who seek to breathe new life into them? Ought we, instead, to take nihilism seriously and unmask the "will to power" which supposedly lies behind all systems of reason?

It would be misleading, at least right now, to suggest that we can distill in any definitive way what the new postmodern perspective on structure and agency is from proposals for reviews of postmodern geographic research (see in particular Gregory 1989; Soja 1989; Dear 1988, 1994). The literature does, however, provide a few hints of some of the conceptual elements or fragments that might contribute to a postmodern perspective on structure and agency. One such element is the notion of the duality of structure and agency, which, simply put, implies that structures and agency are mutually constituted and simultaneous or coexistent (i.e., structures are only created and re-created through the practices of agents and the practices of agents are always shaped by the structures of authority and power to which people's practices give rise). Gregory (1989a: 354) argues that this notion of duality, central to Giddens's work on structuration, challenges dualistic conceptions of the causal relation between structure and agency and society and space. The duality thesis therefore helps to challenge linear, temporal accounts of social phenomena by insisting that spatiality, or the way in which agency and structure combine in particular places, is central to the course of social change. Despite protestations to the contrary, these basic premises of the duality thesis are not peculiar to postmodern social theory, but have been fundamental to both feminist and Marxist conceptions of social change (in the geographic literature, see Kobayashi and Mackenzie, eds., 1989; Walker 1985; Peet and Thrift 1989; Soja 1979, 1985, 1989). Like these other research traditions, then, a postmodern reconceptualization of structure and agency would emphasize that the spatiality of structuration, or the uneven development of social relations, experiences, and capacities for action, plays a central role in determining whether and how prevailing patterns of power and privilege will be perpetuated and challenged in particular places by giving rise to significant differences in social conditions (e.g., the extent to which industry is dominated by capitalist social relations) and ways of life (e.g., the political forms that working-class and feminist organizing has taken) between places. Where a postmodern conception of structure and agency would presumably differ from these other approaches in the geographic literature is in a relatively greater emphasis on social conditions of being (as opposed to becoming) as the key to understanding social experience and change. That is to say, an emphasis on how the postmodern condition of rapid change, shifting and fragmented cultural imagery, multiple and overlapping social mechanisms of discipline and regulation, and the differentiation of political struggles and social landscapes helps to perpetuate social power and privilege (even as its social forms and mechanisms are transformed) and individualizes and fragments experiences of social power and change. Unlike dialectical conceptions of social change, which focus on the transformative potential of particular modes of social organization and practice (e.g., on how difficulties in Fordist production encouraged the development of post-Fordist production relations and techniques), the postmodern perspective stresses the indeterminacy of social outcomes: contemporary changes in cities and regions are as likely to signal social stasis as transformation. Gregory's (1989a, 1989b) use of Giddens's, Habermas's, Foucault's, and Hägerstrand's work as bases for a new postmodern human geography points toward such a reconceptualization of human agency, structure, and social change, although the premises and details of such an approach have yet to be spelled out in the geographic literature.

Like feminism and Marxism, postmodernism also promises to alter our conceptions of structure and agency through the critique of existing views of scientific knowledge and explanation. In contrast to positivist and neopositivist views of science as objective and value free, these critical perspectives recognize that scientific knowledge and practices are socially constructed and value laden. It follows that science often serves to perpetuate the interests of the economic and political elite at the expense of subordinate groups such as the working class and women (Harvey 1984; Massey 1991; Bondi 1990b). Feminism and postmodernism also share a concern for overcoming dualisms in scientific thought (e.g., personal-political, subjective-objective, subject-object) that falsely oppose particular aspects of social experience and change and in so doing encourage mis-specification of the processes leading to particular social outcomes. With feminism, the emphasis has been on affirmation that personal experience is socially constructed and politically relevant and that women's subjective knowledge is of key importance in critical accounts of social change (both in terms of rejecting positivist claims of scientific objectivity and of insisting on the validity and importance of women's accounts of social processes) (Mackinnon 1989; Harding 1991).

Nonfeminist postmodernism, in contrast, has combined skepticism about the enlightenment project of objective scientific knowledge with an emphasis on the fragmentary, shifting, and ephemeral nature of knowledge and experience. The latter condition not only precludes any total or certain understanding of social phenomena, but, at least in more extreme versions of postmodernism, implies that people's capacities to make sense of social processes are as limited by the complexity and pace of social change (i.e., their condition of being) as by the structure and exercise of power (Dews 1987; Soja 1989; Harvey 1989; Ross, ed., 1988). In moderation the postmodern critique provides a useful corrective to the worst pretensions of modern science. It reminds us, for example, that advances in scientific knowledge or understanding are halting, contradictory, fragmented, and often illusory rather than linear and cumulative, and it recognizes that in our struggles to better understand social change, our reach frequently exceeds our grasp. We must therefore look to the puzzles and silences in our understanding if we hope to develop a better critical understanding of the causes of contemporary social conditions and the prospects for change. This is a key message, for example, of Soja's (1989: ch. 9) provocative geographic essay "Taking Los Angeles Apart." Here, Soja concentrates on the conundrums in Los Angeles's development and in people's attempts to understand that development. What is it that is so mesmerizing about the "dream machine" (entertainment industry), for instance, that its image often masks the complex and diverse industrial landscapes of Los Angeles? How is it that this metropolis, which has so long defied the conceptions and categorizations of urban theory, seems to epitomize so many facets of contemporary urban development and change? What are we to make of the numerous and multiple forms of protection and surveillance at work in an urban landscape that so successfully conveys messages of freedom, choice, and the fulfillment of desires and dreams?

In different ways, then, the Marxist, feminist, and postmodern critiques of science remind us that scientific discourses and practices play an important role in limiting people's capacities to act as agents of social change and in per-petuating prevailing power relations or structures. Science not only helps to structure or constitute human agency, it is also the product of human agents who act under conditions of social inequality and flux—conditions that too often silence and marginalize the voices and practices of dissent. Ironically, for example, feminist perspectives and concerns have been notably absent from recent proposals for postmodern geographic inquiry and marginalized within applied research in critical social geography (see Bondi 1990b; Massey 1991).

Contemporary Approaches to Conceptualizing Structure and Agency

Recent debates have enriched and broadened the conceptions of structure and agency used in geographic research and promise to stimulate significant advances in the future. In concluding this discussion of conceptual approaches in critical social geography, I outline the key features of contemporary Marxist and socialist-feminist perspectives on structure and agency as exemplars of two of our most fully developed approaches. As indicated above, however, it is im-portant to bear in mind that these approaches have evolved through close di-alogue with other critical traditions (notably, humanism, structuration theory, and postmodernism), and they will continue to do so in response to critiques offered from these and other perspectives.

Contemporary Marxist and socialist-feminist conceptions of structure and agency in the geographic literature are characterized by relatively inclusive views of the social relations constituting the structure of society and by a non-deterministic view of the role of structural forces in social change, that is, by an emphasis on how social structure limits rather than directly determines so-cial action and experience (for elaboration and illustration, see Edel 1981; Esping-Anderson et al. 1976; Wright 1979; Chouinard and Fincher 1987; Chouinard 1990b, 1994a; Bowlby, Lewis, McDowell, and Foord 1989). A case in point is the response of Marxist geographers to critiques of class re-ductionism or essentialism (particularly from a feminist perspective). Their work has gradually, but increasingly, acknowledged that gender, ethnicity, and race play as vital a role as class relations in the division and exercise of power in industrial and postindustrial cities and regions and that definitions of social structure must be broadened accordingly (Massey 1983, 1984; Mc-Dowell 1983; Bowlby 1984; Bowlby, Lewis, McDowell, and Foord 1989; Rose 1989; Fincher 1989; Nelson 1986; Jackson 1988). This is not to say that all Marxist geographers are attentive to the role of gender and race (on the con-trary, much work remains relatively gender and race blind), nor that Marxists and feminists necessarily agree on how to conceptualize the role of gender in social processes (as, for example, debates in *Antipode* indicate: Foord and Gregson 1986; McDowell 1986; Knopp and Lauria 1987; Gier and Walton 1987; Johnson 1987), but Marxist and socialist-feminist geographers do increasingly concur on the need for inclusive conceptions of structure and agency that recognize that social processes are mediated by gender, ethnicity, sexuality, and ability as well as class (Chouinard and Grant 1995).

The dialogue between Marxist and feminist geographers has given rise to a continuum of perspectives on structure and agency. At one end are Marxist conceptions that regard class relations as the fundamental determinants of social power and hence of structural limits to human action, while acknowledging that gender and other nonclass social relations play contingent roles in shaping the course and outcome of social processes, such as class conflict over changes in industrial production or state programs in particular places. Society, then, is conceptualized as necessarily structured by class inequalities and only contingently so by nonclass relations such as gender and race. Examples of such an approach include Massey (1983, 1984), Smith and LeFaivre (1984), Chouinard (1989a), and Harvey (1989).[2] Smith and LeFaivre (1984), for example, argue for a class analysis of gentrification which treats gentrification as the outcome of redevelopment pressures associated with capital accumulation in the urban built environment but recognizes as well that the gentrification process encompasses and transforms the whole range of social relations that sustain a way of life within particular neighborhoods (e.g., relations of kinship and ethnicity, traditions of mutual aid, and political organizing).

Toward the midpoint of the continuum are conceptualizations of structure and agency that imply that both class and gender are necessary to the power structure of industrial and postindustrial societies and that these social relations therefore intertwine to shape the course and outcome of such processes as local state development, gentrification, back office relocation, transformations in urban form and functions, and women's political struggles (Fincher 1989; Rose 1989; Nelson 1986; Mackenzie 1988; Kofman and Peake 1990; McDowell 1986). Human agency is, therefore, necessarily constrained by both class and gender. McDowell (1986), for example, has argued for a class-based explanation of women's subordination, which treats the gender division of labor (e.g., women's material dependence on male breadwinners during periods of pregnancy and infant care) as the outcome of contradictory pressures within advanced capitalist societies to facilitate capitalist appropriation of surplus labor in the short term while simultaneously ensuring the reproduction of wage laborers in the long term. The perpetuation of male authority over women within the exploited classes helps to ensure that women will continue to perform necessary, unpaid domestic labor within the home (e.g., child care, meal preparation, cleaning) and be available as a relatively docile, low-paid pool of wage labor for capitalist businesses and state agencies.

At the other end of the continuum are socialist-feminist conceptions of structure and agency that define social structure and the structural limits to human action primarily in terms of gendered power relations. This approach regards patriarchal gender relations as the central cause of gender inequality and women's oppression; the class relations of capitalism and the processes to which these give rise are either treated as the general historical context in which these gender divisions arise, rather than as causal forces that shape gender relations and roles, or they are not explicitly considered at all. An example of the former approach is Bowlby's (1984) account of the ideologies shaping retail planning in Britain. An example of the latter approach is Brownhill and Halford's (1990) discussion of feminist struggles to promote women's interests within local government in Britain. In explaining why only certain local authorities adopted women's initiatives during the 1980s Brownhill and Halford (1990: 411) write: "Evidence suggests that the reason why only certain local authorities chose to set up *women's* initiatives arises from variations in local gender relations, which in turn are connected to variations in feminist political activity and ultimately in distinctive local policy outcomes." Similarly, their account of the barriers or blockages to women's initiatives within the local state focuses on the patriarchal nature of local state relations:

> Bringing about positive changes for women continues to face the same old problems. All kinds of political forums and institutions appear to house vested male interests. Particular concepts of power, government and bureaucracy associated with the local state are male-biased and resistant to feminist social change. . . . Neither is community politics a political haven for women. . . . It is another of the interconnections that the very same blocks, particularly in the shape of male power and the definition of issues as politically important, have been shown to operate outside the state as well. (Brownhill and Halford 1990: 412)

In addition to these various positions in debate, contemporary conceptualizations of structure and agency in Marxist and feminist research have been characterized by a growing interest in social identities and how these are formed in the course of living within specific places and through particular daily relations and even struggles (Massey 1992; Chouinard 1995). This interest in how ways of being translate into place-specific ways of living and constructing social relations reflects concerns to further problematize agency (e.g., to recognize diversity in subjective knowledges). These concerns are in part a response to postmodernism's destabilization of universal conceptions of knowledge and identity. They are also indicative of a more general shift toward conceptions of structure and agency that emphasize diversity in the living of social relations of power and the consequences of that diversity for social change.

Conclusions: Structure, Agency, and Geographic Research

What are the advantages and limitations of these several conceptions of structure and agency for geographic research? In this concluding section I outline some of the ways in which they have advanced our understanding of social change and the challenges that remain.

Conceptions of structure and agency that recognize the role of gender and other nonclass social relations in social change have contributed to more supple and nuanced accounts of the complex causality of the geography of capitalist societies (see Edel 1981 for a discussion of the differences between complex causal and other Marxist explanations of urban phenomena). Significant advances in conceptualizing and explaining the uneven development of state institutions, procedures, and regulations between regions and localities have been made. For example, Duncan and Goodwin (1988) show how the uneven development of local state institutions and programs in Britain is linked to particular local conditions and relations of political struggle against central state authority (e.g., differential responses to the Thatcher regime's policies of intervention in local state activities through such measures as rate capping and abolition). Duncan, Goodwin, and Halford (1988) demonstrate as well the significance of local gender relations and traditions of political organizing around women's issues in shaping collective struggles to advance women's rights and welfare through the local state. In my own work on the evolution of assisted housing programs in postwar Canada and experiences of co-op housing programs in particular localities (Chouinard 1990b, 1990c) I argue that the uneven development of state programs, procedures, and social relations must be understood as the outcomes both of changing conditions of capitalist accumulation, social regulation, and state formation in specific periods and of the diverse ways in which these structural limits to state development are manifested and experienced in particular localities as a result of differences in local state intervention in housing issues, the local housing market, and the politics of community organizing around housing and redevelopment issues. An important advantage of such nondeterministic explanations of the geography of the state is their emphasis on the role of human agency in transforming state institutions, policies, and procedures. They encourage, for instance, close attention to how local experiences of state policies, procedures, and struggles constrain or enhance people's capacities for collective opposition to prevailing power relations in and against the state (Chouinard and Fincher 1987; Chouinard 1989b, 1989c, 1990d).

Among the challenges facing geographers who wish to apply these more flexible conceptions of structure and agency in their research, three are particularly pressing. First is the need for better theories of processes of social marginalization, oppression, and exclusion. As noted above, analysts increasingly concur that gender, race, ethnicity, and class relations are interrelated causes of social power and oppression in contemporary capitalist societies. It is, however, one thing to recognize that these interrelations exist and quite another to sort out how these relations intertwine to produce particular social outcomes (e.g., to specify the range of processes through which a gendered division of domestic labor is produced within the home). Debate continues in the geographic literature on, for example, the extent to which women's oppression can be explained in terms of the role of gender divisions in sustaining the reproduction of wage labor. Socialist-feminists argue that the subordination of women by men plays a necessary, central role in facilitating the appropriation of surplus labor by capital (e.g., via women's roles as unpaid domestic laborers in the home) and that it is in women's role in reproduction that class and gender combine to perpetuate women's oppression. Other analysts contend that women's oppression cannot be explained quite so directly by the dynamics of capitalism—that patriarchy is sustained as well by processes, such as the construction of women as objects of male sexuality and violence, which cannot be explained solely in terms of the requirements of specific modes of production and reproduction (see in particular the 1986 and 1987 exchanges in *Antipode*). Such debates are indicative of important ambiguities in current conceptualizations of the processes contributing to the marginalization, oppression, and exclusion of disadvantaged social groups and of the need to develop theoretical perspectives that do not require an a priori reduction of the causes of social oppression to a single category of social relations (e.g., class).

Such perspectives would recognize the multiple origins and forms of social oppression in contemporary societies and that it is in part through fragmentation of social identities and roles on the basis of class, gender, race, ethnicity, physical and mental abilities, age, and religious/political beliefs that social regulation and oppression are realized and sustained. This recognition does not necessarily require acceptance of the radical eclecticism in social theory and explanation that is currently fashionable among critical social geographers (see, for example, Knox 1991, Ley 1991, and Fincher's 1983 discussion of the inconsistencies of eclecticism). It does, however, require acceptance of the idea that processes of marginalization, oppression, and exclusion are sustained by a multiplicity of social relations in contemporary capitalist societies—social relations that derive from precapitalist and capitalist modes of social organization as well as from movements prefiguring new power relations and ways of life (such as socialism and feminism).

A second challenge is to further explore the role of subjective experiences in shaping human agency and capacities to contest the existing social structure. Recent studies that focus on class and gender formation (i.e., the translation of specific experiences of social change into class and gender positions and roles and propensities for social action) offer promising steps in this direction (Fincher 1989; Rose 1989, 1990; Mackenzie 1988; Chouinard 1989a; Moss 1989).

A third and very important challenge is to avoid the temptation to erect new, exclusionary accounts of structure and agency in our struggles to overcome the limitations of existing critical perspectives. Feminist geographers have quite rightly taken to task recent Marxist and postmodern proposals for geographic research for failing to seriously engage feminist insights on the central role of gender relations in social change and on how Western science works to silence voices of dissent (Massey 1991; Bondi 1990). It is equally important, however, to acknowledge that feminist geography does not somehow transcend or develop outside these problems of engagement and silencing (it is undoubtedly true that feminist work is in some respects carried on outside dominant male projects—see Christopherson 1989—but it does not follow from this that the research is therefore free of such difficulties). Further engagement with nonmainstream feminisms (e.g., black as opposed to white middle-class feminism) is necessary, for instance, if feminist geographers are to develop relatively nonexclusionary accounts of the causes and consequences of women's oppression. Similarly, continued serious engagements with nonfeminist radical geographic analyses are essential if feminists are to avoid gender reductionism in their analyses of causes and consequences of social oppression. It is vital as well to take feminist critiques of universality seriously and admit the real silences in existing socialist-feminist accounts of geographic change—the voices of disabled women are notably absent, for instance. The point here is not that feminists are especially likely to fall into the trap of erecting new, exclusionary orthodoxies; in fact, they are probably among the least likely. The point is rather that at times of especially vigorous debate and enthusiasm for new ways of rethinking structure and agency it is particularly easy to adopt categorical or dichotomous ways of thinking (us-them, gender-blind/gender-sensitive, reductionist-expansive, exclusionary-inclusionary) that not only polarize debate, but also convey the (false) message that one's chosen research perspective is free of the old problems and dilemmas.

As the preceding comments suggest, Marxist and socialist-feminist geographic research have made major conceptual and empirical contributions to more flexible, critical conceptions of the nature of structure and agency and their role in geographic change. Thanks to these advances, we are beginning to understand the complex ways in which gender and class intertwine to shape urban and regional change, that transformations in the form and function of cities have been shaped as much by gendered social divisions in the workplace, home, and community as they have been by class inequalities in the control of production and conditions of everyday life (see Mackenzie 1988 for a fascinating argument along these lines with respect to the geographic evolution of Canadian cities). We are also better able to understand how the fragmentation of social relations and roles that accompanies the uneven development of regulatory institutions and practices (e.g., state agencies) serves to limit, contain, and deflect collective challenges to prevailing power relations and forms of social oppression and exclusion under capitalism. Many exciting challenges in refining Marxist and socialist-feminist conceptions of structure and agency remain. These include, for example, the development of more inclusionary theories of social oppression and marginalization and further exploration of the impacts of male-defined sexuality and social norms on people's experiences of urban and regional change and their capacities to contest social oppression. Such work may help us explain how urban and regional spaces come to be socially and spatially constructed in ways that exclude, marginalize, and victimize people on the basis of gender, class, age, race, physical and mental abilities, sexual preference, and other characteristics, and doing so will help us work toward more democratic and humane societies.

Although many challenges remain, critical analyses of structure, agency, and geographic change have made impressive advances since the early 1970s. The on-going debates about structure and agency, in combination with increasingly innovative applied research, suggest that geographers will continue making important strides throughout the 1990s and will play a significant role in developing novel approaches to structure and agency in the social sciences.

Notes

1. By "critical," I refer to approaches that are self-consciously aware of prevailing social relations and conditions and that are concerned with demonstrating how this societal context influences the distribution of social power and human welfare, i.e., approaches that treat the organization of society as a key causal force in the distribution of power between social groups and the social outcomes of urban and regional change. Clark and Dear (1981) capture the difference between mainstream and critical social theories of the state by distinguishing between "theories of the state in capitalism" and "theories of the capitalist state," respectively.

2. Harvey (1989) does, however, acknowledge the need to treat relations such as gender as omnipresent components of power structures and social practices (355).

References

Althusser, L. 1969. *For Marx.* London: Penguin.

———. 1971. *Lenin and philosophy and other essays.* New York: Monthly Review Press.

Althusser, L., and E. Balibar. 1970. *Reading Capital.* London: New Left Books.

Anderson, P. 1980. *Arguments within English Marxism.* London: New Left Books and Verso.

———. 1983. *In the tracks of historical materialism.* London: Verso.

Bondi, L. 1990a. Landscapes of change: Masculinity and femininity in the city. Paper presented at the Annual Meeting of the Association of American Geographers, Toronto, Canada, 19–22 April.

———. 1990b. Feminism, postmodernism, and geography: Space for women? *Antipode* 22: 156–67.

Bondi, L., and L. Peake. 1988. Gender and the city: Urban politics revisited. *Women in cities: Gender and the urban environment,* ed. J. Little et al., 21–40. London: MacMillan.

Bowlby, S. 1984. Planning for women to shop in postwar Britain. *Environment and Planning D* 2: 179–99.

Bowlby, S. A., L. Lewis, L. McDowell, and J. Foord. 1989. The geography of gender. *New models in geography,* 2 vols., ed. R. Peet and N. Thrift, vol. 2, 157–75. London: Unwin Hyman.

Breitbart, M. 1972. Advocacy in planning and geography. *Antipode* 4: 64–68.

Brownhill, S., and S. Halford. 1990. Understanding women's involvement in local politics: How useful is a formal/informal dichotomy? *Political Geography Quarterly* 9: 396–414.

Castells, M. 1979. *The urban question.* Cambridge, Mass.: MIT Press.

Chouinard, V. 1989a. Class formation, conflict, and housing policies. *International Journal of Urban and Regional Research* 13: 390–416.

———. 1989b. Explaining local experiences of state formation: The case of cooperative housing in Toronto. *Environment and Planning D* 7: 51–68.

———. 1989c. Social reproduction and housing alternatives: Cooperative housing in postwar Canada. In *The power of geography*, ed. J. Wolch and M. Dear, 222–37. London: Unwin Hyman.

———. 1989d. Transformations in the capitalist state: The development of legal aid and legal clinics in Canada. *Transactions of the Institute of British Geographers* N. S. 14: 329–349.

———. 1990a. Rethinking Marxist geography: Advances and challenges. Paper presented to the Annual Meeting of the Association of American Geographers, Toronto.

———. 1990b. The uneven development of capitalist states: Theoretical proposals and an analysis of postwar changes in Canada's assisted housing programs. *Environment and Planning* A 22: 7–18.

———. 1990c. The uneven development of capitalist states: 2—The struggle for cooperative housing. *Environment and Planning* A 22: 1441–54.

———. 1990d. State formation and the politics of place: The case of community legal aid clinics. *Political Geography Quarterly* 9: 23–38.

———. 1994. Geography, law, and legal struggles: Which ways ahead? *Progress in Human Geography* 18(4): 415–40.

———. N. d. Challenging law's empire: Ontario's legal aid clinics. Unpublished manuscript.

Chouinard, V., and R. Fincher. 1983. A critique of "Structural Marxism and human geography." *Annals of the Association of American Geographers* 73: 137–46.

———. 1987. State formation in capitalism: A conjunctural approach. *Antipode* 19: 329–353.

Chouinard, V., and A. Grant. 1995. On being not even anywhere near the project: Ways of putting ourselves in the picture. *Antipode* 27: 137–66.

Christopherson, S. 1989. On being outside "the project." *Antipode* 21: 83–89.

Clark, G., and M. Dear. The state in capitalism and the capitalist state. In *Urbanization and urban planning in capitalist society*, ed. M. Dear and A. Scott, 45–62. London: Methuen.

Dear, M. 1981. Social and spatial reproduction of the mentally ill. In *Urbanization and urban planning in capitalist society*, ed. M. Dear and A. Scott, 481–500. London: Methuen.

———. 1988. The post-modern challenge: Reconstructing human geography. *Transactions of the Institute of British Geographers* N. S. 13: 1–13.

———. 1994. Postmodern human geography: A preliminary assessment. *Erkunde* 48: 2–13.

Dear, M., and A. Moos. 1986. Structuration theory in urban analysis 2: Empirical application. *Environment and Planning A* 18: 351–73.

Dear, M., and A. Scott, eds., 1981. *Urbanization and urban planning in capitalist society.* London: Methuen.

Dews, P. 1987. *Logics of disintegration: Poststructuralist thought and the claims of critical theory.* London: Verso.

Duncan, J., and D. Ley. 1982. Structural Marxism and human geography: A critical assessment. *Annals of the Association of American Geographers* 72: 30–59.

Duncan, S., and M. Goodwin. 1988. *The local state and uneven development.* Oxford: Polity Press.

Duncan, S., M. Goodwin, and S. Halford 1988. Policy variations in local states: Uneven development and local social relations. *International Journal of Urban and Regional Research* 12: 107–128.

Edel, M. 1981. Capitalism, accumulation, and the explanation of urban phenomena. In *Urbanization and urban planning in capitalist society,* ed. M. Dear and A. Scott, 19–41. London: Methuen.

Esping-Anderson, G., R. Friedland, and E. O. Wright. 1976. Modes of class struggle and the capitalist state. *Kapitalistate* 4/5: 186–220.

Eyles, J. 1981. Why geography cannot be Marxist: Towards an understanding of lived experience. *Environment and Planning A* 12: 1371–88.

Fincher, R. 1981. Local implementation strategies in the urban built environment. *Environment and Planning A* 13: 1233–52.

———. 1983. The inconsistency of eclecticism. *Environment and Planning A* 15: 607–22.

———. 1987. Space, class, and political processes: The social relations of the local state. *Progress in Human Geography* 11: 496–516.

———. 1989. Class and gender relations in the local labor market and the local state. In *The power of geography: How territory shapes social life,* ed. J. Wolch and M. Dear, 93–117. London: Unwin Hyman.

———. 1991. Caring for workers' dependents: Gender, class, and local state practice in Melbourne. *Political Geography Quarterly* 10: 356–81.

———. 1993. Women, the state and the life course in urban Australia. In *Full circles: Geographies of women over the life course,* ed. C. Katz and J. Monk, 243–63. London: Routledge.

Foord, J. and N. Gregson. 1986. Patriarchy: Towards a reconceptualization. *Antipode* 18: 186–211.

Foster, J. 1977. *Class struggle and the industrial revolution.* London: Methuen.

Giddens, A. 1981. *A contemporary critique of historical materialism.* London: Macmillan.

————. 1984. *The constitution of society.* Cambridge: Polity Press.

Graham, J. 1988. Post-modernism and Marxism. *Antipode* 20: 60–66.

Gregory, D. 1989a. The crisis of modernity? Human geography and critical social theory. In *New Models in Geography,* 2 vols., ed. R. Peet and N. Thrift, 2: 348–85. London: Unwin Hyman.

————. 1989b. Areal differentiation and post-modern human geography. In *Horizons in human geography,* ed. D. Gregory and R. Walford, 67–96. Totowa, New Jersey: Barnes and Noble.

Gregory, D., and R. Walford, eds. 1989. *Horizons in human geography.* Totowa, N. J.: Barnes and Noble.

Gregson, N. 1986. On duality and dualism: The case of structuration and time geography. *Progress in Human Geography* 10: 184–205.

Grier, J., and J. Walton. 1987. Some problems with reconceptualising patriarchy. *Antipode* 19: 54–58.

Harding, S. ed. 1987. *Feminism and methodology.* Bloomington and Indianapolis: Indiana University Press and Milton Keynes Open University Press.

————. 1991. *Whose science? Whose knowledge?* Ithaca, N. Y.: Cornell University Press.

Harvey, D. 1973. *Social justice and the city.* Baltimore: Johns Hopkins University Press.

————. 1978. Labor, capital and class struggle around the built environment in advanced capitalist societies. In *Urbanization and conflict in market societies,* ed. K. R. Cox, 9–37. Chicago: Maaroufa Press.

————. 1982. *The limits to capital.* Chicago: University of Chicago Press.

————. 1987. Three myths in search of a reality in urban studies. *Environment and Planning D* 5: 367–76.

————. 1989. *The condition of postmodernity.* Oxford: Blackwell.

Harvey, D., and L. Chatterjee. 1974. Absolute rent and the structuring of space by governmental and financial institutions. *Antipode* 6: 22–36.

James, P. E., and G. J. Martin. 1981. *All possible worlds: A history of geographical ideas,* 2d ed. New York: John Wiley and Sons.

Jessop, B. 1982. *The capitalist state.* Oxford, England: Martin Robertson and Company.

Jackson, P. 1988. Social geography: Social struggles and spatial strategies. *Progress in Human Geography* 12: 263–69.

Johnson, L. 1987. Patriarchy and feminist challenges. *Antipode* 19: 210–15.

Knopp, L., and M. Lauria. 1987. Gender relations and social relations. *Antipode* 19: 48–53.

Knox, P. 1991. The restless urban landscape: Economic and sociocultural change and the transformation of metropolitan Washington, D.C. *Annals of the Association of American Geographers* 81: 181–209.

Kobayashi, A., and S. MacKenzie, eds. 1989. *Remaking human geography.* London: Unwin Hyman.

Kofman, E., and L. Peake. 1990. Into the 1990s: A gendered agenda for political geography. *Political Geography Quarterly* 9: 313–36.

Ley, D. 1991. The inner city. In *Canadian cities in transition*, ed. T. Bunting and P. Filion, 313–48. Oxford, England: Oxford University Press.

Mackenzie, S. 1988. Building women, building cities: Toward gender sensitive theory in the environmental disciplines. In *Life spaces*, ed. C. Andrew and B. Moore, 13–30. Vancouver: University of British Columbia Press.

———. 1989. Restructuring the relations of work and life: Women as environmental actors, feminism as geographical analysis. In *Remaking human geography*, ed. A. Kobayashi and S. Mackenzie, 40–61. London: Unwin Hyman.

Mackinnon, C. 1989. *Toward a feminist theory of the state.* Cambridge, Mass.: Harvard University Press.

Massey, D. 1983. Industrial restructuring as class restructuring: Production decentralisation and local uniqueness. *Regional Studies* 17: 73–89.

———. 1984. *Spatial divisions of labor: Social structures and the geography of production.* London: Methuen.

———. 1991 Flexible sexism. *Environment and Planning D* 9: 31–57.

McDowell, L. 1983. Towards an understanding of the gender division of urban space. *Environment and Planning D* 1: 59–72.

———. 1986. Beyond patriarchy: A class–based explanation of women's subordination. *Antipode* 18: 311–21.

Miles, A. and G. Finn, eds. 1989. *Feminism: From pressure to politics*, 2d ed. Montreal: Black Rose Books.

Moos, A. and M. Dear. 1986. Structuration theory in urban analysis 1: Theoretical exegesis. *Environment and Planning A* 18: 231–52.

Moss, P. 1993. Gender formation in waged labor processes. Unpublished doctoral dissertation, Department of Geography, McMaster University.

————. 1989. Production and reproduction in the commodification of domestic labor. Unpublished doctoral research proposal, Department of Geography, McMaster University.

Nelson, K. 1986. Labor demand, labor supply and the suburbanization of low wage office work. In *Production, work and territory*, ed. A. J. Scott and M. Storper, 149–71. Boston: Allen and Unwin.

Paris, C. 1974. Urban renewal in Birmingham, England: An institutional approach. *Antipode* 6: 7–15.

Peake, L. 1990. Race, gender, and household survival strategies: The spatial reproduction of social inequality. Research seminar, Department of Geography, McMaster University.

Peet, R. 1977. The development of radical geography in the United States. *Progress in Human Geography* 1: 64–87.

Peet, R., and J. V. Lyons. 1981. Marxism: Dialectical materialism, social formation, and the geographic relations. In *Themes in geographic thought*, ed. M. E. Harvey and B. P. Holly, 187–205. London: Croom Helm.

Peet, R., and N. Thrift, eds. 1989. *New models in geography*, 2 vols. London: Unwin Hyman.

Poulantzas, N. 1974. *Classes in contemporary capitalism*. London: New Left Books.

————. 1976. The capitalist state: A reply to Miliband and Laclau. *New Left Review* 95: 63–83.

————. 1978. *State, power, and socialism*. London: New Left Books.

Pred, A. 1983. Structuration and place: On the becoming of a sense of place and structure of feeling. *Journal for the Theory of Social Behaviour* 13: 45–68.

————. 1984a. Place as historically contingent process: Structuration and the time–geography of becoming places. *Annals of the Association of American Geographers* 74: 279–97.

————. 1984b. Structuration, biography formation, and knowledge: Observations on port growth during the late mercantile period. *Environment and Planning D* 2: 251–76.

Rose, D. 1989. A feminist perspective of employment restructuring and gentrification: The case of Montreal. In *The power of geography*, ed. J. Wolch and M. Dear, 118–38. London: Unwin Hyman.

————. 1990. Collective consumption revisited: Analyzing modes of provision and access to childcare services in Montreal, Canada. *Political Geography Quarterly* 9: 353–80.

Ross, A. ed. *Universal abandon?: The politics of postmodernism.* Minneapolis: University of Minnesota Press.

Saunders, P., and P. Williams. 1986. The new conservatism: Some thoughts on recent and future development in urban studies. *Environment and Planning D* 4: 393–99.

———. 1987. For an emancipated social science. *Environment and Planning D* 5: 363–500.

Sayer, A. 1989a. On the dialogue between humanism and historical materialism in geography. In *Remaking human geography,* ed. A. Kobayashi and S. Mackenzie, 206–26. London: Unwin Hyman.

———. 1989b. The "new" regional geography and problems of narrative. *Environment and Planning D* 7: 253–76.

Smith, N. 1979. Toward a theory of gentrification: A back-to-the-city movement by capital, not people. *Journal of the American Planning Association* 45: 538–48.

———. 1987. Rascal concepts, minimalizing discourse, and the politics of geography. *Environment and Planning D* 5: 377–83.

Smith, N., and M. LeFaivre. 1984. A class analysis of gentrification. In *Gentrification, displacement and neighbourhood revitalization,* ed. J. Palen and B. London, 43–64. Albany, N. Y.: State University of New York Press.

Soja, E. 1980. The sociospatial dialectic. *Annals of the Association of American Geographers* 70: 207–25.

———. 1989. *Postmodern geographies: The reassertion of space in critical social theory.* London: Verso.

Thompson, E. P. 1969. *The making of the English working class.* London: Penguin.

———. 1978. The poverty of theory or an orrery of errors. In *The poverty of theory and other essays,* 1–120. New York and London: Monthly Review Press.

Thrift, N. 1983. On the determination of social action in space and time. *Environment and Planning D* 1: 23–57.

Walker, R. A., and D. A. Greenburg. 1982a. Postindustrial and political reform in the city: A critique. *Antipode* 14: 17–32.

———. 1982b. A guide for the Ley reader of Marxist criticism. *Antipode* 14: 38–43.

Warf, B. 1990. The reconstruction of social ecology and neighbourhood change in Brooklyn. *Environment and Planning D* 8: 73–96.

Williams, R. 1980. Base and superstructure in Marxist cultural theory. *Problems in materialism and culture*. London: Verso (orig. pub. *New Left Review*, vol. 82, 1973).

Wolch, J., and M. Dear, eds. 1989. *The power of geography: How territory shapes social life*. London: Unwin Hyman.

Wright, E. O. 1979. *Class, crisis, and the state*. London: Verso.

————. 1983. Giddens' critique of Marxism. *New Left Review* 138: 11–36.

15

Feminism and Human Geography

Mona Domosh

Unlike many of the other conceptual terms that have entered geographical discourse in the past twenty years (Marxism, structuralism, postmodernism), *feminism* provides neither a methodology nor a theory for human geography, although methodological and theoretical stances have been derived from it. Rather, feminism as it was originally introduced to geography had a far more radical goal—it provided a political basis for a critique of the practices of geography, practices that had allowed for the invisibility of women as both practitioners in the field and objects of inquiry. Unlike other such terms, *feminism* was not a mode of analysis borrowed from some other social science where its implications had already been thought through; rather, it developed out of the direct political imperatives of the women's liberation movement of the 1960s, a movement that based its politics on personal experiences. As Robin Morgan wrote in 1970 in the landmark book *Sisterhood is Powerful,*

> Women's liberation is the first radical movement to base its politics—in fact, create its politics—out of concrete personal experiences. We've learned that those experiences are not our private hang-ups. They are shared by every woman, and are therefore political. The theory, then, comes out of human feeling, not out of textbook rhetoric. That's truly revolutionary, as anyone knows who's ever listened to abstract political speeches. (Morgan 1970: xvii–xviii)

Morgan was giving full voice to the slogan developed out of the 1960s women's movement—that the personal is political. Taken unambiguously, the slogan was indeed revolutionary. It implied a blurring of categories of

411

thinking that had been kept separate throughout much of contemporary Western thinking—the division between the personal/private and public worlds and between the domestic realm and the political realm. This separation had allowed the personal world to be thought of as natural, not subject to the same contingencies as the political, public world. By blurring these heretofore separate categories feminists hoped to show how personal lives were as subject to political and social negotiation as was the economy or the state, thereby opening up the personal, private world to political scrutiny and action.

Not all of the sectors of the women's movement interpreted the slogan so vigorously, least of all those in the academy, particularly geography. The first efforts to address the problem of the "missing female geographer" (Zelinsky 1973) developed out of a slightly different emphasis in feminist thought, and it is therefore important here to outline briefly the historical context of feminism and its developments in the late 1960s and 1970s.

The feminist movement of the 1960s was in many respects a new creation. The ferment of activity that characterized the early years of the century seemingly ended with the passage of the Nineteenth Amendment granting women the vote. In the following decades little activity in the area of women's rights was apparent, but that began to change in the post-World War II years. For many women the war years provided them with the first opportunity to participate in the paid labor force and to gain some degree of economic independence, but that empowerment was short-lived. The ideological commitment to a particular type of family structure (the nuclear family) and role for women within that structure (as a mother and housewife) became explicit after the war, when many government policies actively supported programs that it saw as essential for the return to the traditional family. Through both propaganda and effective legislation the federal government made clear that women's place was indeed in the home. In order to strengthen the postwar economy and provide jobs, education, and housing for the returning GIs, the government enacted policies that provided low-interest housing loans and free higher education for the returning soldiers. With such government support and with the development of the Levittown-type, mass-produced housing projects, residential construction in the new suburban areas boomed (Hayden 1985). The new middle-class suburb of this era embodied the ideology of the traditional family as it replicated and further supported the separate spheres of workplace and domestic life.

The message of Betty Friedan's *The Feminine Mystique*, published in 1963, was aimed directly at the women in these suburbs, and the book has been credited with the reawakening of interest in feminism in America (Nicholson 1986). Friedan gave voice to many of these women's dissatisfaction with their restricted lives as she uncovered and exploded the myth of the happy housewife. This dissatisfaction led many of these middle-class white women to join the paid workforce, and there they were confronted directly with the institutional barriers to equal employment opportunities, equal pay, and other more subtle but no less powerful personal forms of sexism. It was this double malaise—a dissatisfaction with the role of housewife and a recognition of the structures that kept women out of other arenas of life—that precipitated the contemporary women's movement.

As that movement began to take shape in the mid-1960s, it became apparent that what was meant by feminism and its political agenda was not unambiguous, and by the 1970s at least three different strains of feminist thought were identifiable. Liberal feminism developed out of the need to eliminate the structural barriers that stood in the way of women entering the nondomestic world. Its agenda was established with the formation of the National Organization of Women (NOW) in 1966 and the bill of rights that the group endorsed. Included in those demands was the passage of the Equal Rights Amendment, enforcement of sex discrimination laws in employment, guarantees of maternity leave rights, and provisions for child care centers. The major concern here was to make it easier for women to participate in nondomestic activities, and the emphasis was on changes in the legal system and the powers of the state. Although later on this strain of political thought in feminism would concern itself more with personal issues, such as reproductive rights and pornography, its major emphasis continued to be with changing the structures of the state, not of the family or economy. It is from within this particular line of thinking that geography first entered into the feminist discussion, as some of its practitioners began to examine the institutional barriers that had prevented women from entering the field. Geography's interest in feminism has since converged with other important types of feminism that are outlined here.

Radical feminism began with a dissatisfaction on the part of women active in NOW who found that the organization was not attacking the root causes of sexism, which they felt rested in the larger political and social system. Instead of focusing attention on changing laws, as liberals did, radical feminists focused their attention on changing how people lived their personal lives. Their critique led to an understanding of how the roles of femininity and masculinity structured situations in which women were always inferior.

> The norms embodied in femininity discouraged women from developing their intellectual, artistic, and physical capacities. It dissuaded women from thinking of themselves and from being thought of by others as autonomous agents. Whereas "masculinity" embodied certain traits associated with adulthood, such as physical strength, rationality, and emotional control, "femininity," in part embodied traits associated with childhood, such as weakness and irrationality. (Nicholson 1986: 28)

Such interest in the construction of sex roles inevitably led to concern for the family, where those roles were initially played out. The political agenda took a distinctly personal turn as radical feminists began to explore the cultural construction not only of femininity and masculinity, but of sexuality and personal relationships.

The third strain of feminism developed out of the Marxist/socialist political movement of the late 1960s and 1970s. Although the relationship between Marxism and feminism has always been an ambivalent one, the analysis of the origins of a class-based society that Marxism provided did afford valuable insights into the origins of gender divisions of labor and the evolution of a hierarchical societal structure where women had less power than men. Socialist feminists view the patriarchal system as part of a more general social structure that is characterized by a class system and therefore see patriarchy not as a stable, unchanging concept, but as one that varies through time and place. Race, class, and gender are all seen as variables in systems of dominance and oppression. Strict Marxist analysis relies, however, on economic explanations of oppression and thereby looks to fundamental changes in the economic system to eradicate inequalities in the state and in the family. Such a focus has been at the root of the dissatisfaction with Marxism of many feminists, who claim that gender divisions of society are not derived from the economy, but are equally fundamental to societal structures. This debate continues and is apparent in geography.

These different strains of feminism are all visible in geography, and they serve as organizing categories for this essay.

Feminism in the Academy

As a theory originally derived from personal experiences and from political movements, feminism entered the academy on shaky ground; yet the women's liberation movement of the 1960s had succeeded in raising awareness of the pervasiveness of sexism in society, and it soon became apparent that such sexism was mirrored in scholarship. Women were either invisible in scholarly writing, or they were somehow distorted by the male-defined disciplines. The first task of feminist scholars, then, became the identification of male bias in the methods, theories, and results of research (Dubois et al. 1985). It was in history that one of the first full critiques of disciplinary traditions was undertaken (Gordon 1972). Women had been rendered invisible in history because what had been defined as subjects worthy of the historians' attention were invariably male defined — wars, politics, and activities of the public sector. Women had traditionally participated in the more private world of the family and of community life, subjects that had been accorded far less stature in the historical record. This recognition led to a critique of one of the bases of history, the notion of periodization. Kelly-Gadol showed that the traditional markers of historical periods were based on male activities, that the periods were differentiated by the changing status of men, and that women's status oftentimes was not changed in the same direction (1975). Other, similar critiques could be found, for example, in anthropology (Slocum 1975), philosophy (Garside 1971), and literature (Showalter 1971).

From this basis, feminist scholarship began to expand beyond the level of critique into theory construction. Much of the original theoretical focus concerned the nature and causes of women's oppression. For example, anthropologists began to question the origins of women's oppression, with two different theories emerging as explanatory. The first followed a Marxian framework and looked for the sources of women's oppression in the economic conditions of society. The second considered women's child-bearing capacity as the source of oppression, thereby arguing that women's oppression was not dependent on external factors such as the economy, but on the conditions of their own physical being. Both theories were found unsatisfactory—the first because it suggested that sexual and gender relations were secondary to economic relations in structuring society; the second because it posited women's "natural" condition as the source of oppression, thereby accepting the "naturalness" of a particular family and sexual structure in society. Gayle Rubin was the first to suggest an alternative to these theories. She traced the history of women's oppression to the development of a "sex gender system," which, as she explained it, is the "set of arrangements by which a society transforms biological sexuality into products of human activity, and in which these transformed sexual needs are satisfied." (Rubin 1975: 159). Rubin thus questioned not only the naturalness of gender relations, but also of sexual relations, challenging the notion of an unmediated division between male and female and therefore of obligatory heterosexuality.

Taken together, the development of these theories and the debates that they elicited represent one of the most provocative theoretical constructions in the academy and indicate the power of feminist theory. This concern with the forces of women's oppression and liberation provides a unifying theme in feminist scholarship. For DuBois et al., this concern "underlies all feminist scholarship, implicitly or explicitly, and provides a common framework and language for scholars in different disciplines and for intellectuals within and outside the academy" (1985: 87). The notion of women's oppression was, however, originally derived from political discourse, not from any disciplinary tradition "within the academy" (1985: 87). No one discipline could adequately theorize a concept that requires insights derived from cultural, economic, social, and psychological studies. This emphasis on understanding women's oppression, therefore, meant that much feminist scholarship became interdisciplinary. Throughout the 1970s and 1980s feminist theories began to focus not only on the origins of women's oppression, but on the construction of sexist ideology and how it perpetuates and legitimizes women's oppression and on the interaction between the public and private spheres, since this separation parallels the hierarchical separation of the sexes in the modern world (DuBois et al. 1985).

Feminism in geography shares this common concern with understanding women's oppression—first, with the oppression of women within the discipline of geography itself and, second, with women's oppression as it operates in the geographic world.

Historical Context of Geography

The politics of consciousness-raising groups and women's self-help clinics did not accord readily with the standards of "hard" science practiced by the social sciences in the early 1970s. Logical positivism in geography took the form of the quantitative revolution, a revolution that was meant to place mainstream geography within the confines of a "proper" science. Value neutrality guided research methodology, and the goal of such research was the prediction of geographical processes. The world view created and legitimized by such practices privileged the universal over the specific, the constant over the changing, and the certain over the ambiguous. Theory that was derived from a politics of feeling, of the specificity of concrete personal experiences, was completely outside the prevailing norms of social science as it was practiced in the 1960s. In addition, as Hanson and Monk have pointed out, positivism is a "method that tends to preserve the status quo" (Monk and Hanson 1982: 12). Because of its explicit attempt to separate values from scientific research, positivism was certainly not conducive to any feminist political agenda.

Because it was kept out of the mainstream, feminism was at times allied with Marxism, particularly in the early 1970s, and many of the first feminist articles were published in *Antipode* (see Burnett 1973; Hayford 1974). Both of these outsider positions were political by nature, but their agendas were quite different. As I have already pointed out, the Marxist emphasis on the economy as the arena for social change relegated the analysis of the family and personal relationships to a derivative position. The feminist agenda thus was not of prime importance to Marxists, and, as Seager points out, by the late 1970s "women in geography (as in the women's movement at-large) were largely disenchanted with the very male and often misogynist left-wing" (Seager 1992: 315).

In addition, there were profound differences between Marxism and feminism as critical modes of inquiry. As hostile as Marxism was to the prevailing conservativeness of geographical discourse in the late 1960s and early 1970s, it did not provide any real epistemological or methodological threat to the status quo of geographical inquiry. Marxist analysis, in fact, fit the prevailing scientific assumptions and methods of geography; it shared in the world view that privileged the universal over the specific and provided explanations of social worlds based on certain governing laws. Certainly, the conclusions Marxists drew as to the causes of social problems were far from the mainstream, yet, although Marxism as a mode of analysis differed from the mainstream, it did not force a qualitative break from it. Feminism, however, contained the potential for such a break, as did other new modes of thinking that were being introduced into geography in the 1970s, such as phenomenology and existentialism. These more humanistic ways of thinking emphasized individuals and their decisions, thus opening the way for studies of personal lives, feelings, and values. Much of the contemporary feminist literature in geography emerged from this particular context—but I am getting ahead of the story here, because the original feminist impetus in geography concerned the very political question of why there were so few women practitioners in the field, not necessarily why geography was hostile to feminist theory. Although recent critiques of science have shown how the two issues are fundamentally related (Harding 1986), for the sake of clarity I will keep them separate.

Women in Geography

Liberal feminism as a political movement forced an awareness of the lack of women in geography and the particular biases within the discipline that had exacerbated the more general societal inequalities. Zelinsky's "missing female geographer" (1973) raised a series of issues about the practitioners and practices of geography.

> The weak showing of the female geographer does not necessarily reflect any inherent weakness of intellect or character. The immediate causes are the institutional rules, traditions, and biases, usually unspoken and unwritten, of the organizations in which they are trained and employed. And the ultimate culprit is the sexist structure of the larger social system, with its very easy, highly divergent socialization of the two sexes, a theme that would require several major volumes for adequate treatment. (1973: 104)

A delineation of those traditions, rules, and biases that Zelinsky referred to has since become a focus of work in feminist geography, although it was not for ten years or so after this that feminists began to study the issue in detail.

Mildred Berman's 1984 article outlining her personal experiences as a professional geographer touched on many of the explicit as well as subtle sexist practices of the discipline, and Janice Monk's (1989) study of women in geographic institutions from 1900 to 1950 shows how pervasive sexism was and is in geography.

Certainly, sexism was a reflection of larger societal inequalities, yet there were and are practices particular to geography that served to create an overwhelmingly male atmosphere. For example, the discipline's traditional associations with fieldwork—in both the Sauerian tradition and the regional geography approach of Hartshorne—served to exclude women. Although women explorers in the late nineteenth and early twentieth centuries had gained some degree of authority in geography by their claims for the insights of personal experiences, and had therefore staked their claim to an early form of fieldwork, the codification of fieldwork as scientific activity at the turn of the century had systematically excluded women (Birkett 1989; Middleton 1982). As Stoddart points out, by the end of the nineteenth century "the systematic and organized accumulation of knowledge during planned investigations became the central objective" (1986: 150), and the context of women's lives precluded such investigations. Denied their one source of authority in geography, women remained outside the academic walls of the discipline throughout most of the nineteenth and early twentieth centuries. By the mid-twentieth century, when systematic fieldwork was theoretically considered open to women, social constraints continued to deter most of them. The same male club atmosphere in which such early professional organizations as the Royal Geographical Society and the American Geographical Society were fostered pervaded the field camps and trips of graduate schools of geography. Such practices, combined with the more general institutional biases, prevented most women from entering the professional academy. In addition, as I already have pointed out, geography's association with logical positivism in the 1970s served to discourage women who were interested not in mathematical, abstracted models, but in fostering social change.

Geography of Women

Following the work done in allied fields such as history and anthropology, feminist geographers very early turned their attention to the geography of women, delineating the reasons that women and their worlds had been ignored as objects of inquiry. After reading most of the geographic literature in the 1970s, it would have been easy to conclude that the world was populated only by men—that they were the only ones to create places and structure spaces. Feverish activity by feminists in geography led to a series of studies that tried to compensate for this huge gap in the geographic literature by making the world of women visible (Zelinsky, Monk, Hanson 1982; Mazey and Lee 1983; Holcomb 1984). Many of the early studies were influenced by Marxist theory and thereby used a materialist analysis to criticize geographic models for not including women (Burnett 1973; Hayford 1974). This led to a series of studies of urban structure that included the world of women—women as decisionmakers in the urban setting (McDowell 1983), as factory workers (Christopherson 1983), and as urban decisionmakers in transportation planning (Hanson and Pratt 1988; Pratt and Hanson 1988). The so-called humanistic/historical side of geography led to landscape studies of the traditional domain of women—the home and its design, use, and meaning (Loyd 1981; Seager 1988). These were landscapes that had been ignored by traditional cultural geographers, who considered the step into the interior of the home beyond their domain. A capstone to this work, a series of atlases that graphically depicted the world of women, appeared in the mid-1980s (Seager and Olson 1986; Gibson and Fast 1986; Shortridge 1987).

In 1982 Hanson and Monk summarized many feminist concerns by outlining how sexism had infiltrated the content, method, and purpose of geographic inquiry, and their analysis stands as one of the most comprehensive explanations of women's invisibility in geography. Their goals in writing the piece indicate the type of feminism prevalent at the time. "Although we encourage an awareness of gender differences and of women's issues throughout the discipline now (so that the geography of women does not become 'ghettoized'), we would like to see gender blurred and then erased as a line defining inequality" (Hanson and Monk 1982: 19–20). Hanson and Monk hoped eventually to incorporate gender and women's issues into geographic theory. The goal was implicitly guided by a political philosophy of liberal feminism — that with a recognition of women's rights and the elimination of unequal practices, sexism would be eradicated. Their goal, then, was to eliminate sexist practices and to include the world of women in geographic theory.

Feminist Theory in Geography

A more radical stance was taken by some geographers who looked at gender as a fundamental category not only of our social world, but of our ways of thinking and knowing that world. Here, the emphasis shifts from women as objects of study to women as active knowers and as subjects of inquiry, the goal being the articulation of theory itself from the perspective of women's experiences. This radical stance required an examination of those experiences, of how it is that the cultural construction of gender shapes our personal, social, and political reality. In geography this meant examining how women's lives shape their experience and/or perception of environments, their design and creation of places, their definition and use of cultural resources, and their construction of geographic knowledge.

Inspired by such works as Annette Kolodny's *The Land Before Her* (1984), geographers began to examine women's perceptions of the American West. Janice Monk's and Vera Norwood's *The Desert is No Lady* (1988) portrays how women's experiences of place (the American Southwest) constitute a way of knowing and imbuing the world with meaning that is different from men's: "The essays offer new visions of women's engagement with the landscape and a fresh assessment of their part in defining the meaning of the region within American culture" (Monk and Norwood 1988: 2). Jeanne Kay (1990) has looked at the history of women's encounter with the American frontier, suggesting that women's experiences tell a far less heroic story than do men's experiences. Close studies of women's lives and particularly their work in the agricultural sector of the Third World has forced a reassessment of development theories and strategies for economic aid (Momsen and Townsend 1986). Suzanne's Mackenzie's book *Visible Histories* (1989) relates the stories of women living in postwar Brighton, highlighting their active role in shaping the postwar urban environment. These women's stories suggest the inseparability of work from home and of private from public, thereby calling into question a basic assumption of traditional geographic theory.

The relatively recent discussions within geography and the other social sciences concerning what has come to be called the condition of postmodernity have raised issues that in many senses dovetail with those raised by feminist theory. Postmodernism has forced a questioning of our deeply embedded ways of thinking and has exposed previously hidden assumptions about how we know and represent our geographic world. Although the relationship between feminism and postmodernism is often seen as ambivalent (Nicholson 1990), and many cautions have been issued from feminists concerning the politics of postmodernism (Mascia-Lees et al. 1989; Bondi and Domosh 1992), its overarching critical stance toward modernity and transcendent forms of knowledge has made it a natural ally of feminism. Postmodern thinking in geography has opened the doors of discussion to the issue of representation, to critiques of universal and transcendent forms of knowing, and to an awareness of the situatedness of all knowledge claims (see chapter 16).

From the perspective of women's experiences, feminist geographers have begun to show how much geographic thinking and theory construction has been not only sexist, in that it supports a society dominated by men, but phallocentric, as it posits a masculine way of thinking as universal and subordinates the feminine to that of the "other" (Rose 1993). This critique of geographic knowledge construction is supported by work in other fields, particularly anthropology, sociology, and the philosophy of science (Harding 1986, 1991; Mascia-Lees 1989). Critiques in geography include discussions of its professional practices (Domosh 1991; Blunt and Rose 1994) and its theories of economic development (Momsen and Townsend 1987), resource use (Katz 1991), environmental development (Monk and Norwood 1987), and landscape settlement (Kay 1991).

Geographers have also begun to examine the social construction of the norms of masculinity and femininity (Jackson 1991; Pile 1991; Bondi 1990). These components of the human experience are seen as integral to an understanding of how we perceive and construct our material reality, of how we come to understand and represent the geographic world. Although it has become a central interest of feminists in other fields, the exploration of the experience of sexuality and its role in shaping our landscapes has not yet been addressed explicitly in geography, as Liz Bondi has pointed out (Bondi 1992). Her analysis of the sexual metaphors and stereotyping of gentrification design and planning suggests that the human experience of sexuality is certainly implicated in landscape creation, thereby challenging us to further explore this arena of human experience.

The Future of Feminist Theory and Human Geography

Although the development of feminist theory in geography is a relatively recent phenomenon, feminist social theory in general constitutes one of the most vigorous reconceptualizations of our social realities, and I close this essay with a discussion of several strands of thought in feminist social theory that geographers are beginning to explore.

The first issue focuses on the politics of identity and difference. The radical strain in feminism based much of its theory and politics on the notion of the distinctiveness of the category *woman*, using it to posit a separate and active voice for women. As Pratt and Barrett have pointed out (Pratt 1991; Barrett 1989), however, there are multiple sources of discontent with the concept of a feminist identity, that is, with the notion that some essential factors constitute the category *woman*. One critique, derived from postmodern thought, suggests that the positing of one feminist identity ignores the historical and spatial specificity of social life. The suggestion of a unified womanhood does little to alter the belief in a gender hierarchy; it simply substitutes *woman* for the all-knowing *man*. The second source of discontent stems from women who have been marginalized from society on bases other than gender — race, class, or sexual orientation. For these women gender serves as only one, and oftentimes not the most important, source of oppression. The feminism of white, Anglo, privileged women does not speak to their concerns. Women experience the power relations embedded in gender categorization differently. These critiques of a feminist identity have led to the deconstruction of a single gender identity and have left many wondering about the fate of a feminist politics. Without an identifiable category *woman*, what forms the basis of action?

Judith Butler, in her provocative book *Gender Trouble* (1990), positions a feminist politics on different grounds. She problematizes the opposition implicit in the concept of identity, that is, the opposition between a subject, or agent, and the discursive actions of that subject. In other words, she is engaged in a critique of the idea of identity that posits a prediscursive self. By so doing, Butler questions the foundational aspects of identity, arguing that it is constituted through repetitive actions that signify identity. As she states: "The foundationalist reasoning of identity politics tends to assume that an identity must first be in place in order for political interests to be elaborated and subsequent political action to be taken. My argument is that there need not be a 'doer behind the deed,' but that the 'doer' is variably constructed in and through the deed." (Butler 1990: 142). The basis for feminist politics is not therefore a global, natural, feminist identity, but rather the processes through which gender is constructed. The task becomes one of identifying what practices of signification have enabled those processes, of locating those processes in time and place, and of working toward alternative "practices of repetition that constitute identity and, therefore, present the imminent possibility of contesting them" (Butler 1990: 147).

According to Butler, this opens up new worlds to political scrutiny and presents possibilities for altering our local realities that were not possible with a foundational view of identity. Instead of leaving us without a basis for feminist politics, the recognition of the processes that constitute our differences makes everyday politics more of a reality: "The deconstruction of identity is not the deconstruction of politics; rather, it establishes as political the very terms through which identity is articulated" (Butler 1990: 148).

Such discussion among feminists recasts many of the debates in social theory and the implications of space in those theory constructions. Close examinations of where and how feminine and masculine identities and actions have been articulated through time and space would bring under scrutiny an entire, unexamined range of geographies. How have gender identities been articulated in different places and different eras? How have landscapes and places participated in that articulation? What interactions with the physical environment have been shaped by the practices of gender identity?

The other issue integral to feminist theory that geographers have begun to investigate is the nature of the distinction between the private and the public spheres of life. This debate is not entirely new—socialist feminists have been examining the changing historical conditions of, and relationships between, the reproductive (private) and productive (public) spheres of the economy—but the debate has been refocused on gender issues. For feminists the distinction between the private and public spheres poses a fundamental dilemma: How to reconcile our suspicion of the ways our modern world has viewed the relation of family, state, and economy—"that the divisions between these spheres are not as rigid as we are led to believe and that conceiving them in such a manner obscures the realities of women's lives" (Nicholson 1986: 11)—with our known reality in which those divisions are facts of life that need to be reckoned with. According to Linda Nicholson, the way out of this dilemma is to adopt a historical approach, wherein a narrative can help explain how those different spheres of social activity (family, state, economy) emerged from common occurrences and only under particular sets of circumstances developed into distinct spheres. As she argues:

> Because what now appear as separated spheres share common origins and interrelated histories, there are connections which the new, if still partial, fact of separation has helped to obscure. For example, if we recognize that once upon a time, the political and the familial were interconnected in the institution of kinship—a beginning modern liberalism has obscured through its contract theory of the origins of the state—then we can make comprehensive contemporary feminism's awareness of the patriarchal, and thus political, component of the contemporary family, and its awareness of the patriarchal, and thus gendered component of the contemporary state. (Nicholson 1986: 11)

An historical approach thus offers us a view of these three categories of social analysis—the family, the state, and the economy—as not necessarily distinct, but as aspects of human life that have "been made distinct at specific historical moments" (Nicholson 1986: 12).

What is so important about this discussion is that it allows feminist theory to see how gender differences have been historically constructed and perpetuated through these three areas of social analysis that have heretofore constituted our understanding of our social worlds. Although I cannot do justice here to the full scope of Nicholson's discussion, I suggest that the historical approach she uses is eminently geographical as well. For example, there is a geography as well as a history of the separation of the private sphere from the public sphere, a separation that had profound implications for the status of women, and it is up to feminist geographers to investigate this fairly unknown territory. Sallie Marston has begun to explore this avenue of research, showing how the conceptualization of citizenship in the early American nation was linked to related notions of gender roles and the gendering of public and private life. This set of beliefs, she argues, acted as a "foundation for the construction of the early American national community and, as a consequence, the political geography of social life" (1990: 457). Because most social theory has obscured the circumstances under which spheres of social activity have become distinct, a geographical analysis would help us understand the particular circumstances and context for the separation of domestic space, personal space, private space, and public space throughout different times and places. By analyses of this sort we might begin to understand how the distinction between men and women came to be seen as determinant of status and then to apply that understanding in the construction of a forum for political action.

References

Barrett, Michele. 1989. Some different meanings of the concept of "difference": Feminist theory and the concept of ideology. In *The difference within: Feminism and critical theory*, ed. Elizabeth Meese and Alice Parker, 37–48. Philadelphia: John Benjamins.

Berman, Mildred. 1984. On being a woman in American geography: A personal perspective. *Antipode* 6: 61–66.

Birkett, Dea. 1989. *Spinsters abroad: Victorian lady explorers*. Oxford: Basil Blackwell.

Blunt, Alison, and Gillian Rose, eds. 1994. *Writing women and space: Colonial and postcolonial geographies*. New York: Guilford Press.

Bondi, Liz. 1990. Landscapes of change: Masculinity and femininity in the city. Paper presented at the Association of American Geographers' meeting, Toronto.

———. 1992. Gender symbols and urban landscapes. *Progress in Human Geography* 16: 157–70.

Bondi, Liz, and Mona Domosh. 1992. Other figures in other places: On feminism, postmodernism, and geography. *Environment and Planning D: Society and Space* 10: 199–213.

Burnett, Pat. 1973. Social change, the status of women, and models of city form and development. *Antipode* 5: 57–62.

Butler, Judith. 1990. *Gender trouble: Feminism and the subversion of identity*. New York: Routledge.

Christopherson, Susan. 1983. The household and class formation: The changing social economy of Ciudad Juarez. *Environment and Planning D: Society and Space* 1: 323–328.

Domosh, Mona. 1991. Toward a feminist historiography of geography. *Transactions of the Institute of British Geographers* N. S. 16: 95–104.

DuBois, Ellen Carol, et al. 1985. *Feminist scholarship: Kindling in the groves of academe*. Urbana: University of Illinois Press.

Friedan, Betty. 1963. *The feminine mystique*. New York: Norton Press.

Garside, Christine. 1971. Can a woman be good in the same way as a man? *Dialogue* 10: 534–44.

Gibson, Anne, and Timothy Fast. 1986. *The women's atlas of the United States*. New York: Facts on File.

Gordon, Linda, et al. 1972. A review of sexism in American historical writing. *Women's Studies* 1: 133–58.

Hanson, Susan, and Geraldine Pratt. 1988. Spatial dimensions of the gender division of labor in a local labor market. *Urban Geography* 9: 173–93.

Harding, Sandra. 1986. *The science question in feminism*. Ithaca, N. Y.: Cornell University Press.

————. 1991. *Whose science? Whose knowledge? Thinking from women's lives*. Ithaca, N. Y.: Cornell University Press.

Hayden, Dolores. 1985. *Redesigning the American dream: The future of housing, work, and family life*. New York: W. W. Norton.

Hayford, Alison. 1974. The geography of women: An historical introduction. *Antipode* 6: 1–19.

Holcomb, Briavel. 1984. Women in the city. *Urban Geography* 5: 247–54.

Jackson, Peter. 1991. The cultural politics of masculinity: Towards a social geography. *Transactions of the Institute of British Geographers* N. S. 16: 199–213.

Katz, Cindi. 1991. Sow what you know: The struggle for social reproduction in rural Sudan. *Annals of the Association of American Geographers* 81: 488–514.

Kay, Jeanne. 1991. Geography and mythos: Or, Joseph Campbell meets Preston James. Paper presented at the Association of American Geographers' meeting, Miami.

Kelly-Gadol, Joan. 1976. The social relations of the sexes: Methodological implications of women's history. *Signs* 1: 809–24.

Kolodny, Annette. 1984. *The land before her: Fantasy and experience of the American frontier*. Chapel Hill: University of North Carolina Press.

Loyd, Bonnie. 1981. Women, home, and status. In *Housing and identity*, ed. James Duncan. London: Croom Helm.

Marston, Sallie. 1990. Who are "the people"?: Gender, citizenship, and the making of the American nation. *Environment and Planning D: Society and Space* 8: 449–58.

Mascia-Lees, F. E. et al. 1989. The postmodernist turn in anthropology: Cautions from a feminist perspective. *Signs* 15: 1–29.

Mazey, Mary Ellen, and David Lee. 1983. *Her space, her place: A geography of women.* Washington, D.C.: Association of American Geographers.

Mackenzie, Suzanne. 1989. *Visible histories: Women and environments in a post-war British city.* Montreal: McGill-Queen's University Press.

McDowell, Linda. 1983. Towards an understanding of the gender division of urban space. *Environment and Planning D: Society and Space* 1: 73–87.

Middleton, Dorothy. 1982. *Victorian lady travelers.* Chicago: Academy Chicago.

Momsen, Janet Henshall, and Janet Townsend, eds. 1987. *Geography of gender in the Third World.* London: Hutchinson.

Monk, Janice. 1989. Women geographers and geographic institutions, 1900–1950. Paper presented at the 1989 Association of American Geographers' meeting, Baltimore.

Monk, Janice, and Susan Hanson. 1982. On not excluding half of the human in human geography. *Professional Geographer* 34: 11–23.

Monk, Janice, and Vera Norwood, eds. 1987. *The desert is no lady: Southwestern landscapes in women's writing and art.* New Haven: Yale University Press.

Morgan, Robin. 1970. *Sisterhood is powerful.* New York: Random House.

Nicholson, Linda. 1986. *Gender and history.* New York: Columbia University Press.

———, ed. 1990. *Feminism/postmodernism.* New York: Routledge.

Pile, Stephen. 1991. Masculinity, otherness and the drive for geographical knowledge. Paper presented at the Institute of British Geographers' conference, Sheffield.

Pratt, Geraldine, and Susan Hanson. 1988. Gender, class, and space. *Environment and Planning D: Society and Space* 6: 15–35.

———. 1991. Feminist politics: The danger of difference, the place of geography. Paper presented at the Association of American Geographers' meeting, Miami.

Rose, Gillian. 1993. *Feminism and geography: The limits of geographical knowledge.* Minneapolis: University of Minnesota Press.

Rubin, Gayle. 1975. The traffic in women. In *Toward an anthropology of women*, ed. Rayna Rapp Reiter, 157–210. New York: Monthly Review Press.

Seager, Joni. 1988. Father's chair: Domestic reform and housing change in the Progressive era. Doctoral dissertation, Clark University.

———. 1992. Women deserve spatial consideration: (Or geography like no one ever learned in school). In *The Knowledge Explosion*, ed. Dale Spender and Cheris Kramerae, 213–24. New York: Pergamon Press.

Seager, Joni, and Anne Olson. 1986. *Women in the world: An international atlas*. London: Pluto Press.

Showalter, Elaine. 1971. Women in the literary curriculum. *College English* 32: 855–62.

Shortridge, Barbara G. 1987. *Atlas of American women*. New York: Macmillan.

Slocum, Sally. 1975. Woman the gatherer: Male bias in anthropology. In *Toward an anthropology of women*, ed. Rayna Rapp Reiter, 36–50. New York: Monthly Review Press.

Zelinsky, Wilbur. 1973. The strange case of the missing female geographer. *Professional Geographer* 25: 101–6.

———. 1973. Women in geography: A brief factual account. *Professional Geographer* 25: 151–65.

Zelinsky, Wilbur, Janice Monk, and Susan Hanson. 1982. Women and geography: A review and prospectus. *Progress in Human Geography* 6: 317–66.

16

Postmodernism in Human Geography

Nancy Duncan

The literatures on postmodernity and postmodernism have grown rapidly over the past decade. These have become fashionable topics and scholars from a wide range of disciplines within the social sciences and the humanities are busily exploring the implications for their fields. The term *postmodernism* is often used rather loosely, some seeing it as an emerging phase of history or as a new cultural system, while others see it more narrowly as a scholarly discourse, a set of ideas that radically challenges modernism, an intellectual movement that itself has been defined in diverse ways. In order to retain this useful distinction, I call the former *postmodernity*, the latter *postmodernism*. Of the former I ask, How might we distinguish it as an era from modernity and premodernity? Might these be seen as coexisting cultural systems? The relationships between the latter and poststructuralism, post-Marxism, and deconstruction are matters of contention. Is postmodernism as an intellectual movement neoconservative, anarchic, nihilistic? Can it be assimilated into Western Marxism or other modern schools of thought often seen by postmodernists as master narratives?

The first two parts of this chapter provide overviews of the literature on postmodernity and postmodernism in the humanities and social sciences. I distinguish between postmodernity as an emerging cultural or societal condition that is seen as reflective of ongoing transformations in the world's economic and sociopolitical systems and postmodernism as a set of strong epistemological and ontological claims.

The last part of this paper examines some examples from the growing geographic literature on postmodernity and postmodernism. While postmodernity and its relation to post-Fordism and postindustrial society are of major concern, especially for geographers interested in political economy, questions of postmodernism as an intellectual movement have also become prominent in the field. The conclusion suggests that whether or not there are any good grounds for positing the arrival of postmodernity, postmodernism is an increasingly influential intellectual position that, when taken in its strongest form, challenges many of the presuppositions of most contemporary academic practice. I end with some caveats about the epistemological, ontological, political, and ethical problems that attend an uncritical adoption of these postmodernist views.

Postmodernity

Fredric Jameson (1984) is perhaps the best known of the writers who have formulated a notion of postmodernity[1] as a societal condition or era within which postmodernism and poststructuralism are sets of ideas and values constituting its dominant cultural component.[2] He has had a noticeable influence on a number of geographers who are interested in drawing causal links between the political economy of multinational capitalism, space, and cultural change. Jameson sees postmodernism as a pervasive global cultural force that cannot be transcended by an individual. Within the era of postmodernity there is no possibility of achieving critical distance because we are all (critics, political activists, and moralists and his Third World "Others" alike) so "immersed in or penetrated by postmodernist space" that the "luxury of old-fashioned ideological critique, the indignant moral denunciation of the other, becomes unavailable" (Jameson 1988: 86).

Jameson is particularly interested in the role of what he terms new experiences of space or "hyperspace" in which we become disoriented and lose our perspective and thus the ability to position ourselves cognitively in the "great global multinational and decentered communicational network in which we find ourselves caught as individual subjects" (Jameson 1984). It is this loss, Jameson claims, that leads to the obliteration of critical distance. Possibly because he always insists on historicizing, he has not forfeited the future possibility of resisting the global penetration of capitalism and its cultural logic, which is postmodernism.[3]

Jameson sees postmodernity as a stage of cultural production produced by late capitalism—a "cultural dominant" controlled by the structures of multinational capitalism. Following Ernest Mandel, he sees postmodernism as the latest stage of capitalism. Accordingly, he argues that postmodernism represents a radical break from an earlier cultural episteme beginning in the late 1950s or early 1960s and crystallizing about 1973 (Jameson 1984: xx).

In this new economic era, cultural forms, signs, and representations are produced and consumed as is any other commodity. This commodification, according to Jameson, pervades all cultural forms of contemporary postmodern society: film, television, advertising, and other productions of postmodernity.[4] Furthermore, according to Jameson, postmodernism is so pervasive and dominant that individuals cannot escape its logic—thus the abolition of critical distance mentioned above.

"Reading off" culture—that is, understanding its meanings and roles— from the stages of capital requires specification of the causal relation if we are to avoid what Mike Davis (1988: 80) has called, with reference to Jameson, a "return to essentialism and reductionism with a vengeance." Doubtless Jameson's notion of the relationship between intellectual discourse and the mode of production is more subtle and complex than Davis implies; furthermore, Jameson does acknowledge the necessity of specifying the connections, and, as we shall see below, there are several geographers, David Harvey being a prime example, who have attempted to do precisely that. Jameson's main point, however, is that the disappearance of privileged viewpoints, the instability of meaning by which signifiers and their signifieds are only fleetingly related, the loss of a sense of history, the crisis of representation, and the fragmentation of human subjectivity are characteristics of late capitalist society.

Jameson, however, has been forced into some rather unconvincing verbal gymnastics to defend his attempts to assimilate postmodernism with Western Marxism, which is clearly a modernist philosophy. He has acknowledged that his concept of postmodernism is a totalizing one and, as we shall see below, postmodernism itself rejects what are referred to as metanarratives or grand totalizing theories. These, of course, include Marxism, as Jameson admits. Certain geographers as well fall equally uncomfortably into a similarly contradictory eclecticism.

Postmodernism

One way of describing postmodernism as an intellectual movement is to point out what it is not. Postmodernism is not concerned with the origins of the term itself, nor is it concerned with periodizing postmodernity. Origins and periods constitute a modernist problematic that is contrary to the spirit of postmodernism. Postmodernism regards the question of origins and its corollary (the author as a free, creative source) as dubious and the notion of a unified or coherent historical period as suspect. Postmodernism rejects definition by binary opposition, opposing totalizing or essentializing modes of thought; hence, the oppositions *modernism* and *postmodernism*, as well as *modernity* and *postmodernity*, are themselves seen as problematic. Because postmodernism assumes the instability of meaning, it becomes difficult to define postmodernism from within the discourse itself.

Postmodernism's dismissal of genesis notwithstanding, most studies of this intellectual movement do try to locate its origins. Some say it started (*avant la lettre*) with Hegel; others find its beginnings in the nihilism of Nietzsche. Habermas suggests that it has not yet begun, that the eighteenth-century Enlightenment project that launched modernism remains unfinished and that the abandonment of the project would be premature. Lyotard argues precisely the opposite, that postmodernism can be considered the nascent stage of modernism[5]—and thus we have the celebrated Habermas-Lyotard debate.[6]

The dispute rages on. Is postmodernism a departure from modernism or merely one of its many manifestations? (On this point, see Huyssen 1986: 207; Graff 1979, Lyotard 1984: 79; and Jencks 1986: 7.) Because modernism is often defined principally by its valorization of new perspectives, its proponents continually seek out new ideas to replace currently held orthodoxy; postmodernism as a departure from modernism might then seem to be a redundant concept because it is merely the latest manifestation of modernism. Proponents of the philosophically stronger versions of postmodernism would argue, however, that they do not intend to replace any current orthodoxy but instead wish to destabilize the modernist progression from one orthodoxy to another.

Ihab Hassan, who along with Charles Jencks is largely responsible for the popularity of the term in the 1970s, claims that it has been a subterranean current since the eighteenth century and has resurfaced in the twentieth, and furthermore, "we have created in our mind a model of postmodernism, a particular typology of culture and imagination, and have proceeded to 'rediscover' the affinities of various authors and different moments with that model" (Hassan 1990: 121). He describes this as "reinventing" our ancestors.

The various versions of postmodernism owe their differences, in part, to the many different modernisms in opposition to which they are defined. *Modern* is sometimes viewed as a temporal category referring to that which is contemporary. Other times, the modern is regarded more generally as an oppositional attitude. Irving Howe (1970: 3), for example, distinguished the modern from the merely contemporary, characterizing modernity as "an unyielding rage against the official order." The dilemma of modernism, he argues, is that it must "always struggle but never quite triumph, and then after a time, must struggle in order not to triumph" (1963: 4). Hal Foster (1983: ix) says that modernism has triumphed but that "its victory is a Pyrrhic one—no different than defeat, for modernism is now largely absorbed."

Marshall Berman (1988: 17) suggests that history has rendered modernism inert, that is to say that the modernist rage has been co-opted. The nineteenth century, he argues, represented modernism's most creative and revolutionary period, "when a modern public can remember what it is like to live, materially and spiritually, in worlds that are not modern at all" (1988: 17). The capacity for self-critique and self-renewal, for a prelapsarian age, remains a possibility, however. Berman says that "postmodernist social thought pours scorn on all the collective hopes for moral and social progress, for personal freedom and public happiness, that are bequeathed to us by the modernists of the eighteenth century Enlightenment" (1988: 9). For Berman "the book is far from closed on the 'grand narrative(s)'" of modernism, however (1988: 12); he believes that modernism is as self-critical and ironic as postmodernism is thought to be, and he holds out hope for a reappropriation of its revolutionary potential.

Postmodernism is sometimes seen as a jaded, albeit sophisticated, declaration of resignation and political impotence, an exhaustion of the Enlightenment's boundless optimism. Postmodernism, some argue, opposes not modernism itself, but its institutionalization and canonization as well as the ensuing loss of its critical, oppositional edge (e.g., Newman 1985: 27–35).

Charles Jencks (1975, 1986), who first wrote about postmodernism in 1975, devoted a monograph to the movement with particular reference to architecture. He defines postmodernism more narrowly than most. After distinguishing between late, ultra-, and neomodernisms, he points out that what passes for postmodernism is in fact an exaggerated or "agonistic" modernism. Unlike some who regard postmodernism as heir to the transgressive impulse of the modern avant-garde, Jencks rejects a critical role for postmodernism. According to Jencks, postmodernism as defined by writers such as Foster, Jameson, Lyotard, Baudrillard, and Hassan is committed to novelty and is unconcerned with the past, tradition, continuity, or pluralism. He thus claims that what they refer to as postmodern is actually modern or, more precisely, late modern. Jencks redefines postmodernism as merely a style of cultural production associated with tradition, ornament, and pluralism, with "semantics, convention, historical memory, metaphor, symbolism, and respect for existing cultures" (Jencks 1986: 34–35).

Jencks's architectural version of postmodernism has been regarded by some as neoconservative or, as Foster (1985: 28) puts it, ahistorical in its "pop-historical imagery." Some have dismissed postmodernist architecture as an eclectic appropriation and reshuffling of cultural and historical imagery torn from its contexts (Foster 1985: 28).

Nevertheless, in art and architecture many of postmodernism's proponents have seen it as critical of modernist works. Modernist architecture is viewed as elitist, cold glass and steel monuments to capitalism, while postmodernist architecture is seen as a more populist alternative.[7] By "learning from Las Vegas" (Venturi, Brown, and Izenour 1977) postmodernist architects are expected to be more sensitive to the needs and tastes of ordinary people. However, although some have suggested that postmodernist architecture with its parodic references to historical styles is critical, Hal Foster disagrees, suggesting that in fact "culture is treated as so many styles" and that postmodern architecture "plays upon responses that are already programmed" (Foster 1985: 28). He argues that the historical references incorporated into architecture are curiosities, souvenirs, so many commodities to be consumed, and as such lead not to a "sharpened awareness of difference (social, sexual, artistic, etc.) but to a stagnant condition of indiscrimination not to resistance but to retrenchment" (Foster 1985: 31).

According to Foster, postmodernism is not necessarily populist at all. He suggests that through the use of superficial historical references or "cliches," postmodern architecture "stratifies as it juxtaposes, and condescends as it panders (some will get this, it says, some that). Though it wishes to paper over social differences, it only pronounces them along with the privileges that underlie them" (Foster 1985: 29).

In anthropology postmodernism is quite different. It largely concerns the crisis of representation as it is faced by some of those who are currently engaged in ethnographic writing. In this literature postmodernism tends to be seen as an ethical and political problem of speaking on behalf of others who are assumed to be unable to represent themselves. Only a few such as Tyler (1986, 1987) have paid more than fleeting attention to the difficult issues and implications of the impossibility of representing reality with any degree of certainty. Instead, authors such as James Clifford, George Marcus, Michael Fisher, and others[8] debate the problem of the ethnographer's right and ability to represent cultural Others. They argue for texts that provoke other voices and avoid strong authorial control. These anthropologists also criticize most Western writings about other cultures to show how power relations between societies are reinforced through these representations and how polyvocality may be a step in the direction of solving the problem of representation as they define it.

Adding to the confusion over postmodernism is the fact that, while there is a clear break between postmodernism and modernism in architecture, it is somewhat less clear in literary and social theory, and much more difficult to discern in literature. Each field thus tends toward its own dominant version of postmodernism, which may be only tenuously related to other versions.

Postmodernism in literature is often associated with a constellation of ideas that includes deconstruction. It emphasizes certain ideas that challenge modernism, but, unlike modernism, it does not break with ideas of the past in order to replace them with the new. It is neither progressive nor authoritative; progress is denied, as is the author as an active agent. It is critical but in a particular, deconstructive way, working through rereadings of the texts of modernism. As Hugh Silverman (1990: 1) asserts, it explores the limits that modernist works set on their own projects. "Its significance is to marginalize, delimit, disseminate, and decenter the primary (and often secondary) works of modernist and premodernist cultural inscriptions." By this he means that postmodernism is not the latest period within intellectual history, but an attitude that arises out of modernism and that challenges some of the dominant metanarratives of modernism—ideologies such as those of humanism, progress, and rationality that underlie the Enlightenment project. Silverman says that postmodernism is "fragmented, discontinuous, multiple, and dispersed. Where modernism asserts centering, focusing, continuity—once the break with tradition has already occurred—postmodernism decenters, unframes, discontinues, and fragments the prevalence of modernist ideals" (Silverman 1990: 5).

Is postmodernism the "cultural logic of late capitalism" (Jameson 1984)? Is it the cultural politics of the Other? Is it the decline of western imperialist metanarratives? Or is it, as I am tempted to suggest, an extreme philosophical position that may trouble some by its logical elegance but few in their practical everyday experience?

The arguments and counterarguments about postmodernism are confusing because of the diversity of definitions and interpretations of both postmodernism and modernism. The debates over whether postmodernism is a continuation of the modernist avant-garde or, as Habermas argues, the abandonment of modernism's emancipatory project are not merely a matter of commentators talking past one another or the results of definitional difference. The divergent points of view reflect fundamental differences on many issues, the most important of which is antifoundationalism, the key proposition underlying definitions of postmodernism.

Although some have argued that the prefix suggests continuity with modernism, this is a contentious issue. I would argue on the contrary that *post-* implies the rather grand claim of a break between discourses. It is difficult to imagine a clear break from the highly fluid and progressive intellectual position that modernism represents. In fact, radical antifoundationalism is the only criteria in any of the definitions of postmodernism that has impressed me as providing a sufficiently dramatic departure from modernism to warrant the prefix.

Postmodernism in the sense of radical antifoundationalism is a relativist thesis that in its very strongest form involves ontological claims concerning the nature of human phenomena or, in some formulations, reality in general. It can be contrasted with foundationalism defined as an epistemological and ontological perspective entailing a bipolar truth value—truth and falsity. It usually assumes that guarantees of truth about a reality existing independently of our knowing are worth pursuing; in other words, that there can be foundations upon which we can base judgments concerning truth and falsity where truth and falsity are logically independent of culture, power, or paradigms (see Fish 1989: 342; Bernstein 1983: 8–12.) The latter, however, can be seen within modernism as epistemological constraints that inevitably influence our understandings and interventions in the world. There are thus versions of foundationalism that assume the possibility of discovering truth while acknowledging the likelihood of fallibility. As I discuss below in reference to a paper by Andrew Sayer (1992), much of modernist thought is foundational only in this weaker sense.

Strong claims for antifoundationalism entail some form of either epistemological relativism or ontological relativism or both. In the case of epistemological relativism there is no possibility of grounding judgements about better or worse interpretations or explanations. This form of relativism is not widely held, and it should be said that this form makes a much stronger claim than that of cultural relativism,[9] which is generally seen as reasonable in contemporary liberal societies. In the case of ontological relativism it is assumed that phenomena are inherently underdetermined by our theories. In fact, it is sometimes thought that they are also inherently alterable by interpretation alone. The signifier-signified relation is seen as ontologically unstable rather than merely epistemologically undeterminable. Contradiction, incoherence, and indeterminacy are seen as actual characteristics of the world, rather than merely a matter of our human perceptual limitations; there is no notion of objective truth even as an ideal, if unobtainable, standard.

As we have seen above, however, many postmodernists in architecture and anthropology subscribe to the somewhat less rigorous formulation of antifoundationalism as implied in Lyotard's famous "incredulity toward metanarratives." By this they mean to oppose the idea of universal, timeless truths.[10] Accordingly, postmodernists assume that there are human histories, but no human nature. This view is usually characterized by a concern with difference, the Other, untranslatability of languages, incommensurability of world views, incongruent paradigms, radical historicism, and the impossibility of progress. This tends to be a strong ontological as well as an epistemological thesis.

Because all versions of antifoundationalism deny the possibility of escaping from our discourses in order to directly study the real world, the conclusion is often drawn that we must abandon the notions of truth, rationality, science, and realism.[11] Antifoundationalism is most threatening, however, when it entails a rejection of any criteria on which to judge human actions. This is seen to undermine the foundations of any progressive form of politics. It is thus feared that arguments against such evils as Nazism must be forfeited in the absence of a privileged position from which to launch a critique.

Habermas, who has devoted his career to establishing a foundation for critical theory, believes that postmodernism cannot be assimilated to any progressive political program because of its antifoundationalism. The form of foundationalism he wishes to retain assumes rationality as the bedrock on which to found emancipation from oppression, and, thus, he cannot accept postmodernism.

As we have seen, the many postmodernisms include some that are strong and some that are weak (in the sense of being less philosophically rigorous). Some are merely passing styles, such as postmodernism in architecture, which is fast being eclipsed by deconstructivism. Other postmodernisms, however, such as those in the realm of social and political thought are not as easily naturalized as part of a seemingly inevitable process of one fashion replacing another. Instead, these offer less commodified, more fundamental challenges to modernism.

Consequently, we may ask whether postmodernism as an epistemology is wholly dependent. Is there no positive project? Where modernism creates anew, does postmodernism only deconstruct? Does the fragmentation of cultural texts assume prior wholeness? Does the decentering presuppose a once-centered subject? In its parasitic relationship with modernism, postmodernism has no ground of its own to stand on; it is in its strongest formulations radically antifoundational, and this, philosophically speaking, is its most important characteristic, one that some geographers tend to lose sight of.

Postmodernism and Postmodernity in Geography

Geographers who have taken up the postmodern challenge generally believe, as I do, that the discipline should not be isolated from the debates that rage all around us in the social sciences and the humanities. Although most geographers who have considered postmodernism closely are skeptical of many of its claims, some may not have been cautious enough in their attempts to assimilate it to Marxist or other types of modernist thought. These attempts "recuperate"[12] the theory in ways that ignore the logic of postmodernism; and it is recuperation, as many postmodernists see it, that is to be avoided above all other sins.

This review considers three influential books and a number of articles by geographers who have given explicit attention to the issues of postmodernism. In reviewing each of these, I point out where the authors have clearly separated these issues, where they have conflated them, and where they have adopted the stronger or weaker claims of postmodernism. I begin with David Harvey's *Condition of Postmodernity* (1989), which analyzes postmodernity as a societal condition; I then consider several books and papers that, in attempting to look at both postmodernity and postmodernism, often conflate the two; finally, I consider other geographers who apply postmodernist thought in their writings. Some of these geographers subscribe to looser definitions than others. As might be anticipated from comments above, I find myself in agreement with the perspective of many of these geographers, while maintaining that they recuperate postmodernism in ways that make it no longer defensible as a position clearly differentiated from modernism. While respectful of the strong claims of those few such as Ulf Strohmayer and Matthew Hannah who take a more clearly postmodern position defined as antifoundationalism (I concede that they best deserve the label), I find myself uncomfortable with the radicalism of their position. Lastly, I review a paper by Andrew Sayer that effectively argues that realism is able to retain the important insights of postmodernism without falling into the trap of radical antifoundationalism defined as relativism.

I devote the most attention to David Harvey's (1989) text because his is the most significant contribution to the larger literature on postmodernity as an era; similarly, I give close attention to Strohmayer and Hannah's (1992) paper because it best exemplifies a clear defense of postmodernism in its strong sense.

I present Harvey's argument in some detail in order to show that the cultural aspects of postmodernity have not simply been "read off" from economic transformations; he has instead attempted to elucidate the linkages and, to some degree, provide causal explanations. Harvey offers a cautious assessment of the significance and political-economic causes of recent cultural changes, arguing that these changes are superficial and do not represent a new form of postcapitalist society. He traces the history of modernism as originating in the eighteenth-century Enlightenment project—a highly complex cultural movement characterized by a tension between progressive or revolutionary values and an optimistic search for universal truths under which to subsume the notions of moral progress, justice, equality, and human emancipation. Harvey observes that modernist optimism has been shattered in the twentieth century with its two world wars, Hitler's Germany, Stalin's Russia, the experience of Hiroshima and Nagasaki, and the threat of nuclear annihilation (1989: 13). The modernist quest for human emancipation is undermined by the modernist scientific urge to dominate nature and rationalize the bureaucracy and the workplace. He claims that this urge entails a logic that leads to the oppression of human beings.

Harvey describes the modernist movement as complex and full of tensions arising from the complicated reactions and counterreactions to conditions of production, circulation, and consumption as they have intensified over the years since the revolutions of 1848. His sophisticated and plausible arguments for the links between culture and economy set the scene for the causal analysis of the transition to postmodernism and changes in the world economy.

Harvey's fairly linear account of the transition to postmodernity may be explained by the fact that he relates it to such specific, datable events as the recession of 1973, the oil crisis of the early 1970s, and the breakdown of the Bretton Woods Agreement.[13] These were manifestations of the decline of the Fordist regime of accumulation, its associated mode of social and political regulation, and the rise of a new regime of flexible accumulation and its mode of regulation.

Fordism was the regime of accumulation associated with modernism. Fordism, as the application of a scientific system for increasing labor productivity, entailed an entirely new concept of the economy in which mass consumption was linked to mass production, a new politics of labor control, and a new aesthetics and psychology of a rationalized, modernist, and populist democratic society (1989: 126). The Fordist worker was a new type of person having more income and more leisure time for consuming the mass-produced goods of this system.

World War II helped to rationalize industry and technology, while postwar industrial production, suburbanization, state investment in postwar reconstruction, and expansion of transportation and communication infrastructures all served to stimulate the economic boom that created an increasingly homogeneous mass world market (1989: 132). Organized labor, large corporate capital, and the nation-state achieved a balance of power in class relations during the postwar period that, as Harvey puts it, provided a "tense" but fairly stable basis for Fordism and economic growth (1989: 133).

As the Fordist regime broke down in the late 1960s and early 1970s and as the hegemony of the United States in the world financial system began to decline, the rigidities inherent in the infrastructure and labor commitments of mass-production systems began to surface as growth in consumer markets declined. Monetary policy was employed to salvage the system but at the cost of dangerous inflation, which would eventually sink the post-war boom.

A new flexibility has since been introduced into production and consumption processes. Service-sector employment has increased dramatically in the United States while new industrial regions have arisen in such places as the "Third Italy," the NICs (newly industrializing countries), and various silicon valleys. Among the most important characterizations of this new regime of flexible accumulation is a significantly higher degree of "time-space compression," which allows employers much more flexibility and mobility and thus greater power in relation to labor. Trade-union power has been significantly reduced with increasing levels of unemployment and the emergence of segmented labor markets. Flexible patterns of work have been established that are characterized by more part-time, temporary, subcontracted, and female unskilled workers. Workers are forced to become more mobile and adaptable. Just-in-time delivery systems, small-batch production, a return to sweatshops and working at home, and growth in the underground economy characterize the flexible mode of accumulation. Women who are employed on a part-time basis are prime targets for exploitation and are often used to replace full-time male workers.

With changing production structures and the need for what Harvey calls accelerated turnover time in consumption have come new emphases on the creation of and the immediate response to rapidly changing fashions, the commodification of information, the production of spectacles, and more customized products.

Harvey argues that "the more flexible notion of capital emphasizes the new, the fleeting, the ephemeral, the fugitive, and the contingent in modern life, rather than the more solid values implanted under Fordism" (1989: 171). He also talks of a "general shift from more collective norms and values that were hegemonic at least in working-class organizations and other social movements of the 1950's and 1960's, towards a much more competitive individualism as the central value in an entrepreneurial culture that has penetrated many walks of life" (1989: 171).

New, highly sophisticated financial systems operating on a global scale have facilitated, even initiated, a new regime of flexible accumulation. Harvey argues that with this more global perspective comes a new, postmodernist experience of time and space. Here we can see clearly the working out of the proposition that there are material links between political economic and cultural processes (1989: 201).

During the period that Harvey associates with postmodernist thought and flexible accumulation there has been what he calls "an intense phase of time-space compression that has had a disorienting and disruptive impact on political-economic practices, the balance of class power, as well as upon cultural and social life" (1989: 284). One of the most prominent of the new organizational forms of production associated with this new phase of capitalism is the acceleration of turnover time. These new forms require a concomitant acceleration in exchange and consumption of commodities and services.

The manipulation of fashions for mass markets, once limited to clothing but now extended to children's games, music styles, and videos, has resulted in commodities with increasingly shortened lifespans. Similarly ephemeral are such services as various forms of entertainment: rock concerts, spectacles, happenings, and visits to museums or health clubs. All have very short consumption life spans as compared to durable goods.

The increased velocity of fashions has been accompanied by capitalist penetration of many sectors of cultural production. Ideas and ideologies have been commodified, distinctions between advertising and other cultural productions have been blurred (art as advertising and advertising as art), and politics has been "aestheticized"—by which Harvey means that political issues are reduced to images, subjects for cultural producers to package and commodify, and cultural values and place-bound identity are accentuated while global issues have been relatively de-emphasized. All of this Harvey associates with the new regime of flexible accumulation without, however, claiming any simple causal links between the cultural and the economic.

Promotional images of products or political agendas (localism, nationalism, separatism, national or cultural heritage, etc.) have become integrated into the practices of cultural production to a greater extent than ever before. Affirming the analyses of postmodern society by Baudrillard and Jameson, Harvey (1989: 289) suggests that the images (usually based on money, sex, and power) themselves are ephemeral commodities. Their utility comes from the way in which they accelerate turnover time. The premium placed on disposability and novelty and the use of electronic banking and "plastic money" have further hastened the rate of turnover in production and consumption.

The "annihilation of space through time" as an important characteristic of postmodern times is evident in the dizzying variety of commodities now available worldwide, creating a veritable pastiche of the global geographic diversity that can be experienced as a simulacrum (1989: 300). Harvey (1989: 301), paraphrasing Iain Chambers, observes that "a strong sense of 'the Other' is replaced by a weak sense of the 'others.'"

The irony of postmodernism, in Harvey's view, is the creation of place-bound identities through the commodification and marketing of local or national traditions, the escape from contemporary ephemeral culture to traditional values, and the celebration of local histories through the packaging of images, the creation of simulacra or pastiches of historical places. Local history is museumified, transformed into a spectacle for public consumption, and romanticized by the erasure of all "traces of oppressive class relations" (1989: 303).

Harvey thus regards postmodernity and the effects of time-space compression as the historical-geographical condition of contemporary society. He even applauds certain aspects of postmodern social scientific practice; these include a renewed concern for difference and otherness (of race, gender, and religion) and the recognition that image production and aesthetic practices are important objects of study. Furthermore, he suggests that some of his views are consistent with postmodernism—that a concern with space and the geography of power should be an important aspect of historical materialism and that historical-geographical materialism is not a set of universal truths (1989: 357).

He rejects, however, what he considers to be postmodernism's privileging of aesthetics over ethics, of the politics of place and localism over the realities of the internationalism of capitalism, and its rejection of Marxism as a modernist metatheory. He believes that insofar as metatheory is open-ended and dialectical, it can be appropriated for politically and intellectually responsible practice.

Harvey dissents from postmodernism's strongest and most philosophically rigorous claim, the epistemology of antifoundationalism. He contributes instead an analysis of the postmodern condition, that is, postmodernity as an era. Whereas his rather general statements about some of the cultural characteristics of late capitalism may ring true, especially in the Anglo-American context with which he is most familiar, any causal connections drawn from the economy to the very specific philosophical propositions of antifoundationalism in postmodern thought would of course be much less convincing. I do not think he intends to make any such claims; but, of course, given the often very loose interpretations of postmodernism and the conflation of its many definitions that exist in the literature, Harvey's book could be read in this way by less careful followers. Too easy a dismissal of these philosophical claims as complicit with capitalism might follow, and Harvey does little to caution against this.

Edward Soja's *Postmodern Geographies* (1989) makes the case for "the reassertion of space in critical theory." His aims are twofold: to analyze the condition of postmodern society with particular reference to the post-Fordist landscapes of Los Angeles and to experiment with postmodern styles of exposition. He begins, for example, with a postscript that is intended by its placement before the text to "shake up the normal flow of linear text to allow other more lateral connections to be made (1989: 1). He ends the book with two experimental chapters on Los Angeles in which the style of writing is intended to capture the "simultaneity" of a highly spatialized postmodern city through lateral mappings that make it possible to read in a nonlinear fashion.

For Soja the key to postmodern geographies is the superiority of spatial over historicist forms of explanation. Quoting John Berger, Soja writes that "it is space more than time that hides consequences from us" (Soja 1989: 23). He continues: "[R]elations of power and discipline are inscribed into the apparently innocent spatiality of social life" (1989: 7). One of Soja's aims in the book is emancipation from "the temporal prison house of language and similarly carceral historicism of conventional critical theory" to the freedom of "an interpretative human geography, a spatial hermeneutic" (1989: 12). He characterizes contemporary society after Foucault, as an "epoch of simultaneity" (quoted in Soja 1989: 10). Insofar as these diagnoses are correct, then geography as the spatial science is now more central than ever to the study of contemporary society. Unfortunately, it is not made entirely clear why spatiality is a peculiarly postmodern problematic.

Several of the distinguishing features of postmodernism are missing from Soja's book, the most important of which, philosophically, is antifoundationalism. Although Soja (1989: 223) conveys the ambiguous and seemingly contradictory nature of a city such as Los Angeles, whose "splendidly idiographic and enticingly generalizable features" are depicted from various levels of abstraction in a "freed association of reflective and interpretative field notes," he nevertheless portrays the city as an objective reality about which there may be more or less accurate descriptions and explanations. His descriptions would be perfectly commendable were they a realist geography admitting of the ambiguous and contradictory nature of its subject matter. They are some distance, however, from the radical relativism and antifoundationalism of postmodern thought.

Similarly, Soja's appeals for the supremacy of one perspective, the spatial, are characteristically unpostmodern. His words give him away. Phrases such as "pulling away deceptive ideological veils" and "a postmodern politics of demystification" (1989: 5) are anathema to postmodernism. To be sure, the possibility of a postmodern politics is hotly debated, but the concept of demystification is clearly foundational in that it presupposes an objective reality that has been mystified and that can be unveiled. These are modernist terms that originate in Marxism, a metadiscourse by any meaningful definition of either of the terms. Metadiscourses or metatheories, of course, are rejected by postmodernists. Soja clearly retains his commitment to Western Marxism and hopes to assimilate it to postmodernism, a task that, I would argue, is impossible. This is not to suggest that Marxists cannot benefit from taking up certain postmodern challenges, such as the deconstruction of their own taken-for-granted assumptions; however, I would argue that it is unlikely that any strong postmodern position could also be called Marxist. Marxist thought utilizing postmodern insights would ultimately have to recuperate these in order to remain Marxist in any sense of that term as it is now known.

Soja's goal of reconstructing geography along postmodernist lines (1989: 74) belies the fact that Soja is not really a postmodernist. This, as I have indicated above, is because postmodernism, at least in its stronger, more distinctive sense, is not a positive project.

Soja's postmodernism invokes a curious cast of authorities as "pioneers of postmodern geography." (Note that the appeal to authority is another of postmodernism's casualties.) Most of them in fact explicitly reject postmodernism or, at least, would not identify themselves with the label: John Berger, Ernest Mandel, Marshall Berman, and David Harvey (their books are critiques of postmodernism), Nicos Poulantzas, Anthony Giddens, and Henri Lefebvre (no Lyotard or Baudrillard or even a Jencks here). Fredric Jameson is included, but as I have argued, he also falls prey to the same temptation to adopt postmodernism while retaining Marxism, nor is there a postmodernist perspective evident in the weaker sense of polyvocality, of allowing other voices to speak (Los Angelenos, for example).

Despite the promises in the preface and postscript, much of the book is conventional historical narrative (see, for example, its chapter 7 on the history of urban and regional restructuring, which is interesting and informative but not postmodern). As narrative tends to structure writing diachronically rather than synchronically, a spatialized exposition, as Soja himself discusses, is very difficult to construct. The closest he comes is in the two chapters on Los Angeles, especially his last and most experimental chapter, in which he attempts to describe Los Angeles spatially by making "lateral connections" between the spaces of the city. Here he faces the problem, long recognized by geographers, that it is difficult to capture synchronic spatial relations in writing, which, being linear, lends itself more readily to historical description and explanation. Soja says that the "spatiality of Los Angeles is stubbornly simultaneous, but that what we write down is successive" (1989: 247). He captures the problem eloquently in speaking of Los Angeles.

> [I]ts spatiality challenges orthodox analysis and interpretation, for it seems too limitless and constantly in motion, never still enough to encompass, too filled with "other spaces" to be informatively described. Looking at Los Angeles from the inside, introspectively, one tends to see only fragments and immediacies, fixed sites of myopic understanding impulsively generalized to represent the whole. To the more far-sighted outsider, the visible aggregate of the whole of Los Angeles churns so confusingly that it induces little more than illusionary stereotypes. (1989: 222)

Soja then offers what he calls "a succession of fragmentary glimpses, a freed association of reflective and interpretative field notes" (1989: 223).

Regardless of whether his inclusion of spatiality would qualify his work as postmodernist or whether Soja's book is postmodernist for any other reason, it can be seen as a contribution to the literature on the geography of postmodernity. Soja's book makes some valuable points on the history of geographically uneven development as it unfolds during the history of capitalism (see especially its chapter 7). He also makes the very important point that geographically uneven development is not simply a historically contingent outcome of capitalism, but a necessity for capitalism's very survival.

Despite his abstract arguments for space as causative, which occasionally sound too much like the "spatial separatism" he himself criticizes, his actual use of spatial concepts (regions, places, and locales) in his empirical analyses is unobjectionable. In other words, Soja's book is valuable and interesting as an experiment in a spatialized writing style and as a more conventional political economy of postmodernity.

Philip Cooke in his book *Back to the Future: Modernity, Postmodernity, and Locality* (1990) provides an excellent and easily accessible overview of modernity and postmodernity. Like Harvey, he appears well versed in the ideas of postmodernism as they pertain to various fields including postmodern literature and architecture. He recognizes, more clearly than Soja and many other geographers, that postmodernism can have a subversive purpose, mainly in the form of deconstruction, but no positive or progressive program, (1990: 96). Like Harvey, he applauds the attention to the cultural, racial, and female Other, but again recognizes that this is manifested less in a progressive program than in "the interrogation of texts, seeking their hidden modes of domination, looking, for example, for their local exclusions on questions of gender, ethnicity, geography and so on" (1990: 96).

One of the useful distinctions that Cooke is keen to make is that between reactionary antimodernism and postmodernism. He says that the coincidental rise of neoconservativism, especially in Britain and the United States, and postmodernism has encouraged certain writers such as Jameson, Terry Eagleton, and Mike Davis to posit reductionist, causal connections between the two (1990: 113).

Cooke distinguishes between reactionary antimodernism and postmodernism. On the one hand, he cites the critique of modern architecture by the Prince of Wales as pure revivalism (1990: 104–5) and thus an example of antimodernism; on the other hand, he regards postmodernism as an internal critique of modernism that "leaves the main edifice intact" (1990: 198). He does, however, warn of the danger of postmodernism "tipping over into reactionary anti-modernism," as when postmodernist architecture forgets its parodic, critical function and becomes merely populist and reactionary in its attempts to recreate the human scale of traditional architectural forms.

Cooke further distinguishes neoconservativism as a political stance from antimodernism. By emphasizing the rights of the individual and supporting a promarket ideology, the neoconservative critique of twentieth-century modernism draws on an early-modern conception of citizenship rights. It calls for a return to the "minimalist, nightwatchman state securing the legal and institutional rules which enable competitive exchange to function in the markets of labour, products, and services" (1990: 135). Proponents then attempt to reverse the history of twentieth-century struggles for a definition of citizenship that goes beyond mere property rights to include social, welfare, and civil rights.

While this type of neoconservative politics is based on competitive individualism, an earlier modernism, the reactionary antimodernism of Prince Charles and his fellow critics, such as Quinlan Terry, is based on nostalgia for feudal, paternalistic links between the nobility and a peasantry (1990: 134), a form of noblesse oblige in architecture and planning. This antimodernism thus differs significantly from the neoconservative politics of both Reagan and Thatcher as well as from the postmodern critique.

One of the attractions of postmodernism in Cooke's view is its emphasis on the local dimension of thought and practice. He sees themes such as locality, difference, local discourses, a recognition of the Other, and a critique of monolithic values as relevant to a geography that emphasizes place specificity. He points to the influence of Foucault's notion of local discourses on postmodern social theory and Lyotard's notion of local as opposed to grand or universalizing narratives. While these are often associated with postmodernism in its philosophically weaker sense, I question whether they cannot also be seen as modernist. Postmodernist architecture, Cooke points out, draws its inspiration from local and marginalized cultures and in this way differs from the "austere universalism of modernist aesthetics" (1990: 114). As noted above, modernism and postmodernism in architecture refer to different styles, and I do not object to these terms. I caution, however, against the easy leaps of thought that can accompany wide-ranging discussions of many different types of postmodernism. Even when the author understands the differences, the reader may be less certain, especially given the many confusing discussions in the literature.

Post-Fordist flexibility in production and the failures of centralized bureaucracy draw attention to the idea of locality. Cooke suggests that "the postmodern critique of modernity points in one very clear direction, towards a decentralist continuation of the project of modernity" (1990: 179). Accordingly, he argues that the notions of postmodernism as a set of ideas challenging modernism on the one hand and postmodernity as a societal condition on the other need to be taken very seriously by geographers. Ultimately, however, Cooke sees postmodernism merely as a critique of modernism's timeworn but essentially viable and salvageable positive project.

It might be added that while Harvey and Cooke refuse to accept modernism's demise, the differences in their views are often striking. While Cooke welcomes the revival of localities research in geography, David Harvey is uncomfortable with this prospect.[14]

Although Michael Dear has expressed reservations about postmodernism in social science, he has associated himself with the movement by writing prominent agenda-setting articles on the subject (1986, 1988). In these he neither wholeheartedly endorses nor rejects any particular version of postmodernism. Like Soja, he seems anxious to attach it to a politically progressive agenda. While acknowledging the relativism of postmodernism as an intellectual position, he fails to take this most important aspect as seriously as I have suggested it should be taken. The very title of one of his articles, "The Postmodern Challenge: Reconstructing Human Geography" (1988), would suggest a failure to acknowledge the radically antifoundational and deconstructive character of the (non)perspective.

Dear rejects what he calls the "anything goes" school of tolerant eclecticism. He also appears distressed at the lack of consensus in the field, but the value that he places on consensus and unity in a field of study suggests a very modernist attitude. Although he applauds the "incredulity towards metanarratives" characteristic of postmodernism, like many other geographers he fails to confront the radical nature of claims made by Lyotard. While it is reasonable to modernists and postmodernists alike to reject grand universalizing theory (if by that it is meant that there are no social theories that apply everywhere at all times), the claim is actually far more controversial than that.

The notion of postmodern reconstruction (1988: 267) is, I suggest, a contradiction in terms, and in fact Dear's own characterization of postmodernism suggests this as well. Symptomatic of his confusion over whether to accept or reject postmodernism is Dear's observation that "a postmodern social theory deliberately maintains the creative tensions between all theories in its search for *better* interpretations of human behavior" (emphasis added; 1988: 271). This idea, that a postmodern social theory searches for better (as in closer to the truth) explanations, directly contradicts the postmodernist rejection of privileging any one explanation over any other. Conversely, Dear aptly observes that "one is not obliged to become a postmodernist in order to accept the challenge of postmodernism" (1988: 272). His attraction to hermeneutics and structuration theory is quite reasonable, provided that these are not ascribed to postmodernism.

Derek Gregory (1988, 1989) takes up the postmodern challenge by exploring the questions postmodernism poses for the field. Like Soja, Dear, and Cooke, he discusses some exciting prospects for geography's central role in an interdisciplinary postmodernist debate because of the concern that both sides have with space, place, and landscape. Gregory offers a diluted version of postmodernism when he speaks of a "sensitivity" to cultural and place differences, whose "integrity" must be retained (1988). From a postmodern perspective concepts such as *integrity* and *unity* are suspect. Gregory's weak definition of postmodernism affords opportunities for the recovery of areal differentiation through the recognition of the unique qualities of human action in particular places. These sensitivities would satisfy the requirements of a postmodern geography as long as they are not supported by a totalizing discourse such as Marxism (Gregory 1988: 78).

In Gregory's opinion the new ethnography offers an interesting development in postmodernism, but ethnography's claims of admitting other voices — voices of cultural and historical Others — represent one of the weaker theses of postmodernism. A strong postmodernism would assume conversely that these other voices were untranslatable and therefore unavailable to the social scientist for whom they are Other. In allowing other voices Gregory raises further questions of representation and authorial control, but what would polyvocality in geographic writing look like? Could it be achieved in such a way as to justify some role for the social scientist or would it constitute the death of the social scientist as author? If the latter, can we justify a role for the social scientist in the evocation rather than the representation of the Other? Or does postmodernism's rejection of representation radically subvert the possibility of social science?

David Ley (1987) and Caroline Mills (1988) are examples of geographers who define postmodernism principally in terms of the architectural styles and planning principles of postmodernity. In this they owe much to the formulations of Jencks and the architectural perspective on postmodernism that some have labeled antimodern. Ley associates modernism with rationality and postmodernism with romanticism — rationalism and romanticism being the two major ideologies he identifies in Western culture. He sees modernism and postmodernism as two competing political ideologies, rather than as two different epochs. This is evident in his identification of architectural styles in two Canadian landscapes, both built during the 1970s and 1980s. In this case the modern landscape happens to have been built somewhat after the postmodern one. He argues that the modern landscape reflects the ideology of modernism just as the postmodernist landscape reflects postmodernism.

Interestingly, Ley associates the modern rather than the postmodern landscape with neoconservatism. In this he follows the architects and architectural critics rather than postmodernists in other fields. The postmodern, he notes, is the product of the ideology of liberal reform; it reacts against the placelessness created by modernist styles. The modern, meanwhile, represents a reaction against the welfare state in favor of the free enterprise values of big business. Unlike others who see the antimodernism of postmodern architectural styles as nostalgic and neoconservative, Ley sees it as politically progressive, a fusing of aesthetics, social justice, local history and culture, and ecology. Livability, he says, is substituted for the highest and best use in purely economic terms. Ley's depiction of postmodernism as humanistic thus contrasts sharply with other definitions of postmodernism as antihumanist.

Mills writes about a landscape adjacent to those described by Ley. She suggests that a similar but more ambiguous ideology is represented in this somewhat later version of a postmodern landscape. She finds a resistance to the corporate vision of the environment and a promotion of cultural diversity and livability as strongly manifested values. Her analysis of this landscape, however, conforms more closely to other analyses of postmodernity (e.g., Jameson, Baudrillard, Harvey, and Soja) in its emphasis on the highly commodified urban culture and skillfully packaged historical styles offered by the promoters of this landscape. She draws the link between strategies of capital accumulation and gentrification as product differentiation (1988). We see here the aestheticization of politics through the cooptation of oppositional ideologies in the advertising and selling of a cultural product.

In the case of Ley and Mills postmodernism is analyzed as a landscape and architectural style that is generated within a particular stage of capitalism rather than adopted as an intellectual position (although this style clearly has political connotations with which they might or might not choose to identify). In this, of course, Ley and Mills also adopt one of the weaker definitions of postmodernism, thus avoiding the confusion of those who are not clear about whether they espouse postmodernism and, if so, whether they accept the philosophically stronger or weaker version.

Ulf Strohmayer and Matthew Hannah provide us with one of the best examples of postmodernism as antifoundationalism. Their article "Domesticating Postmodernism" (1992) warns of the intellectual dishonesty of recuperating postmodernism back into modernism. They honestly confront the impossibility of representing reality in language—that is, the radical undecidability in the relation between signifieds and signifiers. Citing Wittgenstein, they see this relation as merely a matter of assumption based in repetition: "with 'repetition' preceding 'identity' any claim *about* reality is as much an outcome of conceptual labour as it is a re-enacting of a taken-for-granted connectedness. And into the silences of these acceptances the most effective of all sources of power becomes inscribed: rule following, methodological common sense or tradition" (1992: 35). Strohmayer and Hannah then go on to say that deconstruction is the analysis of this common sense: "a reading of conceptual language against the grain of representational trust, deconstruction radically negates any possibility of extratextual stable references" (1992: 36). Examining the link between language and reality, they observe that "descriptive language no matter how precise and exhaustive, can never succeed in anchoring itself to a reality; it can only move 'sideways' through the realm of words . . . this does not imply that there is no truth, but rather that if there is, we are incapable of pinning it down" (1992: 36). The postmodern challenge, then, as they see it, is a matter of justification. How do we justify our representations? On what grounds do we claim our expertise?

Strohmayer and Hannah show that the various tactics used by those who take up the postmodern challenge are largely unsuccessful—unsuccessful principally because they fail to take up the challenge with the seriousness that it requires. The most common stances are dismissive. The laziest and all too common response is to reject postmodernism outright as a fad. Others restate the claims of postmodernism in absurdly simplistic terms, for example, "there is no truth." "The straw figure phrases are made to appear inexplicable: how could somebody have said that? How ridiculous! There must be some larger context which explains such claims. The larger context which then 'presents itself' is the historical evolution of relations of production and reproduction under capitalism" (1992: 39). Strohmayer and Hannah then counter with a more defensible restatement of postmodernism as a belief in the idea that "if there is truth, we are incapable of recognizing it as such with any certainty" (1992: 39).

Another tactic cited by the authors is a somewhat more sophisticated sociology of knowledge approach such as Harvey's. Seeing postmodernism as a product of late capitalism, it is assumed to be conservative and is dismissed on the basis of this rather tenuous causal connection. Strohmayer and Hannah counter that "terms such as 'pastiche,' 'difference,' and 'the sliding of the signifier' emerged from debates within philosophy whose particular features have been anything but exhaustively determined by the nonphilosophical context" (1992: 40–41). This rejection of a sociology of knowledge (social context as relevant to the truth of propositions) is a standard position in Anglo-American analytic philosophy—one that stands in opposition to continental power/knowledge formulations of the problem such as Foucault's, yet, in the absence of a convincing portrayal of the causal links between the fine details of postmodern thought and late capitalism, I am tempted to agree with their point.

Strohmayer and Hannah identify other tactics as assimilationist. By this they mean that attempts to deal with the relativism of postmodernism are followed by attempts to reconstruct critical social science. As examples they point to Dear (1988), Soja (1988: 1–2), and Gregory (1988: 88). By allowing the possibility of local truth and legitimacy of place-specific studies, geographers believe not only that they can escape the sins of universalizing, which they understand postmodernism as rejecting, but also that they can legitimate geography as a more prestigious discipline. Strohmayer and Hannah argue, however, that even "local truths" do not escape the problem of representation, because, being linguistic, they cannot demonstrate their own truthfulness. "The problem of representation hounds communication at every scale . . . every consensus, even at a local scale conceals the problem only through an exercise of power" (1992: 51). This potentially devastating thesis cannot be avoided without, as Strohmayer and Hannah say, drawing an arbitrary line beyond which relativism is prohibited from crossing (1992: 51). If I understand them correctly, the problem of postmodernism's antifoundationalism can never be resolved within language.

If we geographers are to remain content with our profession and continue to approach our political lives with any degree of confidence, how then are we to take up the postmodern challenge with the seriousness it demands? Strohmayer and Hannah's solution seems curious. In order to retain intellectual honesty in regard to the postmodern problematic (and it seems to me they do this better than most other geographers whose work I have reviewed), they seem to adopt what Andrew Sayer calls a diurnal and a nocturnal philosophy. They acknowledge quite sensibly that political activity continues regardless of the angst of intellectuals grappling with the problems of philosophy. They imply that they too have lives outside of their writings and they too engage in politics. I can agree that this is in fact what happens and, furthermore, that nonaction is as political as action and, hence, that politics is inescapable—but how can they retain intellectual honesty when they cannot justify their politics, when they admit that judgments of right and wrong are ungroundable and that imposing one's political convictions on others is fascist (1992: 48)? How can they talk of a radical responsibility that does not even attempt to justify itself in political theory or any external guidance? Is this radical individualism? And is it possible to achieve? Can we act outside of language and socially constituted discursive structures? They say that we have to make choices and that these will be at some level arbitrary; is this not akin to drawing a line beyond which relativism may not cross—the line in this case dividing academic from other kinds of practice?

Strohmayer and Hannah point out that critical academics spend more time and effort than most people "trying to match language to reality," but that this effort "fails utterly to move us beyond the inherent limitations of language"(1992: 53). As they imply, if ideas of rigor and cumulative accuracy are illegitimate, these will fail to distinguish us from less disciplined folk. They argue that "prior to any interpretative effort, our sensibilities drive us to disgust, offense and objection" (1992: 53). Does this mean that they subscribe to some sort of phenomenological prediscursive political intuition? Or, as Sayer has suggested, simply a pragmatic diurnal philosophy? I assume that their great concern with intellectual honesty would lead them toward formulating some sophisticated version of the former rather than the latter. I, for one, am skeptical of how they will achieve this.

Andrew Sayer in his "Postmodernist Thought in Geography: A Realist View" (1992) makes a very convincing argument that there is a type of antifoundationalism that is not relativist in its premises. We can conclude from his paper that it is possible to retain some of the valuable insights of postmodernism but reject some of the more paralyzing implications of relativism. He argues that modernist critical social science, geography included, does not need foundationalism. He favors a kind of nonrelativist, but nonetheless antifoundational, realism. In fact, Sayer goes so far as to argue that most everyone is, and has been, antifoundationalist. In order to substantiate this claim, he defines foundationalism as a belief that ultimate foundations for knowledge can be found and absolute truth can be established. This he regards as a crude and long discredited version of objectivism. Sayer's point is intriguing, but his equation of foundationalism and objectivism may be too crude. If we define foundationalism more broadly to include (often assumed) qualifications as to fallibility, we could place most people in the foundational camp. I think that the importance of Sayer's point, however, lies in the fact that postmodernists also define foundationalism in such a narrow way that few would support it. The unwary then might be won over to the side of postmodernism if the only other alternative presented was a relativist form of antifoundationalism.

Sayer goes on to define antifoundationalism as the recognition that there is no escaping "the available knowledge/discourses to see how they compare with the reality to which they claim to refer" (1992: 2). Sayer thinks that where realists and the many others who do not believe in a privileged access to reality part company with postmodernists is in their reaction to their shared belief in their own fallibility. Sayer thinks that the postmodernists overreact, "flipping" to the other extreme by "refusing all talk of truth or falsity," denying "any kind of correspondence between thought and the world," asserting that "we do not 'discover' things, but socially or discursively constitute them," refusing "all distinction between fiction and fact" and claiming that "signifiers do not refer to any real objects, but 'float free'" (1992: 3). In conjunction with these beliefs, Sayer notes that postmodernists also posit the incommensurability of local discourses.

For Sayer, the idea of certain truth or fact is highly problematic. He also accepts that, while we can discover things in our world, we often constitute them in our discourses conceptually as objects with certain socially constructed relationships; and, while he undoubtedly recognizes a certain degree of instability in the signifier-signified relation, he does argue that relative stability in this relation is not only achievable, but is a precondition of social life and communication. Nevertheless, despite any similarities between his realism and Strohmayer and Hannah's postmodernism, Sayer clearly thinks that their relativism is extreme and does not follow from antifoundationalism per se.

Sayer is critical of Strohmayer and Hannah's (1992: 36) claim that there can be no vertical relationship between language and reality, only a horizontal move through language (see above); "it doesn't follow from this that there can be no vertical relationship, only that the relationship can't be explained except through horizontal moves within language" (1992: 8), to which he adds that "it is, of course, no surprise that explanations are unavoidably linguistic" (1992: 8). Relative stability, of course, is not absolute stability or certainty with respect to vertical relationships. Sayer's solution to this problem is thus pragmatic; concepts may be practically adequate for the time being. If there is a rough relationship (which certainly can entail ambiguity) between the structure of the world and the structure of discourse, then this will enable us to do a whole range of things successfully (1992: 8). It will also place constraints on us that relativists claim not to be bound by. Sayer's belief is that, if some postmodernists such as Strohmayer and Hannah are not satisfied with the idea of practical adequacy in their nocturnal philosophies, they certainly would appear to be in their diurnal practices!

Conclusion

Soja's (1987) title phrase "the postmodernization of geography" and Dear's (1988: 272) contention that "we are all postmodernists now" are indicative of the geographers' enthusiasm for, but their frequent failure to acknowledge the philosophical rigor of postmodernism. Postmodernism's radical critique presents a serious challenge to geography. It involves coming to grips with a critique that can never be directed from any sustained, coherent position.

A postmodern political position is at once radical and yet impotent in any of the usual senses of progressive or constructive politics.[15] Nothing is sacred: no hegemony above criticism, no proposition unproblematic from the (non)perspective of postmodernism. Herein lies its strength. Every proposition and political position must be problematized, denaturalized, and, ultimately, undermined. It would seem, however, that not everything can be questioned at once, but that whatever perspective we adopt for the purpose of critique would be an apt target for postmodernist subversion.

It is difficult to understand why geographers should be so flattered by the attention some postmodernists outside the field pay to their objects of study — place and space (especially as these are usually used metaphorically) — that they would want to adopt postmodernism and in so doing take on board all of the relativistic baggage that comes with postmodernism's epistemology. Others seem to be trying to co-opt postmodernism's prestige by flirting with, while not wholeheartedly accepting, its radical antifoundationalism and relativism.

If geographers accept postmodernism's challenge, it may be most beneficial to adopt only its unrelentingly critical attitude and turn the critique back on itself. In addition to being more sensitive to difference (cultural or intellectual), we would use difference to undermine our own interpretative complacency, and we might employ postmodernist tools such as deconstruction to replicate the critical energy of postmodernism. If, however, this makes us postmodernists (and I submit that it does not), it would be a weak form of postmodernism.

As geographers, we will continue with our analyses of postmodernity, and doubtless these will assume political, methodological, and theoretical viewpoints other than those of postmodernism. In the end the study of postmodernity is a very broadly defined project, and having been influenced by some of postmodernism's concerns, we may wish to remain skeptical about the use of such totalizing descriptive categories as *postmodernity* itself.

Notes

I would like to thank John Agnew, Stuart Corbridge, Jim Duncan, Joanne Sharp, Ulf Strohmayer, and Judy Walton for their comments on the first draft of this chapter.

1. Jameson uses the term *postmodernism* to mean a societal condition or era; I prefer the term *postmodernity*.

2. In fact, he sees the relationship as being so close that "every possible position on postmodernism in culture whether apologia or stigmatization, is an implicitly or explicitly political stance on the nature of multinational capitalism today" (Jameson 1984: 55).

3. On this, see Young (1990: 111).

4. In his analysis Jameson is indebted to Baudrillard's (1975, 1981) analysis of the political economy of the sign and the writings of Guy Debord (1977).

5. This is not to reverse the chronological order implied in the term *postmodernism* but rather to question the assumption of progress in chronological time. Lyotard (1984: 79) says that postmodernism is a part of modernism and that to become modern a work must first be postmodern. He says that postmodernism is modernism in its nascent state. In this he seems to be saying not only that modernism happens to have lost its critical edge, but that it has by definition—to be modern is to have domesticated or institutionalized the revolutionary impulse. According to Lyotard, it is postmodernism that is unstable and transgressive. In this sense Lyotard's postmodernism could be considered similar to avant-garde or revolutionary modernism. In contrast to Lyotard, Fredric Jameson argues that, although the radical break between modernism and postmodernism does not involve a complete change of content (thus we find many elements of postmodernism in the earlier modernist period), it involves a restructuring of its elements such that the ones that were subordinant become dominant, and some of the oppositional elements of modernism, those that scandalized the moderns, have become normalized and "emptied of their subversive power" (Jameson 1983: 124).

6 See Habermas 1975, 1983, 1990; Lyotard 1984; and Rorty 1986.

7. Jencks (1986) states that Team Ten, Jane Jacobs, Robert Venturi, and the Advocacy Planners attacked "orthodox modern architecture" for its elitism. His view of populism, however, seems quite limited as evidenced by his quotation of John Barth that the ideal postmodernist author "may not hope to reach and move the devotees of James Michener and Irving Wallace — not to mention the lobotomized mass-media illiterates," but may hope to reach beyond the professional devotees of high art (1986:6).

8. Many of those whose names are most closely associated with the "new anthropology" are represented in the volumes by Clifford and Marcus (1986) and Clifford (1988).

9. Cultural relativism here refers to the liberal notions of tolerance and pluralism. It is the idea that the many cultures of the world are equally valid in their own terms. Ethnocentrism is thus a common charge against those who criticize other cultures.

10. Although such arrogant language may not always be used, it can be shown that many modernist truth claims, in fact, assume universality and ahistoricity, although rarely infallibility.

11. Again, see Sayer (1992) for an argument that realism offers a middle way between radical postmodern antifoundationalism and naive empiricism.

12. The term *recuperate* is used by certain postmodernists in a negative sense to mean the appropriation or (often unintentional) reformulation of a theory or concept in such a way as to reduce its critical edge or philosophical rigor. Often, this recuperation involves the retranslation back into "common sense" or taken-for-granted terms within a discourse that is allegedly being rejected.

13. Harvey is not as vulnerable as Jameson to the charge of inconsistency when he employs a conventional narrative style or appeals to a metanarrative. This is because Harvey, unlike Jameson, explicitly rejects a postmodernist position. Instead, he claims to analyze postmodernity as a societal condition.

14. See, for example, the debates in *Antipode* in 1986 and *Society and Space* in 1987 between Harvey, Cooke, Neil Smith, Nigel Thrift, Andrew Sayer, and others over local versus global, which tends to get conflated with other dualisms such as necessary/contingent, abstract/concrete, and empirical/theoretical. It could be argued that there are no fundamental differences between these authors that could not be solved with clearer definitions and a little less passion, but there is no space here to pursue that debate.

15. For two interesting analyses of the possibility of postmodern politics, see Arac (1986) and Hutcheon (1989).

References

Aglietta, Michel. 1979. *A theory of capitalist regulation: The U.S. experience.* New York: Verso.

Arac, Jonathan, ed. 1986. *Postmodernism and politics.* Minneapolis: University of Minnesota Press.

Baudrillard, Jean. 1975. *The mirror of production*. St. Louis: Telos Press.

———. 1981. *For a critique of the political economy of the sign*. St. Louis: Telos Press.

Berman, Marshall. 1988. *All that is solid melts into air: The experience of postmodernity*. New York: Penguin Books.

Bernstein, Richard, 1983. *Beyond objectivism and relativism: Science, hermeneutics, and praxis*. Philadelphia: University of Pennsylvania Press.

Clifford, James, and George Marcus, eds. 1986. *Writing culture: The poetics and politics of ethnography*. Berkeley: University of California Press.

———. 1988. On ethnographic authority. In *The predicament of culture*. Cambridge, Mass.: Harvard University Press.

Cooke, Philip. 1990. *Back to the future: Modernity, postmodernity, and locality*. London: Unwin Hyman.

Davis, Mike. 1988. *Reshaping the U.S. left: Popular struggles in the 1980s*. New York: Verso.

Dear, Michael. 1986. Postmodernism and planning. *Environment and Planning D: Society and Space* 4: 367–84.

———. 1988. The postmodern challenge: Reconstructing human geography. *Transactions of the Institute of British Geographers* N.S. 13: 262–74.

Debord, Guy. 1977. *Society of the spectacle*. Detroit: Black and Red.

Fish, Stanley. 1989. *Doing what comes naturally*. Durham, N. C.: Duke University Press.

Foster, Hal. 1983. Postmodernism: A preface. *The anti-aesthetic: Essays on postmodern culture*, ed. Hal Foster, iv-xvi. Seattle: Bay Press.

———. 1985. *Recodings: Art, spectacle, cultural politics*. Seattle: Bay Press.

Graff, Gerald. 1979. *Literature against itself*. Chicago: University of Chicago Press.

Gregory, Derek. 1988. Areal differentiation and post-modern human geography. In *Horizons in human geography*, ed. D. Gregory and R. Walford, 67–96. London: Macmillan.

———. 1989. The crisis of modernity? Human geography and critical social theory. In *New models in geography*, 2 vols., ed. Richard Peet and Nigel Thrift, 1: 348–85. London: Unwin Hyman.

Habermas, Jurgen. 1975. *Legitimation crisis*. Boston: Beacon Press.

———. 1983. Modernity: An incomplete project. In *The anti-aesthetic: Essays on postmodern culture*. ed. Hal Foster, 3–15. Seattle: Bay Press.

————. 1990. *The philosophical discourse of modernity*, trans. F. Lawrence. Cambridge, Mass.: MIT Press.

Harvey, David. 1989. *The condition of postmodernity.* Oxford: Basil Blackwell.

Hassan, Ihab. 1980. The question of postmodernism. *Bucknell Review*, 25: 117–26.

Howe, Irving. 1970. *The decline of the new.* New York: Harcourt Brace and World.

Hutcheon, Linda. 1989. *The politics of postmodernism.* New York: Routledge.

Huyssen, Andreas. 1986. *After the great divide: Modernism, mass culture, postmodernism.* Bloomington: University of Indiana Press.

Jameson, Fredric. 1983. Postmodernism and consumer society. In *The antiaesthetic: Essays on postmodern culture*, ed. Hal Foster, 111–26. Seattle: Bay Press.

————. 1984. Postmodernism, or the cultural logic of late capitalism. *New Left Review* 146: 53–92.

Jencks, Charles. 1975. The rise of postmodern architecture. *Architecture Association Quarterly* 4: 3–14.

————. 1986. *What is postmodernism?* New York: St. Martin's Press.

Ley, David. 1987. Styles of the times: Liberal and neoconservative landscapes in inner Vancouver. *Journal of Historical Geography* 13: 40–56.

Lyotard, Jean-Francois. 1984. *The postmodern condition: A report on knowledge*, trans. G. Bennington and B. Massumi. Minneapolis: University of Minnesota Press.

Mills, Caroline. 1988. Life on the upslope: The postmodern landscape of gentrification. *Environment and Planning D: Society and Space* 6: 169–89.

Newman, Charles. 1985. *The postmodern aura.* Evanston, Ill.: Northwestern University Press.

Rabinow, Paul. 1986. Representations are social facts: Modernity and postmodernity in anthropology. In *Writing culture: The poetics and practices of ethnography*, ed. James Clifford and George Marcus, 234–61. Berkeley: University of California Press.

Rorty, Richard. 1986. Habermas and Lyotard on postmodernity. In *Habermas and modernity*, ed. R. Bernstein, 161–76. Cambridge, Mass.: MIT Press.

Sayer, Andrew. 1992. Postmodernist thought in geography: A realist view. Research Paper Number 6, Geography Laboratory, University of Sussex.

Silverman, Hugh. 1990. Introduction: The philosophy of postmodernism. In *Postmodernism — philosophy and the arts*, ed. H. Silverman, 1–9. New York: Routledge.

Soja, Edward. 1987. The postmodernization of geography: A review essay. *Annals of the Association of American Geographers* 77: 289–96.

————. 1989. *Postmodern geographies: The reassertion of space in critical social theory*. London: Verso.

Strohmayer, Ulf, and Matthew Hannah. 1992. Domesticating postmodernism. *Antipode* 24: 29–55.

Tyler, Stephen. 1986. *Writing culture: The poetics and politics of ethnography*. Berkeley: University of California Press.

————. 1987. *The unspeakable: Discourse, dialogue, and rhetoric in the postmodern world*. Madison, Wis.: University of Wisconsin Press.

Venturi, Robert, Denise Brown, and Steven Izenour. 1977. *Learning from Las Vegas*. Cambridge, Mass.: MIT Press.

Young, Robert. 1990. *White mythologies: Writing history and the West*. New York: Routledge.

Index

Abbott, A., 42
aboriginal drained-field cultivation, 175
Abrahms, Philip, 336
absolute motion, 11
absolute space, 11, 13
absolute time, 50
adaptive dynamics ecology, 162–63, 174, 175, 180; and human-environment relations, 176; of indigenous peoples, 175; of peasant farming systems in Ecuador, 175
Africa, 217, 219
African historical geography, 44
agency, 133, 336. *See also* structure and agency
"Agency of Man on the Earth," 133, 233
Agnew, John A., 114n2
agrarian economy, 245
agrarian innovation, 340, 342, 347n5, 347n12
agrarian transformation in southern Sweden, 336
agricultural hinterland, 329
agricultural landforms, 175
Agricultural Origins and Dispersals, 106, 167, 233
agriculture, 233–34, 238–40, 242–354, 301–2, 329–34, 335–38. *See also* agrarian innovation, agro-

ecology, ecology, Thünen model of agrarian land use
agroecology, 86, 180
Althusser, L., 388
Amazon, 177, 179
Amedeo, D., 38
American anthropology, 104
American Geographical Society, 137
American Geography: Inventory and Prospect, 66, 86
American past, radical interpretations of, 49
American political behavior, 339
American Revolution, 344
Anderson, Kay, 114n2
Anderson, P., 388
animation in map representation, 289
antecedent boundary, 222
Anthropogeographie, 104
anthropology, 107, 111, 171, 434, 436
antifoundationalism, 435, 436
antimodernism, 445
Anuchin, Dmitrii, 101
a priorism, 335
Aquinas, St. Thomas, 191
Arcadia, of Virgil, 78
archaeology, 54
architecture, 433, 434, 436, 437
archival sources, 141

About the Contributors

EDMUNDS V. BUNKŠE is Associate Professor of Geography at the University of Delaware. He is a historian of ideas concerning human nature and the environment. Most recently he has coproduced films for Latvian Television on cultural themes (1993–1995), edited a special *GeoJournal* issue (1994) on the Baltic states, and published the essay, "The Postindustrial City as Exile and Its Possible Consequence for Sense of Place" (R. B. Singh, ed., *The Spirit and Power of Place*, Geographic Society of India, 1994).

ANDREW F. BURGHARDT is Professor Emeritus of Geography at McMaster University, Hamilton, Ontario, Canada. His publications in political and historical geography have dealt with the origins of cities and changes in administrative areas and in early transportation. Recently he contributed to the *Canadian Historical Atlas* (University of Toronto Press, 1993).

VERA CHOUINARD is Associate Professor of Geography at McMaster University, Ontario, Canada. Her interests include philosophy, social theory, the political economy of the state and cities, and struggles for social change. She is the author of various articles concerned with social theory and geography, state formation, and struggles over cooperative housing, legal services, and rights for the disabled. Her most recent publication is "Geography, Law and Legal Struggles: Which Ways Ahead?" (*Progress in Human Geography* 18 [1994]: 415–440).

MICHAEL R. CURRY is Assistant Professor of Geography at the University of California, Los Angeles. His primary interest is the relationship between the development of geographic ideas and technologies and the practice of geography. He is the author of various articles on the subject, and of *The Work in the World: Putting the Geographical Work in its Place* (University of Minnesota Press, forthcoming).

MONA DOMOSH is Associate Professor of Geography at Florida Atlantic University. Her research focuses on the historical geography of American cities, particularly how gender identities are constituted in urban landscapes. She is coeditor of *Gender, Place and Culture: A Journal of Feminist Geography*.

NANCY DUNCAN is Adjunct Assistant Professor of Geography at Syracuse University. She is the author of various articles on political and cultural geography. At present she is editing a book on geographies of gender and sexuality and writing a book with James Duncan on the politics of exclusion.

CARVILLE EARLE is Professor of Geography at Louisiana State University. He is the author of various articles and books on the historical geography of the United States, most recently *Geographical Inquiry and American Historical Problems* (Stanford University Press, 1992), and editor of the *Annals of the Association of American Geographers*.

DAVID HORNBECK is Professor of Geography at California State University, Northridge. He is the author of *California Patterns* (Mayfield Press, 1984) and the past president of the Western Social Science Association and the California Mission Association. He has published numerous articles and chapters on the historical geography of the American West.

MARTIN S. KENZER teaches upper-division geography courses in the interdisciplinary College of Liberal Arts (in Davie, Florida) as well as graduate seminars in the Geography Department (in Boca Raton) of Florida Atlantic University. His interests include the history and philosophy of geography, regional geography, and refugees around the world. He is author of numerous books and articles.

JOHN U. MARSHALL is Professor of Geography at York University, Ontario, Canada. His principal interests lie in urban and economic geography with special reference to the growth dynamics and functional differentiation of regional systems of cities. He is a former editor of *The Canadian Geographer* and the author of *The Structure of Urban Systems* (University of Toronto Press, 1989).

KENT MATHEWSON is Associate Professor of Geography at Louisiana State University. Field studies have taken him to Latin America and Oceania. He has published on cultural ecology, landscape archaeology, and the history of geography. He has authored and edited volumes including: *Irrigation Horticulture in Highland Guatemala* (Westview Press, 1984); *Culture, Form, and Place* (Geoscience Publications, 1993); and *Re-reading Cultural Geography* (University of Texas Press, 1994).

PHILLIP C. MUEHRCKE is Professor of Geography at the University of Wisconsin at Madison. He is author of various articles and books on cartography, including *Elements of Cartography* (John Wiley and Sons, 1995) and *Map Use: Reading, Analysis and Interpretation* (JP Publications, 1992). He is interested in cartographic thought and communication, with focus on the map-environment relationship.

KENNETH ROBERT OLWIG is Associate Professor at the Humanities Research Center, Menneske og Natur, at Odense University. He publishes both in English and the Scandinavian languages, and is the author of *Nature's Ideological Landscape: A Literary and Geographic Perspective on its Development and Preservation on Denmark's Jutland Heath* (George Allen & Unwin, 1984).

CHRISTINE M. RODRIGUE is Associate Professor of Geography and Planning at California State University, Chico. Her work focuses on the structuring of human response to risk, as seen in a prehistoric context in her 1992 *Professional Geographer* article, "Can Religion Account for Early Animal Domestications? A Critical Assessment of the Cultural Geographic Argument, Based on Near Eastern Archaeological Data," and in a contemporary setting in her 1993 *California Geographer* article, "Home with a View: Chaparral Fire Hazard and the Social Geographies of Risk and Vulnerability."

LESTER B. ROWNTREE is Professor of Geography and Director of Environmental Studies at San Jose State University in California. His research interests are global environmental issues, environmental change, and landscape studies. Besides authoring various research articles, he is a coauthor (with Terry Jordan and Mona Domosh) of *The Human Mosaic: A Thematic Introduction to Cultural Geography* (Harper Collins, 1994).

JONATHAN M. SMITH is Assistant Professor of Geography at Texas A&M University. He is coeditor of the book *Re-Reading Cultural Geography* (University of Texas Press, 1994) and of the annual *Philosophy and Geography*. His principal interest is in the connection between ethical systems, spatial concepts, and cultural landscapes.

LAKSHMAN YAPA is Associate Professor of Geography at Pennsylvania State University. His principal interests lie in economic geography, poverty, development, postmodern discourse theory, and GIS.

KARL S. ZIMMERER is Associate Professor of Geography at the University of Wisconsin at Madison. He is the author of numerous articles on biodiversity and soil resources in Latin America and the Andes and on ecological thought in geography. His book, *Changing Fortunes: Biodiversity and Peasant Livelihood in the Peruvian Andes*, is forthcoming with the University of California Press (1995).